End-User Computing, Development and Software Engineering:

New Challenges

Ashish Dwivedi
University of Hull, UK

Steve Clarke
University of Hull, UK

Managing Director:	Lindsay Johnston
Senior Editorial Director:	Heather Probst
Book Production Manager:	Sean Woznicki
Development Manager:	Joel Gamon
Development Editor:	Heather Probst
Acquisitions Editor:	Erika Gallagher
Typesetters:	Mackenzie Snader
Print Coordinator:	Jamie Snavely
Cover Design:	Nick Newcomer, Greg Snader

Published in the United States of America by
Information Science Reference (an imprint of IGI Global)
701 E. Chocolate Avenue
Hershey PA 17033
Tel: 717-533-8845
Fax: 717-533-8661
E-mail: cust@igi-global.com
Web site: http://www.igi-global.com

Library of Congress Cataloging-in-Publication Data

End-user computing, development, and software engineering: new challenges / Ashish Dwivedi and Steve Clarke, editor.
p. cm.
Includes bibliographical references and index.
Summary: "This book explores the implementation of organizational and end user computing initiatives and provides foundational research to further the understanding of this discipline and its related fields"--Provided by publisher.
ISBN 978-1-4666-0140-6 (hardcover) -- ISBN 978-1-4666-0141-3 (ebook) -- ISBN 978-1-4666-0142-0 (print & perpetual access) 1. End-user computing. 2. Software engineering. I. Dwivedi, Ashish N. II. Clarke, Steve, 1950-
QA76.9.E53E4623 2012.
005.1--dc23

2011045621

British Cataloguing in Publication Data
A Cataloguing in Publication record for this book is available from the British Library.

All work contributed to this book is new, previously-unpublished material. The views expressed in this book are those of the authors, but not necessarily of the publisher.

List of Reviewers

Akhilesh Bajaj, *The University of Tulsa, USA*
Peter Baloh, *University of Ljubljana, Slovenia*
Mary Brabston, *The University of Manitoba, Canada*
Randy Bradley, *The University of Tennessee, USA*
Linda L. Brennan, *Mercer University, USA*
Janice Burn, *Edith Cowan University, Australia*
Tom Butler, *University College Cork, Ireland*
Terry A. Byrd, *Auburn University, USA*
Govidarajala Chitibabu, *Delaware State University, USA*
Katherine M. Chudoba, *Utah State University, USA*
Carol Clark, *Middle Tennessee State University, USA*
Paul Cragg, *University of Canterbury, New Zealand*
Lizette de Wet, *University of the Free State, South Africa*
Judy Drennan, *Queensland University, Australia*
James P. Downey, *University of Central Arkansas, USA*
Evan W. Duggan, *University of Alabama, USA*
Jeanette Eriksson, *Blekinge Institute of Technology, Sweden*
TerryAnn Glandon, *University of Texas at El Paso, USA*
Chitibabu Govidarajala, *Delaware State University, USA*
Mary Granger, *George Washington University, USA*
Nicole Haggerty, *Richard Ivey School of Business, USA*
Ranida B. Harris, *Indiana University Southeast, USA*
Bassam Hasan, *The University of Toledo, USA*
Ciara Heavin, *University College Cork, Ireland*
Richard Herschel, *St. Joseph's University, USA*
Yujong Hwang, *DePaul University, USA*
I.M. "Jim" Jawahar, *Illinois State University, USA*
Allen C. Johnston, *University of Alabama at Birmingham, USA*
Arnold Kamis, *Bentley College, USA*
Rex Karsten, *University of Northern Iowa, USA*
Terry Kidd, *Texas A&M University, USA*
Stefan Koch, *University of Economics and BA, Austria*
Eija Korpelainen, *Helsinki University of Technology, Finland*

Associate Editors

Table of Contents

Section 2
Approaches, Frameworks and Techniques for End-User Computing

Section 3
End-User Computing: Evidence from Practice

Detailed Table of Contents

Section 1
End-User Computing: Innovations and New Understanding

The Resource-Based View (RBV) has become one of the most popular ways to examine the impact of IT on firm performance. An increasing number of researchers are using the theoretical underpinning of the RBV to ground their research in investigating this relationship. This paper follows in this tradition by developing multidimensional measures for two dimensions of IT capability, inside-out IT capability and spanning IT capability. In this regard, the authors relate these dimensions to firm performance as profit ratios and cost ratios. Inside-out capability is the IT resources deployed from inside the firm in response to market requirements and opportunities. However, spanning IT capability involves both internal and external analysis and is needed to integrate the firm's inside-out and outside-in IT competences. This study also makes an exploratory comparative assessment of the relative impact of inside-out IT capability and spanning IT capability, while analyzing the differences on the impact of IT capability in diverse types of organizations. Finally, the authors give evidence that different dimensions of IT capability may have different effects on performance measures.

Communities of practice have been heralded as a powerful knowledge management tool, especially for geographically disparate workgroups. Research into knowledge management (KM) in healthcare organizations is a needed research focus, given that differences exist in knowledge and knowledge management processes between healthcare and other organization types. The research presented in this paper examines the effectiveness of communities of practice as a knowledge sharing tool in a large and geographically disparate healthcare organization. Findings suggest that job role affects community

The article presents and analyzes data from a case study in customer-initiated software product development. We have observed and participated in system development activities in a commercial software house (company) over a period of two years. The company produces project-planning tools for the oil and gas industry, and relies on interaction with customers for further development of its products. Our main research question is how customers and professional developers engage in mutual development mediated by shared software tools (products and support systems). We have used interviews with developers and customers as our main source of data, and identified the activities (from use to development) where customers have contributed to development. We analyze our findings in terms of co-configuration, meta-design and modding to name and compare the various stages of development (adaptation, generalization, improvement request, specialization, and tailoring).

In this article, we present WOAD, a framework that was inspired and partly validated within a 2-year observational case study at a major teaching hospital. We present the WOAD framework by stating its main and motivating rationales, outlining its high-level architecture and then introducing its denotational language, LWOAD. We propose LWOAD to support users of an electronic document system in declaratively expressing, specifying and implementing content- and event-based mechanisms that fulfill coordinative requirements and make users aware of relevant conditions. Our focus addresses (a) the user-friendly and yet formal expression of local coordinative practices based on the work context; (b) the promotion of awareness of both these conventions and the context to enable actors to quickly respond; (c) the full deployment of coordination-oriented and context-aware functionalities into legacy electronic document systems. We give examples of LWOAD mechanisms taken from the case study and discuss their impact from the EUD perspective.

This descriptive single case study examines the process and implications of the self-determined adoption of an internet-based meeting system in a global company. Self-determination theory and structuration theory are used as theoretical lenses to understand the adoption and use of an ICT system. The data were collected using qualitative semi-structured interviews with eleven system users and analyzed using a content analysis approach. The research shows that the self-determined adoption of ICT systems has benefits like user motivation and satisfaction. Problems in such adoption relate to users' experiencing uncertainty regarding the organizational legitimization of the system and support for its use. Employees and organizations are likely to benefit from self-determined adoption because it promotes employees' motivation and initiative-taking. However, a shared understanding of self-determination and organizational support for it are required.

Course management systems (CMSs) enable institutions to engage users efficiently, increase enrollment without major facilities investments, and serve geographically dispersed student markets on an ongoing basis. The full benefits of technology cannot be realized if faculty do not adopt the new technology and use it to achieve their instructional design objectives. From a faculty perspective, pedagogical usability of the software is an important factor affecting technology adoption and effective implementation. Pedagogical usability is measured using Chickering and Gamson's seven principles of good educational practice. In a distance learning context, this paper provides an initial exploratory study of how faculty perceptions of CMS software characteristics like content re-configurability, interaction re-configurability, and modularity design help faculty implement good pedagogical principles. Additionally, a model is presented that links CMS software design characteristics like content re-configurability, interaction re-configurability, and modularity design with the pedagogical usability assessments of faculty. This model is tested using a sample of 56 faculty members using WebCT at a mid-western university.

End-user programming has become ubiquitous; so much so that there are more end-user programmers today than there are professional programmers. End-user programming empowers—but to do what? Make bad decisions based on bad programs? Enter software engineering's focus on quality. Considering software quality is necessary, because there is ample evidence that the programs end users create are filled with expensive errors. In this paper, we consider what happens when we add considerations of software quality to end-user programming environments, going beyond the "create a program" aspect of end-user programming. We describe a philosophy of software engineering for end users, and then survey several projects in this area. A basic premise is that end-user software engineering can only succeed to the extent that it respects that the user probably has little expertise or even interest in software engineering.

The first decade of the World Wide Web predominantly enforced a clear separation between designers and consumers. New technological developments, such as the participatory Web 2.0 architectures, have emerged to support social computing. These developments are the foundations for a fundamental

Preface

One of the major challenges that faces managers is how to make effective decisions based on the data at hand. It is acknowledged that the selection of a particular direction is both constrained and influenced by the availability of data, the ability to transform data into information and then to make recognition of it by deriving knowledge from information. Modern day organisations are facing a deluge of data and information whilst simultaneously lacking knowledge. The 20th century has witnessed a business environment where revolutionary technologies have resulted in new products and reduced product lifecycles. Thus the twin forces of economic and technological revolutions have put organisations under pressure to adopt innovative information management practices so as to be in a position to adapt swiftly to the new business environment (Dwivedi, Wickramasinghe, Bali, & Naguib, 2008; Sieloff, 1999).

Technological innovations relating to workflow and groupware systems in conjunction with the growth of the WWW has brought about a radical transformation in the way organisations can interact internally and externally. These new ways of collaboration have resulted in organisations deluged with information to an unprecedented degree resulting in data/information overload (Sieloff, 1999). The widespread use of Internet applications using client server architecture and web browsers has further increased exponentially our ability to draw on information in ways not previously possible.

LINKAGE BETWEEN INFORMATION AND COMMUNICATION TECHNOLOGY, INFORMATION MANAGEMENT, AND END-USER COMPUTING

Information And Communication Technology (ICT) has been be defined as a "family of technologies used to process, store and disseminate information, facilitating the performance of information-related human activities, provided by, and serving both the public at-large as well as the institutional and business sectors" Salomon and Cohen (1999) in (Zhang, Van Donk, & Van der Vaart, 2011). According to Antonelli, Geuna, and Steinmueller (2000) advances in ICT are changing the ways in which organisations carry out their core processes and, more importantly, organise their processes for creating, classifying and accumulating new knowledge. They observe that:

1. ICTs have made it easier to transfer information. Through the use of ICTs, organisations are in a position to combine their internal tacit knowledge with the knowledge of external parties (suppliers etc). In some cases, this also helps organisations to overcome geographical barriers.
2. Modern ICTs are the result of the amalgamation of a number of diverse scientific and technological advances. They have drawn upon the best from different and distinct scientific and technological

fields with the end product being totally different and possessing a very rich knowledge base. When these ICTs are used in different domains they are therefore able to provide new ways of generating or applying knowledge.

3. Modern ICTs that provide support for simulation etc in combination with their ability to access and draw broad trends from a wide variety of data sources can assist organisations in elucidating new forms of quasi-codified knowledge.
4. Modern ICTs, through the use of powerful and diverse general purpose software and algorithms, have increased the economic value of codified knowledge which consequently has further accelerated the rate of codification.
5. The evolution of ICTs has also impacted on organisational structures with the old model of vertical integration in an organisation being rendered obsolete. Innovative organisational structures based upon quasi-vertical integration are becoming the norm. Large Research and Development (R&D) laboratories are being replaced with internal networks of small units (both internal and external).
6. ICTs are serving as a means of bringing together highly localised knowledge which was traditionally inaccessible.

According to Rabkin and Tingley (1999) in 1999 about fifty percent of American households owned a computer and about forty percent of all American adults had access to the Internet. One of the new challenges brought about by the ICT revolution is that consumers' expectations with regard to the speed of service have increased exponentially. Contemporary consumers are technologically proficient and are used to a very fast response time (in IT terms). It is expected that, in the future, companies who are unable to meet consumers high expectations may not survive (Rabkin & Tingley, 1999).

According to Antonelli, Geuna and Steinmueller (2000) advances in ICT are changing the way organisations carry out their core processes and, more importantly, organise their process for creating, classifying and accumulating new knowledge. Antonelli, Geuna and Steinmueller (2000, pp.73) have observed that throughout the twentieth century "the central goal of technology management has been to align the mass production of artifacts and knowledge". They support this contention by stating that, after the end of the Second World War, a number of Organisation for Economic Cooperation and Development (OECD) economies (including the USA) started large scale public funding for R&D activities which, in many cases, amounted to over 50% of the total R&D expenditure. This was in sheer contrast to the period preceding the second world war when public R&D funding was severely limited.

Antonelli, Geuna and Steinmueller (2000) go on to argue that this approach led to creation of an extremely complex research network that was composed of both public and private actors (people and organisations). Concurring with this, we offer the example of the Internet which was financed by Defense Advanced Research Projects Agency (DARPA) (Talbot, 2001).

The Internet was partly financed by DARPA primarily for USA defence purposes but later spawned to civilian purposes. This validates the contention expressed above that the most important goal of technology management has been to align the mass production of artifacts and knowledge processes. Dertouzos writing in Talbot (2001, pp.50) mentions that DARPA can be said to have had a return on investment in the region of 1,000 to one, or in business terms 100,000 percent. He further mentions that some of its most significant success have been "ethernet, the ARPAnet… major advances in computer aided design, especially of very-large-scale integration (VLSI) circuits, speech-understanding systems and many other key contributions in computer science and AI". Dertouzos believes that DARPA has been responsible for about fifty percent of the major innovations that have made IT what it is today.

Figure 1. Evolution of Information Management

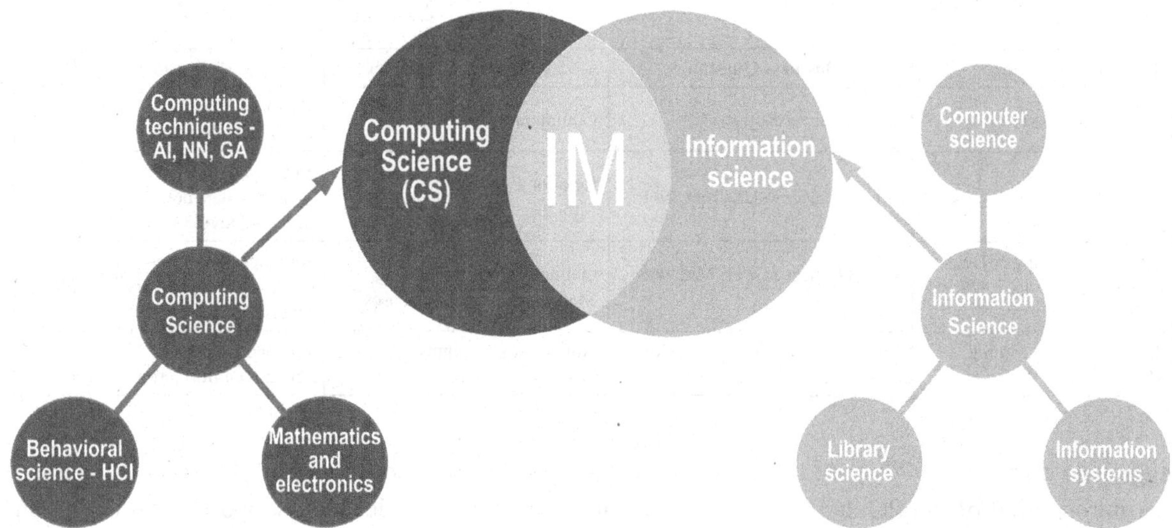

Information Management (IM) has been in existence for over 4000 years. The earliest known attempts at information management have been traced to the ancient city of Ebla in Syria where texts dating back approximately 4000 years illustrate attempts to record and organise information (Pearlson & Saunders, 2003). Whilst the phenomenon of Information Management has not changed, the tools and techniques used to enable the process of Information Management have changed. To better understand the relevance of the change in Information Management and its relationship to End User Computing, it is important to understand the nature of the components of the Information Management processes. Information Management in the 20th century has been defined by the evolutions in Information Technology and Computing Science paradigms. Information management can be defined as: "The economic, efficient and effective coordination of the production, control, storage, retrieval and dissemination of information from external and internal sources, in order to improve the performance of the organisation" (Best, 2010)

A common point in most definitions of Information Technology (IT) is that IT refers to the application of technology to carry out the capture, storage, retrieval, analysis, and communication of information. IT has its origins in the domain of information sciences which itself is a cluster of separate but related branches of knowledge (see Figure 1), including computer science, information systems, and library science (Pyle & Illingworth, 1996). Similarly definitions of Computing Science (CS) state that it includes the study of computers and its underlying principles and use. It incorporates computing techniques, such as simulation and artificial intelligence (Dwivedi et al., 2008). The interaction between Computing Science (CS) and Information Science (IS) created the IM concept (see Figure 1). Table 1 traces how the evolution in Information Management products has impacted upon organisation decision-making over the last forty years.

It is possible to draw a link between the evolution of computing technologies in business and its organisational impact. In the 1960s, the centralised mainframe architecture (see Table 1) became the industry norm and was typically used for electronic data processing. Organisations that adopted this architecture were characterised as being "data heavy at the bottom and data management systems were used to keep the data in check" (Grover and Davenport, 2001, pp.5). The main objective behind them was to provide information for decision-making. Information was presented using database concepts to

Table 1 Stages in the Evolution of Information Management. Adapted from (Dwivedi et al., 2008; Pilot Software Inc, 1999)

Evolutionary Stage	Business Question	Enabling Technologies	Features
Data Collection (1960s)	Breast Cancer worldwide?	Computers, tapes, disks	Retrospective Static data delivery
Data Access (1980s)	Breast Cancer in UK from 1960?	Relational databases Structured Query Language	Retrospective Dynamic data delivery at record level
Data warehousing & Decision support systems (early 1990s)	Breast Cancer in West Midlands from 1960?	Online analytic processing Multidimensional databases	Retrospective Dynamic data delivery at multiple levels
Intelligent Data Mining (late 1990s)	Incidence Breast Cancer in Coventry next year? Why?	Advanced algorithms, Multiprocessor computers	Prospective Proactive information delivery

aggregate data. The 1970s saw the advent of management information systems. The 1980s witnessed the introduction of the PC and saw its subsequent application as a decision support system. This in conjunction with user friendly fourth generation languages, and distributed informational control gave the end users the ability to cater to their own unstructured data and information needs" (Grover & Davenport, 2001). The mid to late 1980s witnessed the coming of age of strategic information systems which were characterised by organisations adopting a proactive approach to information and systems. This facilitated the development of competitive advantage and its subsequent deployment for achieving organisational objectives. A major catalyst for the above was "the emergence of the Internet and related technologies that provided a potent mechanism for efficiently allowing access to a rich repertoire of information using multimedia channels" (Grover and Davenport, 2001, pp.6).

The evolution in Information Management practices and processes as detailed above has meant that the introduction of information systems into organizations will generally cause a change in behaviour of the actors who interact with various components of Information Management practices and processes, i.e. it will cause a change in human behaviours. Substantial research aimed at understanding crucial factors which contribute to or hinder acceptance and utilization of information systems (IS) exists, and it is widely acknowledged that changing human behaviour is a complex issue and is often regarded as being "obtrusive and distracting". Incorporation of End-user perspectives is often regarded as a possible solution to this dilemma (Oinas-Kukkonen, Hohtari, & Pekkola, 2010).

However, incorporation of End-user perspectives is quite complex. This is primarily due to the inability to have a clear boundary for what the term "End-user perspective" represents. Over two decades ago, (Galletta & Hufnagel, 1992) had noted that, "although the term 'EUC policy' is widely used in the MIS literature, a clear definition of it has not been stated". O'Donnell and March (1987) have noted that there are there are numerous taxonomies in the literature addressing the meaning of the term "end-user", and "that the categories are either loosely defined and overlapping so that categorization is difficult, or too specific, leaving some classes undefined" (O'Donnell & March, 1987).

Consequently, key concepts such as End-User Computing, End-User Development, and Usability all are related concepts which fall within the boundary of 'End-user perspective'. End-User Computing has been defined as "direct interaction with application software by managerial, professional, and operating level personnel in user departments" (Torkzadeh & Lee, 2003), whilst (Alavi, 1985) has noted that End-user computing "means that the user of the results of the computing also creates the software specifications necessary to effect the computing itself".

End-User Development has been defined as a set of methods, techniques, and tools that allows users of software systems, who are acting as non-professional software developers, at some point to create, modify or extend a software artefact (Lieberman, Paternò, & Wulf, 2006). Wang, Doll, and Deng (2010) have noted that Usability has been conceptually defined and operationally measured in multiple ways, with definitions of usability extend from high-level conceptualizations to more focused descriptions that include notions of user relevance, use efficiency, user attitude, which has resulted in a scenario wherein a key issue facing usability researchers and practitioners alike is which metrics can best measure the construct of usability itself (Wang, Doll, & Deng, 2010).

In-order to provide Information Technology educators, researchers, and practitioners a concise summary on the theory and practice of organizational and end user computing, as editors, we have structured current publications from the Journal of Organizational and End User Computing in three sections titled as "End-User Computing: Innovations and New Understanding" (Section 1), Approaches, Frameworks and Techniques for End-User Computing (Section 2), and "End-User Computing: Evidence from Practice" (Section 3).

ORGANISATION OF THIS BOOK

Section 1 (End-User Computing:Innovations and New Understanding) has five chapters which discuss the new Innovations that are characterising the domain of End-User Computing. Chapter 1 (Contrasting IT Capability and Organizational Types: Implications for Firm Performance) by Byrd and Byrd discusses how the Resource-Based View (RBV) has become one of the most popular ways to examine the impact of IT on firm performance. They argue that increasing number of researchers are using the theoretical underpinning of the RBV to ground their research in investigating this relationship. The authors develop multidimensional measures for two dimensions of IT capability, inside-out IT capability and spanning IT capability, make an exploratory comparative assessment of the relative impact of inside-out IT capability and spanning IT capability, while analyzing the differences on the impact of IT capability in diverse types of organizations.

Chapter 2 (Utilization and Perceived Benefit for Diverse Users of Communities of Practice in a Healthcare Organization) by Walczak and Mann argues that Communities of Practice have been heralded as a powerful knowledge management tool, especially for geographically disparate workgroups. They examine the effectiveness of communities of practice as a knowledge sharing tool in a large and geographically disparate healthcare organization. They authors note that the findings suggest that job role affects community members' perceptions of the benefit and impact of communities of practice as well as their participation in such communities. Chapter 3 (Culturally Compatible Usability Work: An Interpretive Case Study on the Relationship between Usability Work and Its Cultural Context in Software Product Development Organizations) by Livari analyzes how organizational culture is intertwined with usability work in software (SW) development organizations. The author notes that Usability is an important quality characteristic of software products and systems, but the development of usability is challenging in SW development. The empirical results suggest that differences exists in how usability work is modified and interpreted in the organizations with divergent cultural contexts, those advocating different motives and practices for usability work.

Chapter 4 (Studying the Documentation of an API for Enterprise Service-Oriented Architecture) by Myers, Jeong, Xie, Beaton, Stylos, Ehret, Karstens, Efeoglu and Busse notes that almost all software today is written using application programming interfaces (APIs). The authors report the results of a user study of the online documentation of a large and complex API for Enterprise Service-Oriented Architecture (eSOA), which showed that the participants' background influenced how they navigated the documentation. Lack of familiarity with business terminology was a barrier for developers without business application experience.

The last chapter in Section 1 - Chapter 5 (Mutual Development: The Software Engineering Context of End-User Development) by March and Andersen presents and analyzes data from a case study in customer-initiated software product development. The main research question is how customers and professional developers engage in mutual development mediated by shared software tools (products and support systems). The authors report their findings in terms of co-configuration, meta-design and modding to name and compare the various stages of development (adaptation, generalization, improvement request, specialization, and tailoring).

Section 2 (Approaches, Frameworks and Techniques for End-User Computing) consisits of six chapters which presents novel approaches in the domain of End-User Computing. Chapter 6 (WOAD: A Framework to Enable the End-User Development of Coordination-Oriented Functionalities) by Cabitza and Simone present WOAD - a framework that was inspired and partly validated within a 2-year observational case study at a major teaching hospital. The WOAD framework addresses (a) the user-friendly and yet formal expression of local coordinative practices based on the work context; (b) the promotion of awareness of both these conventions and the context to enable actors to quickly respond; (c) the full deployment of coordination-oriented and context-aware functionalities into legacy electronic document systems.

Chapter 7 (Self-Determined Adoption of an ICT System in a Work Organization) by Korpelainen, Vartiainen and Kira examines the process and implications of the self-determined adoption of an internet-based meeting system in a global company. Self-determination theory and structuration theory are used as theoretical lenses to understand the adoption and use of an ICT system. The research shows that the self-determined adoption of ICT systems has benefits like user motivation and satisfaction. Employees and organizations are likely to benefit from self-determined adoption because it promotes employees' motivation and initiative-taking.

Chapter 8 (A Model of System Re-Configurability and Pedagogical Usability in an E-Learning Context: A Faculty Perspective) by Wang, Doll and Deng uses the example of course management systems (CMSs) to discuss how and why the full benefits of technology cannot be realized if faculty do not adopt the new technology and use it to achieve their instructional design objectives. From a faculty perspective, pedagogical usability of the software is an important factor affecting technology adoption and effective implementation.

Chapter 9 (End-User Software Engineering and Why it Matters) by Burnett highlights why end-user programming has become ubiquitous. In this chapter, the authors consider what happens when we add considerations of software quality to end-user programming environments, going beyond the "create a program" aspect of end-user programming. The authors describe a philosophy of software engineering for end users, and then survey several projects in this area. A basic premise is that end-user software engineering can only succeed to the extent that it respects that the user probably has little expertise or even interest in software engineering.

Chapter 10 (End User Development and Meta-Design: Foundations for Cultures of Participation) by Fischer notes that whilst the first decade of the World Wide Web predominantly enforced a clear separation between designers and consumers, new technological developments, such as the participatory Web 2.0 architectures, have emerged to support social computing. These developments are the foundations for a fundamental shift from consumer cultures (specialized in producing finished goods) to cultures of participation (in which all people can participate actively in personally meaningful activities).

Chapter 11 (Investigating Technology Commitment in Instant Messaging Application Users) by Wang and Datta observes that although much research in the IS field has examined IS adoption, less is known about post-adoption behavior among IS users, especially when competing alternatives are available. Incorporating commitment theory from social psychology and management science literature, the authors propose an IS continuance model that explains why some IS technologies enjoy continued use after adoption and others are often relegated to the basement as shelfware. The model is empirically tested in the context of instant messaging software. Results show a strong support for the model and explicate commitment differentials among users across different brands of instant messaging software.

Section 3 (End-User Computing: Evidence from Practice) consists of six chapters and builds upon the preceding sections and presents lessons from current and previous End-User Computing implementations. Chapter 12 (Appropriation Infrastructure: Mediating Appropriation and Production Work) by Stevens, Pipek and Wulf taking the case of the BSCWeasel groupware, discusses how End User Development offers technological flexibility to encourage the appropriation of software applications within specific contexts of use. The empirical results from the BSCWeasel project demonstrate the impact of such an infrastructure on the appropriation and design process. It is argued that the social construction of IT artifacts should be tightly integrated in the material construction of IT artifacts in bridging design and use discourses.

Chapter 13 (Entering the Clubhouse: Case Studies of Young Programmers Joining the Online Scratch Communities) by Kafai, Fields and Burke argue that previous efforts in end-user development have focused on facilitating the mechanics of learning programming, leaving aside social and cultural Actors equally important in getting youth engaged in programming. The authors as part of a 4-month long ethnographic study, followed two 12-year-old participants as they learned the programming software Scratch and its associated file-sharing site, scratch.mit.edu, in an after-school club and class. The chapter focusses on the role that agency membership, and status played in their joining and participating in local and online communities of programmers.

Chapter 14 (Enterprise Systems Training Strategies: Knowledge Levels and User Understanding) by Coulson, Olfman, Ryan and Shayo observe that Enterprise systems (ESs) are customizable, integrated software applications designed to support core business processes. The authors report their experiments demonstrated that training involving the tool-conceptual knowledge level leads to superior mental models, compared with training oriented toward lower knowledge levels, as expressed in the recollection and communication of ES concepts.

Chapter 15 (The Influence of Perceived Source Credibility on End User Attitudes and Intentions to Comply with Recommended IT Actions) by Johnston and Warkentin provides a conceptual model for explaining the influence of source credibility on end user attitudes and behavioral intentions to comply with organizationally motivated, recommended IT actions within a decentralized, autonomous environment. The findings suggest that the elements of source competency, trustworthiness, and dynamism are significant determinants of attitudes and behavioral intentions to engage in recommended IT actions. These findings reveal the importance of these elements of effective communication in persuading end users to follow recommended IT activities and advance IT acceptance and adoption research through the application of persuasive communication theory to the domain.

Chapter 16 (Organizing End-User Training: A Case Study of an E-Bank and its Elderly Customers) by Oinas-Kukkonen, Hohtari and Pekkola describes a qualitative case study of how the end-user training in an e-Bank was organized, and how the training was delivered to its elderly customers. The authors argue that an approach that integrates the end-user training with the system's development improves organizational implementation. As a result, this chapter makes practical suggestions about the issues related to organizing end-user training. The last chapter of the book - Chapter 17 (A Path Analysis of the Impact of Application-Specific Perceptions of Computer Self-Efficacy and Anxiety on Technology Acceptance) by Hasan and Ahmed notes that perceptions of computer self-efficacy (CSE) and computer anxiety are valuable predictors of various computer-related behaviors, including acceptance and utilization of information systems (IS). The authors add that although both factors are purported to have general and application-specific components, little research has focused on the application or system-specific component, especially in IS acceptance contexts. The results demonstrated that the direct impacts of application CSE and application anxiety on perceived ease of use and perceived usefulness were almost equal, but in opposite directions.

We hope that you, the academics, practitioners, managers, and students who access this volume, will enjoy reading these contributions as much as we have, and will find within them issues of interest and value for your own practice and research.

Ashish N. Dwivedi
Hull University, UK

Steve Clarke
Hull University, UK

October 2011

REFERENCES

Alavi, M. (1985). End-user computing: The MIS managers' perspective. *Information & Management*, *8*(3), 171–178. doi:10.1016/0378-7206(85)90046-1

Antonelli, C., Geuna, A., & Steinmueller, W. E. (2000). Information and communication technologies and the production. *distribution and use of knowledge, Int. J. Technology Management*(20), Nos. 1-2.

Best, D. P. (2010). The future of information management. *Records Management Journal*, *20*(1), 61–71. doi:10.1108/09565691011039834

Dwivedi, A. N., Wickramasinghe, N., Bali, R. K., & Naguib, R. N. G. (2008). Designing intelligent healthcare organizations with KM and ICT. *International Journal of Knowledge Management Studies*, *2*(2), 198–213. doi:10.1504/IJKMS.2008.018321

Galletta, D. F., & Hufnagel, E. M. (1992). A model of end-user computing policy: Context, process, content and compliance. *Information & Management*, *22*(1), 1–18. doi:10.1016/0378-7206(92)90002-W

Grover, V., & Davenport, T. H. (2001). General perspectives on knowledge management: Fostering a research agenda. *Journal of Management Information Systems, 18*(1), 5–21.

Lieberman, H., Paternò, F., & Wulf, V. (2006). *End user development.* Dordrecht: Springer. doi:10.1007/1-4020-5386-X

O'Donnell, D. J., & March, S. T. (1987). End-user computing environments — Finding a balance between productivity and control. *Information & Management, 13*(2), 77–84. doi:10.1016/0378-7206(87)90012-7

Oinas-Kukkonen, H., Hohtari, S., & Pekkola, S. (2010). Organizing End-User Training: A Case Study of an E-Bank and its Elderly Customers. *Journal of Organizational and End User Computing, 22*(4), 95–112. doi:10.4018/joeuc.2010100105

Pearlson, K. E., & Saunders, C. S. (2003). *Managing and Using Information Systems: A Strategic Approach.* Wiley.

Pilot Software Inc. (1999). An introduction to data mining. Retrieved 4 March 2002, from http://www.umich.edu/~cisdept/bba/320/1999/fall/pilot-software.html

Pyle, C. I., & Illingworth, V. (1996). *Dictionary of computing.* Oxford University Press.

Rabkin, B., & Tingley, M. (1999). Tech-savvy customers want quick response. *National Underwriter, 103*(40), 12–13.

Salomon, I., & Cohen, G. (1999). *ICT and urban public policy: does knowledge meet policy. Serie Research Memoranda.* Amsterdam: Faculteit der Economische Wetenschappen en Econometrie, Vrije Universiteit Amsterdam.

Sieloff, C. (1999). If only HP knew what HP knows: The roots of knowledge management at Hewlett-Packard. *Journal of Knowledge Management, 3*(1), 47–53. doi:10.1108/13673279910259385

Talbot, D. (2001). DARPA'S disruptive technologies. *Technology Review, 104*(8), 42–50.

Torkzadeh, G., & Lee, J. (2003). Measures of perceived end-user computing skills. *Information & Management, 40*(7), 607–615. doi:10.1016/S0378-7206(02)00090-3

Wang, J., Doll, W. J., & Deng, X. (2010). A Model of System Re-Configurability and Pedagogical Usability in an E-Learning Context: A Faculty Perspective. *Journal of Organizational and End User Computing, 22*(3), 66–81. doi:10.4018/joeuc.2010070104

Zhang, X., Van Donk, D. P., & Van der Vaart, T. (2011). Does ICT influence supply chain management and performance?: A review of survey-based research. *International Journal of Operations & Production Management, 31*(11), 1215–1247. doi:10.1108/01443571111178501

Section 1
End-User Computing:
Innovations and New Understanding

Chapter 1
Contrasting IT Capability and Organizational Types:
Implications for Firm Performance

Terry Anthony Byrd
Auburn University, USA

Linda W. Byrd
Auburn University, USA

ABSTRACT

The Resource-Based View (RBV) has become one of the most popular ways to examine the impact of IT on firm performance. An increasing number of researchers are using the theoretical underpinning of the RBV to ground their research in investigating this relationship. This paper follows in this tradition by developing multidimensional measures for two dimensions of IT capability, inside-out IT capability and spanning IT capability. In this regard, the authors relate these dimensions to firm performance as profit ratios and cost ratios. Inside-out capability is the IT resources deployed from inside the firm in response to market requirements and opportunities. However, spanning IT capability involves both internal and external analysis and is needed to integrate the firm's inside-out and outside-in IT competences. This study also makes an exploratory comparative assessment of the relative impact of inside-out IT capability and spanning IT capability, while analyzing the differences on the impact of IT capability in diverse types of organizations. Finally, the authors give evidence that different dimensions of IT capability may have different effects on performance measures.

INTRODUCTION

Two distinct research streams have emerged in the study of the relationship between information technology (IT) and firm performance (Barua & Mukhopadhyay, 2000). One stream uses production economics (Brynjolfsson & Hitt, 1996; Loveman, 1994; Roach, 1987) and the other stream focuses more on "process-oriented" models of IT value (Byrd & Turner, 2001; Cron & Sobol, 1983; Harris & Katz, 1991; Weill, 1992). Results from early studies in both streams generally found no significant relationship between IT and firm performance (Loveman, 1994; Roach, 1987;

DOI: 10.4018/978-1-4666-0140-6.ch001

Weill, 1992). More recent studies in both streams, however, yield results that are in contrast with the earlier studies. These recent studies report a positive link between IT and firm performance (Barua & Lee, 1997a; Bharadwaj et al., 1999a; Hitt & Brynjolfsson, 1996; Lee & Barua, 1999; Menon et al., 2000; Mukhopadhyay et al., 1997; Rai et al., 1997). Three reviews of these results are Barua and Mukhopadhyay (2000), Melville, Kraemer, and Gurbaxani (2004), and Piccoli and Ives (2005).

During the 1980s, many researchers and practitioners advocated using IT as a source of competitive advantage (Clemons & Row, 1991; King et al., 1989; Neo, 1988; Porter & Millar, 1985). During this same time and into the 1990s, companies such as Wal-Mart, FedEx, and American Airlines were touted as companies that had gained competitive advantage through the use of so-called strategic information systems (SISs) (Kettinger et al., 1994; Reich & Benbasat, 1990; Sabherwal & King, 1995). SISs were reputed to change the goals, operations, products, or environmental relationships of organizations to help them gain an advantage, at least temporarily, over other their chief competitors.

However, despite empirical evidence that IT can give competitive advantage, many observers still remain skeptical. One prominent example of this skepticism is the publicity and notoriety of an article by Carr where he proclaims that "IT Doesn't Matter" (Carr, 2003). In the article, he argues that IT is ubiquitous and available to all organizations much like electricity or other utilities. Since IT is equally available to everyone, it cannot be a source of competitive advantage, according to Carr. He asserts that IT can be easily copied and replicated and, therefore, is deprived of any ability to confer competitive advantage and differential benefits.

In differing with Carr, authors of two recent review articles reason IT can indeed give a competitive advantage if the focus is placed on certain IT resources (Piccoli & Ives, 2005; Wade & Hulland, 2004). Using the resource-based view (RBV) of the firm (Barney, 1991; Barney, 2001), these articles explain how certain types of IT resources can meet the criteria set forth in the RBV theory for resources that give sustained competitive advantage. The RBV view states that organizational resources can provide sustained competitive advantage if they are (1) economically valuable; (2) relatively scarce, (3) causally ambiguous, (4) difficult to imitate, or (5) socially complex (Barney, 1991; Teece et al., 1997).

Several recent IT studies utilize the RBV when examining the competitive value of IT capability to business (Bhatt & Grover, 2005; Kearns & Lederer, 2003; Ravichandran & Lertwongsatien, 2005). The findings from these studies are generally favorable establishing that IT capabilities can lead to better firm performance and to competitive advantage. For example, Kearns and Lederer (2003) report that strategic alignment between the IT plan and the business plan is related to competitive advantage. Likewise, Bhatt and Grover (2005) find another IT capability, IT business experience, has a significant positive effect on the competitive advantage in business firms.

Bharadwaj (2000) and Santhanam and Hartono (2003) both use more comprehensive measures of IT capability as they examine the relationship between IT capability and several profit ratios and cost ratios. However, their measure of IT capability suffers because it is monolithic and does not differentiate between different dimensions. Studies such as Wade and Hulland (2004) note that IT capability is really composed of different dimensions (such as inside-out, spanning, and outside-in) that can have different effects on performance variables of an organization. One of the contributions of this study is to look inside the "black box" of IT capability to determine if these different dimensions have different effects on the profit and cost ratios that have been used in these previous studies. Additionally, we explore how these different dimensions produce distinct effects on firm performance in diverse types of

Figure 1. The conceptual research model

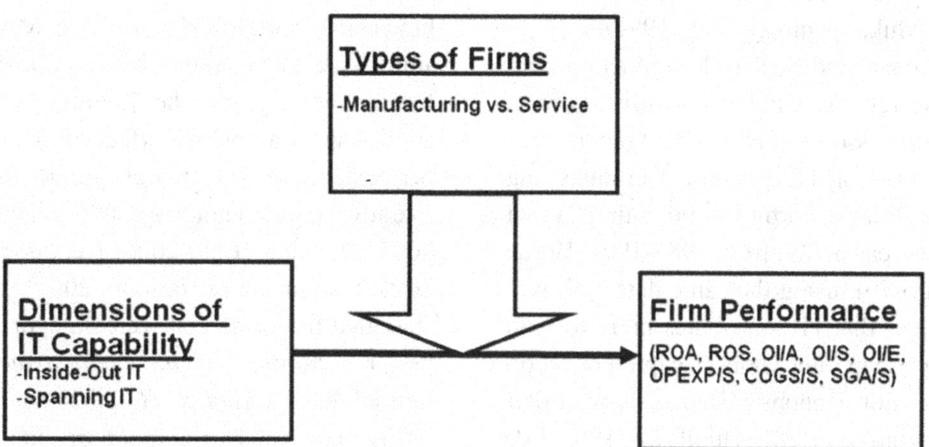

organizations. The effects of IT capability are examined in manufacturing firms and contrasted with the effects in service firms. The differences of the two IT dimensions in these organizations are analyzed and discussed. The conceptual model for this study is shown in Figure 1.

THEORETICAL CONSIDERATIONS

IT and Firm Performance Research

Early studies examining the relationship between IT and firm performance focus primarily on the link between IT investment and firm performance. Cumulative results from early studies investigating the relationship between IT investment and performance metrics are plagued with ambiguities and inconsistencies. The early process-oriented studies include studies from Bender (1986), and Cron and Sobol (1983). Studies exploring the relationship between IT investment and firm performance continued to show inconsistent results into the late 1980s and early 1990s (Harris & Katz, 1991; Weill, 1990; Weill, 1992). For example, Weill (1992) surveys 33 small and medium-sized valve manufacturing firms regarding their IT investment and their relationship to organizational performance. Collecting data that accounted for 6 years of indicators for each company, Weill finds that transactional IT investment has a positive relationship with firm performance, that strategic IT investment has a negative relationship to firm performance, and that informational IT investment has no relationship to firm performance.

During this same time period, the results from economics-based studies matched the disappointing results from the process-oriented studies. In fact, it was the dismal results from this stream of research that prompted Roach (1988, 1991) to coin the term "productivity paradox" for the lack of evidence of positive returns from the investment in IT. For example, Loveman (1994), using data that included IT capital, non-IT capital, labor and inventory of 60 large strategic business units find that contribution from IT expenditures is actually slightly negative in his study.

Recent work on the value of IT has been much more encouraging. Research in both the process-oriented studies and the economics-based studies indicates that some of the pessimism about the value of IT that followed the results of the early studies was perhaps unwarranted. Barua, Kriebel, and Mukhopadhyoy (1995) report positive IT effects on capacity utilization and inventory turnover. Other process-oriented studies show similar positive returns on IT investment (Bharadwaj et al., 1999a; Mukhopadhyay et al., 1997).

More recent evidence from production economics research has also been positive. For example, Brynjolfsson and Hitt (1996) report huge positive returns on IT investment in analyzing data from 380 large Fortune 1000 with data that cover a five-year period from 1987-1991. Barua and Lee (1997b), using the same data as Loveman, discover that IT contributes more to firm performance than either non-IT capital or labor. Other production economics studies show similar positive findings (Hitt & Brynjolfsson, 1996; Lee & Barua, 1999; Rai et al., 1997).

The Resource-Based View and IT Performance

The RBV of the firm is one of the newer theories that is used to better understand the link between IT and firm performance. The RBV focuses on the characteristics of firm resources that are necessary to give a firm sustainable competitive advantage. Barney (1991) defines firm resources as "all assets, capabilities, organizational processes, attributes, information, and knowledge controlled by a firm that enable the firm to conceive of and implement strategies that improve its efficiency and effectiveness" (p. 101). A company enjoys a competitive advantage when firm resources enable some valuable strategies or processes that are not duplicated by competitors (Barney, 1991). A sustainable competitive advantage adds the requirement that the firm resources enabling the strategies or processes cannot be easily or quickly duplicated by competitors (Barney, 1991). Firm resources that are valuable, inimitable, scarce, or imperfectly mobile within a firm are likely to give an organization a sustainable advantage over its competitors (Barney, 1991). The use of the RBV is very well established in the strategic management literature.

The RBV has been adopted by a growing number of IT studies to serve as a theoretical foundation to better understand the relationship between IT and firm performance. Most of these studies are fairly recent, being published in the last five or six years. The general results of these studies show a positive effect of IT on different performance variables that are proxies for competitive advantage (Bharadwaj, 2000; Bhatt & Grover, 2005; Dehning et al., 2003; Kearns & Lederer, 2003; Santhanam & Hariono, 2003). Bharadwaj state that the firms that were categorized as superior performers by *InformationWeek*, a trade journal, have higher profit ratios and lower cost ratios than matched competitors not identified as such. In her article, she attributes these results to the superior IT performers having a higher IT capability than its competitors. Santhanam and Hartono extend Bharadwaj's study and find that the superior IT performers had higher profit ratios and lower cost ratios than all of the firms in their respective industry. Bhatt and Grover report that IT business experience and the ability of the IT group to understand business are positively related to measures of competitive advantage. Ravichandran and Lertwongsatien (2005) use a path model to show that IT support for core competencies positively affects return on assets and return on sales. Dehning and Stratopoulos (2003) state that superior IT managerial skills lead to a longer duration of sustained competitive advantage.

This study adds to the RBV literature by contrasting the effects of different dimensions of IT capability on several profit ratios and cost ratios used in the Bharadwaj study and in the Santhanam and Hartono study. In this way, this research builds upon these studies by examining two different dimensions of IT capability. Instead of looking only at the overall IT capability of firms, this study breaks up this capability and contrasts the effects of these different dimensions on the same ratios used in previous studies. Using these same performance measures will help in comparing the outcomes across the studies and help build a comparable research stream.

Hypotheses

From this review, it seems very clear that IT can and does impact the competitive advantage in many firms. However, it is also clear that different dimensions of IT may have different effects on firm performance in firms. Wade and Hulland (2004) divide IT capability into three dimensions: inside-out, spanning, and outside-in. Two of these, inside-out and spanning, are inspected in this study. The inside-out IT capability is "deployed from inside the firm in response to market requirements and opportunities, and tend to be internally focused (e.g., technology development, cost controls)" (p. 111). The spanning IT capability involves "both internal and external analysis and is needed to integrate the firm's inside-out and outside-in IT competences (e.g., managing IT/business partnerships, IT management and planning)" (p. 111). The outside-in IT capability, which is not investigated in this study, is "externally-oriented, placing an emphasis on anticipating market requirements, creating durable customer relationships, and understanding competitors (e.g., market responsiveness, managing external relationships)" (p. 111). The absence of outside-in IT capability in this study should not be perceived as this construct being less important than the other two. All three are important and should be studied and examined by scholars in this stream of research. However, it is likely that inside-out and spanning IT capabilities are the most prevalent in today's organizations (Tallon et al., 2000).

The combination of these dimensions has been shown to increase profit ratios and decrease cost ratios in organizations, thus possibly providing a competitive advantage (Bharadwaj, 2000; Santhanam & Hariono, 2003). Hitt, Wu, and Zhou (2002) reveal that adopters of large-scale IT resources like enterprise resource planning (ERP) software have a significant advantage over non-adopters in many firm performance measures like labor productivity, return on assets (ROA), inventory turnover, return on equity (ROE), profit margin, asset turnover, and Tobin's q.

To set a baseline for this study and to compare with the results of these previous studies, the relationships between IT capability and the firm performance measures used in these two previous studies are investigated. With these previous studies as evidence, the first two hypotheses are presented:

H1: Superior IT capability will significantly increase profit ratios.

H2: Superior IT capability will significantly decrease cost ratios.

In considering the possibility that any or all of these dimensions as expressed by Wade and Hulland can yield a competitive advantage, one must first understand what the most likely outcome from developing the capability in each of the three areas. In other words, what firm performance measures are most likely to be associated with which specific dimension of IT capability? If these associations are known, it can help firms know which IT dimension to focus more organizational resources on to get the best outcomes. For example, if a company's business strategy is centered on minimizing costs, it is best to invest more into the IT dimension that best supports that strategy.

There are likely differences in the effects of the IT dimensions as reported in Wade and Hulland. Bharadwaj, and Santhanam and Hartono use profit ratios and cost ratios as measures of firm performance. These same measures are used in this study. However, unlike Bharadwaj and Santhanam and Hartono, this study purposes that different dimensions of IT capability will have different effects on the profit ratios and the cost ratios. That is, with these two dimensions of IT capability, one will have a greater effect on profit ratios and the other will have a greater impact on cost ratios.

There is some evidence from the IT literature that different dimensions of IT capability may have effects on different performance aspects of the organization (Sethi & King, 1994; Tallon et al., 2000; Weill, 1992). It is logical to assume that the differences in inside-out IT and spanning IT may prompt differences in the impact on firm performance measures. Inside-out IT capability consists of resources such as information systems (IS) infrastructure, IS technical skills, IS development, and cost effective IS operations. The IS infrastructure is made up of telecommunications, computer hardware, complementary software such as operating systems and utilities, and organizational data quality (Byrd, 2001). The IS technical skills are associated with the skills and knowledge of the IT professionals that are appropriate for managing the existing IS infrastructure and the IT applications in a firm (Bharadwaj, 2000; Wade & Hulland, 2004). IS development is related to the development of new IT applications. It also involves the experimentation with new technologies and the ability to discover new technological trends (Wade & Hulland, 2004). The cost effective IS operations is related to the capability to "provide efficient and cost-effective IS operations on an ongoing basis" (Wade & Hulland, 2004) (p. 115). Organizations with low cost IS operations may be able to have a distinct advantage over other firms if those firms can not readily match this capability. Some of the costs related to this factor might be maintenance costs, downtime of critical IT resources, and costs of the development and implementation of IT applications, especially those that are critical to the business strategies of the firm.

Spanning IT capability in Wade and Hulland's typology consists of IS-business partnerships, IS planning, and change management. Wade and Hulland explain that these IS-business partnerships are referred to as strategic alignment (Chan et al., 1997), synergy (Bharadwaj, 2000; Javenpaa & Leidner, 1998), assimilation (Armstrong & Sambamurthy, 1999), and partnership (Bharadwaj et al., 1999b) by other researchers. IS planning and change management are components of IT managerial skills and refer to that ability to plan, manage, organize, control and direct IT resources within the firm. IT managerial skills include tasks such as establishing IT standards, managing IT-enabled change, and formulating the requirements for future change and growth.

The inside-out IT capability seems to be more related to operational efficiency. In fact, one of the factors in this construct, cost effective IS operations, by definition is associated with lower costs of a major expense item in a company, the IS operations. The immediate impact of the measures of inside-out IT capability is likely to be on the internal operations of the firm. There is ample evidence that the technologies that make up the inside-out IT capability affect operational efficiency and lower costs. Banker, Kauffman, and Morey (1990) use data envelopment analysis (DEA) to illustrate that a new cash register point-of-sale and order-coordination technology (part of a new IS infrastructure) called "Positran" helps reduce input material costs in their chain of restaurants. Byrd and Turner (2001) report that technical IT skills impact efficiency measures in their study.

The studies of Brynjolfsson and Hitt (e.g., Brynjolfsson & Hitt, 1996; Hitt & Brynjolfsson, 1996) indicate that inside-out IT capabilities have a major impact on increasing efficiency in organizations. However, there has been very little evidence that inside-out IT capability affects profitability in organizations and thus gives sustained competitive advantage. In fact, Hitt and Brynjolfsson present evidence that indicates that inside-out IT capability does not positively affect profitability measures. Similarly, Bhatt and Grover's results strengthen the belief that the quality of the inside-out IT capability is not significantly related to competitive advantage in firms. They find no evidence of a relationship between IT infrastructure and a measure of competitive advantage in the firms they surveyed.

Although these studies do seem to support the speculation of Mata, Furest, and Barney (1995) that technologies that make up inside-out IT capability do not generally impact sustained competitive advantage, these IT resources do seem to have a positive effect on organization by increasing the efficiency, thus lowering costs. Therefore, inside-out IT capability is expected to have an impact on the cost ratios but not the profit ratios. This leads to the following hypotheses:

H3: Superior inside-out IT capability will significantly decrease cost ratios.
H4: Superior inside-out IT capability will not significantly increase profit ratios.

Contrary to research of inside-out IT capability, the literature on spanning IT capability has been more encouraging on its relationship to profitability measures. Chan et al. (1997) give details of their study on the relationships between strategic alignment and profitability measures. They note a positive, but weak, link between strategic IT alignment and firm profitability in their study. Byrd, Lewis, and Bryan (2006) find evidence of a link between strategic alignment and profits as do Sabherwal and Chan (2001).

Strategic alignment should help firms focus their IT investments toward more transformative applications (Lim et al., 2004). With the business aligned with IT, companies are better able to create more innovative IT applications that can change existing business models and introduce radical new challenges for competitors. Such IT applications are often disruptive and can move entire industries from established positions. Innovators of such transformative IT applications have been shown to produce positive, abnormal profits (Dehning et al., 2003).

Strategically aligned planning efforts facilitate fast delivery of business initiatives that can lead to higher profits in organizations (Ross et al., 1996). Enterprise-wide IT planning and change management that focus on strategic business projects involve IT managers more in business strategy and processes. One common problem with IT managers in trying to deliver strategic IT resources is the difficulty of matching the IT resources with business plans because IT managers are outside the executive level in many firms and are unaware of key organization-level plans (Sabherwal, 1999). Including IT managers and their IT planning tasks as part of the overall business planning of the organization will likely eliminate this possibility. IT managers that are knowledgeable about business goals and objectives are better able to continually innovate with IT around these goals and objectives and thus keep their firms ahead of the competition (Lim et al., 2004; Sabherwal, 1999). Additionally, IT managers and business managers that are working together in close harmony will be better able to anticipate their future needs and improve strategic actions through the use of IT (Nelson & Cooprider, 1996; Reich & Benbasat, 2000). This evidence and these arguments lead to the next hypothesis.

H5: Superior spanning IT capability will significantly increase profit ratios.

The link between superior spanning IT capability and cost ratios is more uncertain. There is very little doubt that aligning IT strategy and architecture with business strategy and architecture is an expensive undertaking, one that will initially increase costs in a firm. The time needed to align and, ultimately, to integrate these organizational resources are enormous and involve highly paid members of the company. However, in the long run, these increased expenses from the planning and management of these resources may be offset by decreases in other areas of IT spending. Aligning IT with business aids in the implementation of companywide IT standards and interoperable systems that minimize redundancy and increase compatibility and connectivity. Less redundancy and more compatibility and connectivity should help reduce costs by reducing the number of standards and systems that need to be supported by the IT function. Closer alignment between IT planning and business planning should facilitate more rational investments in IT and reduce wasteful spending on IT (Henderson & Sifonis, 1988). Spending on IT resources can be more focused and centrally controlled yet still retain some flexibility within the business functions.

Although there is some reason to believe that spanning IT capability may increase costs, there seems to be more evidence that, at least in the long run, the effect of spanning IT capability will reduce costs in an organization. A multi-year view of the performance measures is taken in this study and, therefore, it is proposed that spanning IT capability will reduce the cost ratios in this study.

H6: Superior spanning IT capability will significantly decrease cost ratios.

One can conclude that from the hypotheses H3 and H5 that spanning IT capability will have a greater impact on profitability than inside-out capability. This is suggested by Wade and Hulland when they note that, generally, the spanning IT capability tends "to have somewhat greater value, be rarer (but less appropriable), be more difficult to imitate or acquire through trade, and have fewer strategic substitutes" (p. 122). Therefore:

H7: Spanning IT capability will have a greater impact on increasing profit ratios than inside-out IT capability.

On the other hand, the evidence for the greater effect on cost ratios seems to be a little more uncertain since both types of capability are expected to decrease costs. However, the evidence for inside-out IT capability is stronger than the evidence for spanning IT capability. In fact, as argued, it is not clear cut if the spanning resources will even have an effect. The evidence for the inside-out capability is strong since almost all studies that examine the effects of the resources of this capability find a positive relationship with organizational efficiency. Because of this evidence, the following hypothesis is given:

H8: Inside-out IT capability will have a greater impact on decreasing cost ratios than spanning IT capability.

Manufacturing Firms versus Service Firms

Manufacturing firms and service firms have different characteristics and may be affected by IT capability differently (Stevenson, 2005). In manufacturing firms, the output is tangible with high uniformity in both input and output. Service firms, on the other hand, have intangible output with low uniformity of both input and output. The labor content in the output of manufacturing firms is low while the labor content in service firms is high. Customer contact in manufacturing firms is low as their products are usually sold to distributors and middlemen before reaching the final customer. Service firms typically have high customer contact. The measurement of productivity and other types of evaluation is easier in manufacturing firms than services firms because the input and output are tangible. Productivity is measured by the ratio of output to input. Both of these measures are usually easier to determine in a manufacturing firm than a service firm because of the tangible nature of the input and output. The opportunity to examine and to correct problems with quality before delivery to the customer is higher in manufacturing firms than service firms (Stevenson, 2005).

There are at least two reasons that IT capability may show a greater effect on performance in the manufacturing firms in this study's sample as opposed to the service firms. First, all the firms in this sample are large firms. Manufacturing firms of this size are likely to use either mass production or mass customization in their production processes. Either type of production – think automobile manufacture or computer manufacture – will have processes that depend on computerized machines and equipment. Although these machines and equipment are extremely expensive, they also create very low unit production cost thus yielding economies of scale. The computerization in manufacturing tends to be directly involved in the production process and not depend as much on humans to act as intermediaries in delivering the output. Direct service outputs through technology such as self checkout at retail establishments and customer service through ATMs in the banking industry are growing. Yet it seems that most of the IT investment in service firms is used to support employees in delivering service outputs to customers. The use of the technology is more indirect in rendering service output and probably will not have the same impact as the more targeted technologies found in manufacturing firms.

It would also seem to be easier to plan for IT spending in manufacturing firms and align technology with the goals of the organization. Since the output is tangible and the uniformity of the input and output of manufacturing firms is relatively high compared to service firms, the uncertainty involved in IT planning and alignment with business goals should be less. Productivity measurements and evaluations are simpler in manufacturing firms making for more efficient and targeted purchases of technology. The organizational processes in manufacturing firms, which are likely technology driven, are apt to be more patentable than in service firms (Stevenson, 2005). This adds a layer of protection against duplication and can more readily be a source of sustainable competitive advantage for these types of firms. From these arguments, it would seem that IT capability would have more impact in manufacturing firms than in service firms. The characteristics of manufacturing firms seem to complement those of IT capability better than service firms. Based on these arguments, the following hypothesis is given:

H9: IT capability will have a greater impact on firm performance in manufacturing firms than in service firms.

RESEARCH METHODOLOGY

Content Validity for the IT Factors

The collection of data for this study was done before the publication of the Wade and Hulland typology for IT capability. However, the concepts associated with IT capability and IT performance has been around for more than two decades. The original intent for this study was to develop and test measures for IT capability and IT performance. Fortunately, the concepts from the investigation associated with this study fit very well into two of the dimensions of IT capability articulated by Wade and Hulland.

To develop items for the factors in the study, an extensive content analysis of IT performance literature was performed using a twenty year period. Databases that contain periodical indices in business and social science (ABI/INFORM and Wilson Social Science Directory, respectively) were searched using relevant terms (e.g., IT infrastructure) along with results oriented IT terms like information systems (IS)/IT capability, IS/IT performance, IS/IT productivity, and IS/IT success. The top IT academic journals (*Information Systems Research, MIS Quarterly, Journal of MIS, Communications of the ACM, Decision Sciences*, and *Management Science*) were reviewed specifically for years not contained in the indices. Scholarly books and monographs that had the stated criteria in their titles were also included.

Using the sources from the literature, explicit characteristics of each factor were extricated and noted. Three MIS faculty members reviewed the lists in an iterative fashion until agreement was reached on the characteristics of the factors. They were no further involved in the study. The characteristics provided the foundation for items used on the measurement instrument developed in the second round of the research methodology. The objective was to determine various aspects of each IT factor and to represent them in the questionnaire.

Pre-Test

A pre-test with seven faculty members and eight PhD students at a major university in the Southeast was performed. The participants were asked to complete the initial questionnaire and then to review and comment on both its content and appearance. The respondents' comments on the questionnaire were reviewed and appropriately consolidated into the instrument. For example, two questions were dropped from the "hardware/OS" factor because participants' comments indicated that the questions did not fit very well. The overall format was revised in line with their suggestions.

Pilot Test

Several large IT intensive companies were contacted to help pilot test the instrument. A contact person in each participating firm was asked to distribute the pilot test packet to IT managers in their firms. The pilot test packet included a cover letter explaining the research objectives, the questionnaire, and a stamped, return-addressed envelope. The IT managers included IT project managers, IT functional managers (e.g., application development, database management), and senior IT managers. Participants were asked to complete the instrument and to provide comments regarding the wording of the items, especially understandability and lack of ambiguity (Kerlinger, 1986). Additionally, the managers were asked to comment on the overall appearance and organization of the instrument.

The responses from the pilot study suggested only minor cosmetic changes. No additional questions were dropped. Since there were only minor changes suggested and with the further review of two other University faculty members, the instrument was deemed ready to be sent to a large sample to gather data to evaluate the validity and reliability of the instrument and evaluate the hypotheses. The items for each IT factor used in this paper are shown in Table 1.

Data Collection

The companies used in this study were a subset of a group of companies surveyed for a larger study. For the original, larger sample of companies, a mailing list of top computer executives was compiled from the *Directory of Top Computer Executives*. Due to the difference in profit motive for profit and non-profit firms, all public hospitals, public educational institutions, governmental agencies, and other non-profit organizations were eliminated from consideration as sample participants. For-profit firms typically have a greater incentive to optimize all of their resources including IT than non-profit or governmental firms do. Companies selected for the population also had to have 50 or more IT employees. This increased the probability that the companies would have at least a basic level of IT resources. About 3,000 companies in the Directory were qualified according to these criteria.

Once the population was decided upon, random numbers were generated for each firm and the firms were sorted in ascending numerical order. The qualified population of about 3,000 firms was divided into homogeneous strata based on industry type and placed in each type in ascending numerical order. The number of entries needed for each industry category to achieve a sample size of 1,000 firms yet maintains the population proportion of the Directory was calculated. For example, if there were 300 health services companies (one-tenth of the total population) in the population of firms, the first 100 firms (one-tenth of the total sample) in this industry were chosen for the overall sample of 1000. In this way, the ratio to total firms in the sample relative to the population was maintained

Table 1. List of items used in study (All items measured on 7-point Likert scale)

Code	ITEMS IN QUESTIONNAIRE
Heading	***The following statements describe the efficiency with which the information technology development and operations process use assigned resources (equipment, staff, materials, money) to provide information technology to your firm. Please CIRCLE THE NUMBER that best reflects the degree to which you disagree or agree with each statement.***
	(HDO: Hardware and Operating Systems)
HDO1	Hardware and operating systems are available for use 24 hours per day, 7 days a week.
HDO2	Hardware and operating systems response time are adequate to keep users satisfied.
HDO3	Hardware and operating systems exhibit high degree of reliability.
HDO4	Hardware and operating systems uptime are comparable to available user time.
	(COM: Communication Systems)
COM1	Communications systems are available for use 24 hours per day, 7 days a week.
COM2	Communications systems response times are adequate to keep users satisfied.
COM3	Communications systems exhibit high degrees of reliability.
COM4	Communications systems uptimes are comparable to available user time.
	(CEF: Cost Efficient Operations)
CEF1	Development budget cost goals are met.
CEF2	Operating budget goals are met.
CEF3	Development projects are completed on time.
	(BAI: Business Application Integration)
BAI1	Business applications software is readily available to users.
BAI2	Business applications software is integrated across all functional areas within the business unit to enable data exchange.
BAI3	Data is fully integrated between business applications.
BAI4	Communications systems are integrated (data/text/image/video) to enable efficient internal organizational interactions.
Heading	***The following statements describe those characteristics of information produced by information technology that potentially impact on decision making in your firm. CIRCLE THE NUMBER that best reflects the degree to which you disagree or agree with each statement.***
	(DAQ: Data Quality)
DAQ1	Users receive reports in a timely manner.
DAQ2	Users receive accurate information output.
DAQ3	Users receive current information output.
DAQ4	Users receive complete (thorough) information output.
DAQ5	Users receive reliable information output.
DAQ6	Users receive relevant information output.
DAQ7	Data integrity is maintained throughout the organization.
Heading	***The following statements refer to your information technology department's activities and how they compare to those of key competitors. Please CIRCLE THE NUMBER that best describes how your information technology compares with your firm's competitors regarding:***
	(ITD: IT Technical Skills and Development)
ITD1	Hardware and operating systems performance
ITD2	Business applications software performance
ITD3	Communications services efficiency
ITD4	Communications services performance

continued on following page

Table 1. continued

ITD5	Applications development cycle time
ITD6	End user support
ITD7	Information technology investments and expenditures
ITD8	Software maintenance efficiency
Heading	***The following statements describe the extent to which information technology contributes to facilitating your firm's achievement of its goals. Please CIRCLE THE NUMBER that best reflects the extent to which you disagree or agree with each statement.***
	(ITP: Information Technology Planning and Change)
ITP1	Information technology department's planning supports your firm's ability to keep up with changing technology.
ITP2	Long-term data infrastructure plans exist and are followed.
ITP3	Long-term network infrastructure plans exist and are followed.
ITP4	Long-term strategy plans ensuring adequacy of enterprise-wide processing capabilities exist and are followed.
ITP5	Information technology's services evolve to meet your firm's changing needs and capabilities.
Heading	***The following statements refer to the extent to which the information technology department's plans and objectives are aligned with your firm's business objectives and strategy. Please CIRCLE THE NUMBER that best describes how well the information technology department is aligned with the firm regarding:***
	(STA: Strategic Alignment)
STA1	Alignment between the information technology department's strategic plan and your firm's business strategic plan.
STA2	Range of products and services your information technology department delivers to your firm.
STA3	Alignment between information technology investments and expenditures and business objectives and priorities.
STA4	Allocation of resources between existing systems and new systems to reflect the firm's business objectives.
STA5	Integration of information technology in production planning and control.

HDO, COM, CEF, INT, DAQ, and ITP anchored on 7-point Likert scale from "Strongly Disagree" to "Strongly Agree."
ITD anchored on 7-point Likert scale from "Very Inferior to" to "Equal to" to "Very Superior to."
STA anchored on 7-point Likert scale from "Not Well Aligned" to "Very Well Aligned."
Note: The label for each factor (e.g., HDO) was not a part of the questionnaire. They are used here to define the acronyms.

for every industry. Thus, a proportional, stratified random sample of fairly large, for-profit firms was developed and utilized.

Three mailings of the research instrument were made to the companies with each about a month apart. The individual at each firm designated as the top IT executive was targeted as the questionnaire recipient. As Segars and Grover (1998) determined in their study on similar IT organizational resources, the top IT executive is the most knowledgeable individual in the company to give aggregate information about the IT resources at this level of analysis. The use of the top IT executive as the key informant to report on organizational IT resources in a survey is commonplace in the IT literature.

A total of 225 completed questionnaires were returned from the three mailings, approximately a third of the total from each mailing. This resulted in a response rate of 22.5% of the original 1000 firms targeted. Chi-square analysis of the industry distribution of the respondents showed no difference from the industry distribution of the sample and the population (which was the same as explained in the preceding paragraph). The respondents were divided into three groups based on the time that the questionnaires were received. Since the respondents fell into three fairly equal groups based on their response to the first, second, or third mailing, this was relatively easy to do. ANOVA analysis showed no difference among the three groups on any of the IT factors used in the study and on size. These Chi-square and ANOVA tests suggest the absence of response bias in the returned questionnaires relative to the overall sample.

Sub-Sample of Respondents in COMPUSTAT

Of the 225 responding organizations in this survey, 104 of the companies were found in the COMPUSTAT database. The COMPUSTAT database carries financial data for a 20-year period on many of the publicly traded companies in the United States. Of the 104 companies, financial data on 94 companies (the other had data that were marked as NA or not available) were found. The same eight measures from COMPUSTAT that were used in Bharadwaj (2000) and Santhanam and Hartono (2003) were also used in this study. These measures were:

Profit Ratios: Return on Sales (ROS), ROA, operating income to assets (OI/A), operating income to sales (OI/S), and operating income to employees (OI/E).

Cost Ratios: Cost of goods sold to sales (COGS/S), selling and general administration expenses to sales (SGA/S), and operating expenses to sales (OPEXP/S).

These measures are chosen to facilitate comparison with the stated past research on IT capability. Such comparisons help researchers to continually build a stream of research and promote the building of a knowledge base in that stream. Additionally, these measures are commonly used in strategic studies in several different research disciplines such as management (e.g., Huselid, 1995) and operations management (e.g., Mohrman et al., 1995).

The data for this survey were collected in 1998. Each performance measure used in this study represents the average of that measure over a three-year time period from 1998 to 2000 taken from the COMPUSTAT database. Wade and Hulland discuss the importance of considering extended time periods in RBV studies. Although the IT data were taken only at a single point in time (in 1998), there is ample evidence that IT resources like spanning IT and inside-out IT are not likely to change quickly (Brynjolfsson et al., 1994; Wade & Hulland, 2004; Weill et al., 2002). Piccoli and Ives (2005) proclaim that IT infrastructure, an inside-out IT resource, is likely to have a five to seven year development time. Cross, Earl, and Sampler (1997) follow British Petroleum for six years as the company changed its IT department from one with characteristics that were associated with low capability to one with characteristics that were typically associated with high capability. This transformation was not immediate but happened slowly over the six year period. Harkness, Kettinger, and Segars (1996) report on an even longer transformation of IT resources at Bose Corporation from 1985 to 1995, a ten year period, as the firm moved from functional processes to cross functional processes. From these studies, one can easily see that IT capabilities simply do not change very quickly. Therefore, although the IT data were collected only once, it is likely that the levels of these IT resources were consistent over at least the next two to three years. Additionally, the effects of current IT resources are likely to have effects for at least the next two to three years (Brynjolfsson et al., 1994).

The three-year average measures of the 94 companies were standardized by using competitors in the same respective four-digit SIC industry code as each of the companies in the COMPUSTAT set for the time period of 1998-2000. A z-score was calculated for each company using the other companies in that company's industry as references to determine how well each company in this set performed within its own industry over the three year period for each of the performance ratio. The use of four-digit SIC codes is well accepted in organizational studies as a way to standardize for industry effects (e.g., Byrd & Marshall, 1997).

Table 2. Characteristics of study sample

Characteristics of the Respondent	Sub-Sample in COMPUSTAT
I. Average number of years worked in the company	14.5
A. Job Title:	
Chief Information Officer	41.5%
Information Services Director	43.6%
Other	14.9%
III. Characteristics of the Company	
A. Number of Employees	
Between 251 and 1,000	3.2%
Between 1,000 to 5,000	35.1%
Over 5,000	61.7%
B. Gross Revenue (in millions)	
$50 to $250	6.2%
$251 to $500	11.7%
$501 to $1,000	19.3%
Over $1,000	62.8%
C. Industry Group	
Manufacturing	34.0%
Insurance	5.3%
Health Services	4.3%
Financial	9.6%
Retail/Wholesale	13.8%
Utilities	2.1%
Other	26.6%

Wade and Hulland note that in past IT value studies using performance ratios, there was no sense of comparativeness. They state that the performances of companies need to be compared relative to their competitors. For example, take a company, XCOMP, that has a three-year average ROA of 20% and another company, YCOMP, which has a three-year average ROA of 10%. If the raw numbers are examined, it looks as if XCOMP is outperforming YCOMP. However, if the ROAs of the competitors in XCOMP's industry are growing at a three-year average of 80% and the ROAs of the competitors in YCOMP's industry are growing at a three-year average of 5%, it appears now that YCOMP is the better performer over that time period. By producing z-scores that indicate how companies are performing compared to their competitors, a "richer and more complete" picture of true performance is established.

To examine any difference between the set of companies found in COMPUSTAT and the responding companies not in COMPUSTAT, an ANOVA was performed comparing the COMPUSTAT set of companies (94 companies) with the set of companies that were not used found in COMPUSTAT (131 companies) using each IT factor (e.g., hardware/OS, data quality) as the criterion variable. There is no statistical difference between the two sets of companies on any of the IT measures (p-values from.128 to.728).

There is, however, a difference between the size of the COMPUSTAT set and the remaining set of companies on both sales and number of employees (p-values.026 and.032, respectively). From this analysis, it can be determined that the firms in the sub-sample (COMPUSTAT) group are significantly larger than the set of companies not found in COMPUSTAT.

The demographics for the sample of 94 firms used in this study are presented in Table 2. The Chief Information Officer (CIO) or the Information Services Director (ISD) completed 85% of the survey questionnaires. Other respondents identified themselves as vice presidents of IT, vice presidents of information systems, general managers of IT, and global vice presidents of information services. More than 62% of the firms had at least $1 billion in sales with a similar percentage of companies employing more than 5,000 people. The sample consisted of 34% manufacturing firms, 14% retail/wholesale firms, 10% financial firms, and about 5% insurance companies, with lower percentages of other types of firms.

The companies were classified into manufacturing firms or service firms from the responses to a question about the primary business activity of the company. Using these responses, 32 firms were categorized as manufacturing and 38 as service. The designation for the industry type for the other firms in the sample was either not given or did not fall neatly into either category.

RESULTS

There are eight factors in the two set of IT resources. The inside-out IT resources consist of hardware/OS quality (HDO), communications systems quality (COM), cost efficient operations (CEF), IT technical skills and development (ITD), business application integration (BAI) and data quality (DAQ). The spanning IT resources are made up of IT planning and change (ITP), and strategic alignment (STA).

Reliability

The reliabilities of all the measures are good with values well over.70 for all the measures with many in the.8 and.9 ranges. Reliability is "the degree to which the observed measures the 'true' value and is 'error-free' (Hair et al., 1994, p. 9). For example, if the same metrics are asked repeatedly, the more reliable measures will be more consistent (Hair et al., 1994). Reliability was measured using Cronbach's alpha.

Convergent Validity and Discriminant Validity

Convergent validity and discriminant validity was evaluated with five different methods. The PLS confirmatory analysis yields loadings for all the measures. All of the loadings for the items on their respective latent variables are above the threshold of.7 except for two instances. One item for Business Integration is at.67 and one item for IT Technical Skills and Development is at.67. Both are close enough to.7 to remain as part of the latent variable. Second, the average variance explained (AVE) for each of the latent variables is greater than.5: Hardware and Operating Systems (AVE=.66); Communication Systems (AVE=.77); Cost Efficient Operations (AVE =.76); Business Application Integration (AVE =.69); Data Quality (AVE =.72); IT Technical Skills and Development (AVE =.51); Information Technology Planning and Change (AVE =.75) and Strategic Alignment (AVE =.71). Third, all of the AVEs for these latent variables are greater than any of the cross-correlations. Fourth, all of the correlations between the latent variables are also well below the.9 threshold. This suggests that all of these latent variables are distinct from each other. Fifth, an exploratory factor analysis was performed on all of the items. The items load on their respective latent variables with very little cross-loadings. In the few cases of cross-loadings, the loadings on the items for the expected latent variables are always

Figure 2. The relationship model tested in this study

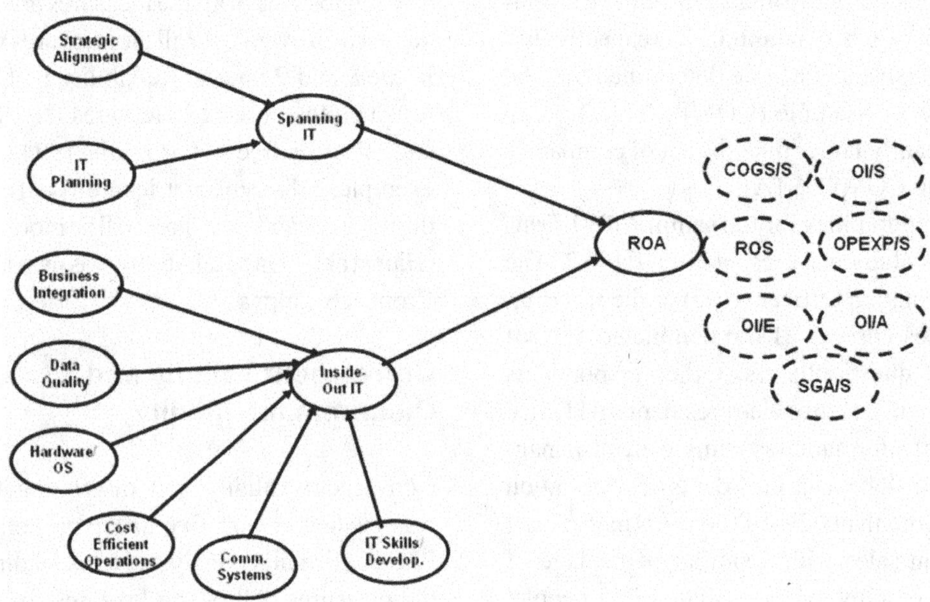

higher than any other loadings. These five tests suggest that the data exhibit adequate convergent validity and discriminant validity.

Results of Hypothesis Testing

The relationship models were evaluated using Partial Least Squares (PLS). PLS is ideal for small sample sizes like the ones in this study (Chin, 1998). A PLS run was done for each performance measure as the dependent variable and both dimensions of capability as the independent variables (see Figure 2). The same procedure was used for manufacturing and service firm groups. In PLS, the statistical significance of the paths was determined by using bootstrap resampling. Two runs of 1000 resamples for each of the models were completed. The significance level used is.05.

In the PLS models, both inside-out IT capability and spanning IT capability are modeled as second-order formative constructs. These were modeled as formative variables because the first order factors are not expected to co-vary together. The relationship models were also run with the IT measures as reflective variables to see if the relationships between IT and the ratios varied. The relationships did not change substantially. This technique is also used in Chwelos, Benbasat, and Dexter (2001). To test H1 and H2, the two IT capability measures were combined into a formative third-order factor of IT capability. This third-order factor was set up as a formative measure because the inside-out and spanning measures are not expected to co-vary. The results of all the model runs are shown in Table 3.

To make the outcomes for the hypotheses easier to determine and to evaluate, the results from the PLS model runs are presented in Table 4. The results of the PLS runs for H1 and H2 generally support the hypotheses that higher IT capability is related to higher profit ratios and lower cost ratios. The only measure that was not significant was COGS/S. H3 and H4 are supported as inside-out IT capability is significantly related to two of the three cost ratios but is not with any of the profit ratios. H5 is supported since

Table 3. Relationship Indicators and R^2 Values

ALL FIRMS IN THE SAMPLE								
	ROA	ROS	OI/E	OI/S	OI/A	OPEXP/S	COGS/S	SGA/S
Both IT	.36*	.31*	.26*	.43*	.26*	-.45*	-.04	-.22*
R^2	.13	.10	.08	.19	.09	.20	.02	.09
Spanning	.40*	.24*	.25*	.31*	.18	-.16	.24*	.14
Inside-out	-.05	-.01	.01	.03	.15	-.32*	.19	-.39*
R^2	.16	.10	.08	.19	.10	.20	.03	.10
MANUFACTURING FIRMS IN THE SAMPLE								
	ROA	ROS	OI/E	OI/S	OI/A	OPEXP/S	COGS/S	SGA/S
Spanning	.40*	.61*	.36*	.17	-.01	.05	.04	.15
Inside-out	.11	-.12	.10	.46*	.31*	-.71*	-.15	-.50*
R^2	.24	.27	.20	.36	.15	.45	.02	.15
SERVICE FIRMS IN THE SAMPLE								
Spanning	.34*	-.02	.26*	.35*	.25*	-.23	-.52*	.40*
Inside-Out	-.06	.11	-.08	.07	.03	-.18	.50*	-.65*
R^2	.10	.03	.05	.16	.08	.14	.15	.22
Cohen's f^2	.15	.25	.16	.24	.08	.36	.13	.09

spanning IT capability was significantly related to all of the profit ratios except OI/A. H6 is not generally supported since spanning IT is significantly related to only COGS/S and not with OPEXP/S and SGA/S. Since spanning IT is related to most of the profit ratios and inside-out IT was not, H7 is supported because of the higher impact of spanning IT on profitability. From the results, inside-out IT capability has the greater impact on the cost ratios thus supporting H8.

The effects of IT capability seem to be more profound in manufacturing firms with the results of the PLS runs for the manufacturing firms and the service firms. Spanning IT capability has much greater impact in manufacturing firms according to the R^2's that are generated in the runs. Although

Table 4. Summary of support for the hypotheses in the study

Hypothesis	Support
H1: Superior IT capability will significantly increase profit ratios.	Supported
H2: Superior IT capability will significantly decrease cost ratios.	Supported
H3: Superior inside-out IT capability will significantly decrease cost ratios.	Supported
H4: Superior inside-out IT capability will not significantly increase profit ratios.	Supported
H5: Superior spanning IT capability will significantly increase profit ratios.	Supported
H6. Superior spanning IT capability will significantly decrease cost ratios.	Supported
H7: Spanning IT capability will have a greater impact on increasing profit ratios than inside-out capability.	Supported
H8: Inside-out capability will have a greater impact on decreasing cost ratios than spanning IT capability.	Supported
H9: IT capability will have a greater impact on firm performance in manufacturing firms than in service firm.	Supported

the spanning IT capability is generally significant for the profit ratios in both types of firms, the R^2 values in the manufacturing firms are much greater. The outcome for the cost ratios are mixed between the two types of firms although the greater impact is tilted toward the manufacturing firms.

To more formally evaluate the differences between the relationships of IT capability and the firm performance measures in this study, Cohen f^2 was calculated. The results in Table 4 confirm the observations in the paragraph above. For the profitability measures, effect sizes are medium to large for the relationships thus supporting a difference in manufacturing and service firms. The effect size for the total expense measure is large again supporting a difference between the two types of firms. From these results, H9 is supported.

DISCUSSION

This study is grounded in the RBV framework. The purpose of this study is to examine the value of two dimensions of IT capability that are identified by Wade and Hulland as possibly impacting firm performance. Additionally, the study investigates how the type of firm may influence the relationship between the IT capability and firm performance. A distinctive contribution of this paper is to break IT capability down into two different dimensions according to an accepted typology and compare these types in their relationships with measures of firm performance. The study also reveals how the type of firms, for example, manufacturing or service, may alter these relationships. Previous IT capability studies have not compared these differences pertaining to the specific type of firm.

First, to establish a baseline for other aspects of this study, the effects of IT capability on firm performance measures are examined. The findings here are similar to those in Bharadwaj and Santhanam and Hartono. IT capability has a significantly positive impact on profit ratios and a significantly negative impact on cost ratios, similar to those found in these two previous studies. In these two previous studies, IT capability is measured indirectly by utilizing companies that have been rated as IT leaders by *InformationWeek* and comparing them to companies not in the list but in the same respective industry as each of the leaders. Both of these papers made solid contributions to the IT value literature using the RBV framework. However, as Santhanam and Hartono note, to continue progress in this crucial area, standardized measures must be developed and utilized. They state "such a measure could provide a systematic and theoretically derived multidimensional assessment of a firm's IT capability" (p. 151). This study contributes to the IT value literature by answering this call and developing preliminary measures for two dimensions of IT capability, spanning IT capability and inside-out IT capability.

This study illustrates the importance of considering IT dimensions in investigating its relationship with firm performance. The inside-out IT capability has a significant impact on cost but not generally on the profits. On the other hand, spanning IT capability has a significant impact on profits but not generally on cost (except the COGS/S). This finding is key because it helps researchers and practitioners to understand that the focus of IT investment should be targeted on a specific dimension of capability if a particular outcome is highly desired. For example, a company that is interested in reducing costs must focus a major portion of its IT investment on inside-out IT capability. This does not mean that this company can simply ignore spanning IT capability but it does mean that an extra emphasis must be placed on the inside-out IT capability if a goal of lower costs is a priority.

Wade and Hulland propose that spanning IT capability may yield more of sustained competitive advantage than inside-out IT capability. In their argument, they suggest that spanning IT capability is more difficult to duplicate than inside-out IT capability and will therefore yield a greater, and perhaps longer, competitive advantage. This proposition seems to be confirmed by the results in this study. Spanning IT capability has its greater impact on the profits of the firm which are more important in the long run than just reducing costs. Competitive advantage is usually related more to sustained profits in a firm than to lowering costs. Higher profits can result from reducing costs but are more likely sustained by expanding existing markets and exploring new ones. It would seem that spanning IT capability has a greater impact on these types of organizational capabilities than inside-out IT and would result in a better chance for competitive advantage.

The impact of IT capability in manufacturing firms is greater than the impact in service firms according to these results. This is a fairly unexplored area of research in IT value. After searching the major journals, no studies comparing the impact of different dimensions of IT capability in manufacturing firms to the impact in service firms were discovered. The characteristics of manufacturing firms may be more congruent with those of existing IT than the characteristics of service firms. In manufacturing firms, IT has been more directly involved with the critical processes of these organizations, that is, manufacturing products. Many of these processes do not involve human participation because automation in these firms shoulders the majority of the production processes. The manufacture of a tangible product also allows more certainty in planning and aligning business and technology. The results of this study support this notion since the spanning IT capability in manufacturing firms has greater impact on the very important profit ratios than in service firms.

Managers in service firms can likely learn something from these results. Although their output from their operations may be intangible, managers in service firms should try to better standardize their organizational processes and make better use of IT to increase its impact. Gaining more knowledge about organizational processes and capabilities should also help in planning for IT and aligning these processes and capabilities with IT. Good management should be combined with IT capability to give optimal results (Banker et al., 2006). This seems extremely important in service firms where the link between IT and organizational processes and capabilities may not be as obvious as in manufacturing firms.

LIMITATIONS AND FUTURE RESEARCH

Like all studies examining complex organizational phenomena, this study had several limitations. The first is that the data for the study were collected prior to the publication of the IT capability typology by Wade and Hulland. The data were mapped into two of the dimensions instead of developed directly from the typology itself. Although the original intent of both this investigation and Wade and Hulland seem to be congruent, once could still argue that the data were "forced" into the typology. However, the concepts and measures seem to match very well especially for an initial empirical examination of this phenomenon using multidimensional factors. Future studies should, of course, improve upon these measures by using the Wade and Hulland typology more directly.

The sample consists of very large US corporations, generally members of the Fortune 2000. Therefore, it may be difficult to generalize the results here to small and medium sized firms. In the same way, it may be problematic to generalize the findings to exclusively foreign corporations, large or small. Finally, on the same note, the findings may not apply to large or small public organizations. Future researchers should create samples using these types of firms in their research projects and compare their findings with the ones here.

Future Research

The one omission from this study is a construct for the outside-in IT resources. Of course, the creation of a measure for this construct should be the starting point in any future research studies investigating IT resources using the RBV, along with improving the measures used in this study as indicated earlier. The development and examination of a measure for outside-in IT resources would complete the typology that Wade and Hulland promote. The results of a survey using the outside-in IT resources combined with the spanning IT resources and inside-out IT resources introduced in this study would allow for a fuller evaluation of IT capability and its relative value.

The measures for IT capability could be used to assess the state of IT in organizations periodically over some time frame in longitudinal studies. This study provided some evidence that IT capability does have an effect over at least a three year time period. A better way to gauge the extended effect of IT resources is to collect data every three or four years in the same organizations and analyze how the relationships between IT and firm performance have changed over time. This type of analysis would give a clearer and more robust picture where more knowledge will be created.

The sample sizes for the analyses for the different types of organizations, entrepreneurial, formal, manufacturing, and service, were relatively small. However, PLS is a fairly robust analysis tool and typically can handle samples sizes smaller than the ones used in this study (Majchrzak et al., 2005). Future researchers should examine these relationships with larger sample sizes to confirm the findings in this study.

CONCLUSION

This study confirms the work of Bharadwaj, and Santhanam and Hartono in showing that IT capability can lead to better performance in firms and be a source of competitive advantage. In addition to the information given in these previous studies, empirical evidence presented in this study reveals that different dimensions of IT capability will have different effects on performance measures used. The results demonstrate that inside-out IT capability had its greater effects on costs while spanning IT capability has its greater impact on profits. Furthermore, this study illustrates how IT capability can have different impacts in diverse types of organizations. For example, the impact of IT capability was significantly more influential in manufacturing firms than in service firms. This demonstrates that researchers must be aware that the types of firm can make a difference when trying to determine the value of IT capability in future studies.

REFERENCES

Armstrong, C. P., & Sambamurthy, V. (1999). Information Technology Assimilation in Firms: The Influence of Senior Leadership and IT Infrastructures. *Information Systems Research*, *10*(4), 304–327. doi:10.1287/isre.10.4.304

Banker, R. D., Bardham, I. R., Chang, H., & Lin, S. (2006). Plant Information Systems, Manufacturing Capabilities, and Plant Performance. *Management Information Systems Quarterly*, *30*(2), 315–337.

Banker, R. D., Kauffman, R. C., & Morey, R. C. (1990). Measuring Gains in Operational Efficiency from Information Technology: A Study of the Positran Deployment at Hardee's Inc. *Journal of Management Information Systems*, *7*(2), 29–54.

Barney, J. B. (1991). Firm Resources and Sustained Competitive Advantage. *Journal of Management*, *17*(1), 99–120. doi:10.1177/014920639101700108

Barney, J. B. (2001). Is the Resource-Based View a Useful Perspective for Strategic Management Research? Yes. *Academy of Management Journal*, *26*(1), 41–56. doi:10.2307/259393

Barua, A., Kriebel, C. H., & Mukhopadhyay, T. (1995). Information Technologies and Business Value - an Analytic and Empirical-Investigation. *Information Systems Research*, *6*(1), 3–23. doi:10.1287/isre.6.1.3

Barua, A., & Lee, B. (1997a). An Economic Analysis of the Introduction of an Electronic Data Interchange System. *Information Systems Research*, *8*(4), 398–422. doi:10.1287/isre.8.4.398

Barua, A., & Lee, B. (1997b). The Information Technology Productivity Paradox Revisited: A Theoretical and Empirical Investigation in the Manufacturing Sector. *International Journal of Flexible Manufacturing Systems*, *9*(2), 145–166. doi:10.1023/A:1007967718214

Barua, A., & Mukhopadhyay, T. (2000). Information Technology and Business Performance: Past, Present, and Future. In Zmud, R. W. (Ed.), *Framing the Domains of IT Management: Projecting the Future through the Past* (pp. 65–84). Cincinnati, OH: Pinnaflex Educational Resources, Inc.

Bender, D. H. (1986). Financial Impact of Information Processing. *Journal of Management Information Systems*, *3*(2), 22–32.

Bharadwaj, A. S. (2000). A Resource-Based Perspective on Information Technology Capability and Firm Performance: An Empirical Investigation. *Management Information Systems Quarterly*, *24*(1), 169–196. doi:10.2307/3250983

Bharadwaj, A. S., Bharadwaj, S. G., & Konsynski, B. R. (1999a). Information Technology Effects on Firm Performance as Measured by Tobin's q. *Management Science*, *45*(7), 1008–1024. doi:10.1287/mnsc.45.7.1008

Bharadwaj, A. S., Sambamurthy, V., & Zmud, R. W. (1999b). IT Capabilities: Theoretical Perspectives and Empirical Operationalization. In *Proceedings of the 20th International Conference on Information Systems*, Charlotte, NC (pp. 378-385).

Bhatt, G. D., & Grover, V. (2005). Type of Information Technology Capabilities and Their Role in Competitive Advantage: An Empirical Study. *Journal of Management Information Systems*, *22*(2), 253–277.

Brynjolfsson, E., & Hitt, L. (1996). Paradox Lost? Firm-level Evidence on the Returns to Information Systems Spending. *Management Science*, *42*(4), 541–558. doi:10.1287/mnsc.42.4.541

Brynjolfsson, E., Malone, T. W., Gurbaxani, V., & Kambil, A. (1994). Does Information Technology Lead to Smaller Firms. *Management Science*, *40*(12), 1628–1644. doi:10.1287/mnsc.40.12.1628

Byrd, T. A. (2001). Information Technology, Core Competencies, and Sustained Competitive Advantage. *Information Resources Management Journal*, *14*(2), 27–36.

Byrd, T. A., Lewis, B. R., & Bryan, R. W. (2006). The Leveraging Influence of Strategic Alignment on IT Investment: An Empirical Examination. *Information & Management*, *43*(3), 308–321. doi:10.1016/j.im.2005.07.002

Byrd, T. A., & Marshall, T. E. (1997). Relating Information Technology Investment to Organizational Performance: A Causal Model Analysis. *Omega-International Journal of Management Science*, *25*(1), 43–56. doi:10.1016/S0305-0483(96)00040-0

Byrd, T. A., & Turner, D. E. (2001). An Exploratory Analysis of the Value of the Skills of IT Personnel: Their Relationship to IS Infrastructure and Competitive Advantage. *Decision Sciences*, *32*(1), 21–54. doi:10.1111/j.1540-5915.2001.tb00952.x

Carr, N. G. (2003). IT Doesn't Matter. *Harvard Business Review*, *81*(5), 41–49.

Chan, Y. E., Huff, S. L., Copeland, D. G., & Barclay, D. W. (1997). Business Strategic Orientation, Information Systems Strategic Orientation and Strategic Alignment. *Information Systems Research*, *8*(2), 125–150. doi:10.1287/isre.8.2.125

Chin, W. W. (1998). The Partial Least Squares Approach to Structural Equation Modeling. In Marcoulides, G. A. (Ed.), *Modern Methods for Business Research* (pp. 295–336). London: Lawrence Erlbaum.

Chwelos, P., Benbasat, I., & Dexter, A. S. (2001). Research Report: Empirical Test of an EDI Adoption Model. *Information Systems Research, 12*(3), 304–321. doi:10.1287/isre.12.3.304.9708

Clemons, E. K., & Row, M. C. (1991). Sustaining IT Advantage: The Role of Structural Differences. *Management Information Systems Quarterly, 15*(3), 275–292. doi:10.2307/249639

Cron, W. L., & Sobol, M. G. (1983). The Relationship Between Computerization and Performance: A Strategy for Maximizing the Economic Benefits of Computerization. *Information & Management, 6*, 171–181. doi:10.1016/0378-7206(83)90034-4

Cross, J., Earl, M. J., & Sampler, J. (1997). Transformation of the IT Function at British Petroleum. *Management Information Systems Quarterly, 21*(4), 401–423. doi:10.2307/249721

Dehning, B., Richardson, V. J., & Zmud, R. W. (2003). The Value Relevance of Announcements of Transformational Information Technology Investments. *Management Information Systems Quarterly, 27*(4), 637–656.

Hair, J. F., Anderson, J. C., Tatham, R. L., & Black, W. C. (1994). *Multivariate Data Analysis*. Upper Saddle River, NJ: Prentice Hall.

Harkness, W. L., Kettinger, W. J., & Segars, A. H. (1996). Sustaining Process Improvement and Innovation in the Information Services Function: Lessons Learned at the Bose Corporation. *Management Information Systems Quarterly, 20*(3), 349–368. doi:10.2307/249661

Harris, S. E., & Katz, J. L. (1991). Organizational Performance and IT Investment Intensity in the Insurance. *Organization Science, 2*(3), 263–295. doi:10.1287/orsc.2.3.263

Henderson, J. C., & Sifonis, J. G. (1988). The Value of Strategic IS Planning: Understanding Consistency, Validity, and IS Markets. *Management Information Systems Quarterly, 12*(2), 187–200. doi:10.2307/248843

Hitt, L. M., & Brynjolfsson, E. (1996). Productivity, Business Profitability, and Consumer Surplus: Three Different Measures of Information Technology Value. *Management Information Systems Quarterly, 20*(2), 121–142. doi:10.2307/249475

Hitt, L. M., Wu, D. J., & Zhou, X. (2002). Investment in Enterprise Resource Planning: Business Impact and Productivity Measures. *Journal of Management Information Systems, 19*(1), 71–98.

Huselid, M. A. (1995). The Impact of Human Resource Management Practices on Turnover, Productivity, and Corporate Financial Performance. *Academy of Management Journal, 38*(3), 635–672. doi:10.2307/256741

Javenpaa, S. L., & Leidner, D. E. (1998). An Information Company in Mexico: Extending the Resource-Based View of the Firm to A Developing Country Context. *Information Systems Research, 9*(4), 342–361. doi:10.1287/isre.9.4.342

Kearns, G. S., & Lederer, A. L. (2003). A Resource-Based View of Strategic Alignment: How Knowledge Sharing Creates Competitive Advantage. *Decision Sciences, 34*(1), 1–26. doi:10.1111/1540-5915.02289

Kerlinger, F. N. (1986). *Foundations of Behavioral Research*. New York: Harcourt Brace Jovanovich.

Kettinger, W. J., Grover, V., Subashish, A. H., & Segars, A. H. (1994). Strategic Information Systems Revisited: A Study in Sustainability and Performance. *Management Information Systems Quarterly, 12*(3), 31–58. doi:10.2307/249609

King, W. R., Grover, V., & Hufnagel, E. H. (1989). Using Information and Information Technology for Sustainable Competitive Advantage: Some Empirical Evidence. *Information & Management, 17*, 87–93. doi:10.1016/0378-7206(89)90010-4

Lee, B., & Barua, A. (1999). An Integrated Assessment of Productivity and Efficiency Impacts of Information Technology Investments: Old Data, New Analysis and Evidence. *Journal of Productivity Analysis*, *12*(1), 21–43. doi:10.1023/A:1007898906629

Lim, J. H., Richardson, V. J., & Roberts, T. L. (2004). Information Technology Investment and Firm Performance: A Meta-Analysis. In *Proceedings of the Thirty-Seventh Hawaii International Conference on System Sciences*, HI (pp. 1-10).

Loveman, G. W. (1994). An Assessment of the Productivity Impact of the Information Technologies. In Allen, T. J., & Scott Morton, M. S. (Eds.), *Information Technology and the Corporation of the 1990's: Research Studies* (pp. 84–110). New York: Oxford University Press.

Majchrzak, A., Beath, C. M., Ricardo, L., & Chin, W. W. (2005). Managing Client Dialogues During Information Systems Design to Facilitate Client Learning. *Management Information Systems Quarterly*, *29*(4), 653–672.

Mata, F. J., Fuerst, W. L., & Barney, J. B. (1995). Information Technology and Sustained Competitive Advantage: A Resource-Based Analysis. *Management Information Systems Quarterly*, *19*(4), 487–505. doi:10.2307/249630

Melville, N., Kraemer, K., & Gurbaxani, V. (2004). Information Technology and Organizational Performance: An Integrative Model of IT Business Value. *Management Information Systems Quarterly*, *28*(2), 283–321.

Menon, N. M., Lee, B., & Eldenburg, L. (2000). Productivity of Information Systems in the Healthcare Industry. *Information Systems Research*, *11*(1), 83–92. doi:10.1287/isre.11.1.83.11784

Mohrman, S. A., Tenkasi, R. V., Lawler, E. E. III, & Ledford, J. G. G. (1995). Total Quality Management: Practice and Outcomes in the Largest US Firms. *Employee Relations*, *17*(3), 26–41. doi:10.1108/01425459510086866

Mukhopadhyay, T., Lerch, F. J., & Mangal, V. (1997). Assessing the Impact of Information Technology on Labor Productivity: A Field Study. *Decision Support Systems*, *19*(2), 109–122. doi:10.1016/S0167-9236(96)00044-9

Nelson, K. M., & Cooprider, J. G. (1996). The Contribution of Shared Knowledge to IS Group Performance. *Management Information Systems Quarterly*, *20*(4), 409–429. doi:10.2307/249562

Neo, B. S. (1988). Factors Facilitating the Use of Information Technology for Competitive Advantage: An Exploratory Study. *Information & Management*, *15*(4), 191–201. doi:10.1016/0378-7206(88)90045-6

Piccoli, G., & Ives, B. (2005). Review: IT-Dependent Strategic Initiatives and Sustained Competitive Advantage: A Review and Synthesis of the Literature. *Management Information Systems Quarterly*, *29*(4), 747–776.

Porter, M. E., & Millar, V. E. (1985). How Information Gives You Competitive Advantage. *Harvard Business Review*, *64*(4), 149–160.

Rai, A., Patnayakuni, R., & Patnayakuni, N. (1997). Technology investment and business performance. *Communications of the ACM*, *40*(7), 89–97. doi:10.1145/256175.256191

Ravichandran, T., & Lertwongsatien, C. (2005). Effect of Information Systems Resources and Capabilities on Firm Performance: A Resource-Based Perspective. *Journal of Management Information Systems*, *21*(4), 237–276.

Reich, B. H., & Benbasat, I. (1990). An Empirical Investigation of Factors Influencing the Success of Customer-Oriented Strategic Systems. *Information Systems Research*, *1*(3), 325–347. doi:10.1287/isre.1.3.325

Reich, B. H., & Benbasat, I. (2000). Factors That Influence the Social Dimension of Alignment Between Business and Information Technology Objectives. *Management Information Systems Quarterly*, *24*(1), 81–113. doi:10.2307/3250980

Roach, S. (1987). *America's Technology Dilemma: A Profile of the Information Economy*. New York: Morgan Stanley.

Roach, S. (1988). Technology and the Service Sector: The Hidden Competitive Challenge. *Technological Forecasting and Social Change*, *34*(4), 387–403. doi:10.1016/0040-1625(88)90006-6

Roach, S. (1991). Services Under Siege - The Restructuring Imperative. *Harvard Business Review*, *69*, 82–91.

Ross, J. W., Beath, C. M., & Goodhue, D. L. (1996). Develop Long-Term Competitiveness Through IT Assets. *Sloan Management Review*, *38*(1), 31–42.

Sabherwal, R. (1999). The Relationship Between Information System Planning Sophistication and Information System Success: An Empirical Assessment. *Decision Sciences*, *30*(1), 137–166. doi:10.1111/j.1540-5915.1999.tb01604.x

Sabherwal, R., & Chan, Y. E. (2001). Alignment between Business and IS Strategies: A Study of Prospectors, Analyzers, and Defenders. *Information Systems Research*, *12*(1), 11–33. doi:10.1287/isre.12.1.11.9714

Sabherwal, R., & King, W. R. (1995). An Empirical Taxonomy of the Decision-Making Processes Concerning Strategic Applications of Information Systems. *Journal of Management Information Systems*, *11*(4), 177–214.

Santhanam, R., & Hariono, E. (2003). Issues Liking Information Technology Capability to Firm Performance. *Management Information Systems Quarterly*, *27*(1), 125–143.

Segars, A. H., & Grover, V. (1998). Strategic Information Systems Planning Success: An Investigation of the Construct and its Measurement. *Management Information Systems Quarterly*, *22*(2), 139–163. doi:10.2307/249393

Sethi, V., & King, W. R. (1994). Development of Measures to Assess the Extent to Which an Information Technology Application Provides Competitive Advantage. *Management Science*, *40*(12), 1601–1627. doi:10.1287/mnsc.40.12.1601

Stevenson, W. J. (2005). *Operations Management*. New York: McGraw-Hill.

Tallon, P. P., Kraemer, K., & Gurbaxani, V. (2000). Executives' Perceptions of the Business Value of Information Technology: A Process-Oriented Approach. *Journal of Management Information Systems*, *16*(4), 145–173.

Teece, D. J., Pisano, G., & Shuen, A. (1997). Dynamic Capabilities and Strategic Management. *Strategic Management Journal*, *18*(7), 509–533. doi:10.1002/(SICI)1097-0266(199708)18:7<509::AID-SMJ882>3.0.CO;2-Z

Wade, M., & Hulland, J. (2004). The Resource-Based View and Information Systems Research: Review, Extension, and Suggestions for Future Research. *Management Information Systems Quarterly*, *28*(1), 107–142.

Weill, P. (1990). Strategic Investment in Information Technology - an Empirical- Study. *Information Age*, *12*(3), 141–147.

Weill, P. (1992). The Relationship Between Investment in Information Technology and Firm Performance: A Study of the Valve Manufacturing Sector. *Information Systems Research*, *3*(4), 307–333. doi:10.1287/isre.3.4.307

Weill, P., Surbramani, M., & Broadbent, M. (2002). Building IT Infrastructure for Strategic Agility. *Sloan Management Review*, *44*(1), 57–66.

This work was previously published in Journal of Organizational and End User Computing, Volume 22, Issue 4, edited by M. Adam Mahmood, pp. 1-23, copyright 2010 by IGI Publishing (an imprint of IGI Global).

Chapter 2
Utilization and Perceived Benefit for Diverse Users of Communities of Practice in a Healthcare Organization

Steven Walczak
University of Colorado Denver, USA

Richard Mann
Cardinal Health, USA

ABSTRACT

Communities of practice have been heralded as a powerful knowledge management tool, especially for geographically disparate workgroups. Research into knowledge management (KM) in healthcare organizations is a needed research focus, given that differences exist in knowledge and knowledge management processes between healthcare and other organization types. The research presented in this paper examines the effectiveness of communities of practice as a knowledge sharing tool in a large and geographically disparate healthcare organization. Findings suggest that job role affects community members' perceptions of the benefit and impact of communities of practice as well as their participation in such communities.

INTRODUCTION

Rising healthcare costs, increasing demand, an increase in the practice of evidence-based medicine (EBM), and the flood of healthcare information now available through the Internet to both consumers and service providers are affecting both the utilization of information technology and the implementation of knowledge management (KM) processes (Walczak, 2003; Ward et al., 2006). Improved quality of care in the medical domain is an overriding strategic goal of most healthcare organizations (Sandars & Heller, 2006). Addition-

DOI: 10.4018/978-1-4666-0140-6.ch002

ally, KM is seen as a process to facilitate knowledge acquisition and knowledge distribution to achieve this goal (Sandars & Heller, 2006).

The traditional focus of KM in an organizational setting is primarily one of knowledge capture and encoding (Foy, 1999). However, the utilization of knowledge assets in healthcare typically requires a focus on knowledge acquisition or sharing and innovation through knowledge creation.

One knowledge management tool that may help to facilitate knowledge acquisition and distribution is the community of practice (Choi & Lee, 2003). A community of practice is defined as an organic and self-organized group of individuals who are dispersed geographically or organizationally but communicate regularly to discuss issues of mutual interest (Becerra-Fernandez, 2004). The utilization of communities of practice (CoPs) has been particularly advocated for knowledge sharing across distributed facilities, (Choi, 2006). CoPs are seen as key components of both organizational learning (Plaskoff, 2003) and knowledge management (Wenger, 2004). Implementation of IT-enabled CoPs in health care settings has been proposed as a means to generate dynamic learning communities (Conner, 2005) and foster more robust and higher quality learning in health care settings (Choi, 2006). This paper will examine virtual/electronic and hybrid CoPs across a large national healthcare provider network to gather empirical evidence regarding the efficacy of CoPs for knowledge sharing and utilization within geographically distributed healthcare organizations. Virtual CoPs are CoPs that are conducted electronically, typically using a synchronous web-based interface for participants to meet simultaneously even though not collocated. Asynchronous discussion groups may also be employed to facilitate CoP interactions when simultaneous meetings are not feasible.

Three questions will form the core of the exploratory research design:

1) If CoPs are intentionally created within healthcare organizations, will healthcare workers utilize them as a knowledge resource?
2) Are CoPs perceived by healthcare workers to be effective in fostering knowledge sharing?
3) Are there differences in how CoPs are utilized that are dependent on healthcare job function?

In other words, will hospital and healthcare workers utilize CoPs and if they do are the CoPs effective at producing knowledge sharing within a large distributed health care organization. The last question examines the diverse nature of job roles within healthcare and asks if CoPs may be beneficial to all healthcare workers regardless of job function or does some aspect of the job role within healthcare make CoPs more useful to specific types of workers. If qualitative differences are identified, then this may signal future KM-oriented research to account for variations in utilization due to job function within organizations.

LITERATURE REVIEW ON COPS AND KM IN HEALTHCARE

CoPs were first formally defined as a business process and knowledge management methodology in the early 1990's (Lave & Wenger, 1991), which indicates that knowledge and utilization of CoPs is close to two decades old. The actual practice of CoPs most likely preceded their formal definition (Nunamaker & Chen, 1990). Since CoPs have been around for a while (Lee & Valderrama, 2003), is there in fact a need to examine CoP usage in healthcare settings?

The Need for CoPs in Healthcare

Recent research (Ghosh & Scott, 2005) has indicated that significant differences exist between healthcare organization and other types of organizations, specifically technical support, with regard to KM processes and KM effectiveness. Information technology solution developers need to account for the differences between organizational processes and medical treatment processes, which is currently lacking in information management IT tools (Lenz & Reichert, 2007).

Further evidence indicates that user population and organizational context may dramatically effect the utilization of organizational learning technologies (Ong et al., 2004). The increasing utilization of EBM necessitates access to consistently accurate information regarding prior evidence on specific medical illnesses and traumatic conditions (Booth et al., 2007; von Lubitz & Wickramasinghe, 2006; Wright et al., 2007). Gabbay and le May (2004) provide empirical evidence that evidentiary methods are established and confirmed through participation in CoP networks. Additional evidence implies that effective knowledge sharing is a prerequisite to effective decision making in medical domains (Boissel et al., 2004; Brooks & Scott, 2006). Furthermore, the ability of individuals to integrate knowledge and consequently transform it into practice is a measure of the competence of healthcare workers (von Lubitz & Wickramasinghe, 2006). CoPs have been proposed as a means for enhancing both professional practice and judgment (Parboosingh, 2002). However, how information is disseminated remains a critical question for healthcare domains (Mulrow & Lohr, 2001). Therefore knowledge sharing is going to continue being a critical topic for knowledge management processes within medical domains.

Various researchers and reports have indicated not only an ever increasing information overload with regard to medical information (Hall & Walton, 2004), but the desire of physicians and other healthcare workers to utilize information technology to facilitate information search and retrieval (Skinner, 2004; Tang & Ng, 2006). However, the utilization of the world wide web (WWW) as a medical information resource requires effective evaluation mechanisms since the WWW contains a high percentage of either misleading or wrong information (Lorence & Abraham, 2006; Tang & Ng, 2006; VanBiervliet & Edwards-Shafer, 2004; Walczak, 2003). Therefore healthcare workers must be able to rely on other "trusted" sources of knowledge for clinical decision making. Communities of practice may be used to enable the development of information consensus (Gabbay et al., 2003) and shared context (Garavan et al., 2007) across diverse organizations and thus provide trusted knowledge resources, especially within geographically disperse organizations.

Continual learning is a paradigm in healthcare communities, with many healthcare workers required to earn continuing education credits to maintain certification. Furthermore, organizational learning is a prerequisite to agile organizations. Learning processes within organizations frequently occur within informal knowledge sharing networks (Chen & Edgington, 2005; Dupouët & Yildizoğlu, 2006), such as those offered through CoPs. Furthermore, interaction with peers, possibly through CoPs in a distributed environment, is a primary method for physician learning (Parboosingh, 2002).

Aspects of CoPs

The concept of the community of practice is evolving, having started with the idea of sharing stories in an informal setting to grow into organizationally mandated knowledge sharing groups (Østerlund & Carlile, 2005; Zboralski et al., 2006) that enable the organization to leverage community knowledge to improve organizational competencies and inspire innovations. From an organizational and knowledge sharing perspective, CoPs originated as self-organizing groups of individuals that share a common interest and meet in person or virtually to share information (Lave & Wenger, 1991). Organizations soon realized the power of CoPs as an organizational learning methodology and began to instantiate

Table 1. Properties of CoPs

CoP Property	Supporting Literature
Alignment with business goals	Choi, 2006; Vestal, 2003, 2006; Conner, 2005 (contradicts this idea)
Appointed (skilled) leader	Choi, 2006; Garavan et al., 2007; Lee & Valderrama, 2003; Vestal, 2003
Well defined knowledge sharing process/rules	Hung & Chen, 2003; Hung et al., 2006; Vestal, 2003
Technology to support knowledge sharing	Bieber et al., 2002; Dubé et al., 2005; Hung & Chen, 2003; Parboosingh, 2002; Vestal, 2003
Topic agenda	Choi, 2006; Vestal, 2003
Open vibrant community	Conner, 2005 (don't exclude people); Hung et al., 2006; McDermott, 1999 (need for autonomy)
Shared context within community	Brown & Duguid, 1998, 2001; Conner, 2005; Hung et al., 2006
Community size	Kohlbacher & Mukai, 2007 (< 20 members)
Trust	Choi, 2006; Garavan et al., 2007
Metrics to evaluate CoP performance, periodic review	Lee & Valderrama, 2003; McDermott, 2002; Vestal, 2003, 2006; Zboralski et al., 2006
Recognition plan for members, incentives for participation	Lee & Valderrama, 2003; Pardo et al., 2006; Stevens, 2000; Vestal, 2003
Providing a feedback loop	Lee & Valderrama, 2003

formal CoPs to address business concerns using this more informal paradigm (Storck & Hill, 2000). These organizationally mandated CoPs may have been called by various names such as strategic communities, knowledge communities, or the traditional CoP name, but in essence their construct and activity mimicked the less formal interest-based CoPs.

Various researchers have tried to define the critical aspects or properties of a CoP within this changing landscape as well as processes for empowering CoPs to succeed in their respective goals. Table 1 presents a brief summary of these properties with the corresponding supporting literature.

With the increase in formal or intentional creation of CoPs within organizations, the alignment of CoP goals with organizational objectives is becoming much more commonplace and required to justify the creation of an organizationally sponsored CoP. In fact, periodic re- alignment with strategic business goals has been recommended (Vestal, 2006). However, within the healthcare community it is also critically important to accurately recognize the domain of the community, since most members will be impassioned about their specific domain (e.g., diabetic care or thoracic surgery) as opposed to a more general process improvement domain (Conner, 2005), which may signal a significant departure from the strategic alignment of more traditional business sponsored CoPs.

Many organizations now recognize CoPs as organizational assets that accrue benefit to the organization, especially by being able to overcome slow-moving traditional hierarchies (Lesser & Storck, 2001). However, intentional CoPs have not been highlighted in the academic literature and additional empirical evidence and case studies are needed to evaluate the organizational benefits of and roadblocks for intentional CoPs (Garavan et al., 2007). Metrics or other means to evaluate the benefit of CoPs are becoming more important, especially in the cost-cutting paradigm of medical domains. Since the product of CoPs is largely intangible: the transfer of expert knowledge and

Figure 1. Community participation levels and roles (Q = questions, A = answers)

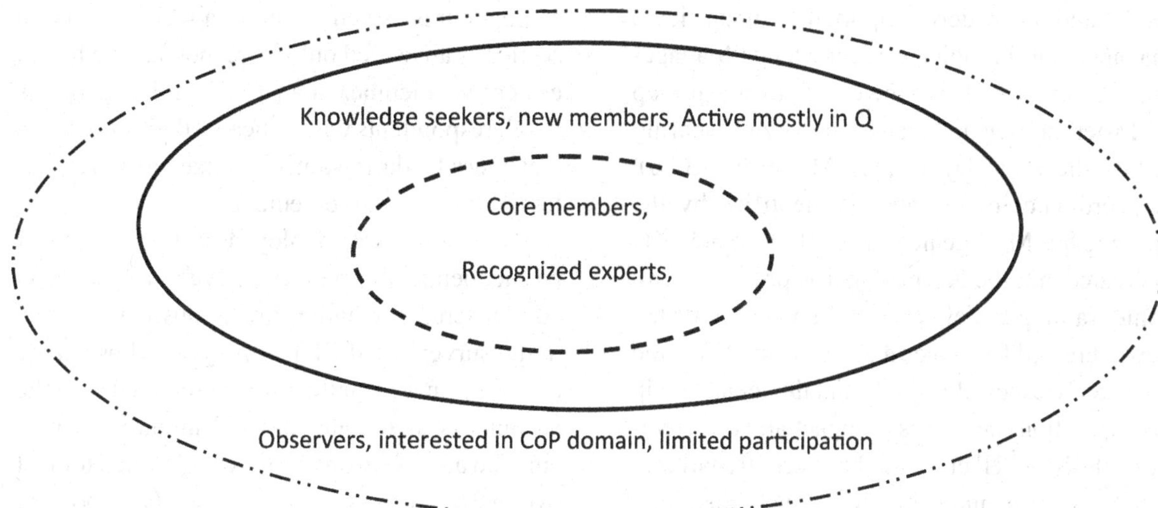

accurate evidence for EBM and possibly facilitating social interactions and connections amongst domain experts, the measurement of benefit to the organization may be problematic (Zboralski et al., 2006). The financial impact on an organization from CoP outcomes is especially difficult to measure (Zboralski et al., 2006).

Finally, though not listed in Table 1 as a property of CoPs, is the nature of how community members interact with and learn from the CoP. Different levels of participation have been recognized by numerous researchers (e.g., Barton, 2005; Dupouët & Yildizoğlu, 2006; Hung et al., 2006; Lave & Wenger, 1991; Wenger, 1998) and may be particularly relevant for healthcare-based CoPs, due to varying levels of expertise within the healthcare organization for specific CoP domains. Figure 1 displays the concept of varying levels of participation.

A real world exploratory evaluation of CoPs in a large national healthcare provider will provide empirical evidence for the essential properties of CoPs required in healthcare settings. Furthermore, insights into the three research questions listed in the Introduction section and specifically, healthcare worker perceptions of the value of CoPs as a knowledge sharing mechanism will be gathered through an exploratory survey of CoP participants.

HEALTHCARE COP CASE STUDY

The focus of the research presented in this article will be on evaluating the efficacy and perceived usefulness of IT-enabled virtual and hybrid (combination of virtual and face-to-face) CoPs in a large multi-state national healthcare provider. The development and utilization of intentional CoPs at a leading health care system, Catholic Health Initiatives (CHI, 2005), will provide the empirical framework for analyzing the three research questions.

As of year-end 2008, CHI had hospitals in 77 communities in 20 states, with National headquarters in Denver, and employs 68,000 employees with total revenues of \$7.7 billion (CHI, 2008). One of their earlier Core Strategy Priority Objectives included the implementation of an advanced clinical information system, creation of a Learning Management System infrastructure and a knowledge transfer methodology that supports innovation (CHI, 2005).

CoPs at CHI are called knowledge communities (KCs) and are widely supported by upper level management through their Knowledge Management Team, which is viewed as a critical step to foster participation and knowledge sharing within the KCs (Dymock & McCarthy, 2006). A coordinator or manager is identified by the Knowledge Management Team before any KC is created and the KC manager is provided with some training to help ensure the viability of the newly created KC. Once a KC is formed, it is the manager's responsibility to maintain (membership and operation) and assess (impact and effectiveness) the KC. CHI currently has over 50 chartered KCs. The large number of KCs helps to address the diverse needs of such a varied population of potential users. Additionally, the large number of electronically available KCs might encourage wider participation in KCs by the CHI network for healthcare providers. Increases in network size have been shown to be proportional to increases in knowledge sharing potential within an organization (Tang et al., 2008).

A means for facilitating CoP functionality within an organization is to survey potential and actual CoP members (Vestal, 2006), with this approach taken in this exploratory research. An exploratory survey to investigate the three research questions mentioned in the Introduction section was developed. Questions for the survey (shown in the Appendix) were taken and adjusted to fit the healthcare domain from previously validated survey tools, specifically: (Bock et al., 2005; Chau & Hu, 2001, 2002; Ryu et al., 2003; Yi et al., 2006). The demographic questions in the first part of the survey were placed to assist in classification of job roles for answering research question 3 and to determine if the type or size of the employing healthcare facility would affect responses. Additional face validity of the modified questions was determined by having the Knowledge Management Team at CHI approve the survey purpose and contents. The survey is divided into three sections. The first section asks for demographic information and whether the respondent is currently part of a KC. The second section is answered only by respondents who are currently a member of a KC. The third section is for all respondents who indicated their job level is managerial, administrative, or executive, regardless of their KC involvement.

The survey was deployed on the website of an independent survey firm, WebSurveyor, and administered by emailing invitations to participate in the survey to all CHI employees whose name appeared on any mailing lists associated with the various KCs. A total of 1757 invitations were emailed and 449 responses were obtained for just over a 25% response rate. Of the 449 responses, 71.94% or 323 respondents indicated that they were currently participating in a KC.

Responses were balanced between urban and rural hospitals and the percentage of participation from different hospital sizes, as measured by bed count, was similar, with very large healthcare facilities (more than 250 beds) having the greatest quantity of responses. Responses were analyzed in aggregate and also separated by either role or level of position within CHI. The breakout for the role of all 449 respondents is displayed in Figure 2. With respect to level of position, the majority of respondents (71%) indicated that they were at the supervisor level or higher administrative roles, with the remaining 29% in staff roles split evenly between clinical and support staff. The job role information helps to clarify this finding since 57% of respondents indicated serving in clinical roles, but many of these individuals function above the staff level.

The length of service question shows that the survey respondents and by inference the CHI healthcare community at large is invested in their relationship with their employer. The majority of respondents, 57%, indicated that they had been with either CHI or their current hospital for more than 10 years.

The level of participation in knowledge communities by each of the different job roles is

Figure 2. CHI KC survey respondent roles

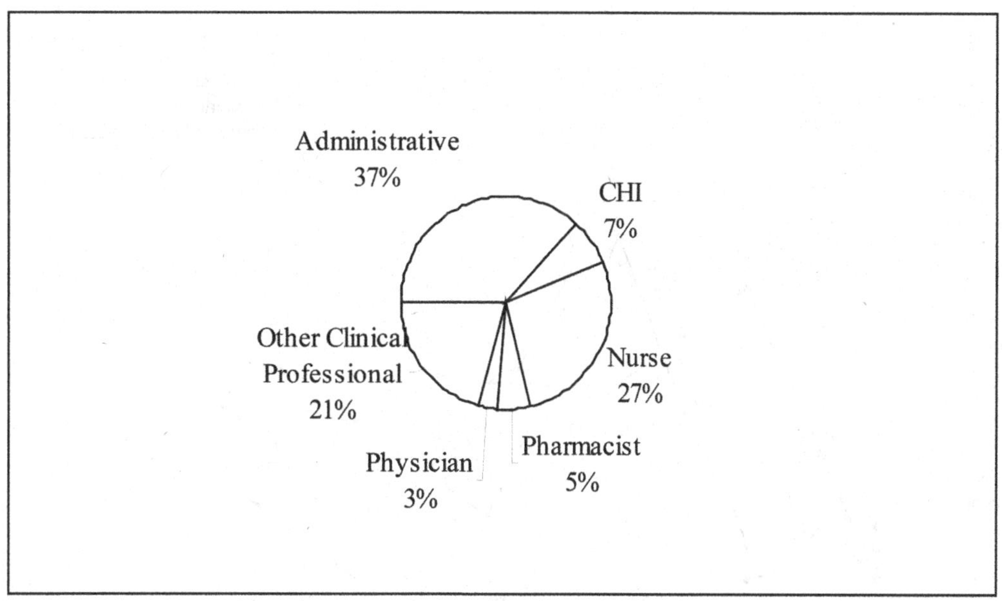

shown in Figure 3. Figure 3 specifically shows the different levels of access (ranging from no access, 0, to 25 or more times) for each job role as a percentage of the respondents from that role. Interestingly, 14 of the 323 respondents that indicated that they are part of a KC also indicated that they had not yet actually participated in any KC activities (e.g., from Figure 3, 10% of the responding pharmacists and 8% of the administrative respondents had not participated in any KC). This may be due to the survey respondent having just been invited to participate in a KC and then answering the survey before they actually had an opportunity to become involved in the KC or alternately they have participated in KCs in the past, but just not within the past 6 months. The time period of 6 months was chosen to capture only recent utilization of the KC by the member, but this quantity of time is arbitrary.

The average participation in KCs by different job roles is examined to see if job role differences may encourage or discourage utilization of KCs for knowledge sharing. Since the number of participants by job role varies quite a bit, each job role is converted to a percentage for presentation in Figure 3, by dividing the number of respondents for each job role at a particular participation level by the total number of respondents for that job role. Therefore, each line in Figure 3 is representative of the respondents from a specific job role and the percentage for each line totals 100 percent.

The role group with the highest average participation is the CHI role (which designates CHI organizational members not affiliated with a specific hospital) followed closely by the pharmacist role, with each group having an average participation response slightly higher than 7-12 times over the past 6 months. The other four job role groups all averaged participation in the middle of 2-6 and 7-12 times over the last 6 months; with the administrative group being highest in this second tier of active KC participants. Only the physician group indicated that every member of this group had participated in a KC at least once within the past 6 months.

The largest portion of each job role's population for most all of the job roles visited a KC

Figure 3. Participation in Knowledge Communities by job role

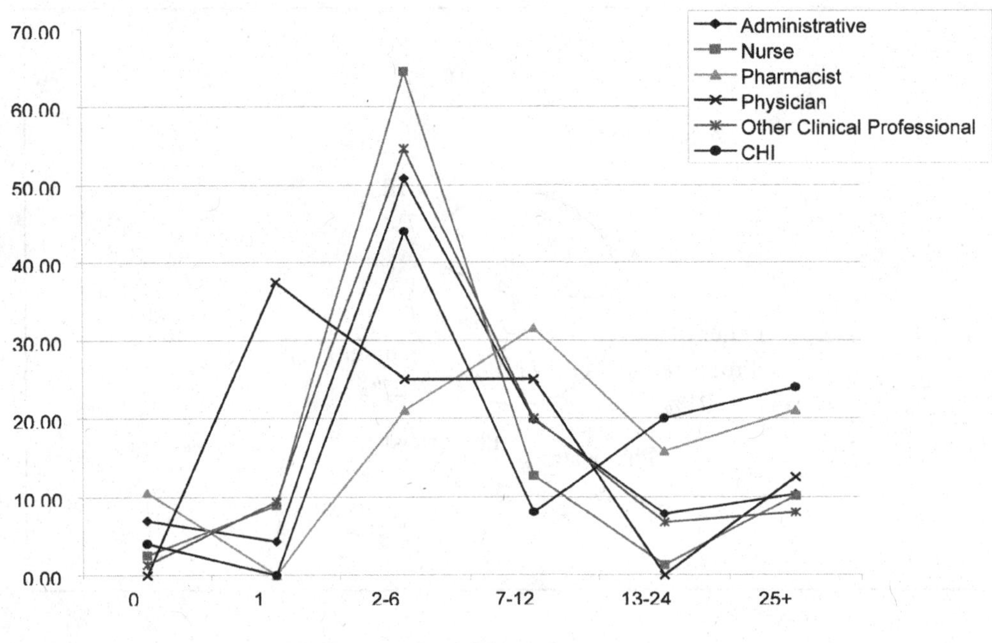

from 2 to 6 times during the past 6 months. The two groups that did not fit this pattern were the pharmacist group which had the largest portion of their group visiting KCs 7 to 12 times and the physicians group that had the largest portion of their group only visiting a KC once over the previous 6 months.

The average response for each of the 23 Likert scale questions administered in Section 2 of the survey, for all KC participants, is displayed in Table 2. Each of the questions is further categorized into a specific construct to which that question is targeted. The constructs include: Intention (Int), Environment (Env), Control (Cont), Attitude (Att), Productivity (Pr), and Normative (Norm). These constructs are derived from the concepts put forward by Bock et al. (2005) based on the Theory of Reasoned Action and later extended and codified in the unified model of technology acceptance (Venkatesh et al., 2003). A graph of the average responses for questions asked of all KC participants is displayed in Figure 4.

The highest overall average response is for the Int10 variable and represents KC participants' willingness to share knowledge with fellow participants. Recent research has indicated that willingness to share knowledge is a critical factor for knowledge diffusion within an organization (Huang et al., 2007).

All KC participants were additionally asked an open-ended question to explore actual benefits gained from KC participation. Open-ended questions are expected in exploratory research to gain insights into the qualitative dimensions impacting the research (e.g., Bellini & Vargas, 2003). A total of 156 responses were received to the open-ended question. Of these, 119 provided specific detailed examples of significant time and/or money savings resulting from knowledge received from participating in a KC. Therefore, measurable and tangible benefits were attributed to knowledge sharing through one of the KCs for 36.8% (119 of 323 survey respondents) of the

Table 2. Average survey response for Section 2, KC participants

Question	Construct	Avg. Response
I belong to external professional groups that encourage the sharing of knowledge.	Norm1	4.26
I try to share knowledge with colleagues through involvement in CHI Knowledge Communities.	Int2	4.15
It is difficult to connect with CHI colleagues about knowledge that I need.	Env3	3.31**
I am expected to share knowledge with CHI colleagues.	Cont4	3.87
I intend to share knowledge within CHI Knowledge Communities more frequently in the future.	Int5	3.88
Most colleagues who are important to me share their knowledge with others through CHI Knowledge Communities.	Norm6	3.59
Knowledge sharing is easy to do within CHI Knowledge Communities.	Env7	3.56
Inside CHI and email are effective ways to share knowledge.	Env8	4.02
I am not required to share knowledge within the CHI Knowledge Communities.	Cont9	2.96**
I make an effort to share knowledge with colleagues when they ask.	Int10	4.36
I can easily find best practices within CHI Knowledge Communities.	Env11	3.29
It is difficult for me to share knowledge frequently.	Att12	3.00**
I am able to easily find people with specific expertise within CHI Knowledge Communities.	Env13	3.23
I have implemented best practices that originated from within CHI Knowledge Communities.	Pr14	3.36
Knowledge sharing through CHI Knowledge Communities is valuable to me.	Att15	4.12
CHI encourages the sharing of knowledge.	Norm16	4.20
Participating in a CHI KC:		
Helps me do my job better.	Pr17	3.96
Saves (has saved) me significant time on programs or projects.	Pr18	3.55
Saves (has saved) me significant money on programs or projects.	Pr19	3.29
Reduces time needed to solve problems.	Pr20	3.66
Decreases rework (avoids reinventing the wheel).	Pr21	3.81
Helps me to avoid costly mistakes.	Pr22	3.54
Is a valuable part of being within the CHI system.	Pr23	4.11

**Adjusted because they are negatively stated.

KC participants, thus supporting the perceived productivity benefits of KCs within CHI.

Section 3 of the survey is only administered to those individuals indicating that their level is managerial or higher in the organization. Recall though, that 71% of the respondents perceived their role as being at this level within the CHI organization. The average responses to the 4 Likert scale questions asked of managers or other administrators are displayed in Table 3.

Each administrator was also asked 2 open-ended questions to explore perceived benefits of KCs from a managerial perspective and managerial support for knowledge sharing through the various KCs. Visible managerial support for participation in KCs may be viewed as a prerequisite to achieving actual participation (Dubé et al., 2005; Goh, 2003; Nahm et al., 2004).

A word count-based qualitative analysis is performed to cluster responses (LaPelle, 2004) with respect to the open-ended survey questions evaluating the perceived benefits of KCs. A total of 364 comments were received (some surveys contained multiple comments). Within the 364 comments, 9 were negative and did not see a benefit from the KCs. However, from the remaining 355

Figure 4. Average responses to survey construct questions

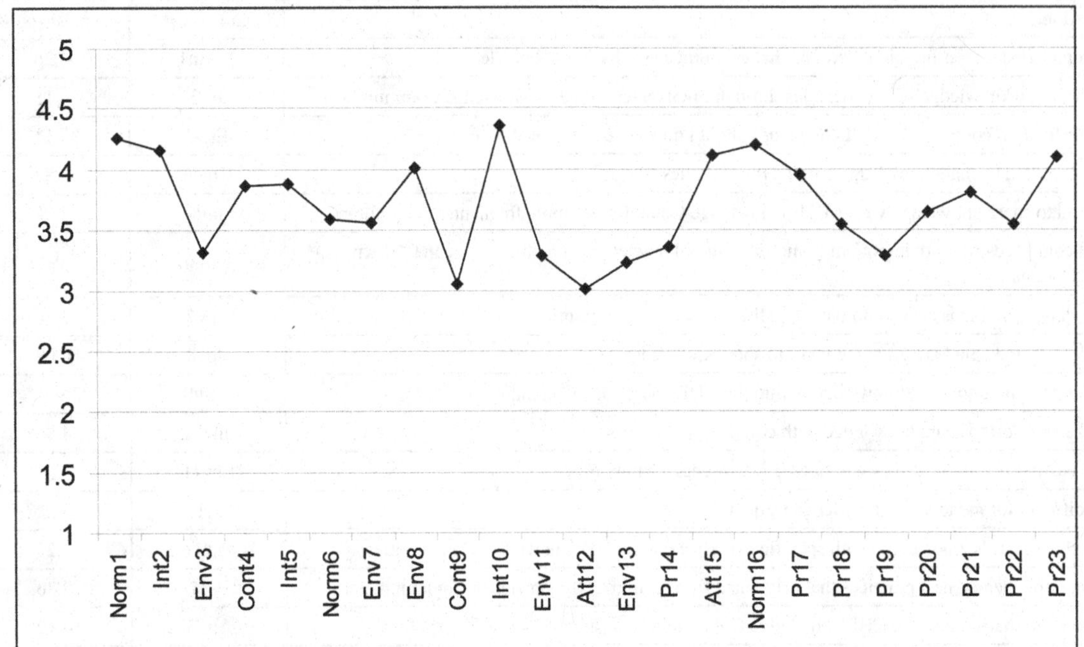

positive comments 333 of these referred to specific benefits achieved and credited at least in part to knowledge and resource sharing through the KCs. The specific benefits cited were organized into the following categories, based on the qualitative analysis: documents and policies (29 comments), people and peer access (63 comments), resource sharing (10 comments), information sharing (99 comments), best practices (98 comments), problem solving strategies (19 comments), and cost savings (15 comments).

The other open-ended question administered to managerial level KC members asked how they encouraged staff to participate in KCs, showing managerial support for the KCs. Of the 247 responses, 54 indicated that support of staff was N/A (not applicable) to them, perhaps due to a small department with no other staff present, and 13 indicated a negative response to enabling staff based on the theme cookbook for this question. The remaining 180 responses that indicated specific support for staff utilization of the KCs for knowledge sharing, just over 56.1% indicated providing encouragement to employees and 43.4% indicated that they provided employees with time or other resources in order to participate in KCs.

Table 3. Average responses for Section 3, managerial perceptions of knowledge communities

Question	Average Response
KCs result in positive benefits for the organization.	4.22
Positive, definable impact resulting from staff participating in a KC.	3.75
Knowledge-sharing through KC should be rewarded.	3.94
I encourage my staff to participate in KCs.	3.86

Table 4. Open comments by all survey participants

Comment Classification	Percentage of open comment respondents (*N* = 180).
Didn't know that KC existed	4.44%
Wanted additional training on use of KCs	6.67%
Thought system was too complex or needed a better user interface	4.44%
Thought sharing process should be better defined	1.11%
Recommended a cost justification (or cost benefit analysis)	1.11%
Indicated a lack of management support	1.67%
Wanted more clinical staff participating or invited to participate	1.67%
Insufficient time (during job) to participate effectively	4.44%
Suggested new KC topics	2.22%
Negative (didn't think KCs worked or were useful)	1.67%
Positive (both general and specific positive comments)	75.56%

ANALYSIS AND DISCUSSION

Each of the three questions from the Introduction will be examined individually with respect to the survey results. The first research question is: If CoPs are intentionally created within healthcare organizations; will healthcare workers utilize them as a knowledge resource?

The first indicator that healthcare workers are willing to utilize CoPs (or KCs) is the percentage of respondents that indicated that they did in fact participate in a KC, which was 323 out of 449 or almost 72%. Now this value is subject to selection bias, due to the selection of employees who had in some way been associated with a KC, but still indicates a willingness to utilize the KCs. A total of 180 respondents left a comment to an open-ended question, answered by all survey participants regardless of KC participation. The majority of these comments, 75.56%, are rated as very positive regarding the perceived usefulness of KCs. Table 4 displays the frequency of concerns or suggestions regarding KCs from this open-ended question. Note that a single respondent could have listed multiple suggestions for a KC.

The four main reasons given by respondents for reasons why they felt the KCs were underutilized are: need for additional training, the system was either too complex (difficult to navigate) or the user interface needed to be simplified, respondent had insufficient time during their normal work process to adequately utilize KC s, and finally that the respondent didn't know that KCs existed. Hence, it appears that CHI could quickly increase KC utilization through two simple steps. First, advertise the KCs and their corresponding effectiveness for knowledge sharing, perhaps by sharing KC participants' success stories. Second, training courses should be developed to show KC participants how to effectively navigate through the various KC resources available, locate desired information or contacts, and share information with co-workers. Adequate training may also subsequently help to reduce the number of participants under-utilizing the KCs due to the complexity of the system or inherent problems associated with the user interface/navigation system. One of the negative responses indicated that traditional web search engines provided easier to locate information, but an increase in the perceived ease of use through training may change this perception.

A limitation of the current research is in the lack of an age demographic for the survey. While tenure at CHI or individual hospitals was measured, this may not accurately reflect differences in age. Younger users of CoPs traditionally prefer more IT technical methods of communication and may not have the same perceptions on lack of ease of use as older members (Yamazaki, 2004).

The insufficient time to fully utilize the KC system may be associated with the perception of a lack of managerial support for the KCs and participation in KCs. As indicated in the discussion following Table 3, only 43% of the managers that indicated they provided support to staff did so through allocating of time or other resources specifically for participating in KCs. This indicates that the perceived lack of managerial support is well founded in actual practice by the managers. This supports the "lack of management support" reason given by some of the open comment respondents for not making full use of KCs. Management support of CoPs is critical factor for the success of CoPs (Dubé et al., 2005; Goh, 2003; Nahm et al., 2004). While overall support of the KCs is proclaimed as a strategic goal for CHI and they are attempting to integrate KCs as an institutional formalism (Dubé et al., 2005), development of specific management initiatives that include allocating time as a resource for employees is inferred to be able to create user enthusiasm and greater utilization of the KCs for knowledge sharing (Dymock & McCarthy, 2006).

The indication that specific new KCs were desired indicates that further utilization of the KC processes could be gained by intentionally creating those additional KC topics that are viewed as being under-served by the current communities This may be associated with an increase in perceived usefulness, since the newer KCs would be more targeted at the domain specific interest areas of many participants. While CHI already has over 50 KCs, recall that within medical domains, the community focus must be perceived as relevant to a specific role or domain as opposed to a more business-oriented objective (Conner, 2005).

The next research question is: Are CoPs effective in fostering knowledge sharing (as perceived by the users in a healthcare setting)? Social capital theory, which claims that social relations have worth and attempts to provide explanations for how this worth is calculated and enhanced among the actors in social networks (Lin, 2001), provides the explanation for the primary motivations for sharing knowledge in a KC (Bock et al., 2005; Inkpen & Tsang, 2005; Rohde et al., 2007; Wasko & Faraj, 2005). Among these knowledge sharing motivators are individual motivators such as reputation or status within the organization, structural motivators such as being centrally connected to a majority of the other members in the group, cognitive motivators such as self-perception as an expert in the field and a need to give back to the organization after a long tenure, and finally relational motivators such as the anticipation of reciprocal knowledge sharing from other members at some point in the future (Ardichvili et al., 2003; Wasko & Faraj, 2005).

The intention to share knowledge variables from the survey provide the most direct support for the efficacy of KCs for fostering knowledge sharing. The three intention variables have an overall average response of 4.13, indicating a strong perceived intention to share knowledge. The highest response value for the entire survey is for the variable INT10. Since the question indicates that employees will share knowledge via a KC when asked, this implies a social component through interaction with the question asker. This desire or need for a social aspect may derive from one or more of the identified motivators: individual (through the perception that by responding to a "tough" question reputation will increase), cognitive (increases self-perception as expert by being asked as a source of knowledge and may satisfy perceived need to "give back" to the organization), structural (feeling more connected to the question asker), and relational (through an implied reciprocal expectation from the question asker).

Figure 5. Preliminary model of knowledge community factors affecting productivity

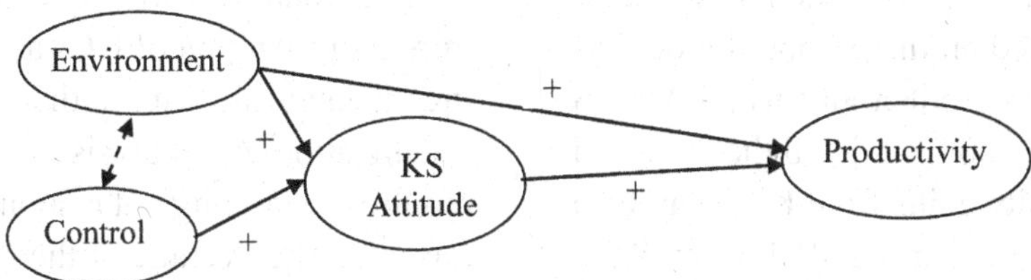

One response to the open-ended question at the end of the survey helps illustrate the interplay between individual and cognitive motivators for knowledge sharing in the KCs. The response, "fairly new in my position … when asked for policies or information, I am not comfortable with sharing at this point because I'm not sure that my policies represent best practice … as I mature in the position my feelings should change," indicated that the individual did not yet share knowledge because they were new to the position (cognitive: did not rate their expertise as high and did not feel they had sufficient tenure) and were not sure they could adequately make a contribution (individual: status within the organization).

A different and perhaps better evaluation of the knowledge sharing potential for the KCs would be in the subsequent utilization or application of knowledge to facilitate solving a real business problem (Gabbay et al., 2003). The productivity variables from the survey and the managers-only responses indicate that knowledge gained from participating in KCs has been beneficial with respect to both time and money savings directly attributed to KC activity. A preliminary model that links together the desire of individual's to share knowledge via the KCs with subsequent productivity gains attributed to the KCs is shown in Figure 5. Figure 5 also includes Environment and Control factors which have been widely shown in the literature to affect willingness to participate in KM practices (Bock et al., 2005; Chau & Hu, 2001, 2002; Ryu et al., 2003; Yi et al., 2006). The dashed bi-directional arrow between the Environment and Control indicates that some interaction between these two factors is expected, but the specific direction is unknown and may even be variable between individuals.

The Environment and Control constructs shown in the exploratory model of Figure 5 are adapted to fit the knowledge sharing in a medical domain from previously validated constructs (Bock et al., 2005; Venkatesh et al., 2003). Some of the variables used to measure the KS Attitude construct represent social persuasion effects from social capital theory (McFarland & Hamilton, 2006). The reliabilities of the variable groupings defining each construct in Figure 5 were evaluated utilizing Cronbach's alpha, with values shown in Table 5. The alpha values for Productivity, Environment and KS Attitude all indicate reasonable internal consistency and are thus viewed as reliable. The.625 alpha for the Control construct indicates only minimally adequate reliability, which may indicate the need for addi-

Table 5. Factor reliability evaluation using Cronbach's alpha

Construct	Cronbach's Alpha
Environment	**.821**
KS Attitude	**.780**
Control	.625
Productivity	**.919**

tional variables/measurements of control in future experiments.

A SEM (structural equation modeling) factor analysis is performed on the proposed model of KC contributions to productivity using AMOS 6.0 to gain an initial confirmation if the proposed model of productivity gains from KCs may be a reliable model for evaluating ROI from KCs. AMOS is a graphical tool that facilitates the construction of SEM models (Bacon, 1997). SEM models explore the underlying relationships between latent variables and constructs and also account for unreliability in response data (Bacon, 1997; Hsu, 2007). Exploratory SEM-based factor analysis enables this analysis without predefining any a priori relationships between the observed data and the latent variables (Brown, 2006). Other tools such as LISREL or PLS could also have been used for this purpose. Fit indexes and chi-square values are shown in Table 6 for the proposed model.

The χ^2 at 3.382 shows a good fit between the data and the proposed model (with a *p*-value <.001). Although the χ^2 is generally considered the most robust goodness of fit indicator, other evaluation criteria should simultaneously be used (Schermelleh-Engel et al., 2003). Recommended values for other goodness of fit indexes indicate that these various indexes (e.g., CFI, GFI, and NFI) should all have a value >.90 and the RMSEA indicates a good fit below.05, an adequate fit between.05 and.08, and a mediocre fit between.08 and.10 (Hu & Bentler, 1999; Schermelleh-Engel et al., 2003). While the RMSEA indicates a mediocre fit, the most of the other fit indexes fall below the suggested heuristics, with the exception of the CFI which is above the suggested.90 cutoff. However, it should be noted that the utilization of absolute cutoff values, especially in social science research, has been questioned and the absolute values for cutoffs are frequently debated and adjusted to fit the current modeling situation (Marsh et al., 2004), thus the near.90 values for the GFI and NFI may in this case indicate a reliable model, but further investigation is clearly required.

The final research question is if job role impacts utilization of KCs as a knowledge sharing mechanism within the broader healthcare organization. An analysis of job role differences requires separating out responses with respect to job role. The average of the section 2 responses from current members of a KC with respect to job role is displayed in Table 7, with the overall average responses from Figure 4 included. Table 7 indicates that there are differences between job role utilization and perceived benefits from the KCs and this appears to be split into at least two distinct groups, with one group of three job roles being very close to the overall average for all questions and the other groups being more distinct.

From Table 7, it may be seen that administrators, nurses, and other clinical professionals all had average responses nearly identical to the overall average and thus were very similar. This is not surprising since these three groups constitute 85 percent of the respondents, but what is surprising is the high degree of similarity between these three job role groups. The largest differences between job role groups came from the physician job role followed by both the pharmacist and CHI organizational members. To further analyze the perceived differences in responses between job roles, 15 *t* tests were performed to determine if the average responses between the different job roles for the 23 Likert-style questions had any differences (thus giving a uniform 22 degrees of freedom for all tests). One *t* test paired

Table 6. Fit indexes for proposed model of productivity from KCs

X^2 / df	3.382
GFI	.880
NFI	.873
CFI	.907
RMSEA	.089

Table 7. Average response values by job role for survey questions

Survey Question	Administrator	CHI	Nurse	Pharmacist	Physician	Other Clinical Professional	Overall
Norm1	4.348	4.120	4.114	4.053	4.500	4.240	4.260
Norm6	3.548	3.400	3.443	3.684	3.125	3.627	3.582
Norm16	4.200	4.160	4.152	4.263	3.625	4.187	4.197
Int2	4.209	4.240	4.038	4.000	4.125	4.133	4.150
Int5	3.791	4.040	3.835	3.789	3.750	3.987	3.878
Int10	4.374	4.520	4.380	4.158	4.375	4.253	4.359
Env3	3.417	3.160	3.215	3.421	2.500	3.387	3.309
Env7	3.522	3.560	3.557	3.579	2.875	3.533	3.557
Env8	4.026	4.040	3.962	3.842	3.500	3.933	4.016
Env11	3.400	2.680	3.253	3.421	2.625	3.267	3.289
Env13	3.322	2.880	3.177	3.316	2.625	3.253	3.228
Cont4	3.904	4.280	3.696	3.947	3.250	3.840	3.866
Cont9	2.939	2.880	3.127	2.895	3.625	3.107	3.044
Att12	3.139	2.920	2.987	2.632	3.000	3.013	3.003
Att15	4.122	4.080	4.076	4.105	3.750	4.160	4.119
Pr14	3.452	2.800	3.228	3.684	2.750	3.360	3.352
Pr17	3.991	3.840	3.863	4.000	3.500	3.907	3.953
Pr18	3.595	3.280	3.513	3.895	2.750	3.547	3.547
Pr19	3.319	3.080	3.225	3.632	2.875	3.213	3.291
Pr20	3.681	3.520	3.550	3.842	2.875	3.573	3.646
Pr21	3.862	3.680	3.725	4.105	3.125	3.787	3.804
Pr22	3.474	3.280	3.550	3.684	3.250	3.520	3.539
Pr23	4.164	4.200	3.963	4.105	3.375	4.040	4.103

for two sample means is performed for comparing each job role against every other job role. The t values are displayed in Table 8.

As a case example, the differences between nurses (similar to all average responses) and physicians (the most different from average responses) will be examined. What would cause different utilization of KCs by physicians versus nurses? Typically nurse schedules are very time demanding and recall that time was indicated as a major factor needed to improve KC participation across various job roles. Over 37% of these time constraint responses were from nurses. Due to the time commitment required to share and actively participate in the KCs, nurses may view the KCs as more of a performance support tool, which is not an uncommon response to a new knowledge management methodology (Kimble & Hildreth, 2005), to look up current best practices for treatment protocols.

This does not mean that the other consistent average users, administration and other clinical professionals, utilize the KCs as performance support tools, but highlights the need for further investigations to determine how specific job role groups are utilizing the KCs and means for improving their perceived benefit (productivity) and increasing their participation. Previous research has indicated that tool design and required time for utilizing the tool are both significant factors for

Table 8. t test values for comparison of differences between job roles average responses

	Administration	CHI	Nurse	Physician	Pharmacist
CHI	2.608 ***				
Nurse	4.237 ***	-0.852			
Physician	5.378 ***	3.653 ***	4.776 ***		
Pharmacist	-0.266	-1.984 *	-2.340 *	-4.167 ***	
Other Clinical	2.126 *	-1.950 *	-3.365 ***	-5.311 ***	1.217

*** significant at $p < .001$; ** significant at $p < .01$; * significant at $p < .05$.

new information technology adoption in healthcare domains (Van Schail et al., 2004).

Physicians compared to nurses should be examined using the social capital perspective. While they certainly should have the cognitive motivators (e.g., viewing themselves as having expertise in their domain), it may be that other motivators are weak or absent. For example, relational motivators may be missing if the physician feels that there is a lack of reciprocal information or that they will not be able to take advantage of reciprocal information in the future or they are already receiving desired information from another community. While it would normally be expected that individual motivations are adequately present, i.e., seeking reputation or status in the community, this may in fact be missing or even serve as a deterrent since new diagnostic and treatment protocols are frequently being discovered and debated. It may be that a physician would prefer to only share information after a large number of trials have been performed to gather sufficient evidence, thus supporting the foundations of evidence-based medicine. The main set of variables where physicians consistently ranked lower than everyone was for the productivity variables, indicating that they might already have desired information from other sources, especially since physicians were the highest average response with respect to belonging to other professional groups or communities. Although, physicians appear to be less captivated by the utility or perceived usefulness of the KC system, they did consistently respond with the main group averages in respect to their willingness to share knowledge (the intention variables).

Adding the Job Role Construct, which is a categorical construct, into the proposed model of evaluating the productivity improvements achieved from KC participation produces the new model shown in Figure 6 with fit indexes displayed. Since this is an exploratory model, factor influence values are not produced by the AMOS software package used to generate the fit indexes. The ± symbol is used to indicate that the effect is expected to vary depending on the specific job role.

In general the chi-square still indicates a good fit between the survey data and the new model, the CFI fit index is still acceptable, and the RSMEA value has improved to indicate an adequate fit. The GFI and NFI indexes are still lower than desired. The improvement in the RMSEA as well as the acceptable fit shown by the chi-square and CFI tests imply that adding in a job role construct does not degrade the model and might in fact improve its overall fit (with respect to the RMSEA), indicating that at least for healthcare knowledge management research: the construct of job role should be accounted for in future research.

One additional possible evaluation of job role effects is possible by examining the responses of the various job roles that indicated managerial level responsibility within the organization. Figure 7 displays the job role average responses to the managerial perceptions of KC effectiveness and

Figure 6. New preliminary model incorporating the job role construct

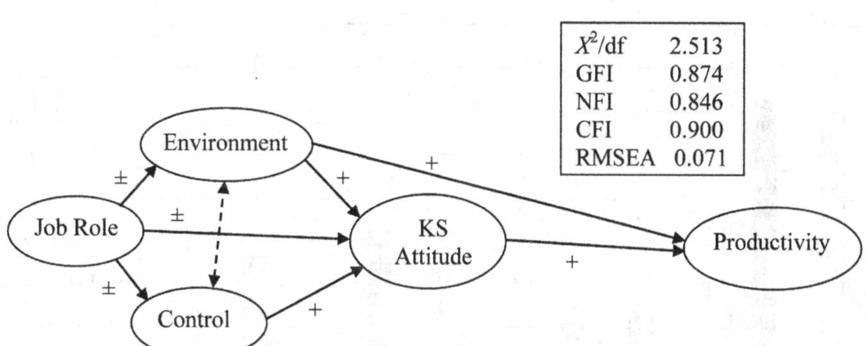

motivation strategies that were listed in Table 3. The overall pattern of the responses is similar for all job roles, except for the CHI organization-level members who saw a diminished need to reward knowledge sharing behavior. Interestingly, the groups that were above average for motivating knowledge sharing behaviors through specific rewards were all clinical professionals: physicians, pharmacists, nurses, and other clinical professionals, while the CHI and administrator roles were both below average on this survey item.

Managers serving in a pharmacist role saw the greatest productivity benefits and impact from the utilization of KCs, followed closely by the CHI organizational level members. Physicians with managerial level responsibility also saw overall benefits from KCs to the organization, but were much closer to the average for obtaining definable impact from staff participating in KCs. Finally, it may be seen that with the exception of encouraging staff in some way to participate in KCs, the administrative role had the lowest values, though still very positive, for perceived benefits and impact as well as rewarding sharing behaviors by staff. This may be a result of not having metrics or effective metrics for defining the contributions of KC, since these types of benefits are often intangible. The development of specific metrics to evaluate KC contributions to the organization could increase the administrative perceptions of benefit and definable impact from the various KCs.

One aspect of the KCs implemented at CHI is not evaluated in the survey, but bears some discussion, specifically with respect to how KCs (or CoPs) may be expected to achieve maximum knowledge transfer in medical domains. Consistent with the approach to developing hybrid CoPs suggested by various researchers (Kimble & Hildreth, 2005; Yamazaki, 2004), many CHI KCs have annual or periodic face-to-face meeting between KC members. While the virtual/electronic nature of the KCs at CHI is necessary and an optimal design due to the geographically distributed nature of the organization and the need for knowledge sharing across traditional organizational boundaries (Dubé et al., 2005; Lesser & Storck, 2001; Pardo et al., 2006), the physician-oriented KCs specifically need to operate in either face-to-face or hybrid modes (using both virtual and face-to-face meetings) to ensure and increase physician participation through emulation of other professional CoPs. Face-to-face meetings may prove impractical for some of the KCs due to the geographic dispersion, in which case webinars or other virtual face-to-face meetings could be set up to supplement the current KCs.

Figure 7. Average responses to managerial perceptions of KC by role type

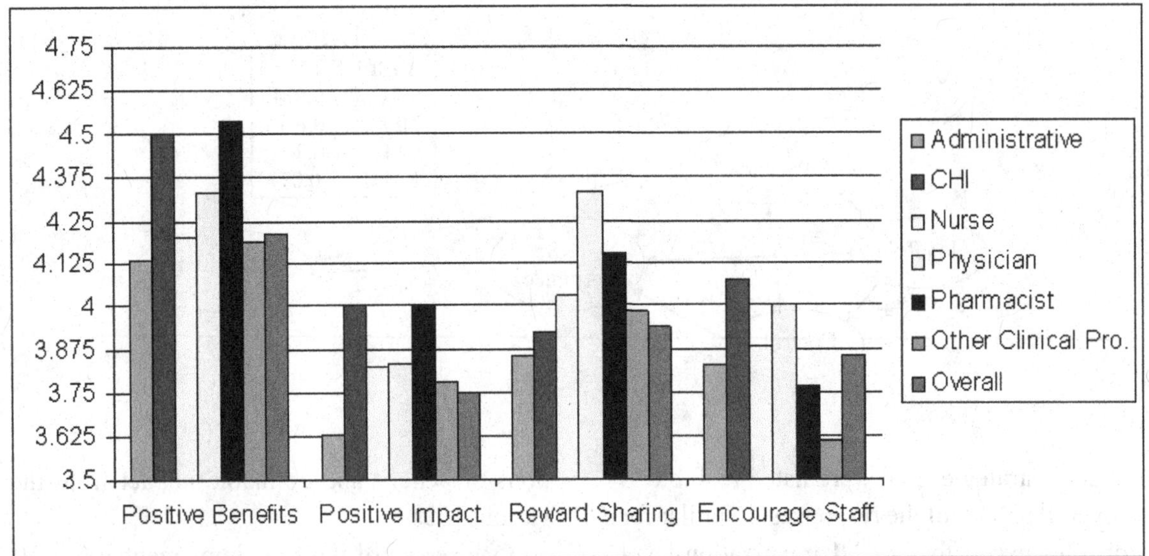

CONCLUSION AND FUTURE RESEARCH

Although differences in the requirements for and benefits of knowledge management systems between healthcare and other service oriented organizations have been identified (Ghosh & Scott, 2005; Lenz & Reichert, 2007), there is a need for empirical evaluation of specific information technology tools including communities of practice applied in healthcare settings. The utilization of IT-enabled virtual and hybrid communities of practice, or knowledge communities, as a means to drive knowledge sharing in a healthcare setting is evaluated at a very large national healthcare provider, Catholic Health Initiatives. CHI utilizes intentionally created virtual communities that are launched (Garavan et al., 2007) and managed by a knowledgeable and trained leader (Choi, 2006; Lee & Valderrama, 2003; Vestal, 2003). While specific motivations employed by management to engage KC members were not collected in the survey, other than through open-ended question responses, it appears that the majority of managerial-level respondents found motivation of employees to be either already implemented or a desired future process (Lee & Valderrama, 2003; Pardo et al., 2006; Stevens, 2000; Vestal, 2003).

The large number of KCs (over 50) is able to provide alignment with strategic business goals through some of the communities (Choi, 2006; Vestal, 2003, 2006) while other communities are able to address more domain relevant knowledge sharing which is seen as being critical in healthcare settings (Conner, 2005; Dubé et al., 2005). The very large network of virtual KCs should serve to increase knowledge sharing across the organization (Tang et al., 2008). Since the KCs are provided electronically/virtually, this overcomes knowledge sharing barriers in widely distributed organizations and in heavily compartmentalized organizations (Ardichvili et al., 2003; Bieber et al., 2002; Dubé et al., 2005; Hung & Chen, 2003; Parboosingh, 2002; Vestal, 2003).

Additionally the communities are open (Conner, 2005; Hung et al., 2006), semi-autonomous (McDermott, 1999), initially have KC manager specified topics (Choi, 2006; Vestal, 2003), and have a shared context (Brown & Duguid, 1998, 2001; Conner, 2005; Hung et al., 2006). Thus it appears that the definition, management and application of KCs at CHI satisfy most of the recommended practices for CoPs, shown in Table 1, in a more general business sense.

A possible barrier to participation that was identified through the survey was lack of knowledge about the KCs and more specifically how to use them effectively. If additional training on the utilization of the KCs and how to more effectively find desired knowledge is developed, then this would consequently increase the utilization of the KCs within CHI and would satisfy the recommendation to have a well defined knowledge sharing process (Hung & Chen, 2003; Hung et al., 2006; Vestal, 2003).

Because of the differences in knowledge management between IT service industries and medical provider industries identified by Ghosh and Scott (2005), a significant need exists to examine IT-enabled KM practices in medical domains. This article extends research in this area, but additional research is still needed to extend empirical evidence of IT-based KM practices and to perhaps extend this further to novel applications of CoPs in medical domains that include healthcare consumers such as that demonstrated by Winkelman and Choo (2003).

This exploratory survey research has several limitations, but since it is meant to be exploratory, these limitations may be overcome by future research. The first limitation is that the survey provides only a snapshot view of KC participation and perceived benefits. While the survey participation lasted for 6 weeks, each participant's answers reflect a single moment in time for that specific participant. It may prove worthwhile to return and perform similar surveys annually; especially as training or other participation improvement strategies are implemented to gain a longitudinal understanding of the development of KCs within the organization. While the survey did provide a feedback mechanism to KC participants, a regularly administered survey as suggested would provide a more effective and ongoing feedback mechanism (Lee & Valderrama, 2003) to determine the need for and effectiveness of continuing KC process improvements.

The design of the survey was meant to require a minimal amount of time to complete so as not to be intrusive in the normal workflow of KC participants. This design constraint therefore, necessarily limited the amount of knowledge that could be acquired. An example of a new piece of information that would be included in a future survey would be not only the number of times a KC member participated in a KC over the past 6 months, but additionally how much time on average was spent during each visit to a KC. It may be possible to collect such information automatically, which would alleviate the need to acquire it in a survey. Such information might provide additional insights into the time constraint limitations as well as utilization of the KCs for performance support versus knowledge sharing. Another piece of information that may have helped distinguish the need for correlating the specific knowledge interests of medical workers (Lenz & Reichert, 2007) could have been acquired by asking questions to identify how well existing KCs match specific domain interests of the participants. Other additional parameters for the survey and model of productivity are as yet to be determined and these additional parameters to better define KC needs and requirements within medical domains are a goal for future research.

Another significant finding of the reported exploratory research is the impact of job role on KC utilization and corresponding perceptions of effect on productivity. These findings highlight the need for future research to account for differences in job role.

Finally, this research has supported previous research indicating that social capital theory is a driver behind employee participation in networks or CoPs. Additionally, the relationship of several social capital theory aspects have been tied to a proposed TAM like model and hopefully this will lead to additional future investigations of model combinations, especially in social-behavioral oriented research such as knowledge management processes.

ACKNOWLEDGMENT

We are very grateful to Catholic Health Initiatives for allowing us to survey their employees and perform this exploratory research. Special thanks to Colleen Elliott, the Director of Knowledge Management at CHI and to Holly Pendleton, Knowledge Manager, who was invaluable in assisting with collection of information on KC practices at CHI and establishing the web survey protocols. We would also like to thank several of the anonymous reviewers and editors at *JOEUC*, whose comments and suggestions helped to clarify and improve the presentation of our research.

REFERENCES

Ardichvili, A., Page, V., & Wentling, T. (2003). Motivation and barriers to participation in virtual knowledge-sharing communities of practice. *Journal of Knowledge Management*, *7*(1), 64–77. doi:10.1108/13673270310463626

Bacon, L. D. (1997). *Using Amos for structural equation modeling in market research*. Retrieved from ftp://hqftp1.spss.com/pub/web/wp/AMOSMRP.pdf

Barton, A. J. (2005). Cultivating Informatics Competencies in a Community of Practice. *Nursing Administration Quarterly*, *29*(4), 323–328.

Becerra-Fernandez, I., Gonzalex, A., & Sabherwal, R. (2004). *Knowledge Management: Challenges, Solutions and Technologies*. Upper Saddle River, NJ: Prentice Hall.

Bellini, C. G. B., & Vargas, L. M. (2003). Rationale for Internet-Mediated Communities. *Cyberpsychology & Behavior*, *6*(1), 3–14. doi:10.1089/109493103321167929

Bieber, M., Engelbart, D., Furuta, R., Hiltz, S. R., Noll, J., & Preece, J. (2002). Toward Virtual Community Knowledge Evolution. *Journal of Management Information Systems*, *18*(4), 11–35.

Bock, G.-W., Zmud, R. W., Kim, Y.-G., & Lee, J.-N. (2005). Behavioral Intention Formation in Knowledge Sharing: Examining the Roles of Extrinsic Motivators, Social-Psychological Forces, and Organizational Climate. *Management Information Systems Quarterly*, *29*(1), 87–111.

Boissel, J.-P., Amsallem, E., Cucherat, M., Nony, P., & Haugh, M. (2004). Bridging the gap between therapeutic research results and physician prescribing decisions: knowledge transfer, a prerequisite to knowledge translation. *European Journal of Clinical Pharmacology*, *60*(9), 609–616. doi:10.1007/s00228-004-0816-2

Booth, J., Tolson, D., Hotchkiss, R., & Schofield, I. (2007). Using action research to construct national evidence-based nursing care guidance for gerontological nursing. *Journal of Clinical Nursing*, *16*(5), 945–953. doi:10.1111/j.1365-2702.2007.01773.x

Brooks, F., & Scott, P. (2006). Exploring knowledge work and leadership in online midwifery communication. *Journal of Advanced Nursing*, *55*(4), 510–520. doi:10.1111/j.1365-2648.2006.03937.x

Brown, J. S., & Duguid, P. (1998). Organizing Knowledge. *California Management Review*, *40*(3), 90–111.

Brown, J. S., & Duguid, P. (2001). Knowledge and organization: A social-practice perspective. *Organization Science*, *12*(2), 198–213. doi:10.1287/orsc.12.2.198.10116

Brown, T. A. (2006). *Confirmatory Factor Analysis for Applied Research*. New York: Guilford Press.

Chau, P. Y. K., & Hu, P. J.-H. (2001). Information Technology Acceptance by Individual Professionals: A Model Comparison Approach. *Decision Sciences, 32*(4), 699–718. doi:10.1111/j.1540-5915.2001.tb00978.x

Chau, P. Y. K., & Hu, P. J.-H. (2002). Investigating healthcare professionals' decisions to accept telemedicine technology: an empirical test of competing theories. *Information & Management, 39*(4), 297–311. doi:10.1016/S0378-7206(01)00098-2

Chen, A. N. K., & Edgington, T. M. (2005). Assessing Value in Organizational Knowledge Creation: Consideration for Knowledge Workers. *Management Information Systems Quarterly, 29*(2), 279–309.

CHI (Catholic Health Initiatives) Corporate Website. (2005). Retrieved December 21, 2006, from http://www.catholichealthinit.org/body.cfm?id=37785&action=detail&ref=1634

CHI (Catholic Health Initiatives) Corporate Website. (2008). Retrieved January 22, 2009, from http://www.catholichealthinit.org/default.cfm

Choi, B., & Lee, H. (2003). An empirical investigation of KM styles and their effect on corporate performance. *Information & Management, 40*(5), 403–417. doi:10.1016/S0378-7206(02)00060-5

Choi, M. (2006). Communities of practice: an alternative learning model for knowledge creation. *British Journal of Educational Technology, 37*(1), 143–146. doi:10.1111/j.1467-8535.2005.00486.x

Conner, M. (2005). Communities of practice in health care: a personal reflection. *Work Based Learning in Primary Care, 3*(4), 347–350.

Dubé, L., Bourhis, A., & Jacob, R. (2005). The impact of structuring characteristics on the launching of virtual communities of practice. *Journal of Organizational Change, 18*(2), 145–166. doi:10.1108/09534810510589570

Dupouët, O., & Yildizoğlu, M. (2006). Organizational performance in hierarchies and communities of practice. *Journal of Economic Behavior & Organization, 61*(4), 668–690. doi:10.1016/j.jebo.2004.07.011

Dymock, D., & McCarthy, C. (2006). Towards a learning organization? Employee perceptions. *The Learning Organization, 13*(5), 525–536. doi:10.1108/09696470610680017

Foy, P. S. (1999). Knowledge Management in Industry. In Liebowitz, J. (Ed.), *Knowledge Management Handbook*. Boca Raton, FL: CRC Press.

Gabbay, J., & le May, A. (2004). Evidence based guidelines or collectively constructed "mindlines?" Ethnographic study of knowledge management in primary care. *British Medical Journal, 329*(7473), 1013–1017. doi:10.1136/bmj.329.7473.1013

Gabbay, J., le May, A., Jefferson, H., Webb, D., Lovelock, R., Powell, J., & Lathlean, J. (2003). A case study of knowledge management in multi-agency consumer-informed 'communities of practice': implications for evidence-based policy development in health and social services. *Health: An Interdisciplinary Journal for the Social Study of Health. Illness & Medicine, 7*(3), 283–310.

Garavan, T. N., Carbery, R., & Murphy, E. (2007). Managing intentionally created communities of practice for knowledge sourcing across organisational boundaries. *The Learning Organization, 14*(1), 34–49. doi:10.1108/09696470710718339

Ghosh, B., & Scott, J. E. (2005). Comparing knowledge management in health-care and technical support organizations. *IEEE Transactions on Information Technology in Biomedicine*, *9*(2), 162–168. doi:10.1109/TITB.2005.847202

Goh, S. C. (2003). Improving organizational learning capability: lessons from two case studies. *The Learning Organization*, *10*(4), 216–227. doi:10.1108/09696470310476981

Hall, A., & Walton, G. (2004). Information overload within the health care system: a literature review. *Health Information and Libraries Journal*, *21*(2), 102–108. doi:10.1111/j.1471-1842.2004.00506.x

Hsu, M. K. (2007). *Structural equation modeling with Amos*. Retrieved from ftp://hqftp1.spss.com/pub/web/wp/Amos and SEM in the Services Sector.pdf

Hu, L.-T., & Bentler, P. M. (1999). Cutoff Criteria for Fit Indexes in Covariance Structure Analysis: Conventional Criteria versus New Alternatives. *Structural Equation Modeling*, *6*(1), 1–55. doi:10.1080/10705519909540118

Huang, N.-T., Wei, C.-C., & Chang, W.-K. (2007). Knowledge management: modeling the knowledge diffusion in community of practice. *Kybernetes*, *36*(5-6), 607–621. doi:10.1108/03684920710749703

Hung, D., & Chen, D.-T. (2003). Learning within the context of communities of practice: a re-conceptualization of tools, rules, and roles of the activity system. *Educational Media International*, *39*(3-4), 247–255.

Hung, D., Chen, D.-T., & Koh, T. S. (2006). The reverse LPP process for nurturing a community of practice. *Educational Media International*, *43*(4), 299–314. doi:10.1080/09523980600926267

Igbaria, M., Zinatelli, N., Cragg, P., & Cavaye, A. L. M. (1997). Personal Computing Acceptance Factors in Small Firms: A Structural Equation Model. *Management Information Systems Quarterly*, *21*(3), 279–305. doi:10.2307/249498

Inkpen, A. C., & Tsang, E. W. K. (2005). Social Capital Networks and Knowledge Transfer. *Academy of Management Review*, *30*(1), 146–165.

Kimble, C., & Hildreth, P. (2005). Dualities, distributed communities of practice and knowledge management. *Journal of Knowledge Management*, *9*(4), 102–113. doi:10.1108/13673270510610369

Kohlbacher, F., & Mukai, K. (2007). Japan's learning communities in Hewlett-Packard Consulting and Integration. *The Learning Organization*, *14*(1), 8–20. doi:10.1108/09696470710718311

LaPelle, N. (2004). Simplifying Qualitative Data Analysis Using General Purpose Software Tools. *Field Methods*, *16*(1), 85–108. doi:10.1177/1525822X03259227

Lave, J., & Wenger, E. (1991). *Situated Learning: Legitimate Peripheral Participation*. Cambridge, MA: Cambridge University Press.

Lee, J. Sr, & Valderrama, K. (2003). Building Successful Communities of Practice. *Information Outlook*, *7*(5), 28–32.

Lenz, R., & Reichert, M. (2007). IT support for healthcare processes – premises, challenges, perspectives. *Data & Knowledge Engineering*, *61*(1), 39–58. doi:10.1016/j.datak.2006.04.007

Lesser, E. L., & Storck, J. (2001). Communities of Practice and organizational performance. *IBM Systems Journal*, *40*(4), 831–841. doi:10.1147/sj.404.0831

Lin, N. (2001). *Social Capital*. Cambridge, UK: Cambridge University Press.

Lorence, D., & Abraham, J. (2006). Comparative Analysis of Medical Web Search Using Generalized vs. Niche Technologies. *Journal of Medical Systems*, *30*(3), 211–219. doi:10.1007/s10916-005-7990-y

Marsh, H. W., Hau, K.-T., & Wen, Z. (2004). In Search of Golden Rules: Comment on Hypothesis-Testing Approaches to Setting Cutoff Values for Fit Indexes and Dangers in Overgeneralizing Hu and Bentler's (1999) Findings. *Structural Equation Modeling*, *11*(3), 320–341. doi:10.1207/s15328007sem1103_2

McDermott, R. (1999). Why Information Technology Inspired But Cannot Deliver Knowledge Management. *California Management Review*, *41*(4), 103–117.

McDermott, R. (2002). Measuring the impact of communities. *Knowledge Management Review*, *5*(2), 26–29.

McFarland, D. J., & Hamilton, D. (2006). Adding contextual specificity to the technology acceptance model. *Computers in Human Behavior*, *22*(3), 427–447. doi:10.1016/j.chb.2004.09.009

Mulrow, C. D., & Lohr, K. N. (2001). Proof and policy from medical research evidence. *Journal of Health Politics, Policy and Law*, *26*(2), 249–266. doi:10.1215/03616878-26-2-249

Nahm, A. Y., Vonderembse, M. A., & Koufteros, X. A. (2004). The impact of organizational culture on time-based manufacturing and performance. *Decision Sciences*, *35*(4), 579–607. doi:10.1111/j.1540-5915.2004.02660.x

Nunamaker, J. F., Jr., & Chen, M. (1990). Systems Development in Information Systems Research. In *Proceedings of the Twenty-third Annual Hawaii International Conference on System Sciences* (Vol. 3, pp. 631-640).

Ong, C.-S., Lai, J.-Y., & Wang, Y.-S. (2004). Factors affecting engineers' acceptance of asynchronous e-learning systems in high-tech companies. *Information & Management*, *41*(6), 795–804. doi:10.1016/j.im.2003.08.012

Østerlund, C., & Carlile, P. (2005). Relations in Practice: Sorting Through Practice Theories on Knowledge Sharing in Complex Organizations. *The Information Society*, *21*(2), 91–107. doi:10.1080/01972240590925294

Parboosingh, J. T. (2002). Physician Communities of Practice: Where Learning and Practice Are Inseparable. *The Journal of Continuing Education in the Health Professions*, *22*(4), 230–236. doi:10.1002/chp.1340220407

Pardo, T. A., Cresswell, A. M., Thompson, F., & Zhang, J. (2006). Knowledge sharing in cross-boundary information system development in the public sector. *Information Technology Management*, *7*(4), 293–313. doi:10.1007/s10799-006-0278-6

Plaskoff, J. (2003). Intersubjectivity and community building: learning to learn organizationally. In Easterby-Smith, M., & Lyles, M. A. (Eds.), *The Blackwell Handbook of Organizational Learning and Knowledge Management* (pp. 161–184). Oxford, UK: Blackwell Publishing.

Rohde, M., Klamma, R., Jarke, M., & Wulf, V. (2007). Reality is our laboratory: communities of practice in applied computer science. *Behaviour & Information Technology*, *26*(1), 81–94. doi:10.1080/01449290600811636

Ryu, S., Ho, S. H., & Han, I. (2003). Knowledge sharing behavior of physicians in hospitals. *Expert Systems with Applications*, *25*(1), 113–122. doi:10.1016/S0957-4174(03)00011-3

Sandars, J., & Heller, R. (2006). Improving the implementation of evidence-based practice: a knowledge management perspective. *Journal of Evaluation in Clinical Practice, 12*(3), 341–346. doi:10.1111/j.1365-2753.2006.00534.x

Schermelleh-Engel, K., Moosbrugger, H., & Müller, H. (2003). Evaluating the Fit of Structural Equation Models: Tests of Significance and Descriptive Goodness-of-Fit Measures. *Methods of Psychological Research Online, 8*(2), 23–74.

Skinner, B. (2004). Web alert: news and views within healthcare -- managing the information overload. *Quality in Primary Care, 12*(4), 289–292.

Stevens, L. (2000, October). Incentives for Sharing. *Knowledge Management*, 54-60.

Storck, J., & Hill, P. (2000). Knowledge diffusion through strategic communities. *Sloan Management Review, 41*(2), 63–74.

Tang, F., Mu, J., & Maclachlan, D. L. (2008). Implication of network size and structure on organizations' knowledge transfer. *Expert Systems with Applications, 34*(2), 1109–1114. doi:10.1016/j.eswa.2006.12.020

Tang, H., & Ng, J. H. K. (2006). Googling for a diagnosis? Use of Google as a diagnostic aid: internet based study. *British Medical Journal, 333*(7579), 1143–1145. doi:10.1136/bmj.39003.640567.AE

Van Biervliet, A., & Edwards-Shafer, P. (2004). Consumer Health Information on the Web: Trends, Issues, and Strategies. *Medsurg Nursing, 13*(2), 91–96.

Van Schaik, P., Flynn, D., Van Wersch, A., Douglass, A., & Cann, P. (2004). The acceptance of a computerized decision-support system in primary care: A preliminary investigation. *Behaviour & Information Technology, 23*(5), 321–326. doi:10.1080/0144929041000669941

Venkatesh, V., Morris, M. G., Davis, G. B., & Davis, F. (2003). User Acceptance of Information Technology: Toward a Unified View. *Management Information Systems Quarterly, 27*(3), 425–478.

Vestal, W. (2003). Ten traits for a successful Community of Practice. *KM Review, 5*(6), 6.

Vestal, W. (2006). Sustaining: communities of practice. *KM World, 15*(3), 8–40.

von Lubitz, D., & Wickramasinghe, N. (2006). Network centric healthcare and bioinformatics: Unified operations within three domains of knowledge. *Expert Systems with Applications, 30*(1), 11–23. doi:10.1016/j.eswa.2005.09.069

Walczak, S. (2003). A Multiagent Architecture for Developing Medical Information Retrieval Agents. *Journal of Medical Systems, 27*(5), 479–498. doi:10.1023/A:1025668124244

Ward, M. M., Jaana, M., Behensky, J. A., Vartak, S., & Wakefield, D. S. (2006). Clinical Information System Availability and Use in Urban and Rural Hospitals. *Journal of Medical Information Systems, 30*(6), 429–438.

Wasko, M. M., & Faraj, S. (2005). Why Should I Share? Examining Social Capital and Knowledge Contribution in Electronic Networks of Practice. *Management Information Systems Quarterly, 29*(1), 35–57.

Wenger, E. (1998). *Communities of practice: Learning, meaning, and identity*. Cambridge, UK: Cambridge University Press.

Wenger, E. (2004). Knowledge management as a doughnut: Shaping your knowledge strategy through communities of practice. *Ivey Business Journal, 68*(3), 1–8.

Winkelman, W. J., & Choo, C. W. (2003). Provider-sponsored virtual communities for chronic patients: improving health outcomes through organizational patient-centered knowledge management. *Health Expectations*, *6*(4), 352–358. doi:10.1046/j.1369-7625.2003.00237.x

Wright, R. W., Brand, R. A., Dunn, W., & Spindler, K. P. (2007). How to Write a Systematic Review. *Clinical Orthopaedics and Related Research*, *455*, 23–29. doi:10.1097/BLO.0b013e31802c9098

Yamazaki, H. (2004). East Meets West in Japanese Communities: Combining face-to-face with virtual communications in CoPs. *KM Review*, *7*(2), 24–27.

Yi, M. Y., Jackson, J. D., Park, J. S., & Probst, J. C. (2006). Understanding information technology acceptance by individual professionals: Toward an integrative view. *Information & Management*, *43*(3), 350–363. doi:10.1016/j.im.2005.08.006

Zboralski, K., Salomo, S., & Gemuenden, H. G. (2006). Organizational Benefits of Communities of Practice: A Two-Stage Information Processing Model. *Cybernetics and Systems*, *37*(6), 533–552. doi:10.1080/01969720600734461

APPENDIX

KC Effectiveness Survey

The following brief survey has been developed in coordination with the (deleted for blind review) program. We are in the process of defining measures of the effectiveness of knowledge community initiatives within CHI. All responses are anonymous. The survey should take less than 10 minutes to complete. Your participation is appreciated!

Section 1 – Demographics (Everybody Answers)

What is your role?

- Physician
- Nurse
- Pharmacist
- Other Clinical Professional
- Administrative
- Corporate CHI, not assigned to a specific hospital

Please specify the level of your position.

- Executive
- Director/Manager/Supervisor
- Clinical Staff
- Support Staff

The hospital I work in is

- Rural
- Urban

Hospital bed size is:

- 1-99
- 100-250
- >250

I have been with CHI for

- 0-1 year
- 1-3 years
- 3-5 years
- 5-10 years
- >10 years

CHI Knowledge Communities include activities such as collaboration communities, Inside CHI and Live Meeting..Do you currently participate in one or more CHI Knowledge Communities? (Yes, No)

Conditional Page Break: *The participant doesn't see these instructions. This is an automatic transfer.*

- If yes (to CHI KC question above), go to next section
- If no & answered Executive or Dir/Mgr/Sup, go to section 3
- If no & did not answer Executive or Dir/Mgr/Sup, go to end

Table 9.

1. I belong to external professional groups that encourage the sharing of knowledge.					
2. I try to share knowledge with colleagues through involvement in CHI Knowledge Communities.					
3. It is difficult to connect with CHI colleagues about knowledge that I need.					
4. I am expected to share knowledge with CHI colleagues.					
5. I intend to share knowledge within CHI Knowledge Communities more frequently in the future.					
6. Most colleagues who are important to me share their knowledge with others through CHI Knowledge Communities.					
7. Knowledge sharing is easy to do within CHI Knowledge Communities.					
8. The CHI computerized systems for posting and retrieving information are an effective way to share knowledge					
9. I am not required to share knowledge within the CHI Knowledge Communities.					
10. I make an effort to share knowledge with colleagues when they ask.					
11. I can easily find leading / best practices within CHI Knowledge Communities.					
12. It is difficult for me to share knowledge frequently.					
13. I am able to easily find people with specific expertise within CHI Knowledge Communities.					
14. I have implemented leading / best practices that originated from within CHI Knowledge Communities.					
15. Knowledge sharing through CHI Knowledge Communities is valuable to me.					
16. CHI encourages the sharing of knowledge					

Section 2 – Knowledge Sharing

Answer the questions in Table 9 about knowledge sharing within CHI on a scale of 1 (strong disagreement) to 5 (strong agreement).

Strongly Strongly
Disagree Neutral Agree
1 2 3 4 5

Answer the questions in Table 10 about Participation in CHI Knowledge Communities on a scale of 1 (strong disagreement) to 5 (strong agreement).

Participating in a CHI KC…

Strongly Strongly
Disagree Neutral Agree
1 2 3 4 5

Table 10.

1. Helps me do my job better.					
2. Saves (has saved) me significant time &/or money on programs or projects.					
3. Reduces time needed to solve problems.					
4. Decreases rework (avoids reinventing the wheel).					
5. Helps me to avoid costly mistakes.					
6. Helps me to be more connected and to feel part of the CHI organization.					
7. Is a valuable part of being within the CHI system.					

How many times have you shared knowledge with colleagues in external professional groups in the past 6 months (via email, online communities, chat boards, knowledge repository, conference call, meeting, etc.)?

- None
- Once
- 2-6 times
- 7-12 times
- 13-24 times
- >24 times

How many times have you participated in CHI Knowledge Community activities in the past 6 months (via email, online communities, chat boards, knowledge repository, conference call, meeting, etc.)?

- None
- Once
- 2-6 times
- 7-12 times
- 13-24 times
- >24 times

Please describe a situation where significant time &/or money was saved (or loss avoided) as a result of knowledge sharing within a CHI knowledge community:

Conditional Page Break: *The participant doesn't see these instructions. This is an automatic transfer.*

- ◦ If answered Executive or Dir/Mgr/Sup, go to section 3
- ◦ Otherwise, go to end

Section 3 – Management (Only Those Who Are Executive / Manager / Supervisor or Director Answer This Section)

Answer the questions in Table 11 about CHI Knowledge Communities on a scale of 1 (strong disagreement) to 5 (strong agreement).

Table 11.

1. CHI Knowledge Communities are valuable and result in positive benefits for the organization.					
2. There is a positive, definable impact resulting from my staff participating in CHI Knowledge Communities.					
3. Employee knowledge-sharing through CHI Knowledge Communities should be rewarded.					
4. I encourage my staff to participate in CHI Knowledge Communities.					

Strongly Strongly
Disagree Neutral Agree
1 2 3 4 5

What specific benefits do you see resulting from CHI Knowledge Communities?
How do you encourage and enable your staff to participate?

Section 4 – Conclusion/End

All participants, please add any comments or thoughts about knowledge-sharing or knowledge communities at CHI.

This work was previously published in Journal of Organizational and End User Computing, Volume 22, Issue 4, edited by M. Adam Mahmood, pp. 24-50, copyright 2010 by IGI Publishing (an imprint of IGI Global).

Chapter 3
Culturally Compatible Usability Work:
An Interpretive Case Study on the Relationship between Usability Work and Its Cultural Context in Software Product Development Organizations

Netta Iivari
University of Oulu, Finland

ABSTRACT

This paper analyzes how organizational culture is intertwined with usability work in software (SW) development organizations. Usability is an important quality characteristic of software products and systems. However, the development of usability is challenging in SW development. Organizational culture has been argued to affect usability work in SW development organizations, thus, this paper takes a culture-oriented approach in the analysis of usability work in two SW development organizations operating in the product development context. First, based on a literature review, a definition of usability work is offered. An interpretive view of organizational culture, acknowledging its recent critique, is then introduced and utilized in the empirical analysis. The empirical results suggest that differences exists in how usability work is modified and interpreted in the organizations with divergent cultural contexts, those advocating different motives and practices for usability work. Finally, the importance of understanding the cultural context into which usability work is introduced is emphasized, and it is argued that culturally compatible strategies to usability work should be adopted.

DOI: 10.4018/978-1-4666-0140-6.ch003

1. INTRODUCTION

This paper examines how organizational culture and usability work are intertwined in software (SW) development organizations operating in the product development context. Generally, usability is an important quality characteristic of a software products and systems (Gulliksen et al., 2006; ISO 9241 1998; ISO 13407 1999). Especially the field of Human Computer Interaction (HCI) has addressed the development of usable software products and systems in approaches such as Usability Engineering (UE) and User-Centered Design (UED) (Iivari, 2006a; Kujala, 2003; Mayhew, 1999b; Nielsen, 1993; Rosson & Carroll, 2002). Within the field of HCI, a widely cited definition of usability specifies it as 'the extent to which a product can be used by specified users to achieve specified goals with effectiveness, efficiency and satisfaction in a specified context of use' (ISO 9241 1998). Also Information Systems (IS) research has emphasized the importance of usability: it has been praised as an essential element in technology acceptance (Davis, 1989) and diffusion of innovations (Rogers, 1995). The Technology Acceptance Model, widely utilized in IS research, defines as relevant aspects in the acceptance process to be perceived usefulness – "the degree to which a person believes that using a particular system would enhance his or her job performance"; and perceived ease of use – "the degree to which a person believes that using a particular system would be free of effort" (Davis, 1989, p. 320). The theory of diffusion of innovations is another widely used theory within the IS field. The perceived usefulness is very similar to the relative advantage construct in the theory of diffusion of innovations, the perceived ease of use resembling very closely the complexity construct (cf., Rogers, 1995). One can conclude that the importance of usability (as well as usefulness) is accepted within the both research fields, the field of HCI, however, providing also practical guidance for developing usability. Therefore, in this paper, HCI literature on developing usability is reviewed, as a result of which the concept of *usability work* is defined.

Afterwards, an interpretive view of organizational culture as *continuous spinning and re-spinning of the fragile webs of meaning* (cf., Ortner, 1999) is introduced, and the paper examines usability work and its cultural context in SW development organizations operating in the product development context. Product development refers to the development of commercial, generic SW for external use, the SW being targeted at large user population that might be unknown until the product is on the market (Carmel, 1997; Carmel & Sawyer, 1998; Grudin, 1991a; Grudin & Pruitt, 2002; Keil & Carmel, 1995; Kujala, 2007). One can argue that in this context an ideal is that "anonymous and un-locatable designers (…) deliver technological solutions to equally de-contextualized and consequently un-locatable users", an ideal which can be labeled as "design from nowhere", which is "closely tied to the goal of construing technical systems as commodities that can be stabilized and cut loose from the sites of their production long enough to be exported *en masse* to the sites of their use" (Suchman, 2002, p. 95). The product development context is a new and less studied context in IS research; but it is the context in which the field of HCI emerged (Grudin, 1991a). In the IS literature the traditional context has been custom IS development (Grudin, 1991a; Markus & Mao, 2004), but new trends – e.g. package installations, outsourcing, web information systems – have emerged (Markus & Mao, 2004), making the product development context and its challenges relevant also for the IS community.

HCI research has assigned the responsibility of the development of usability to a group of specialists variably called usability, UCD, UE or human factors specialists in the literature (Aucella, 1997; Bias & Reitmeyer, 1995; Borgholm & Madsen, 1999; Bødker & Buur, 2002; Fellenz, 1997; Gulliksen et al., 2006; Iivari, 2006a; Iivari,

2006b; Tudor, 1998). Generally, there is a lot of HCI literature offering guidance for developing usability, but the literature is fragmented and without shared terminology. However, from here on in this paper, these specialists will be called usability specialists and their work usability work. It has already been revealed that their work is very challenging in product development context as well as elsewhere (Bloomer & Croft, 1997; Boivie et al., 2006; Borgholm & Madsen, 1999; Bødker & Buur, 2002; Carmel & Sawyer, 1998; Gulliksen et al., 2006, Iivari, 2006a; Iivari, 2006b; Kujala, 2007; Mayhew, 1999a; Mayhew, 1999b; Rosenbaum et al., 2000). A culture-oriented approach is taken in the analysis of usability work in SW product development organizations. The effects of organizational culture on different kinds of IS phenomenon has been a very popular and also a current topic (Gallivan & Srite, 2005, Leidner & Kayworth, 2006). Existing HCI literature suggests that organizational culture may affect usability work in SW development organizations (Bloomer & Croft, 1997; Catarci et al., 2002; Hutchings & Knox, 1995; Iivari, 2006a; Mayhew, 1999a; Rosenbaum et al., 2000). However, these studies generally do not report on how they defined or empirically analyzed culture. In addition, it has been argued that culture is a very complex concept, and there are many controversies in both defining and applying it – in IS literature, organizational studies as well as in anthropology (Alvesson, 1990; Avison & Myers, 1995; Kroeber & Kluckhohn, 1952; Smircich, 1983). Therefore, a careful analysis of the existing research on organizational culture is needed as a basis of this research effort.

Based on the discussion, the specific research questions examined in this paper are formulated the following way. The research effort examines: 1) what is organizational culture and how should one study it; 2) what is usability work; and 3) what is the relationship between organizational culture and usability work – how can one characterize it? As a summary, the research effort is motivated by the following arguments: usability is an important quality characteristic of software products and systems, development of usability is a challenge, organizational culture may affect the development of usability, however, there are controversies related to defining both the concept of organizational and usability work, due to which a review of the related literatures is needed before empirically examining the relationship. As a result of empirical examination, this paper identifies two alternative and allegedly culturally compatible ways of organizing usability work in software product development organizations.

The paper is organized as follows. The next section reviews the literature on usability work. The third section discusses the concept of organizational culture. The fourth section presents the cases involved in this study and the procedures of data gathering and analysis. The ensuing sections outline the results of the empirical examination and discuss their implications. The final section summarizes the key findings, outlines their limitations, and suggests paths for future work.

2. USABILITY WORK

This section reviews HCI literature on usability work. As mentioned, the literature assumes usability specialists to take care of usability in the development. The development of usability necessitates understanding who are the intended users, what are their goals regarding the use of the system, and in what kind of context of use the system will be used (cf., ISO 9241, 1998). Furthermore, the solution is to be designed so that the users can achieve their goals with effectiveness, efficiency and satisfaction (cf., ISO 9241, 1998). It is assumed that *users are configured* – i.e., the users are defined and delineated, and the parameters for their work practices are established – already during development (Grint & Woolgar, 1997). The developers always inscribe predictions about the world into technological artifacts: they produce projected, anticipated users with specific competencies, motives, tastes and aspirations, and define the relationships between the object and the actors in the use setting (Akrich, 1992). In order to ensure that the resulting solution is usable for the user, one could assume that it is of paramount importance to 'know the users'. Indeed, the HCI literature maintains the usability specialists are to 'know the users' and based on that, to 'represent the users' in the development (Cooper & Bowers, 1995). The term *represent* implies that user participation in the development is indirect; i.e., user influence is exerted through these intermediaries (cf., Mumford, 1983). In this paper the focus is on *representing* in a political sense, in which representing denotes one person standing for another, having delegated authority (http://www.m-w.com). Usability specialists are expected to act as user representatives, who are to have knowledge about the users and to stand for the user population in the development. Next we review in more detail what is included in this work.

As mentioned, the field of HCI arose in the product development context, in which the focus was initially on the generic aspects of HCI and on the look and feel of the SW (Grudin, 1991a; Grudin, 1991b). The goal was to produce analytical models and general principles for HCI design. However, psychology and experimental research-based HCI was soon criticized, and the focus shifted to fields such as sociology and anthropology, and consequently, to field methods and ethnographic analyses (Bannon, 1991; Cooper & Bowers, 1995; Karat, 1997; Rosson & Carroll, 2002). Currently, empirical inquiries related to users, their goals and work practices, and the context of use are strongly advocated in HCI textbooks (e.g., Beyer & Holtzblatt, 1998; Cooper, 1999; Mayhew, 1999b; Nielsen, 1993; Rosson & Carroll, 2002). However, analytical models and general design principles have also preserved a legitimate position within the field of HCI: for example usability inspection methods, that do not necessitate user participation, but instead the expertise of the inspectors relying on HCI guidelines and heuristics, are still popular (e.g., Mayhew, 1999b; Nielsen & Mack, 1994; Nielsen, 1993). Therefore, in the HCI literature the authority to represent the users is to be based on empirical investigations and/or on general state-of-the-art HCI knowledge. In either case, the usability specialists are to represent the users also in the presentational sense, in which *representing the user* refers to the crafting of representations of users and their work for making users and their work visible for development (Suchman, 1995).

Furthermore, the focus has turned to the role of HCI in the design process and to the relationship between HCI and designers (Cooper & Bowers, 1995). At first, the role of usability specialists was restricted to assurance testing at the end of the development process (Karat, 1997; Rosson & Carroll, 2002). They were in an informative or consultative role - allowed to act as providers of information or to comment on predefined design solutions (cf., Damodaran, 1996). However, later on it was acknowledged that usability specialists should be in a participative role; actively taking part in the design process, having decision-making power regarding the solution (cf., Damodaran, 1996). Furthermore, usability specialists have been positioned as facilitators between users and designers (Kyng, 1998). Related to this, the background is in the participatory design (PD) tradition (Greenbaum & Kyng, 1991). The PD-oriented literature argues that the usability specialists - if needed at all – are to support and facilitate cooperation between users, designers and usability specialists and make everyone comfortable with taking part in the design process (Bødker & Buur, 2002; Kyng, 1998).

However, the designers have also been postulated as a critical target group. Cooper and Bowers (1995) argue that HCI research wants to make its results usable to the designers, who are postulated as users of the results. Indeed, it is also strongly emphasized that designers and usability specialists should cooperate in order for the work of the usability specialists to influence the design (Aucella, 1997; Billingsley, 1995;

Bloomer & Croft, 1997; Fellenz, 1997; Grudin, 1991a; Grudin, 1991b; Tudor, 1998). It is argued that project teams should perceive usability specialists as team members and allies (Aucella, 1997; Bias & Reitmeyer, 1995; Fellenz, 1997; Mayhew, 1999a; Mayhew, 1999b; Rosenbaum et al., 2000). A part of recent HCI literature suggests that design solutions should be produced solely by the professional usability specialists, who are to have the power and authority to produce solutions that suit the users (e.g., Cooper, 1999; Iivari, 2006b; Muller & Carey; 2002). They are expected to act as the configurers of the users, who have 'knowledge about the user' and general state-of-the-art HCI knowledge, through which they are well-equipped to produce suitable solutions for the users (Iivari, 2006b).

Furthermore, regarding this facilitator role, the role of usability specialists has been extended to include selling usability to the larger organizational context, i.e. they are to act as spokespeople for users in their company. Usability specialists are to act as change agents with political skills, making their organizations more user-centric: they are to initiate cooperation with many different groups involved in 'configuring the user', e.g., marketing, training and documentation, and tailor their message to languages each target group understands (Beyer & Holtzblatt, 1998; Billingsley, 1995; Bloomer & Croft, 1997; Cooper, 1999; Hutchings & Knox, 1995; Grudin, 1991b; Mayhew, 1999a; Mayhew, 1999b; Rosenbaum et al., 2000). Management is also postulated as an important target group (Beyer & Holtzblatt, 1998; Bias & Reitmeyer, 1995; Billingsley, 1995; Cooper, 1999; Grudin, 1991b; Fellenz, 1997; Mayhew, 1999b; Nielsen, 1993). Furthermore, there are usually different kinds of change and improvement initiatives in organizations, and usability specialists should be perceived as allies also in terms of these initiatives (Bloomer & Croft, 1997; Mayhew, 1999a).

It is also argued that usability work should contribute to the business success of the development organization (Beyer & Holtzblatt, 1998; Bloomer & Croft, 1997; Cooper, 1999; Fellenz, 1997; Mayhew, 1999a; Mayhew, 1999b; Rosenbaum et al., 2000). Usability specialists should ensure that their work makes sense from the business perspective and is related to achieving key business goals (Beyer & Holtzblatt, 1998; Bloomer & Croft, 1997; Cooper, 1999; Fellenz, 1997). Consideration of cost-benefit tradeoffs is also recommended, since they may play a major role in the adoption of usability methods (Mayhew, 1999b; Nielsen, 1993; Vredenburg et al., 2002).

In this discussion, the ideology of managerialism is evident. Management goals are postulated as the main motivators of usability work. This orientation emphasizes profit maximization, work intensification, and competitive advantage achievable through usability (cf., Asaro, 2000; Hirschheim & Klein, 1989; Spinuzzi, 2002). The aim is to improve the design process (identify user requirements, validate design options, deal with changes in requirements) and/or facilitate implementation (ensure follow-up, overcome resistance, ensure acceptance) (cf., Nandhakumar & Jones, 1997). Generally, usability work aims at functional empowerment of the users, which maintains that workers should be able to do their job effectively and efficiently (Clement, 1994).

Finally, the concept of *usability work* is defined and summarized in Table 1. Usability work refers to the work of the usability specialists aiming at functional empowerment of the users. However, there are also other motives for usability work, outlined in Table 1. In carrying out usability work, it is assumed that there needs to be 'knowledge about the user' as a basis while 'configuring the user' and the gaining of this knowledge is to be organized by the usability specialists. However, there are differences in what is included in this work. The usability specialists are to represent the user in a political and presentational sense, to take part in the 'configuration of the user' in informative, consultative, participative or configurer role, and to facilitate cooperation among other 'configurers of the user'.

Table 1. Defining usability work: why and how it is to be carried out

Aspect	Usability work
Why	- Functional empowerment of users - Profit maximization, work intensification, competitive advantage, improving design process, facilitating implementation
How	- Users represented by usability specialists, indirect user participation o In political sense: acting as 'user representatives', the legitimacy resting on empirical inquiries and 'state-of-the-art HCI knowledge' o In presentational sense: crafting representations of users and their work - Informative, consultative, participative or configurer roles for usability specialists - Usability specialists facilitating cooperation among the configurers of the user

3. ORGANIZATIONAL CULTURE

3.1 Approaches to Organizational Culture

The concept of culture is derived from the tradition of cultural anthropology, in which the concept and studies on culture have been traditional focuses of study. The concept is central within the discipline; but despite this, the concept is not clearly defined one (Kroeber & Kluckhohn, 1952; Lett, 1987). Nevertheless, the symbolic school especially has had a central position in cultural anthropology (Lett, 1987; Ortner, 1999; Smircich, 1983). The symbolic school postulates culture as a system of shared symbols or meanings, with researchers seeking out local interpretations in order to reveal cultural meanings from the native's point of view (Geertz, 1973; Lett, 1987; Smircich, 1983). Geertz, a famous anthropologist from the symbolic school, states that "man is an animal suspended in webs of significance he himself has spun, I take culture to be those webs, and the analysis of it to be therefore not an experimental science in search of law but an interpretive one in search of meaning" (Geertz, 1973, p. 5).

However, there are several approaches within which organizational culture studies have been carried out (Czarniawska-Joerges, 1992; Iivari, 2006a; Smircich, 1983). The approaches can be labeled as comparative, clinical and interpretive (Iivari, 2006a), of which only the interpretive approach relies on the tradition of cultural anthropology and its methods. The comparative approach, on the other hand, postulates culture as an independent, explanatory variable (Ouchi & Wilkins, 1985; Smircich, 1983). Culture is perceived as measurable traits or dimensions that can be compared; the measurement relying on some kind of typology of organizational culture, which is assumed to be applicable to all organizations studied (Iivari, 2006a). The researchers aim at deriving cause and effect relationships (Iivari, 2006a). This approach has been very popular among the organizational culture researchers in the IS context. These studies have revealed the importance of cultural compatibility; they have proposed compatible culture types for different kinds of technologies (e.g., Ahadi, 2004; Harrington & Ruppel, 1999; Ruppel & Harrington, 2001) as well as compatible implementation strategies for different culture types (e.g., Pliskin et al., 1993; Ruppel & Harrington, 2001).

The clinical approach, furthermore, views culture as a manipulable, controllable, dependent variable that is to be modified by some treatment to achieve desired ends (Iivari, 2006a). Therefore, it is assumed that cultures can be managed and intentionally changed. Culture is seen as an adaptive mechanism, which can be guided and controlled for better adaptation or even as a managerial tool to be utilized in the pursuit of excellence (Alvesson, 1990; Czarniawska-Joerges, 1992; Gallivan & Srite, 2005; Iivari, 2006a; Leidner & Kayworth,

2006; Schein, 1985). Also this approach has been utilized a lot in organizational culture studies in the IS context. The studies have defined ideal cultures that should be, and according to the studies can be, aimed at, and offered guidance on how to manipulate cultures towards the ideal state (e.g., Cabrera et al., 2001; Fok et al., 2001; Harper & Utley, 2001; Kanungo et al., 2001).

Finally, as mentioned, the interpretive approach relies on the tradition of cultural anthropology, and is the 'traditional, generally accepted' approach on culture inquiry. Cultures are assumed to be socially produced and they are to be approached from the native's point of view. Ethnography is postulated as the main method for data gathering; the researchers should spend long periods of time in organization and participate in the daily activities with the culture members in order to understand the culture in depth, without predefined categories restricting data gathering (Czarniawska-Joerges, 1992; Iivari, 2006a). It is also assumed that cultures can not be designed or intentionally managed (Alvesson, 1990; Czarniawska-Joerges, 1992; Gallivan & Srite, 2005; Iivari, 2006a; Leidner & Kayworth, 2006). Culture studies in the IS context have been carried out quite extensively also within this approach. These studies focus on the interpretations and meanings attached to technologies; they are interpreted and reinterpreted in the cultural context in an emergent process of sense making (e.g., Brown, 1995; Davison & Martinsons, 2002; Dent, 1991; Dube & Robey, 1999; Kaarst-Brown & Robey, 1999). Furthermore, the dynamics between the technology and the context are highlighted from the opposite point of view also: the effects on the cultural context are brought up. Technologies are perceived of being capable to produce new forms of cultural knowledge and to change the cultural context in a reciprocal relationship (Brown, 1995; Dent, 1991; Dube & Robey, 1999; Kaarst-Brown & Robey, 1999). The studies also emphasize the need to tailor the technology so that it is compatible with the context (e.g., Brown, 1995; Davison & Martinsons, 2002).

Both the comparative and clinical approaches can be criticized as relying on very naïve notions of culture: the comparative approach views culture as a variable, the clinical approach even as a designable, manipulable variable (Iivari, 2006a). The instrumental, utilitarian aspects that are the most distinctive features of the clinical approach make this approach even more problematic than the comparative approach - these aspects contradict the notion of culture developed within anthropology, and are in sharp contrast with the ethical concerns culture studies within cultural anthropology share (Iivari, 2006a). Both approaches seem to rely on rather mechanistic assumptions about organizations and people. Especially naïve are the assumptions about culture and people being directly manipulable. Furthermore, it has been warned that causal relations between organizational culture and consequences of technology should be questioned (Robey & Azevedo, 1994). Probably this applies also to usability work. Therefore, in this research effort the interpretive approach was selected as suitable for the analysis of culture, which is thus viewed as a symbolic system guiding the behavior of the cultural members.

3.2 Reformulating the Interpretive Approach to Culture

Also the interpretive approach to culture, however, has been criticized recently. The view of culture as a static, shared pattern or whole has been questioned (Borofsky, 1994; Clifford & Marcus, 1986; Fox, 1991; Keesing & Strathern, 1998; Ortner, 1999). Researchers have brought up that cultures are always plural and open to interpretations, due to which they should not be viewed as fixed sets of shared meanings, but instead as fragmented, emergent, pluralistic phenomena - if culture is seen as a system of meanings, one should at least acknowledge that the meanings are continuously negotiated and struggled over (Borofsky, 1994;

Clifford & Marcus, 1986; Fox, 1991; Keesing & Strathern, 1994; Ortner, 1999; Weedon, 2004). People continuously spin the fragile webs of meanings, and focus should thus be on meaning-making, not on the system (Ortner, 1999). Actually, the concept of *cultural* should be preferred instead of the concept of culture, since the viewpoints presented above, as well as *cultural* highlight the fragmented, emergent nature of culture - if the concept of culture is used, then the phenomenon is already essentialized and reified (Borofsky, 1994; Clifford & Marcus, 1986; Keesing & Strathern, 1994; Ortner, 1999). Similarly, the simplistic view of organizational culture as a harmonious, static, shared entity should be abandoned and instead, organizational culture should be seen as contested, changing and emergent, and meanings constantly recreated and negotiated in organizations (Avison & Myers, 1995, Czarniawska-Joerges, 1992; Robey & Azevedo, 1994).

Therefore, this paper adopts the interpretive view of culture, acknowledging the recent critique. Instead of analyzing culture's effects on a variable labeled as usability work, this paper analyzes the process of negotiating and modifying usability work and its cultural context. It is assumed that usability work might be culturally modified in the SW development organizations. In this paper the cultural context, the process and the end result of this modification are under examination. The concept of *cultural* (in organizations) is used to refer to the symbolic system of meanings, but this system is perceived to consist of continuous spinning and re-spinning of the fragile webs of meaning (Ortner, 1999). Therefore, the Geertzian tradition is supplemented with more recent research on interpretive culture inquiry (Fox, 1991; Ortner, 1999). In IS research, interpretive culture inquiries have been popular (e.g., Dent, 1991; Dube & Robey, 1999; Kaarst-Brown & Robey, 1999), but the recent critique presented within cultural anthropology has not yet been acknowledged. The continuous spinning and re-spinning of the fragile webs of meanings is related to the joint enterprise, shared practice, mutual relationships and collective identity (Lave & Wenger, 1991; van Maanen & Barley, 1985; Wenger, 1998). With respect to cultural identity, it is important to acknowledge that identity is always relational: it is defined in relation to what one is not - identity always has its "other," from which difference is manifested (Weedon, 2004). One should focus on the construction of the notions of *we* and *the other* (Weedon, 2004). Furthermore, the spinning of the fragile webs of meaning is also related to the joint enterprise of the community, related to which the community shares and constantly refines its practice that supports the enterprise (Lave & Wenger, 1991; van Maanen & Barley, 1985; Wenger, 1998).

4. RESEARCH DESIGN

In this research effort we utilized a case study method, in which one examines "a phenomenon in its natural setting, employing multiple methods of data collection to gather information from one or few entities (people, groups, or organizations). The boundaries of the phenomenon are not clearly evident at the outset of the research and no experimental control or manipulation is used" (Benbasat et al. 1987: 370). More specifically we utilized an interpretive case study method, in which the researchers assume that our "knowledge of reality is gained only through social constructions", and attempt to understand and make sense of the world, not to explain in the predictive sense (Klein & Myers, 1999, p. 69). The meanings attached to the phenomenon studied are focused upon (Denzin & Lincoln, 2000). Theories are used only as sensitizing devices; the aim is not to falsify them as is the case in the positivist case studies (Klein & Myers, 1999). In an interpretive case study the goal is to capture the native's point of view, to produce thick descriptions, and to gain thorough understandings of particular cases (Denzin & Lincoln, 2000; Klein & Myers, 1999). However, also interpretive research aims at generalizations; the particularities in the empirical material should be related to more abstract categories, and the "unique instances" observed in the cases should be related to the "ideas and concepts that apply to multiple situations" (Klein & Myers, 1999, p. 75). The generalizations are to be viewed as "explanations of particular phenomena derived from empirical interpretive research in specific IS settings, which may be valuable in the future in other organizations and contexts" (Walsham, 1995, p. 79).

The interpretive case study method is suitable when studying how organizational culture and usability work are intertwined in the product development context. In focus are the meanings connected to usability work and its cultural context, and their co-construction. The reciprocal process of negotiating and modifying usability work and its cultural context was examined in two organizational settings. Access to the settings was gained through a research project that dealt with the facilitation of usability work in SW development organizations. The project included action research -oriented researchers developing methods for usability work in close cooperation with the organizations. In addition, the project included qualitative, interpretive research–oriented researchers empirically examining usability work and its cultural contexts in the settings. The aim of this part of research was to examine the context and the process of usability work as it naturally unfolds, documenting it as much as possible. We observed these issues for three years time, thus gaining a long-term insight into the evolving negotiation and modification of the cultural context and usability work. We adopted the role of an outsider observer rather than an involved researcher, having no direct personal stake in the outcomes and interpretations (Walsham, 1995). We did not go native to the extent that the study could be called ethnographic. However, the research material has been gathered over a period of three years and during that time, even though we were not active agents involved in the activities in the field, we visited the field intensively.

4.2 Case Description

Two cases were involved in this study. They involve the product development units from two SW development companies operating in Finland. Unit A is part of a large global corporation, whose responsibility is user-interface (UI) SW development. There are approximately 30 employees in the unit. Most of them are SW designers, whose responsibilities include designing, coding and testing the SW. They work in large-scale product development projects which involve personnel from several organizational units. There is also a team of usability specialists (4 persons) in the unit. The first usability specialist had been hired a couple of years prior to the research effort.

Unit B, on the other hand, is a product development unit of a small-to-medium-sized SW house. The unit has 25 employees. Unit B's responsibility is product development. The unit is divided into two teams; a development team and a development services team. Most of the employees on the development team are SW designers. Few designers focus specifically on UI development. The development services team contains expertise in, for example, testing, documentation, usability and graphical design. Unit B has a long history of usability work; usability testing began in the early 1990s. There had been a large team of usability specialists and graphical designers in the unit; the number had been cut down, however. During the data gathering, there was one usability specialist left in the unit.

The cases were chosen to provide examples of interesting polar types. To make the process of interest clearly observable, cases involving polar types and extreme situations are recommended (Eisenhardt, 1989). These two cases provided interesting examples of two polar types, since unit A is part of a large, global corporation, whereas unit B is part of a small SW house. In addition,

Table 2. Methods and informants in data gathering

Data Gathering Method	Informants, Unit A	Informants, Unit B
Process assessment	10	9
Organizational culture surveys	30	21
Interviews	4	4
Workshop 1	3	5
Workshop 2	6	7

the units' backgrounds in usability work clearly differed, from over a decade (unit B) to only a couple of years (unit A). Insights provided by Poltrock and Grudin (1994) regarding user participation in large, hierarchical organizations, and by Carmel and Sawyer (1998) regarding user participation in companies developing packaged SW characterized by entrepreneurial, individualistic milieus and immature processes indicate that the differences mentioned above might have some implications on usability work. Since there is not much research on organizational factors affecting usability work, the site selection had to rely on the above-mentioned factors.

4.3 Data Gathering

The research material was gathered over a 3-year period in the early 2000s by utilizing multiple methods for data gathering (see Table 2). The material was gathered while conducting process assessments in the units and while supporting the units in usability work by offering workshops and training. In the process assessments we interviewed the personnel of the units about their ways of working in a selected project, and evaluated whether usability work was carried out in the projects. Afterwards, we presented the results to the personnel of the units and gathered feedback. Furthermore, we organized different kinds of workshop and training sessions related to usability work in the units. In addition, we held regular meetings with the personnel of the units, discussing the current state of the project and planning for the future. Memos from the meetings, interview transcripts from the assessments, the assessment reports, units' internal documentation related to their ways of working, and all e-mail correspondence with the personnel of the units were saved for the purposes of the research. The research team also kept field notes after all joint events.

We also gathered primarily cultural data from the units. First we delivered organizational culture surveys to the personnel of the units. The personnel filled in the questionnaires in a weekly meeting. We produced a report on the survey results for each unit, after which we interviewed the personnel and gathered feedback from the survey results. First we interviewed the usability specialists of the unit. We then interviewed people whose work was directly related to the unit's core mission. The usability specialists together with their managers decided the interviewees. With both types of interviewees we discussed the cultural context in the unit and the position of usability work in the unit. After the interviews we produced a report on the interview results for the units. We then organized workshop sessions in the units, in which we again focused on cultural context and the position of usability work in the units. In these sessions we discussed and evaluated the interview results. Finally, we organized additional workshop sessions in which the results gained though the different techniques for data gathering were compared and contrasted with the results of other units. In addition, before the workshop sessions we went through all the memos, e-mails, field notes, and assessment reports produced in relation to each unit. From this material we listed the usability activities carried out in the units, reported problems related to these activities and preferences for future actions that the units had expressed. We presented this material to also allow the personnel to comment on the material. In both workshop sessions, again, the company representatives selected the participants: usability specialists, designers as well as managers were invited for hearing the results and commenting on them. The interviews and workshop sessions were all tape-recorded and the tapes transcribed.

4.4 Data Analysis

The analysis of qualitative data has been argued to be the most difficult and least codified phase of the interpretive research: the researchers have a large amount of data that is not mechanically manipulable (Eisenhardt, 1989; Walsham, 1995). The ideal in interpretive research is that there is no theory under consideration during the data gathering and analysis. This, however, is impossible, since researchers' prior knowledge and assumptions always shape the investigation, and actually, it has been argued that prejudice, prejudgment, and prior knowledge are a necessary starting point for our interpretations (Denzin & Lincoln, 2000; Klein & Myers, 1999). Interpretive research seeks emic meanings – meanings held by the people within the case studied (Denzin & Lincoln, 2000). However, Geertz reminds us that: "all anthropological writings are interpretations of interpretations. What we call our data are really our own constructions of other people's constructions of what they and their compatriots are up to." (Geertz 1973, p. 9) Interpretive practice is therefore always artistic, political, and creative (Denzin & Lincoln, 2000). In interpretive research the researcher must be acknowledged as a central instrument in the data gathering and analysis, and that the research material is socially constructed through the interaction between the researcher and the researched. With this in mind, researchers should carefully reflect on their position, on the relationship to the ones researched, and on the whole research process (Denzin & Lincoln, 2000; Klein & Myers, 1999; Schwandt, 2000; Walsham, 1995).

The data analysis proceeded in different phases. During the culture analysis, we categorized the findings from the interview after each interview. The categorization was inductive and based on empirical data. Case study write-ups were produced and commented on by the interviewees and by the workshop participants. The workshop participants also commented on the material having to do with the position of usability work in their unit that was presented in the second workshop sessions. Therefore, the technique of member checking was utilized extensively in this research effort, adding thereby to the credibility of the results. The research subjects have had numerous opportunities to evaluate the research results. Their comments have also been taken into account in the following phase of inquiry. Another reason for utilizing the member checking technique was to make use of previously-gathered data as a basis for reflection for the following data gathering effort. The case study write-ups also succeeded in initiating reflection of the cultural members, thus forming a good basis for more in-depth investigation.

Afterwards, we adopted a social constructivist epistemological stance, which rejects a "naïve realist view of representation" (meaning realism – "meanings are fixed entities that can be discovered") and the notion of language as a discloser of meaning (Schwandt, 2000, pp.197-200). A weak version assumes that there still are better and worse interpretations, but a strong version rejects even that notion, maintaining that all statements are produced by particular interpreters and should be analyzed with suspicion (Schwandt, 2000). We adopted the weak version of social constructivism, which emphasizes the socially constructed nature of research and research material. The empirical material was seen to capture a process of meaning construction and a process of representa-

Table 3. Analytical framework outlining aspects of cultural context and usability work

Cultural context	Usability work
- Collective identity and joint enterprise (who are we and what are we supposed to be up to?) - Shared practice (how are we supposed to carry out our work?) - Mutual relationships (how are we supposed to relate to each other?)	- Shared practice of usability work (how to carry out usability work?) o Usability specialists represent the users in political and presentational sense o Informative, consultative, participative, configurer roles for usability specialists o Facilitating cooperation among the configurers of the user - Motives for usability work (why to carry out usability work?); o Functional empowerment of users o Profit maximization, work intensification, competitive advantage, improving the design process, facilitating the implementation

tion. The interview material and the field notes capture attempts to produce representations by the cultural members of themselves and of their organization. Therefore, the material doesn't tell "the truth", but it tells how the natives' are representing themselves. It was not meaningful to try to derive objective facts of culture, usability work and the relationship between them, but instead to focus on the process and the end result of co-construction. The aim was not to try to provide "true descriptions", but negotiated and socially constructed representations of usability work in two SW product development organizations. In the analysis, the focus was on co-constructed meanings characterizing the cultural context (see section 3) and usability work (see section 2). The analytical framework used as a sensitizing device is summarized in Table 3.

5. EMPIRICAL EXPLORATIONS

There is a group of four usability specialists of unit A (Usability specialist A1-4). In addition to the usability specialists, the manager of the unit (Manager A) has often emphasized usability work. The remaining personnel are SW designers responsible for the UI SW labeled the "*manager UI*". In the citations, this part of the personnel is represented by three SW designers (Designer A1-3) and two team leaders (Team leader A1-2). In unit B there currently is only one usability specialist left in the unit (Usability specialist B), but both a team leader (Team leader B1) and a manager (Manager B) are former usability specialists. The usability specialist and graphical designers are on the service team, which is represented in the citations by a graphical designer (Graphical designer B), the usability specialist, and their team leader (Team leader B1). The development team is represented by two SW designers (Designer B1-2) and their team leader (Team leader B2). In addition, two executives have participated in the workshop sessions (Executives B1-2).

5.1 The Cultural Context

The joint enterprise of unit A is to produce functionally-correct "*manager UI*" within set schedules. Control, monitoring, measurement and tight deadlines are used to characterize their practice supporting the enterprise. The personnel emphasize their work environment as a part of a big, bureaucratic organization: "*it [the unit] is a big, bureaucratic organization, because our company is big. We have this bureaucracy here to make sure everything functions. We have clear rules and ISO standards and audits and everything else connected to that. The guidelines are very powerful.*" (Usability specialist A1) In this context 'control mechanisms set the pressures' and 'constant monitoring, measuring and controlling is normal project work': "*yes, we try to work in a controlled manner and according to the plan. We have goals and we follow them up*" (Team leader A1).

Here we have a quality organization which perceives quality within a rules-oriented approach. Numerical things are highlighted, bugs and stuff like that. We have quality plans and report the bugs and follow the projects. [...] We have these control mechanisms, and they are very powerful. If you try to compete with them, and you are not in the control mechanisms, then you are left out. Because these control mechanisms set the pressures. (Usability specialist A1)

Controlling, constant controlling and monitoring, it's part of normal project work (Team leader A1)

In this context the personnel trust their management to 'take care of people': "*our leader is a father figure. I think this describes very well the leadership in our unit [...] He takes care of people*" (Usability specialist A1). "*They just appear [decisions], and I have never wanted to participate in that, because we can give comments if we want, if something is missing or needed. But it is good that someone else has already thought them through [laugh]. [...] You can participate, if you want, and our boss always asks us for comments*" (Usability specialist A1). "*We must be [satisfied], because we don't complain. We don't give comments or participate [in decision-making] [laugh]*" (Designer A2). The personnel are not interested in participating in decision-making, and harmonious social relationships are emphasized. When asked about the type of worker that is respected, the response is that "*everyone is respected, that is the starting point. We all are valued workers.*" (Team leader A1) Furthermore, it is emphasized that: "*of course you can give constructive criticism, but you should never be mean*" (Usability specialist A1).

In this unit the designers are responsible for designing, coding and testing the "*manager UI*". Therefore, it is the sole responsibility of the designers to configure the user. However, configuring the user is not considered as an explicit or important task by the designers': "*our work involves a lot of investigation of new things. Most of our time is spent on investigating things when we are designing new things and new interfaces. When someone has thought of a new part for the system, then we have to investigate how it affects our part of the system. Most of our time is spent on investigating things. Quite little time is spent on coding or on designing the UI*" (Designer A3).

In unit B, on the other hand, the joint enterprise is "*engine*" and associated "*services*" development. Most of the personnel are responsible for the development of the "*engine*": "*it [the engine] is there at the bottom. It of course needs to be okay. Almost all of our developers work with [the engine]*" (Designer B). A couple of designers focus specifically on UI, i.e. "*service*", development. However, "*engine*" development is considered the most valued type of development: "*service development is less valued, because our core competence is in the hard core, it is in the engine*" (Team leader B1). Furthermore, "*here has not been much service development. We don't have that tradition here. We haven't even had a strong team here who would have developed them. We have only had a few individuals and they have been quite alone here.*" (Manager B) In addition, the "*engine*" developers separate their work from the "*service*" development: "*these Java coders, quite many of them have a strong opinion that they don't touch the UIs. Someone else has to do that. They won't do it. And this reflects their professionalism. They have different types of design problems*" (Team leader B2). The usability specialist and graphical designers complain that their service team is less valued:

The developers outrank us, the servants, who serve the developers (Usability specialist B)

Truly, we have a feeling that the service people are second rate people. We are, our history is technocratic, and technology is appreciated here. Even though we talk about user-centeredness and multidisciplinary teams and competence [...] I understand that the engine is important; it has to be there. But when we compete for the resources, it is always the engine that wins. (Team leader B1)

Well yes, but the engine is always needed. (Team leader B2)

The joint enterprise of this unit is characterized as innovative technological development. The unit is to be "*at the cutting edge of technological development*" (Team leader B2). Related to this, "*in development, well, the developers respect innovativeness. It depends on who is capable of innovating*" (Team leader B1). Especially respected is a BOA team: "*we have this team of three people, BOA, board of architects. They are developers, or actually I think their job title is architect*" (Designer B1). "*They are this kind of trio, technology trio. They have actually implemented the engine*" (Team leader B1). Therefore, in this unit respect needs to be earned, and it is earned through innovating at the 'cutting edge of technological development'.

The practice of supporting the enterprise is further characterized by freedom, experimentation and taking initiative. People are trusted and allowed to take the initiative:

We do what we want. We have this traditional culture. [A product] wouldn't have been invented if we had obeyed the managers. But people did it in the lab. And finally, something came out. It's the same thing here; we do it in secret. And I have said many times that don't give the permission, we will do it in secret anyway [laugh]. [...] We are encouraged to take initiative. It's like "do what you want if you are capable and have the resources for it, do whatever you want." (Team leader B1)

However, the problem is that the work is not supported enough. The employees have to assume much responsibility for their work themselves:

We don't control people; people are trusted [...]. But there is a problem. We have not been forbidden to do, but not concretely supported, either. It's just that it's enough that we do things. They [management] think it's enough and we take care of it by ourselves. (Team leader B1)

Doesn't this apply to many things here? (Executive B2)

Yes. To everything. "(Team leader B1)

Furthermore, with respect to mutual relationships, respect needs to be earned and harmonious relationships are not emphasized. Instead: "*there are strong personalities and blood-and-thunder fights (in the unit)*" (Team leader B1). The management also receives harsh feedback:

Two things have traditionally been very difficult here. One is decision-making and the other is communicating decisions. And a third one, which is connected to these two, is that if decisions are made, it is problematic to follow them up. [...] When certain large-scale decisions need to be made at the managerial level, things are left undecided. [...] Things are left on their own and then things just drift along. (Designer B1)

5.2 The Shared Practice of Usability Work

Representing the User - in the Political Sense

The responsibility of the usability specialists in unit A is to represent the users in a political sense. The usability specialists have organized usability evaluations and carried field studies observing and interviewing the users, on which basis they can claim to know the user. Based on their knowledge, they are expected to comment on the design solutions the designers produce, from the users' perspective: "*Yes, we all know that we need to ask for comments from the usability specialists in the design phase.*" (Designer A3) "*Yes, a coder cooperates with a usability specialist, who provides the guidelines. Then you don't have to figure out everything by yourself. You don't have that much responsibility for the decisions made during the design and implementation. You can ask how this should be done. This way it's visible. The usability specialists check out whether the design is good.*" (Designer A1)

However, the usability specialists complain they cannot affect the design much:

At this moment we can't trust that the projects know at what time they should contact us. We must follow the situation and control it and push ourselves into the projects. (...) The latest experiences have revealed that if a project is in the early phase, it seems like they actually reject our involvement. They say you don't have to peep in here yet, we are doing nothing yet. (Usability specialist A3)

Therefore, the role of the usability specialists in unit A is mainly consultative. It is up to the designers to ask for comments while configuring the user.

The usability specialists represent the users in a political sense also in unit B. They can also claim to know the user through the field studies and usability evaluations they have carried out. However, in this unit, the participative role of the usability specialists is emphasized. Both the graphical designers and the usability specialists have taken an active role in configuring the user. Collaboration between usability specialists, graphical designers and UI developers is underlined: "*it is pair work. Either a visualist and a usability person, or a usability person and a UI developer, like Mary, this kind of pair sits together using the same computer and works together.*" (Usability specialist B) It is assumed that the knowledge of the usability specialists affects the design only if the usability specialists and designers actively cooperate: "*The most relevant way to do it is to do it together and think aloud at the same time. Then the knowledge spreads.*" (Manager B)

This is not only few people's job, but everyone should understand what user-centeredness means and how much I should apply those principles and in which part of my job. [...] I think it is better that everyone knows a little about it than that we have a dozen usability specialists and the rest of the personnel know nothing about it. Because in this situation, it is a battlefield. Or there should be a developer and a usability specialist doing things together all the time. But in this situation, the developer becomes a usability specialist almost naturally (Team leader B1)

Furthermore, the usability specialists might be even in the configurer role (configuring the user) in this unit: "*When we think of how the next generation product development project is managed, the specification starts when I [former usability specialist] and Susan [usability specialist] do the functional specification. And the APIs are specified according to that. (...) It's not anything like vague assistance. The whole thing starts from the specification and that is in the project plan.*" (Manager B) "*I'm the project manager, or help in that.*" (Usability specialist B) "*You are the right hand*" (Team leader B1). The usability specialists make many important decisions during this specification work. Furthermore, a former usability specialist was nominated as a manager in the unit (i.e. Manager B):

I think it is very important from the point of view of user-centeredness that our manager is a usability specialist, that there is that kind of competence. [...] This user-centered viewpoint kind of affects other things in secret. I think it is strategically very important that a usability specialist was nominated as a manager [...] She can affect that usability is considered among other things. (Team leader B1)

Representing the User in Presentational Sense

The task of representing the users in presentational sense is in an important position in unit A. The usability specialists have utilized many strategies in making the users and their work visible to the designers. Based on their field study data, they have produced a Context of Use description – a document describing the users, their tasks and the environment in which the system is used. In addition, they have videotaped the field studies and the tapes are available to the designers. Furthermore, they have created a persona (described e.g. in Cooper 1999) called *Eric* - a hypothetical user - to make users more visible to the designers. They have also presented the material at team meetings to make users (and *Erics*) visible. However, representing the users in presentational sense has proven problematic. The designers have criticized Eric for being "*too stupid*" (Usability specialist A1) and dismissed him as "*a special case, which we don't need to serve*" (Usability specialist A2). Furthermore, the documents and the videotapes that the usability specialists have produced tend to be ignored by the designers.

Also, in unit B, the usability specialists have represented the users in a presentational sense: they have presented the results of field studies and usability tests to the designers. However, in unit B this work has been deemed inefficient: "*I think that it is quite difficult here sometimes. Here are many developers that do what they want. They don't follow the guidelines produced, even though they were good and reasonable.*" (Designer B2) "*I have also understood that people do it when you together with them discuss and agree on things. But it seems to be very unpleasant situation that someone else has made the decision and you should search for some kind of guidelines and do according to them.*" (Team leader B1) Therefore, the emphasis has shifted to other strategies: "*Earlier we tested a lot. First we tested, then we had this guideline phase and now we focus on specifications.*" (Team leader B1) Specifications refer to the situation, in which the usability specialists are actively taking part in projects during the specification phase as the configurers of the user.

Facilitating Cooperation among the Configurers of the User

Unit A has been involved in the development of a new SW process model in which usability work is incorporated. According to the process model, the context of use should be specified, usability requirements defined, and prototyping and formal usability testing carried out in the projects. (Project documentation A.) The personnel rely on the process model to incorporate usability work into the projects: "*it should tackle the hurry phase [caused by tight deadlines] of the projects. These things are done before the hurry phase. (...) When it's known from the beginning what is to be done, it's done at a much earlier phase and it's done well.*" (Manager A)

Now, when the new process is being implemented, now these [usability activities] are planned, and then you have permission to do them and time to do them, they are included in the schedules. Earlier they were not included in the project plans and schedules. It was very difficult to order projects to do them. Then they usually said that 'no way, we'll finish this release and then think about it'. It was difficult in the later phase of the project, if it was not planned in the beginning (Team leader A1)

The designers view controlling as 'part of normal project work', for which reason: "*if usability work can be measured and controlled, then it's more natural, then its just part of your job.*" (Team leader A1) The usability specialists also prefer this controlling strategy: "*when you bring usability orientation into an organization you have to be a police in the beginning. The designers don't have the knowledge needed in their head, and you have to act as a police*" (Usability specialist A3).

Furthermore, the work in the unit alone cannot ensure the usability of the product. Cooperation with other units is necessary. The usability specialists have initiated cooperation and presented their material to other units. However, this work "*can't influence much*" (Usability specialist A3) and involving other units, is, altogether "*extremely painful and persevering job. You must proceed slowly and take small steps. You can't change the direction of a ship of this size very fast.*" (Manager A)

In unit B, as mentioned, the usability specialists act in the participative or even in the configurer role in the development. This strategy is seen in a positive light: "*this user-centered viewpoint kind of affects other things in secret*" (Team leader B1), and "*the developer becomes a usability specialist almost naturally*" (Team leader B1). Therefore, the goal of the usability specialists in this unit is to sneak in their knowledge, the designers not even noticing this influence. In addition, the usability specialists employ influential positions as facilitators of cooperation inside the entire company: "*It [knowledge of user-centeredness] spreads through my and Ellen's [former usability specialists] personalities. We forcibly talk about user-centeredness when they [sales and marketing] want to hear what we do.*" (Team leader B1) "*Here the discussions between development and marketing happen through me. The developers don't discuss directly with marketing and marketing doesn't contact the developers directly. I function as a mediator. [...] You need to sit down and talk with them [sales] and listen to them. They tell things by using their own jargon and then I have to translate it into the jargon the developers understand. I function as an interpreter.*" (Manager B)

5.3 The Motives for Usability Work

Unit A motivates usability work by postulating it as improving the design process:

It is problematic to get money and permission from the projects to do this, it's not easy to get permission to spend money on doing usability (Team leader A2)

Yes, if we think of these things separately. But if we think of it from the viewpoint of our everyday job, the question is do we get permission to do a quality job [laugh]? (Usability specialist A3)

Yes, do they allow us to stop the projects from wasting their time and effort? [...] I don't think in the long run usability work costs a lot in the projects. And afterwards you save money through high-level usability. (Manager A)

Unit B, on the other hand, highlights usability work as a selling argument and an image factor:

From the viewpoint of the image of the company, one of our goals is to be a pioneer. (Executive B2)

This is visible also in the way the usability issues have been acknowledged. We were the first ones who started it. It's not only related to the technology. (Manager B)

I think it has been a selling argument and a thing that we have had, but not necessarily the competitors. We have been the most progressive in this respect. (Team leader B1)

In SW development companies of this size, there might not be even this, what we have. You should always proportion these things. Here at least it has a clear position. (Executive B3)

And we have the will. (Executive B2)

The usability specialists are afraid that usability work is used only as an image factor and a selling argument in their company: "*I admit that it is valued here, my and Ellen's [usability specialist] work is valued in this firm, but it is like: "it is*

Table 4. Two strategies for usability work in two product development organizations

	Unit A	**Unit B**
Identity and Joint Enterprise	A product development unit producing functionally correct manager UI within set schedules	A product development unit staying at the cutting edge of technological development, a pioneer
Shared Practice	Manager UI development the only real job, relies on controlling, monitoring and measuring; control mechanisms and processes in place and useful	Engine development the only real job, relies on ad hoc ways of working, innovating, experimenting and taking initiative
Mutual Relationships	'We are all valued workers', harmonious relationships important	Competent, innovative people respected, 'blood and thunder fights'
Motives for Usability Work	Improves the design process	Is used as a selling argument, image factor, influencing strategic decision making
Practice of Usability Work	Usability specialists represent the users in political sense in informative and consultative roles, representing the user in presentational sense important, controlling strategy for designer involvement	Usability specialists represent the users in political sense in participative and configurer roles, sneaking in strategy for designer, sales and marketing involvement

enough that you are here [laugh]." It is like mere talk was enough" (Team leader B1). Nevertheless, also they emphasize that usability work should contribute to business and the strategic level decision making. They advocate '*proactive product and business planning and strategy development influenced by a user-centered approach*' (Project documentation B), and argue that "*here the most important targets for improvement are not related to making the position of the usability specialists better or their work easier, but they are related to the strategic level, [...] related to decision-making, for example when you are deciding what to include in the next release.*" (Manager B).

6. DISCUSSION

This section summarizes the empirical results and discusses their implications on IS research.

6.1 Summary of the Empirical Results

This paper examined the how organizational culture and usability work are intertwined in the SW product development context. First, the concept of usability work was defined to make sense of the fragmented HCI literature on developing usability. Afterwards, an interpretive approach to culture acknowledging its recent critique was selected as appropriate for the empirical analysis. This analysis was subsequently carried out in two SW development organizations operating in the product development context. Table 4 summarizes the findings related to the cultural context and the strategies for usability work identified in the cases. The cultural context was analyzed by searching for co-constructed, shared meanings attached to 1) collective identity and the joint enterprise, 2) shared practice; and 3) mutual relationships. Usability work was analyzed by searching for co-constructed, negotiated meanings attached to 1) why to carry out usability work; and 2) how to carry out usability work.

The results show that there is a multiplicity of meanings attached to usability work in practice. Usability work has been interpreted as an image factor and a selling argument, as controlling the designers to do quality job, and as sneaking in, through collaboration. The results suggest that there are similarities in the ways usability work has been modified in these two product development units; more interestingly, there are also clear differences. The differences are related to both why and how usability work is carried out. In unit

A, usability specialists have concentrated on crafting representations of users and their work. Furthermore, they have been assigned a consultative role in configuring the user; they are to act as user representatives, commenting on predefined design solutions. In involving the designers, the usability specialists have adopted a controlling strategy that aims at forcing projects to carry out usability work. Usability work is seen as improving the design process, i.e. it is used for money saving purposes. In unit B, on the other hand, the usability specialists emphasize cooperation with the designers. Configuring the user is postulated as a multidisciplinary, cooperative process, in which usability specialists take actively part. Usability work is to sneak in. That is, usability work is to influence decisions and design solutions through usability specialists employing influential positions in their organization and through active cooperation with the designers, without the other people even noticing the influence. Usability work is motivated as an image factor and as a selling argument to be utilized in profit making.

6.2 Implications on IS Research

As mentioned, in the IS literature it has been noticed that new, challenging IS context have emerged, for example enterprise resource-planning package implementations, web information systems and outsourced development (Markus & Mao, 2004). This paper examines the challenging product development context, in which the user population tends to be large and scattered around the world, which might be the case also in the above mentioned contexts. In this paper the focus is particularly on usability work in this context. The HCI research has traditionally addressed this development context and emphasized the importance of usability. However, usability work is still challenging, in product development context as well as elsewhere, and there also currently is a lack of empirical HCI research addressing this challenge. In custom IS development, usability work and the usability specialists 'representing the user' in the development have not been considered very critical, since the user population has traditionally been identifiable and easily approachable, for which reason direct or representative user participation has been feasible (Mumford, 1983). In the new, challenging IS contexts in which the user population might be unknown or very difficult to get in touch with (Markus & Mao, 2004), usability specialists and their work may increase in importance. These 'user representatives' speak on behalf of the users, based on their knowledge about the user. They know the user through empirical usability testing and field studies (interviewing and observing the users). They also have general state-of-the-art HCI knowledge that they can utilize in commenting and improving the design solutions. The results of this study suggest, however, that the position of the usability specialists might still be problematic. There is a risk that their work does not have any effects on how the users are configured. This study describes two alternative ways to organize usability work in the product development organizations. These ways are not suggested as ideals, but as ones encountered in the empirical material, providing, nevertheless, suggestions on how to realize usability work in practice.

One might argue that both organizations seem to advocate aspects of usability work that are compatible with their cultural context. In unit A, the usability specialists introduce usability work through controlling, measuring and monitoring which is argued to resemble 'normal project work' in the unit; in unit B, on the other hand, the usability specialists try to sneak in, and are careful of not commanding people to do things against their will, since the personnel are used to 'doing what they want', 'people are trusted' and they are 'allowed to take initiative'. Existing IS research on organizational culture also maintains that compatibility between organizational culture and technology is a very important criterion for success - the technology is to be tailored to be compatible with the target culture (e.g., Brown, 1995; Davison & Martinsons, 2002; Gallivan & Srite, 2005; Leidner & Kayworth, 2006; Pliskin et al., 1993; Ruppel & Harrington, 2001). Part of the HCI literature also supports this view in arguing that one should rely on different strategies for usability work in different contexts, there being no one-size-fits-all (e.g., Aucella, 1997; Bloomer & Croft, 1997; Iivari, 2006a; Tudor, 1998). Based on the results of this study and the existing literature, therefore, one could argue that the cultural context might affect which aspects of usability work are emphasized. Cultural context might support and reinforce certain aspects of usability work. Consequently, the results can be interpreted to suggest that, in different cultural contexts, different (compatible) strategies, methods and tools are adopted related to usability work. This interpretation implies that the cultural characteristics succeed in explaining the aspects of the usability work adopted. Thus, one might be able to explain and predict how usability work will be modified and tailored in different cultural contexts.

Clearly, more research is needed to determine the relationship between culture and usability work. This paper provides contextual information for future research to be able to analyze whether the patterns discovered in this study appear in organizations with similar characteristics. An interesting observation is that unit A resembles the case organization described by Poltrock and Grudin (1994): the unit is part of a large, hierarchical organization that highlights project schedules, a mature SW process and controlling, monitoring and measuring as normal project work. It can also be argued that, in terms of its development process and cultural milieu, unit A resembles custom IS development organizations as described by Carmel and Sawyer (1998). Unit B, on the other hand, is part of a small SW house having similar characteristics with companies operating in the context of packaged SW development described by Carmel and Sawyer (1998), in which time-to-market pressure, immature processes and entrepreneurial and individualistic cultural milieu are typical. Unit B also seems to have a history of supporting individuality, initiative and innovativeness. Clearly, usability work has been modified in different ways in these two differing contexts, but future research is needed in order to be able to generalize the results.

All in all, different positions can be identified for conceptualizing the relationship between organizational culture and usability work. The positions can be characterized by using the distinctions of realism vs. nominalism and determinism vs. voluntarism. The realist, deterministic position "implies that reality is predictable and at least in principle manipulable, prescribable and designable" (Iivari & Hirschheim 1996, p. 553); human beings are postulated as responding to external events in a mechanistic or even deterministic way (Burrell & Morgan, 1979). The nominalist, voluntarist position, on the other hand, views "social phenomena largely as emergent and not directly designable" (Iivari & Hirschheim, 1996, p. 553); the human agent is viewed as a creator of the environment and as a controller rather than as controlled (Burrell & Morgan, 1979). With respect to the latter position, technological determinism is rejected and interpretive flexibility highlighted (e.g., Grint & Woolgar, 1997; Gallivan & Srite, 2005; Leidner & Kayworth, 2006; Robey & Azevedo, 1994). This study and its culture conception can be associated with the nominalist, voluntarist position that implies that the relationship between culture and usability work is a continuous, dynamic process in which mechanistic, universal, context-free guidance will probably not work – at least as it is supposed to work. Also, part of the literature on usability work supports this while arguing that different meanings can be attached to usability work in practice (Artman, 2002; Catarci et al., 2002). This study and the literature above both suggest that usability work – when it is introduced into organizations – will be interpreted and reinterpreted in the cultural context in an emergent process of sense making.

7. CONCLUSION

This paper has conceptualized usability work in the SW product development context. The concept of usability work aims at being useful both for the HCI and IS research communities for making sense of and classifying the heterogeneous literatures addressing the development of usability. In addition, this paper has introduced an interpretive view of culture as continuous spinning and re-spinning of the fragile webs of meaning (Ortner, 1999), which recognizes the recent critique of the traditional interpretive view of culture. The paper has also utilized this culture conception in the empirical analysis of usability work in the cultural context of SW product development organizations. Although interpretive culture inquiries have been popular in IS research, the recent critique presented within cultural anthropology has not yet been acknowledged. The research design and epistemological assumptions adopted in this study are in line with the introduced interpretive culture conception. Other culture researchers may benefit both from the review of different approaches utilized in organizational culture studies as well as from the description of the application of this particular conception in practice in this research effort.

The empirical results offer to the reader a description of two alternative ways on how to organize usability work in SW development organizations. The results suggest that there are differences in how usability work is modified and interpreted in the organizations with divergent cultural contexts, those advocating different motives and practices for usability work. The results can be interpreted to imply that culturally compatible strategies to usability work should be adopted in differing cultural contexts.

There are a number of implications for practice. First of all, the reader gains an understanding of what is involved in usability work and why should one hire usability specialists for taking care of it. Usability work may contribute by saving money (i.e., improving the design process) or by making profit (i.e. as an image factor, selling argument). The usability specialists contribute to the development through 'representing the users' based on their knowledge about the users. They are expected to know the users through empirical inquiries (typically through usability testing and field studies including interviewing and observing the users) and through general state-of-the-art HCI knowledge gained through their education. They are expected to deliver their knowledge to the development by informing the designers, by commenting on predefined design solutions, by actively taking part in the design process or by themselves acting as the configurers of the users, producing the design solutions.

Second, it is argued that sensitivity to cultural issues in relation to usability work is important. The problem of selecting a culturally-suitable strategy for usability work is raised. Practitioners introducing usability work into their organization can benefit from the insights presented in this paper. Two different ways of organizing usability work have been outlined. One can assign informative and consultative roles to the usability specialists, who then concentrate on commenting on design solutions and on representing the user in the presentational sense to the designers. In addition, the controlling strategy forcing projects to carry out usability work could be adopted. However, one can also assign participative and even configurer roles to the usability specialists, who then actively cooperate with the designers. The usability specialists could try to sneak in, i.e., usability work influencing decisions and design solutions through usability specialists employing influential positions in their organization and through active cooperation with designers, marketing, sales etc., without others even noticing the influence. Both strategies seem to work in their particular contexts.

This paper advocates the nominalist, voluntarist position for conceptualizing the relationship between organizational culture and usability work. Mechanistic, universal, context-free strategies for usability work seem to rely on naïve notions of culture and change in organizations. The complexity related to this phenomenon should be acknowledged, even though one might never be able to control or directly manipulate the process. Furthermore, this paper argues that cultural context might explain the aspects of the usability work adopted. If this is the case, one might, in the future, be able to explain and predict how usability work will be modified and tailored in different cultural contexts. However, more research on the matter is needed.

In terms of the limitations of this study, the paper is based on the analysis of only two cases. This type of analysis should be carried out in more varying contexts employing a larger amount of cases. Furthermore, the influence of divergent organizational subcultures and occupational communities should be addressed. The representational practices of the usability specialists, and especially their role in serving particular (managerial) purposes, should also benefit from further analysis. Moreover, the natives of this study are the personnel of the SW product development organizations – not the end users themselves. The end users are only represented in the development, not actually present in the development. As a result, their voices are not heard in this study. However, it would be an interesting topic of another study to listen to the voices of the users in a situation in which they are represented in the development by a group of specialists who are not the users themselves. Finally, avenues for further work include also a further analysis of the relationship between culture and usability work in SW development organizations. Follow-up data related to usability work should be gathered from the cases – this paper provides understanding gained during a three year long glimpse into the dynamic, continuous process of modifying and interpreting usability work in SW development organizations.

REFERENCES

Ahadi, H. (2004). An Examination of the Role of Organizational Enablers in Business Process Reengineering and the Impact of Information Technology. *Information Resources Management Journal*, *17*(4), 1–19.

Akrich, M. (1992). The De-Scription of Technical Objects. In Bijker, W., & Law, J. (Eds.), *Shaping Technology/Building Society. Studies in Sociotechnical Change* (pp. 205–224). Cambridge, MA: The MIT Press.

Alvesson, M. (1990). On the Popularity of Organizational Culture. *Acta Sociologica*, *33*(1), 31–49. doi:10.1177/000169939003300103

Artman, H. (2002). Procurer usability requirements: negotiations in contract development. In O. Bertelsen, S. Bødker, & K. Kuutti (Eds.), *Proceedings of the second Nordic conference on Human-computer interaction* (pp. 61-70). New York: ACM Press.

Asaro, P. (2000). Transforming Society by Transforming Technology: the science and politics of participatory design. *Accounting. Management and Information Technologies*, *10*(4), 257–290. doi:10.1016/S0959-8022(00)00004-7

Aucella, A. (1997). Ensuring Success with Usability Engineering. *Interaction*, *4*(3), 19–22. doi:10.1145/255392.255395

Avison, D., & Myers, M. (1995). Information systems and anthropology: an anthropological perspective on IT and organizational culture. *Information Technology & People*, *8*(3), 43–56. doi:10.1108/09593849510098262

Bannon, L. (1991). From human factors to human actors: The role of psychology and human-computer interaction studies in system design. In J. Greenbaum & M. Kyng (Eds.), *Design at Work. Cooperative Design of Computer Systems* (pp. 25-44). Mahwah, NJ: New Jersey: Lawrence Erlbaum Associates.

Benbasat, I., Goldstein, D., & Mead, M. (1987, September). The Case Study Strategy in Studies of Information Systems. *Management Information Systems Quarterly*, 368–386.

Beyer, H., & Holtzblatt, K. (1998). *Contextual Design: Defining Customer-Centered Systems*. San Francisco, CA: Morgan Kaufmann Publishers, Inc.

Bias, R., & Reitmeyer, P. (1995). Usability Support Inside and Out. *Interaction*, *2*(2), 29–32. doi:10.1145/205350.205355

Billingsley, P. (1995). Starting from Scratch: Building a Usability Program at Union Pacific Railroad. *Interaction*, *2*(4), 27–30. doi:10.1145/225362.225366

Bloomer, S., & Croft, R. (1997). Pitching Usability to Your Organization. *Interaction*, *4*(6), 18–26. doi:10.1145/267505.267510

Bødker, S., & Buur, J. (2002). The Design Collaboratorium – a Place for Usability Design. *ACM Transactions on Computer-Human Interaction*, *9*(2), 152–169. doi:10.1145/513665.513670

Boivie, I., Gulliksen, J., & Göransson, B. (2006). The lonesome cowboy: a study of the usability designer role in systems development. *Interacting with Computers*, *18*(4), 601–634. doi:10.1016/j.intcom.2005.10.003

Borgholm, T., & Madsen, K. (1999). Cooperative Usability Practices. *Communications of the ACM*, *42*(5), 91–97. doi:10.1145/301353.301438

Borofsky, R. (Ed.). (1994). *Assessing Cultural Anthropology*. New York: McGraw-Hill, Inc.

Brown, A. (1995). Managing Understandings: Politics, Symbolism, Niche Marketing and the Quest for Legitimacy in IT Implementation. *Organization Studies*, *16*(6), 951–969. doi:10.1177/017084069501600602

Burrell, G., & Morgan, G. (1979). *Sociological Paradigms and Organizational Analysis. Elements of the Sociology of Corporate Life*. London: Heinemann Educational Books Ltd.

Cabrera, A., Cabrera, E., & Barajas, S. (2001). The key role of organizational culture in a multi-system view of technology-driven change. *International Journal of Information Management*, *21*(3), 245–261. doi:10.1016/S0268-4012(01)00013-5

Carmel, E. (1997). American Hegemony in Packaged Software Trade and the "Culture of Software". *The Information Society*, *13*(1), 125–142. doi:10.1080/019722497129322

Carmel, E., & Sawyer, S. (1998). Packaged software development teams: what makes them different? *Information Technology & People*, *11*(1), 7–19. doi:10.1108/09593849810204503

Catarci, T., Matarazzo, G., & Raiss, G. (2002). Driving usability into the public administration: the Italian experience. *International Journal of Human-Computer Studies*, *57*(2), 121–138. doi:10.1016/S1071-5819(02)91014-1

Clement, A. (1994). Computing at Work: Empowering Action By 'Low-level Users'. *Communications of the ACM*, *37*(1), 52–63. doi:10.1145/175222.175226

Clifford, J., & Marcus, G. (Eds.). (1986). *Writing culture: the poetics and politics of ethnography*. Berkeley, CA: University of California Press.

Cooper, A. (1999). *The inmates are running the asylum: Why high-tech products drive us crazy and how to restore the sanity*. Indianapolis, IN: Sams.

Cooper, C., & Bowers, J. (1995). Representing the users: Notes on the disciplinary rhetoric of human-computer interaction. In Thomas, P. (Ed.), *The Social and Interactional Dimensions of Human-Computer Interfaces* (pp. 48–66). Cambridge, MA: Cambridge University Press.

Czarniawska-Joerges, B. (1992). *Exploring Complex Organizations. A Cultural Perspective*. Newbury Park, CA: Sage Publications.

Damodaran, L. (1996). User involvement in the systems designs process - a practical guide for users. *Behaviour & Information Technology, 15*(16), 363–377. doi:10.1080/014492996120049

Davis, F. (1989). Perceived usefulness, perceived ease of use, and user acceptance of information technology. *Management Information Systems Quarterly, 13*(3), 319–340. doi:10.2307/249008

Davison, R., & Martinsons, M. (2002). Empowerment or enslavement? A case of process-based organizational change in Hong Kong. *Information Technology & People, 15*(1), 42–59. doi:10.1108/09593840210421516

Dent, J. (1991). Accounting and Organizational Cultures: A Field Study of the Emergence of a New Organizational Reality. *Accounting, Organizations and Society, 16*(8), 705–732. doi:10.1016/0361-3682(91)90021-6

Denzin, N., & Lincoln, Y. (2000). Introduction: The Discipline and Practice of Qualitative Research. In Denzin, N., & Lincoln, Y. (Eds.), *Handbook of Qualitative Research* (2nd ed., pp. 1–34). Thousand Oaks, CA: Sage.

Dube, L., & Robey, D. (1999). Software Stories: Three Cultural Perspectives on the Organizational Practices of Software Development. *Accounting. Management and Information Technologies, 9*(4), 223–259. doi:10.1016/S0959-8022(99)00010-7

Eisenhardt, K. (1989). Building Theories from Case Study Research. *Academy of Management Review, 14*(4), 532–550. doi:10.2307/258557

Fellenz, C. (1997). Introducing Usability into Smaller Organizations. *Interaction, 4*(5), 29–33. doi:10.1145/264044.264047

Fok, L., Fok, W., & Hartman, S. (2001). Exploring the relationship between total quality management and information systems development. *Information & Management, 38*(6), 355–371. doi:10.1016/S0378-7206(00)00075-6

Fox, R. (Ed.). (1991). *Recapturing Anthropology. Working in the Present*. Santa Fe, NM: School of American Research Press.

Gallivan, M., & Srite, M. (2005). Information Technology and Culture: Merging Fragmented and Holistic Perpectives of Culture. *Information and Organization, 15*(2), 295–338. doi:10.1016/j.infoandorg.2005.02.005

Geertz, C. (1973). *The interpretation of cultures: selected essays*. New York: Basic Books.

Greenbaum, J., & Kyng, M. (Eds.). (1991). *Design at Work. Cooperative Design of Computer Systems*. Mahwah, NJ: Lawrence Erlbaum Associates.

Grint, K., & Woolgar, S. (1997). *The Machine at Work. Technology, Work and Organization*. Cambridge, MA: Polity Press.

Grudin, J. (1991a). Interactive Systems: Bridging the Gaps between Developers and Users. *IEEE Computer, 24*(4), 59–69.

Grudin, J. (1991b). Systematic Sources of Suboptimal Interface Design in Large Product Development Organizations. *Human-Computer Interaction, 6*(2), 147–196. doi:10.1207/s15327051hci0602_3

Grudin, J., & Pruitt, J. (2002). Personas, Participatory Design and Product Development: An Infrastructure of Engagement. In T. Binder, J. Gregory, & I. Wagner (Eds.), *Proceedings of Participatory Design Conference* (pp. 144-161). Palo Alto, CA: CPSR.

Gulliksen, J., Boivie, I., & Göransson, B. (2006). Usability professionals – current practices and future development. *Interacting with Computers, 18*(4), 568–600. doi:10.1016/j.intcom.2005.10.005

Harper, G., & Utley, D. (2001). Organizational Culture and Successful Information Technology Implementation. *Engineering Management Journal, 13*(2), 11–15.

Harrington, S., & Ruppel, C. (1999). Practical and value compatibility: their roles in the adoption, diffusion, and success of telecommuting. In P. De & J. DeGross (Eds.), *Proceedings of the 20th International Conference of Information Systems* (pp. 103-112). Atlanta, GA: AIS.

Hirschheim, R., & Klein, H. (1989). Four Paradigms of Information Systems Development. *Communications of the ACM, 32*(10), 1199–1216. doi:10.1145/67933.67937

Hutchings, A., & Knox, S. (1995). Creating Products - Customer Demand. *Communications of the ACM, 38*(5), 72–80. doi:10.1145/203356.203370

Iivari, J., & Hirschheim, R. (1996). Analyzing information systems development: a comparison and analysis of eight IS development approaches. *Information Systems, 21*(7), 551–575. doi:10.1016/S0306-4379(96)00028-2

Iivari, N. (2006a). 'Representing the User' in Software Development – A Cultural Analysis of Usability Work in the Product Development Context. *Interacting with Computers, 18*(4), 635–664. doi:10.1016/j.intcom.2005.10.002

Iivari, N. (2006b). Understanding the Work of an HCI Practitioner. In A. Morch, K. Morgan, T. Bratteig, G. Ghosh, & D. Svanaes (Eds.), *Proceedings of fourth Nordic Conference on Human Computer Interaction* (pp. 185-194). New York: ACM.

International Standard ISO 13407. (1999). *Human-centered design processes for interactive systems.* Geneva, Switzerland: International Organization for Standardization.

International Standard ISO 9241-11. (1998). *Ergonomic requirements for office work with visual display terminals (VDT)s - Part 11 Guidance on usability*. Geneva, Switzerland: International Organization for Standardization.

Kaarst-Brown, M., & Robey, D. (1999). More on Myth, Magic and Metaphor. Cultural Insights into the Management of Information Technology in Organizations. *Information Technology & People, 12*(2), 192–217. doi:10.1108/09593849910267251

Kanungo, S., Sadavarti, S., & Srinivas, Y. (2001). Relating IT strategy and organizational culture: An empirical study of public sector units in India. *The Journal of Strategic Information Systems, 10*(1), 29–57. doi:10.1016/S0963-8687(01)00038-5

Karat, J. (1997). Evolving the Scope of User-Centered Design. *Communications of the ACM, 40*(7), 33–38. doi:10.1145/256175.256181

Keesing, R., & Strathern, A. (1998). *Cultural Anthropology. A Contemporary Perspective* (3rd ed.). Fort Worth, TX: Harcourt Brave College Publishers.

Keil, M., & Carmel, E. (1995). Customer-Developer Links in Software Development. *Communications of the ACM, 38*(5), 33–44. doi:10.1145/203356.203363

Klein, H., & Myers, M. (1999). A Set of Principles for Conducting and Evaluating Interpretive Field Studies in Information Systems. *Management Information Systems Quarterly, 23*(1), 67–94. doi:10.2307/249410

Kroeber, A., & Kluckhohn, C. (1952). *Culture: a critical review of the concepts and definitions*. Cambridge, MA: Harvard University Press.

Kujala, S. (2003). User involvement: a review of the benefits and challenges. *Behaviour & Information Technology, 22*(1), 1–16. doi:10.1080/01449290301782

Kujala, S. (2007). Effective user involvement in product development by improving the analysis of user needs. *Behaviour & Information Technology*, *27*(6), 457–473. doi:10.1080/01449290601111051

Kyng, M. (1994). Scandinavian Design: Users in Product Development. In B. Adelson, S. Dumais, & J. Olson (Eds.), *Proceedings of the Conference on Human Factors in Computing Systems* (pp. 3-9). New York: ACM.

Kyng, M. (1998). Users and computers: A contextual approach to design of computer artifacts. *Scandinavian Journal of Information Systems*, *10*(1-2), 7–44.

Lave, J., & Wenger, J. (1991). *Situated learning: Legitimate peripheral participation*. Cambridge, MA: Cambridge University Press.

Leidner, D., & Kayworth, T. (2006). A Review of Culture in Information Systems Research: Towards a Theory of IT-Culture Conflict. *Management Information Systems Quarterly*, *30*(2), 357–399.

Lett, J. (1987). *The Human Enterprise. A Critical Introduction to Anthropological Theory*. Boulder, CO: Westview Press Inc.

Markus, M., & Mao, Y. (2004). Participation in Development and Implementation - Updating an Old, Tired Concept for Today's IS Contexts. *Journal of the Association for Information Systems*, *5*(11-12), 514–544.

Mayhew, D. (1999a). Strategic Development of Usability Engineering Function. *Interaction*, *6*(5), 27–34. doi:10.1145/312683.312706

Mayhew, D. (1999b). *The usability engineering lifecycle: a practitioner's handbook for user interface design*. San Francisco, CA: Morgan Kaufmann Publishers, Inc.

Muller, M., & Carey, K. (2002). Design as a Minority Discipline in a Software Company: Toward Requirements for a Community of Practice. In [CHI Letters]. *Proceedings of the Conference on Human Factors in Computing Systems*, *4*(1), 383–390.

Mumford, E. (1983). *Designing Human Systems for New Technology. The ETHICS Method*. Manchester, UK: Manchester Business School.

Nandhakumar, J., & Jones, M. (1997). Designing in the Dark: the Changing User-Developer Relationship in Information Systems Development. In J. DeGross & K. Kumar (Eds.), *Proceedings of the 18th International Conference of Information Systems* (pp. 75-86). Atlanta, GA: AIS.

Nielsen, J. (1993). *Usability engineering*. Boston, MA: Academic Press.

Nielsen, J., & Mack, R. (Eds.). (1994). *Usability inspection methods*. New York: John Wiley & Sons.

Ortner, S. (Ed.). (1999). *The Fate of Culture. Geertz and Beyond*. Berkeley, CA: University of California Press.

Ouchi, W., & Wilkins, A. (1985). Organizational Culture. *Annual Review of Sociology*, *11*, 457–483. doi:10.1146/annurev.so.11.080185.002325

Pliskin, N., Romm, T., Lee, A., & Weber, Y. (1993). Presumed Versus Actual Organizational Culture: Managerial Implications for Implementation of Information Systems. *The Computer Journal*, *36*(2), 1–10. doi:10.1093/comjnl/36.2.143

Poltrock, S., & Grudin, J. (1994). Organizational Obstacles to Interface Design and Development: Two Participant – Observer Studies. *ACM Transactions on Computer-Human Interaction*, *1*(1), 52–80. doi:10.1145/174630.174633

Robey, D., & Azevedo, A. (1994). Cultural Analysis of the Organizational Consequences of Information Technology. *Accounting. Management & Information Technology*, *4*(1), 23–37. doi:10.1016/0959-8022(94)90011-6

Rogers, E. (1995). *Diffusion of Innovations* (5th ed.). New York: Free Press.

Rosenbaum, S., Rohn, J., & Humburg, J. (2000). A Toolkit for Strategic Usability: Results from Workshops, Panels, and Surveys. In *Proceedings of the Conference on Human Factors in Computing Systems (CHI Letters)* (Vol. 2, No. 1, pp. 337-344). New York: ACM.

Rosson, M., & Carroll, J. (2002). *Usability Engineering: Scenario-based Development of Human-Computer Interaction*. San Francisco, CA: Morgan-Kaufman.

Ruppel, C., & Harrington, S. (2001). Sharing Knowledge through Intranets: A Study of Organizational Culture and Intranet Implementation. *IEEE Transactions on Professional Communication*, *44*(1), 37–52. doi:10.1109/47.911131

Schein, E. (1985). *Organizational culture and leadership* (2nd ed.). San Francisco, CA: Jossey-Bass.

Schwandt, T. (2000). Three Epistemological Stances for Qualitative Inquiry: Interpretivism, Hermeneutics, and Social Constructionism. In Denzin, N., & Lincoln, Y. (Eds.), *Handbook of Qualitative Research* (2nd ed., pp. 189–214). Thousand Oaks, CA: Sage Publications Inc.

Smircich, L. (1983). Concepts of Culture and Organizational Analysis. *Administrative Science Quarterly*, *28*(3), 339–358. doi:10.2307/2392246

Spinuzzi, C. (2002). A Scandinavian Challenge, a US Response: Methodological Assumptions in Scandinavian and US Prototyping Approaches. In *Proceedings of the 20th annual international conference on Computer documentation* (pp. 208-215). New York: ACM.

Suchman, L. (1995). Making Work Visible. *Communications of the ACM*, *38*(9), 56–64. doi:10.1145/223248.223263

Suchman, L. (2002). Located accountabilities in technology production. *Scandinavian Journal of Information Systems*, *14*(2), 91–105.

Tudor, L. (1998). Human Factors: Does Your Management Hear You? *Interaction*, *5*(1), 16–24. doi:10.1145/268986.268989

van Maanen, J., & Barley, S. (1984). Occupational communities: Culture and control in Organizations. In Staw, B., & Cummings, L. (Eds.), *Research in Organizational Behavior 6* (pp. 287–365). Greenwich, CT: JAI Press.

Vredenburg, K., Mao, J., Smith, P., & Casey, T. (2002). A survey of user-centered design practice. In [CHI Letters]. *Proceedings of the Conference on Human Factors in Computing Systems*, *2*(1), 471–478.

Walsham, G. (1995). Interpretive case studies in IS research: nature and method. *European Journal of Information Systems*, *4*(2), 74–81. doi:10.1057/ejis.1995.9

Weedon, C. (2004). *Identity and Culture: Narratives of Difference and Belonging*. New York: Open University Press.

Wenger, E. (1998). *Communities of Practice. Learning, Meaning, and Identity*. Cambridge, MA: Cambridge University Press.

This work was previously published in Journal of Organizational and End User Computing, Volume 22, Issue 3, edited by M. Adam Mahmood, pp. 40-65, copyright 2010 by IGI Publishing (an imprint of IGI Global).

Chapter 4
Studying the Documentation of an API for Enterprise Service-Oriented Architecture

Brad A. Myers
Carnegie Mellon University, USA

Sae Young Jeong
Carnegie Mellon University, USA

Yingyu Xie
Carnegie Mellon University, USA

Jack Beaton
Nokia, Inc., USA

Jeff Stylos
Carnegie Mellon University, USA

Ralf Ehret
SAP, AG, Germany

Jan Karstens
SAP, AG, Germany

Arkin Efeoglu
SAP, AG, Germany

Daniela K. Busse
SAP Labs, LLC, USA

ABSTRACT

All software today is written using application programming interfaces (APIs). We performed a user study of the online documentation of a large and complex API for Enterprise Service-Oriented Architecture (eSOA), which identified many issues and recommendations for making API documentation easier to use. eSOA is an appropriate testbed because the target users include high-level business experts who do not have significant programming expertise and thus can be classified as "end-user developers." Our study showed that the participants' background influenced how they navigated the documentation. Lack of familiarity with business terminology was a barrier for developers without business application experience. Both groups avoided areas of the documentation that had an inconsistent visual design. A new design for the documentation that supports flexible navigation strategies seems to be required to support the wide range of users for eSOA. This paper summarizes our study and provides recommendations for future documentation for APIs.

DOI: 10.4018/978-1-4666-0140-6.ch004

1 INTRODUCTION

"Service-Oriented Architecture" (SOA) is a way to structure large and distributed software systems, where services communicate over a network with the client and with other services, and can be combined into composite applications. Increasingly, companies are providing their operations, which may previously have required installing a custom application, as services on the Web, so they can be accessed from a browser. Enterprise SOA (eSOA) is focused specifically on supporting business processes across an enterprise by reusing existing services. When an eSOA application is being planned and developed, many kinds of people are involved. For example, business process experts, who might be titled "Solution Architects," are knowledgeable about the business context but may not necessarily be professional programmers, and are often responsible for identifying and selecting which services will be used. These users might therefore be classified as "end-user developers" (Wulf, Paterno, & Lieberman, 2006). Specifications they write might then be passed to professional programmers, who are responsible for writing code that uses the actual services. Therefore, the documentation and some of the tools must be accessible to both business process experts and professional programmers.

In a service-oriented architecture, code on the user's machine communicates with a remote service using messages across the Internet. When using Web services, the communication is usually encoded in XML, and the format of the messages might be described using a WSDL (Web Services Description Language) file, which has been formalized by the World Wide Web Consortium (e.g., http://www.w3.org/TR/wsdl).

As part of the "Natural Programming Project" (Myers, Pane, & Ko, 2004), we are interested in a whole range of usability issues around programming. Recently, we have begun to focus on the usability of libraries, frameworks, toolkits, and other application programming interfaces (APIs) (Ellis, Stylos, & Myers, 2007; Stylos, Faulring, Yang, & Myers, 2008; Stylos & Myers, 2008). APIs are crucial since most of modern development of all kinds involves finding, understanding, and connecting pre-built items, from small library calls to large-scale components. Enterprise SOA APIs are particularly interesting to study, because they can be large and complex, and therefore expose interesting issues of scale, and because they often target a wide range of developers.

Our previous research has shown that programming using eSOA APIs is not simple when the APIs are providing access to powerful business functionality (Beaton, Jeong, Xie, Stylos, & Myers, 2008; Beaton, Myers, Stylos, Jeong, & Xie, 2008). Some barriers we identified included long names for services, different behaviors of services due to different business behavior, parameters of the services as hierarchies of objects with complex dependencies driven by internal, not exposed, business logic, and lack of example code (Beaton, Jeong, et al., 2008; Beaton, Myers, et al., 2008). The current paper presents the results of a user study of the usability of the online documentation provided by SAP for their enterprise SOA product.

In summary, our results are that when navigating eSOA API documentation, users with business backgrounds did better, and they experienced the most benefit from process component documentation. The process component documentation provides diagrams showing the architecture of an eSOA API in terms of service interfaces, the service operations they contain, and the business objects to which they are connected. All users avoided sites with visual designs that were inconsistent with their starting pages. Developers without business application experience were unfamiliar with business terminology and so they focused on searching and scanning for individual terms with limited success. Based on these results, we recommend that documentation provide flexible ways to navigate for different users with different backgrounds. This study also inspired new documentation tools, which we briefly summarize at the end of this paper.

2 RELATED WORK

Some of the first work on applying usability principles to APIs comes out of Microsoft, focused on specific APIs (Clarke, 2004). Inspired by this, we began working on the usability of API design patterns (Ellis et al., 2007; Stylos & Clarke, 2007; Stylos & Myers, 2008), and the barriers to programming faced by end-user developers, which includes the difficulties of identifying and understanding the appropriate resources in the documentation, which we called "Selection Barriers" (Ko, Myers, & Aung, 2004).

We also reported on our previous studies of the usability of eSOA APIs for programming. We identified many barriers for installing and using the eSOA development environments, including issues with generating the stubs that will interface between the user's code and the XML messages that are required to communicate over the Web, and issues with the long and confusing names of the services (Beaton, Myers, et al., 2008). In a second study, we asked experienced programmers to use four services which had already been identified for them (Beaton, Jeong, et al., 2008). The current study complements these other works by focusing on the task of finding the services in the first place.

Many other people have provided recommendations and guidelines for APIs, but most of these are just based on the writer's intuitions or personal experience, rather than usability studies with users. For example, API designers with experience building the Java (Bloch, 2001) and Microsoft.NET (Cwalina & Abrams, 2005) APIs have published API design guidelines. For SOA, (Jones, 2006) lists anecdotal common mistakes made when developing SOA architectures, such as problems caused by service hierarchies that are either too fine-grained or too coarse-grained. Recently, a new group has formed around API usability (see http://www.apiusability.org).

Focusing on documentation in general, Purho adapted Nielsen's 10 heuristics to apply to documentation (2000). Friendly (1995) applied an informal methodology of user testing to JavaDoc, which is automatically generated from a Java project, and derived clear and succinct recommendations for future API documentation designers. Unlike JavaDoc, the eSOA documentation we studied contains a large amount of hand-created content and addresses a larger, more complex framework.

Others have focused on the internal documentation for projects, focusing on the software developers themselves (e.g., Forward & Lethbridge, 2002), but this is not relevant for understanding how documentation for external users should be designed.

3 METHODOLOGY

3.1 Participants

Based on the success of our earlier studies (e.g., Stylos & Clarke, 2007), we decided to use an informal lab study with users who were representative of the target populations for the eSOA API. Since we were told by SAP that the target API was designed for developers with a wide range of expertise and background, we selected some experienced programmers with little business background, and some experienced business end-user developers with little programming background, and some in between. We did not include experienced SAP developers in order to identify initial learnability issues with the documentation. Overall, we had 8 participants, all of whom were male Masters students at our university, although all but one of them had work experience before returning to school (see Table 1). The age ranged from about 25 to 35. None of the participants had ever seen the specific documentation Web site we

Table 1. Characteristics of the participants in the user study, and whether the search feature was available when they performed the study. Participant p2 had the most extensive business application experience

	p1	p2	p3	p4	p5	p6	p7	p8
Years of Work Experience	3	3	3	1	0	2	1	2.5
Business Application Experience	yes	YES	yes	yes	no	no	no	no
Years Programming Experience	2	3	3	4	2	5	4	2.5
Were able to use Search				yes				yes

were testing, and none had used the API that the documentation was for. Of the eight participants, four had significant experience with business application development using business software such as SAP, PeopleSoft and Oracle. All four of these participants had experience with Enterprise Resource Planning (ERP), which is one of the major areas of business software. Participant p2 had the most business application experience, having used the SAP development environment and SAP's programming language called ABAP. The last 4 participants had no experience with business applications. Three of the participants had moderate to extensive programming experience with Java (4 years or more), and the others had some experience. All of the participants except p2 were enrolled in a Web Services course, but our study was performed before they had gotten very far along. This means that the participants all had an interest in SOA and had been introduced to some of the terms. Thus, we feel that subject p5 could be representative of new hires who might be assigned to do SOA work, p6-p8 might be representative of system integrators, p2 represents an all-around expert, and p1, p3 and p4 be representative of Solution Architects who have moderate knowledge of both business and programming. The experiment lasted about 2 hours, and the participants were each paid $20.

3.2 Tasks

The task for this study was to use the documentation to find the specific services necessary to perform a "Create Sales Order" operation. The participants did not use any programming tools such as an Interactive Development Environment (IDE) and did not have to produce any code. They were shown the introductory page of the documentation Web site and were given a brief tutorial (about 10 minutes) describing the document layout including the various ways to navigate away from the front page. We told participants that they should consider themselves to be high-level architects in a company that was planning to implement a new sales order system using an existing ERP system. They should find the services needed to create a sales order, starting from the string names of a buying company, a selling company, and a product. They did not need to actually implement an application; they only needed to identify the correct services so that another developer could later implement the system. They were given about 2 hours to finish all tasks.

One challenging part of this task was that when participants read the "Create Sales Order" service documentation, they would discover that this service does not take string names for the seller, product and buyer, but instead takes IDs, which the participants had to find other service calls to look up. Therefore, successful task completion required finding four services we refer to here as "Create Sales Order," "Find Customer," "Find Supplier," and "Find Product" (although the actual names were much longer and less clear). Participants were not told in advance about the need for multiple inter-related services. Discovering that

Figure 1. Different possible navigation paths

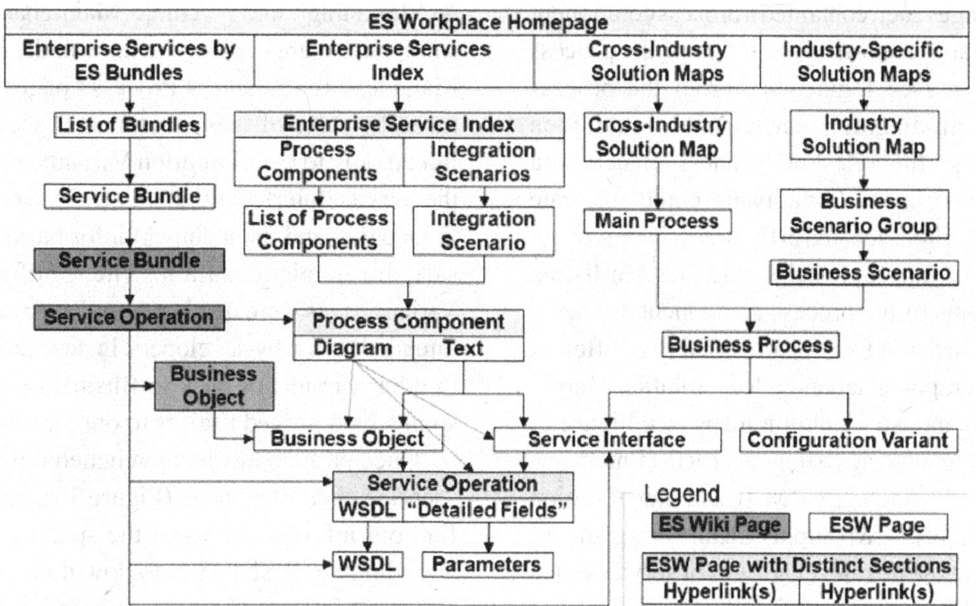

inter-related services were necessary from the documentation was an essential part of the task.

During the study, we used the "think-aloud" protocol (Nielsen, 1993), in which participants are encouraged to talk continuously to the experimenter, because we were interested in gaining insights as to what participants were thinking while performing the task. In order to be able to gain as much useful information from each participant as possible, after seeing enough confusion to confirm that the participant was experiencing a usability breakdown, we would offer help so the participant would not remain stuck on one problem for the entire session. We wanted to know why problems occurred, not the length of delays. However, explicit help was relatively rare because it was difficult to give advice without giving away the whole solution.

3.3 Context: SOA Documentation

The participants used the actual then-released (February 2008) online documentation of SAP's eSOA product called the "ES Workplace," which is described below. Based in part on the results of our study, SAP has since improved the site significantly, and many parts now no longer match what the participants saw.

There are several different paths that participants could use to navigate from the starting page down to the pages of individual service operations (see Figure 1). One path grouped services into Enterprise Service (ES) "Bundles" that collected together a set of services that are often used together. The ES Bundles navigation path was implemented using a user-editable wiki, so that users of the documentation could add and update the bundles to show what services were actually used together in practice. Since this navigation path led to a wiki, the visual formatting of these pages was quite different from other parts of the documentation Web site. The bundles contained a list of service operations, and from there, users could eventually navigate down to the individual services, at which point they would leave the wiki and return to the previous "normal" format.

A second path used the Enterprise Service Index, which listed business "process components" in alphabetical order. The Process Component pages each contained a process component diagram and a textual description of the process component (see Figure 3a). From the process component diagram, participants could then navigate to the relevant business objects and service interfaces. Participants could navigate using hyperlinks located in the process component diagram or in a table below the diagram listing the contents of the process component as text.

The third and fourth paths used two different kinds of graphical tables called "Solution Maps." The cross industry solution maps (see Figure 2) provided categories such as ERP (Enterprise Resource Planning), CRM (Customer Relation Management), SCM (Supply Chain Management), and then at the next level, groups of services such as "Analytics," "Financials," and "Sales and Service." The industry solution maps provided categories like "Retail," "Airlines," or "Oil & Gas," and then groups of services such as "Sales & Marketing" and "Vehicle Maintenance." As shown in Figure 1, all of the links in the Solution Maps lead to "Business Process" pages. Unfortunately, some of these Business Process pages linked only to Configuration Variants, and not to the Service Interfaces that link to Service Operations pages and the technical information necessary for implementation. The Configuration Variant pages were dead ends and apparently not intended for use by developers. Instead they linked to other variants or back to Business Processes, so this path proved useless to our participants.

Once participants had navigated down to the "service operation" page (Figure 3b), they could find out information about the specific service, including the WSDL files to download. On each of the service operation pages, there was a hyperlink to a separate "Detailed Field" page with collapsible tree hierarchies of the input and output

Figure 2. Cross industry solution map for ERP

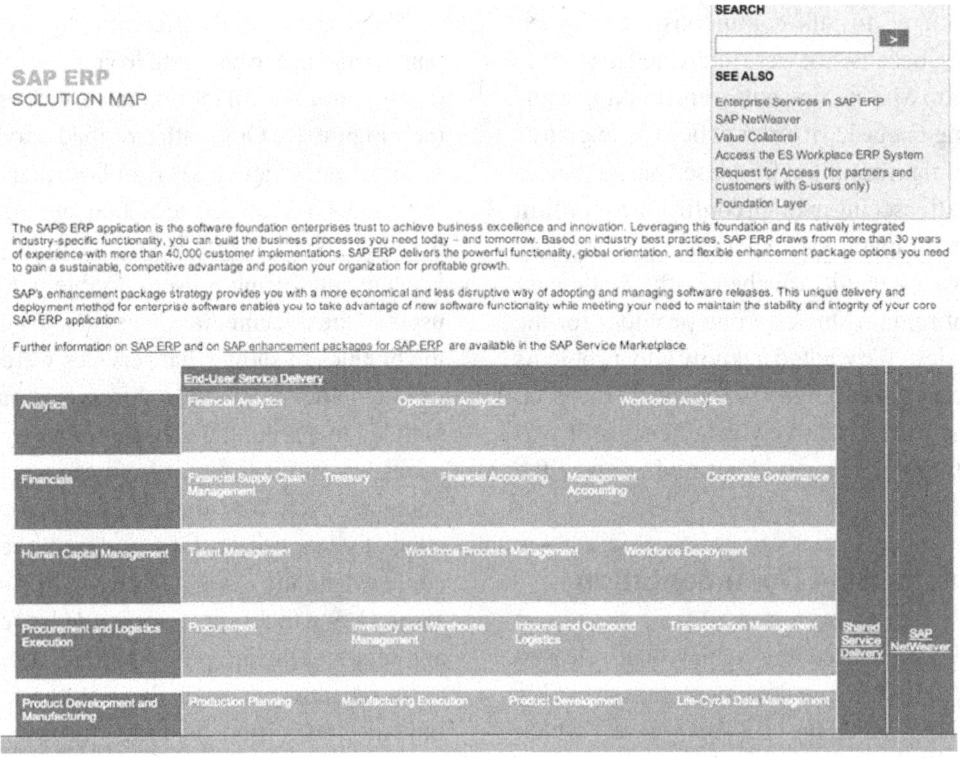

SEARCH

SAP ERP
SOLUTION MAP

SEE ALSO

Enterprise Services in SAP ERP
SAP NetWeaver
Value Collateral
Access the ES Workplace ERP System
Request for Access (for partners and customers with S-users only)
Foundation Layer

The SAP® ERP application is the software foundation enterprises trust to achieve business excellence and innovation. Leveraging this foundation and its natively integrated industry-specific functionality, you can build the business processes you need today – and tomorrow. Based on industry best practices, SAP ERP draws from more than 30 years of experience with more than 40,000 customer implementations. SAP ERP delivers the powerful functionality, global orientation, and flexible enhancement package options you need to gain a sustainable, competitive advantage and position your organization for profitable growth.

SAP's enhancement package strategy provides you with a more economical and less disruptive way of adopting and managing software releases. This unique delivery and deployment method for enterprise software enables you to take advantage of new software functionality while meeting your need to maintain the stability and integrity of your core SAP ERP application.

Further information on SAP ERP and on SAP enhancement packages for SAP ERP are available in the SAP Service Marketplace

	End-User Service Delivery					Shared Service Delivery	SAP NetWeaver
Analytics	Financial Analytics	Operations Analytics	Workforce Analytics				
Financials	Financial Supply Chain Management	Treasury	Financial Accounting	Management Accounting	Corporate Governance		
Human Capital Management	Talent Management	Workforce Process Management	Workforce Deployment				
Procurement and Logistics Execution	Procurement	Inventory and Warehouse Management	Inbound and Outbound Logistics	Transportation Management			
Product Development and Manufacturing	Production Planning	Manufacturing Execution	Product Development	Life-Cycle Data Management			

Figure 3. (a) Process component view page for the accounting process component which includes a diagram and text below the diagram (not shown). (b) Service operation page for create sales order.

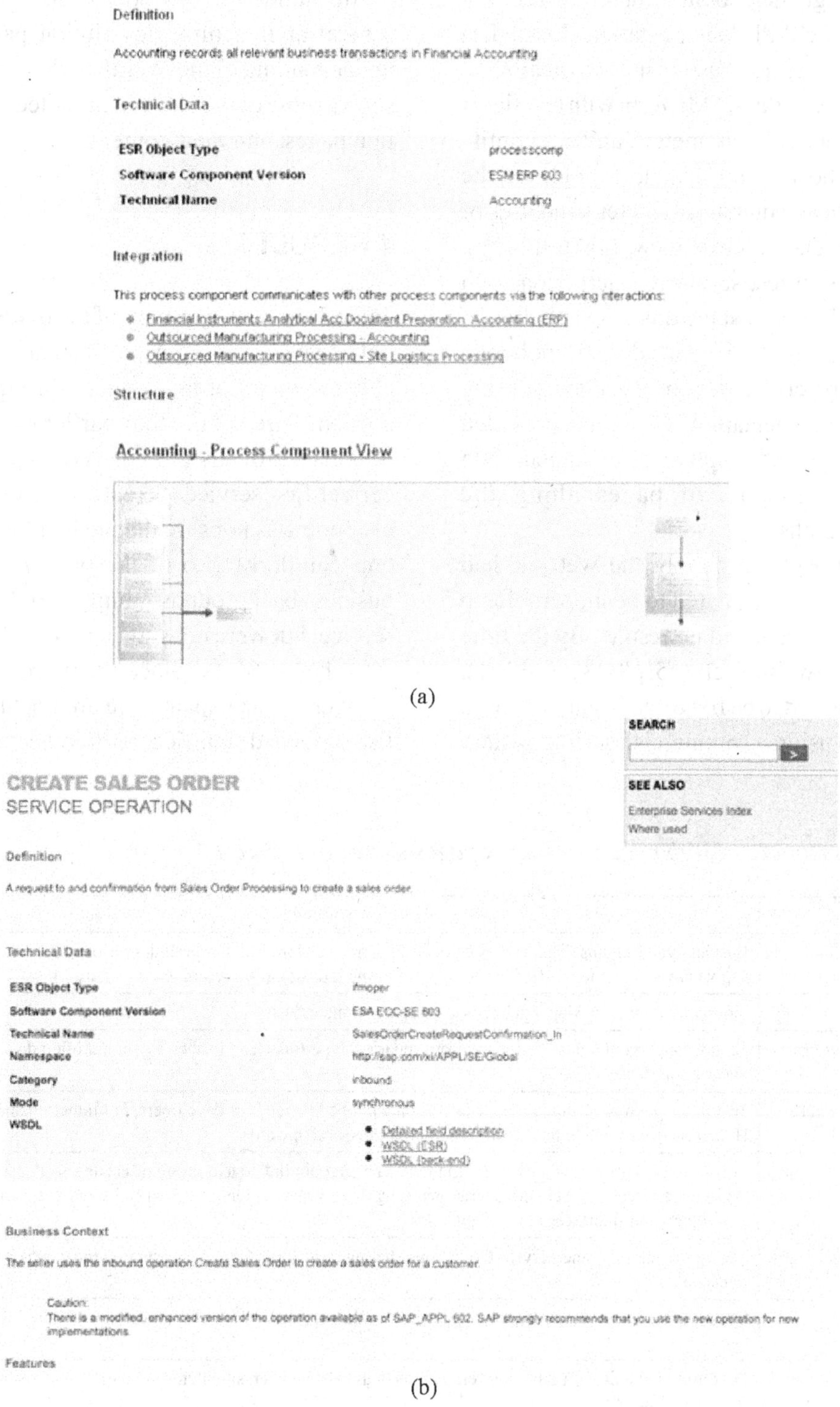

Definition

Accounting records all relevant business transactions in Financial Accounting

Technical Data

ESR Object Type	processcomp
Software Component Version	ESM ERP 603
Technical Name	Accounting

Integration

This process component communicates with other process components via the following interactions:

- Financial Instruments Analytical Acc Document Preparation Accounting (ERP)
- Outsourced Manufacturing Processing - Accounting
- Outsourced Manufacturing Processing - Site Logistics Processing

Structure

Accounting - Process Component View

(a)

SEARCH

SEE ALSO

Enterprise Services Index

Where used

CREATE SALES ORDER

SERVICE OPERATION

Definition

A request to and confirmation from Sales Order Processing to create a sales order.

Technical Data

ESR Object Type	ifmoper
Software Component Version	ESA ECC-SE 603
Technical Name	SalesOrderCreateRequestConfirmation_In
Namespace	http://sap.com/xi/APPL/SE/Global
Category	inbound
Mode	synchronous
WSDL	• Detailed field description • WSDL (ESR) • WSDL (back-end)

Business Context

The seller uses the inbound operation Create Sales Order to create a sales order for a customer.

Caution:
There is a modified, enhanced version of the operation available as of SAP_APPL 602. SAP strongly recommends that you use the new operation for new implementations.

Features

(b)

parameters for calling the service. Since the Web services can be accessed from a variety of programming languages, coding examples were not provided in the API documentation. Instead, a browser-based service "testing jig" was available, implemented using an HTML form with text fields to input the service's parameters, and a "submit" button. By showing all available fields of the complex input and output parameter structures of the Web services in a tree view, this testing jig allowed users to test service consumption with real values. However, at the time, the only link to the testing jig was provided inside a "Handbook" PDF guide hyperlinked from the main starting page of the documentation. This guide provided an end-to-end walkthrough of the documentation site and screenshots of pages along the navigational paths.

When we began this study, the Web site had a search box, but it appeared to be inoperable, in that all searches returned no results. By the time we ran the last two subjects (p5, p8—see Table 1), the search seemed to be fixed and began working. (A hazard of using a commercial on-line system for a study—one cannot guarantee all participants will have the identical system!)

In summary, the documentation provided several architectural description pages to help understanding of the overall architecture. Table 2 shows some of the different architectural description pages, and their content.

4 RESULTS

Table 3 shows a summary of the overall results—only two of the eight participants (25%) were able to find all of the services during the 2-hour session. Three of the four participants with business backgrounds (75%) were able to find the correct first service ("create sales order"), however one was not sure that he had found the right one. Similarly, two of the participants without business backgrounds found the right sales order service, but were not sure, and none found any of the other services. Since there are such a small number of participants, we are not able to establish statistical significant differences between the

Table 2. Descriptions of Web page content for pages shown in Figure 1

Documentation	Content
Solution Map	Business value chains displayed as colorful diagrams. Colored bars hyperlink to processes and scenarios. May apply across industries (ERP, CRM, etc.) or for one industry. (Oil, Retail, etc.) (Figure 2)
Scenario Group	Similar to a Solution Map, but specific to a part of one industry.
Main or Business Process, Scenario	Text description of a business process or scenario. Hyperlinks lead further down, but often do not link to Service Interfaces.
Configuration Variant	Text description of business use cases that may not be intended for developers, but rather business analysts. Hyperlinks go only to other Configuration Variants, and upwards.
Process Component	This page contained both a diagram and text. The diagram linked to a group of Business Objects, and all Service Interfaces and Service Operations using those Business Objects. Text links below the diagram went to the Objects and Interfaces only. (Figure 3a)
Service Interface	Text hyperlinks to some Service Operations sharing a Business Object, which may have one or more Service Interfaces.
Service Operation	Description of a service operation. Hyperlinks to the service WSDL and parameters. (Figure 3b)
Business Object	Description of a distinct business "entity" (such as a sales order, supplier, etc.) with links to Service Operations acting upon it.
WSDL	XML file that describes the service in machine-readable form.

Table 3. Starting and rally points for the participants (using page categories from Figure 1), and success of participants on finding the 4 services

	p1	p2	p3	p4	p5	p6	p7	p8	Total
Was able to use Search				**yes**				**yes**	
First Entry Point	**M**	**M**	**M**	**I**	**M**	**M**	**I**	**S**	
Other Rally Points	**I,P**	**I,P**	**B**	**L,P**	**M,B**	**I,P**	**L,P**	**M,P**	
Found Correct Service Operation:									
Create Sales Order	**X**	√	√	√-	**X**	√-	**X**	√-	**62.5%**
Find Customer Service	**X**	√	√	**X**	**X**	**X**	**X**	**X**	**25%**
Find Supplier Service	**X**	√	√	**X**	**X**	**X**	**X**	**X**	**25%**
Find Product Service	**X**	√	√	**X**	**X**	**X**	**X**	**X**	**25%**

Key: **M**=Solution Map; **S**=Search; **I**= ES Index, **P**=Process Component, **L**=List of Process Components, **B**=Business Process √=Success; √- =Success but not sure; **X**=Failure

two groups, although the trend is striking. From our observations and the think-aloud comments of the participants, we were able to understand the participants' strategies and barriers at a much more detailed level.

4.1 Paths through the Documentation

Given the four starting entry points for navigating from a home page (Figure 1), participants were confused with which one to use, and spent significant time reading text on the home page to try to figure this out. The main page did not explain the motivations and goals of the four different paths, leaving participants confused about why there were multiple choices and which might be the most useful. This confusion made participants feel frustrated right at the beginning. Table 3 summarizes where the participants started.

An interesting observation was the use of what we call *rally points* by participants while navigating through unfamiliar areas (see Table 3). Participants would choose a path, go down that path until they decided whether or not it was worth continuing, and then return to an earlier page multiple times. Participant's selection of a rally point indicated a level of certainty that the navigation up to that point, at least, was correct.

Figure 4 summarizes the paths of all of the participants when trying to find the Create Sales Order Service. Each row represents a type of Web page, as described in Table 2. Each circle represents Web pages that the participant visited, with the size of the circle representing how long the participant stayed at that page. In Table 3 and Figure 4, we can see that the page at which the participant started was a natural rallying point at first, but participants would move the rally point around as they gained and lost confidence in the usefulness of various paths through the documentation.

Most participants showed a tendency to choose the Solution Maps as a starting point (as shown in Table 3), but five of the participants changed to the Enterprise Service Index after failing to use the solution maps. The Enterprise Service Index page only provided process component lists and integration scenario lists in alphabetical order. In the process component lists, there were prominent business software categories such as CRM, ERP, SCM and SRM. Participants with business application backgrounds used the "Enterprise Service Index" pages as a rally point, and when they found the "Sales Order Processing" component

Figure 4. Summaries of the navigational paths of all of the participants when trying to find the Create Sales Order service. The sizes of the circles represent the amount of time spent at web pages of the type in the first column.

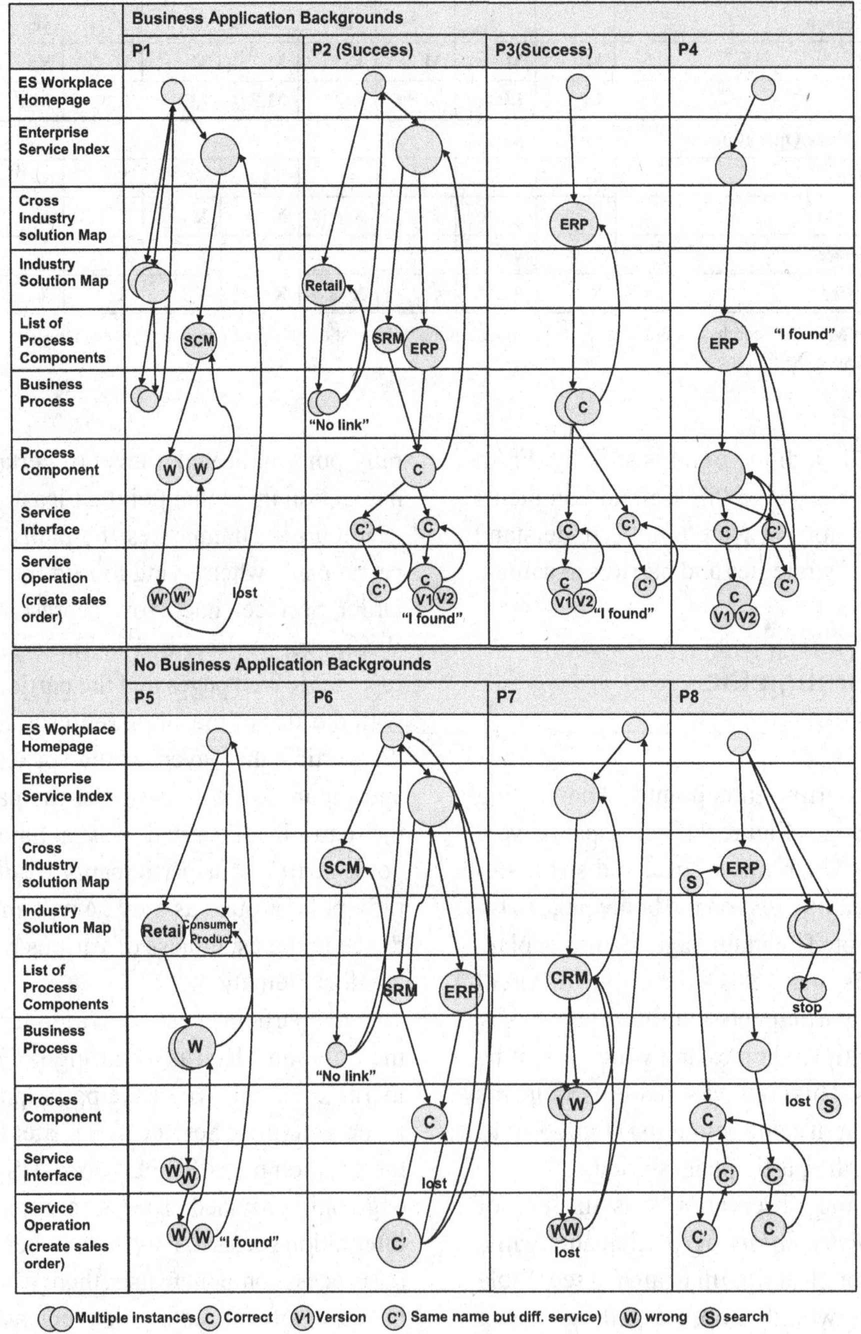

in the ERP and SRM category, they felt they were on the right track. Most participants were frustrated by new and unfamiliar terms and acronyms, but participants without business application backgrounds were particularly confused by the large number of prominent acronyms such as ERP,

CRM, SCM, SRM and other business-specific terms that they did not understand.

When participants navigated to the Enterprise Service Bundles page (which was a wiki), they were surprised by the different look and feel of this part of the Web site, and felt they must have gone astray, so they quickly back-tracked. None of the participants made use of the Bundles pages, so they do not appear in Figure 4.

Participants spent a lot of time trying to use the solution maps (Figure 2). Some participants selected cross industry solution map, possibly because they were not told about any specific industry in the task instructions, but others guessed an industry they thought might be appropriate, and used an industry-specific map. However, the participants without business backgrounds had difficulties in using the any of these solution maps to navigate further due to the unfamiliar terminology and the large number of choices making a brute-force systematic search difficult. However, half of the participants without business backgrounds used a map page as a rallying point (see Figure 4). In the think-alouds, the participants expressed a desire to understand the "big picture," and the solution maps seemed to provide a good overview. The business-background participants understood the category names such as ERP and SRM, and their sub-grouping such as "Financials," "Retail," and so forth, but even these participants often only had experience with some of the categories and sub-groupings. However, all participants were confused by classifications with similar names like "Sales," "Sales Execution," "Sales Order," and "Sales & Service" in the solution maps.

4.2 Process Component View

The Process Component view shows one or more related business objects and services (see Figure 3a). For example, in the "Sales Order Processing" process component view, the user can navigate to the "Ordering In" and "Ordering Out" service interfaces and the "Sales Order" business objects. The page was composed of two parts: a diagram, and a table. The diagram displayed business objects as small blocks and service interfaces as large blocks that held groups of smaller blocks representing service operations. The service operations were connected to the business objects they acted upon with arrows. The titles of the blocks acted as hyperlinks to the appropriate business object, service interface, and service operation pages. Due to the large number of objects to be shown in the diagram, the font of the elements was extremely small and yet horizontal and vertical scrolling was still needed.

In spite of these barriers, some participants spent an extensive amount of effort trying to understand the diagrams. Many of the participants found this view to be a good rallying point, since it provides a well-organized collection of related items to explore. However, some of the participants who were familiar with UML notation (Unified Modeling Language) mentioned that they would have preferred UML class diagrams, which have a standard notation for classes and their relationships.

Another cause for confusion was that the system provided many similar-sounding services in the process component view, and even multiple versions of the same service with similar names such as "Create Sales Order V1," "Create Sales Order V2," and "Check Sales Order Creation." Participants could not find any relevant information to differentiate different versions of services from the process component view. The participants had to drill down to the service operation level for each, to try to determine which should be used. If the user could recognize the differences among these different services at the process component view, this would have saved significant time and confusion.

Beneath the diagram, a table contained text descriptions and hyperlinks to many of the same locations as the diagram, with the exception of the service operations.

4.3 Service Descriptions

In the tasks we gave the participants, it was important to investigate the input and outputs of the various services. However, this was difficult to verify from the detailed service pages. Only three participants were able to find the "buyerID," "sellerID" and "materialID" parameters for the "Create Sales Order" service operation, which was crucial to determining what other services were needed.

Other problems with understanding the services included unfamiliar technical terms such as synchronous and asynchronous mode and inbound and outbound messages. The participants did not find any explanations of these terms in the documentation, although they are pervasive throughout all services. Some of the details of the operation, such as which fields were required versus optional, were actually not documented anywhere except in the generated WSDL XML files themselves, which were too long and difficult to read to serve as effective documentation.

The detailed page for each service listed three classes of messages: input message, output message and fault message, which participants did not understand. In fact, only input messages are relevant (messages that go "in" to the server), but this was not explained anywhere.

In general, many participants found the correct target service, but then were unsure whether it was correct or not, and continued searching. For example, Table 3 and Figure 4 show that participants p4, p6 and p8 found a service operation to create a Sales Order, but then navigated away and kept looking. There were multiple versions and the participants were not confident which service operation should be used.

4.4 Using Search

As mentioned above, the search box was present for all participants, but only began working for the last two (Table 1). All of the participants expressed a desire to use search to try to find the services. In general, if the participants knew the name of what they wanted, they preferred to use search, and the participants for whom search worked often returned to try searching when they were lost. Participants often tried to search for phrases we used in the instructions, such as "create sales order," "selling company," "buying company" and "product," but these were not helpful, and then participants tried related terminology such as "agency," "supplier," "customer," and so forth. In general, participants were not successful at using search because there were always either no results or too many matching results. Even the most experienced participants had difficulty mapping the "product" in the instructions with the actual term used in the parameter and service names, which was "material."

When search began working, the results were presented grouped by the various API documentation types shown in Table 2, such as solution map pages, process component view pages, and service operation pages. This grouping proved helpful to participants, and made it easy to find the appropriate process components and business objects when they recognized them in the results. However, since there were often too many search results, and the listing was in alphabetical order, often participants missed the answer even when it was included.

4.5 Individual Strategies

By performing a detailed time analysis of each participant, we were able to break down their activities into various categories. We identified four categories of activities, with two opposing strategies in each:

- Focusing on scanning textual descriptions ("Scan text") vs. focusing on scanning process diagrams ("Scan diagrams").
- Trying to understand how to use the Web site by reading the provided PDF docu-

Figure 5. Strategies the participants tried, and how well each strategy worked

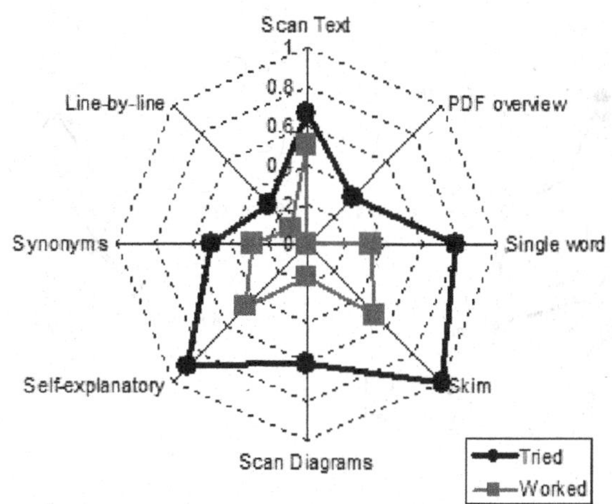

mentation ("PDF overview"), or just by looking through the Web site itself, relying on the Web site to be self-explanatory ("Self-explanatory"). Five participants found the PDF document but three of them did not use it, because it was a separate document.

- Browsing the documentation with a single specific key word in mind from the task instructions, such as "buyer" ("Single word"), or else using a set of interrelated synonyms ("Synonyms").
- Skimming the documentation focusing on only the prominent text, such as the headers ("Skim"), or systematically reading the pages line-by-line ("Line-by-line").

We then analyzed each of the participants, looking for whether they tried to use each of these strategies, and whether it worked for them. Note that each participant might have used different strategies at different times. Figure 5 provides a radar chart averaged over all participants for the strategies. The opposing strategies are shown at opposite ends of each line. The outer black line (connecting the circles) shows the average of whether this was used or not (where 1 would mean everyone used it, and 0 would mean no one used it). The inner red line (connecting the squares) shows our estimate of how successful this strategy was.

Figure 5 makes it clear that participants were split on using text and diagrams, they strongly preferred the documentation to be self-explanatory, rather than using the PDF overview, more tried single words rather than synonyms, and everyone skimmed, but only a few systematically read line-by-line. As for the success of these strategies, by-and-large, the success seemed to mostly correlated with participants' expectations (they used a strategy about as much as it was successful, so the two lines go in and out together), with the notable exception of the diagrams—as discussed above, many participants wanted to use these, but they did not work out for them. Another notable result is that the PDF overview was surprisingly unhelpful.

Figure 6 provides the same data broken down by whether the participants had business background or not. In terms of what they tried, it is clear that the non-business participants did not use synonyms (because they did not know the other terms that might be related), and the non-business participants were more systematic, trying to extract more meaning from the pages (whereas the business participants were more likely to be able to

Figure 6. Breakdown for participants who had (a) and did not have (b) business backgrounds

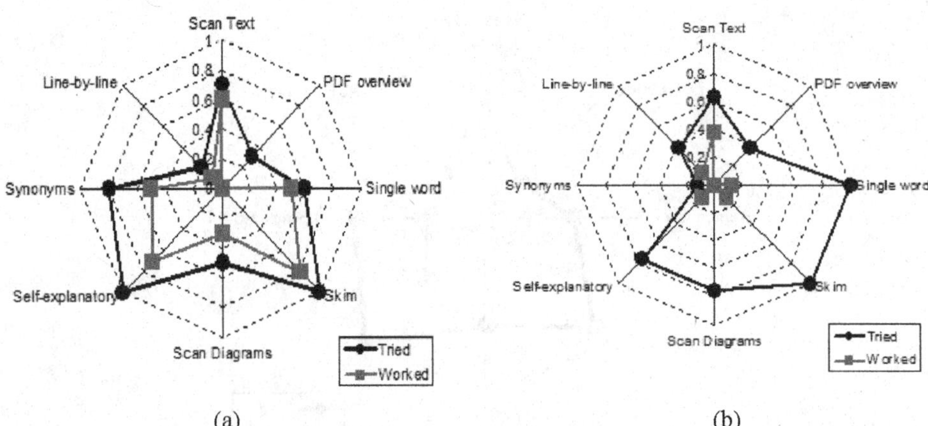

pick up the meaning from skimming). It is clear that few strategies worked for the participants without business backgrounds, and only scanning the text was overall successful.

5 THREATS TO VALIDITY

There are many reasons why the results of this study may not generalize. First, we only used a small number of participants, and we were not able to get statistically significant results about their different behaviors. Most of the results reported here are impressions and informal analyses based on our observations of their behaviors, barriers and successes. The participants are also not necessarily representative of the target population for the documentation. eSOA APIs may be used only by people with some business background or people who have specific, relevant training. For example, SAP offers various training courses that would have explained many of the fundamental terms about which the participants were confused. Our participants were all completely unfamiliar with the documentation or the API.

The experimental set-up may have also biased the results. In real life, users would have more than 2 hours to perform tasks, and they would likely go to more experienced colleagues for help when they were stuck, which was not an option in this study. Also, our task was much simpler than real-world eSOA tasks.

6 DISCUSSION

As with other usability analyses (Nielsen, 1993), when multiple user-study participants in even a small sample have difficulty with something, it is highly likely that a portion of the larger target audience will also have trouble, so the documentation is likely to be improved by eliminating the barriers reported here.

The differences in strategies and success between the people with business experience and those without are also interesting. These can mainly be attributed to the differences in their ability to understand the many terms and acronyms used in the documentation. Participants with business backgrounds were aware of inter-related business concepts and terminology, and so understood more explanations on the Web site. The navigational strategies were also very different between the two groups.

Of the four ways to navigate to the service operation, the ES index was found to be most useful to many developers, who then used the process component diagrams as a rally point. The graphical solution maps were frequently used by all participants, but tended to lead developers to the wrong services. The frequent use of the maps and process diagrams strongly suggests that a good diagram of the system is important to users. The presence of the many alternative navigation paths without sufficient explanation or description was itself a barrier to participants, since they had to investigate which one to use.

This study particularly focused on identifying services based on their input/output characteristics, but this turned out to be surprisingly difficult to determine from the documentation. Our previous study showed that understanding the dependencies among the parameters is also a key barrier to developers (Beaton, Jeong, et al., 2008), since which parameters are required and which are optional depends on the values supplied for other parameters. This means that more attention is needed on documenting the parameters of services, where it is possible. It might not always be possible because some services deal with highly customizable business processes. Customers can set up the system for their special business needs and therefore the behavior of the services can change from customer to customer. So a "Create Sales Order" service can be used in a simple retail scenario, where you just buy 100 pencils, as well as in the aerospace industry when you can order 20 Airbus A380 airplanes, which have quite different requirements.

A consistent look and feel for the documentation was found to be important. When participants encountered the different format of the wiki, they immediately backtracked without studying the new location. As a result, the grouped services on the wiki went unseen and unused by all of the participants.

The names of services and their types were found to be a problem. We observed one participant confused with several versions of "Create Sales Order V1" and "V2," the differences service interfaces of the same name with "In" and "Out" appended, and also with the difference between the "Synchronous" and "Asynchronous" versions of the same service. Another problem was the length and construction of the names themselves, which some participants found confusing (for example, SalesOrderERPCreateRequestConfirmation_In_V1).

7 IMPLICATIONS FOR DESIGN

How can the documentation be designed to best serve developers across the whole spectrum? Improvements in the usability of the documentation are clearly necessary if users such as our participants are to succeed. For the EUD community, focusing on having high-quality documentation is crucial, since EUDs are likely to be less willing to participate in training classes yet are just as likely to need to use large APIs. We are happy to report that many of these recommendations have been implemented in the current version of the SAP documentation, and others are being investigated for future versions.

Based on our observations and user study results, we recommend the following as documentation guidelines:

- **Consistent Look-and-Feel:** Overall, the entire documentation Web site should have a consistent, yet unique, format, so that developers who leave the path know it instantly, and developers who find a useful area do not backtrack. This may mean that more developer participation in a wiki might occur if its format is not visibly different from the rest of the API documentation.
- **Provide an Overall Map:** When we ourselves were trying to understand the SAP documentation before we ran the user study, we created early versions of Figure 1 and Table 2, which we found very help-

ful. Having such information at the front of the documentation Web site would likely benefit users.

- **Explain Starting Points:** It is important to make the purpose of various starting points clear. It seems that some of the paths on the eSOA documentation may be targeted at different classes of users, such as Business Experts versus developers. Alternatively, they might be used for different tasks. Users would benefit from a better explanation of *why* there are multiple paths, and how they are intended to be used.
- **Provide a "Bread Crumb Trail":** Users were often lost in the documentation. Providing a trail that shows where they are in the documentation structure, and the main nodes along the path to that page, would be helpful. However, the documentation is a graph and not a tree because some locations are in multiple paths (e.g., the same service may be used by multiple industries). This means that the trail will have to be careful to differentiate multiple possible paths to the current page, hopefully highlighting the path actually used.
- **Support Use of Rally Points:** In addition to the bread crumbs, there could be other support for users to backtrack to well-known pages that are serving as "rally points." For example, we created a prototype which included an always-visible bookmark list into which the user could easily save pages while continuing navigation, and then these could serve as shortcuts for navigating back to a rally point. Another idea is to provide pages which *other* users or the system designers have identified as useful rally points, to support a kind of "crowd-sourcing."
- **Integrate "How-To-Use" Information:** We discovered that although a PDF guide explained how the documentation could be used, users were reluctant to leave their browsing to read a document in an external format, so the explanations should be in HTML format, hyperlinked to the documentation. Even better would be if the documentation was self-explanatory, with explanations integrated with the main documentation content, so there would be no need for separate documents explaining how to use the API documentation. For example, pop-ups or special hyperlinks might explain "What is this?" for items that users may not be familiar with.
- **Effective Search:** The participants for whom search did not work were unhappy, so a good search facility needs to be part of all documentation. Since participants tried to search on all aspects of services, all parts of the API should be included in the search, including the parameter names and types, and the documentation of the names and types. It should be easy to navigate from data types to the fields that use those types. In order to reduce the size of the answers, the search should allow users to qualify what they are looking for (e.g., limit the answers to service operations). The grouping of the search results into categories is a good idea, but each result should be presented in a way that is easy to understand, so the user does not need to navigate into each result item to see if it is the desired one or not. Support should also be provided for "near miss" search terms, by returning results for the appropriate term that is used in the implementation (such as "material") when a synonym understood by the users is entered (such as "product").
- **Provide Familiar Diagram Formats:** Our participants expected UML class diagrams or other well-known architectural presentations to help them understand the services. Users should be surveyed on what formats

they will find familiar before the decision is made to create new formats.

- **Balance of Diagrams and Text:** Some participants focused on diagrams showing the relationships among services, so these need to be clear and concise, with appropriate labels that are understandable yet not too big. At the same time, other users skipped the diagrams in favor of text, so both should be supported.
- **Curtail User Focus on Esoteric Terminology:** Specialized terminology for specialized users and use cases is absolutely necessary in API documentation. However, we observed that participants who are exploring tend to focus on unfamiliar terms, even if they are unnecessary as part of their task, and so waste time while increasing their level of confusion and frustration. However, most users will (at least eventually) be familiar with the terminology, so it is important that any definitions or other help not interfere with expert use. It is also important that users be able to quickly tell what parts of the document are important to them, so they can skip large parts (and any unfamiliar terminology in those parts). Quick definition of unfamiliar terms might be achieved with "What is this?" links or pop-ups, as described above.
- **Explain Crucial Terminology:** Participants could not find the correct services in our study without understanding the difference between synchronous and asynchronous services, or the meaning of "in" and "out" services. To the extent that all users must understand certain "esoteric" terminology, make sure it is clearly explained, or even better, use more generally-understood terms so less explanation is needed.
- **Make the Parameters for Services More Prominent:** Participants cited the parameters of the service signature as the main indicators of the usefulness of a service. Therefore, parameters should be given a prominent position in the description of a service operation. Our previous research showed that the distinction between optional and required parameters, and parameters used to call the service and those filled in by the service as return values was not clear to developers (Beaton, Jeong, et al., 2008). This needs to be particularly well explained, and certainly not left to be deduced from the WSDL files, which are XML and difficult to read.
- **Support Comparing Services:** There are many similar services, and participants needed to compare services to find out the differences. In the current system, sometimes they needed to open up the low-level WSDL files and try to manually determine the differences. Instead, direct comparisons and explanations should be available to differentiate services. For example, side-by-side visualizations of two services might emphasize the differences in parameters or actions. If a service is an updated version of another service, the modification dates and differences should be clear with cross-links and explanations of when each might be used.
- **Clear Names for Services:** The user should be able to recognize what a service does by its name. If there are multiple versions, it should be clear why there are multiple versions, and whether they are all intended to be useful (vs. some being deprecated, for example), and which one should be selected.
- **Present Related Services:** The documentation should describe related services and business objects. For example, to create a sales order required providing three different parameters that were returned by other services. Listing each of these pa-

rameters and services could help the user understand and find related services. The Bundles idea in the current documentation may help with this goal, but we are not able to comment on how well it works because our participants did not try the Bundles.

- **Provide Code Examples:** While Web services are often advertised for their ability to be consumed in any programming language, this does not excuse the provider from showing sample code snippets. Even if it is not possible to provide example code in every target language, then it is still useful to provide some examples (at least in the most high priority target language or languages) rather than none. It should be noted that standardization across similar services will mean that fewer examples need to be provided, because a pattern that works for one service should also work for its "sibling" services.
- **Online Service Testing:** Developers who want to see how a service works before starting to program may benefit from an interactive way to provide parameters and run the service. The current SAP documentation does have such a "Test" function, where users can try out a service and see what it returns for various parameters. This kind of online service testing can have a positive effect on developers' understanding of Web service consumption. It has the potential to display required and optional parameters, and allow users to verify their understanding of the service. However, without valid test data to use as parameters, the user may never be able to get a useful return value. Therefore, the testing mechanism should be combined with multiple examples, and cross-linked to other services that might return the kinds of values required for the service to operate correctly. Furthermore, once the user has configured a test call interactively, it would be useful if there was some way to generate code in the desired target language that would do the same thing.
- **New Organizations for Hierarchical Browsing:** In their think-alouds, we noticed that various participants, especially the ones without business experience, seemed to be trying to navigate based on different starting points and hierarchies. For example, some participants seemed to be trying to find particular operations (verbs) first (such as "create" or "find"), then the objects on which those operations occurred (the nouns), and finally, other parameters of the operation (adverbs such "by what" the find should get the object, or "using what" to create the object). This inspired the design of the Apatite documentation tool (see next section). The current documentation does allow users to start from a business object and find all of its services, or to get a global list of services, but these are always organized alphabetically. Since the services are named based with the affected business object at the front of the name (e.g., SalesOrderERPCreate RequestConfirmation_In_V1), both lists are essentially noun first. Allowing a sort by operation (sorting all the "create" service operations together) might be helpful.

8 NEW DOCUMENTATION TOOLS

Inspired in part by this study, along with our other studies, we created two new documentation tools. Although inspired by eSOA documentation, the initial implementation and target for these new tools is Java, in order to be able to develop and test them with a wide variety of people.

The Jadeite tool (Stylos et al., 2009) (http://www.cs.cmu.edu/~jadeite) emphasizes the most commonly used items using larger font sizes, allows users to add items that seem to be miss-

Figure 7. The Jadeite documentation tool displays packages (top left) and classes (bottom left) with different font sizes based on popularity, and allows users to add new methods (like read()) which are not in the API as "placeholders" to show how to perform that operation (http://www.cs.cmu.edu/~jadeite).

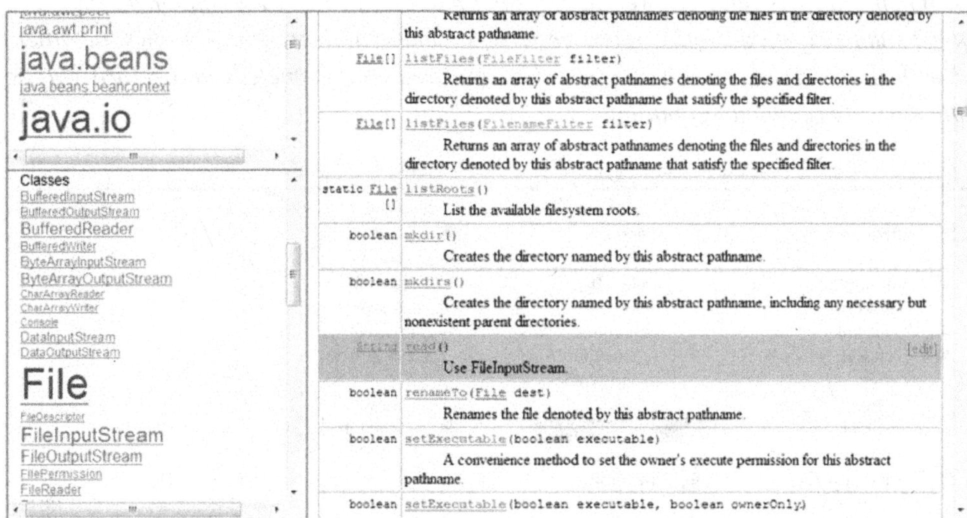

ing from the documentation along with a cross-reference for how to perform what that item would do (as a form of "crowd-sourcing"), and automatically searches the Web to provide code examples (see Figure 7). An evaluation showed that programmers were about three times faster at performing common tasks with Jadeite than with standard Javadoc.

The Apatite tool (http://www.cs.cmu.edu/~apatite) supports browsing of APIs in a different way by finding the items that are associated with a selected item. When an item is selected in the first column (see Figure 8), Apatite displays related packages, classes, and methods in the second column. Motivated by the observation in our eSOA study that users sometimes wanted to start from the actions instead of the object types, Apatite allows users to start from an action (verb) such as "add" (see Figure 8) and find all the classes that implement that method. If a method is selected, Apatite will show the other methods that are often used with a selected method, to help with the problem of finding how to perform common composite operations. For example, this might help with the task of our eSOA study: to use multiple services together to create the sales order. Apatite also shows which classes are used as parameters and return values of that method.

The initial display shows four or fewer items in each category, but the user can easily see more by clicking on the "+" icon. If an item is selected in the second or subsequent columns, then new columns are added that show items associated with all of the previous selections. The text field at the top of each column allows the items to be filtered by keywords. A tooltip on each item shows details of the relationships and of the selected item, and clicking on the "?" takes the user to the detailed JavaDoc documentation.

9 FUTURE WORK AND CONCLUSION

This informal study is just the beginning of a long investigation into improvements that can be made to API documentation. We are currently working on interesting new designs to see how we can make

Figure 8. The Apatite documentation tool allows users to start from any package, class or method, but also from an action (verb) or property, and navigate to all the associated items. Here, the second column shows the most popular 4 classes that implement an "add" action (out of 362 classes which implement an "add"). When "List" is selected, we see the top 4 methods in List that implement add. The tool-tip shows a quick summary of addNotify. If a user selects a method, then Apatite shows the other methods often used with that method, and the classes that are used as parameters and return values for that method (http://www.cs.cmu.edu/~apatite).

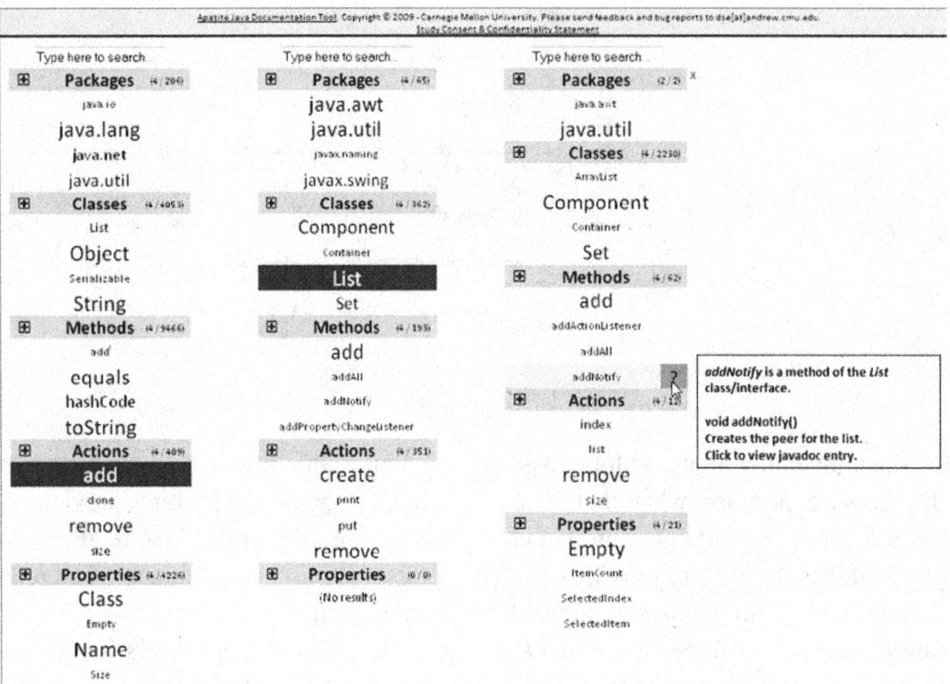

documentation even easier to search and browse, and how to make the important information more salient. We will continue to evolve the Jadeite and Apatite tools described in the previous section, along with new tools.

Meanwhile, SAP is continuing to improve their APIs and the documentation for them. We plan to repeat this study with the new designs to see what problems have been solved, and if there are any new problems introduced. In the new study, it will be interesting to investigate more classes of users, from Business Expert EUDs with little programming experience to experienced programmers, and hopefully get some non-university participants from local businesses. It would also be useful to compare people who are expert users of the system and documentation to the novice users on which we focused in this study. Good documentation should also be efficient for experts, as well as helpful for novices.

In addition to providing insights into how to improve the current documentation, these kinds of studies can provide generalizable knowledge that is useful for all documentation writers for all kinds of systems, since many of the challenges will be similar. Since all programmers, from EUDs to novices and to professionals, spend significant time trying to understand and use APIs, improvements to documentation can have significant impacts on the overall usability of the system as a whole.

ACKNOWLEDGMENT

This article is revised from: Sae Young Jeong, Yingyu Xie, Jack Beaton, Brad A. Myers, Jeff Stylos, Ralf Ehret, Jan Karstens, Arkin Efeoglu, Daniela K. Busse, "Improving Documentation for eSOA APIs through User Studies", Second International Symposium on End User Development (IS-EUD'2009), March 2-4, 2009. Siegen, Germany. Springer-Verlag, LNCS 5435, pp. 86-105. This work was performed while the first five authors were all at Carnegie Mellon.

For help with this article, we thank many people at SAP (especially Paul Hofmann, Dan Rosenberg, Ike Nassi, Claudius Fischer, Bernhard Drittler, and Oliver Schmidt) and the participants for sharing in user study. This research was partially funded by a grant from SAP and partially by NSF under grants ITR-0325273 through the EUSES Consortium, and CCF-0811610. Opinions, findings and conclusions or recommendations expressed in this material are those of the authors and do not necessarily reflect those of the NSF or SAP.

REFERENCES

Beaton, J., Jeong, S. Y., Xie, Y., Stylos, J., & Myers, B. A. (2008, September 15-19). Usability challenges for enterprise service-oriented architecture APIs. In *Proceedings of the the 2008 IEEE Symposium on Visual Languages and Human-Centric Computing (VL/HCC '08)*, Herrsching am Ammersee, Germany (pp. 193-196). Washington, DC: IEEE Computer Society.

Beaton, J., Myers, B. A., Stylos, J., Jeong, S. Y., & Xie, Y. (2008). Usability evaluation for enterprise SOA APIs. In *Proceedings of the 2nd International Workshop on Systems Development in SOA Environments (SDSOA 2008, ICSE 2008)*, Leipzig, Germany, (pp. 29-34). ACM Publishing.

Bloch, J. (2001). *Effective java programming language guide*. Reading, MA: Addison-Wesley.

Clarke, S. (2004). Measuring API usability. *Dr. Dobb's Journal, May 2004*, S6-S9.

Cwalina, K., & Abrams, B. (2005). *Framework design guidelines*. Upper-Saddle River, NJ: Addison-Wesley.

Ellis, B., Stylos, J., & Myers, B. (2007, May 19-27). The factory pattern in API design: A usability evaluation. In *Proceedings of the 29th International Conference on Software Engineering (ICSE 2007)*, Minneapolis, MN (pp. 302-312). Washington, DC: IEEE Computer Society.

Forward, A., & Lethbridge, T. C. (2002, November 8-9). The relevance of software documentation, tools, and technology: A survey. In *Proceedings of DocEng 2002*, McLean, VA (pp. 26-33). ACM Publishing.

Friendly, L. (1995, June 1-2). The design of distributed hyperlinked programming documentation. In *Proceedings of the International Workshop on Hypermedia Design*, Montpellier, France, (pp. 151-173). London: Springer.

Jones, S. (2006). *SOA anti-patterns*. Retrieved from http:// www.infoq.com/ articles/ SOA-anti-patterns

Ko, A. J., Myers, B. A., & Aung, H. H. (2004, September 26-29). Six learning barriers in end-user programming systems. In *Proceedings of the IEEE Symposium on Visual Languages and Human-Centric Computing*, Rome, Italy (pp. 199-206). Washington, DC: IEEE Computer Society.

Myers, B. A., Pane, J. F., & Ko, A. (2004). Natural programming languages and environments. *Communications of the ACM, 47*(9), 47–52. doi:10.1145/1015864.1015888

Nielsen, J. (1993). *Usability engineering*. Boston: Academic Press.

Purho, V. (2000). Heuristic inspections for documentation-10 recommended documentation heuristics. *STC Usability SIG Newsletter, 6*(4).

Stylos, J., Busse, D. K., Graf, B., Ziegler, C., Ehret, R., & Karstens, J. (2008, September 15-19). A case study of API design for improved usability. In *Proceedings of the the 2008 IEEE Symposium on Visual Languages and Human-Centric Computing (VL/HCC'08),* Herrsching am Ammersee, Germany (pp. 189-192). Washington, DC: IEEE Computer Society.

Stylos, J., & Clarke, S. (2007, May 19-27). Usability implications of requiring parameters in objects' constructors. In *Proceedings of the 29th International Conference on Software Engineering (ICSE 2007),* Minneapolis, MN (pp. 529-539). Washington, DC: IEEE Computer Society.

Stylos, J., Faulring, A., Yang, Z., & Myers, B. A. (2009, September 20-24). *Improving API documentation using API usage information*. Paper presented at the 2009 IEEE Symposium on Visual Languages and Human-Centric Computing (VL/HCC'09), Corvallis, OR. (pp. 119-126).

Stylos, J., & Myers, B. A. (2008, November 9-14). The implications of method placement on API learnability. In *Proceedings of the 16th ACM SIGSOFT Symposium on Foundations of Software Engineering (FSE 2008),* Atlanta, GA (pp. 105-112). ACM Publishing.

Wulf, V., Paterno, F., & Lieberman, H. (Eds.). (2006). *End user development*. New York: Springer.

This work was previously published in Journal of Organizational and End User Computing, Volume 22, Issue 1, edited by M. Adam Mahmood, pp. 23-51, copyright 2010 by IGI Publishing (an imprint of IGI Global).

Chapter 5
Mutual Development:
The Software Engineering Context of End-User Development

Anders I. Mørch
University of Oslo, Norway

Renate Andersen
University of Oslo, Norway

ABSTRACT

The article presents and analyzes data from a case study in customer-initiated software product development. We have observed and participated in system development activities in a commercial software house (company) over a period of two years. The company produces project-planning tools for the oil and gas industry, and relies on interaction with customers for further development of its products. Our main research question is how customers and professional developers engage in mutual development mediated by shared software tools (products and support systems). We have used interviews with developers and customers as our main source of data, and identified the activities (from use to development) where customers have contributed to development. We analyze our findings in terms of co-configuration, meta-design and modding to name and compare the various stages of development (adaptation, generalization, improvement request, specialization, and tailoring).

INTRODUCTION

The goal of the research reported here is to identify areas where end-user development (EUD) and professional software development meet and interact. We have observed and participated in development activities in a commercial software house (referred to as company) over a period of two years. We propose a model of the activities, which we refer to as mutual development. The model consists of the 5 sub-processes, which connects EUD and professional development.

DOI: 10.4018/978-1-4666-0140-6.ch005

Motivation

There are two levels of software development: specific and general, represented by the activities of amateur (end-user) and professional developers, respectively. When they interact in a mutually beneficial way a new opportunity for innovation emerges that extends the boundaries of what can be accomplished with in-house driven innovation (Victor & Boynton, 1998). We call this model *"inside-out"* and the model advocated in this chapter *"outside-in."* Inside-out innovation is initiated by professional developers and technology managers, that is, technological innovation, whereas outside-in is driven by external events, a type of innovation that originates outside professional communities by end users (Fischer, 2002) and customers (von Hippel, 2005). They are amateur (non professional) developers who act on behalf of specific needs and by creating ad hoc modifications to "finished" products. The mutual dependency between technological and user-driven innovation can be exemplified by the development of Levi's blue jeans. In 1873 Jacob Davis and Levi Strauss invented to rivet (copper nail) the pocket corners on men's working pants to make them stronger. The two men were granted a patent on this, which is widely recognized as the invention of the blue jean. It is an example of technological innovation. Later on, in 1937 the rivets (copper nails) were removed on the back pockets (first sewn so that they were hidden, and during the Second World War removed to save metal). The hiding and removal of the rivets were in response to consumers who complained that the rivets scratched furniture and saddles. This was a user-driven innovation triggered by various external events that modified a technological invention into a more useful design (Levi Strauss & Co., 2009). It serves as a motivating example for the topic of this article, which is about mutual development: the integration of end-user development and professional software development.

Mutual development is based on a technique for participatory design (PD) known as mutual learning (Bratteteig, 1997). Mutual learning is a technique for users to learn about software design from professional developers, and developers learning the professional (workplace) language of domain-expert users. Mutual development takes this a step further in that the shared knowledge established during mutual learning serves as platform for end-user development. The goal is not only to support collaboration between developers and users (as in PD), but also to empower them with new tools and new forms of organization. This is arguable easier when there are two distinct levels of development, one for software engineers and another for end-user developers. Rich communication channels to connect them can stimulate formalizing ad hoc modifications into software artifacts, and a good process of collaborative design can transform an end-user developed solution into a commercial product feature (Mørch, Nygård, & Ludvigsen, 2009). Users will be increasingly motivated to participate in end-user development when the activity has impact beyond a local solution.

The Case

The company is engaged in commercial software development in the area of project planning and management and provides consultancy services in using its tools. At present, the company employs 25–30 people, but they intend to grow and is concurrently expanding their staff and searching for new markets. In fact, the company is recognized as a major player in the business of project planning tools. They have several hundred customers and they have long-term commitments with many of them. One of their recent products is an add-on to Microsoft Project.

The main market has been the Nordic oil and gas industry. To expand into new markets, particularly building and construction, the company has started to modify and improve its knowledge man-

Figure 1. Researchers' development activity: Snapshot from a design workshop, example of a customer interaction scenario, and screenshot of Web prototype depicting an iterative systems development process.

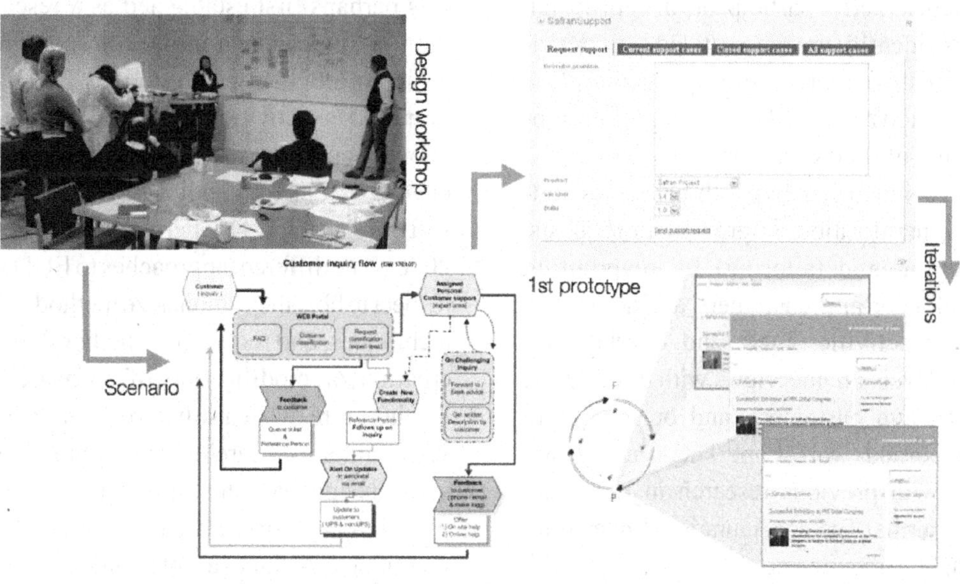

agement practices regarding customer relations. As researchers, we were invited by the company to give advice for how to improve knowledge management practices with customers.

The company is known for their customer initiated product development approach, that is, close interaction with customers to develop tailor-made solutions (Andersen, 2008; Nygård & Mørch, 2007). Customers are encouraged to report problems, innovative use, and local development to the company. This has been stimulated through long-term relationships (maintenance contracts) and user forums (online and F2F). Each year the company hosts a large showcase where customers are invited, and developers provide communication and information sharing tools for customer interaction. This started with the telephone, then supplemented by email, later extending to a Helpdesk interface, then a Customer Relationship Management (CRM) system, and most recently a Web 2.0 prototype created by the research team (Nedic & Olsen, 2007).

The background for the Web prototype was to design a portal to organize the rapid growth of information and to improve the communication within the company and towards its customers. The company experienced expansion of the working staff, as well as in the customer base. Because the requirements for the Web portal were uncertain, the development demanded a lot of communication and collaboration between us, as developers, and the company. We used a combination of agile methodology (rapid prototyping interspersed with company feedback) and participatory design (involving users in design). The agile approach helped is to identify the necessary technological foundations needed for the realization of the running prototype. Techniques from participatory design, in particular design workshops helped us to gain a better understanding of the components to be made. An overview of these techniques is shown in Figure 1. It shows, the steps of the researchers' system development activity: design workshop, scenarios, and iterative Web development.

Our main research question and objective is how there is mutual development between customers and professional developers, mediated by software products and ICT support systems. By *mutual development* we mean that both professional developers and end users contribute to development as active participants in both design and use. We identify the range of end-user development activities (from use to design) taking place in the interaction between the company's developers and some of their customers.

We have identified five sub-processes (adaptation, generalization, improvement requests, specialization, and tailoring) by pinpointing what developers and customers are doing and where their activities meet and overlap. We base our analysis on interviews with developers, consultants, and customers, and on data from a video-recorded workshop. The findings are compared with previous research in EUD and analyzed in terms of co-configuration (Engeström, 2004, 2007), meta-design (Fischer, Giaccardi, Ye, Sutcliffe, & Mehandjiev, 2004; Fischer & Scharff, 2000) and modding (Jeppesen, 2004; Jeppesen & Molin, 2003). The goal is to identify the interdependencies of EUD and professional development and to construct a model for their mutual development.

The rest of the article is organized as follows. It starts with an overview of EUD. Next, we present a survey of research in the intersection of EUD and software development. Then we present three theoretical perspectives on EUD. We analyze our findings by comparing with the three perspectives. At the end we summarize our findings and suggest some directions for further research.

END-USER DEVELOPMENT

End-user development is an umbrella term for research and development in end-user tools for application development. This originated with research that dealt with technological and organizational issues of an emerging field, such as end-user programming in spreadsheets and tailorable systems (Mehandjiev & Bottaci, 1998). Most recently, Web application development has introduced a new line of R&D that shares many similarities with EUD (e.g., mashups, Yahoo pipes). However, EUD was perhaps first established as a research field with its own agenda in the European EUD-Net project (2002-3), which defines EUD as "a set of methods, activities, techniques, and tools that allow people who are non-professional software developers, at some point to create or modify a software artifact" (Lieberman, Paterno, & Wulf, 2006). The different approaches to EUD vary with respect to how they emphasize methods, activities, techniques, and tools, and whether they focus on creation or modification of software artifacts. Furthermore, what a software artifact means also varies among researchers. Software tools, source code, design diagrams, application units, and application development environments have been mentioned. As an example, end-user tailoring is about methods, activities, techniques, and tools for adaptation and further development of existing software applications based on direct activation of tailoring tools from the applications' user interface (Mørch, 1995; Wulf & Golombek, 2001).

EUD is multidisciplinary and its rationale (the "why" of EUD) has multiple dimensions: human-computer interaction (HCI), software engineering, and organizational use. From a human-computer interaction perspective, EUD is about leveraging the deployment of easy-to-use ICT and turning them into easy-to-further-develop systems (Costabile, Foglia, Fresta, Mussio, & Piccinno, 2003; Lieberman et al., 2006; Mørch, Stevens, Won, Klann, Dittrich, & Wulf, 2004; Wulf, Pipek, & Won, 2008). From a software engineering perspective, EUD is supportive of the trend of producing generic applications (Bansler & Havn, 1994; Mørch, 1996). By "generic" is meant multifunctional, domain independent, or application generators, that is, specialized functionality that can be configured to different user needs (Åsand & Mørch, 2006), or domain independent tools like groupware and generic drawing programs, or "under designed" design environments that support users in creating new applications (Fischer et al.

2004; Fischer & Scharff, 2000). For example, a groupware system can provide different users with different access rights to shared objects (Stevens & Wulf, 2002). From the perspective of organizational use, the rationale for EUD is associated with the user diversity found in organizations employing advanced ICT. Users have different cultural, educational, training, and employment backgrounds. They are novice and experienced computer users (e.g., super user), ranging from the young to the mature, and they have many different abilities and disabilities (Åsand & Mørch, 2006; Costabile et al. 2003; Mehandjiev, Sutcliffe, & Lee, 2006).

SOFTWARE ENGINEERING CONTEXT OF EUD

EUD interrelates with software development in multiple ways, but (to the best of our knowledge) there are few studies that have examined EUD in terms of boundary crossing of two types of organizations (developer and customer). We survey the related work below.

Stevens and Wulf (2002) presented a case study of inter-organizational cooperation from the steel industry in Germany. They analyzed the relationship between two engineering offices and a steel mill to identify patterns of cooperation that can serve as requirements for new designs. They found that there was tight coupling across organizational boundaries, but also competition between the units. EUD was proposed in terms of a component-based framework for tailoring a groupware application at runtime. The focus was on flexible access control for sharing material stored in electronic repositories among the interacting units. The new access mechanisms could be decomposed and integrated and the users were able to realize new access mechanisms that did not already exist in the groupware. By decomposing application components into simpler ones and assembling the parts into new compounds (intermediate building blocks) and applications, users can modify existing applications and create new ones, without accessing the underlying program code (Wulf et al., 2008).

Eriksson and Dittrich (2007) identified the reasons why tailoring should be integrated with software development. In a case study of a Swedish telecom provider, they found it was possible to provide end-user developers with the means to tailor not only individual applications, but also the infrastructure in which applications are integrated. According to the authors, this is an area that might change faster than applications, especially in rapidly changing business contexts. To support this form of tailoring in the organization, they studied tailoring needs to coordinate better with software development activities. In another study, Dittrich and Vaucouleur (2008) found that customization practices of an ERP system they studied at several sites were at odds with software engineering practices, resulting in a discrepancy in terms of integrated environments for end-user development.

In a case study in an accounting company in Norway, the activities of end user developers were followed and analyzed using Activity Theory (Åsand & Mørch, 2006). The authors show how the company successfully initiated a program to train super users (Kaasbøll & Øgrim, 1994) in conjunction with introducing a new software application, Visma Business (VB). The research was formulated to address how super users engage in EUD activities in order to achieve an efficient use of VB, and how EUD activities were organized. In terms of organization, there was a certain division of labor within the company: 1) between the regular users and the super users, 2) between the super users and the application coordinator (acting as local developer), and 3) between the application coordinator and the professional developers. It was also interesting to find a new role for a local developer. This person's responsibility was primarily to perform EUD activities at a general level, to work closely with some of the more experienced super users in the offices, and to communicate with the professional developers outside the company. This person generalized the results of useful EUD activities and made local solutions available throughout the company.

Explicit and implicit channels for communication between developers and users for the purpose of end user development have been proposed in a variety of contexts, especially in the area of CSCW. For example Mørch and Mehandjiev (2000) demonstrated that design rationale integrated with a tailor-enabled application could support indirect communication between developers and users and thus help end user developers to further develop their applications. Along the same lines, Stevens and Wiedenhöfer (2006) developed a wiki-based help system for communication and information sharing to be integrated with standalone applications. It provides online help to a community of users and thus enhances communication between developers and users with the affordances of Web 2.0. The authors claim this form of integration creates a more seamless transition between the use context and the resolution of problems due to the familiarity users have with Wiki-based systems (Stevens & Wiedenhöfer, 2006).

CONCEPTS FOR ANALYSIS

We analyze our findings in terms of three theoretical perspectives on end-user development in order to account for a broad array of relevant concerns, ranging from computer science to application domains to organization of work: meta-design, modding, and co-configuration.

SER Model and Meta-Design

SER (Seeding, Evolutionary growth, Reseeding) is a process model for integrating end-user development with software engineering (Fischer & Ostwald, 2002). It is different from user-centered design in HCI (e.g., prototyping) and from software engineering (e.g., specification driven methods). It has more in common with aspects of participatory design in that the SER model describes a sociotechnical environment for tailorable applications to be used over an extended period of time. It postulates that systems that evolve over a sustained time span must continually alternate between periods of unplanned evolutions by end users (evolutionary growth), and periods of deliberate restructuring and enhancement (reseeding), involving users in collaboration with designers (Fischer & Ostwald, 2002).

The SER model makes a distinction between design time and use time, which distinguishes developers' activity from users' activity. Integrating these two types of software development activities is the aim of meta-design: a framework to provide end users with tools that allow them to tailor and further develop professional tools in their own context (Fischer et al., 2004; Fischer & Scharff, 2000). Meta-designers use their creativity to develop sociotechnical environments in which other (less technical oriented) users can be creative in their own areas of expertise. Meta-design as viewed from a software engineering viewpoint defines flexible design spaces for end-user developers. Examples are tailoring languages, application frameworks and EUD tools integrated with applications. This means the users interested in being active contributors should be supported in exploring an application's potential for being incorporated in new activities, and evolving its functionally to support new needs (Fischer et al., 2004). To the extent this can be accomplished without end users having detailed knowledge of programming, meta-design becomes a powerful framework and perspective for EUD.

The SER model has influenced the mutual development model we present below. In particular, we elaborate on evolutionary growth and reseeding and the dynamic interaction between them in the company we studied.

Modding

Modding is when users modify products by themselves, without the direct intervention of professional developers. The term is a slang expression derived from the word modify that refers to the act of modifying a piece of software or hardware, originally conceived in the gaming industry. Modding is an alternative way of including customers in product development processes. Modding can be seen to combine EUD and participatory design, in that it combines the inclusion of customers in both early and later stages of product development, depending on the customer's needs. By adopting this activity, modding can be seen as extending the design environment approach to EUD (Fischer & Scharff, 2000; Mørch et al., 2004; Wulf et al., 2008) by making it possible for customers to promote an array of ideas, needs and tentative solutions in the early stages of product development, even before a given framework exists.

The outcomes of modding, called mods, range from minor alterations to very extensive variations of the original product (Jeppesen, 2004; Jeppesen & Molin, 2003). An example of modding from the gaming industry is when hardcore players create hacks and figure out how to develop software add-ons to twist games' parameters, such as the creation of a "No Jealousy" patch, which lets characters have more than one lover without either one getting jealous (Knight, 2008). What is even more interesting is how the original product serves as a platform for further modding for customers.

Modding as an alternative approach to including customers in product development processes is a noteworthy concept since it engages the customer in different stages of the product development process. Modding is based on further development of an already existing platform. However, this must not be misunderstood. It does not mean the narrowing down of product development to simply be further development of already existing products, as is often the case with tailorable applications and evolutionary application development (Mørch, 1996). On the contrary, it appears that already existing products may be "opened up" by end-user contributions in terms of generating new ideas for functionality, new features, and even new products. In many ways, it is the concrete (executable) applications rather than the more abstract application frameworks and tailoring languages that best serve as a platform for end-user development (Mørch, 1996).

Co-Configuration

Engeström (2004, 2007) adopted the term co-configuration from Victor & Boynton (1998) to enhance the theory of expansive learning in order to address a new form of work that involves user participation from customers and employees in the development of products. Co-configuration implies both a new form of work and a new way of learning. Engeström draws on the empirical findings of a broadband telecommunications firm in Finland, focusing on learning as joint creation of new knowledge and new practices by multiple stakeholders (Engeström, 2004). Engeström, building on Victor and Boynton (1998), defines co-configuration as an emerging historical type of work with the following general characteristics (Engeström, 2004):

- Adaptive and adaptable customer products or services, or more typically integrated product-service combinations
- A continuous relationship of mutual exchange between customers, producers, and the product-service combinations
- Continuous co-configuration and customization of the product-service- customer relationship over lengthy time periods
- Active customer involvement and input in the co-configuration work
- Multiple collaborating producers that need to operate together in networks within or between organizations,

- Mutual learning from interactions between the parties involved in configuration actions.

From this description, we can understand the term co-configuration as a type of work that includes active participation from customers in developing their products. It provides a rationale for why companies should pay attention to EUD and user driven innovation, namely to establish closer connections with its customers. One of the characteristics of co-configuration work is the great degree of customer participation required in order for it to work. For example, when developing project planning software to fit in a user organization, it is important to include users as participants in the process since they are the ones who know best the work tasks to be supported. However, not all companies will benefit by such a strategy. For example, to what degree is the company dependent on involvement from customers? What happens if some customers do not see the value of being part of such co-configuration work? To what degrees do the customers actually participate? To what degree is it reasonable to expect that customers will continue to participate over lengthy time periods? It is probably realistic to assume that in today's world of mass consumption the majority of end users will not want to design or contribute to further development of the products they use (Fischer, 2002). We chose to focus on those customers who took an active part in the case we report.

Researchers in information systems have used terms like super user (Åsand & Mørch, 2006; Kaasbøll & Øgrim, 1994) and boundary spanner (Volkoff, Strong, & Elmes, 2002) for a similar role as "active user." They share the view that these people help to broaden participation and democratize the design process (Kanstrup & Christiansen, 2006), and study them by drawing on insights derived from empirical data gathered from user organizations, like we have done in this article.

Method

Our objective is to construct a model of mutual development between customers and professional developers as seen from a EUD perspective. In the area of software development, participatory design (Bratteteig, 1997; Ehn & Kyng, 1991; Kanstrup & Christiansen, 2006), directed observation (e.g., Norman, 2008), and strategic ethnography (Pollock & Williams, 2008) are plausible methods for addressing the objective. Directed observation means to seek out and analyze the workarounds, hacks, and clever improvisations active users and ordinary people create at work and at home (Norman, 2008). Strategic ethnography is longitudinal studies following artifacts (packaged software) as they evolve over time within developer organizations and across organizational boundaries to the organizations developers interact with (Pollock & Williams, 2008).

We adopted a case study approach and designed it to extend our own previous efforts by treating the interaction of two organizations (developer and customer) as the unit of analysis (Åsand & Mørch, 2006; Nygård & Mørch, 2007). We identify the sub-processes of the product development process studied. EUD is one component in this picture, but not the only one. By presenting the whole picture we wish to provide a comprehensive view of mutual development, which we present as different stages of activity, using examples and theoretical analyses to justify our claims. We used a qualitative approach as part of a case study. In addition, we used video and audio recorders to gather data. Moreover, we used open-ended interviews, focus groups and participant observations.

CATEGORIZING DATA

This section will elaborate on how the intermediate terms used to describe mutual development emerged as a result of analysis done while screening and analyzing data. The form of analysis used is "template analysis," which is the process whereby "the researcher produces a list of codes (a template) representing themes identified in their textual data" (King, 1994). This is both a top-down and bottom up process. Below, we have named some terms, more precisely the different stages of mutual development, representing different themes identified in the empirical findings. After identifying these themes, the data was analyzed with this in mind, using these themes as a template. King distinguishes three features in template analysis: defining codes, hierarchical coding and parallel coding (King, 1994).

Defining codes is to label a section of text with a code in order to index it as relating to a theme or issue in the data that the researcher has identified as important to his or her interpretation (King, 1994). We had the research questions in mind the first time we went through the data, but in the second round of selecting data we categorized it accordingly. The categorization of "outer loop" and "inner loop" were used as "high-level codes," and may be connected with what King defines as hierarchical coding. These terms were used in the analysis and correspond to the terms "outside in" and "inside out," which is used elsewhere in the article.

Hierarchical coding "is codes that are arranged hierarchically with groups of similar codes clustered together to produce more general higher order codes" (King, 1994). The high-level codes of "inner loop" and "outer loop" roughly clustered the data into two different terrains, one about customer-initiated development activity (outer) and the other about software engineering (inner). This was done deliberately to create an overview of the data. Knowing that our area of interest was mostly on the "outer loop" product development process, the data was analyzed again for topics within this domain. It was found that within the interviews there existed some sub-processes of outer loop product development. They were identified as Adaptation, Generalization, Tailoring, Improvement Request and Specialization. Using these terms or codes as a template, the data was searched again in order to support these sub-processes with empirical evidence.

Parallel coding is when the same segment of data is classified within two (or more) different codes at the same level (King, 1994). In one instance, the same set of data excerpts was classified within the intermediate code "outer loop" and the lower order code Specialization, which is a stage within the inner loop product development. Therefore, parallel coding was used in this context.

DATA AND ANALYSIS

At the end of the coding we ended up with the following five sub-processes (stages) of customer-initiated product development:

- **Adaptation:** Adaptation is when a customer requests an improvement to an existing product and the company chooses to fulfill the request. It becomes an Adaptation just for this customer. Sometimes, the customer has to pay for this, sometimes not.
- **Generalization:** Generalization occurs when a new version of an existing product is released and is available to more than one customer.
- **Improvement Request:** This is when customers request the company for extra functionality, report bugs and usability problems, and is viewed from the customers' perspectives.
- **Specialization:** Specialization is when the professional developers at the company create in-house builds. This is common in large-scale and longitudinal software development projects. This could potentially result in new features, but most often it entails refining the product, reorganizing program code, and removing bugs.
- **Tailoring:** Is about active end users who make adaptations on their own.

We justify these stages using the data extracts and analysis below. The two first extracts define basic issues (types of process) that resurface in the other extracts and in the analyses. The last three extracts represent four of the five stages.

Excerpt 1: Types of Improvement Request

In the first excerpt, the focus is on how a developer (informant) judges the Improvement Requests of the customer. This includes making a power decision as to what kinds of Improvement Requests to consider. The power to judge whether or not a customer Improvement Request should be accepted lies in the hands of the company's professional developers. This excerpt does not go into detail about how exactly these Improvement Requests enter the company, but it does elaborate in what way the customers ask for Improvement Requests.

Informant: Often when they (the customers) want Improvement Requests they ask me if I can make a change (to the existing product), according to some needs they have. In addition they put it (the Improvement Request) into a list we have on the Internet. We receive a lot of Improvement Requests and some of them are actually such good ideas that we want to integrate them into our products. And there are other ideas that are really bad. There are also some ideas that are not so good (but they are doable), therefore we incorporate them if they pay for it. When doing this we make special libraries for that particular customer. Then this does not become a part of the system (the product).

Improvement Requests turned out to be an important activity for communication with the company, requiring less technical expertise than Tailoring. Excerpt 1 is an example of how customers propose changes to the company's products without doing any local development. Excerpt 1 shows that an Improvement Request is one of the prerequisite sub-processes of Adaptation. It is when a professional developer creates a new feature for an already existing product in accordance with the customer's demands. At the end of this excerpt, the informant introduces the theme of how they get good, possible (doable) and bad ideas for further development. If an idea is labeled good it is accepted as is. When an idea is categorized as possible it means that the idea is plausible, but will not become a part of the general product. It might be accepted under contract (with payment), and turns into a local Adaptation. Finally, an idea labeled bad is rejected outright. Implicit in this example is the assumption that the company's employees are the ones who judge whether the Improvement Requests are good, possible or bad and have the freedom to make those distinctions.

As seen from a meta-design and SER perspective (Fischer & Ostwald, 2002; Fischer & Scharff, 2000), Excerpt 1 may be interpreted as an example of boundary crossing, namely that submitting, receiving and handling of improvement request cross the boundary of two organizations (customer and developer). It also indicates some of the decisions that have to be made before the "evolutionary growth" of an application at a specific site can be accepted into the "reseeding" phase by company developers. In this way, Improvement Requests can help to bridge the gap between EUD and professional development.

The data in Excerpt 1 may have some commonalities with Engeström's (2004, 2007) notion of co-configuration. Item number two in the definition of co-configuration (see Integrated EUD) is about the mutual exchange between customers, producers and the product-service combinations (Engeström, 2007). Mutual exchange can be seen in this excerpt as well, between the customers issuing requests to the company and the professional developers handling these requests. The exchange for customers is getting the development they want, while the company receives money for performing the development (or more satisfied customers).

If a request is categorized as good or possible, the next stage of Adaptation takes place. During the second stage of Adaptation terms like patch, build and version become relevant, which we discuss below.

Excerpt 2: Types of Generalization

This is part of an interview one of the researchers had with one of the developers. The informant explains the software deployment (packaging) terms patch, build and version as part of an elaborated answer to a question about improvement requests:

Informant: There are three levels: we have a so-called patch, which is a quick fix to some sort of a problem. This is being sent out to the customer, which is a (solution) right there and then. After the customer installs the patch, he tests if it works and then the problem is fixed. After a while, when we have made enough patches like this, we find new errors and the customers find errors and then we make a new complete program. That is what we call a build. On top of this, we have something we call versions; they could be (called) 3.4, 3.5, 3.5.1. They have more content and much more functionality.

Patch, build and version are the developers' responses to customers forwarding Improvement Requests in the Adaptation stage, which again can lead to Specialization and Generalization. Patch is understood as a quick fix to a problem. Patches are packaged extensions that fit specific versions. For example, if Word is being used to write some text and one's references in EndNote are lost each time text is converted into PDF, the company could be contacted. They will fix it and send back a so-called patch, which is small program (a software component) that may be installed on the computer and linked with the main program, and the problem is fixed. Builds result if the company has had many quick fixes, similar to the example with Word, and 2nd order problems emerge (i.e., problems connected to the compatibility of patches). Then they create a build, which is a compiled program. Builds are associated with Specialization. Finally, a new version is both an extension and a generalization. It is an extension (improvement) of a build, and a generalization when a new version is made available to new customers and to the existing customers when they are due for an upgrade according to their contract. Generalization is a borderline activity between inside-out and outside-in product development.

In Excerpt 2 it is evident that to a large extent, software development at the company proceeds with the SER model, as Fischer describes (Fischer & Ostwald, 2002). Excerpt 2 has a lot in common with the example Fischer uses to explain the reseeding phase, where open source software systems take some time to evolve, aided by using local (user created) extensions and the integration of patches (evolutionary growth), but eventually require major reorganizing in order to incorporate the patches and extensions in a coherent fashion (reseeding) (Fischer & Ostwald, 2002). In the company it happened like this: First the product evolves locally as a result of patches created in response to customer requests, and when this becomes unwieldy the company's professional developers create a build. Lastly, when the modifications become too numerous or are judged to be useful (good) for other (potential) customers, the developers create a new version of the product. However, Fischer does not distinguish between build and version. He uses the term reseeding for all developer activity associated with reorganizing multiple adaptations (patched systems) into unified (seamless) versions. Due to the complexity of this activity, it is useful to distinguish the multiple sub processes (types) of reseeding and the interaction between evolutionary growth and reseeding.

Excerpt 3: Improvement Request and Adaptation

Excerpt 3 below illustrates how the Improvement Requests, as elaborated in the excerpt above, are differentiated. It also shows what is meant by Adaptation.

Question: So, the rationale for a given upgrade lies with a specific customer, which means that a customer can be a part of setting the standards for what other customers receive?

Answer: Mm, but if what one customer suggests is far off, then we just make a local adaptation for that specific customer.

Question: So, this becomes a new version for you then?

Answer: What we have in addition to every menu choice is a so-called user option, it is placed in an "own" library, which can be linked, and allows us to do further product development.

What triggered the statement above is that one of the interviewers asked how the company develops their products. In sentence number two, the informant answers that if the customer's request is "far off" they just make an Adaptation for this particular customer, as long as the customer pays for it. As mentioned above, this corresponds with an Improvement Request labeled possible. Excerpt 3 shows how an Improvement Request labeled good may become available to all customers. The informant acknowledges after some hesitation and with elaboration that the customers are to some extent "defining" what other customers receive of product upgrades. They do this by suggesting Improvement Requests and other customer-initiated activities such as Tailoring. However in most cases Improvement request that are responded to by an Adaptation, providing a custom-made product for this customer by using patches or user options with the current released version of the product. In the last sentence in Excerpt 3, the informant explains what is meant by (local) Adaptation. It is associated with a patched system installation that can be continually adapted (further developed) by user options that are deployed in a separate package (own library). When installed in the system, it appears as a separate menu with items for the various user options.

Excerpt 4: Generalization

The above excerpt introduced the term "user option," which is a special kind of patch. The related terms user option, patch and new version will be clarified in Excerpt 4 below. The excerpt illustrates the generalization process.

Question: Do you have other examples of customers initiating new functionality to the product?

Answer: Yes, we have done it for BuildingCompany and ABB... (two large European engineering and consultancy companies)

Question: What sort of new functionality did they want?

Answer: Yes, well, it is. I don't remember - it was years ago. I know that when they bought the product they had specific requirements that were originally not part of the product. But we wrote it into the contract as the functionality they wanted.

Question: Ok, so it was a part of the contract?

Answer: Yes, they wanted it within a specific time period. Their requirements were rather demanding regarding what they wanted us to make.

Question: Was it an add-on specifically made for BuildingCompany or..

Answer: No, it became a part of the product. Yes, it started as a patch, what we call a user option.

The informant underlines that a request for new functionality eventually became part of the company's general product portfolio and was made available to all their customers. It is an example of Generalization. It becomes clear that in this situation the request for new functionality that Building Company asked for was something specific they needed. The company wrote their demands into the contract. This excerpt reiterates a point made above, that good Improvement Requests would be incorporated into the next version of one of their products.

The transition from Adaptation to Generalization is evident in Excerpt 4 since it describes an activity that involves one specific product (Planner) based on interaction with specific customers (Building Company in particular). The product has developed from small local extensions (patches and user options) to a basic core (in-house) version to a new (released) version where generally useful local adaptations are incorporated into the new release. We interpret the last sentence of the excerpt to mean a step-wise integration into the product (from specific to general) along three steps. It is associated with the combination of the utterance of "No" and "Yes" that signify a contradiction and disruptive (non incremental) transition (from Adaptation to Generalization). 1-2) Yes, it started as a special type of patch (user option), which is Adaptation, 3) no, it was only later incorporated into the product, which is Generalization. Adaptation represents the two first steps. First, the extra functionality BuildingCompany asked for is a user option, which means it is only available for this specific customer. Second, they want to make this available for later use, so they make a patch that the other customers can access upon demand, for example via the company's Web pages. Third, when there is a new version of the product, the extra functionality (patches and user options) have been incorporated in the product and therefore made available to potentially all customers. In other words, we may say that there is a gradual development of the company's products over the years, many of which are based on local development initiatives and Improvement Requests to generalized versions and back to new initiatives for further development, as new user contexts appear.

Fischer and Ostwald's SER model (Fischer & Ostwald, 2002) suggests mutual dependency of evolutionary growth and reseeding, and this is supported by the findings reported here, namely that use time activity (Improvement Requests) can trigger design-time (Generalization) activity. It is also related to SER in a more indirect way, in that Adaptation as a user-oriented design-time activity can lead to Generalization.

Jeppesen underlines how a defining characteristic of modding is how "final mods often are freely revealed," meaning that no users are excluded from using the new modified version" (2004). In the same way as final mods are freely available, the Adaptations made to products based on some customers' ideas become available for all customers in the Generalization stage, when the suggestions from customers are accepted and integrated into a new version of the product, as shown in the excerpt above.

Excerpt 5: Tailoring

Excerpt 5 shows how customers locally adjust a software product by end-user programming to create their own extensions. Excerpt 5, from an interview with a customer in the building industry, shows a customer stating that he has adjusted the product himself by writing code in the domain-specific language SQL.*Question: Have you requested any wishes or needs for local adaptations?*

Answer: No, we have not got any special adaptations of the products (from the company). The reason for this is because I knew a great deal about SQL from earlier experience; therefore I managed to find a shortcut (of how to do it myself). I do not know the whole structure of the system, but it is available through ordinary documentation. There you get the whole (database) table structure and that has made it possible for me to find a shortcut through Access (a proprietary database management system) and allowed me to make some special (local) adaptations.

Question: So, in reality you have made your own adaptations to the products?

Answer: Yes, you may say that.

This excerpt illustrates Tailoring, which is the sub-process that most closely resembles EUD as a standalone activity. Microsoft Office Access is used in conjunction with one of the company's project planning tools for data storage.

In the first sentence of this excerpt the customer states that the company has not adjusted the products for them. It is discovered that the reason for this is because the customer has made some adaptations to the product himself. He has tailored the product. This was possible for the customer because the products are well documented. In addition, because this customer was familiar with SQL, a high-level database query language, it was natural for him to fix the problem himself to suit his needs. This excerpt is an example of what we refer to as Tailoring. In Tailoring, the customer actually locally adapts the product without any company involvement. This might mean creating a small program to work around an inefficient solution as shown in this excerpt.

The reason the customer is able to tailor the product himself is because he is an expert project manager and is interested in learning how to work around a problem or inefficient solution when it appears. In other words, he is a super user. As an example, he describes how he can access and reorganize database tables as he sees fit and in a way that meets his organization's needs. The cost of this is his time and the skills required for programming, albeit simplified with a database query language like SQL compared to programming languages like Java. The advantage is that he will be able to see results of his ideas implemented relatively quickly as compared to the turnaround time when ideas for change are submitted to the company via improvement requests. The interviewer asks if this is a way of doing local adaptation, and he confirms that his SQL programming can be perceived as such. If Tailoring is followed with an Improvement request, tailoring might contribute to further development at the general levels, as was illustrated in the previous excerpt.

In previous work, end-user tailoring has been described as evolutionary application development (Mørch, 1996. That work ignored the connection between end-user tailoring and professional development or reseeding, but explored the design space of evolutionary growth. According to the mutual development model, this understanding must be extended. Based on the data reported here, tailoring is better conceived of as *evolutionary design*, in the sense that the local (customer) solution serves as a design for a general (company) solution. Therefore we can say, as our title proclaims, software engineering provides a context for end-user development.

The findings reported in this section have been condensed and depicted in the mutual development model shown in Figure 2. Excerpt 1 can be seen as clarifying the informants' perception of the terms good, possible and bad. Excerpt 2 has a similar role for the terms patch, build and version (user options are further distinguished in Excerpts 3 and 4). Excerpt 3 also underlines the processes of Improvement Request and Adaptation, which are related in that one feeds into the other. Excerpt 4 exemplifies the stage of Generalization. It illustrates how a product becomes available to all customers. Finally, Excerpt 5 illustrates Tailoring by showing how a customer with some programming knowledge modified the product himself. It should be stressed that we have focused on the

Figure 2. Different stages of mutual development: developer activity and customer activity co-evolve; the arrows indicate dependencies. Specialization is not addressed in this article because it does not interrelate directly with end-user activities. Similarly Adaptation and Generalization contain software engineering activities that are not addressed, for example restructuring code for optimization, and re-writing a system in a new programming language.

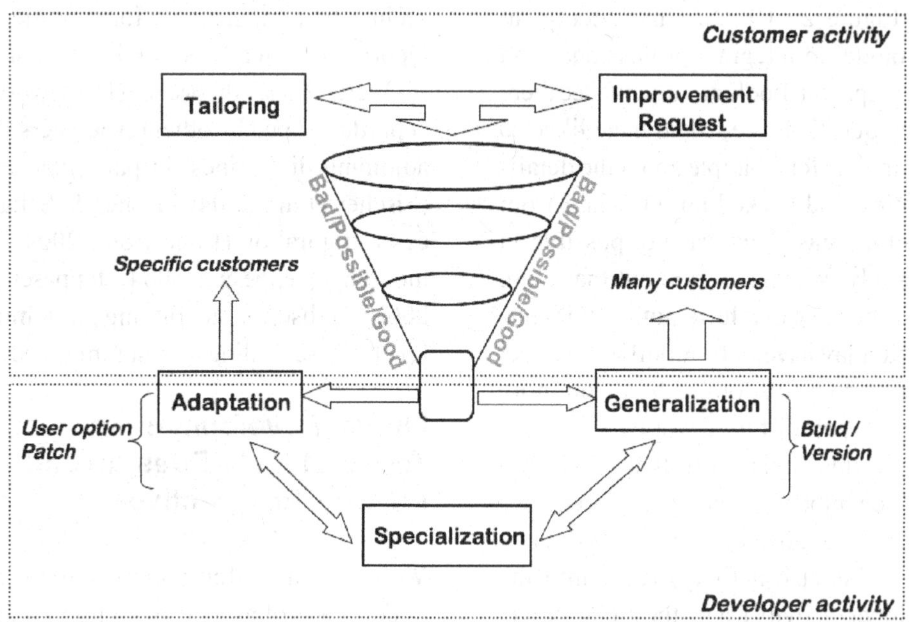

activities that involve end users (customer activity) and multiple perspectives on developer-user interaction. We do not yet have sufficient data to illustrate the Specialization stage.

GENERAL DISCUSSION AND DIRECTIONS FOR FURTHER WORK

Our main research question and objective is how there is mutual development between customers, professional developers mediated by software products and ICT support systems in the company we studied. Our findings points to the components of the product development process studied. It was found that within the interviews there existed some sub-processes of mutual development (initially formulated during the preliminary analysis as customer-initiated product development) (Andersen, 2008; Mørch et al., 2009). They were identified as Adaptation, Generalization, Improvement Request, Specialization, and Tailoring.

We have shown five interview excerpts to justify our claims that illustrate how the products in the company evolve in the zones between different activity systems by developers' interaction with customers. On one end it is initiated by customers' improvement requests and locally developed solutions. On the other it is initiated and responded to by developers with specialized and locally adapted instances, which may later generalize into features of stable products. It goes through an elaborated process of specialization (refinement), adaptation (domain orientation) and generalization (one too many instances), starting with a stable (non optimal) product version that is gradually improved by local extensions, user options, and patches. At some point this configuration becomes unwieldy and the system is re-built. The new system may be introduced as a new version of the product if it will benefit the company. Interaction between the stages is bidirectional because new versions may lead to new local development and improvement requests, which repeat the process.

The components of mutual development are depicted in Figure 2. It is our first attempt to construct a model to integrate professional and end-user development. Looking back, we see there are additional questions we would have liked to ask our informants, for example about the details of the activities, and backed up with data from additional informants. This was not possible in the current study. We cannot rule out that there may be sub-processes that have not been identified, some that may have to be modified, and yet others that need to be elaborated based on more research. This is part of future work.

In spite of this, it is clear that EUD and professional development are interdependent, and represent two different activity systems, one (customer-initiated activity) feeds into the other (developer activity) and they co-evolve. When considering these two activity systems they are arguable most easily distinguished by their objects of activity: The customer activity system is oriented towards project planning in large organizations, whereas the developer activity system is oriented towards improving the products and the support systems and searching out new markets for the products. Even though there are obvious differences in activity motives, the products (i.e., the user interfaces) and support systems are common in the two activity systems, and act as boundary objects (Star & Griesemer, 1989). The company benefits from the close connection and interdependency with its customers in two ways. First, developers in the company rely on input from customers for continuation of its products and services through maintenance and support contracts. Second, innovative ideas for new products will attract new customers. This is to some extent a result of the company's small size and its operation in niche markets. On the other hand, customers also benefit from the interdependency. They rely on the company for the most advanced project planning tools in the market, training and consultancy services, the ability to interact with the company's developers, and last but not least the pleasure they get from seeing their suggestions for modification being incorporated in a later version of a product.

We have used theoretical frameworks and concepts developed by other researchers in EUD and adjoining disciplines, in particular meta-design (Fischer et al., 2004; Fischer & Scharff, 2000), co-configuration (Engeström, 2004, 2007), and modding (Jeppesen, 2004; Jeppesen & Molin, 2003) to discuss our findings at a more general level. These findings are summarized as follows.

Mutual Development in Terms of Meta-Ddesign and the SER Perspective

We have identified customers who are active, either as designers of aspects of solutions or as producers of new ideas. The developers in the company adapt the products in accordance with customers' needs, sometimes in collaboration with the active customers, and these are the main methods to further develop the products. The project planning tools the company develops thus evolve as a result of being used in specific contexts, and it is the interaction between active customers and professional developers that is the driving force of evolutionary development.

Mutual Development in Terms of Co-Configuration

Both customers and professional developers gain from customer-initiated product development. Some of the customers forward Improvement Requests and the company and handling this forms a sort of network to distribute labour according to areas of concern. A network is more flexible than a hierarchy to handle the many unanticipated requests. Some customers are active in the product

Figure 3. Customers who want to become end-user developers of a product need to interact with professional developers in the company manufacturing the products (enterprise). This is illustrated by three stages of interaction: Passive customers (consumers), active customers (end-user developers), and expert customers (in-house developers). Our study focused on the second stage, which required a distinction of levels of development: specific (EUD) and general (professional development).

development process, and the customer-initiated product development is a continuous process lasting for a long time (up to several years). When customers and professional developers interact in intimate ways to develop products, they can be considered collaborators.

Mutual Development in Terms of Modding

Changes made to the company's products by users vary in complexity. There are changes made solely by users, and some modifications become available to all customers. Customer-initiated product development motivates technical-minded users. Customers suggesting or designing new features of a product in a way "open it up" for further development. There are channels for communication between users like the company's annual customer forum. When customers develop new features, it can be seen as a decentralized development activity.

Finally, mutual development can be compared with two other ways of organizing interaction between users and developers in a customer oriented enterprise (Figure 3). The three ways are identified as stages of "entering the enterprise": *black box*, *grey box*, and *white box*, respectively, highlighting the degree of customers' interaction with IT developers in the enterprise, and its visibility to the outside world in terms of this.

DIRECTIONS FOR FURTHER WORK

Our results can furthermore be extended, compared and applied along directions advocated by researchers in user-driven innovation, participatory design, and evolution of technology.

Users can be creative and contribute to development without developing anything, and end-user development is often triggered by *innovative use* of a tool as a first step to address a breakdown in use. Norman (2008) suggests workarounds and hacks as two techniques people draw on in everyday situations when coping with difficult-to-use tools. Many companies are starting to realize that innovation can arise not only from the IT department, but also from the interaction with partners, suppliers, and customers.

Eric von Hippel, a pioneer and long-time champion of studying users as innovators in product development coined the term user-driven innovation. He has introduced a method for identifying sources of innovation, following "lead users" (von Hippel, 2005). Many of the innovations he has studied originated with lead users' novel use of an existing product or an adaptation of a product based on knowledge of a related product. The example I gave in the beginning of this article, the story behind the disappearance of the rivets (copper nails) on the back pockets of Levi's 501 jeans illustrates the power of the combination active user participation and a system that take advantage of active users' creative ideas. We called this process *outside in* because it starts with external events and requires an elaborate process of from ideation to realization compared with inside-out (professional developers') technological innovation. We also showed that outside in contains inside out as a sub-process and as such can be seen as the more general form of innovation.

To compare our work on mutual development with previous work and emerging trends we sketch three models for the integration of EUD and processional development:

1. *Tailorable systems*: EUD support is built into commercial (standard) software applications in the form of components, APIs, templates, integrated development environments, customization forms, small languages, and so forth. Using the languages and tools, end-user developers can customize, integrate, extend, and configure the applications. The aim of this model is to support users in creating their own local adaptations of a standard system. Users are not considered partners in the design process when products are updated. Locus of control is in the developer organization, which is only slightly decentralized with EUD-enabled applications. This model can be positioned somewhere between the first and second stage of Figure 3, with a unidirectional arrow from the enterprise to the end-user developer.
2. *Mutual development*: EUD is a local development activity that is distinct from professional development as with Tailorable systems, but in close interaction with it. EUD and professional development are interdependent, one feeds into the other and they co-evolve. The developer organization is dependent on user participation for continuation of its products, for example, due to small size, continuation of specialized products, maintenance and consultation contracts. Data to support this model was presented in this article. It is depicted as the middle (second) stage in Figure 3.
3. *User manufacturing:* EUD is an autonomous activity and not part of a commercial enterprise and distribution network. It resembles open source development, and has been made possible with recent application development environments for Web 2.0. Control is distributed, through the network of end-user developers. When complexity increases to a threshold outside the control of end-user developers, core developers will be given a central role in organizing the joint development efforts. This model is not depicted in Figure 3, since it departs from conventional (commercial) manufacturing.

The user manufacturing model of integrating EUD and professional development is an area that deserves more attention in the future, since it is new and requires more research in order to identify to what extent end-user developers can make use of the tools provided for participation (e.g., Fischer, this issue), what business models (if any) can be provided, and what strategies are needed to ensure that user manufacturing will resist the competition from the more established and centralized models of integrated EUD (1 and 2 above). Model 3 is currently associated with Web 2.0 and social networking technologies. However, there is a bumpy road from social interaction to (end-user) development, as we know from previous research in PD.

Based on a study of user driven innovation in an open source community von Hippel (2001) observed "the ability of user communities to develop and sustain exceedingly complex products without any manufacturer involvement is remarkable." He identifies the conditions that favor user innovation and explores how circumstances evolve, sometimes to include commercial manufacturers and sometimes not (von Hippel, 2001). When commercial manufactures are included in the loop, the resulting inter-organization activity structure can be compared with "mutual development." When commercial manufactures are not included in the loop, the resulting organization can be compared with the emerging "user manufacturing" model. Aided by the Internet and Web 2.0 applications to support communication and information sharing and most recently "mashing" (combining existing Web 2.0 applications to create new ones), this model has the potential to attract new interest in end-user development due to the enormous success of this platform to attract self-motivated contributors (Floyd, Jones, Rathi, & Twindale, 2007). To leverage this potential for end-user tailoring and evolutionary design is an area for further research in EUD.

In their study, Douthwaite, Keatinge and Park (2001) state the following "as technology and system complexity increase so does the need for interaction between the originating R&D team and the key stakeholders (those who will directly benefit and be penalized from the innovation)." This is a hypothesis we believe applies to software development as well. It implies when software products increase in complexity, the interaction between developers and customers must proportionally increase in order to successfully manage further development and sustain the product. Otherwise, users will seek out other products that are simpler to use. The reason for increasing customer interaction as complexity unfolds is that a successful technology represents a synthesis of the developers and key stakeholder activity systems, and creating this synthesis requires more iteration and negotiation as complexity increases (Douthwaite et al., 2001). This is a hypothesis that ought to be explored in software evolution as well, in particular when end-users are enabled by EUD environments and rich feedback channels to more experienced developers.

ACKNOWLEDGMENT

The members of the KIKK project at InterMedia, University of Oslo: Shazia Mushtaq, Damir Nedic, Kathrine Nygård, and Espen Olsen contributed to the ideas and systems presented here. Anne Moen and Sten Ludvigsen gave us constructive feedback throughout the processes of the research and writing. The project is part of KP-Lab (Knowledge Practices Laboratory), and supported financially by the European Commission's contract FP6-2004-IST-4 027490. This article is an extended version of Andersen and Mørch (2009).

REFERENCES

Andersen, R. (2008). *Customer-initiated product development: A case study of adaptation and co-configuration*. Unpublished masters' thesis, University of Oslo, Norway.

Andersen, R., & Mørch, A. I. (2009, March 2-4). Mutual development: A case study in customer-initiated software product development. In V. Pipek, M. B. Rosson, B de Ruyter, & V. Wulf (Eds.), *End-User Development: Proceedings of the 2nd International Symposium on End-User Development,* Siegen, Germany (LNCS 5435, pp. 31-49).

Åsand, H.-R., & Mørch, A. I. (2006). Super users and local developers: The organization of end-user development in an accounting company. *Journal of Organizational and End User Computing, 18*(4), 1–21.

Bansler, J. P., & Havn, E. (1994, May 30-31). Information systems development with generic systems. In W. Baets (Ed.), *Proceedings of the 2nd European Conference on Information Systems,* Nijenrode, the Netherlands (pp. 30-31). Nijenrode University Press.

Bratteteig, T. (1997, August 9-12). Mutual learning: Enabling cooperation in systems design. In K. Braa & E. Monteiro (Eds.), *Proceedings of the 20th Information Systems Research Seminar in Scandinavia,* Hankø, Norway (pp. 1-20). Department of Informatics, University of Oslo, Norway.

Costabile, M., Foglia, D., Fresta, G., Mussio, P., & Piccinno, A. (2003, October 28-31). Building environments for end-user development and tailoring. In *Proceedings of the IEEE Symposium on Human Centric Computing Languages and Environments,* Auckland, New Zealand (pp. 31-38). Washington, DC: IEEE Computer Society.

Dittrich, Y., & Vaucouleur, S. (2008, May 13). Practices around customization of standard systems. In L.-T. Chen et al. (Eds.), *Proceedings of the 2008 International Workshop on Cooperative and Human Aspects of Software Engineering,* Leipzig Germany (pp. 37-40). ACM Publishing.

Douthwaite, B., Keatinge, J. D. H., & Park, J. R. (2001). Why promising technologies fail: The neglected role of user innovation during adoption. *Research Policy, 30*(5), 819–836. doi:10.1016/S0048-7333(00)00124-4

Ehn, P., & Kyng, M. (1991). Cardboard computers: Mocking-it-up or hands-on the future. In J. Greenbaum & M. Kyng (Eds.), *Design at work: Cooperative design of computer systems* (pp. 169-195). Hillsdale, NJ: Lawrence Erlbaum.

Engeström, Y. (2004). New forms of learning in co-configuration work. *Journal of Workplace Learning, 16*(1-2), 11–21. doi:10.1108/13665620410521477

Engeström, Y. (2007). Enriching the theory of expansive learning: Lessons from journeys toward co-configuration. *Mind, Culture, and Activity, 14*(1-2), 23–29.

Eriksson, J., & Dittrich, Y. (2007). Combining tailoring and evolutionary software development for rapidly changing business systems. *Journal of Organizational and End User Computing, 19*(2), 47–64.

Fischer, G. (2002). Beyond "couch potatoes:" From consumers to designers and active contributors. *First Monday, 7*(12). Retrieved July 15, 2009, from http://firstmonday.org/issues/issue7_12/fischer/index.html

Fischer, G. (This issue). End-user development and meta-design: Foundations for cultures of participation. *Journal of Organizational and End User Computing.*

Fischer, G., Giaccardi, E., Ye, Y., Sutcliffe, A. G., & Mehandjiev, N. (2004). Meta-design: A manifesto for end-user development. *Communications of the ACM, 47*(9), 33–37. doi:10.1145/1015864.1015884

Fischer, G., & Ostwald, J. (2002, June 23-25). Seeding, evolutionary growth, and reseeding: Enriching participatory design with informed participation. In T. Binder, J. Gregory, & I. Wagner (Eds.), *Proceedings of the 2002 Participatory Design Conference,* Malmo, Sweden (pp. 135-143). Palo Alto, CA: CPSR.

Fischer, G., & Scharff, E. (2000, August). Meta-design: Design for designers. In D. Boyarski & W. A. Kellogg (Eds.), *Proceedings of the 3rd International Conference on Designing Interactive Systems,* New York (pp. 396-405). ACM Publishing.

Floyd, I. R., Jones, M. C., Rathi, D., & Twidale, M. B. (2007, January 3-7). Web mash-ups and patchwork prototyping: User-driven technological innovation with Web 2.0 and open source software. In *Proceedings of the 40th Annual Hawaii International Conference on System Sciences,* Big Island, HI (pp. 86-96). Washington, DC: IEEE Computer Society.

Jeppesen, L. B. (2004). *Profiting from innovative user communities: How firms organize the production of user modifications in the computer industry* (Working Papers 2003-2004). Copenhagen, Denmark: Copenhagen Business School, Department of Industrial Economics and Strategy.

Jeppesen, L. B., & Molin, M. J. (2003). Consumers as co-developers: Learning and innovation outside the firm. *Technology Analysis and Strategic Management, 15*(3), 363–384. doi:10.1080/09537320310001601531

Kaasbøll, J., & Øgrim, L. (1994). Super-users: Hackers, management hostages or working class heroes? A study of user influence on redesign in distributed organizations. In P. Kerola, A. Juustila, & J. Järvinen (Eds.), *Proceedings of the 17th Information Systems Research Seminar in Scandinavia,* Syöte, Finland (pp. 784-798). Department of Information Processing Science, University of Oulu, Finland.

Kanstrup, A. M., & Christiansen, E. (2006, October 14-18). Selecting and evoking innovators: Combining democracy and creativity. In A. Mørch, K. Morgan, T. Bratteteig, G. Ghosh, & D. Savanaes (Eds.), *Proceedings of the 4th Nordic Conference on Human-Computer Interaction,* Oslo, Norway (pp. 321-330). ACM Publishing.

King, N. (1994). Template analysis. In G. Symon & C. Cassell (Eds.), *Qualitative methods and analysis in organizational research: A practical guide* (pp. 118-134). London: Sage.

Knight, W. (2008). *Supernatural powers become contagious in PC game.* Retrieved April 28, 2008, from http://www.newscientist.com/article.ns?id=dn6857

Levi Strauss & Co. (2009). *History of the Levi's 501 jeans.* Retrieved June 14, 209, from http://www.levistrauss.com/Downloads/history_of_levis_501_jeans.pdf

Lieberman, H., Paterno, F., & Wulf, V. (Eds.). (2006). *End-user development: Empowering people to flexibly employ advanced information and communication technology.* New York: Springer.

Mehandjiev, N., & Bottaci, L. (Eds.). (2004). End-user development [special issue]. *Journal of End User Computing, 10*(2).

Mehandjiev, N., Sutcliffe, A. G., & Lee, D. (2006). Organisational views of end-user development. In H. Lieberman, F. Paterno, & V. Wulf (Eds.), *End user development: Empowering people to flexibly employ advanced information and communication technology* (pp. 371-399). New York: Springer.

Mørch, A. (1996). Evolving a generic application into a domain-oriented design environment. *Scandinavian Journal of Information Systems, 8*(2), 63–90.

Mørch, A. I. (1995, July 3-7). Application units: Basic building blocks of tailorable applications. In B. Blumenthal, J. Gornostacv, & C. Unger (Eds.), *Proceedings of the 5th International Conference on East-West Human-Computer Interaction,* Moscow, Russia (LNCS 1015, pp. 45-62).

Mørch, A. I., & Mehandjiev, N. D. (2000). Tailoring as collaboration: The mediating role of multiple representations and application units. *Computer Supported Cooperative Work, 9*(1), 75–100. doi:10.1023/A:1008713826637

Mørch, A. I., Nygård, K. A., & Ludvigsen, S. R. (2009). Adaptation and generalisation in software product development. In H. Daniels, A. Edwards, Y. Engestrom, T. Gallagher, & S. R. Ludvigsen, (Eds.), *Activity theory in practice: Promoting learning across boundaries* (pp. 184-205). London: Routledge.

Mørch, A. I., Stevens, G., Won, M., Klann, M., Dittrich, Y., & Wulf, V. (2004). Component-based technologies for end-user development. *Communications of the ACM, 47*(9), 59–62. doi:10.1145/1015864.1015890

Nedic, D., & Olsen, E. A. (2007). *Customizing an open source web portal framework in a business context: Integrating participatory design with an agile approach.* Unpublished master's thesis, University of Oslo, Norway.

Norman, D. A. (2008). Workarounds and hacks: The leading edge of innovation. *Interaction, 15*(4), 47–48. doi:10.1145/1374489.1374500

Nygård, K. A., & Mørch, A. I. (2007, November 5-9). The role of boundary crossing for knowledge advancement in product development. In T. Hirashima, U. Hoppe, & S. S. C. Young (Eds.), *Proceedings of the 15th International Conference Computers in Education,* Hiroshima, Japan (pp.183-186). Amsterdam, The Netherlands: IOS Press.

Pollock, N., & Williams, R. (2008). *The biography of the enterprise-wide system or how SAP conquered the world.* London: Routledge.

Star, S. L., & Griesemer, J. R. (1989). Institutional ecology, translations, and boundary objects: Amateurs and professionals in Berkeley's Museum of Vertebrate Zoology. *Social Studies of Science, 19*(3), 387–420. doi:10.1177/030631289019003001

Stevens, G., & Wiedenhöfer, T. (2006, October 14-18). CHIC - a pluggable solution for community help in context. In A. Mørch et al. (Eds), *Proceedings of the 4th Nordic Conference on Human-Computer Interaction,* Oslo, Norway (pp. 212-221). ACM Publishing.

Stevens, G., & Wulf, V. (2002, November 16-20). A new dimension in access control: Studying maintenance engineering across organizational boundaries. In E. F. Churchill, J. McCarthy, C. Neuwirth, & T. Rodden (Eds.), *Proceedings of the 2002 Conference on Computer Supported Cooperative Work (CSCW 2002),* New Orleanes (pp. 196-205). ACM Publishing.

Victor, B., & Boynton, A. C. (1998). *Invented here: Maximizing your organization's internal growth and profitability.* Boston: Harvard Business School Press.

Volkoff, O., Strong, D. M., & Elmes, M. B. (2002, August). Between a rock and a hard place: Boundary spanners in an ERP implementation. In D. R. Banker, H. Chang, & Y.-C. Kao (Eds.), *Proceedings of the 8th Americas Conference on Information Systems,* Dallas, TX (pp. 958-962). Atlanta, GA: Association for Information Systems.

von Hippel, E. (2001). Innovation by user communities: Learning from open-source software. *MIT Sloan Management Review, 42*(4), 82–86.

von Hippel, E. (2005). *Democratizing innovation.* Cambridge, MA: MIT Press.

Wulf, V., & Golombek, B. (2001). Direct activation: A concept to encourage tailoring activities. *Behaviour & Information Technology*, *20*(4), 249–263. doi:10.1080/01449290110048016

Wulf, V., Pipek, V., & Won, M. (2008). Component-based tailorability: Enabling highly flexible software applications. *International Journal of Human-Computer Studies*, *66*(1), 1–22.

This work was previously published in Journal of Organizational and End User Computing, Volume 22, Issue 2, edited by M. Adam Mahmood, pp. 36-57, copyright 2010 by IGI Publishing (an imprint of IGI Global).

Section 2

Approaches, Frameworks and Techniques for End-User Computing

Chapter 6
WOAD: A Framework to Enable the End-User Development of Coordination-Oriented Functionalities

Federico Cabitza
Università degli Studi di Milano-Bicocca, Italy

Carla Simone
Università degli Studi di Milano-Bicocca, Italy

ABSTRACT

In this article, we present WOAD, a framework that was inspired and partly validated within a 2-year observational case study at a major teaching hospital. We present the WOAD framework by stating its main and motivating rationales, outlining its high-level architecture and then introducing its denotational language, LWOAD. We propose LWOAD to support users of an electronic document system in declaratively expressing, specifying and implementing content- and event-based mechanisms that fulfill coordinative requirements and make users aware of relevant conditions. Our focus addresses (a) the user-friendly and yet formal expression of local coordinative practices based on the work context; (b) the promotion of awareness of both these conventions and the context to enable actors to quickly respond; (c) the full deployment of coordination-oriented and context-aware functionalities into legacy electronic document systems. We give examples of LWOAD mechanisms taken from the case study and discuss their impact from the EUD perspective.

THE NEED FOR EUD IN DIGITIZING DOCUMENT-MEDIATED COOPERATIVE WORK

The fact that documents are ubiquitous means to support work activities is well known. Their initially undifferentiated role has been more recently investigated and articulated to understand why documents, which are so natural and widespread, still create problems when they are transformed into digitized counterparts, not only when electronic documents are used as stand-alone artifacts but, above all, when they are parts and components of an electronic document system (Braa & Sandahl, 2000; Sellen & Harper, 2003). Therefore, they mediate collaboration between

DOI: 10.4018/978-1-4666-0140-6.ch006

actors. The solution to this paradox calls for stronger involvement of users in the definition and maintenance of functionalities that support them in accomplishing their duties and coordinating their actions. These functionalities closely relate to how users read and write their paper-based artifacts and to the often implicit conventions that regard the use and interpretation of documents. A very inspiring domain in which to motivate this claim and highlight requirements for a EUD-based solution is the health-care domain. In this domain, investment policies in ICT are usually focused on what are called secondary purposes, that is, rationalizing care provision for cost savings and standardizing reporting to enable clinical research and business intelligence. This leads to the design of Electronic Patient Records (EPR) where document structures and functionalities are aimed at supporting information inscription and use according to data quality and usability criteria (Cabitza & Simone, 2006), which tend to neglect (or heavily overlook) the primary purposes (Berg & Goorman, 1999) of doctors and nurses: namely keeping track of the patient's illness trajectory, supporting discussion on clinical cases, information exchange in shift hand-over, order handling and care reporting for accountability issues. The additional effort of articulation work on the clinical record is then usually left to practitioners; often as well as the burden of reconfiguring their coordinative practices once their habitual paper-based artifacts have been digitized (Winthereik & Vikkelso, 2005).

In this context, document templates and masks are usually imposed on practitioners from above, irrespectively of their coordinative needs. Even in the best case where documents are cooperatively and participatorily defined, they tend to be given to actors just once, which would neglect the frequent tuning activities and adjustments that coordinative mechanisms require for their negotiated and participated nature (Divitini & Simone, 2000; Schmidt & Simone, 1996).

Our observational studies in two wards of a large provincial hospital in Northern Italy confirmed other reports from the CSCW literature (e.g., Berg, 1999; Fitzpatrick, 2004; Heath & Lu, 1996) on how practitioners try to reconcile primary and secondary purposes on the artifacts of daily use to make them useful both to store and retrieve information but also to support mutual learning, knowledge sharing and coordination of caring activities. To this aim, actors define, renegotiate and evolve ad-hoc practices, peculiar conventions, and agreed interpretations that are local and unique to their work settings.

Our research question is then how to facilitate this local management in a sustainable way. The paper aims to give a contribution in this direction by presenting a design-oriented framework that has been deeply influenced and partially validated in our field study in the above mentioned hospital (Cabitza & Simone, 2007). In fact, the development of the framework has been intertwined with the incremental analysis of the setting and with its validation. This trajectory is not completed but currently covers the main part of the research path: namely, i) understanding the kind of functionalities users need to take full advantage of their documental systems; ii) identifying a way to express the functionalities in a compositional, incremental and flexible manner; iii) defining an architecture where the functionalities can then be implemented, validated and, above all, maintained and kept aligned with the ever-changing needs and conventions of a community of users.

The next sections describe two main components of the framework—the architecture and language—and illustrates the field study and the rich real-life conventions on which we tested the framework. Then, Section 5 discusses the main findings of the case study, Section 6 illustrates the visual prototype we used as a proof-of-concept of the findings related to mechanism specification, and finally Section 7 sums things up and sheds light on current and future directions of our research in the EUD field (Liebermann, Paternó, & Wulf, 2006a).

THE WOAD FRAMEWORK

Our empirical research involved the Neonatal Intensive Care Unit (NICU) of a major teaching hospital of Northern Italy, where 10 neonatologists and a 25-nurse staff treat approximately 400 critical newborns yearly. We spent an effort of approximately 40 days at their facility where we conducted a series of unobtrusive observations in the ward, had informal talks, undertook individual interviews with key doctors and nurses (especially the head physician and head nurse), and participated in open group discussions with ward practitioners. These interactions were initially used to deal with the "descriptive" part of the research and to reach a reasonable and common language and mutual understanding (Nygaard, 1984). However, almost immediately the need to deal with what practitioners called "local habits and conventions" emerged and especially the need to reflect on how these customs could be effectively supported by a suitable technology. Once questioned about the role of conventions in their daily work, practitioners exhibited the twofold need to rely on an electronic documental system that could be i) constantly aligned to their local coordinative and work conventions; ii) able to support coordination not only with specific and necessarily good-for-all functionalities but could also help users become aware of relevant conditions in the field of work, still leaving users the decision of how to react to those conditions. Then our goal was to support the effort of practitioners to make explicit, symbolic and computable relationships between recurrent patterns of context and conventional ways to cope with that context. To this aim, we addressed the problem of i) how to support actors in describing recurrent conditions of the work context that should call for their attention; ii) how to facilitate actors in formalizing corresponding functionalities that could make them aware of the current context in light of some local and conventional work rule. The main point underlying the WOAD framework is that practitioners themselves can bridge the gap between a functionality and the aptest time to exploit it, if the computer-based support can provide them with unobtrusive and additional information that promotes collaboration awareness Dourish (2001) and evokes in their minds conventional ways to cope with the work context (Cabitza, Sarini, & Simone (2007). This point makes it clear that the event- and data-based mechanisms should trigger the provision at the user interface of what in Cabitza, Simone, and Sarini (2009) and Cabitza and Simone (2009) we called Awareness Promoting Information (API). An API is any annotation, graphical clue, affordance, textual indication that could make actors aware of something closely related to the context of reading and writing. In our interaction with the practitioners we detected thirteen types of API that are described in Cabitza et al. (2009).

The Concept of Active Document

During the requirement collection and preliminary analysis, we observed that the simplest, though powerful, concept that practitioners grasped with fewer equivocations was the one of rule, and its computable counterpart, that is, well-defined and modular *if-then* statement (see Figure 1). This finding heavily influenced how we conceived the WOAD framework (Cabitza & Simone, 2007), an acronym for "Web of Active Documents."

WOAD is a design-oriented framework that we grounded on the concept of "active documental artifact." This concept was first proposed by Divitini and Simone (2000) to refer to data structures capable of assuming an active (i.e., either reactive or proactive) role in mediating information exchange and coordination among cooperative actors. The most notable research on active artifacts in documental settings is the Placeless Document Project developed at PARC (Dourish et al., 2000). Placeless documents were documents that are managed according to their properties, that is, sort of metadata that both describe the

Figure 1. The design-implementation loop inspired by the case study

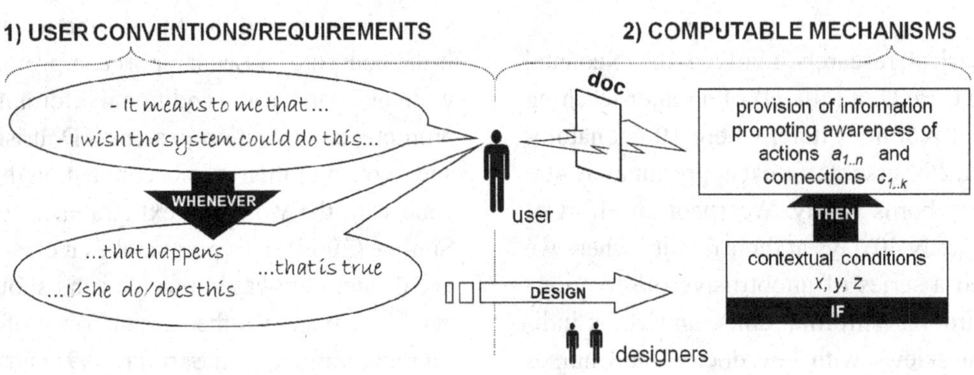

document's content and carry the code to implement elementary functionalities of document use (e.g., automatic backup, logging, transmission).

In the WOAD framework, we extend this idea by considering documents as parts of interconnected document systems that exhibit active behaviors to facilitate the coordination of tasks, the sharing of experiences in a community, and the promotion of awareness of collaborative interactions among users. In WOAD, these behaviors are triggered by the documents' content (and hence by human interaction with documents) and are oriented toward the documents' content, or better yet, toward how to support the access to the content, its use, the ways it is displayed to make it more meaningful, as well as toward how to make a connection between the content and some other document either explicit or tacitly meaningful. For this reason, the behaviors exhibited by WOAD Active Documents are seen as incremental and compositional and regard either intrinsic and data-centered aspects of documents, or community-centered and event-based aspects of documental work.

To this aim, Active Documents are made of smaller "documental widgets," which we call *didgets*, much alike OpenDoc documents were conceived as collections of *parts* (OpenDoc Design Team, 1993), although the objectives of the two proposals are quite different. In fact, a didget is defined as a coherent set of data that are gathered together at design time because they relate to either the same abstract data type (e.g., the patient), the same work activity (e.g., drug prescription), or even the same portion of a paper-based artifact, for example, a table in a record (Cabitza & Simone, 2009). Didgets can be reused in a number of active documents and each of them can be coupled with a number of autonomous and modular *mechanisms*, that is, specialized if-then statements expressed in the WOAD language. These mechanisms represent the (business) logic that regards the specific data structures that didgets tie together and they are the interpretable code that activates document-centered behaviors. For instance, data-centered behaviors can regard the check of the correctness and domain integrity of the values inserted by users into the didget's structures; event-based mechanisms cope with synchronization policies between didgets of different documents; mechanisms that are associated to local conventions and work policies and that affect how data are displayed whenever some specific condition occurs (see left side of Figure 1) are an example of mechanisms reflecting community-oriented conventions. The set of the mechanisms embedded within the didgets of a document constitute the "active" part of an Active Document (as well as of the Web of Active Documents, i.e., the WoAD) that is sensitive and work upon its "passive" part, that is, the data values its didgets contain. Moreover, since

Figure 2. A pictorial representation of a web of active documents. Mechanisms are rules sensitive to data structures of any document.

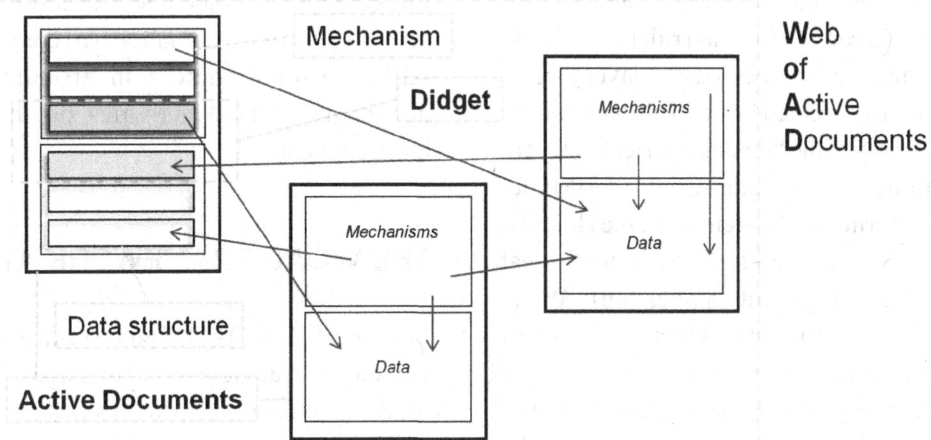

the if-part of mechanisms can be sensitive to the data of other didgets contained in possibly other active documents, didgets are also the logic clue that strings documents together to their WoAD within either an organization or community. This is especially true in the case of documents shared within a community and of rules pertaining to community-wide conventions. In this case, the mechanisms and data structures (i.e., the didgets) that can be used to build (or maintain) a WoAD enable end-users as designers to create local behaviors and conventional cross-links between their documents at compile and even at run time (Cabitza & Simone, 2008).

In summary, the WOAD framework is aimed at facilitating the definition of mechanisms (at the back-end) and affordances (at the front-end) that could evoke in the minds of users pragmatic responses to context on the basis of conventions that are neither formalized nor necessarily externalized. In fact, active documents are proactive in displaying additional clues regarding data but do not prompt users to take any action. They just notify users that a local convention, which associates a certain data in a certain template to a specific situation, has become significant; users are then left free to exploit this indication and strengthen the inclusion of the convention in practice, or just disregard it, while being well aware of the convention at hand.

The WOAD framework encompasses i) a general architecture to design WoADs in cooperative settings where work is mediated to large extent by documents and forms; ii) a denotational language to express reactive mechanisms that relate agreed and socially stratified ways to cope with context with document-mediated functionalities which promote the awareness of how to cope with context; iii) a set of application systems that produce and process the information flow needed to provide the required functionalities and that enable end-users to define and maintain the computational specifications of their requirements. In the following, we give a brief description of the former two components of the WOAD framework as a reference for the subsequent argumentation that involves a specific application system, namely the mechanism editor.

The WOAD Architecture and Language

The WOAD architecture can be seen as the specialization of a common design pattern, the Model-

View-Controller (MVC) (see Figure 3). In fact, the concept of active document makes a typical MVC architecture "content-aware" and oriented to community's conventions and rules. In WOAD active documents are processed by a layer that we call "community-oriented layer." This layer is conceptually on-top-of the "business-oriented layer" that constitutes the regular Controller-Model stack of an Information System (e.g., the Hospital Information System coupled with a traditional Electronic Patient Record application). While this gives access to data, stores them and permits their modification, the community-oriented layer is designed to enrich these same data with API that is generated by a set of mechanisms on the basis of conditions that are expressed over the "passive" portion of documents (bottom side of Figure 3) and possibly over other data coming from either the View layer (e.g., user-driven events) or other third-party context managers (not depicted in Figure 3 for the sake of simplicity). Hence, mechanisms can be seen as simple conditional statements, like if-then rules. In order to execute them, an interpreter (see middle section of Figure 3) matches the mechanisms' antecedent with the data that the Controller fetches from the underlying Model to execute their consequents. These then-parts contain instructions to build specific metadata to be associated with application data; these metadata are RDF statements that associate data fields, values and API types. These metadata are then processed by a Mark-up Tagger (see the top part of Figure 3). This component automatically annotates the Data pages with mark-up tags that are associated to specific style classes so that specific API types can been rendered in terms of specific affordances, icons and text formatting as defined in corresponding style sheets (Styles in Figure 3). Finally, a Layout Engine (e.g., an Internet browser), in the View layer, takes the annotated pages as input, interprets them and displays the final document to the user.

The second component of the WOAD framework is a language called LWOAD that is conceived as an abstract programming interface with which to program mechanisms that: (a) process the content of a document according to local conventions of coordination; (b) convey suitable API to support actors in articulating their document-centered activities on the basis of local conventions.

THE WOAD FRAMEWORK AT WORK

In using the WOAD framework, users are involved in three development stages (see Figure 4): A) identifying the dimensions and attributes suitable to represent relevant states of the context on electronic documents, basically the definition of the didgets' content; B) defining relationships between contextual conditions and the identified palette of APIs to display in active documents, basically the definition of the didgets' mechanisms; C) choosing apt ways to display APIs on active documents; this can be accomplished by associating API types to specific styles of content presentation.

In this paper, we focus on the second aspect (see B in Figure 4) since we had the opportunity to interact with practitioners who had already defined the documents intended to support their work (Cabitza et al., 2007). Therefore, practitioners were interested more in how to make their documents useful and effective by means of suitable API rather than in experimenting with the flexibility of WOAD to define the structure of the documents' content. According to the participatory design approach that has a long tradition in the healthcare domain (Bjerknes & Bratteteig, 1987; Nygaard, 1984) and in the light of EUD, the research challenge was to see if the practitioners found LWOAD usable to define the mechanisms that would generate the desired API. In fact, although LWOAD is a symbolic language that is based on simple constructs such as the rule, it must also comply with strict syntactic constraints, like any other language that a computational

Figure 3. The WOAD architectural pattern

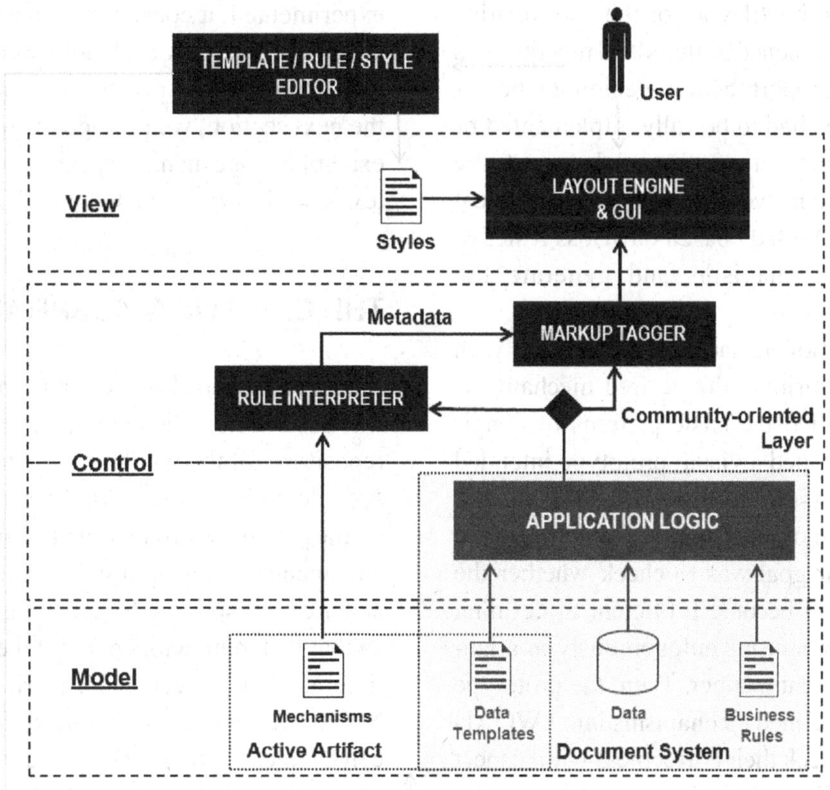

engine can interpret; this made us think that LWOAD was still far from being usable directly by practitioners. For this reason in our study we adopted a two-step approach: first, for each identified coordinative need and convention, we invited the practitioners to indicate both the relevant set of attributes of the domain entities, events and documental data that the computational system should be sensitive to, and what conditions the system should evaluate on these relevant aspects of the work setting in order to activate the desired functionalities. The practitioners expressed the "mechanisms" in natural, tough structured and restricted language, which we translated "on the

Figure 4. The three development phases in the WOAD framework

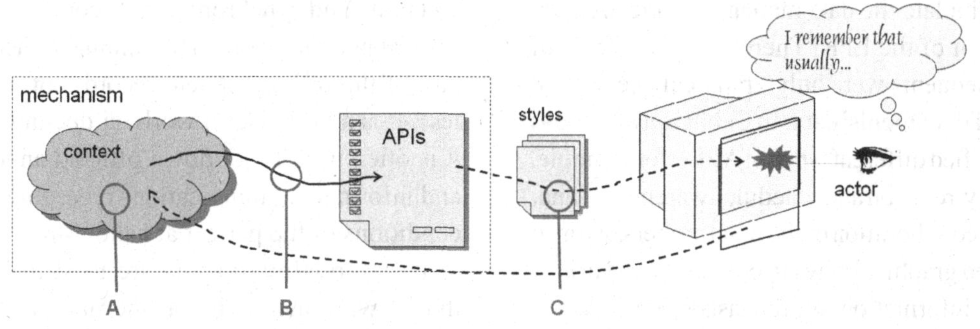

fly" in LWOAD statements. In doing so, we could rapidly convey the "flavor" of the coordinative mechanisms envisioned by the NICU practitioners and we could support them in deciding whether the mechanisms had to be fully implemented or not in the hypothetical final release of the EPR. In this step, we deployed a prototypical interpreter of LWOAD based on JBoss Rules to execute the mechanisms and generate the appropriate metadata.

Once practitioners had become familiar with this way of describing the desired mechanisms and had identified the basic patterns of conditions, we developed a visual prototype intended to be a sort of wizard to support practitioners in the construction of mechanisms (more details in Section 6). Our goal was to check whether the practitioners had become proficient in defining the desired mechanisms autonomously in a language-independent manner. Then, the prototype translated the defined mechanisms into LWOAD constructs to check their correctness with respect to both the application conditions and the desired outputs (Liebermann et al., 2006). Generally, practitioners did not find problems in expressing LWOAD mechanisms, probably for their intrinsic simplicity: antecedents are constituted by fact patterns and Boolean tests; practitioners found it natural to express them as a conjunction of facts that must be true in a given situation. On the other hand, consequents are sequences of WOAD primitives and practitioners mastered them in a relatively short time since our design choice was to limit LWOAD to the expression of functionalities that promote collaboration awareness and do not manipulate the data managed in the archival dimension of the EPR. Therefore, the effects of the consequents were only graphical cues added on top of documents' data. In Cabitza et al. (2009) we classified different types of API—for example, criticality, revision and schedule awareness—and, with the collaboration of the practitioners, we also identified graphical ways to convey these various kinds of information (cf. the task C in Figure 4). Although this latter identification is not completely experimented, it constituted a basis where to get an initial impression of how well the interface could be usable by practitioners on their own. In the next section, we provide the reader with two examples of mechanism specification and the context in which we validated the WOAD approach.

THE CASE OF A HOSPITAL WOAD

The patient record is the main documental artifact used in hospital care, as it is the composite repository for the whole information concerning a single patient stay. During a patient's stay, the whole patient record is split up into several sheets and documents; these are distributed in the ward and are very specific for a certain aspect of care so that different actors can use them at the same time at their convenience. During the study at NICU, practitioners recognized the need to conceive functionalities which were supportive of the conventional ways by which documents were used both to document their work and to mutually articulate their activities with each other.

The Case of Structure-Related Conventions

Due to the fact that clinical data are usually scattered across multiple artifacts in different places, doctors at NICU found it useful to rely on a summary of clinical data that are gathered into one single sheet that they call Summary Sheet (SS); they update the SS quite frequently by taking and synchronizing its content from the official patient record. The summary sheet is not part of the official patient record, but nevertheless, it is a very useful working document since it is often used to jot down offhand annotations and informal communications regarding clinical conditions of the patient at hand. Moreover, due to its informality, doctors are used to bringing the SS with them either as the first page of sets of papers under their arm or even folded in their pocket. Therefore, since the SS is usually the first document doctors have in their hand during their hectic activities, they also use it to jot down clinical data and prescriptions on-the-go, which they will have to replicate into the official record later as a rule of law. Hence, the summary sheet is not only a "passive view" of previously reported data, that is, a view of data fetched by querying multiple tables of a clinical database on the illness course of a single patient. It is also an active entry form, into which practitioners insert data at the point of care and from which they copy data into the official records for the sake of accountability and liability. Doctors were well aware of this twofold functionality that the digital counterpart of the SS should have; therefore, they were willing to express constraints and define conceptual connections between sections and fields of the summary sheet and corresponding sections and fields of the documents compounding the patient record. These connections were seen as symmetrical, that is, equivalent and irrespective of where the original data were actually inserted first. They can be traced back to the class of connections that in Cabitza and Simone (2008) we denoted as enabling "redundancy by duplicated data", in that they make the association explicit between identical data that are reported in two or more documents of the patient record. These sorts of connections regard conventions of production and use of clinical documents: more specifically, they regard how data are organized within templates, what data type are allowed in what field (i.e., syntactic integrity) and also where people fill in data during their situated documental activities. Moreover, these connections are local and conventional both in their definition, and above all, in their use. In fact, it is only on a conventional and context-dependent basis that doctors want summary sheets to be completely compiled after the patient record and, conversely, values reported in the SS first to be fed into the patient record at the proper time.

An example can better illustrate this point. Some members of the NICU staff team expressed the requirement that values on the weight of newborns would be reported in the summary sheet only whenever a newborn was in life-threatening conditions. In fact, only in that case did practitioners deem it necessary to rely on weight data at the point-of-care, in order to calculate drug dosage precisely.

In the other cases, to have these data available on the SS would only result in an unnecessary information overload, and even more annoying, it would undermine the role of the unobtrusive reminder on critical conditions that the presence or absence of weight data in the summary sheet could play at the point of care. Likewise, at NICU, clinical data that are reported in the SS first are often deemed as still provisional; these data are reported there so that colleagues can consider these data but also understand that they are not yet definitive, or even understand they need further verification. The need for doctors to be aware of what is still provisional and hence different from what constitutes an unmodifiable and legal account of accomplished deeds is essential to cooperatively structure the formation of decisions and judgments, as also reported in Hardstone, Hartswood, Procter, Slack, Voss, and Rees (2004).

Figure 5 depicts how we and the practitioners expressed the above mentioned conventions on data replication and criticality awareness in a dedicated and concise LWOAD mechanism. This mechanism has in its antecedent all the relevant aspects of context that are concerned with the coordinative functionality expressed in the consequent. While practitioners expressed this subset of contextual information in their own terms (see Figure 5, top side), we translated the consequent into four conditional elements, that is, namely three patterns and an inequality test (see Figure 5, bottom side). Through its consequent, the mechanism states that two specific fields of the EPR must host the same datum and that the reader must be made aware of the critical conditions of the considered inpatient. Through its antecedent, the mechanism states that this holds only whenever the blood pressure of the inpatient is under a conventional threshold, that is, in critical condition. There is a reason why even an objective and scientific threshold of blood pressure is considered "conventional," and hence specific to the hospital ward or even specific to a single doctor. In fact, doctors told us that the notion of "critical condition" also changes according to a number of contextual aspects that are mostly neglected by monitoring devices: their alarms are most of the time consciously and rightly ignored by expert nurses, as reported in Randell (2004). For this reason, doctors believe that these conditions are utterly difficult to hardwire into procedural application logic in all but the most obvious cases. In fact, criticality—seen along the coordinative dimension as the condition of a patient that calls for a direct and immediate intervention of some practitioner—depends on several anamnestic and physiological elements, on the illness history of the patient, and also on even more situated aspects, like the attitude of attending practitioners and their current workload. Obviously, not all the above often tacit contextual conditions can be immediately and comprehensively externalized into a mechanism and neither should they be: however, as long as recognizing a specific situation has a relevant coordinative value, practitioners can be motivated into characterizing it formally, by relying on some shared and broader conventional interpretation of data combinations or on the mutual acquaintance of the involved actors. In all these cases, the highly incremental structure and computational autonomy of mechanisms (in terms of their inner components and role in the control flow of the application, respectively) can facilitate stakeholders in expressing and updating mechanisms that are quite specific to complex and ever new situations.

Conventions Grounded on Run-Time Connections

The Problem List (PL) is the artifact of the patient record where clinicians enumerate the patient's problems. This list is intended to document all those conditions and events that can be related to clinical hypotheses and procedures. The term "problem" is purposely left vague enough to comprise a number of factors like symptoms, any alterations of vital signs, and all the concomitant pathologies that could affect a patient's hospitalization. The PL is likely to change during the caring process since practitioners are supposed to update its content with respect to the actual improvements or aggravations exhibited by the patient but also with respect to the extent they can consolidate their diagnostic hypothesis. Therefore, the PL is more than a mere list of either concomitant or sequential problems affecting the patient: it is the artifact where doctors represent the main deviations and swerves of illness trajectories, and the results of the epicrises (i.e., summings up) doctors periodically accomplish in evolving and improving their diagnosis on a specific case. The epicrises can result in the need to "cross out" previously unrelated symptoms and substitute them with new comprehensive diagnostic items. On the other hand, changes that regard the acuteness of single problems previously stated are not explicitly represented in the PL. These are rather represented in the Doctors's Diary (DD). The DD is the central repository for the notes that physicians need to write down in order to account for the decisions and interventions they are responsible for, as well as to make impressions, opinions, or just lines of reasoning explicit, either for themselves as a memorandum or as written notes to other colleagues.

The physicians called our attention on how useful it would be for them to be able to make explicit on the record itself the relationships between past problems and new problems as well as between problems of the PL and the daily entries reported

Figure 5. A coordinative mechanism on conventional patterns of data redundancy. Above, as expressed by practitioners in their own terms. Below, how this is translated in terms of LWOAD facts and primitives.

ANTECEDENT:

CONSIDER THE LATEST WEIGHT PARAMETER ON THE SIGN SHEET OF A NEWBORN

CONSIDER HER CURRENT BLOOD PRESSURE AS REPORTED IN THE VITAL SIGN SHEET

TEST WHETHER BLOOD PRESSURE IS LOWER THAN 70mmHg,
I.E., WE HAVE A "CRITICAL CONDITION"

CONSEQUENT:

HAVE THE RIGHT WEIGHT VALUE COPIED INTO THE SIGN SHEET

MAKE ME AWARE OF THE FACT THE NEWBORN IS IN CRITICAL CONDITIONS

```
(antecedent
   (document-fact (record-id ?pr) (name SS) (latest-weight ?lw))
   (document-fact (record-id ?pr) (name VS) (current-weight ?cw) (current-blood-pressure ?bp))
   (patient-fact (name ?name) (patient-record ?pr) )
   (test (< ?bp 70mmHg)))
(consequent
   <write ?lw = ?cw >
   <convey (API-fact (type criticality)) on (document-fact (record id ?pr) (name SS))
                                            for (patient-fact (name ?name)) >)
```

into the DD (see Figure 6). The former capability was seen as a way of reconstructing, or better yet, of making the line of thought explicit by which symptoms have been rationalized into problems and unrelated problems into a precise diagnosis. The latter was seen as a way of facilitating the a posteriori reconstruction of a problem progress from its outset, in order to give indications on how to head the course of clinical interventions toward its conclusion. These requirements point to a relevant coordinative need, besides that of keeping track of relevant phases during the decisional/medical process: in fact, doctors were also, sometimes implicitly, expressing the need to be informed on what problems they should address first and on the way their colleagues had coped with these problems so far.

We then asked practitioners which kinds of relationships they would more naturally employ to join two or more data that are not explicitly correlated by the patient record structure. The result was that practitioners found it more natural to consider relationships as occurring between data entries, either already recorded or still to be recorded on the patient record. In the former case, they pointed out the usefulness to relate data over distributed and different documents; in the latter case, they referred to the capability of drawing relationships between data values and fields yet to fill in, that is between documental activities and articulated work activities still to be performed. While almost any doctor expressed her preference for a number of possible relationships that had small overlaps (if any) with those pointed out by the others, we noticed that when these relationships were actually applied in the field of work, they all blurred into three main categories: causal, temporal and intentional connections Cabitza and Simone (2008). The generic semantics that pertain to the nature of the relationships between a source information and a target information could then be respectively rendered as: (a) "the source because of the target"; doctors would use this connection in order to hint of a strict causal relationship between items of the patient record: for example, the diagnosis "pneumonia"—reported in the PL—can be indicated as cause of the symptom "cough"—reported in

Figure 6. A list-like representation of the mechanism of run-time creation of data connections

```
(antecedent
  (document-fact (name ?f1) (content (entry (id ?e1)))
                     Consider any form in the EPR, e.g. the PL
  (document-fact (name ?f2) (content (entry (id ?e2))))
               and consider any OTHER form in the EPR, e.g. the DD
  (relation-fact  (level instance) (source-entity ?e1) (target-entity ?e2))
          and see if someone has drawn a connection btw their data
)
(consequent
   <convey (API-fact (type inquiry)) on (document-fact (name ?f2)) for ?e2>
)
                then make the reader aware of that connection
```

the DD—as a way to explain the symptom itself. (b) "the source after the target"; doctors would use this connection not only in a strict temporal sense, but also to hint a very weak or just supposed causal relationship: for example, reporting that a skin rash—a symptom from the DD—occurred after having administered a drug—an order reported somewhere else in the PR—would indicate a hypothesized correlation between these two clinical facts. (c) "the source for the target," that doctors would use in order to highlight evidence supporting a particular decision or to make an intention explicit (e.g., that the bacterial culture—an order—has been prescribed to verify the diagnostic hypothesis of pneumonia—an item in the PL).

DISCUSSION ON USER-DRIVEN MECHANISM FORMALIZATION

LWOAD was presented to the clinicians as a sort of specification language with which to implement functionalities of their EPR so that this application would not hinder, but rather foster, patterns of cooperative behaviors. The fact that users could be facilitated in "rapidly having a taste of a functionality" (as suggestively said by an interviewee) called for the twofold requirement that coordinative requirements must be flexibly specified—not to hinder their incremental re-definition—and the corresponding functionalities must be flexibly combined—to fit an ever-changing and necessarily underspecified context.

This stress on flexibility matches the basic goal of LWOAD, to be a language with which to render coordinative requirements not only in a computable and still platform-independent but especially at the desired level of abstraction. This makes mechanisms easy to define and modify by not necessarily expert users, and makes their execution dependent on the current context (in the line of the major tenets of context-aware computing Dourish (2001). In fact, NICU practitioners appreciated the possibility to manage connections that had been explicitly instantiated between data during their daily activities, and not just at the schema level and at compile time. The adopted rule-based approach allows coordinative functionalities to be expressed in terms of reactive and declarative mechanisms. We agree with Wulf, Stiemerling, and Pfeifer (1999) that rule-based programming has some important advantages over procedural programming in grasping and aligning with cooperative work, especially for its data- and event-driven nature. Reactive and declarative mechanisms have been recognized as intuitive for end-users: in fact, they are symbolic statements intended to translate their typical question "... and could I have the system do this, whenever that occurs?" into computable instructions (Pane & Myers, 2006). The declarativeness of these statements allows for the expression and formal specification of what a system should do rather than worrying about how it really accomplishes it at specification time. Declarativeness also allows mechanisms to be written without imposing a strict control flow, which is hardly recognized by clinicians in actual work situations. On the other hand, reactivity allows mechanisms to be written by using circumscribed units of code (i.e., rules) that relate to flexibility in terms of a greater easiness of maintenance due to better modularity and incrementality. For instance, if the NICU practitioners had expressed the need not to be alerted for low blood pressure problems of their inpatients unless in more specific cases than those represented in Figure 5, the antecedent of that mechanism would have been enriched with a new combination of conditional elements: for example, a test to evaluate whether the basal and physiologic blood pressure of the newborn is usually low, or whether she has been already treated for low blood pressure after the onset of the criticality, or even whether the latest drug that had been administered to her normally brings low blood pressure. In the WOAD framework, the progressive tuning of how the application should respond to ever evolving and local needs does not require a major rewriting of the application logic behind the corresponding functionality, but just calls for the addition (or deletion) of specific conditional elements within the mechanism that triggers the provision of criticality API on those critical conditions.

Moreover, defining mechanisms at the desired level of abstraction (instead of imposing a single level as in the traditional procedural approach) allows for better participation of users in the process of modelling and defining formal expressions. Therefore, these formal expressions can reflect how users really see their domain-specific knowledge and functionalities.

Thinking in terms of rules assured NICU clinicians that the whole set of mechanisms, once specified as a whole, is "rescaled" each time into smaller active subsets, that is, those mechanisms whose antecedent is satisfied according to what actors do (as to any other contextual event). This releases practitioners from conceiving an arbitrarily long sequential flow of control in which these kinds of mechanisms are discarded in all cases except in a very specific situation. In our validation at NICU, this flexibility was experienced and appreciated by practitioners, especially in the case of connections that were created at run-time across documents of the patient record, such as the problem list and the doctors' diary.

Finally, taking rules as the basic units of code addresses the flexibility requirement from the combination point of view (Won, Stiemerling, & Wulf, 2006). In fact, in WOAD (as in all rule-based notations) the *if* part of the rule can be as complex as necessary without interfering with the execution of the other rules; on the other hand, the particular kind of action that LWOAD mechanisms trigger, that is, augmenting the interface with graphical cues and indications promoting collaboration awareness, brings down the problem of mutual consistency of the rule set. This kind of consistency often makes the adoption of rule-based specification difficult to be understood and managed by layman users. In order to avoid this problem, WOAD is different from production and expert systems conceived in the AI field to support users' decisions and carry out inferences on available data to produce new data or solutions. In the AI domain, in fact, possibly long chains of rules are usually executed consecutively in order to infer a line of action on the basis of progressively true conditions. This makes the computational system (and its outputs) particularly sensitive to things like the completeness and internal consistence of the initial conditions, the order of rule execution, and the soundness of conflict resolution strategies. Conversely, WOAD adopts the rule-based approach in order to separate functional concerns into single mechanisms (not into chains of their executions); in regard to mechanism design, WOAD applies the principle that the consequent of each mechanism should be expressed as simply as possible, that is, that each mechanism should only address a single and punctual functionality that the system must exhibit against possibly over-detailed and specific contextual conditions. Moreover, the fact that LWOAD primitives used in the mechanisms' consequents do not change data (and hence the state of the world) but rather convey APIs, and the fact that APIs are conceived as strictly decoupled from any specific visual or interaction mode, guarantee that data inconsistency and ambiguities in data presentation are difficult to occur due to mechanisms execution. Moreover, possible conflicts in alerts (e.g., when two mechanisms trigger the same API but with different values) can be "caught" before execution by the mechanism interpreter itself (i.e., by monitoring the execution agenda). If a conflict arises, the system can show it to users as a sign that a particular situation calling for their interpretation and resolution on the basis of their experience and knowledge has happened. This can be useful whenever double checking and redundancy of effort (Cabitza & Simone, 2008) is preferable to compensating coordination breakdowns. For instance, if we assume that each department and community of users has developed its own sets of mechanisms to remind its members of meaningful conventions, the handoff of patients (and associated documentations) across department boundaries can raise unexpected challenges and jeopardize continuity of care especially when things (e.g., information transfer, interventions on patients) are given for granted and conventions of external facilities are transparent to whom takes responsibility for any shared resource. In cases like this, the proper API can help the practitioners of the target department detect and recognize the possible conflict, and can have them ask for the help of their colleagues from the source department in order to cope with the problematic situation.

The EUD literature shows that end-users are characterized by different kinds of abilities and levels of inclination toward the use of formal languages, as required by ICT design. The WOAD Wizard (WW) we used in the second step of our study can contribute to take into account this diversity and, in so doing implement the "gentle slope" in complexity claimed by almost all proposals for EUD (e.g., Liebermann et al., 2006). In fact, it is a graphical tool that users who are less proficient in computable formalization can use to create mechanisms in even a more abstract but less flexible and powerful manner than the direct use of LWOAD. In fact, the WW is intended as a component of the WOAD framework to facilitate i) the creation of document templates through didget composition (template editor); ii) the definition of mechanisms that support the information needs of a WoAD and its community (mechanism editor); iii) the association between API and Cascading Style Sheets (CSS), in order to progressively tune the aptest way to render the additional information that mechanisms produce according to the context (style editor). Due to space constraints, we will only describe the part of mechanism configuration that was presented to the key users of our study to get their preliminary impressions. In this case, the WW was seen as a sort of more abstract (yet less flexible) programming interface to make the notational technicalities of LWOAD transparent to users. Both LWOAD and the WW are proposed to be used by users interchangeably, according to their skills, attitudes and actual needs.

VISUAL PROTOTYPE OF THE WOAD WIZARD

In what follows, we illustrate the WOAD Wizard (WW), the visual prototype that we developed after the requirement analysis. The WW was meant as a proofof-concept for the prospective application that users would use to develop coordinative mechanisms by themselves and associate them to the active documents used within their main application system (see Figure 3). Since mechanisms are but rules, the main idea was to assimilate mechanism development to rule configuration: we then conceived the LWOAD mechanism editor similar to an interactive help utility, much like those provided by email clients to guide users through the configuration of personal filters and mechanisms of message filing. The WW was intended as a sequence of dialog boxes where users could select options and fill in details; each page was endowed with active areas corresponding to the buttons and links of the prospective interface in order to simulate the typical interaction involved in mechanism creation.

In the first window, users have access to the macro-functionalities of the WW (see Figure 7) regarding either mechanism composition or API visualization. In this paper, we do not address the functionalities of API rendering, that is, the association between API types and rendering functionalities (e.g., colors, icons, highlighting, see task C in Figure 4) provided by the documental platform. In regard to mechanism composition, a list of existing mechanisms is displayed in the top frame of the window. Users can read the textual description of each mechanism by selecting the corresponding row: the description is then displayed in the bottom frame (in Figure 7 we report the same mechanism illustrated in Figure 5). From the textual description of a mechanism, users can directly modify its parameters by clicking on the underlined elements (i.e., variables of the mechanism's pattern). Users can also change the structure of the mechanism (clicking on 'change...'); delete it, "activate" it (by checking the corresponding checkbox); and run the mechanism to check its functioning (clicking on 'Run Now...'). If the user clicks on 'New', the WW starts a three-step process; in the first window, the system proposes two options: to create a mechanism from a template, or to compose it from scratch, that is, from a blank template. We will consider this second case. In this case, the system opens a new window in place of the former, like that depicted in Figure 8 (left side, background). From the top frame of this window, the user can select any number of conditions the mechanism should be sensitive to (in its antecedent). In-depth analysis and participatory design sessions have allowed us to list together all the relevant conditions that practitioners wanted to be caught with respect to the records' content, time and clinical context. By selecting a condition from the list, the associated conditional statement is added in the bottom frame. As in the case of the first screen (Figure 7), the user can specify the value of the parameters the mechanism should monitor by clicking on the underlined parts of the statement. In doing so, corresponding input boxes are displayed to let users insert the value (e.g., 70 mmHg, a blood pressure value as in the case reported in Figure 5). If the user wants to specify the document where to check the condition, the system opens a box like that depicted in Figure 8 (right side, foreground).

Here, the user can consult a tree-like schema of the official documentation and select the document(s) (or their inner sections) whose data must be matched with the pattern's values. Once the antecedent of the mechanism has been defined, the wizard proposes a third window (in place of the previous one—see Figure 9) where the user can specify what the system is supposed to do when the conditions are true, that is, the elements of the consequent part. Also in this case, the user can select a number of different actions from the top frame; and then specify a value for each key presented in the textual description in the bottom frame. The list depicted in Figure 9 presents the main options selected by practitioners on a relevance basis during the interviews. The system groups these options together by similar category: for example, API provision, connection definition, data replication and insertion and the like. In the case where the action regards API provision, the user can also insert a textual explanation. This would be displayed on the clinical record only if requested in case a user can not interpret the API clue conveyed. By clicking the button 'Finish', the system creates the mechanism that is executable by the LWOAD interpreter. The strong de-

Figure 7. Screenshot of the mechanism editor, first windows

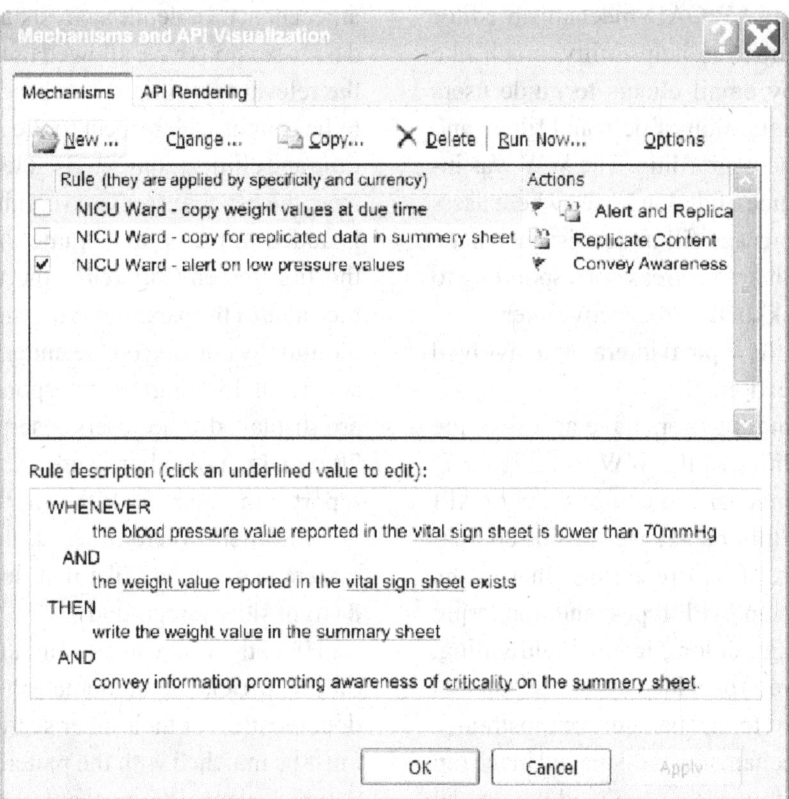

coupling we pursued in the design of the WOAD architecture between cooperative logic and the operational platform allows for the development of other compilers by which to translate LWOAD statements into other rule-based scripting languages.

ROADMAP FOR CURRENT AND FUTURE WORK

The paper illustrates the trajectory we have followed to approach the definition of a framework where layman users can specify mechanisms supporting their cooperation mediated by documental artifacts. In regard to how users should interact with the proposed architecture and system, our research agenda covers the incremental involvement and increasing skills of users: namely, we started having practitioners express conditional mechanisms in natural language (we translated these mechanisms in a platform-independent and abstract denotational language, LWOAD); then we stimulated them to use a graphical application to compose and detail condition-action statements of increasing complexity; lastly, we envision the opportunity to have users autonomously tweak and adjust LWOAD statements created with the former application in case of progressive customization and compliance to local needs. In this study, the choice of a rule-based representation seemed the most suitable one for the different types of flexibility it allows: namely, flexibility in specifying computational mechanisms and in combining them together at execution time.

The empirical findings we gathered so far refer to the healthcare domain and to a hospital setting. In this case, the problem was to endow

Figure 8. Screenshot of the WOAD Wizard for the definition of the mechanism's antecedent

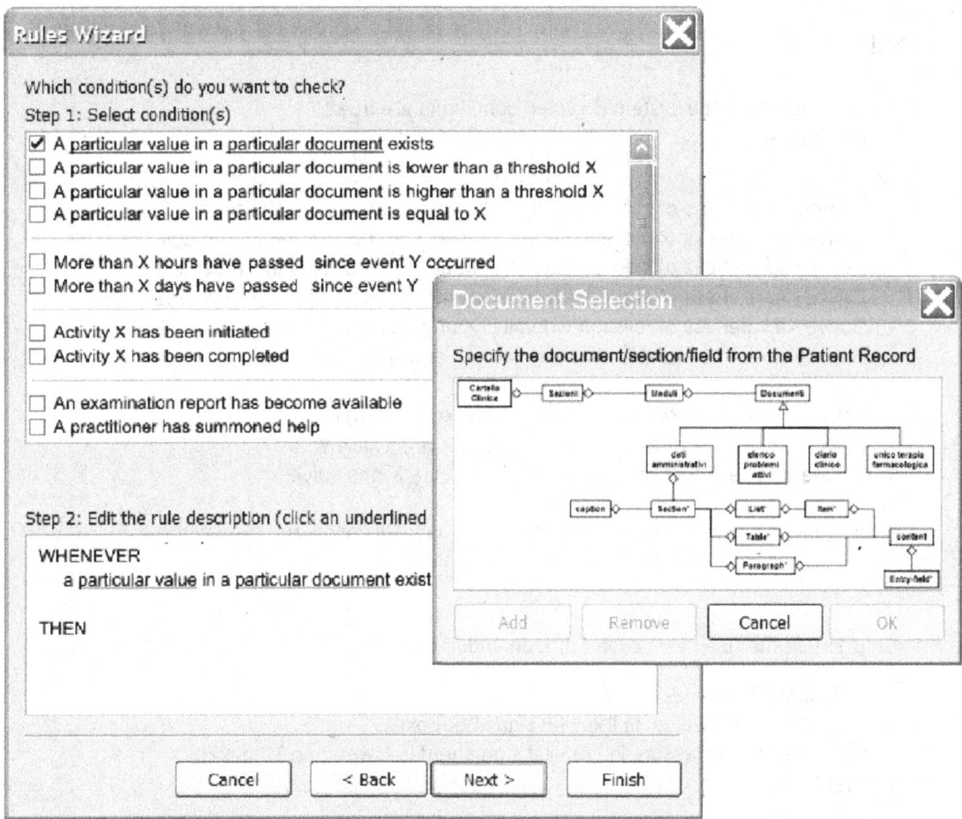

the implementation of an EPR with means that preserve or even support the conventions that practitioners adopt to make their cooperation smooth and seamless. A first natural question regards how much our empirical findings can be generalized to other settings, even within the same domain: we recognize that the involved group of doctors and nurses were extraordinarily helpful in trying and co-developing innovative solutions with computer researchers and professionals; they were extremely motivated in molding any tool that could help them provide a better care and return healthier newborns to their parents. For this reason, scalability and generalization of our proposal is part of our research agenda. Our next activities will also include the full implementation of the interface, informally validated through the visual prototype illustrated in Section 6: our pilot sessions confirm its feasibility as a tool that makes users autonomous in specifying condition-action mechanisms, once the set of patterns has been identified for their antecedents and a rich palette of graphical cues has been proposed as output of their consequents.

This approach however opens a new area of problems: a tool like that depicted in Section 6 interprets EUD more as a flexible kind of customization than as a real development environment (Liebermann et al., 2006). In fact, the predefined set of patterns cannot fulfil the needs of increasingly skilled users wanting to extend the "localization" of the desired support. To fulfil this requirement, users must also have access to the implementation environment: here it is where the WOAD framework and specifically its specification language—LWOAD —can play

Figure 9. Screenshot of the WW for the mechanism's consequent definition

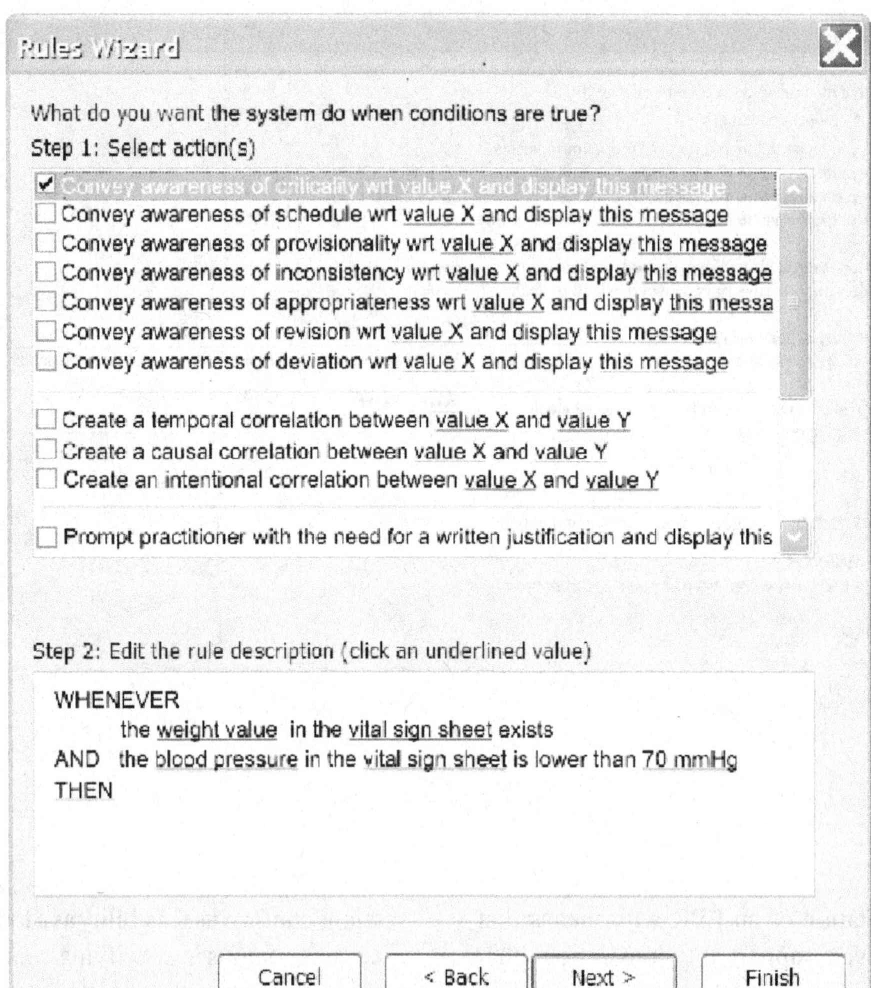

a relevant role for its declarative, abstract and modular approach that divides complex situations into a bunch of supportive functionalities that are invoked reactively with respect to the current context. The first phase of the study showed how (relatively) easily layman users can transform informal rules of their particular setting into executable statements, due to the "isomorphic" nature of the involved representations.

The next step is to allow users to define more general rules by selecting the needed pieces of information to build the antecedent of the rules out of the documents in a natural way. Practitioners proposed a solution that could mimic how users of a spreadsheet copy data from cell to cell just by clicking on them and pasting them where needed. Likewise, users should be able to express contextual conditions from a predefined palette of templates (concerning, for example, time, frequency, iterations, etc.) and specialize them by expressing simple key-value pairs and selecting data structures and data values directly from their documentation. Of course, this additional flexibility would require strong interoperability between the coordinative layer and the archival layer, that is, the EPR, or at least the capability to export and represent suitable views of clinical data, irrespectively of how they are organized and memorized. In our opinion, and on the basis of our interaction with practitioners, this kind of interoperability could bring data presentation strategies to EPR that are more natural and closer to the way practitioners use the current paper-based clinical record fruitfully. This positive mutual influence is the final goal we aim to pursue in our planned interactions with users in the healthcare domain.

ACKNOWLEDGMENT

The work presented in this paper has been partially supported by the F.A.R. 2008. The authors would like to thank the management and the Neonatal Intensive Care Unit personnel of the Alessandro Manzoni Hospital of Lecco for their kind collaboration. In particular, we would like to acknowledge the invaluable help and courtesy of Dr Bellù and Mrs Colombo.

REFERENCES

Berg, M. (1999a). Accumulating and coordinating: Occasions for information technologies in medical work. *Computer Supported Cooperative Work, 8*(4), 373–401. doi:10.1023/A:1008757115404

Berg, M., & Goorman, E. (1999b). The contextual nature of medical information. *International Journal of Medical Informatics, 56*, 51–60. doi:10.1016/S1386-5056(99)00041-6

Bjerknes, G., & Bratteteig, T. (1987). Florence in wonderland. System development with nurses. In G. Bjerknes, P. Ehn, & M. Kyng (Ed.), *Computers and democracy. A Scandinavian challenge* (pp. 279-295). Aldershot, UK: Avebury.

Braa, K., & Sandahl, T. (2000). Introducing digital documents in work practices challenges and perspectives. *Group Decision and Negotiation, 9*(3), 189–203. doi:10.1023/A:1008783106613

Cabitza, F., Locatelli, M., Sarini, M., & Simone, C. (2006, March 13-17). CASMAS: Supporting collaboration in pervasive environments. In *Proceedings of the 4th Annual IEEE International Conference on Pervasive Computing and Communications (PerCom2006)*, Pisa, Italy (pp. 286-295). Washington, DC: IEEE Computer Society.

Cabitza, F., Sarini, M., & Simone, C. (2007, November 4-7). Providing awareness through situated process maps: the hospital care case. In *Proceedings of the 2007 International ACM SIGGROUP Conference on Supporting Group Work (GROUP'07)*, Sanibel Island, FL (pp. 41-50). ACM Publishing.

Cabitza, F., & Simone, C. (2006, October). *"You Taste Its Quality": Making sense of quality standards on situated artifacts*. Paper presented at the 1st Mediterranean Conference on Information Systems (MCIS'06), Venice, Italy. Association for Information Systems.

Cabitza, F., & Simone, C. (2007, September 24-28). "... and do it the usual way": fostering awareness of work conventions in document-mediated collaboration. In *Proceedings of the 10th European Conference on Computer Supported Cooperative Work (ECSCW'07)*, Limerick, Ireland (pp. 24-28). Dordrecht, The Netherlands: Springer.

Cabitza, F., & Simone, C. (2008, June 17-19). Supporting practices of positive redundancy for seamless care. In *Proceedings of the 21st IEEE International Symposium on Computer-Based Medical Systems (CBMS'08)*, Jyväskylä, Finland (pp. 470-475). Washington, DC: IEEE Computer Society.

Cabitza, F., & Simone, C. (2009, June 25-27). Active artifacts as bridges between context and community knowledge sources. In *Proceedings of the 4th International Conference on Communities and Technologies (C&T2009),* Univeristy Park, PA (pp. 115-124). ACM Publishing.

Cabitza, F., & Simone, C. (in press). PRODOC: An electronic patient record to foster process-oriented practices In *Proceedings of the 11th European Conference on Computer Supported Cooperative Work (ECSCW2009),* Vienna, Austria. Dordrecht, The Netherlands: Springer.

Cabitza, F., Simone, C., & Sarini, M. (2009). Leveraging coordinative conventions to promote collaboration awareness. *Computer Supported Cooperative Work, 18*(4), 301–330. doi:10.1007/s10606-009-9093-z

Divitini, M., & Simone, C. (2000). Supporting different dimensions of adaptability in workflow modeling. *Computer Supported Cooperative Work, 9*(3), 365–397. doi:10.1023/A:1008751210054

Dourish, P. (2001). Seeking a foundation for context-aware computing. *Special Issue on Context-Aware Computing HCI Journal, 16*(2), 229–241.

Dourish, P., Edwards, W. K., LaMarca, A., Lamping, J., Petersen, K., & Salsibury, M. (2000). Extending document management systems with user-specific active properties. *ACM Transactions on Information Systems, 18*(2), 140–170. doi:10.1145/348751.348758

Fitzpatrick, G. (2004). Integrated care and the working record. *Health Informatics Journal, 10*(4), 291–302. doi:10.1177/1460458204048507

Hardstone, G., Hartswood, M., Procter, R., Slack, R., Voss, A., & Rees, G. (2004, November 6-10). Supporting informality: Team working and integrated care records. In *Proceedings of the International Conference on Computer Supported Cooperative Work (CSCW '04),* Chicago (pp. 142-151). ACM Publishing.

Heath, C., & Lu, P. (1996, November 16-20). Documents and professional practice: 'Bad' organisational reasons for 'good' clinical records. In *Proceedings of the International Conference on Computer Supported Cooperative Work (CSCW'96),* Boston (pp. 354-363). ACM Publishing.

Lieberman, H., Paternò, F., & Wulf, V. (Eds.). (2006). *End user development*. New York: Springer.

Nygaard, K. (1984). User-oriented Languages. In *Proceedings of the International Conference on Medical Informatics Europe (MIE 1984)* (pp. 38-44). Berlin, Germany: Springer-Verlag.

OpenDoc Design Team. (1993). *OpenDoc technical summary*. Apple Computer.

Pane, J. F., & Myers, B. A. (2006). More natural programming languages and environments. In H. Lieberman, F. Paternò, & V. Wulf (Ed.), *End user development* (pp. 31-50). New York: Springer.

Randell, R. (2004, November 6-10). Accountability in an alarming environment. In *Proceedings of the International Conference on Computer Supported Cooperative Work (CSCW '04),* Chicago (pp. 125-131). ACM Publishing.

Schmidt, K., & Simone, C. (1996). Coordination mechanisms: Towards a conceptual foundation of CSCW systems design. *Computer Supported Cooperative Work, 5*(2-3), 155–200. doi:10.1007/BF00133655

Sellen, A. J., & Harper, R. H. R. (2003). *The myth of the paperless office*. Cambridge, MA: MIT Press.

Winthereik, B. R., & Vikkelso, S. (2005). ICT and integrated care: Some dilemmas of standardising inter-organisational communication. *Computer Supported Cooperative Work, 14*(1), 43–67. doi:10.1007/s10606-004-6442-9

Won, M., Stiemerling, O., & Wulf, V. (2006). Component-based approaches to tailorable systems. In H. Lieberman, F. Paternò, & V. Wulf (Ed.), *End user development* (pp. 115-141). New York: Springer.

Wulf, V., Stiemerling, O., & Pfeifer, A. (1999). Tailoring groupware for different scopes of validity. *Behaviour & Information Technology*, *18*(3), 199–212. doi:10.1080/014492999119084

This work was previously published in Journal of Organizational and End User Computing, Volume 22, Issue 2, edited by M. Adam Mahmood, pp. 1-20, copyright 2010 by IGI Publishing (an imprint of IGI Global).

Chapter 7
Self-Determined Adoption of an ICT System in a Work Organization

Eija Korpelainen
Helsinki University of Technology, Finland

Matti Vartiainen
Helsinki University of Technology, Finland

Mari Kira
Helsinki University of Technology, Finland

ABSTRACT

This descriptive single case study examines the process and implications of the self-determined adoption of an internet-based meeting system in a global company. Self-determination theory and structuration theory are used as theoretical lenses to understand the adoption and use of an ICT system. The data were collected using qualitative semi-structured interviews with eleven system users and analyzed using a content analysis approach. The research shows that the self-determined adoption of ICT systems has benefits like user motivation and satisfaction. Problems in such adoption relate to users' experiencing uncertainty regarding the organizational legitimization of the system and support for its use. Employees and organizations are likely to benefit from self-determined adoption because it promotes employees' motivation and initiative-taking. However, a shared understanding of self-determination and organizational support for it are required.

INTRODUCTION

The implementation of Information and Communication Technology (ICT) systems is often described as a predetermined and controlled process. This paper documents an ICT system implementation process of a very different sort; we had an unexpected opportunity to study implementation as an organic and decentralized process. This opportunity came up while we were conducting a preliminary study for a research project focusing on the user and organizational factors and outcomes in ICT system adoptions.

DOI: 10.4018/978-1-4666-0140-6.ch007

As appropriate in a preliminary study, we used exploratory interview questions that allowed the interviewees to broadly describe their experiences of why and how an ICT system was put into use, what problems and benefits the system brought along with it, how the system was used in the company, how the system assisted learning at work, and what kind of user support was available. An important interest area was the emergent learning processes, both during the initial adoption and eventual day-to-day use of an ICT system.

After the whole research project was finished, one observation from this preliminary study remained unexplained. In this particular implementation process, addressing the adoption of an internet-based meeting system, most interviewees expressed satisfaction with the way the system was introduced, and they stated that the system was adopted successfully and in good spirits. According to the literature, such smooth adoption processes are rare, and the adoption of an ICT system often causes problems, especially in terms of user resistance (Adams, Berner, & Wyatt, 2004; Chen & Lou, 2002; Jiang, Muhanna & Klein, 2000; Klaus, Wingreen, & Blanton, 2007; Nunamaker, 1997; Orlikowski, 1993). This led us to explore further this successful adoption process in which the users interviewed expressed their willingness to use the system.

These explorations indicated that the users voluntarily adopted the internet-based meeting system and their interests guided its adoption and use. There was little organizational communication concerning the system, and many actually learned about the system from a peer. Each user was allowed to decide freely whether to use the system or not, and also to decide the purpose of its use. In short, the organization provided an ICT system for its employees and provided some information on different possible reasons for utilizing it, but allowed the users to decide if the system was beneficial for their work and whether or not to utilize it. Because of these characteristics of the adoption process, we started to call it self-determined adoption. Self-determined ICT system adoption thus means a process in which the system users decide on whether and how to adopt the system; the users also coordinate their own learning processes during the adoption in terms of learning strategies, resources, and situations. They also assess and control the outcomes of the adoption process and experience themselves as autonomous in the process (cf., Deci & Ryan, 2000; Knowles, 1975).

We therefore had in our hands a special single case of a self-determined ICT system adoption process that left the users satisfied with the system and motivated to use it. To describe this self-determined adoption process analytically and more formally, we articulated two new research questions and completely reanalyzed the data set (see Hinds, Vogel, & Clarke-Steffen, 1997; Thorne, 1994) to respond to two questions:

1) How does the self-determined adoption of an ICT system proceed?
2) What possibilities and problems do the users perceive in the self-determined adoption and use of an ICT system?

There are several descriptions of and models for the introduction and adoption of ICT systems in the literature. Most often, the models depict an implementation process proceeding step by step from the scanning of organizational needs to a full and effective use of technology in daily practices (see e.g., Cooper & Zmud, 1990; Kwon & Zmud, 1987; see also Orlikowski & Hofman, 1997, for the critique and an alternative view to change). This is the prevailing view of an ICT implementation process. However, the initial analysis of our case indicated that the adoption process in question could not be described as such a predetermined step-by-step process: an alternative theoretical framework was needed to capture the dynamics of the case. We found that the insights of Barley and Tolbert (1997), DeSanctis and Poole (1994), and Giddens (1984) concerning structuration theory and institutional change resonated in our case. Therefore, we decided to use their approaches as preliminary theoretical concepts (cf., Yin, 2003a) when describing our case.

A further element of theory relevant to our case was the autonomy or self-determination of the system users. An opportunity for self-determination, or autonomous regulation of one's activities, has a powerful impact on an individual's behavior and development (Deci & Ryan, 2000; Knowles, 1975). Having recognized the system users' autonomy in the case, we applied the self-determination theory to understand their reactions to the adoption process and the outcomes of that process.

The article is organized as follows: first, we present the two alternative models of the organizational implementation of ICT systems; second, we review the self-determination theory and consider its implications for ICT adoption. The paper then proceeds to our empirical case study of the self-determined ICT adoption process in a global technology company. Finally, we discuss the users' opportunities for self-determined behavior in ICT system adoption processes and the consequences of this self-determination. We conclude the paper by discussing our findings and outlining the practical and theoretical implications of a self-determined adoption of ICT systems.

Implementation of ICT Systems in Organizations – Two Alternative Approaches

The organizational implementation of an ICT system refers to "all activities related to deployment and adoption of a new technology, namely requirements specification, acquisition and/or design and development, installation, training and internalisation of routines for effective utilization" (Munkvold, 2003, p. 3). The adoption refers to individual acceptance and willingness to use the system. The implementation of an ICT system entails two adoption processes at the same time, namely, the adoption of technology and the adoption of new ways of working. The technological aspect of the adoption is usually rather straightforward, as employees are instructed and respectively learn the details of a system (i.e., which buttons to press). The technological tool, however, makes possible and demands new working methods, and it is more common to encounter problems when users start to learn and apply the new ways of doing their work (West, Waddops, & Graham, 2007; Wheeler, Dennis, & Press, 1999). A key challenge in ICT system implementation processes is, therefore, that users need to learn new ways to perform their daily work, communicate (Andriessen, 2003), teach (West et al., 2007), and study. They cannot only start to use the system, but they also have to internalize new ways of working and thinking. During this process, users may also develop novel ways of using the system (DeSanctis & Poole, 1994; Orlikowski, 1993), not anticipated by the system designers.

The relevant literature distinguishes users' acceptance of a system as a vital characteristic of an implementation process. The way users assess the costs and benefits from the system affects their acceptance of the system and their decision on whether to use it (e.g., Davis, 1989; Venkatesh, Morris, Davis, & Davis, 2003). If users perceive the benefits offered by a system as being few, they will not accept it, even if the system developers thought that the system would be suitable for the work. Additionally, the match between the system and the tasks affects the users' acceptance of the system. Grudin (1989, 1994) argues that designers and managers often misjudge users' perceptions on the benefits of the use of the system. For example, these decision-makers see the potential benefits from their own point of view, but fail to consider whether subordinates will be able to perceive the direct benefits of the system. The decision-makers also tend to underestimate the amount of work the adoption requires from the users. Nevertheless, successful user adoption of an ICT system is vital as it enhances the productive use of the system

Table 1. The model of an ICT system implementation process (based on Cooper & Zmud, 1990; reviewed by Munkvold, 2003; Kwon & Zmud, 1987) [1]

Stages	Activities
1.) Initiation	Scanning organization needs and ICT solutions
2.) Organizational adoption	Negotiations to get organizational backing for novel ICT implementation
3.) Organizational adaption	Developing, installing, and maintaining the ICT system. Developing new organizational procedures. Training users both in the new procedures and in the use of ICT
4.) User adoption and acceptance	Including the members of the organization to use the technology
5.) Established use	Use the ICT system is encouraged among employees as a normal activity
6. Infusion	The intended benefits of the technology are obtained through effective use of the technology.

(Andriessen, 2003; Grudin, 1994; Ehrlich, 1987; Kwon & Zmud, 1987; Orlikowski, 1993).

An organizational ICT system implementation process is usually conceptualized as a series of stages (see e.g., Orlikowski & Hofman, 1997). Kwon and Zmud (1987) developed a six-stage model of an ICT system implementation process (see Table 1). The model is based on the organizational change and innovation and technological diffusion literature. The stages replicate Lewin's (1952) change model from unfreezing to change and to refreezing. The model covers an implementation process from the scanning of organizational needs to a full and effective use of the technology in daily practices. Munkvold (2003) states, however, that an actual implementation process is rarely linear, but iterative, and the different stages partly overlap (Cooper & Zmud, 1990). The strength of the model is that it helps to understand comprehensively the different stages, the activities connected to each stage, and the prominence of each stage in an ICT implementation process.

However, alternative models for organizational change and especially for ICT implementation are also beginning to merge. These models challenge the neat step-wise progression of a planned change and pay more attention to the unpredictable and emergent nature of social change (see e.g., Orlikowski & Hofman, 1997). In this paper, we propose that building on structuration theory, it is possible to outline such an alternative model for the ICT implementation. Structuration theory is founded on Giddens' (1984) conceptualizations of social processes as involving reciprocal interaction between human actors and institutions (loosely speaking, Giddens calls these 'structures'). Barley and Tolbert (1997) define institutions as "shared rules and typifications that identify categories of social actors and their appropriate activities or relationships" (p. 96). Human actions are thus enabled and constrained by institutions (the accepted ways of doing things). At the same time, the institutions emerge – over time – from human actions (Orlikowski, 1992) that create and establish ever-new shared rules and typifications. Institutions, therefore, are created, maintained, and changed through action. According to structuration theory, the potential for both stability and change exists in any social situation: human actions may promote change while institutions promote stability.

Figure 1 depicts an ICT system implementation as a process of human actions and institutional change based on Barley and Tolbert (1997) and DeSanctis and Poole (1994). The model considers emerging and existing discrepancies between the concrete activity level and the more abstract institutional level. In the model, the *realm of institutions*

Figure 1. Model of institutional change in the context of ICT-systems (based on Barley & Tolbert, 1997) (© 1997, SAGE Publications, used with permission) (see also DeSanctis & Poole, 1994).

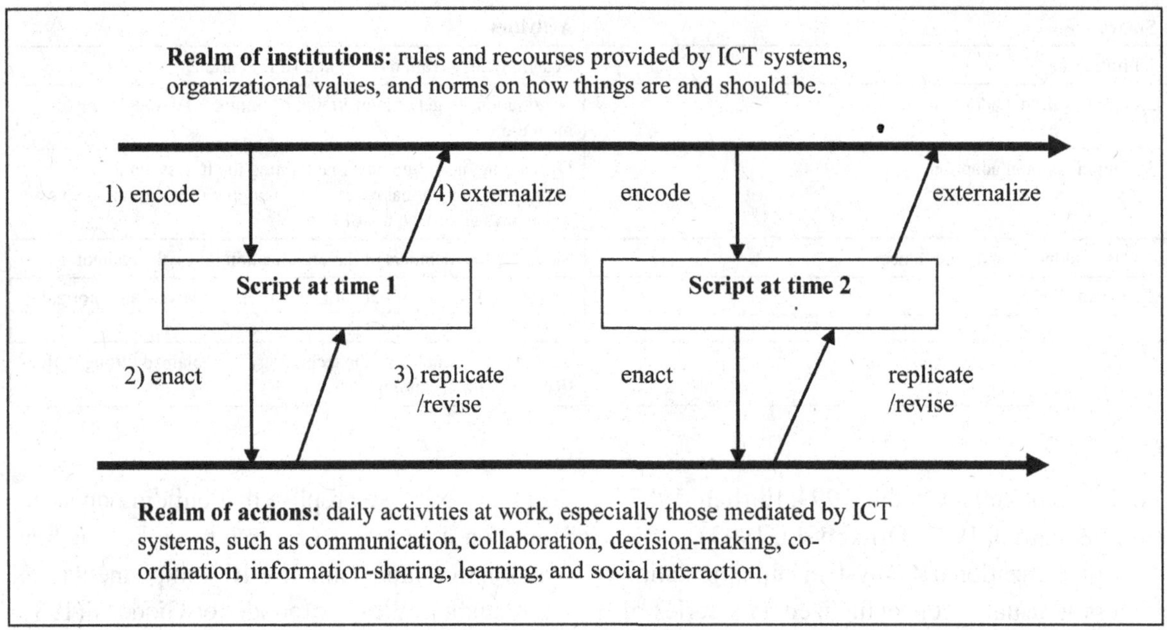

refers to values, rules and norms on how things are and how they should be. ICT systems offer specific types of rules, resources, and capabilities, and govern how information can be managed by their users (DeSanctis & Poole, 1994). Values, norms, and recourses provide employees with an understanding of the environment they operate in (Furumo & Melcher, 2006), and show how they should act as members of a particular community. The *realm of actions* refers to daily activities at work (Kira & Forslin, 2008), especially those mediated by ICT systems. The model suggests that institutionalization is a continuous process, and the operations can be observed only through time. The bold horizontal arrows in the figure stand for the temporality of the two realms of the social structure, namely institutions and actions.

The realms of institutions and actions 'communicate' via *scripts*. Barley and Tolbert (1997) define scripts as behavioral regularities; however, scripts may also be viewed as shared mental models that underlie behaviors. In Figure 1, a script refers to a mental model - a subcase of a schema - which describes a characteristic sequence of events in a particular setting (Gleitman, Fridlund, & Reisberg, 1999). For example, a script may be a mental model of the correct way of working.

The first arrow refers to the *encoding* of institutional principles in the scripts to be used in specific situations. Encoding takes place in socialization as individuals internalize rules and interpretations of behavior appropriate for particular settings (Berger & Luckmann, 1967). The second arrow refers to action, in which individuals *enact* these scripts in their activities, for example when employees use an ICT system to perform daily work tasks. The third arrow refers to the choice of individuals: if they choose a different way, they *revise* the script, and if they choose the institutionalized way, they *replicate* the script. Barley and Tolbert (1997) state that a change in an organization's environment is often needed for employees to collectively question and revise scripted patterns of behavior; otherwise, actors are likely to replicate them. For example, changes in technology, such as the development and availability of new ICT-based tools, or changes in business conditions, such as economic downturns, increase the probability of individuals transforming a script.

The last arrow refers to the *externalization* of the patterned behaviors and interactions produced while posing questions and making innovations. Revised scripts may change the shared assumption of how things should be done, and these revised actions may become institutionalized. Most importantly for our purposes, new ways of using ICT systems discovered in daily activities may impose changes on institutionalized rules and beliefs.

Structuration theory has recently gained interest in information systems research (Jones & Karsten, 2003; 2008; Poole & DeSanctis, 2004). Two influential applications in information systems research are adaptive structuration theory, in which the impact of ICT systems on organizational change is examined (DeSanctis & Poole, 1994), and the structurational model of technology, in which structuration theory is used to theorize aspects of the information systems research field (Orlikowski, 1992, 2000; Orlikowski & Robey, 1991). Many researchers have also used structuration theory in the context of the organizational implementation of information systems (see e.g., Barley, 1986; DeSanctis, Poole, Dickson, & Jackson, 1993; Kouroubali, 2002; Walsham, & Han, 1993). These articles often use interpretive case analysis in order to illustrate the theory. However, the existing literature usually focuses on examining and explaining how social actions and structures affect the introduction and adoption of information technology in organizations. None of these studies address the dynamic process in which individuals actively adopt, enact, replicate, revise, and/or reject the institutionally grounded meanings and purposes of ICT systems. In this article, structuration theory is used to describe how people – through their daily actions and choices – can change scripts and institutionalized assumptions rather than only being confined by them. We were not able to find other articles in which the Barley and Tolbert (1997) model (Figure 1) was used to describe an implementation process of an ICT system as an institutional change in an organization.

The alternative ICT implementation models presented in Table 1 and Figure 1 can be examined in parallel. The stages from 'Initiation' to 'Organizational adaptation' in Table 1 may be carried out by the managers and system designers as planned but, from the phase 'User adoption and acceptance' on, such linear process may be interrupted. While users are exploring and learning to use the system, and also performing work tasks in the realm of actions, they may choose different ways of acting than those suggested by the existing institutional rules, resources, and values. The users may choose unplanned actions for many reasons but, in most cases, a contextual change is a strong trigger. Eventually, if carried out consistently, the unplanned ways of acting may revise the existing script and change the shared assumptions as to how things should be and should be done. The institutional realm may also start to change.

Self-Determination in the Implementation Process of ICT Systems

An implementation of an ICT system always entails both organizational and individual change. As employees adopt a new system, they need to learn its use, and the use of the system also changes their work. In a change process, it is important to consider what motivates people to change, and how this motivation can be influenced by others. Motivation concerns energy, direction, persistence, and all aspects of activation and intention to do something, for example to utilize technologies (Ryan & Deci, 2000). Theories on self-determination (Deci & Ryan, 2000), self-direction (Knowles, 1975), and decision latitude or autonomy (Karasek, 1979) offer an important perspective on human motivation. These theories point out that, for motivation to form, individuals need to be able to regulate their activities. For example, in the field of educational research, self-determination or self-direction has been shown to lead to motivated and effective learning. During self-directed learning, students take the initiative, diagnose their learning needs, formulate learning goals, identify resources for learning, select and implement learning strategies, and evaluate learning outcomes (Knowles, 1975). The learners take responsibility for their learning to construct a meaningful learning process (Garrison, 1997).

The self-determination theory of Deci and Ryan (2000) draws a distinction between autonomous motivation and controlled motivation. Autonomy or self-determination refers to acting with a sense of volition and experiencing the possibility of choice. Ryan and Deci show that self-determination induces interest in an activity and excitement about it, and boosts confidence, performance, persistence, and creativity. On the contrary, controlled motivation builds on the pressure to engage in socially expected actions and/or actions that are not an end in them, but only a means to reach something else, e.g., rewards (Deci, Ryan, & Koestner, 1999; Gagné & Deci, 2005). Activities connected to controlled motivation can lead to amotivation or a total lack of motivation, as the person has few chances to regulate his/her behavior and experience the goals of his/her activity as being meaningful. The possibility of self-determination therefore supports employees' motivation at work, while the lack of this possibility undermines motivation and full engagement in work activities (see also Sundholm, 2000).

On the basis of such research, we propose that self-determination is also an important enabler in the implementation and use of an ICT system. The first approach to an ICT implementation, presented in Table 1, can be characterized as stable and predetermined. The user adoption and acceptance stage does not take self-determination into account very significantly: the developers of this model (Cooper & Zmud, 1990; Kwon & Zmud, 1987) notice that users do not adopt and accept new tools automatically, but they do not discuss that further. Thus, the model pays little attention to the possibility of people rejecting the system or using it in a different way than that intended by the designers and managers. As noted above, such user rejection or revision is likely, as the designers and managers are prone to misjudge users' reactions to the system. Users' desire for self-determination may cause problems if it is not taken into account in the implementation plan. On the contrary, self-determination fits well into the scope of the implementation model presented in Figure 1, which takes into account the fact that users actively enact institutional scripts in their daily work and may either replicate or revise these scripts.

METHODOLOGICAL APPROACH

We used a single special case study to describe the self-determined adoption of an ICT system (Stake, 1994; Yin, 2003b). Siggelkow (2007) argues that a single case can be powerful, when it provides special insights into the phenomenon being studied that other cases would not be able to provide. A transformation in an organization at the level of institutional structures and assumptions is a situation in which a single case study can offer special insights. Indeed, Barley and Tolbert (1997) state that "an enormous amount of luck or prescience are required to recognize an emerging institution and then gather data on relevant, ongoing action and interaction" (p. 100). Thus, we were lucky to come across a single case of a self-determined and successful ICT adoption process where a change in an organization's institutionalized assumptions took place. We identified the case as a special opportunity to describe an ICT adoption process as an institutional change after the data gathering and initial analyses (Hinds et al., 1997; Thorne, 1994). However, it was possible for us to re-examine and re-analyze the case data thoroughly from this particular perspective because the initial interview questions were rather open and all 11 interviewees ended up describing their experiences with the self-determined adoption of ICT.

The study was conducted in a global technology company producing machinery and process technology on a large scale worldwide. At the time of the study, the company was operating in over 50 countries. This study focused on one business area in Finland, where most of the work carried out was office work.

An internet-based meeting system was put into use in 2002. The system made it possible to arrange live internet sessions for meetings or training, and it combined voice and video conferencing. Users participated in sessions by means of a PC connected to the internet. They wore headsets to listen and speak to each other. It was also possible to use a webcam. Among other things, the system supported file-sharing, and it was also possible to record and edit sessions. Data for this study were gathered in 2005 [2]. At the time of the study, almost all the employees in the case company had access to the system, but it was used by only a limited number of employees. All in all, however, about 2500 members of the company's staff (and 500 external actors) had used the system and, each month, between 400 and 500 meetings were arranged. There were about 500 moderators who had the right to involve participants in meetings.

Data Collection and Analysis

A qualitative and interpretive research approach was chosen for the study, which initially was designed to be a preliminary investigation for a larger research project. The data were collected through qualitative interviews. A semi-structured interview protocol was devised, and the order, form, and extent of the questions varied from one interview to another (Miller & Crabtree, 1992). Semi-structured interviews provided freedom for the interviewees to describe the matters they found important while, at the same time, the loosely set themes in the interview protocol ensured that all the important issues were addressed.

Altogether, eleven volunteer office employees were interviewed in 2005, three females and eight males, aged from 28 to 43. The interviewees were selected from three different professions (see Appendix): support and HR persons, operational employees, and middle managers. The aim was to cover different viewpoints on the introduction and adoption of ICT in the company. Three interviewees could be called key informants: they had been involved in the selection and implementation process of the system from the very beginning, they were super users with all rights to use the system, and they trained and supported other users, and developed the use of the system. The rest of the interviewees were ordinary users who had made the decision to adopt and use the system. These ordinary users were on various levels of expertise in the use of the system. One interviewee had used the system only a few times as a participant in a meeting, while some had used the system regularly when organizing and participating in meetings. Three of the ordinary users said that they had had some reservations and doubts concerning the system before actually trying it out. The 11 interviewees, therefore, formed a small but typical group of users (see e.g., Kuzel, 2000; Miles & Huberman, 1994, p. 27; Patton, 1990, p. 169) there were both interviewees who were highly interested in the use of the system and interviewees who had regarded the system with some reservations. Each interview lasted from 45 minutes to 60 minutes.

Organizational documents were also gathered and analyzed in order to get background information: for example, a report on a system test period evaluation conducted in 2002 was studied. At the time of writing of this case study, additional contacts were made with the three key persons to address some specific questions based on the theories of self-determination and institutional change and to clarify some remaining questions from the analysis of the original interviews.

The interviews were conducted by the first author. The interviews were recorded and then professionally transcribed. Content analysis was used to organize and describe the phenomenon being investigated and to express it in a compact form (Miles & Huberman, 1994). The analysis method was selected because it made it possible to sift through large volumes of data in a systematic and objective manner, and it suited the unstructured data (Weber, 1990). The analysis applied the systematic combining approach based on abductive logic (Dubois & Gadde, 2002): we continuously matched theoretical concepts with the empirical reality to form our emerging case description. In practice, the analysis process was conducted in three phases. First, the original interviews were examined from the point of view of self-determined adoption and institutional change theory. These theories were used as preliminary theoretical concepts to set a direction and boundaries for our description of the ICT adoption process (see Yin, 2003a). Second, the data were organized into categories that followed the Barley and Tolbert (1997) model of institutional change. Finally, the categories were further specified and finalized on the basis of this theoretical framework of the study.

To ensure the quality of this qualitative research, we paid special attention to three quality criteria: communicative validity, pragmatic validity, and reliability. Validity relates to the truthfulness of interpretations (Sandberg, 2005). Communicative validity refers to an understanding between the researcher and research participants about what both parties are doing (Apel, 1972). Communicative validity was ensured in two ways in this study: (1) the interviews were conducted in the form of a dialog; the interview questions were elaborated with follow-up questions, such as "Can you give me on example?", and the interviewees were made aware that the researcher was interested in their personal experiences; (2) in the analysis, the aim was to strive for coherent interpretations, which means that the parts of the studied phenomenon must fit the whole and the whole must fit the parts (Sandberg, 2005; Silverman, 2006). Pragmatic validity refers to testing knowledge produced in action (Kvale, 1989). In this study pragmatic validity was ensured by asking follow-up questions in the interviews which constantly embedded the statements in actual situations.

Reliability concerning the procedure for achieving truthfulness in interpretations (Sandberg, 2005) was secured in five ways: (1) the research process has been described carefully (Yin, 2003b), and the theoretical stance from where the interpretation of the results takes place has been expressed clearly (Silverman, 2006); (2) the interviews were recorded and transcribed word by word (Seale, 1999); (3) the data categorizations made by the first author were discussed and confirmed with other researchers in the research group. The other researchers challenged and asked for justification of the emerging categories until the categorization could be considered final (Miles & Huberman, 1994, p. 64); (4) the researchers stayed in contact with the case organization, and checked the findings with the three key informants, (Miles & Huberman, 1994, p. 275); 5) the reliability of analysis was examined by blind check-coding: two persons independently (the first and second authors) classified 18% of the data (Miles & Huberman, 1994, p. 64), and we found 82% agreement in our analyses.

The quality of the secondary analysis of the data set was ensured based on criteria distinguished in earlier literature (e.g., Heaton, 1998; Hinds et al., 1997; Thorne, 1994). Firstly, we reanalyzed our own data, which were recorded and transcribed; the new research questions arose directly from the primary data (e.g., Gladstone, Volpe & Boydell, 2007). Secondly, all the interviewees described their experiences of the phenomenon being studied, and consequently there were no missing data (Hinds et al., 1997; Thorne, 1994). Thirdly, we also reported the main methodological issues regarding the original study, together with the description of the processes in the secondary data (Heaton, 1998).

RESULTS

In this section, we first describe how the self-determined ICT adoption took place in the case company. We then outline the possibilities and problems the users perceived in this process. As we will discuss later on, the adoption of the ICT system in the case company cannot easily be fitted into the traditional ICT adoption process template summarized in Table 1. Instead, the process can be described by discussing its events within the framework of institutional change depicted in Figure 1. We therefore describe the adoption process as progressing from an initial script (Script 1) to a new, emergent script (Script 2) through the interaction between the institutionalized meanings of the system and the daily work activities of its users.

Script 1: The Internet-Based Meeting System is the Means to Train Customers in This Company

In 2002, the internet-based meeting system was put into use, primarily to provide a novel way for customer training and learning. Up until then, customers had participated on location in training provided by the case company; the aim was now to replace this face-to-face training with electronic learning (eLearning), made possible by the internet-based meeting system. The main aim was thus to develop cost-efficient customer training by reducing customer and expert travel. In the background, there was also an idea that the system could be used for the internal meetings of the company's staff.

Realm of institutions. There were several factors in the realm of institutions that directed the implementation process. The system implementation was organized in the same manner as that in which many previous ICT system implementations had taken place in the company. There was plenty of organizational communication on how and how much to use the system. One of the middle managers who were interviewed stated that "pedantic" classroom and internet-based training sessions and seminars were arranged for both employees and customers, and detailed time statistics were kept on the use of the system. At this point, the company sought to apply an implementation process corresponding to Table 1. The company's values and norms held large eLearning projects to be important ('eLearning' was the buzzword of the time); the report on a system test-period evaluation stated that the company had to make use of eLearning in various ways. In line with the generally prevailing enthusiasm for ICT, it was believed that live eLearning sessions increased the quality of learning, because they were interactive, learner-centered, and offered more on-demand knowledge sharing with experts. These assumptions became *encoded* in Script 1 as the project managers and ICT support staff of the company extensively informed other employees about the new meeting system, its use, possibilities, user training, and support functions. The *enactment* of the script took place as the employees in the customer training department familiarized themselves with the system and started to use it as a new tool for customer training.

Realm of action. However, very soon, the tide turned for large eLearning projects in the company. Internet-based customer training was abandoned as the customers did not have the required equipment and facilities, or they were not interested in training via the internet-based meeting system. They preferred traveling to training sessions as it provided an opportunity to be away – for a change – from their usual workplaces. One support person who was interviewed stated that the customer trainers feared that the new system might cost them their jobs or create too high a workload. According to this interviewee, this was one reason for the failure of the adoption of the system. The internet-based training also proved to be more expensive than anticipated. However, a small group of managers and sales people of the company discovered the potential usefulness of the system in replacing face-to-face meetings, and saving travel costs. They discovered that the internet-based meeting system was much more useful than e.g., a videoconferencing system. It was simple and easy to use and made it possible to speak, show material, and work together on a document. All this coincided with the company setting a stricter budget that required reduced travel costs from staff and rationalized time management. Therefore, what initially was a secondary aim for the system – to use it for the company's internal meetings – became the priority. Because of their personal needs and contextual changes, the system users *revised* the script to emphasize the system as a tool for internal meetings rather than for customer training. As the users started to function according to this newly found meaning of the system, they *externalized* it to challenge the institutional assumptions concerning the ICT systems in the company. Customer reluctance, customer trainer fears, and the high costs of internet-based training materials prevented the replication of the script of the use of the system for internet-based customer training, while some IT-enthusiastic managers of the company realized the potential of the system for reducing traveling time and costs in meeting team members in a geographically decentralized company. All the activities, events, and influencing issues at this time in the implementation process are depicted in Figure 2.

Script 2: The Internet-Based Meeting System Can be Used to Arrange Internal Meetings in This Company

A new script started to emerge for the internet-based meeting system. The system was now perceived as a tool for internal internet meetings, with a secondary emphasis on the possibility of using the system in in-house training. The goal was to reduce traveling costs, but also to get the company's expert knowledge to where it was needed. The employees' well-being at work was also emphasized; the system was seen to lead to reduced traveling and, thus, increased leisure time.

Realm of institutions. A profound change took place in how the internet-based meeting system was introduced to its users. The large-scale and formal introduction of a customer training system turned into a small-sized pilot project for an internal meeting system. The key characteristic of the adoption process was to provide users with a tool and let them decide whether the tool was useful for their work. The target was not to put the system into use in the whole company in one go, but to introduce the system gradually, to keep the expenses low, and to let users' experiences expand the use of the system. The new script (Script 2) was made visible, *encoded*, as the project managers and ICT support staff made information available for employees on the system, its use, possibilities, user training, and support functions. This time around, however, colleagues and managers acted as active agents between the organization level and employees by providing information about the system. The emphasis all along was on the fact that the use of the system was voluntary and based on the employees' needs. The *enactment* of the script took place as each employee had the opportunity to decide whether to learn to use the system or not.

Realm of actions. The top management, starting from the managing director, decided to use the internet-based meeting system in internal meetings. This signaled to the employees that the system was useful and beneficial. Furthermore, the benefits and effectiveness of the use of the system were publicized, and statistics about cost savings were shown to the employees. At first, experienced and enthusiastic IT users started to use the system in their meetings. User training, manuals, and other official support activities were available, but users were not interested in using them, because they did not "have time". New, spontaneous ways to use the system emerged at this point; for example, one unit organized in-house product training with the system. In this phase, the users actually *replicated* Script 2, emphasizing the voluntary use of the system in internal meetings. In-house training was also tried out, with good results. The users also chose different roles during the adoption process. Enthusiastic users actively convinced other employees of the usefulness of the system. Experienced users guided novices, who were able to identify these experienced users by using information from the grapevine. These various roles in the system use reflect the users' autonomy, initiative, and self-determination in the use of the system.

Script 1 was, therefore, revised on two levels. The events in the company affected shared mental models on both how to use the system and how to take it in use. The whole process described here led eventually to a change in the realm of institutions: a new way of using the system (as a tool for internal meetings) and a new way of introducing the system to employees (voluntarily, in a self-determined manner) emerged. The events, actions, and influencing issues during the process described above are depicted in Figure 3.

Possibilities and Problems of the Self-Determined Use of an ICT System as Perceived by the Interviewees

Most interviewees perceived many possibilities in the use of the system. For instance, the system allowed employees to travel less and thus have time for other things, meetings became shorter but more efficient, expert knowledge was easily available, and all this allowed users to plan their working days more flexibly. All the interviewees also mentioned that the system would enable considerable savings in travel expenses. In addition, the interviewees described the introduction process as successful, and they also approved of the system as a whole, because it was easy and practical to use. All the interviewees also emphasized, in different ways, how the system allowed them to work more efficiently and in a more meaningful manner. This may also relate to the fact that the interviewees were able to choose for themselves the best possible way to apply the system. All these positive views were shared by the support persons, operational employees, and middle managers alike. In addition, the support persons emphasized that the system allowed them to learn more about modern technology. For example, they explained that the skills they developed when using the system contributed to their general competencies and understanding of computer tools that can enhance communication and interaction. They perceived the system as providing great new opportunities for the company by offering new perspectives on various ways to use ICT tools in the organization. The middle managers, moreover, emphasized that the system allowed more efficient operations to be achieved without the employees' well-being being forgotten. One middle manager, when interviewed again in 2008, deduced that a key reason for the interviewees' positive assessment of the opportunities provided by the system was that they had to think about these possibilities and opportunities more carefully, as they – personally – had to decide whether or not to use the system.

The interviewees also mentioned some problems with the use of the system. They all mentioned problems caused by the unfamiliar communication style and technology. The most disturbing factors in the new ways of communication were a lack of non-verbal communication and immediate feedback, and the technical problems concerning delays with voices and interruptions to internet connections. One operational employee who was interviewed also stated that initial problems and failures in the use of the system might discourage people from sticking with the system. Indeed, one support person and two operational employees said that they were initially afraid to use the system – "How can I handle work tasks virtually? Am I able to handle the technology?" – but became more confident after having tried the system out. The middle managers who were interviewed, furthermore, did not want to use the system for customer contacts or if dealing with sensitive matters with colleagues, because they felt that trust was difficult to achieve via the system. Instead, they used the system only when handling pressing matters with familiar colleagues.

Although all the interviewees were in general satisfied with the system and its introduction, some support persons and operational employees had hoped for more formal advice and support during the adoption process. For example, one support person stated that employees should be systematically trained to use the system so that the threshold to participation in meetings and arranging meetings would be lower. The support persons in general worried about user acceptance: without it, the system would not be used. One operational employee who was interviewed talked about "controlled compulsion", which meant that the organization should promote the system as *the* tool for internal meetings, and also advise and finally even compel employees to use the system. All types of interviewees (i.e., support persons, operational employees, and middle managers alike) also expressed concern about other employees who did not understand how to use this handy and beneficial meeting system. In short, all types of interviewees experienced the system as such a good tool that they would have liked all employees to use it! However, the voluntary, self-determined nature of the adoption of the system did not bring about such quick, widespread adoption, but led to a situation in which there were only a few users at the beginning. One operational employee who was interviewed said that he would use the system more, but it was impossible, because his co-workers did not use it yet.

DISCUSSION AND CONCLUSION

The ICT system adoption described in this article cannot easily be fitted into the traditional ICT adoption process template summarized in Table 1. The company originally devised formal plans for the utilization of the internet-based meeting system to enhance customer training. But the whole implementation process ran into difficulties, because customer preferences, trainer doubts, high costs, and business downturns prevented these plans from being fulfilled. The implementation process was interrupted in Stage 5 of Table 1. The implementation process succeeded, however, after the process was conducted differently: users were left to decide for themselves if they needed the system and how they would use it. The users were able to experience control over their work and freedom of choice in what and how to do their work, and in that way to experience autonomy and be intrinsically motivated. The interviewees' obvious enthusiasm about the system points out that the self-determined adoption truly led to intrinsic motivation. Revision of the initial script in Figure 2 was a crucial point in redirect-

Figure 2. Script 1: The internet-based meeting system is the means to train customers in this company

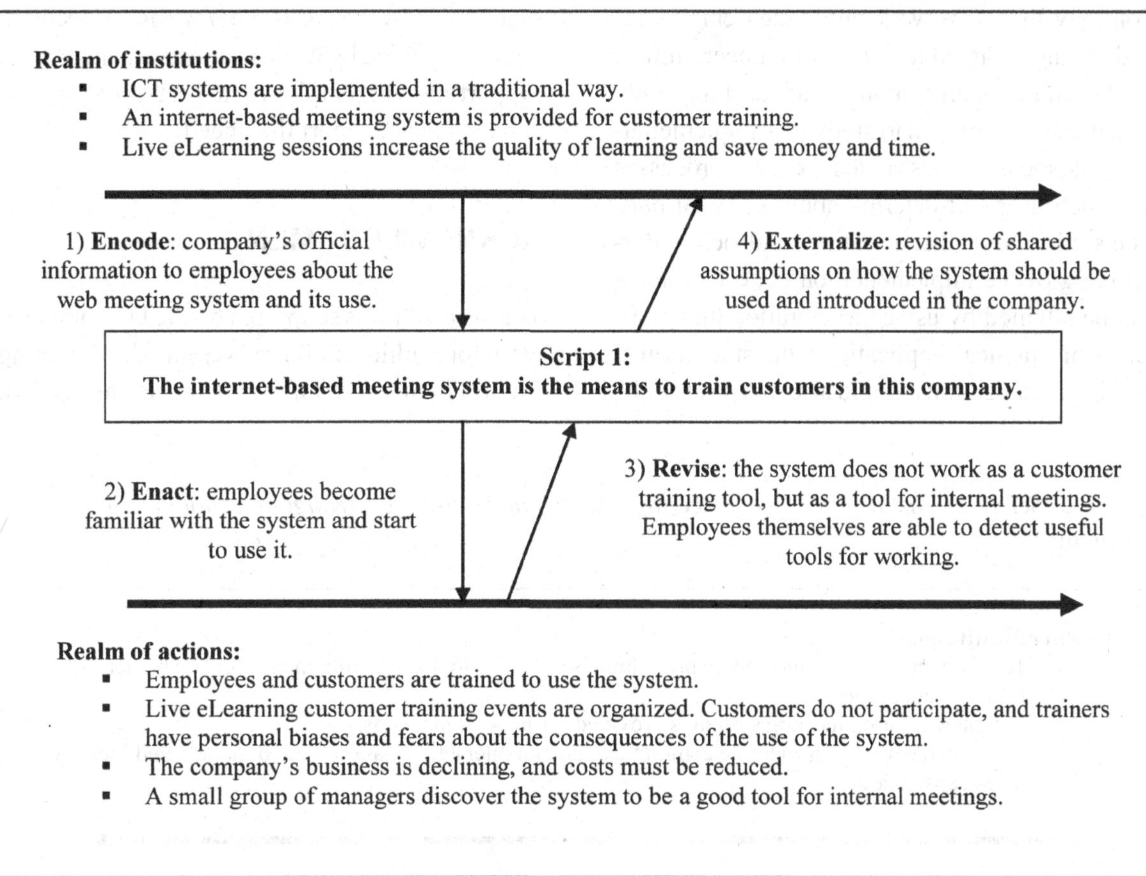

ing the whole implementation process towards new opportunities.

On the basis of the case study, we conclude that the self-determined adoption of ICT systems can have benefits. As employees are able to discover the benefits of the system by themselves and decide whether to use the system, they become motivated and committed. Freedom, voluntariness, and control over one's own work make employees satisfied and reduce user resistance. A self-determined employee may even transcend her work role, and show features of organizational citizenship behavior (Organ, Podsakoff, & MacKenzie, 2006). In the case study, some interviewees had obviously turned into self-appointed advocates of the system and worried that other employees were not reaping the full benefit of the system. A self-determined implementation process may thus lead to a greater probability of success in the adoption and acceptance of an ICT system. Moreover, because the use of the system is based on the real needs of employees' work activities, the organization has invested in a meaningful and useful system.

However, self-determined adoption has problems as well. It is quite an unsystematic process; there are no clear signs for employees that the company considers the system important and beneficial. Employees might not receive consistent information on the system, and therefore they start to wonder whether other employees use the system and what the official recommendations concerning its use are. A slow and unsystematic process may also appear too inefficient and risky from the point of view of management. Self-determined adoption may therefore work only when employees and managers are able to live with uncertainties.

The main theoretical implication of the study is that it seems fruitful to study ICT implementations as socially constructed, organic processes of which user self-determination is a vital part. The study shows that a realistic and rich understanding of the implementation of ICT systems can be attained by using structuration theory. In terms of practical implications, the study points out that organizations should also be open to self-determined processes in the implementation of ICT systems. However, self-determination needs to be accompanied by well-designed organizational support allowing employees to get the information and technical support they need.

ACKNOWLEDGMENT

This research was supported by the Doctoral Program for Multidisciplinary Research on Learning Environments, Finland, and the Finnish Work

Figure 3. Script 2: The internet-based meeting system can be used to arrange internal meetings in this company

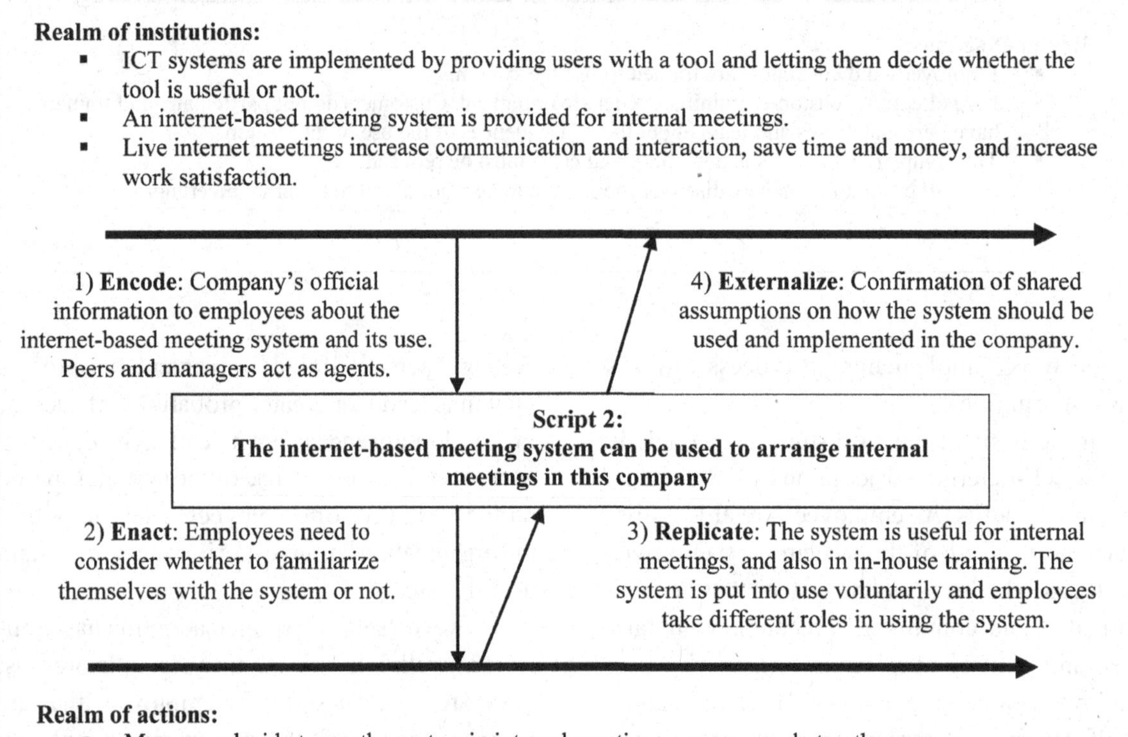

Environment Fund. Mari Kira would like to gratefully acknowledge funding from the Academy of Finland, grant number: 119612.

REFERENCES

Adams, B., Berner, E. S., & Wyatt, J. R. (2004). Best practice. Applying strategies to overcome user resistance in a group of clinical managers to a business software application: A case study. *Journal of Organizational and End User Computing, 16*(4), 55–64.

Andriessen, J. H. E. (2003). *Working with groupware. Understanding and evaluating collaboration technology*. London: Springer.

Apel, K.-O. (1972). The a priori of communication and the foundations of the humanities. *Man and World, 51*, 3–37. doi:10.1007/BF01253016

Barley, S. R. (1986). Technology as an occasion for structuring: Evidence from observations of CT scanners and social order of radiology departments. *Administrative Science Quarterly, 31*, 78–108. doi:10.2307/2392767

Barley, S. R., & Tolbert, P. S. (1997). Institutionalization and structuration: studying the links between action and institution. *Organization Studies, 18*(1), 93–117. doi:10.1177/017084069701800106

Berger, P., & Luckmann, T. (1967). *The social construction of reality*. New York: Doubleday.

Chen, Y., & Lou, H. (2002). Toward an understanding of the behavioral intention to use a groupware application. *Journal of End User Computing, 14*(4), 1–16.

Cooper, R. B., & Zmud, R. W. (1990). Information technology implementation research: A technological diffusion approach. *Management Science, 36*(2), 123–139. doi:10.1287/mnsc.36.2.123

Davis, F. D. (1989). Perceived usefulness, perceived ease of use, and user acceptance of information technology. *Management Information Systems Quarterly, 13*(3), 319–342. doi:10.2307/249008

Deci, E. L., & Ryan, R. M. (2000). The "what" and "why" of goal pursuits: Human needs and the self-determination of behavior. *Psychological Inquiry, 11*(4), 227–268. doi:10.1207/S15327965PLI1104_01

Deci, E. L., Ryan, R. M., & Koestner, R. (1999). A meta-analytic review of experiments examining the effects of extrinsic rewards on intrinsic motivation. *Psychological Bulletin, 125*(6), 627–668. doi:10.1037/0033-2909.125.6.627

DeSanctis, G., & Poole, M. S. (1994). Capturing the complexity in advanced technology use: adaptive structuration theory. *Organization Science, 5*(2), 121–132. doi:10.1287/orsc.5.2.121

DeSanctis, G., Poole, M. S., Dickson, G. W., & Jackson, B. M. (1993). Interpretive analysis of team use of group technologies. *Journal of Organizational Computing, 3*(1), 1–29. doi:10.1080/10919399309540193

Dubois, A., & Gadde, L. (2002). Systematic combining: an abductive approach to case research. *Journal of Business Research, 55*(7), 553–560. doi:10.1016/S0148-2963(00)00195-8

Ehrlich, S. F. (1987). Strategies for encouraging successful adoption of office communication systems. *ACM Transactions on Office Information Systems, 5*(4), 340–357. doi:10.1145/42196.42198

Furumo, K., & Melcher, A. (2006). The importance of social structure in implementing ERP systems: A case study using adaptive structuration theory. *Journal of Information Technology Case and Application Research, 8*(2), 39–58.

Gagné, M., & Deci, E. L. (2005). Self-determination theory and work motivation. *Journal of Organizational Behavior*, *26*(4), 331–362. doi:10.1002/job.322

Garrison, D. R. (1997). Self-directed learning: Toward a comprehensive model. *Adult Education Quarterly*, *48*(1), 18–33. doi:10.1177/074171369704800103

Giddens, A. (1984). *Constitution of society outline of the theory of structuration*. Cambridge, UK: Polity Press.

Gladstone, B. M., Volpe, T., & Boydell, K. M. (2007). Issues encountered in a qualitative secondary analysis of help-seeking in the prodrome to psychosis. *The Journal of Behavioral Health Services & Research*, *34*(4), 431–442. doi:10.1007/s11414-007-9079-x

Gleitman, H., Fridlund, A. J., & Reisberg, D. (1999). *Psychology* (5th ed.). New York: W. W. Norton & Company.

Grudin, J. (1994). Eight challenges for developers. *Communications of the ACM*, *37*(1), 93–105. doi:10.1145/175222.175230

Grudin, J. T. (1989). Why groupware applications fail: problems in design and evaluation. *Office Technology and People*, *4*(3), 245–264.

Heaton, H. (1998). Secondary analysis of qualitative data. *Social Research Update, 22*. Retrieved February 24, 2009, from http://sru.soc.surrey.ac.uk/SRU22.html

Hinds, P. S., Vogel, R. J., & Clarke-Steffen, L. (1997). The possibilities and pitfalls of doing a secondary analysis of a qualitative data set. *Qualitative Health Research*, *7*(3), 408–424. doi:10.1177/104973239700700306

Jiang, J. J., Muhanna, W. A., & Klein, G. (2000). User resistance and strategies for promoting acceptance across system types. *Information & Management*, *37*(1), 25–36. doi:10.1016/S0378-7206(99)00032-4

Jones, M., & Karsten, H. (2003). *Review: Structuration theory and information systems research*. Retrieved February 10, 2009, from http://www.jbs.cam.ac.uk/research/working_papers/2003/wp0311.pdf

Jones, M. R., & Karsten, H. (2008). Giddens's structuration theory and information systems research. *Management Information Systems Quarterly*, *32*(1), 127–157.

Karasek, R. A. (1979). Job demand, job decision latitude, and mental strain: Implications for job redesign. *Administrative Science Quarterly*, *24*(2), 285–308. doi:10.2307/2392498

Kira, M., & Forslin, J. (2008). Seeking regenerative work in the post-bureaucratic transition. *Journal of Organizational Change Management*, *21*(1), 76–91. doi:10.1108/09534810810847048

Klaus, T., Wingreen, S., & Blanton, J. E. (2007). Examining user resistance and management strategies in enterprise system implementations. In *Proceedings of the ACM SIGMIS CPR Conference on Computer Personnel Research*, St. Louis, MO (pp. 55-62).

Knowles, M. S. (1975). *Self-directed learning. A guide for learners and teachers*. Englewood Cliffs, NJ: Prentice Hall.

Kouroubali, A. (2002). Structuration theory and conception-reality gaps: Addressing cause and effect of implementation outcomes in health care information systems. In *Proceedings of the 35th Hawaii International Conference on System Sciences*. Washington, DC: IEEE.

Kuzel, A. J. (2000). Sampling in qualitative inquiry. In Crabtree, B. F., & Miller, W. L. (Eds.), *Doing qualitative research* (2nd ed., pp. 31–44). Thousand Oaks, CA: Sage.

Kvale, S. (1989). To validate is to question. In Kvale, S. (Ed.), *Issues of validity in qualitative research* (pp. 73–92). London: Chartwell Bratt.

Kwon, T. H., & Zmud, R. W. (1987). Unifying the fragmented models of information systems implementation. In Bolan, R. J., & Hirschheim, R. A. (Eds.), *Critical issues in information systems research* (pp. 227–251). New York: John Wiley.

Lewin, K. (1952). Group decision and social change. In Newcombe, G. E., & Hartley, E. L. (Eds.), *Readings in social psychology* (pp. 459–473). New York: Henry Holt.

Miles, M. B., & Huberman, A. M. (1994). *Qualitative data analysis. An expanded sourcebook* (2nd ed.). Thousand Oaks, CA: Sage.

Miller, W. L., & Crabtree, B. F. (1992). Primary care research: A multimethod typology and qualitative road map. In Crabtree, B. F., & Miller, W. L. (Eds.), *Doing qualitative research* (2nd ed., pp. 3–28). Thousand Oaks, CA: Sage.

Munkvold, B. E. (2003). *Implementing collaboration technologies in industry. Case examples and lessons*. London: Springer.

Nunamaker, J. F. Jr. (1997). Future research in group support systems: Needs, some questions and possible directions. *International Journal of Human-Computer Studies*, *47*(3), 357–385. doi:10.1006/ijhc.1997.0142

Organ, D. W., Podsakoff, P. M., & MacKenzie, S. B. (2006). *Organizational citizenship behavior: Its nature, antecedents, and consequences*. Thousand Oaks, CA: Sage.

Orlikowski, W. J. (1992). The duality of technology: rethinking the concept of technology in organizations. *Organization Science*, *3*(3), 398–427. doi:10.1287/orsc.3.3.398

Orlikowski, W. J. (1993). Learning from notes: Organizational issues in groupware implementation. *The Information Society*, *9*(3), 237–250. doi:10.1080/01972243.1993.9960143

Orlikowski, W. J. (2000). Using technology and constituting structures: A practice lens for studying technology in organizations. *Organization Science*, *11*(4), 404–428. doi:10.1287/orsc.11.4.404.14600

Orlikowski, W. J., & Hofman, J. D. (1997). An improvisational model of change management: the case of groupware technologies. *Sloan Management Review*, *38*(2), 11–21.

Orlikowski, W. J., & Robey, D. (1991). Information technology and the structuring of organizations. *Information Systems Research*, *2*(2), 143–169. doi:10.1287/isre.2.2.143

Patton, M. Q. (1990). *Qualitative evaluation and research methods* (2nd ed.). Newbury Park, CA: Sage.

Poole, M. S., & DeSanctis, G. (2004). Structuration theory in information systems research: Methods and controversies. In Whitman, M. E., & Woszczynski, A. B. (Eds.), *The handbook of information systems research* (pp. 206–249). Hershey, PA: IGI Global.

Ryan, R. M., & Deci, E. L. (2000). Intrinsic and extrinsic motivations: classic definitions and new directions. *Contemporary Educational Psychology*, *25*(1), 54–67. doi:10.1006/ceps.1999.1020

Sandberg, J. (2005). How do we justify knowledge produced within interpretive approaches? *Organizational Research Methods*, *8*(1), 41–68. doi:10.1177/1094428104272000

Seale, C. (1999). *The quality of qualitative research*. London: Sage.

Siggelkow, N. (2007). Persuasion with case studies. *Academy of Management Journal*, *50*(1), 20–24.

Silverman, D. (2006). *Interpreting qualitative data* (3rd ed.). Thousand Oaks, CA: Sage.

Stake, R. E. (1994). Case studies. In Denzin, K. N., & Lincoln, Y. S. (Eds.), *Handbook of qualitative research* (pp. 236–247). Thousand Oaks, CA: Sage.

Sundholm, L. H. (2000). *Self-determination in organisational change*. Jyväskylä, Finland: University of Jyväskylä.

Thorne, S. (1994). Secondary analysis in qualitative research: Issues and implications. In Morse, J. M. (Ed.), *Critical issues in qualitative research methods* (pp. 263–279). Thousand Oaks, CA: Sage.

Venkatesh, V., Morris, M. G., Davis, G. B., & Davis, F. D. (2003). User acceptance of information technology: Toward a unified view. *Management Information Systems Quarterly*, *27*(3), 425–478.

Walsham, G., & Han, C. K. (1993). Information systems strategy formation and implementation: The case of a central government agency. *Accounting. Management & Information Technology*, *3*(3), 191–209. doi:10.1016/0959-8022(93)90016-Y

Weber, R. P. (1990). *Basic content analysis*. Beverly Hills, CA: Sage.

West, R. E., Waddoups, G., & Graham, C. R. (2007). Understanding the experience of instructors as they adopt a course management system. *Educational Technology Research and Development*, *55*(1), 1–26. doi:10.1007/s11423-006-9018-1

Wheeler, B. C., Dennis, A. R., & Press, L. I. (1999). Groupware Comes to the Internet: Charting a New World. *The Data Base for Advances in Information Systems*, *30*(3-4), 8–21.

Yin, R. K. (2003a). *Applications of case study research* (2nd ed.). Thousand Oaks, CA: Sage.

Yin, R. K. (2003b). *Case study research: design and methods* (3rd ed.). Thousand Oaks, CA: Sage.

ENDNOTES

1. The name of the model is originally 'Model of information systems implementation process'.
2. The case study thus took place before free internet-based meeting and telecommunicating systems (such as Skype) became widely used.

APPENDIX

Table 1. Participants in the study, their job titles and purpose of use of the system

Job Title	Purpose of use of the system
1. Support persons, who supported other's use of the system	
1.) A customer training designer A, (a key informant of the study)	Participated in small, mostly internal meetings once a week, developed electronic customer training and trained users.
2.) An office assistant	Coordinated global in-house product and sales training (organized training sessions, guided participants, tested web connections) 2-3 times a week
3.) A customer training designer B, (a key informant of the study)	Participated in small internal meetings once a week with colleagues, guided other system users.
4.) A human resource developer	Participated in small internal meetings once a month with colleagues, occasionally supported other employees' use of the system
2. Operational employees, who used the system actively in order not to travel to meetings and training	
5.) A trainer and coordinator of global product training	Provided global in-house product training with the system for many years to a great number of participants at a time (about 300 trainees per year), edited sessions
6.) A global technology coordinator	Participated in global web meetings, participated and trained others with the system in global in-house product and sales training 102 times a week
7.) A product sales director A	Participated in global in-house product and sales training, and internal team meetings every other week
8.) A product sales director B	Participated twice and trained once with the system in global product and sales training and participated a few times in internal web meetings
3. Middle managers, who used the system actively in order not to travel to meetings and training	
9.) A manager in the IT department, the key advocate of the system (a key informant of the study)	Participated in global or internal web meetings every day, trained with the system to some extent, edited sessions, coordinated the implementation of the web meting system
10.) A customer training manager	Participated in internal and global web meetings every other week with groups from the organization's different parts
11.) A manager of a business line	Participated in global executive management team meetings: the team had three web meetings and then one face-to-face meeting

This work was previously published in Journal of Organizational and End User Computing, Volume 22, Issue 4, edited by M. Adam Mahmood, pp. 51-69, copyright 2010 by IGI Publishing (an imprint of IGI Global).

Chapter 8
A Model of System Re-Configurability and Pedagogical Usability in an E-Learning Context:
A Faculty Perspective

Jianfeng Wang
Mansfield University of Pennsylvania, USA

William J. Doll
The University of Toledo, USA

Xiaodong Deng
Oakland University, USA

ABSTRACT

Course management systems (CMSs) enable institutions to engage users efficiently, increase enrollment without major facilities investments, and serve geographically dispersed student markets on an ongoing basis. The full benefits of technology cannot be realized if faculty do not adopt the new technology and use it to achieve their instructional design objectives. From a faculty perspective, pedagogical usability of the software is an important factor affecting technology adoption and effective implementation. Pedagogical usability is measured using Chickering and Gamson's seven principles of good educational practice. In a distance learning context, this paper provides an initial exploratory study of how faculty perceptions of CMS software characteristics like content re-configurability, interaction re-configurability, and modularity design help faculty implement good pedagogical principles. Additionally, a model is presented that links CMS software design characteristics like content re-configurability, interaction re-configurability, and modularity design with the pedagogical usability assessments of faculty. This model is tested using a sample of 56 faculty members using WebCT at a mid-western university.

DOI: 10.4018/978-1-4666-0140-6.ch008

INTRODUCTION

E-learning has become pervasive among educational institutions from K-12 school districts, to community colleges, and to universities. With course management systems (CMSs), these institutions are implementing successful strategies for engaging users, increasing enrollment capacity without making major facilities investment, and serving geographically dispersed student populations. The benefits of e-learning include cost efficiency (Evans & Haase, 2001), easy and convenient 24/7 access from anywhere, scalability, and timeliness (Clarke & Hermens, 2001). The full benefits of e-learning cannot be realized if faculty do not adopt the new technology and fully use it to achieve their course design objectives. To achieve course design objectives, faculty need software that is pedagogically usable e.g., software that helps instructors implement good pedagogical principles in developing and implementing their courses.

Usability theory has been widely examined in computer systems and web-based systems (Nielsen, 1993; Pearrow, 2000; Shneidermann, 1998; Agarwal & Venkatesh, 2002; Palmer, 2002; Venkatesh & Agarwal, 2006; Venkatesh & Ramesh, 2006), but few studies investigate the relevance and applicability of usability concept in the design of digital learning environments (Zaharias, 2005). Agrarwal and Venkatesh (2002) argue that the nature of the application and the type of user should be considered in developing a useful usability metric. The digital learning environment is a unique context for studying usability.

In this unique context, each faculty member assumes the dual roles of application (i.e., on-line course) developer and system user. As course developers, they appropriate the functional and interface features embedded in the software to design the on-line course. As users, they use the system to communicate with students, monitor student activities, and evaluate student performance. Making an e-learning system usable basically involves two aspects: pedagogical usability and technical usability (Melis et al., 2003). Simply put, pedagogical usability aims at supporting the learning process while technical usability involves methods for ensuring a trouble-free interaction with the system. Technical usability is analogous to ease of use. While considerable attention has been focused on the ease of use construct (Lewis, 1995; Tilson et al., 1998; Raquel, 2001; Palmer, 2002), the construct of pedagogical usability of course management software has not been adequately addressed in the extant literature.

This paper focuses on the pedagogical usability of CMSs in an e-learning context. Pedagogical usability is defined as the extent to which the CMS software helps the instructor implement good pedagogical practices. The pedagogical literature suggests Seven Principles (Chickering & Gamson, 1987) of instructional design that are good teaching methods for traditional as well as e-learning courses. Technology contributes to pedagogical objectives if it encourages contact between faculty and students, facilitates cooperation among students, uses active learning techniques, enables prompt feedback, emphasizes time on task, helps communicate high expectations, and respects diverse talents and ways of learning (Chickering & Ehrmann, 1996).

If the power of CMSs is to be fully realized, e-learning technology should be designed to help faculty achieve these pedagogical goals. Based upon the information systems and e-learning literatures, this study provides an initial exploratory model of pedagogical usability of CMSs from a faculty perspective. This model links CMS software design characteristics - content re-configurability (Horton, 2000; Skyrme, 2001; Wild et al., 2002), interaction re-configurability (Kilby, 2001), and modularity design (WebCT Website at www.webct.com; Markus et al., 2002) - with pedagogical usability. This model is tested using a sample of 56 faculty members from an Ohio university.

THEORY DEVELOPMENT AND LITERATURE REVIEW

The notion of usability is a key theme in the human-computer interaction (HCI) literature (Zhang & Li, 2005). Research in the HCI tradition has long asserted that the study of human factors is critical to the successful design and implementation of technological devices. The overarching goal of a majority of the HCI work has been to propose techniques, methods, and guidelines for designing better and more usable artifacts.

Usability

Usability has been conceptually defined and operationally measured in multiple ways (Agarwal & Venkatesh, 2002). Definitions of usability range from the high-level conceptualization incorporated in the ISO 9241 standard (Karat, 1997) to more focused descriptions that include notions of user relevance, efficiency, user attitude, learn-ability, and safety (Lecerof & Paterno, 1998).

Gray and Salzman (1998) succinctly summarize the state of affairs related to the definition of usability noting that "the most important issue facing usability researchers and practitioners alike [is] the construct of usability itself." Bernard et al. (1981) suggest that a "truly usable system must be compatible not only with the characteristics of human perception and action, but, most critically, with the users' cognitive skills in communication, understanding, memory, and problem solving". Lecerof and Paterno (1998) underscore that the most important aspect of usability is contingent upon the actual system. For example, ease of use may be a primary criterion for systems designed for use by children, while efficiency is likely to be major usability goal in the design of banking systems (Agarwal & Venkatesh, 2002). Pedagogical usability may be a major consideration in the design of a CMS for e-learning.

The information systems design literature attempts to identify a set of principles and common practices that will ensure usability. Usability of an information system is equivalent to a set of design principles including: (1) consistency of the interface, (2) response time, (3) mapping and metaphors, (4) interaction style, and (5) multimedia and audiovisual (Nielsen, 1993).

In Web site research, Nielsen (2000) extends these design principles to include: (1) navigation, (2) response time, (3) credibility, and (4) content. This suggests easy-to-use navigation, frequent updating, minimal download times, relevance to users, and high-quality content that takes advantage of capabilities unique to the online medium (Nielsen, 1993). Based on Nielsen's (1993, 2000) works, Palmer (2002) develops and validates a Web site usability metric including download delay, navigability, site content, interactivity, and responsiveness. His study reveals that Web site success is significantly associated with above dimensions of usability. Both the information systems (IS) literature and the Web site research do not directly address the concept of usability in the context of CMSs for e-learning.

Lecerof and Paterno (1998) argue that what constitutes usability is contingent upon both the task for which the system is to be used and the target users. Agarwal and Venkatesh (2002) use a heuristic evaluation procedure for examining the usability of Web sites. They claim that a critical requirement of a useful usability metric is its ability to discriminate across Web sites from different industries and among different types of users. They argue that the salience of usability characteristics varies depending on the user task and industry to which the Web site belongs. Thus, they suggest that the instrumental task goals of a user are key determinants to what they seek from a Web site. Based on Microsoft Usability Guidelines (MUG), the metrics of usability Agarwal and Venkatesh (2002) recommend include content, ease of use, promotion, made-for the medium, and emotion. Thus, usability is a multifaceted concept (Agarwal & Venkatesh, 2002) that depends upon the context.

Figure 1. Multifaceted nature of usability in the e-learning context

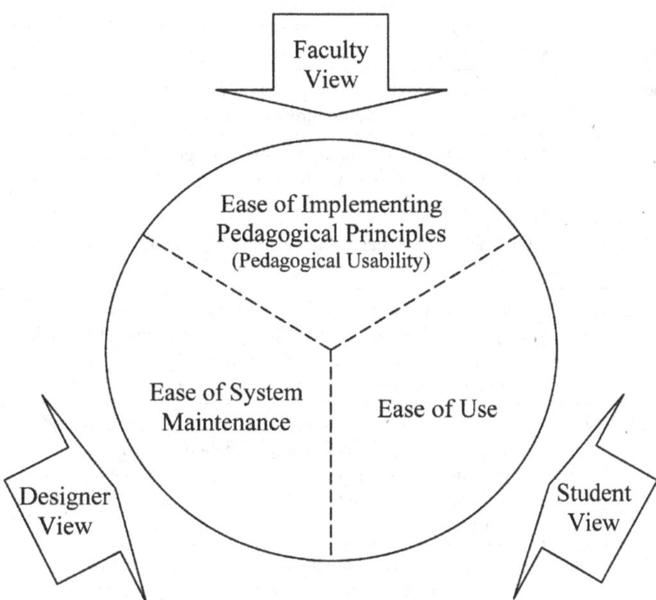

A Faculty Perspective on Usability in an E-Learning Context

In the e-learning context, multiple stakeholders (faculty, students, and software designers) exist and each of these stakeholders has a different perspective for evaluating the usability of CMSs. Thus, usability is not entirely objective in nature, but rather is closely intertwined with the stakeholders' personal interpretation of the artifact and their interaction with the software (Agarwal & Venkatesh, 2002).

The concept of usability from different stakeholder perspectives is depicted in Figure 1. The arrows directed at the circle represent the faculty, student, and software designer view points for evaluating the usability of CMSs. The circle represents the multifaceted nature of usability. Usability can be evaluated from the perspective of whether the system is characterized by ease of implementing effective pedagogical principles, ease of use, and ease of system maintenance. The dotted lines between each facet indicate that each facet is part of an overall usability construct. The arrows point to the primary criterion each stakeholder uses to evaluate usability. For example, pedagogical usability (e.g., whether the system eases faculty implementation of pedagogical principles) may be the primary usability criterion from a faculty perspective.

Silius and Tervakari (2003) use the term "pedagogical usability" to denote whether the tools, content, interface and tasks of the web-based learning environments support various learners to learn in diverse learning contexts, according to selected pedagogical objectives. They divide the pedagogical usability into three main categories: 1. support for organization of the teaching and studying; 2. support for learning and tutoring processes as well as the achievement of learning objectives; and 3. support for the development of learning skills (interaction with other actors, growth of learners' autonomy and self-direction). Tutoring and designed learning processes should

Table 1. Technology's Role in Implementing the Seven Principles of Good Practice

Principles of Good Practice	The Roles Technology Can Play
Good Practice Encourages Student-Faculty Contact	Computer-mediated communication provides faster, more open and more reflective communication.
Good Practice Encourages Cooperation among Students	Computer-mediated communication facilitates group interactions, team problem solving, and community building through chat rooms and discussion forums.
Good Practice Encourages Active Learning	Technology-based simulations allow for greater interactivity and active student engagement in decision making. Primary resources in digital format enhance student scholarly research.
Good Practice Gives Prompt Feedback	On-line quizzes enable students to get immediate feedback on what they know and don't know.
Good Practice Emphasizes Time on Task	Technology can dramatically improve time on task. Technology can help students learn at home or work saving hours otherwise spent commuting to and from campus. Students can spend more time on task by fitting their course work into the work schedule. Students can access important resources easily, saving time.
Good Practice Communicates High Expectations	New technologies can communicate high expectations explicitly and efficiently. E-learning can set powerful learning challenges that drive students to not only acquire information but sharpen the cognitive skills of analysis, synthesis, application, and evaluation. High expectations can be illustrated with samples of excellent, average, and poor performance.
Good Practice Respects Diverse Talents and Ways of Learning	Technology provides the means for instructors to build multiple pathways to learning within the same course by allowing content discussion to be provided in multiple ways. Students can work at their own pace. Student teams can work in study groups without constraints of time and place.

Source: Adapted from Chickering and Ehrmann (1996)

be based on appropriate, context-sensitive learning and teaching models in which motivation, reflection, authenticity, contextualization and transfer are taken into account (Jonassen, 1995; Mezirow, 1997).

Silius and Tervakari (2003) argue that the traditional usability concepts are not adequate in an educational context. A web-based learning environment could be usable in some ways (ease of use), but not pedagogically usable and vice versa, although there could be some overlap in the problems identified (Albion, 1999; Labbate, 1996; Quinn, 1996; Squires, 1997). In CMSs, pedagogical usability is an important consideration in faculty adoption and on-going use decisions.

This study defines pedagogical usability in terms of Chickering and Gamson's (1987) seven principles of good teaching practices. These principles address the teacher's how, not the subject-mater what, of good educational practice. These principles are based on 50 years of educational research on the way teachers teach and students learn. The first column of Table 1 summarizes these seven principles. The rationale for how these seven practices improve learning is explained below.

Encouraging student-faculty contact is the most important factor in student motivation and involvement. Faculty concern helps students get through rough times and keep on working. Encouraging cooperation among students is important because learning is enhanced when it is more like a team effort than a solo race. Working with others often increases involvement in learning. Sharing one's ideas and responding to others' reactions improves thinking and deepens understanding.

Good practice also encourages active learning. Learning is not a spectator sport. Students do not learn much just sitting in class and listening to teachers. Students must talk about what they are learning, write about it, and relate it to past experiences. Active learning helps them make what they learn part of themselves.

Good practice also involves giving prompt feedback. Knowing what you know and don't know focuses learning. Good practice emphasizes time on task. Time plus energy equals learning. There is no substitute for time on task and using the time well. Good practice also communicates high expectations. Expect more and you will get it. Finally, good practice respects diverse talents and ways of learning. People bring many different talents and styles of learning to college. Students need the opportunity to show their talents and learn in ways that work for them.

These seven principles have been used widely to guide course design processes and objectives in traditional classroom environments. They are also valid for e-learning (see The Ohio Learning Network Web site - www.oln.org). The second column in Table 1 describes how technology can help faculty implement these seven principles of good pedagogical practice.

A MODEL OF PEDAGOGICAL USABILITY

From a faculty perspective, the main consideration in evaluating the pedagogical usability of CMSs is whether the software helps them implement the effective pedagogical practices described in Chickering and Gamson's (1987) Seven Principles. In this study, we adopt these widely used Seven Principles to measure the pedagogical usability from a faculty perspective.

Pedagogical usability is a process measure, not an outcome measure. It is the extent to which the system software helps implement good pedagogical practices. It is distinct from outcome measures in distance learning such as cost benefits (Lawhead et al., 1997; Smith, 2001), learner achievements (Benigno & Trentin, 2000), and learning satisfaction (Teh, 1999).

Jackson and Anagnostopoulou (2001) argue that one problem in e-learning is the common juxtaposition of pedagogy and technology. Although the natural tendency is to separate them, faculty should consider pedagogy and technology simultaneously as they design the course and develop the students' on-line learning experience. The diversity of the student needs and instructional objectives suggests that e-learning technology should provide a high level of flexibility to meet varied needs. User interactions with sites that exhibit higher than normal flexibility have been significantly associated with performance improvement (Took, 1990).

The authors contend that it is important to measure system reconfigurability to assess its impact on the pedagogical usability of CMSs. While pedagogical usability is defined in terms of whether the CMSs help the faculty implement good educational practices, our model (see Figure 2) includes aspects of system re-configurability as predictors of pedagogical usability. System re-configurability factors that contribute to faculty perceptions of pedagogical usability are content re-configurability, interaction re-configurability, and modularity design. During on-line teaching, faculty members need to reconfigure CMSs due to the different subject areas and instructional objectives. Thus, reconfigurable CMS software should help teachers with different needs implement good educational practices appropriate for their subject area and student characteristics.

Content Re-Configurability

In this study, content re-configurability is defined as the capability of the software to provide a wide range of options for instructors to load information related to the course. CMSs are a type of web-based system. Prior research on Web site usability found that content and interaction dimensions were important to web site success (Nielsen, 2000; Agarwal & Venkatesh, 2002; Palmer, 2002).

Figure 2. A Model of pedagogical usability in an e-learning context

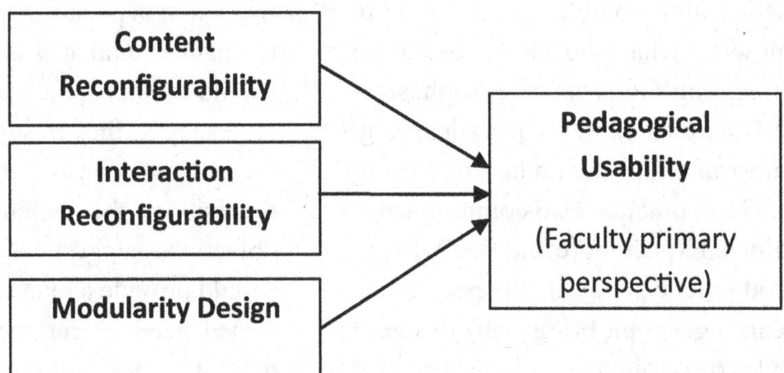

The first step in developing a course is to gather the materials for student use on the content list (Horton, 2000). Content provides the bricks for a virtual pyramid. In e-learning, content might be represented in a Word, Excel, PowerPoint, or PDF format. PowerPoint file may have narrated slides to improve comprehension. Skyrme (2001) suggests that, for certain kinds of information, the use of audio, images, and video enhances student comprehension. Content re-configurability of a CMS enables diverse forms of content to be easily loaded, sequenced, and rearranged to aid the instructional process.

Interaction Re-Configurability

In this research, interaction re-configurability is defined as the capability of the software to enable faculty to set up on-line communication mechanisms or forums. Interaction mechanisms include chat rooms, discussion forums, project groups, on-line submissions, quizzes, on-line simulations, and email. In CMSs, the objectives of these mechanisms are to help students communicate with faculty, cooperate with each other, receive prompt feedback, engage in active learning exercises that require time on task.

A key capability of CMSs is its capacity to support greater interactivity. Kilby (2001) argues that online training often occurs without extensive interaction between members of the class and the trainer. Without careful course design, this could lead to an anti-social environment where learners feel isolated. Interaction re-configurability of a CMS enables faculty to add, modify, or delete mechanisms by which students interact with the course content, the instructor, and other students.

Modularity Design

Modularity design is defined as the capability of the software to use a collection of sequentially arranged pages with a table of contents, built-in navigation links, and optional interactive tools. A typical example of modularity design is a Test or Learning Unit function where instructors do not need to create exams or assignments by reinventing the wheel. This capability is used to create learning modules. A learning module is a convenient way of organizing the student's learning experience. Learning modules are organized into a hierarchy and sequence, where the sequence of pages is the typical route that you want your students to follow.

Such modularity design is a useful means of managing complexity (Ethiraj & Levinthal, 2004). Ulrich and Eppinger (1999) argue that modular design structures are favored over integrated ones when flexibility and rapid innovation are more important than overall performance. In IS design theories, Markus et al. (2002) propose that componentizing everything is an effective principle guiding the IS design of emergent knowledge processing systems. In the e-learning context, new users with situated and emergent needs are continually encountered. Design modularity should be an effective way of responding to these emergent needs by enabling faculty to organize their course materials in a logical order.

Hypotheses Development

The more software system makes it easier for faculty to reconfigure the content of their on-line courses, the more they feel the software can help them implement good instructional practices. In education literature, Heeter (1989) argues that the ease of adding or reconfiguring content is an essential capability of technologies in teaching. In distance learning environment, faculty use multimedia resources, such as URL, pictures, audio/video clips, and animation to enrich course content, and, by this reconfiguration of the Web site, achieve various pedagogical principles of good practice. For example, by enabling faculty to post content in different formats and presentations (e.g., text, simulation, PowerPoint, video clips), the system helps respect diverse talents and ways of learning. Thus, we contend:

H1: The greater the content re-configurability, the greater the pedagogical usability.

Due to the lack of face-to-face contact, many researches emphasize that interaction is an important component of online course design (Chou, 2003; Garrison & Cleveland-Innes, 2005). Based on the results of their empirical study, Garrison and Cleveland-Innes (2005) suggest that interaction must be a specific course design goal. They also suggest that, if deep approaches to learning are to be achieved, interaction must be facilitated and directed in a sustained manner. Holsapple and Lee-Post (2006) find that students desire a human touch such as seeing other students' comments, being able to chat with other students, and interacting with other students in on-line forums. CMSs provide various tools such as discussion boards, feedback forums, chat rooms, email, and team groups to increase the communication and collaboration among teacher-learner, learner-learner, and learner-content (Moore, 1999). Thus, we argue:

H2: The greater the interaction re-configurability, the greater the pedagogical usability.

Most CMSs provide module or unit design functions for instructors. These modules contain self-paced activities like objectives, presentation, discussion topics, quizzes, and assignments. Using these modules, instructors may set up specific navigation patterns and time frames that emphasize time on task and provide avenues for prompt and reflective feedback. Where faculty members wish to make on-the-spot changes to their web sites, Ulrich and Eppinger (1999) argue that modular design structures provide flexibility and enable rapid innovation. This flexibility and rapid innovation enable faculty to easily changes that implement any of the seven principles of good practice. This suggests a third hypothesis:

H3: The greater the modularity design, the greater the pedagogical usability.

METHODOLOGY

To test these hypotheses, the authors examine the literature to generate items and conduct a two round heuristic evaluation procedure to make sure that the items are measuring their corresponding factors among the faculty subjects.

Item Generation

To measure pedagogical usability in a faculty course development context, we adapt the Seven Principles from the pedagogical literature (Chickering & Ehrmann, 1996) – see Table 1. Respondents were asked to identify their opinions concerning the role technology can play in implementing each of the seven principles of good practice. A five-point Likert scale, ranging from 1 (strongly disagree) to 5 (strongly agree), is used to measure pedagogical usability.

Based on the literatures of Web site design, information systems, e-commerce, and the functions and features of WebCT and Blackboard software, items are developed to measure content re-configurability (Powel, 2000; Skyrme, 2001), interaction re-configurability (Barnes & Vidgen, 2001; Raquel, 2001; Agarwal & Venkatesh, 2002; Palmer, 2002), and modularity design (Markus et al., 2002; Thomke & Hippel, 2002; Hippel & Katz, 2002). Respondents are asked to identify their opinions of each statement on a five-point Likert scale, ranging from 1 (strongly disagree) to 5 (strongly agree), to measure these three component factors of system re-configurability.

Heuristic Evaluation Procedure

Kantner and Rosenbaum (1997) observe that heuristic evaluation is one of the most frequently used approaches for evaluating measurement items. Heuristic evaluations are assessments conducted by a small group of evaluators against a pre-established set of guidelines or "heuristics" (Nielsen, 1994). A structured interview questionnaire is developed and processed to (1) assess whether each item reflects its corresponding factor, (2) verify that important aspects of each factor are not omitted, and (3) enable an interviewer to make an assessment of the four factors in the model depicted in Figure 2.

In November 2004, personal interviews were conducted with WebCT users (instructional designers and faculty) from the University of Toledo. First, structured interviews asking about the role and importance of each of the factors were conducted. Then, respondents were asked to answered the questionnaire and describe their thinking out loud as they answered each question. This gave researchers insights into how the respondents viewed the items. It also enabled the interviewer to ask follow-up questions. As a result of these interviews, the items used to measure content re-configurability, interaction re-configurability, and modularity design were modified.

These structured interviews helped the researchers realize that faculty saw the technology as usable to the extent that it could contribute to the course design principles proposed by Chickering and Ehrmann (1996). The ways that information technology can contribute to each principle are illustrated in Table 1.

Later, in February 2005, the revised self-administered questionnaire was distributed to both instructors and instructional designers from two universities - one using Blackboard and another using WebCT. The respondents' opinions and comments were recorded and the questionnaire was modified accordingly. For example, to make the question easier to understand, one original item in content re-configurability was changed from "this software enables me to add *publisher* content to my course" to "this software enables me to add *course* content".

Subjects

In order to test the model in Figure 2, we gathered data from the University of Toledo. The Distance and eLearning Division of this institution sponsored the survey. The CMS used was WebCT. The online questionnaire was sent out to 560 instructors by the director of this division.

Table 2. Descriptive statistics

Variables	Mean	Standard deviation	Alpha
Content re-configurability	3.94	0.80	0.91
Interaction re-configurability	3.60	0.88	0.87
Modularity design	3.74	0.67	0.75
Pedagogical usability	3.83	0.71	0.88

The reason for selecting instructors rather than students relates to the purpose of this study (i.e., to assess the pedagogical usability of CMSs). System re-configurability is only applicable to instructors. Students do not have the authority to alter the system artifact.

Fifty six faculty provided usable responses. This was a ten percent (10%) response rate. Among these 56 respondents, 53.57% used the system for distance learning course, 37.5% for Web-assisted courses, and 8.93% for both.

MODEL TESTING RESULTS

First, the reliability, convergent validity, and discriminant validity of the measures were examined. Finally, the hypotheses were tested using multiple regression.

Measurement Results

The validity of the instrument was examined in terms of internal consistency (i.e., reliability), convergent validity, and discriminant validity (Straub, 1989). Internal consistency was examined using Cronbach alpha's values. Table 2 provides the mean, standard deviation, and Cronbach's alpha values for content re-configurability, interaction re-configurability, modularity design, and pedagogical usability. Most constructs exhibited alpha values greater than 0.87, significantly higher than the threshold value of 0.8 (Nunnaly & Bernstein, 1994). The only exception is modularity design with alpha = 0.75. This suggests that all the variables have adequate reliability for an exploratory study.

Convergent and discriminant validities are examined by an exploratory factor analysis using principal components as the means of extraction and direct oblimin as the method of rotation. For system re-configurability, there are three factors with eigenvalues greater than 1.0. The three factor solution reported in Table 3 represents a simple structure. The items are grouped by their highest (primary) factor loading and listed in descending order. All item-factor loadings are greater than 0.60 on their intended factor. There are no cross loadings greater than or equal to 0.40. The three factors explain 75.19% of the variance of the system re-configurability items. The three constructs exhibit both convergent validity (high item-factor loadings on intended factor) and discriminant validity (low cross loadings). For pedagogical usability, one factor emerges explaining 58.30% of the variance – see Table 4.

Results for Substantive Hypotheses

The Pearson correlation coefficients among the factors are presented in Table 5. The bi-variate relationships indicate that all the variables are significantly correlated with each other at the $p < 0.05$ level. Content re-configurability and interaction re-configurability are significantly correlated with pedagogical usability at the $p < 0.01$ level.

To test hypotheses H1 through H3, the three system re-configurability factors (content, interaction, and modularity) are entered as independent variables into a stepwise linear regression that

Table 3. Factor structure of system re-configurability

No.	Items	Loadings			
Factor: content re-configurability					
1.	This software provides various ways to manage files.	0.94			
2.	This software provides a wide range options for the course content.	0.78			
3.	This software enables me to add course content to my course at any stage of the course design process.	0.69			
4.	This software provides many choices to deliver course content efficiently (e.g. single page, email, discussion, attachment).	0.68			
5.	This software enables me to add various types of files (e.g. images, Flashes, audio).	0.61			
Factor: interaction re-configurability					
6.	This software enables me to set up multiple forums.		0.98		
7.	This software enables me to embed forums in appropriate content areas.		0.85		
8.	This software enables me to set up forums around different topics.		0.80		
Factor: modularity design					
9.	Our online courses use built-in navigation links.			0.91	
10.	Our online courses use optional interactive tools.			0.72	
11.	Modules (or Units) can be incorporated into course design.			0.64	

treated pedagogical usability as the dependent variable. Each independent variable has to produce a significant change in the variance of the dependent variable at the $p < 0.05$ level to be included in the regression equation. The results appear in Table 6.

Content re-configurability is the first factor entered into the step-wise regression model. It explains a highly significant ($p < 0.001$) forty percent of the variance in pedagogical usability. Interaction re-configurability is the second factor entered into the regression. It increases the variance explained by a significant 5% ($p < 0.02$). Modularity design does not enter the step-wise regression in the third step. It does not account for a significant incremental change in R-square.

Table 4. Factor structure of pedagogical usability

No.	Items	Loadings			
1.	In distance learning, this software helps me respect diverse talents and ways of learning				0.82
2.	In distance learning, this software helps me communicate high expectations				0.82
3.	In distance learning, this software helps me encourage contacts between students and faculty				0.79
4.	In distance learning, this software helps me give prompt feedback				0.77
5.	In distance learning, this software helps me develop collaboration and cooperation among students learning (e.g. team work)				0.76
6.	In distance learning, this software helps me use active learning techniques (e.g. simulation)				0.74
7.	In distance learning, this software helps me emphasize time on task				0.62

Table 5. Correlation analysis

Variables	2	3	4
1. Content re-configurability	.57**	.30*	.64**
2. Interaction re-configurability		.35**	.57**
3. Modularity design			.30*
4. Pedagogical usability			

** Correlation is significant at the 0.01 level (2-tailed).
* Correlation is significant at the 0.05 level (2-tailed).

The results show that content re-configurability has a significant impact on pedagogical usability (Beta = 0.47, $p < 0.001$). Thus, H1 is supported. Interaction re-configurability is also found significantly related to pedagogical usability (Beta = 0.30, $p < 0.05$), which supports H2. However, modularity design is non-significant. Thus, H3 is rejected.

DISCUSSIONS AND IMPLICATIONS

The major contribution of this study is to define and operationalize the pedagogical usability concept from a faculty stakeholder perspective in the e-learning context. While it is acknowledged that usability is a complex concept with different meaning for different stakeholders, pedagogical usability is considered the principal concern of faculty. The seven pedagogical principles incorporated in the proposed measure of pedagogical usability are widely used in faculty CMSs training to explain how the computer can help faculty achieve these best pedagogical practices (Chickering & Ehrmann, 1996). If the CMS software can not help the faculty achieve their pedagogical objectives, they may often stay with more traditional in-class methods to generate discussion, encourage team work, etc.

E-learning teaching often involves an emerging process of deliberations as faculty learn how students react to assignments and, thus, change the content of the web site or the way the distance learning site is configured for student use. Faculty members are knowledge workers who often have substantial authority to enact distance learning courses. This enactment requires reconfigurable CMSs to support the reconfiguration task, improve pedagogical usability, and achieve each course's unique learning goals. This paper makes a contribution by providing evidence that content re-configurability and interaction re-configurability of the CMS enhance the pedagogical usability of the software.

Because faculty members assume a dual role in CMSs as both developers and users, there are some limitations in this study that should be taken into consideration. Ease of use has been presented in this paper as a primary concern of student stakeholders. But, ease of use may also be a concern of faculty if the CMS software meets their primary concern of pedagogical usability. Even though

Table 6. Regression results for predicted path relationships

Dependent variable	Independent variables	Beta	R square after entry	p-value
Pedagogical usability	Content re-configurability	0.47	0.40	0.000
	Interaction re-configurability	0.30	0.45	0.017

the faculty perceptions of the re-configurability of the software (i.e., easy to reconfigure) suggests it may be easy to use, it may be useful to make a distinction between the re-configurability of content and interaction and faculty perceptions of the ease by which these reconfigurations are executed. Universities often provide substantial training and technical support to improve faculty software skills and enhance their perceptions of ease of use.

To test the multifaceted nature of usability in an e-learning context, opinions and observations of designer, faculty, and student stakeholders should be examined in future studies. Faculty using WebCT are the subjects of this study. Although other software, such as Blackboard and Angela, may have similar design features, the way these features are enacted by faculty, maintained by designers, or used by students may not be the same, affecting perceptions of system re-configurability and its consequences. Future research should also be designed to collect data from the three stakeholders of CMSs.

Content re-configurability was found the dominant design characteristic which impacts pedagogical usability. This is consistent with the observations by Cole et al. (2000) and Agarwal and Venkatesh (2002) in their Web site researches. Web sites tend to be much more content-focused than traditional software (Powel, 2000). As the Web moves away from a print design background, it has continued to become more and more multimedia-driven. In an e-learning environment, faculty use animation, and audio and video are becoming popular as well. Content re-configurability enables instructors to upload course material in multiple formats, enabling faculty to make online learning lively, effective, and easy for individuals with different talents and ways of learning.

Interaction re-configurability was also found to be a significant predictor of pedagogical usability. An interactive system is one where the users are able to interact directly with the content or with other users of the system (Powel, 2000). Truly interactive systems allow users to manipulate the content itself, and in some cases even add their own content. A CMS that allows a student to post questions for other users to view would also be considered interactive. Based on Horton (2000), the interactive potential of the computer is one of the principal reasons it is used as a medium for instruction. In Web-based instruction, learners actively participate in the learning process: they are presented with an array of choices from which to construct their own path to knowledge and understanding.

Modularity design was not found to be the determinant of pedagogical usability. Although modularity design by itself has significant bivariate relationship with pedagogical usability ($r = 0.30$, $p < 0.05$), this relationship became non-significant in the step-wise regression when we took into account content re-configurability and interaction re-configurability. Because the course design process is situated and emergent, users do not like to become boxed in by e-learning technology. Faculty users require CMSs to be designed to provide more functions to satisfy their growing needs. The modularity design characteristic, on one hand, makes complex systems easier to use. On the other hand, modularity design thwarts the attempt of users with advanced needs. Another reason for this non-significant relationship might be that modularity of design was something that technical people were aware of and could respond to. However, faculty may be less aware of design modularity concepts and provide less reliable answers.

CONCLUSION

E-learning has rapidly advanced from the realm of experimenters and early adopters to a mission-critical component of an institution's educational environment. Many studies have focused on how to design effective CMSs and the effects of web-based systems on learner satisfaction and learning outcomes. These studies are more concerned with the outcomes of distance learning systems (e.g., student learning, cost, 24/7 accessibility) than with the pedagogical practices (i.e., seven principles of good teaching practices) that are computer enabled in distance learning.

In this study, we develop a model of pedagogical usability of CMSs from a faculty perspective. The relationship between software re-configurability and pedagogical usability is explored. The results show that the more reconfigurable the faculty perceive the CMSs, the more they use the system to improve their implementation of the seven principles of good pedagogical practice. To facilitate good pedagogical practices, institutions should choose CMS software with high content and interaction re-configurability.

REFERENCES

Agarwal, R., & Venkatesh, V. (2002). Assessing a firm's Web presence: a heuristic evaluation procedure for the measurement of usability. *Information Systems Research, 13*, 168–186. doi:10.1287/isre.13.2.168.84

Albion, P. R. (1999). Heuristic evaluation of educational multimedia: from theory to practice. In *Proceedings of the 16th annual conference of the Austrasian Society for Computers in Learning in Tertiry Education (ASCILITE)*.

Barnes, S. J., & Vidgen, R. (2001). An evaluation of cyber-bookshops: the WebQual method. *International Journal of Electronic Commerce, 6*(1), 11–30.

Benigno, V., & Trentin, G. (2000). The evaluation of online courses. *Journal of Computer Assisted Learning, 16*, 259–270. doi:10.1046/j.1365-2729.2000.00137.x

Bernard, P. J., Hammond, N. V., Morton, J., & Long, J. B. (1981). Consistency and compatibility in human-computer dialogue. *International Journal of Man-Machine Studies, 15*(1), 87–134. doi:10.1016/S0020-7373(81)80024-7

Chickering, A., & Ehrmann, S. (1996). *Implementing the Seven Principles: Technology as Lever*. AAHE Bulletin.

Chickering, A., & Gamson, Z. F. (1987). *Seven Principles for Good Practice in Undergraduate Education*. AAHE Bulletin.

Chou, C. (2003). Interactivity and interactive functions in web-based learning systems: A technical framework for designers. *British Journal of Educational Technology, 34*(3), 265–279. doi:10.1111/1467-8535.00326

Clarke, T., & Hermens, A. (2001). Corporate developments and strategic alliances in e-learning. *Education + Training, 43*(4), 256-267.

Cole, M., O'Keefe, R. M., & Siala, H. (2000). From the user interface to the consumer interface. *Information Systems Frontiers, 1*, 349–361. doi:10.1023/A:1010009923913

Ethiraj, S. K., & Levinthal, D. (2004). Modularity and innovation in complex systems. *Management Science, 50*, 159–173. doi:10.1287/mnsc.1030.0145

Evans, J. R., & Haase, I. M. (2001). Online business in the twenty-first century: An analysis of potential target markets. *Internet Research: Electronic Networking Applications Policy, 11*(3), 246–260. doi:10.1108/10662240110396432

Garrison, D. R., & Cleveland-Innes, M. (2005). Facilitating Cognitive Presence in Online Learning: Interaction Is Not Enough. *American Journal of Distance Education, 19*(3), 133–148. doi:10.1207/s15389286ajde1903_2

Gray, W. D., & Salzman, M. C. (1998). Damaged merchandise? A review of experiments that compare usability evaluation methods. *Human-Computer Interaction, 13*, 203–261. doi:10.1207/s15327051hci1303_2

Heeter, C. (1989). Implications of New Interactive Technologies for Conceptualizing Communication. In Salvaggio, J. L., & Bryant, J. (Eds.), *Media use in the information age: emerging patterns of adoption and consumer use* (pp. 217–235). Hillsdale, NJ: Lawrence Erlbaum.

Hippel, E. V., & Katz, R. (2002). Shifting Innovation to Users via Toolkits. *Management Science, 48*(7), 821–833. doi:10.1287/mnsc.48.7.821.2817

Holsapple, C. W., & Lee-Post, A. (2006). Defining, assessing, and promoting e-learning success: An information systems perspective. *Decision Sciences Journal of Innovative Education, 4*(1), 67–85.

Horton, S. (2000). *Web Teaching Guide – A Practical Approach to Creating Course Web Sites*. New Haven, CT: Yale University Press.

Jackson, B., & Anagnostopoulou, K. (2001). Making the right connections: Improving quality in online learning. In Stephenson, J. (Ed.), *Teaching and learning online: Pedagogies for new technologies* (pp. 53–66). Sterling, VA: Stylus Publishing.

Jonassen, D. (1995). Supporting communities of learners with technology: A vision for integrating technology with learning in schools. *Educational Technology, 35*(4), 60–63.

Kantner, L., & Rosenbaum, S. (1997). Usability studies of WWW sites: Heuristic evaluation vs. laboratory testing. In *Proceedings of SIGDOC*, Snowbird, UT (pp. 153-160).

Karat, J. (1997). Evolving the Scope of User-Centered Design. *Communications of the ACM, 40*, 33–38. doi:10.1145/256175.256181

Kilby, T. (2001). The direction of Web-based training: A practitioner's view. *The Learning Organization, 8*(5), 194–199. doi:10.1108/EUM0000000005912

Labbate, E. (1996). Usability and pedagogical issues in user interface design. Retrieved from http://www.technosphere.net/usability_in_uid.htm.

Lawhead, P. B., Alpert, E., Bland, C. G., Carswell, L., Cizmar, D., DeWitt, J., et al. (1997). The web and distance learning: What is appropriate and what is not. In *Proceedings of ITiCSE '97 Working Group Reports and Supplemental* (pp. 27-37). New York: ACM.

Lecerof, A., & Paterno, F. (1998). Automatic support for usability evaluation. *IEEE Transactions on Software Engineering, 24*, 863–887. doi:10.1109/32.729686

Lewis, J. R. (1995). IBM computer usability satisfaction questionnaires: psychometric evaluation and instructions for use. *International Journal of Human-Computer Interaction, 7*(1), 57–78. doi:10.1080/10447319509526110

Markus, M. L., Majchrzak, A., & Gasser, L. (2002). A design theory for systems that support emergent knowledge processes. *Management Information Systems Quarterly, 26*, 199–232.

Melis, E., Weber, M., & Andrès, E. (2003). Lessons for (Pedagogic) Usability of eLearning Systems. *World Conference on E-Learning in Corporate, Government, Healthcare, &. Higher Education*, (1): 281–284.

Mezirow, J. (1997). Trasformative learning: theory to practice. In Cranton, P. (Ed.), *Trasformative learning in action: Insights from practice. New Directions for Adult and Continuing Education*. San Franciso, CA: Jossey-Bass Publishers.

Moore, M. G. (1999). Three types of interaction. *American Journal of Distance Education, 3*(2), 1–6. doi:10.1080/08923648909526659

Nielsen, J. (1993). *Usability Engineering*. San Francisco, CA: Morgan Kaufmann.

Nielsen, J. (1994). Heuristic evaluation. In Nielsen, J., & Mack, R. L. (Eds.), *Usability Inspection Methods* (pp. 25–62). New York: John Wiley and Sons.

Nielsen, J. (2000). *Designing web usability*. Indianapolis, IN: New Riders Publishing.

Nunnaly, J., & Bernstein, I. (1994). *Psychometric Theory*. New York: McGraw-Hill.

Palmer, J. W. (2002). Web site usability, design, and performance metrics. *Information Systems Research, 13*, 151–167. doi:10.1287/isre.13.2.151.88

Pearrow, M. (2000). *Web Site Usability*. Rockland, MA: Charles River Media.

Powel, T. A. (2000). *The Complete Reference. Web Design*. New York: Osborne/McGraw-Hill.

Quinn, C. N. (1996). Pragmatic evaluation: Lessons from usability. In *Proceedings of the 13th Annual Conference of the Australasian Society for Computers in Learning in Tertiry Education (ASCILITE)*.

Raquel, B. F. (2001). Using protocol analysis to evaluate the usability of a commercial Web site. *Information & Management, 39*, 151–163. doi:10.1016/S0378-7206(01)00085-4

Shneiderman, B. (1998). *Designing the User Interface: Strategies for Effective Human-Computer Interaction*. Reading, MA: Addison-Wesley.

Silius, K., & Tervakari, A.-M. (2003). The Usefulness of Web-based Learning Environments. The Evaluation tool into the Portal of Finnish Virtual University. In *Proceedings of the International Conference on Network Universities and e-Learning*. Retrieved from http://www.hsh.no/menu/

Skyrme, D. J. (2001). *Capitalizing on Knowledge: from E-business to K-business*. Oxford, UK: Butterworth-Heinemann.

Smith, L. J. (2001). Content and delivery: A comparison and contrast of electronic and traditional MBA marketing planning courses. *Journal of Marketing Education, 23*(1), 35–44. doi:10.1177/0273475301231005

Squires, D. (1997). An heuristic approach to the evaluation of educational multimedia software. In *Proceedings of the Computer Assisted Learning Conference*, University of Exeter, Exeter, UK. Retrieved from http://www/media/uwe.ac.uk/masoud/cal-97/papers/squires.htm

Straub, D. W. (1989). Validating Instruments in MIS research. *Management Information Systems Quarterly, 13*, 147–169. doi:10.2307/248922

Teh, G. P. L. (1999). Assessing Student Perceptions of Internet-based Online Learning Environment. *International Journal of Instructional Media, 26*(4), 397–402.

Thomke, S., & Hippel, E. V. (2002, April). Customers as Innovators – A New Way to Create Value. *Harvard Business Review*, 74–81.

Tilson, R., Dong, J., Martin, S., & Kiele, E. (1998). Factors and principles affecting the usability of four E-commerce sites. In *Proceedings of the 4th Conference on Huamn Factors and the Web*, Basking Ridge, NJ.

Took, R. (1990). Putting Design into Practice: Formal Specification and the User Interface. In Harrison, M., & Thimbleby, H. (Eds.), *Formal Methods in Human-Computer Interaction* (pp. 82–96). Cambridge, UK: Cambridge University Press.

Ulrich, K. T., & Eppinger, S. D. (1999). *Product Design and Development* (2nd ed.). New York: McGaw-Hill.

Venkatesh, V., & Agarwal, R. (2006). Turning visitors into customers: A usability-centric perspective on purchase behavior in electronic channels. *Management Science*, *52*(3), 367–382. doi:10.1287/mnsc.1050.0442

Venkatesh, V., & Ramesh, V. (2006). Web and wireless site usability: understanding differences and Modeling use. *Management Information Systems Quarterly*, *30*(1), 181–206.

Wild, R. H., Griggs, K. A., & Downing, T. (2002). A framework for e-learning as a tool for knowledge management. *Industrial Management & Data Systems*, *102*(7), 371–380. doi:10.1108/02635570210439463

Zaharias, P. (2005). Call for Papers: E-Learning Design and Usability. *ISWorld.*

Zhang, P., & Li, N. (2005). The Intellectual Development of Human-Computer Interaction Research: A Critical Assessment of the MIS Literature (1990-2002). *Journal of the Association for Information Systems*, *6*, 227–291.

This work was previously published in Journal of Organizational and End User Computing, Volume 22, Issue 3, edited by M. Adam Mahmood, pp. 66-81, copyright 2010 by IGI Publishing (an imprint of IGI Global).

Chapter 9
End-User Software Engineering and Why It Matters

Margaret Burnett
Oregon State University, USA

ABSTRACT

End-user programming has become ubiquitous; so much so that there are more end-user programmers today than there are professional programmers. End-user programming empowers—but to do what? Make bad decisions based on bad programs? Enter software engineering's focus on quality. Considering software quality is necessary, because there is ample evidence that the programs end users create are filled with expensive errors. In this paper, we consider what happens when we add considerations of software quality to end-user programming environments, going beyond the "create a program" aspect of end-user programming. We describe a philosophy of software engineering for end users, and then survey several projects in this area. A basic premise is that end-user software engineering can only succeed to the extent that it respects that the user probably has little expertise or even interest in software engineering.

INTRODUCTION

It all started with end-user programming.

End-user programming enables end users to create their own programs. Researchers and developers have been working on empowering end users to do this for a number of years, and as a result, today end users create numerous programs.

The "programming environments" used by end users include spreadsheet systems, Web authoring tools, and graphical languages for creating educational simulations (e.g., Burnett, Chekka, & Pandey, 2001; Lieberman, 2001; Little, Lau, Cypher, Lin, Haber, & Kandogan, 2007; Pane, Myers, & Miller, 2002; Repenning & Ioannidou,

DOI: 10.4018/978-1-4666-0140-6.ch009

Figure 1. U.S. users in 2006 and those who do forms of programming. (This is a summary of data in Scaffidi, Shaw, & Myers, 2005)

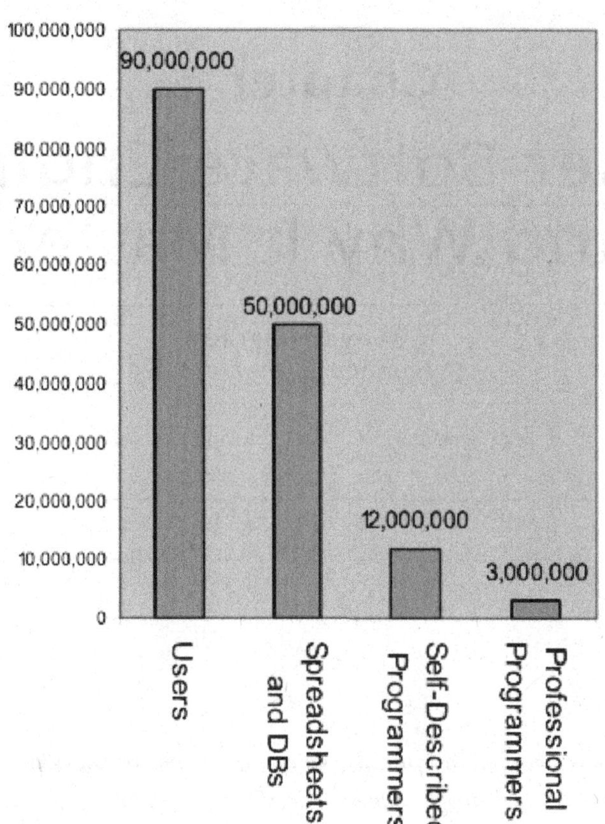

2006). Using these systems, end users create programs in forms such as spreadsheets, dynamic Web applications, and educational simulations. Some ways in which end users create these programs include writing and editing formulas, dragging and dropping objects onto a logical workspace, connecting objects in a diagram, or demonstrating intended logic to the system.

In fact, research based on U.S. Bureau of Census and Bureau of Labor data shows that there are about 3 million professional programmers in the United States—but more than 12 million more people who say they do programming at work, and more than 50 million who use spreadsheets and databases (Scaffidi, Shaw, & Myers, 2005). Figure 1 shows the breakouts. Thus, the number of end-user programmers in the United States falls somewhere between 12 million and 50 million people—several times the number of professional programmers.

Clearly then, end-user programming empowers—it has already empowered millions of end users to create their own software.

Unfortunately, there is a down side: the software they are creating with this new power is riddled with errors. In fact, evidence abounds of the pervasiveness of errors in software end users create (e.g., EUSPRIG, 2009). These errors can have significant impact. For example, one school faced a £30,000 shortfall because values in a budget spreadsheet had not been added up correctly (EUSPRIG, 2009, no. 67). TransAlta

Corporation took a $24 million charge to earnings after a bidding error caused it to buy more U.S. power transmission hedging contracts than it bargained for, at higher prices than it wanted to pay, due to a spreadsheet error (French, 2003). Even when the errors in end-user-created software are non-catastrophic, however, their effects can matter. Web applications created by small-business owners to promote their businesses do just the opposite if they contain broken links or pages that display incorrectly, resulting in client frustration, loss of revenue, and/or loss of credibility. Software resources linked by end users to monitor non-safety-critical medical conditions can cause unnecessary pain or discomfort for users who rely on them. Such problems are ubiquitous in two particularly rapidly growing types of software end users develop: software built using open repositories of shared computational resources (such as public databases, program examples, program templates, entire programs, and portions of programs), and dynamic Web applications.

Thus, the problem with end-user programming is that end users' programs are all too often turning out to be of too low quality for the purposes for which they were created.

A NEW AREA: END-USER SOFTWARE ENGINEERING

A new research area is emerging to address this problem. The area is known as *end-user software engineering* (Burnett, Cook, & Rothermel, 2004), and it aims to address the problem of end users' software quality by looking beyond the "create" part of software development to the rest of the software lifecycle. Thus, *end-user programming* is the "create" part of end-user software development, and end-user software engineering adds consideration of software quality issues to both the "create" and the "beyond create" parts of software development.

More formally, Ko et al. define *end-user software engineering* technologies as "technologies that collaborate with end users to improve software quality" (Ko et al., under review). In essence, end-user programming focuses mainly on how to allow end users to create their own programs, and end-user software engineering considers how to support the entire software lifecycle and its attendant quality issues.

End-user software engineering has similarities to the notion of *end-user development* (Lieberman, Paterno, & Wulf, 2006), but is not quite the same. Lieberman et al. define end-user development as "a set of methods, techniques, and tools that allow users of software systems, who are acting as non-professional software developers, at some point to create, modify, or extend a software artifact" (2006). Thus the notion of end-user development includes elements of the software lifecycle beyond the stage of creating a new program; what end-user software engineering adds to this concept is the consideration of the software's quality.

Our view is that end-user software engineering (done well) is inherently different from traditional software engineering, because simply mimicking traditional approaches seems unlikely to produce successful results. One reason is that end users do not usually have the professional training and background that professional programmers have. Even more important, end users also face different motivations and work constraints than professional programmers (Nardi, 1993). They are not likely to know about quality control mechanisms, formal development processes, modeling diagrams, or test adequacy criteria, and are not likely to invest time learning about such things. This is because in most cases, end users are not striving to create the best software they can; rather, they have their "real goals" to achieve: such as accounting, teaching, managing safety, understanding financial data, or authoring new media-based experiences (Nardi, 1993).

To support these users in pursuing their real goals, the strategy we have used in our own end-user software engineering research has been to gently alert them to potential problems in their programs, to assist them with their explorations into those problems to whatever extent they *choose* to pursue such explorations, and to work within the contexts with which they are familiar. Choice is central to our strategy—only the user knows his or her real goals and socio-organizational context[1]. Thus, our strategy represents a paradigm shift from traditional software engineering and end-user programming research, because it combines in equal measures software engineering foundations with human-computer interaction foundations.

ORGANIZATION

We illustrate the end-user software engineering area with examples of projects that have been conducted by members of the EUSES Consortium (http://eusesconsortium.org), an NSF-funded collaboration of researchers working in the end-user software engineering area. The examples are:

- WYSIWYT and Surprise-Explain-Reward: WYSIWYT is a methodology for supporting systematic testing by end users. Surprise-Explain-Reward is a strategy for enticing end users to engage in software engineering practices such as the testing supported by WYSIWYT. Since WYSIWYT's success depends on Surprise-Explain-Reward, we discuss the two of these works together.
- Debugging Machine-Learned Programs: In recent times, a new kind of "programmer" has entered the mix—machines. These machines, through machine-learning algorithms, automatically create programs on the user's computer, deriving these programs from the user's interaction habits and data history. We discuss a debugging approach and early results for one type of program in this class.
- Gender in End-User Software Engineering: If end-user software engineering is to properly blend HCI-based people-oriented foundations with software engineering foundations, then it must attend to both 50%s of the people who are end users—both the males and the females. We discuss emerging information about gender differences' implications for the design of end-user software engineering tools.

WYSIWYT TESTING AND SURPRISE-EXPLAIN-REWARD

WYSIWYT (What You See Is What You Test) (Rothermel, Burnett, Li, DuPuis, & Sheretov, 2001) supports *systematic testing* by end-user programmers. It has primarily been implemented in the spreadsheet paradigm, so we present it here from that perspective. Its motivation is the following: empirical studies have shown that users often assume their spreadsheets are correct, but even if they try to consider whether there are errors, they do so by looking at the immediate value recalculations they see when they enter or change formulas. This empirical work has shown that this "one test only" feedback is tied to overconfidence about the correctness of their spreadsheets (Wilcox, Atwood, Burnett, Cadiz, & Cook, 1997; Rothermel, Cook, Burnett, Schonfeld, Green, & Rothermel, 2000).

WYSIWYT helps to address this problem. With WYSIWYT, as a user incrementally develops a spreadsheet, he or she can also test that spreadsheet. As the user changes cell formulas and values, the underlying evaluation engine automatically evaluates cells, and the user checks off (validates) resulting values that are correct. Behind the scenes, these validations are used to measure the quality of testing in terms of a dataflow adequacy criterion, which tracks coverage of interactions between cells caused by cell references.

For example, in Figure 2, the user has noticed that Smith's letter grade (row 4) is correct, so the

Figure 2. At any time, the user can test by checking off a value that turned out to be correct, and this test causes borders of the cells involved to become bluer, reflecting coverage of the tests so far

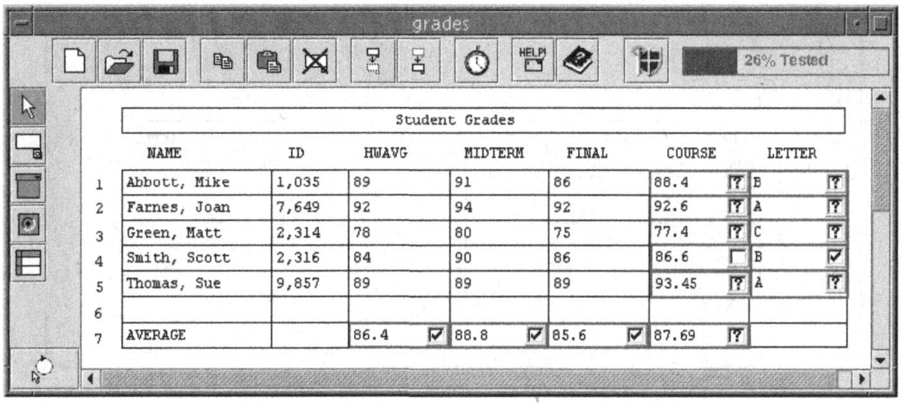

grades — 26% Tested

Student Grades

	NAME	ID	HWAVG	MIDTERM	FINAL	COURSE	LETTER
1	Abbott, Mike	1,035	89	91	86	88.4	B
2	Farnes, Joan	7,649	92	94	92	92.6	A
3	Green, Matt	2,314	78	80	75	77.4	C
4	Smith, Scott	2,316	84	90	86	86.6	B
5	Thomas, Sue	9,857	89	89	89	93.45	A
6							
7	AVERAGE		86.4	88.8	85.6	87.69	

user checked it off. The Average row's values under HWAVG, MIDTERM, and FINAL are also correct, so the user checks them off too. As a result, the cell borders turn closer to blue on a red-blue continuum, in which red means untested, blue means tested, and colors between red and blue (shades of purple) mean partially tested.

But, pause to reflect: Why *should* a user whose interests are simply to get their spreadsheet results as efficiently as possible, choose to spend extra time learning about these unusual new checkmarks, let alone think carefully about values and whether they should be checked off? Let's further assume that these users have never seen software engineering devices before. To succeed at enticing the user to use these devices, we require a strategy that will both motivate these users to make use of software engineering devices and will provide the just-in-time support they need to effectively follow up on this interest.

We call our strategy for enticing and supporting the user down this path Surprise-Explain-Reward (Wilson et al., 2003). The strategy attempts to first arouse users' curiosity about the software engineering devices through surprise, and to then encourage them, through explanations and rewards, to follow through with appropriate actions. This strategy has its roots in three areas of research: (1) research about curiosity (psychology) (Lowenstein, 1994), (2) Blackwell's model of attention investment (Blackwell, 2002) (psychology/HCI), and (3) minimalist learning (educational theory, HCI) (Carroll & Rosson, 1987).

Research into curiosity indicates that surprising a person by violating his or her assumptions can trigger a search for an explanation. The violation of assumptions indicates to the user the presence of something they do not understand. According to the information-gap perspective (Lowenstein, 1994), a revealed gap in the user's knowledge focuses the user's attention on the gap and leads to curiosity, which motivates the user to close the gap by searching for an explanation. This is why the first component of our surprise-explain-reward strategy is needed: to arouse users' curiosity enough, through surprise, to cause them to search for explanations.

Blackwell's model of attention investment (2002) considers the costs, benefits, and risks users weigh in deciding how to complete a task. For example, if a user's goal is to forecast a budget using a spreadsheet, then exploring an unknown feature has perceived costs, perceived benefits, and a perceived risk, such as that using the new feature will waste time or, worse, leave the spreadsheet in a state from which it is difficult (and thus incurs more costs) to recover. The model of attention investment implies that the second component

Figure 3. If the user also notices that a value is incorrect, the user can X it out, and this causes the fault localization algorithm to suggest which cell formulas are most likely to contain the error

grades — 26% Tested

Student Grades

	NAME	ID	HWAVG	MIDTERM	FINAL	COURSE	LETTER
1	Abbott, Mike	1,035	89	91	86	88.4	B
2	Farnes, Joan	7,649	92	94	92	92.6	A
3	Green, Matt	2,314	78	80	75	77.4	C
4	Smith, Scott	2,316	84	90	86	86.6	B
5	Thomas, Sue	9,857	89	89	89	93.45	A
6							
7	AVERAGE		86.4	88.8	85.6	87.69	

(explanation) of the surprise-explain-reward strategy must provide motivation by promising specific rewards (benefits). The third component must then follow through with at least the rewards that were promised.

For example, we instantiate the surprise-explain-reward strategy with the red borders and the checkboxes in each cell, both of which are unusual for spreadsheets. These surprises (information gaps) are non-intrusive: the user is not forced to attend to them if they view other matters to be more worthy of their time. However, if they become curious about these features, they can ask them to explain themselves at a very low cost, simply by hovering over them with their mouse. In this way, the surprise component delivers to the explain component.

The explain component is also very low in cost. In its simplest form, it explains the object in a tool tip. For example, if the user hovers over a checkbox that has not yet been checked off, the tool tip says (in one variant of our prototype): "If this value is right, √ it; if it's wrong, X it. This testing helps you find errors." Thus, it explains the semantics very briefly, gives just enough information for the user to succeed at going down this path, and gives a hint at the reward.

As the above tool tip has pointed out, it is also possible for the user to "X out" a value that is incorrect. For example, in Figure 3, the user has noticed two incorrect values. The system reasons about the backward slice (contributing cells and their values), taking correct values also into account, and highlights the cells in the dataflow path deemed most likely to contain the formula error. In the figure, two cells were X'd out, and those same two are highlighted, but one is highlighted darker than the other, because it was identified as both having a wrong value and as contributing to a second wrong value.

The main reward is finding errors through checking values off and X'ing them out to narrow down the most likely locations of formula errors, but a secondary reward is a "well tested" (high coverage) spreadsheet, which at least shows evidence of having fairly thoroughly looked for errors. To help achieve testing coverage, question marks point out where more decisions about values will make progress (cause more coverage under the hood, cause more color changes on the surface), and the progress bar at the top shows overall coverage/testedness so far.

Our empirical work has shown that the surprise-explain-reward techniques are quite motivating, and do entice users to try the end-user software engineering features and to keep using them (Ruthruff, Phalgune, Beckwith, Burnett, & Cook, 2004; Wilson et al., 2003). Note that these results are necessarily intertwined with the features' effectiveness (functional reward) at actually finding errors, because continued usage would not occur if the features did not genuinely improve effectiveness. Our empirical results have shown strong evidence that these features have indeed improved participants' effectiveness at finding errors. The collection of studies showing this evidence is summarized in Burnett et al. (2004).

The above studies have all been lab studies. In addition, one in-the-field case study of a related commercial product was conducted regarding the adoption decision by an accountant (Subrahmaniyan, Burnett, & Bogart, 2008). That study suggested that the product was a reasonably good match for this user's work practices, and also revealed a collection of real-world advantages and disadvantages the user encountered in experimenting with the software.

DEBUGGING MACHINE-LEARNED PROGRAMS

What if the program that has gone wrong was not written by a human at all? How do you debug a program that was written by a machine instead of a person?

This is the problem faced by users of a new sort of program, namely, one generated by a machine learning system that customizes itself to the user. For example, intelligent user interfaces, recommender systems, and categorizers of e-mail use machine learning to adapt their behavior to users' preferences. This learned set of behaviors is a *program*. These learned programs do not come into existence until the learning environment has left the hands of the machine-learning specialist: they are learned on the user's computer. Thus, if these programs make a mistake, the only one present to fix them is the end user. These attempts to "fix" the system can be viewed as debugging—the user is aware of faulty system behavior, and wants to change the system's logic so as to fix the flawed behavior.

Sometimes correctness is not critical; "good enough" will suffice. For example, a spam filter that successfully collects 90% of dangerous, virus-infested spam leaves the user in a far better situation than having no spam filter at all. However, as the applications of machine learning expand, these programs are becoming more critical. For example, recommender systems that recommend substandard suppliers or incorrect parts, language translators that translate incorrectly, decision support systems that lead the user to overlook important factors, and even e-mail classifiers that misfile important messages could cause significant losses to their users and raise significant liability issues for businesses. For example, this author received an important communication from an executive at a bank, reaching out toward potential future research collaboration. Perhaps because the message came from a bank, it was automatically filed in the spam folder. The message was discovered through sheer luck.

We have begun to investigate how to support end-user debugging of such machine-learned programs. We began with formative studies to understand what end users might want to include in their explanations to a machine, and what style of explanations from a machine might be clear to them (Stumpf et al., 2007). We then built an early prototype, and used it to further explore how end users might problem solve in this type of situation (Stumpf, Sullivan, Fitzhenry, Oberst, Wong, & Burnett, 2008).

These studies produced encouraging results but also revealed issues that led us to rethink our approach to communicating with the user about machine-learned programs. Thus, inspired by the success of the Whyline's support of end-user debugging (Ko & Myers, 2004; Myers, Weitzman, Ko, & Chau, 2006), we designed a method to allow end users to ask Why questions of machine-learned software (Kulesza et al., 2009). Our approach is novel in the following ways: (1) it supports

Table 1. The Why questions (Kulesza et al., 2009) (© 2009 ACM, Inc. Included here by permission.)

Why questions
Why will this message be filed to <Personal>?
Why won't this message be filed to <Bankruptcy>?
Why did this message turn red?
Why wasn't this message affected by my recent changes?
Why did so many messages turn red?
Why is this e-mail undecided?
Why does <banking> matter to the <Bankruptcy> folder?
Why aren't all important words shown?
Why can't I make this message go to <Systems>?

end users asking questions of *machine-learned* programs, and (2) the answers aim at providing suggestions for these end users to *debug* the learned programs.

We have built a prototype of our approach, so that we could investigate both barriers faced by end users when debugging machine-learned programs, and challenges to machine learning algorithms themselves (Kulesza et al., 2009). Our prototype was an e-mail application with several predefined folders. The system utilized a machine-learned program to predict which folder each message in the inbox should be filed to, thus allowing the user to easily archive messages. Our prototype answers the Why questions shown in Table 1.

For example, the answer to Table 1's second question (with dynamically-replaced text in <brackets>) is:

The message will be filed to <Personal> instead of <Bankruptcy> because <Personal> rates more words in this message near Required than <Bankruptcy> does, and it rates more words that aren't present in this message near Forbidden. (Usage instructions followed this text.)

In addition to the textual answers, three questions are also answered visually. These are shown in Figure 4. The bars indicate the weight of each word for predictions to a given folder; the closer to Required/Forbidden, the more/less likely messages containing this word will be classified to this folder.

Figure 5 shows a thumbnail of the entire prototype. The top half is not readable at this size, but it is simply a traditional e-mail program. The bottom middle panel provides visual answers, shown at a readable size in Figure 4.

Using this prototype, we continue to evaluate how well users' problem solving about machine-learned programs is supported with our method. We conducted a formative empirical study to unearth barriers faced by the end user in debugging in this fashion, as well as challenges faced by machine-learning systems that generate the programs that ultimately will be debugged by end users (Kulesza et al., 2009). One of our primary results was that end users faced great difficulty in determining *where* would be the effective places to correct errors—much more so than in than in *how* to do so. The sheer number of these instances strongly suggests the value of providing end users with information about where to give feedback to the machine-learned program, so that they can debug effectively. Another open question is how to ensure that the debugging approach is consistent with users' work practices. The interface shown in this section takes up significant screen space just for debugging, but this may impose too great a cost on a user whose primary mission is to deal with his or her e-mail, not to debug. Further empirically informed iterations with our prototypes are planned to develop approaches that can be shown to align well with users' work practices in the real world.

GENDER IN END-USER SOFTWARE ENGINEERING

Another important result in the Kulesza et al. study (2009) was that gender differences were present in the *number* of barriers encountered, the *sequence* of barriers, and *usage* of debugging

Figure 4. Visual explanations for three Why questions (Kulesza et al., 2009) (© 2009 ACM, Inc. Included here by permission.)

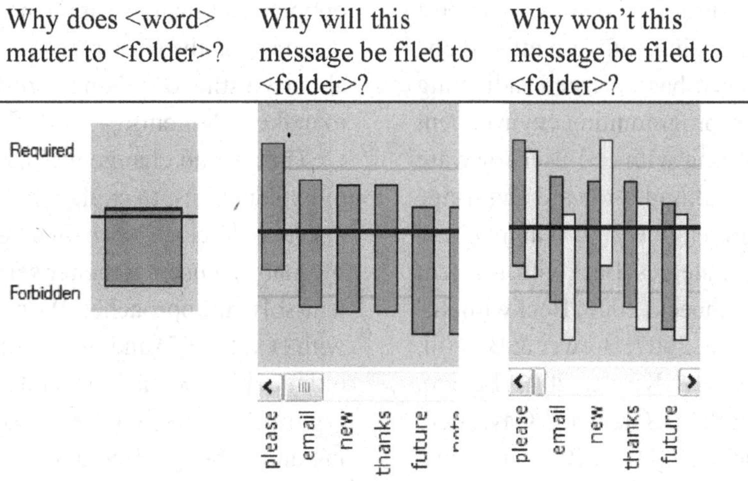

Figure 5. A thumbnail view of the prototype (Kulesza et al., 2009) (© 2009 ACM, Inc. Included here by permission.)

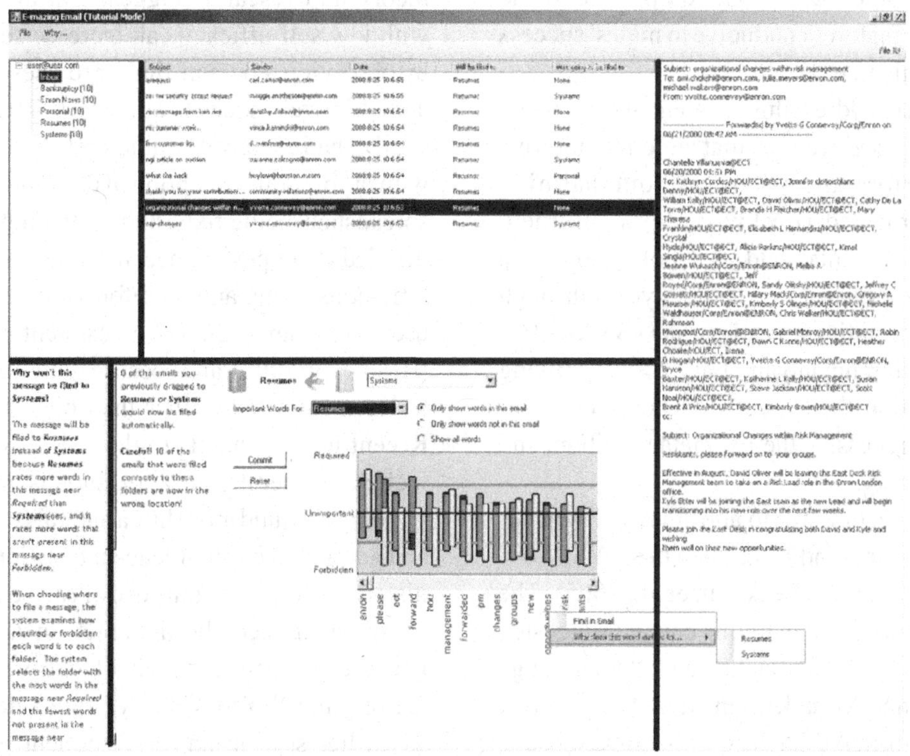

features. This is one of many studies conducted in recent years that show gender differences in how male and female end-user programmers can best be supported in developing software effectively. For example, evidence has emerged indicating gender differences in programming environment appeal, playful tinkering with end-user software engineering features, attitudes toward and usage of end-user software engineering features, and end-user debugging strategies (Beckwith, Burnett, Grigoreanu, & Wiedenbeck, 2006; Beckwith, Inman, Rector, & Burnett, 2007; Brewer & Bassoli, 2006; Kelleher, Pausch, & Kiesler, 2007; Lorigo, Pan, Hembrooke, Joachims, Granka, & Gay, 2006; Rode, Toye, & Blackwell, 2004; Rosson, Sinha, Bhattacharya, & Zhao, 2007; Subrahmaniyan et al., 2008). In essence, in these studies females have been shown to both use different features and to use features differently than males. Even more critically, the features most conducive to females' success are different from the features most conducive to males' success—and are the features least supported in end-user programming environments. This is the opposite of the situation for features conducive to males' success (Subrahmaniyan et al., 2008).

To begin to address this problem, we proposed two theory-based features that aimed to improve female performance—but without harming male performance (Beckwith, Sorte, Burnett, Wiedenbeck, Chintakovid, & Cook, 2005). We evolved these features over three years through the use of formative investigations (Beckwith et al., 2005; Subrahmaniyan et al., 2007), drawing from education theory, self-efficacy theory, information processing theory, metacognition, and curiosity theory.

The first feature was to add "maybe" nuances to the checkmarks and X-marks of the WYSIWYT approach (Figure 6) (Beckwith et al., 2005). The empirical work leading to this change suggested that the original "it's right" and "it's wrong" checkmark and X-mark might seem too assertive a decision to make for low self-efficacy users, and we therefore added "seems right maybe" and "seems wrong maybe" checkmark and X-mark options. The change was intended to communicate the idea that the user did not need to be confident about a testing decision in order to be "qualified" to make judgments.

The second change was a more extensive set of explanations, to explain not only concepts but also to help close Norman's "gulf of evaluation" by enabling users to better self-judge their problem-solving approaches. We proposed it in (Beckwith et al., 2005) and then evolved that proposal, ultimately providing the strategy explanations of Figure 7. Note that these are explanations of testing and debugging strategy, not explanations of software features per se.

The strategy explanations are provided as both video snippets and hypertext (Figure 7). In each video snippet, the female debugger works on a debugging problem and a male debugger, referring to the spreadsheet, helps by giving strategy ideas. Each snippet ends with a successful outcome. The video medium was used because theory and research suggest that an individual with low self-efficacy can increase self-efficacy by observing a person similar to oneself struggle and ultimately succeed at the task. The hypertext version had exactly the same strategy information, with the obvious exception of the animation of the spreadsheet being fixed and the talking heads. We decided on hypertext because it might seem less time-consuming and therefore more attractive to users from an attention investment perspective (Blackwell, 2002), and because some people prefer to learn from text rather than pictorial content. Recent improvements to the video explanations include shortening the explanations, revising the wording to sound more like a natural conversation, and adding an explicit lead-in question to immediately establish the purpose of each explanation.

We evaluated the approach in a controlled laboratory study, in which a Control group used the original WYSIWYT system as described in an earlier section and a Treatment group used

Figure 6. Clicking on the checkbox turns it into four choices whose tool tips say "it's wrong," "seems wrong maybe," "seems right maybe," "it's right" (Beckwith et al., 2005) © 2005 IEEE.

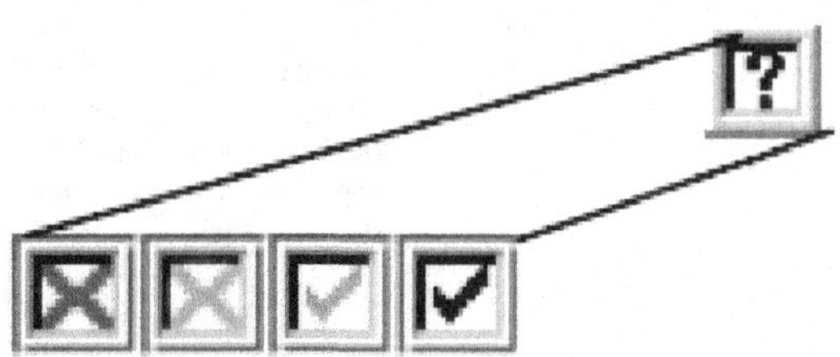

the system with the two changes just described in this section (Grigoreanu et al., 2008). The Treatment females did not fix more bugs than Control females, but we would not expect them to: Treatment females had both lower self-efficacy than Control females and more things to take their time than Control females did. However, taking the self-efficacy and time factors into account reveals that the new features helped to close the gender gap in numerous ways.

First we found that our feature changes reduced the debugging feature *usage* gap between males and females. When we compared the males and females in the Treatment group to their counterparts in the Control group, the feature changes were tied to greater interest among the Treatment group. Compared to females in the Control group, Treatment females made more use of debugging features such as checkmarks and X-marks, and had stronger ties between debugging feature usage and strategic testing behaviors.

Second, we considered playful experimentation with the checkmarks and X-marks (trying them out and then removing them) as a sign of interest. Past studies reported that females were unwilling to approach these features, but that if they did choose to tinker, their effectiveness improved (Beckwith et al., 2006; Beckwith et al., 2007). Treatment females tinkered with the features significantly more than Control females, and this pattern held for both checkmarks and X-marks. Figure 8 illustrates these differences.

Even more important than debugging feature usage per se was the fact that the feature usage was helpful. The total (playful plus lasting) number of checkmarks used per debugging minute, when accounting for pre-self-efficacy, predicted the maximum percent testedness per debugging minute achieved by females in both the Control group and in the Treatment group. Further, for all participants, maximum percent testedness, accounting for pre-self-efficacy, was a significant factor in the number of bugs fixed.

Finally, Treatment females' post-session verbalizations showed that their attitudes toward the software environment were more positive than Control females', and Treatment females' confidence levels were roughly appropriate indicators of their actual ability levels, whereas Control females' confidence levels were not.

Taken together, the feature usage results show marked differences between Treatment females versus Control females, all of which were beneficial to the Treatment females. In contrast, there were very few significant differences between the male groups. Most important, none of the changes benefiting the females showed adverse effects on the males.

These results serve to reconfirm previous studies' reports of the existence of a gender gap related to the software environments themselves

*Figure 7. **(Left): 1-minute video snippets. (Right): Hypertext version (Grigoreanu et al.,** 2008). © 2008 IEEE*

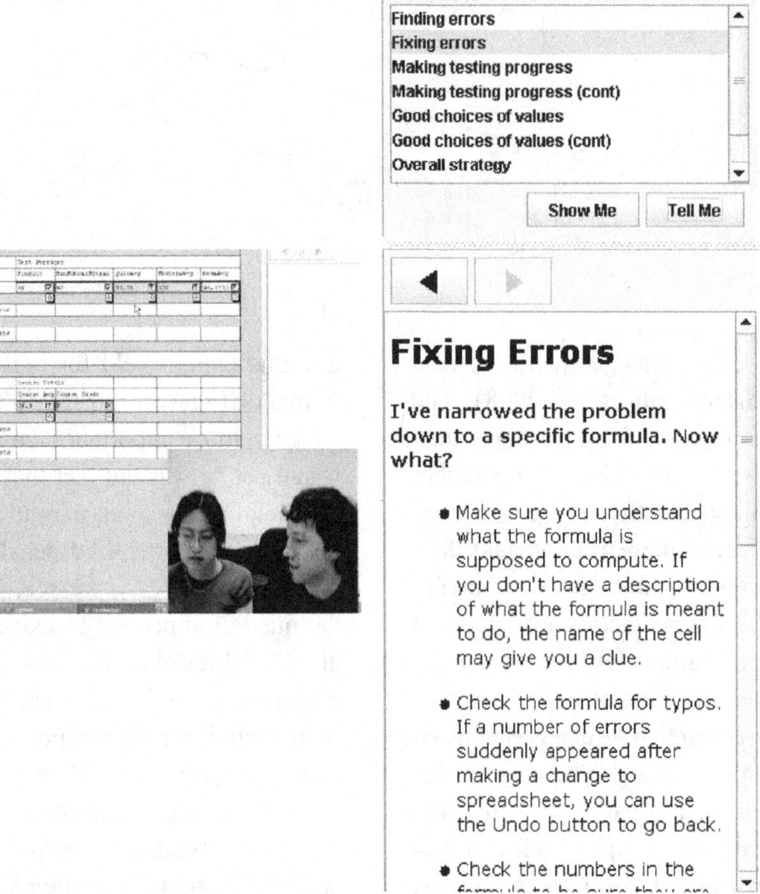

in the realm of end-user programming. However, the primary contribution is that they show, for the first time, that it is possible to design features in these environments that lower barriers to female effectiveness and help to close the gender gap.

THE STATUS OF END-USER SOFTWARE ENGINEERING AS AN AREA

The works presented in this paper are just a few examples of the work that has emerged in the past few years. In fact, the establishment and growth of end-user software engineering has exploded in recent years. Ten years ago, there was only a handful of research activity in end-user development beyond the "create" part of the software lifecycle. In fact, the "create" part (i.e., end-user programming) had dwindled in activity from its earlier heyday. In contrast, in the past five to six years, there has been much research and cross-fertilization among end-user software engineering, end-user development, and end-user programming, with many signs of a research community emerging around the concept of a whole lifecycle of software development that needs to be supported for end-user programmers.

Figure 8. Tinkering with X-marks (left) and √-marks (right), in marks per debugging minute. Note the gender gaps between the Control females' and males' medians. These gaps disappear in the Treatment group (Grigoreanu et al., 2008). © 2008 IEEE

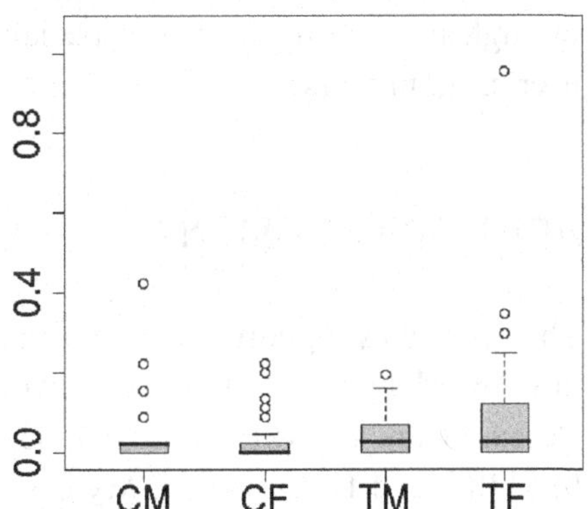

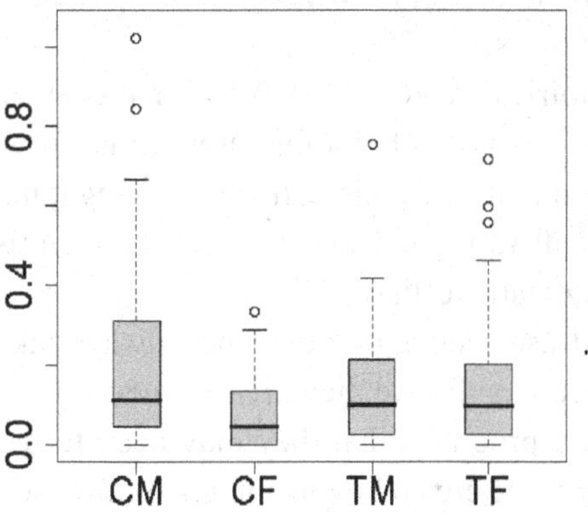

For example, hundreds of papers on these topics have appeared in the last five years. (Nearly 300 have emerged from the EUSES Consortium research group alone, which can be obtained at http://eusesconsortium.org) There have also been about ten conferences and workshops in the past five years, including the five-workshop series on End-User Software Engineering (WEUSE/SEEUP) at CHI, ICSE, and Dagstuhl, SIGs at CHI, and the advent of the End-User Development series of conferences. A special issue of Communications of the ACM on end-user development in 2004 included some papers on this topic, and a special issue of IEEE Software focusing directly on end-user software engineering will appear in fall 2009.

All of this activity shows the interest and activity in this area of work, but there is much more to be done. The field of (traditional) software engineering has decades of research behind it in multiple aspects of software engineering, dealing with quality aspects in lifecycle phases such as requirements, designing, testing, debugging, other forms of maintenance, reuse, software process, and more. These aspects of the software lifecycle phases are all issues in end-user development as well, and may be even more difficult to address given the users' lack of software engineering training. Also, although there has been a substantial amount of empirical work during recent years relating to this topic, most of it has consisted of in-the-lab studies. As the emerging tools become more mature, investigating their use in the field will be very important to understanding how well the approaches align with users' actual work practices. It is therefore clear that the area is still at a beginning, and significant future work is needed.

CONCLUSION

End-user software engineering matters when software quality matters. End-user software engineering takes end-user programming beyond the "create" stage, expanding to consider other elements of the software lifecycle. It matters because sometimes end users' software creations have flaws, and it empowers the end users to do something about these flaws.

This paper has summarized a few key lessons learned in this area. Among the key points were:

- The Surprise-Explain-Reward strategy and its attendant empirical work shows that it is possible to entice end users to use end-user software engineering tools, if the tool is designed to fit seamlessly and incrementally into users' ordinary work practices and tools.

- Empirical work with WYSIWYT showed that it is possible for end users to improve the quality of their software by engaging in software engineering practices such as systematic testing.
- End-user debugging does not always take place in software they created themselves; some programs that they may need to debug were created by machines. In that setting, empirical work has revealed that a particularly important barrier to their success was knowing *where* in the program to devote their efforts.
- Empirical work in spreadsheets revealed significant differences in male and female end-user programmers' usage of end-user software engineering features such as for debugging, with females' less attracted to and supported by many of the features than males. Further empirical work showed that the addition of two relatively small changes, namely the support of nuanced judgments and strategy-oriented support, could make a significant difference in females' usage of and benefit from these features, without introducing disadvantages for the males.

These examples are meant to demonstrate the essence of approaches that blend in equal measure human-computer interaction principles with software engineering knowledge. The primary point of the examples is that end-user software engineering's success rests on respecting end users' real goals and work habits. As the examples illustrate, we do not advocate trying to transform end users into engineers, nor do we propose to mimic the traditional engineering approaches of segregated support for each element of the software life cycle, or even to ask the user to think in such terms. Instead, we advocate promoting systematic ways an end-user programmer can guard against and solve software quality problems through mechanisms meant especially for end-user programmers.

ACKNOWLEDGMENT

This work was supported in part by an IBM Faculty Award, by the Air Force Office of Scientific Research, and by NSF grants ITR-0325273, IIS-0803487, and IIS-0917366. My colleagues and students in the EUSES Consortium contributed in numerous ways to the work summarized here, from making material contributions (as indicated by author lists of papers referenced) to helpful discussions, feedback, and ideas.

REFERENCES

Beckwith, L., Burnett, M., Grigoreanu, V., & Wiedenbeck, S. (2006). Gender HCI: What about the software? *Computer*, *39*(11), 83–87. doi:10.1109/MC.2006.382

Beckwith, L., Inman, D., Rector, K., & Burnett, M. (2007, September 23-27). On to the real world: Gender and self-efficacy in Excel. In *Proceedings of the IEEE Symposium on Visual Languages and Human-Centric Computing (VL/HCC 2007)*, Coeur d'Alene, ID (pp. 119-126). Washington, DC: IEEE Computer Society.

Beckwith, L., Sorte, S., Burnett, M., Wiedenbeck, S., Chintakovid, T., & Cook, C. (2005, September 20-24). Designing features for both genders in end-user programming environments. In *Proceedings of the 2005 IEEE Symposium on Visual Languages and Human-Centric Computing (VL/HCC 2005)*, Dallas, TX (pp. 153-160). Washington, DC: IEEE Computer Society.

Blackwell, A. (2002, September 3-6). First steps in programming: A rationale for attention investment models. In *Proceedings of the 2002 IEEE Symposium on Visual Languages and Human-Centric Computing (VL/HCC 2002),* Arlington, VA (pp. 2-10). Washington, DC: IEEE Computer Society.

Brewer, J., & Bassoli, A. (2006, May 23). Reflections of gender, reflections on gender: Designing ubiquitous computing technologies. In *Proceedings of Gender and Interaction: Real and Virtual Women in a Male World Workshop at AVI 2006,* Venice, Italy (pp. 9-12).

Burnett, M., Chekka, S., & Pandey, R. (2001, September 5-7). FAR: An end-user language to support cottage e-services. In *Proceedings of the IEEE Symposia on Human-Centric Computing Languages and Environments,* Stresa, Italy (pp. 195-202). Washington, DC: IEEE Computer Society.

Burnett, M., Cook, C., & Rothermel, G. (2004). End-user software engineering. *Communications of the ACM, 47*(9), 53–58. doi:10.1145/1015864.1015889

Carroll, J., & Rosson, M. (1987). Paradox of the active user. In J. Carrol (Ed.), *Interfacing thought: Cognitive aspects of human-computer interaction* (pp. 80-111). Cambridge, MA: MIT Press.

EUSPRIG. (2009). *Spreadsheet mistakes news stories*. Retrieved July 19, 2009, from http://www.eusprig.org/stories.htm

French, C. (2003, June 3). TransAlta says clerical snafu costs it $24 million. *Globe and Mail.*

Grigoreanu, V., Cao, J., Kulesza, T., Bogart, C., Rector, K., Burnett, M., et al. (2008, September 15-19). Can feature design reduce the gender gap in end-user software development environments? In *Proceedings of the the 2008 IEEE Symposium on Visual Languages and Human-Centric Computing (VL/HCC'08),* Herrsching am Ammersee, Germany (pp. 149-156). Washington, DC: IEEE Computer Society.

Kelleher, C., Pausch, R., & Kiesler, S. (2007, April 28-May 3). Storytelling Alice motivates middle school girls to learn computer programming. In *Proceedings of the ACM Conference on Human Factors in Computing Systems (CHI 2007),* San Jose, CA (pp. 1455-1464). ACM Publishing.

Ko, A. J., Abraham, R., Beckwith, L., Blackwell, A., Burnett, M., Erwig, M., et al. (2009 under review). The state of the art in end-user software engineering.

Ko, A. J., & Myers, B. (2004, April 24-29). Designing the whyline: A debugging interface for asking questions about program behavior. In *Proceedings of the ACM Conference on Human Factors in Computing Systems (CHI 2004),* Vienna, Austria (pp. 151-158). ACM Publishing.

Kulesza, T., Wong, W., Stumpf, S., Perona, S., White, R., Burnett, M., et al. (2009, February 8-11). Fixing the program my computer learned: Barriers for end users, challenges for the machine. In *Proceedings of the 13th International Conference on Intelligent User Interfaces,* Sanibel Island, FL (pp. 187-196). ACM Publishing.

Lieberman, H. (Ed.). (2001). *Your wish is my command: Programming by example*. San Francisco: Morgan Kaufmann Publishers.

Lieberman, H., Paterno, F., & Wulf, V. (Eds.). (2006). *End-user development*. New York: Springer.

Little, G., Lau, T., Cypher, A., Lin, J., Haber, E., & Kandogan, E. (2007, April 28-May 3). Koala: Capture, share, automate, personalize business processes on the web. In *Proceedings of the ACM Conference on Human Factors in Computing Systems (CHI 2007),* San Jose, CA (pp. 943-946). ACM Publishing.

Lorigo, L., Pan, B., Hembrooke, H., Joachims, T., Granka, L., & Gay, G. (2006). The influence of task and gender on search and evaluation behavior using Google. *Information Processing & Management, 42*(4), 1123–1131. doi:10.1016/j.ipm.2005.10.001

Lowenstein, G. (1994). The psychology of curiosity. *Psychological Bulletin, 116*(1), 75–98. doi:10.1037/0033-2909.116.1.75

Myers, B., Weitzman, D., Ko, A., & Chau, D. H. (2006, April 22-27). Answering why and why not questions in user interfaces. In *Proceedings of the ACM Conference on Human Factors in Computing Systems,* Montreal, Quebec, Canada (pp. 397-406). ACM Publishing.

Nardi, B. (1993). *A small matter of programming: Perspectives on end-user computing*. Cambridge, MA: MIT Press.

Pane, J., Myers, B., & Miller, L. (2002, September 3-6). Using HCI techniques to design a more usable programming system. In *Proceedings of the 2002 IEEE International Conference on Human-Centric Computing Languages and Environments (HCC 2002),* Arlington, VA (pp. 198-206). Washington, DC: IEEE Computer Society.

Repenning, A., & Ioannidou, A. (2006, September 4-8) AgentCubes: Raising the ceiling of end-user development in education through incremental 3D. In *Proceedings of the 2006 IEEE Symposium on Visual Languages and Human-Centric Computing (VL/HCC 2006),* Brighton, UK (pp. 27-31). Washington, DC: IEEE Computer Society.

Rode, J. A., Toye, E. F., & Blackwell, A. F. (2004). The fuzzy felt ethnography - understanding the programming patterns of domestic appliances. *Personal and Ubiquitous Computing, 8,* 161–176. doi:10.1007/s00779-004-0272-0

Rosson, M., Ballin, J., & Nash, H. (2004, September 26-29). Everyday programming: Challenges and opportunities for informal web development. In *Proceedings of the 2004 IEEE Symposium on Visual Languages and Human-Centric Computing (VL/HCC 2004),* Rome, Italy (pp. 123-130). Washington, DC: IEEE Computer Society.

Rosson, M., Ballin, J., & Rode, J. (2005, September 21-24). Who, what, and how? A survey of informal and professional web developers. In *Proceedings of the 2005 IEEE Symposium on Visual Languages and Human-Centric Computing (VL/HCC 2005),* Dallas, TX (pp. 199-206). Washington, DC: IEEE Computer Society.

Rosson, M., Sinha, H., Bhattacharya, M., & Zhao, D. (2007, September 23-27). Design planning in end-user web development. In *Proceedings of the IEEE Symposium on Visual Languages and Human-Centric Computing (VL/HCC 2007),* Coeur d'Alene, ID (pp. 189-196). Washington, DC: IEEE Computer Society.

Rothermel, G., Burnett, M., Li, L., DuPuis, C., & Sheretov, A. (2001). A methodology for testing spreadsheets. *ACM Transactions on Software Engineering, 10*(1), 110–147. doi:10.1145/366378.366385

Rothermel, K., Cook, C., Burnett, M., Schonfeld, J., Green, T., & Rothermel, G. (2000, June 4-11). WYSIWYT testing in the spreadsheet paradigm: An empirical evaluation. In *Proceedings of the 22nd International Conference on Software Engineering,* Limerick, Ireland (pp. 230-239). ACM Publishing.

Ruthruff, J., Phalgune, A., Beckwith, L., Burnett, M., & Cook, C. (2004, September 26-29). Rewarding good behavior: End-user debugging and rewards. In *Proceedings of the 2004 IEEE Symposium on Visual Languages and Human-Centric Computing (VL/HCC 2004),* Rome, Italy (pp. 115-122). Washington, DC: IEEE Computer Society.

Scaffidi, C., Shaw, M., & Myers, B. (2005, September 20-24). Estimating the numbers of end users and end user programmers. In *Proceedings of the 2005 IEEE Symposium on Visual Languages and Human-Centric Computing (VL/HCC 2005),* Dallas, TX (pp. 207-214). Washington, DC: IEEE Computer Society.

Stumpf, S., Rajaram, V., Li, L., Burnett, M., Dietterich, T., Sullivan, E., et al. (2007, January 28-31). Toward harnessing user feedback for machine learning. In *Proceedings of the 12th International Conference on Intelligent User Interfaces,* Honolulu, HI (pp. 82-91). ACM Publishing.

Stumpf, S., Sullivan, E., Fitzhenry, E., Oberst, I., Wong, W., & Burnett, M. (2008, January 13-16). Integrating rich user feedback into intelligent user interfaces. In *Proceedings of the 13th International Conference on Intelligent User Interfaces,* Gran Canaria, Spain (pp. 50-59). ACM Publishing.

Subrahmaniyan, N., Beckwith, L., Grigoreanu, V., Burnett, M., Wiedenbeck, S., Narayanan, V., et al. (2008, April 5-10). Testing vs. code inspection vs.... What else? Male and female end users' debugging strategies. In Proceedings of the *ACM Conference on Human Factors in Computing Systems (CHI 2008),* Florence, Italy (pp. 617-626). ACM Publishing.

Subrahmaniyan, N., Burnett, M., & Bogart, C. (2008, September 16-17). Software visualization for end-user programmers: Trial period obstacles. *ACM Symposium on Software Visualization,* Herrsching am Ammersee, Germany (pp. 135-144). ACM Publishing.

Subrahmaniyan, N., Kissinger, C., Rector, K., Inman, D., Kaplan, J., Beckwith, L., et al. (2007, September 23-27). Explaining debugging strategies to end-user programmers. In *Proceedings of the 2007 IEEE Symposium on Visual Languages and Human-Centric Computing (VL/HCC 2007),* Coeur d'Alene, ID (pp. 127-134). Washington, DC: IEEE Computer Society.

Wilcox, E., Atwood, J., Burnett, M., Cadiz, J., & Cook, C. (1997, March 22-27). Does continuous visual feedback aid debugging in direct-manipulation programming systems? *ACM Conference on Human Factors in Computing Systems (CHI 1997),* Atlanta, GA (pp. 258-265). ACM Publishing.

Wilson, A., Burnett, M., Beckwith, L., Granatir, O., Casburn, L., Cook, C., et al. (2003, April 5-10). Harnessing curiosity to increase correctness in end-user programming. In *Proceedings of the ACM Conference on Human Factors in Computing Systems (CHI 2003),* Fort Lauderdale, FL (pp. 305-312). ACM Publishing.

ENDNOTE

1. For example, a work spreadsheet clearly carries different expectations than a vacation planning spreadsheet. Demonstrating this point, investigations into informal Web developers (Rosson, Ballin, & Nash, 2004; Rosson, Ballin, & Rode, 2005) showed the importance of work versus personal Web development. In these investigations, about half the Web development done by end-user programmers was for work and about half was personal. One of the most important distinguishing characteristics in terms of behaviors, testing attitudes and processes was whether their Web development was done in work contexts.

This work was previously published in Journal of Organizational and End User Computing, Volume 22, Issue 1, edited by M. Adam Mahmood, pp. 1-22, copyright 2010 by IGI Publishing (an imprint of IGI Global).

Chapter 10
End User Development and Meta-Design:
Foundations for Cultures of Participation

Gerhard Fischer
University of Colorado, USA

ABSTRACT

The first decade of the World Wide Web predominantly enforced a clear separation between designers and consumers. New technological developments, such as the participatory Web 2.0 architectures, have emerged to support social computing. These developments are the foundations for a fundamental shift from consumer cultures (specialized in producing finished goods) to cultures of participation (in which all people can participate actively in personally meaningful activities). End-user development and meta-design provide foundations for this fundamental transformation. They explore and support new approaches for the design, adoption, appropriation, adaptation, evolution, and sharing of artifacts by all participating stakeholders. They take into account that cultures of participation are not dictated by technology alone: they are the result of incremental shifts in human behavior and social organizations. The design, development, and assessment of five particular applications that contributed to the development of our theoretical framework are described and discussed.

INTRODUCTION

Cultures are defined in part by their media and their tools for thinking, working, learning, and collaborating (McLuhan, 1964). In the past, the design of most media emphasized a clear distinction between producers and consumers (Benkler, 2006). Television is the medium that most obviously exhibits this orientation (Postman, 1985) and in the worst case contributes to the degeneration of humans into "couch potatoes" (Fischer, 2002) for whom remote controls are the most important instruments of their cognitive activities. In a similar manner, our current educational

DOI: 10.4018/978-1-4666-0140-6.ch010

institutions often treat learners as consumers, fostering a mindset in students of "consumerism" (Illich, 1971) rather than "ownership of problems" for the rest of their lives (Bruner, 1996). As a result, learners, workers, and citizens often feel left out of decisions made by teachers, managers, and policymakers, denying them opportunities in taking active roles in personally meaningful and important problems.

The personal computer can produce, in principle, an incredible increase in the creative autonomy of the individual. But historically these possibilities were often of interest and accessible only to a small number of "high-tech scribes." *End-user development (EUD)* (Lieberman, Paterno, & Wulf, 2006) is focused on the challenge of allowing users of software systems who are not primarily interested in software per se to modify, extend, evolve, and create systems that fit their needs.

What the personal computer has done for the individual, the Internet has done for groups and communities. The first decade of the Internet use was dominated by broadcast models and thereby extended the existing strong separation of "designers" and "users" imposed by existing media. *Meta-design* (Fischer & Giaccardi, 2006) is an evolving framework to exploit computational media in support of collaboration and communication in fostering cultures of participation.

END-USER DEVELOPMENT (EUD)

Familiarity with software applications has become an essential requirement for professionals in a variety of complex domains: architects, doctors, engineers, biochemists, statisticians, and film directors (among many others) all depend on the mastery of various collections of applications (Eisenberg & Fischer, 1994) in their areas of expertise. These applications, to be at all useful, must provide domain professionals with complex and powerful functionality. However, in doing so, these systems likewise increase the cognitive cost of mastering the new capabilities and resources that they offer. Moreover, the users of these applications will notice that "software is not soft"—that is, that the behavior of a given application cannot be changed or meaningfully extended without substantial reprogramming effort.

The need for end-user development is not a luxury but a necessity: computational systems modeling some particular "world" are never complete; they must evolve over time because (1) the world changes and new requirements emerge; and (2) skilled domain professionals change their work practices over time—their understanding and use of a system will be very different after a month and certainly after several years. If systems cannot be modified to support new practices, users will be locked into existing patterns of use.

These problems were recognized early in the context of expert systems and domain-oriented environments as illustrated by the following two examples:

- **Expert systems:** The TEIRESIAS system (Davis, 1984) was a module to support domain professionals to augment the existing knowledge base of a medical expert system; the objective of this component was to establish and support interaction at a discourse level that would allow domain professionals to articulate their knowledge without having to program in LISP.
- **Domain-oriented environments:** The JANUS-MODIFIER system (Fischer & Girgensohn, 1990; Girgensohn, 1992) supported not just human-computer interaction but *human problem-domain interaction* to allow kitchen designers to introduce new components and new critiquing rules into design environments in support of kitchen design.

From a more theoretical perspective, EUD can address the following problems and challenges:

Table 1. A differentiation among related frameworks

Framework	Major Objectives
End-User Programming (EUP)	Empower and support end-users to program (with techniques such as: programming by demonstration, visual programming, scripting languages, and domain-specific languages)
End-User Software Engineering (EUSE)	Add to EUP support for systematic and disciplined activities for the whole software lifecycle (including: reliability, efficiency, usability, version control)
End-User Development (EUD)	Focus on a broader set of developments (e.g., creating 3D models with SketchUp, modifying games); it puts end-users as owners of problems in charge and makes them independent of high-tech scribes
Meta-Design	Define a framework and a design methodology to explicitly "design for designers" by defining contexts that allow end-users to create content; applicable to different contexts and encompasses principles that may apply to programming, software engineering, architecture, urban planning, education, interactive arts, and other design fields
Cultures of Participation	Foster a culture (supported by meta-design) in which people have the opportunity to actively participate in personally meaningful problems in ways and at levels that they are motivated to do so.

- **Ill-defined or wicked problems:** (Rittel & Webber, 1984) cannot be delegated from domain professionals to software professionals, but require the creation of externalizations that talk back to the owner of the problem (Schön, 1983).
- **Breakdowns:** (Fischer, 1994) are experienced by domain professionals and not by the system developers; if domain professionals can respond to these breakdowns without relying on "high-tech scribes," systems will evolve in response to real needs.

Professional programmers and *domain professionals* define the endpoints of a continuum of computer users. The former like computers because they can program, and the latter because they get their work done. The goal of supporting domain professionals to develop and modify systems does not imply transferring the responsibility of good system design to the end-user (Burnett, Cook, & Rothermel, 2004). Generally, normal users will not build tools of the quality a professional designer would, which was recognized as one of the basic limitations of second-generation design methods (Rittel, 1984). However, if a tool does not satisfy the needs or the tastes of the end-users (who know best what these requirements are), then end-users should be able to adapt and evolve the system (Wulf, Pipek, & Won, 2008).

The concepts of end-user programming (EUP), end-user software engineering (EUSE), end-user development (EUD), meta-design, and cultures of participation are related with each other but emphasize different research directions and challenges. The following sections provide a brief description of these frameworks.

A "NEW WORLD" BASED ON CULTURES OF PARTICIPATION

As the research community interested in EUD gathered in 2009 for the *Second International Symposium on End-User Development* (Pipek, Rossen, deRuyter, & Wulf, 2009), an interesting question was: What has changed since the first symposium took place in 2003 (as documented in the book *End-User Development* (Lieberman et al., 2006), which includes a chapter about the future of EUD (Klann, Paterno, & Wulf, 2006))? The major innovation and transformation that emerged between 2003 and 2009 was the *participatory web* (or Web 2.0; O'Reilly, 2006) and social computing (Kellogg, 2007), complementing and transcending the *broadcast web* (or Web 1.0), which dominated the first decade of the Web.

The Web 1.0 model primarily supports Web page publishing and e-commerce, whereas the Web 2.0 model is focused on collaborative design environments, social media, and social networks creating feasibility spaces allowing users to participate rather than being confined to passive consumer roles (Brown, Duguid, & Haviland, 1994).

This transformation represents a fundamental shift from *consumer cultures* (focused on passive consumption of finished goods produced by others) (Postman, 1985) to *cultures of participation* (in which all people are provided with the means to participate actively in personally meaningful activities) (Fischer, 2002; von Hippel, 2005). End-user development is an essential component of this transformation, but its impact is much broader: this transformation represents a change and new opportunities for social production, for mass collaboration, for civic and political life, and for education.

The EUD research community has struggled to make its objectives and techniques known to the world for the past 20 years. The Web 2.0 world has attracted a very large number of contributors that have created a number of success models (including open source software, Wikipedia, Second Life, YouTube, and 3D Warehouse, to name just a few) by breaking down the boundaries between producers and consumers. The research community interested in EUD now has an opportunity to apply its research findings and create a theoretical framework to deeply understand these new developments and evolve them further. This "new world" has established new discourses, including the following:

- Beyond the dichotomy between consumers and producers, new, middle-ground models have emerged such as:
    - **Prosumers:** (Tapscott & Williams, 2006), who are techno-sophisticated and comfortable with the technologies with which they grew up. They have little fear of hacking, modifying, and evolving artifacts to their own requirements. They do not wait for someone else to anticipate their needs, and they can decide what is important for them. They participate in learning and discovery and engage in experimenting, exploring, building, tinkering, framing, solving, and reflecting.
    - **Professional Amateurs:** (Brown, 2005; Leadbeater & Miller, 2008), who are innovative, committed, and networked amateurs working up to professional standards. They are a new social hybrid, and their activities are not adequately captured by the traditional dichotomous definitions of work and leisure, professional and amateur, consumption and production.
    - **Social Production** and **Mass Collaboration:** (Benkler, 2006), which are based on the following facts: (a) a tiny percentage of a very large base is still a substantial number of people; (b) beyond the large quantitative numbers of contributors, there exists a great diversity of interests and passions among users (which can be characterized by the Long Tail (Anderson, 2006)); and (c) while human beings often act for material rewards, they can also be motivated by social capital, reputation, connectedness, and the enjoyment derived from giving things of value away (Fischer, Scharff, & Ye, 2004)
- An emphasis on *open systems* and *open design spaces* (Budweg, Draxler, Lohmann,

Rashid, & Stevens, 2009), which are systems focused on the "unfinished" and take into account that design problems have no stopping rule, need to remain open and fluid to accommodate ongoing change, and for which "continuous beta" becomes a desirable rather than a to-be-avoided attribute.

- The importance of *user-generated content*, in which "content" is broadly defined: (a) creating artifacts with existing tools (e.g., writing a document with a word processor) (Costabile, Mussino, Provenza, & Piccinno, 2009) or (b) changing the tools (e.g., writing macros to extend the word processor as a tool). In specific environments, such as open source software (Fischer, Piccinno, & Ye, 2008), the content is subject to the additional requirement of being computationally interpretable. A particular application domain (E-government Web sites) for user-generated content is described and analyzed in (Fogli, 2009) with an emphasis how to extend content management systems with EUD techniques.
- **Mutual Development:** (see Andersen & Mørch, 2009; Mørch & Andersen, this issue) is a model for how professional developers and end users contribute to development in both design and use. This research identified a range of end-user development activities (from use to design) taking place in the interaction between a software house and some of their customers. It identified five activities (adaptation, generalization, improvement requests, specialization, and tailoring) and describes what developers are doing, what customers are doing and where their activities meet and overlap.
- Moving from guidelines, rules, and procedures to *exceptions, negotiations, and work-arounds* to complement and integrate accredited and expert knowledge with informal, practice-based, and situated knowledge (Orr, 1996; Suchman, 1987; Winograd & Flores, 1986).
- Exploiting the *Long Tail* (Anderson, 2006) of knowledge distribution, allowing people from around the world to engage in topics and activities about which they feel passionate.
- Fostering and supporting richer *ecologies of participation* (Fischer et al., 2008; Preece & Shneiderman, 2009)
- Creating a new understanding of motivation, creativity, control, ownership, and quality (Benkler & Nissenbaum, 2006; Fischer, 2007).

META-DESIGN

Meta-design (Fischer & Giaccardi, 2006) is focused on "design for designers." It creates open systems at design time that can be modified by their users acting as co-designers, requiring and supporting more complex interactions at use time. Meta-design is grounded in the basic assumption that future uses and problems cannot be completely anticipated at design time, when a system is developed. At use time, users will invariably discover mismatches between their needs and the support that an existing system can provide for them. Meta-design contributes to the invention and design of socio-technical environments (Mumford, 1987) in which humans can express themselves and engage in personally meaningful activities. The conceptual frameworks that we have developed around meta-design explore some fundamental challenges including the following:

- How can we support skilled domain workers who are neither novices nor naive users, but who are interested in their work and who see the computer as a means rather than as an end?
- How can we create co-adaptive environments, in which users change because

they learn, and in which systems change because users become co-developers and active contributors?

- How can we deal with the active participation and empowerment in domains whose boundaries blur and dissolve beyond the limits of definite and independent professional domains, practices, and technologies?

Meta-design allows significant modifications when the need arises. It reduces the gap in the world of computing between a population of elite high-tech scribes who can act as designers and a much larger population of intellectually disenfranchised knowledge workers who are *forced* into consumer roles.

The *seeding, evolutionary growth, and reseeding (SER) model* (Fischer & Ostwald, 2002) is an emerging descriptive and prescriptive model in support of meta-design. Instead of attempting to build complete systems at design time, the SER model advocates building *seeds* (in participatory design activities with meta-designers and end-users) that can evolve over time through small contributions of a large number of people (being the defining characteristics of a culture of participation). It postulates that systems that evolve over a sustained time span must continually alternate between periods of planned activity (the seeding phase), unplanned evolution (the evolutionary growth phase), and periods of deliberate (re)structuring and enhancement (the reseeding phase). A seed is something that has the potential to change and grow. In socio-technical environments, seeds need to be designed and created for the *technical* as well as the *social* component of the environment.

To be more specific about the role of meta-designers it is useful to answer the question: *what do they do?* Meta-designers use their own creativity to create socio-technical environments in which other people can be creative. Their main activity shifts from predetermining the meaning, functionality, and content of a system to that of encouraging and supporting end-users to act as designers and engage in these activities. Meta-designers must be willing to share control of how systems will be used, which content will be contained, and which functionality will be supported. They do so with a focus on *underdesign* (Brand, 1995; Habraken, 1972) which:

- Is grounded in the need for "loose fit" in designing artifacts at design time so that unexpected uses of the artifact can be accommodated at use time; it does so by creating contexts and content-creation tools rather than focusing on content alone;
- Avoids design decisions being made in the start of the design process, when everyone knows the least of what is needed;
- Offers users (acting as designers at use time) as many alternatives as possible, avoiding irreversible commitments they cannot undo (one of the drawbacks of overdesign);
- Acknowledges the necessity to differentiate between structurally important parts for which extensive professional experience is required and therefore not be easily changed (such as structure bearing walls in buildings); and components which users should be able to modify to their needs because their personal knowledge is relevant; and
- Creates technical and social conditions for broad participation in design activities by supporting "hackability" and "remixability."

The American Constitution can be considered as one of the biggest success cases for underdesign (Simon, 1996). Written more than 200 years ago and updated by only a small number of amendments, it still serves as a foundation for the United States of America in a world that has changed dramatically.

Figure 1. Different levels of participation and engagement

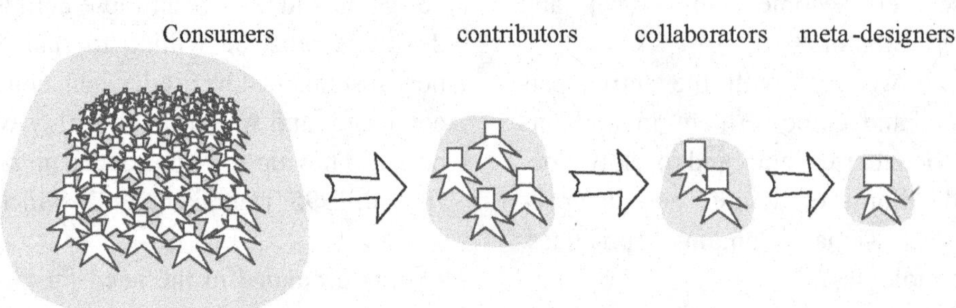

Richer Ecologies of Participation

The traditional notions of developer and user are unable to reflect the fact that many socio-technical environments nowadays are developed with the participation of many people with varied interests and capabilities. Cultures of participation require contributors with diverse background knowledge who require different support and value different ways of participating. Many collaborative design environments serve *only as content management* systems: participants contribute and share their *own* interests and abilities, and additional activities such as critiquing, rating, tagging, deliberating, extending, improving, and negotiating do not take place and are not adequately supported; their value is therefore not sufficiently recognized.

Figure 1 (inspired by the "reader to leader" framework of Preece and Shneiderman, 2009) illustrates a richer ecology underlying cultures of participation by postulating four major roles.

As participants move from left to right, the complexity of their tasks and the amount they have to learn increases. To accept these additional efforts participants must consider these tasks as personally meaningful (Fischer, 2002) and the migration paths need to be supported by a gentle slope system in which the transitions from one level to another level are smooth.

Within one level, these roles can be further differentiated. Early studies (Gantt & Nardi, 1992) already identified that EUP and EUD are more successful if supported by collaborative work practices rather than focusing on individuals. Gantt and Nardi observed the emergence of "gardeners" (also known as "power users" and "local developers"), who are technically interested and sophisticated enough to perform system modifications that are needed by a community of users, but that other end-users are not able, or inclined to perform.

A detailed analysis of open-source software systems (Ye & Fischer, 2007) revealed a variety of different roles: (1) *passive users* (using the system); (2) *readers* (trying to understand how the system works by reading the source code); (3) *bug reporters* (discovering and reporting bugs); (4) *bug fixers* (fixing bugs); (5) *peripheral developers* (occasionally contributing new functionality or features); (6) *active developers* (regularly contributing new features and fixing bugs); and (7) *project leader(s)* (initiating the project and being responsible for its vision and overall direction).

In the SketchUp/3D Warehouse/Google Earth environments, a similar role distribution can be observed: contributors create new models with SketchUp, raters and taggers evaluate and describe these models, and curators organize models in collections and create narratives (see Figure 8).

Motivation, Control, Ownership, Creativity, and Quality

As argued before, understanding and fostering cultures of participation with meta-design requires paying attention to factors from political, economical, and social domains (Fischer, 2007). This section takes a brief look at a few of those factors.

Motivation

Human beings are diversely motivated beings. We act not only for material gain, but also for psychological well being, for social integration and connectedness, for social capital, for recognition, and for improving our standing in a reputation economy. The motivation for going the extra step to engage in EUD was articulated by Rittel (1984, p. 320): "The experience of having participated in a problem makes a difference to those who are affected by the solution. People are more likely to like a solution if they have been involved in its generation; even though it might not make sense otherwise." Meta-design relies on intrinsic motivation for participation and has the potential to influence this by providing contributors with the sense and experience of joint creativity; by giving them a sense of common purpose and mutual support in achieving it; and in many situations, by replacing common background or geographic proximity with a sense of well-defined purpose, shared concerns, and the successful common pursuit of these.

Control

As argued above, meta-design supports users as active contributors who can transcend the functionality and content of existing systems. By facilitating these possibilities, *control* is distributed among all stakeholders in the design process. The importance of this distribution of control has been emphasized as important for architecture (Alexander, 1984, p. 314): "I believe passionately in the idea that people should design buildings for themselves. In other words, not only that they should be involved in the buildings that are for them but that they should actually help design them." Other arguments indicate that shared control will lead to more innovation (von Hippel, 2005): "Users that innovate can develop exactly what they want, rather than relying on manufacturers to act as their (often very imperfect) agents."

Ownership

Our experiences gathered in the context of the design, development, and assessment of our systems indicate that meta-design methodologies are less successful when users are brought into the process late (thereby denying them ownership) and when they are "misused" to fix problems and to address weaknesses of systems that the developers did not fix themselves. Meta-design does work when users are part of the participatory design effort in establishing a meta-design framework, including support for intrinsic and extrinsic motivation, user toolkits for reducing the effort to make contributions, and the seeding of use communities in which individuals can share their contributions.

Social Creativity

Where do new ideas come from in meta-design environments and cultures of participation? The creativity potential is grounded in (1) user-driven innovations, (2) taking advantage of breakdowns as sources for creativity, and (3) exploiting the symmetry of ignorance and conceptual collisions (Fischer, 2000). To increase social creativity requires: (1) *diversity* (each participant should have some unique information or perspective); (2) *independence* (participants' opinions are not determined by the opinions of those around them) (Surowiecki, 2005); (3) *decentralization* (participants are able to specialize and draw on local knowledge) (Anderson, 2006); and (4) *aggregation* (mechanisms exist for turning individual contributions into collections, and private judgments into collective decisions). In addition, participants must be able to express themselves (requiring technical knowledge on how to contribute), must be willing to contribute (motivation), and must be allowed to have their voices heard (control).

Quality

Many teachers will tell their students that they will not accept research findings and argumentation based on articles from Wikipedia. This exclusion is usually based on considerations such as: *How are we to know that the content produced by widely dispersed and qualified individuals is not of substandard quality?*

The online journal *Nature* (http://www.nature.com/) has compared the quality of articles found in the *Encyclopedia Britannica* with Wikipedia and has come to the conclusion that *Wikipedia comes close to Britannica in terms of the accuracy of its science entries.* This study and the interpretation of its findings has generated a controversy, and Doctorow (2006) has challenged the basic assumption that a direct comparison between the two encyclopedias is a relevant issue: "Wikipedia isn't great because it's like the Britannica. The Britannica is great at being authoritative, edited, expensive, and monolithic. Wikipedia is great at being free, brawling, universal, and instantaneous."

There are many more open issues to be investigated about quality and trust (Kittur, Suh, & Chi, 2008) in cultures of participation, including: (1) errors will always exist, resulting in learners acquiring the important skill of always being critical of information rather than blindly believing in what others (specifically experts or teachers) are saying; and (2) ownership as a critical dimension: the community at large has a greater sense of ownership and thereby is more willing to put an effort into fixing errors. This last issue has been explored in open source communities and has led to the observation that "if there are enough eyeballs, all bugs are shallow" (Raymond & Young, 2001, p. 30).

THE UBIQUITY OF META-DESIGN: EXPLORING DIFFERENT APPLICATION DOMAINS

Meta-design transcends end-user development by studying and supporting cultures of participation not only in the area of software artifacts, but in numerous other domains of information and cultural production and it explores different purposes associated with the artifacts under development. In our research, we have explored meta-design (Fischer & Giaccardi, 2006) in the following areas:

- **Design of computational artifacts:** (Lieberman et al., 2006), with an emphasis on customization, personalization, tailorability, end-user modifiability, and design for diversity;
- **Architectural design:** (Brand, 1995), with an emphasis on underdesign and support for an *unself-conscious culture of design* (Alexander, 1964);
- **New models of teaching and learning:** (Brown, 2005; Rogoff, Matsuov, & White, 1998), with an emphasis on learning communities, teachers as meta-designers, and courses-as-seeds (dePaula, Fischer, & Ostwald, 2001). These approaches challenge the assumption that information must move from teachers and other credentialed producers to passive learners and consumers (Illich, 1971);
- **Open source:** (Raymond & Young, 2001), with an emphasis on open source as a success model of decentralized, collaborative, evolutionary development (Scharff, 2002); and

- **Interactive art:** (Giaccardi, 2004), with an emphasis on collaboration and co-creation facilitated by putting the tools rather than the object of design in the hands of users.

In our currently active research, we are further deepening our understanding of meta-design and cultures of participation with the following projects that are described in the following sections:

- *The Envisionment and Discovery Collaboratory, a table-top computing environment supporting stakeholders from diverse backgrounds in face-to-face meetings;*
- *The Memory Aiding Prompting System (MAPS) supporting people with cognitive disabilities and their caregivers;*
- *The "SketchUp+3D Warehouse+ Google Earth" environment in which people from around the world can share 3D models created with SketchUp, and allowing these models to be referenced and displayed in Google Earth;*
- *The SAP Community Network, an example of a successful socio-technical environment consisting of more than one million registered users forming a highly active online community; and*
- *The CreativeIT, a wiki-based environment fostering and supporting the evolving scientific community participating in the NSF Program on "Creativity and IT."*

The Envisionment and Discovery Collaboratory (EDC)

The EDC (Arias, Eden, Fischer, Gorman, & Scharff, 2000) is a long-term research platform that explores conceptual frameworks for democratizing design in the context of framing and resolving complex urban planning by bringing together participants from various backgrounds in face-to-face meetings. The knowledge to understand, frame, and solve such problems does not already exist (Engeström, 2001), but is constructed and evolves during the solution process—an ideal environment to study meta-design and cultures of participation.

The EDC represents a *socio-technical environment* that incorporates a number of innovative technologies, including table-top computing, the integration of physical and computational components supporting new interaction techniques (Eden, 2002), and an open architecture supporting meta-design activities.

Figure 2 shows members of the Boulder City Council and the Regents of the University of Colorado using our table-top computing environment to engage in participatory problem solving and decision making related to urban planning issues that are of concern to all participants.

The vision of the EDC is to provide contextualized support for *reflection-in-action* (Schön, 1983) within collaborative design activities. In our research with the EDC during the last decade, we have observed:

- More creative solutions to problems can emerge from the collective interactions with the environment by *heterogeneous communities* (such as *communities of interest* (Fischer, 2001), which are more diverse than *communities of practice* (Janis, 1972; Wenger, 1998)).
- Boundary objects are needed (Star, 1989) to establish common ground and establish shared understanding for communities of interest.
- Participants must be able to naturally express what they want to say (Myers, Ko, & Burnett, 2006).
- Interaction mechanisms must have a "low threshold" for easy participation and a "high ceiling" for expressing sophisticated ideas (Shneiderman, 2007).
- Participants are more readily engaged if they perceive the design activities as per-

Figure 2. A participatory problem-solving and decision-making environment. the tabletop computing environment supports participation by maximizing the richness of communication among stakeholders in face-to-face interaction, mediated by both physical and computational objects.

sonally meaningful by associating a purpose with their involvement (Brown et al., 1994; Rittel, 1984).

Obstacles to further investigate the above observations rest with the difficulties of democratizing the design of the EDC (von Hippel, 2005) by providing more control to the participants. Each urban-planning problem is *unique*: it has to take into consideration the geography, culture, and population of specific cities. Currently, EDC developers have to customize the system at the source-code level to reflect the specific characteristics of the city and its urban planning problem. In most cases, EDC developers (the meta-designers) do not have sufficient knowledge of the problem and the social context; they do not know which issues are of greatest concern to the city planners and citizens and which conflicts need to be resolved through the EDC system. The domain- and context-specific knowledge is sticky, tacit, and difficult to transfer from local urban planners to EDC developers (Polanyi, 1966).

We are in the process of creating a more powerful meta-design environment, the *Scenario-Design-Kit* (SDK) that will empower participants to dynamically configure the EDC system to fit their specific needs without detailed knowledge of programming.

Figure 3 illustrates a scenario that urban planners would be able to construct with the proposed SDK. Charged with community engagement on a new development, the planners will utilize the SDK to pull together numerous geographic information system (GIS) resources (maps, plans, census data, existing buildings, traffic statistics, etc.) related to a proposed project. Selecting from a number of pre-existing tools, models, and simulations, planners assemble an environment for a series of community meetings allowing neighborhood groups to understand and provide feedback on the impact of new construction.

The EDC interactive table (pane a in Figure 3, used as an action space for citizen participants) will allow them to bring their individual perspectives to the process and collectively interact with the emerging design (for example, sketching

Figure 3. The Integration among the three applications (Portions adapted from: http://sketchup.google.com/3dwarehouse)

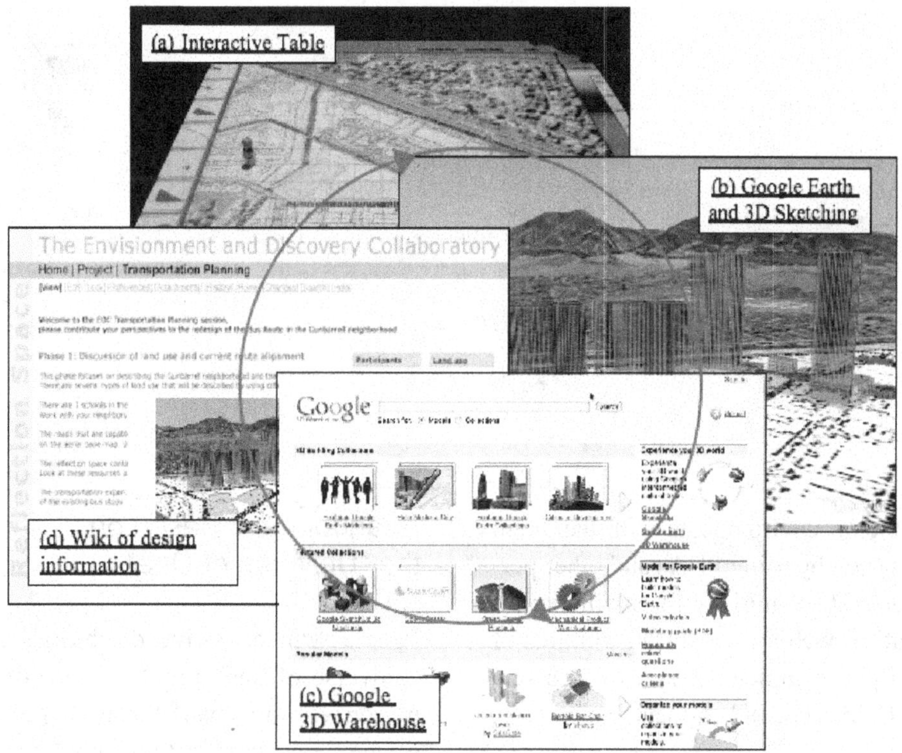

proposed elements). Sketches will be shown in Google Earth as a simple 3D model (pane b) to allow participants to visualize the impacts of the design on neighborhood views and local environments so they can discuss whether a proposed high building would block the view of the mountains from certain neighborhoods. As the process progresses, the crude sketches could be used to locate exemplars in the 3D Warehouse (pane c) or they could be imported to SketchUp to create more complete models to be used in both the action space and the 3D Google-Earth *reflection space* (Schön, 1983).

In addition, the SDK will support creation of wiki spaces (pane d) to host participatory discussion issues surrounding the proposed development. The wiki will be integrated with the EDC interactive table and Google Earth to allow the results of design sessions to be captured and provide access to broader participation by neighbors. The wiki Web sites will serve as reflection spaces and allow those who could not participate in the meeting to view the sketches in Google Earth and provide their comments and ideas as feedback. The collected feedback will then be linked to the project, and future discussions of the development will activate a display of the comments that are contextualized to the design elements.

Another dimension of the EDC research consists of deepening our understanding of and support for the creative processes and technologies needed to integrate *individual and social creativity* (Fischer, Giaccardi, Eden, Sugimoto, & Ye, 2005). The Carretta project (Fischer & Sugimoto, 2006; Sugimoto, Hosoi, & Hashizume, 2004) has integrated and intertwined collective interaction

Figure 4. Meta-Design: Empowering Caregivers to Act as Designers

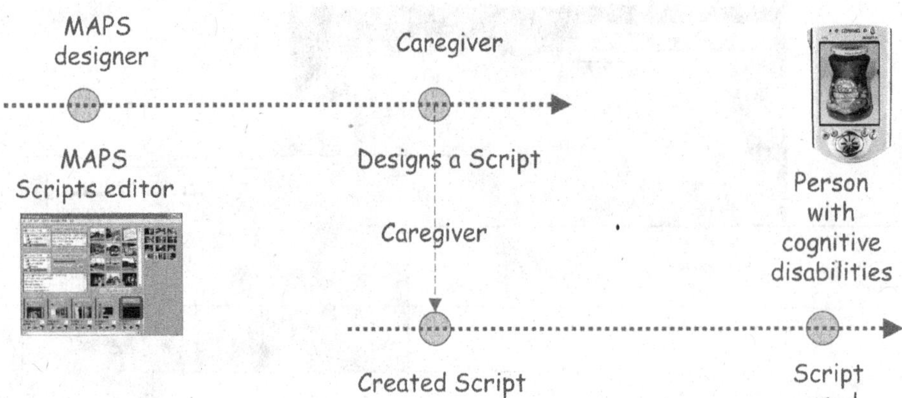

by using tabletop environments with handheld technologies (i.e., by using PDAs and other personal devices). These initial efforts will exploit the participatory Web for supporting cultures of participation that complement face-to-face sessions and activities beyond co-located meetings.

Memory Aiding Prompting System (MAPS)

Individuals with cognitive disabilities are often unable to live independently due to their inability to perform activities of daily living, such as cooking, housework, or shopping. By being provided with *socio-technical environments* (Mumford, 1987) to extend their abilities and thereby their independence, these individuals can lead lives less dependent on others. Our research in this context (Carmien & Fischer, 2008) explored end-user development, meta-design, and cultures of participation by supporting mobile device customization, personalization, and configuration by caregivers and effective use by clients.

Abandonment Based on the "Universe of One"

People with cognitive disabilities represent a "universe of one" problem: a solution for one person will rarely work for another. The "universe of one" conceptualization includes the empirical finding that (1) *unexpected islands of abilities* exist: clients can have unexpected skills and abilities that can be leveraged to ensure a better possibility of task accomplishment; and (2) *unexpected deficits of abilities* exist. Accessing and addressing these unexpected variations in skills and needs, particularly with respect to creating task support, requires an intimate knowledge of the client that *only caregivers* can provide. Currently, a substantial portion of all assistive technology is abandoned after initial purchase and use resulting in that the very population that could most benefit from technology is paying for expensive devices that end up in the back of closets after a short time.

A unique challenge of meta-design in the domain of cognitive disabilities is that the clients themselves cannot act as designers, but the caregivers must accept this role (see Figure 4). Caregivers, who have the most intimate knowledge of the client, need to become the end-user designers. The scripts needed to effectively support users are specific for particular tasks, creating the requirement that the people who know about the clients and the tasks (i.e., the local caregivers rather than a technologist far removed from the action) must be able to develop scripts.

Caregivers generally have no specific professional technology training nor are they interested in becoming computer programmers. This creates the need for design environments with extensive end-user support to allow caregivers to create, store, and share scripts (Fischer, 2006). Figure 5 shows the MAPS design environment for creating complex multimodal prompting sequences allowing sound, pictures, and video to be assembled by using a film-strip-based scripting metaphor. The design environment supports a multi-script version that allows caregivers to present the looping and forking behavior that is critical for numerous task support situations.

The design of MAPS involved three different groups of participants: (1) assistive technology professionals and special education teachers, (2) parents of clients, and (3) professional caregivers. MAPS was tested with representatives of several different groups resulting in the identification of the following requirements for meta-design:

- discover and learn about the client's and caregiver's world and their interactions;
- observe and analyze how tasks and learning of tasks were currently conducted;
- understand and explicate the process of creating and updating scripts;
- comprehend and analyze the process of using the scripts with a real task; and
- gain an understanding of the role of meta-design in the dynamics of MAPS adoption and use.

By designing the MAPS environment to enable script redesign and reuse, caregivers were able to create an environment that matched the unique needs of an individual with cognitive disabilities. MAPS represents an example for democratizing design by supporting meta-design, embedding new technologies into socio-technical environments,

Figure 5. The MAPS design environment for creating scripts

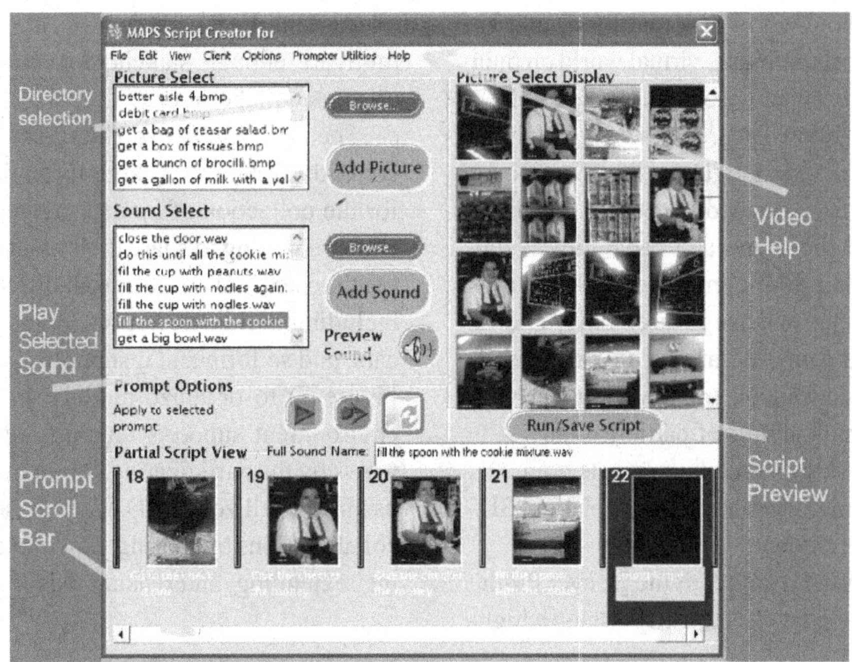

Figure 6. A 3D model developed in SketchUp

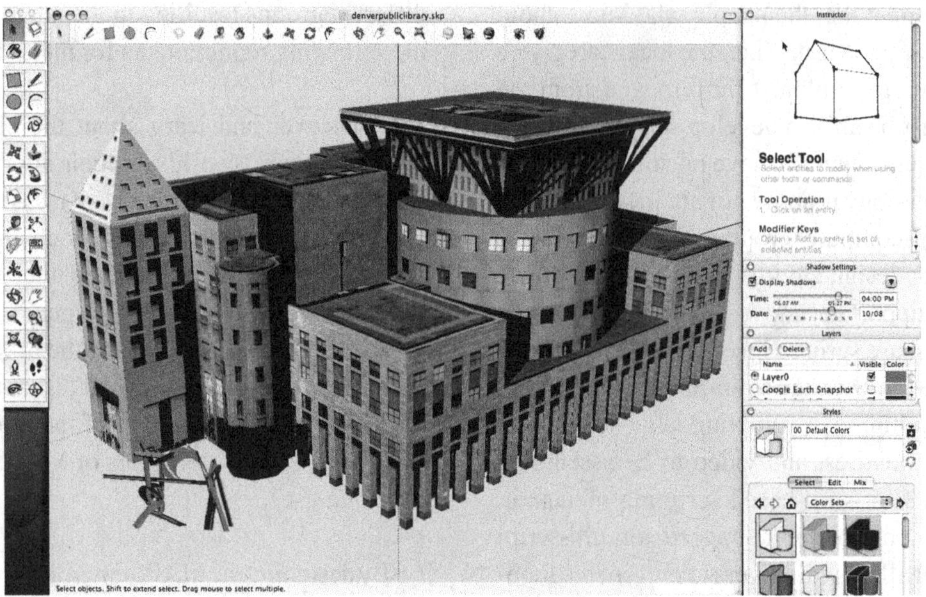

and helping people with cognitive disabilities and their caregivers have more interesting and more rewarding lives.

Modeling the World in 3D: SketchUp, 3D Warehouse, and Google Earth

Having the whole world modeled in 3D and allowing users to explore this virtual world on their computers is the objective behind Google's effort to integrate the following three systems: SketchUp, 3D Warehouse, and Google Earth. The amount of work and local knowledge needed to achieve this is beyond the scope and capability of any locally operating development team. It requires the contributions of a large user base, and as such represents a unique, large-scale example for assessing the conceptual framework underlying meta-design and cultures of participation.

SketchUp (http://sketchup.google.com/) is a highly interactive, direct manipulation 3D-modeling environment.

Figure 6 shows a model of the Denver Public Library developed with SketchUp. Being a high-functionality environment with a "low threshold and high ceiling," developing sophisticated and highly creative models with SketchUp requires a *nontrivial learning effort*. Powerful learning mechanisms for SketchUp are critical to allow everyone who wishes to contribute to learn how to do so. These mechanisms, together with the added value of participation are important to motivate enough stakeholders to contribute to creative collaborations.

The *3D Warehouse* (http://sketchup.google.com/3dwarehouse/) is an information repository for the collection of models created by all users who are willing to share their models. It contains ten thousands of models from different domains, including buildings, houses, bridges, sculptures, cars, and so forth and it supports *collections* (see Figure 7) to organize models. In addition, the environment supports tagging, ratings, and reviews by the participating community. Interested users can utilize the 3D Warehouse for creative collaborations by sharing, downloading, modifying, extending, and reusing existing models.

Google Earth has the capability to show 3D objects that consist of users' submissions that were developed by using SketchUp. Figure 8 shows an example illustrating the interplay of the three systems: the downtown area of the city of Denver in Google Earth, populated by 3D buildings created by users of SketchUp and stored in the 3D Warehouse. The three systems are integrated in the following way: 3D models can be shared by uploading them from SketchUp to the 3D Warehouse, where they can be searched, shared, and re-stored. Models can be downloaded from the 3D Warehouse to SketchUp (for further modification and evolution) and to Google Earth (if the models have a location on Earth) to be viewed by anyone.

In an ongoing collaboration with our partners from the Google Boulder office, we are exploring how to support cultures of participation in the process of modeling the whole world in 3D by pursuing the following research issues:

- Allowing users to act as active contributors to the 3D Warehouse requires extensive learning support to *achieve sufficient mastery* of SketchUp.
- Assessing the effectiveness of different reward structures for motivating users to participate in the collaborative effort to model the whole world. Examples of such incentives include recognition by the community and featuring the best models in the 3D Warehouse and Google Earth,
- Supporting a *richer ecology of participation* including roles such as creators, raters, curators, power users, and local developers, while attending to the diversity and independence of participants.
- Collaborating with Google in its ongoing effort to (1) more tightly integrate the three subsystems to reduce the demands required for participation and (2) facilitate interaction of their systems with other en-

Figure 7. Collections of models in the 3D warehouse (Adapted from: http://sketchup.google.com/3dwarehouse)

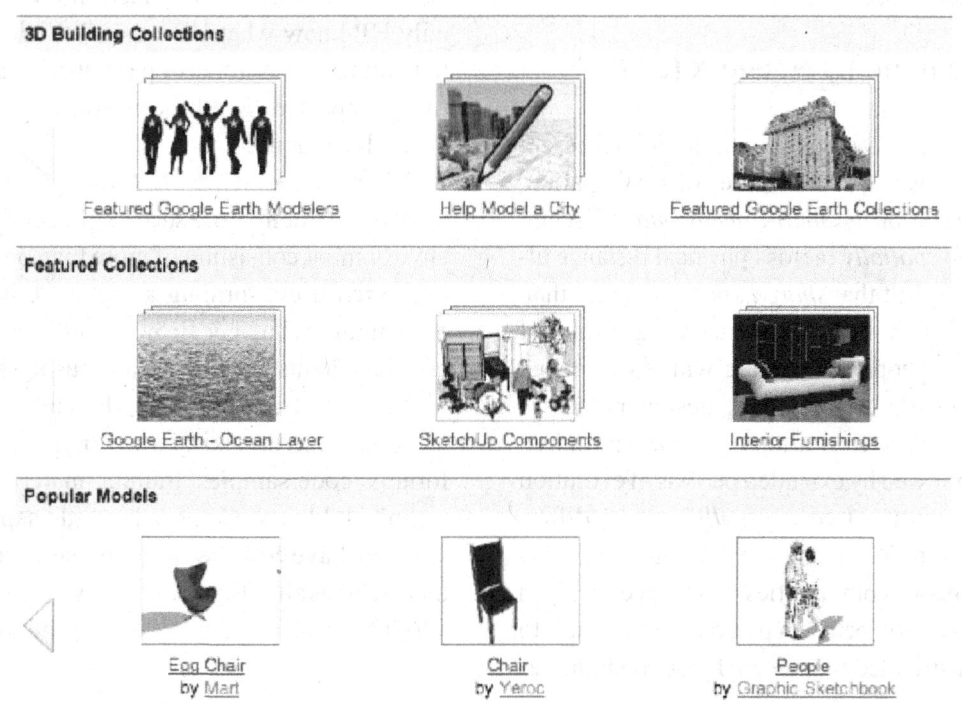

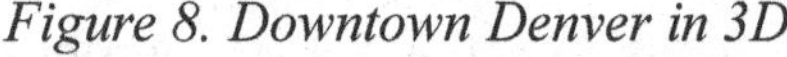

Figure 8. Downtown Denver in 3D

vironments, such as the EDC (see Figure 3), and other 3D environments, such as Second Life.

SAP Community Network (SCN)

Diverse and distributed communities represent important instances of cultures of participation. The distribution is *multi-dimensional* (Fischer, 2005): (1) *spatially* (across physical distance allowing the shift that *shared concern,* rather than shared location, becomes the defining feature of a group of people interacting with each other); (2) *temporally* (across time; design processes often take place over a long period, with initial design followed by extended periods of evolution and redesign); (3) *conceptually* (across different communities, including homogeneous and heterogeneous communities of practice); and (4) *technologically* (between persons and artifacts to support distributed cognition). These communities face the challenge of avoiding the reinvention of knowledge and artifacts already known by someone. This hurdle is articulated in the slogan "If only HP knew what HP knows" (Sieloff, 1999) indicating that cultures of participation are negatively impacted by a lack of awareness of what others have done.

We have studied SCN (Gorman & Fischer, 2009) as an example of a successful socio-technical environment consisting of more than one million registered users forming a highly active online community (Hagel & Brown, 2008) of developers, consultants, integrators, and business analysts building and sharing knowledge about SAP technologies via wikis, expert blogs, discussion forums, code samples, training materials, and a technical library (https://www.sdn.sap.com/irj/sdn). We have collected a comprehensive data set that includes all of the posting activity of more than 120,000 users from June 2003 through May 2008.

Table 2. Statistical features for first response time of the three distributed online communities. The first, second, and third quartile times required for a post from one user to receive a response from another user.

First Response Time	Q1 (25%)	Q2 (Median)	Q3 (75%)
SDN	**6 m**	**23 m**	**3 h 10 m**
Commons	9 m	3 h 56 m	14 h 15 m
Lucene	24 m	1 h 27 m	5 h 51 m

To get a better understanding of processes and dynamics in a culture of participation such as SCN, we have developed an initial analytic framework to measure a number of factors, including attributes such as (1) *responsiveness* (how often and quickly members get responses to their requests), (2) *engagement intensity* (how many helpers and responses are required to answer questions; and (3) *role distribution* (the ratio of users who ask questions to those who answer questions).

Our analysis (Gorman & Fischer, 2009) indicates that we can find patterns in the data that hint toward an environment that is supportive of cultures of participation. The SCN environment provides support and motivation for users to contribute, as can be seen in the time it takes users to receive a response to their post (see Table 2). This time is significantly less than in two other environments we analyzed for comparison, the Open Source communities of Commons and Lucene (Ye & Fischer, 2007). In the SCN the median response time is 23 minutes, less than a third of the time it takes in the second-best environment.

In addition to this *quantitative* analysis, we have engaged in a limited *qualitative* analysis to understand the impact of incentive systems on participation. SCN uses a point system to reward users for their participation, but these features can have negative effects. Points are highly valued, and some users may resort to "gaming the system" to earn points.

CreativeIT Community

The emerging CreativeIT Community, consisting of participants (researchers, artists, graduate students) in the NSF CISE research program on "Creativity and IT" (http://www.nsf.gov/pubs/2007/nsf07562/-nsf07562.htm), is a relatively small community (less than 100 active participants). With the support of NSF grants, we have designed and seeded a wiki-based socio-technical environment (http://swiki.cs.colorado.edu/CreativeIT) to support and foster an evolving scientific community. The unique challenges of this specific community are that people working in interdisciplinary projects or in niches of their disciplines are often isolated in their local environments and unaware of relevant work in other disciplines. The CreativeIT Wiki allows us to assess and collect a variety of data using tools such as Google Analytics as well as our own tools to gain a better understanding of the value of recording implicit interactions and/versus engaging participants in explicit activities (such as tagging, rating, commenting).

Our ongoing research with the CreativeIT Wiki is focused on gaining a deeper understanding on how to support and foster cultures of participation by exploring and analyzing:

- how *awareness mechanisms* will give the participants better sense of overall wiki activities;
- how short- and long-term effects in participation can be achieved through *events* taking place in the wiki (e.g., special pre-

sentations of the most popular contributions or nominations for the most creative participants);

- how *social tools* support participants in finding and connecting to other participants, representing themselves to other researchers, and creating networks of interests can influence user activities;
- how the *social environment* (the number of users, the activities, the level of discussions, and making the environment more *permissive* and unstructured versus more *prescriptive* and structured) will influence social creativity and participation; and
- how *rating systems* allowing participants to rate other people's contributions will increase the trust and interest in existing content.

DRAWBACKS OF CULTURES OF PARTICIPATION

Cultures of participation open up unique new opportunities for mass collaboration and social production, but they are not without drawbacks. One such drawback is that humans may be forced to cope with the burden of being active contributors in *personally irrelevant activities*. This drawback can be illustrated with "do-it-yourself" societies.

Through modern tools, humans are empowered to perform many tasks themselves that were done previously by skilled domain workers serving as agents and intermediaries. Although this shift provides power, freedom, and control to customers, it also has forced people to act as contributors in contexts for which they lack the experience that professionals have acquired and maintained through the daily use of systems, as well as the broad background knowledge to do these tasks efficiently and effectively (e.g., companies offloading work to customers).

Substantially more experience and assessment is required to determine whether the *advantages* of cultures of participation (such as extensive coverage of information, creation of large numbers of artifacts, creative chaos by making all voices heard, reduced authority of expert opinions, and shared experience of social creativity) will outweigh the *disadvantages* (accumulation of irrelevant information, wasting human resources in large information spaces, and lack of coherent voices). Such a determination will depend on creating a deeper understanding of these trade-offs (Carr, 2008; Lanier, 2006).

CONCLUSION

For a couple of decades the rise of digital media has been providing new powers for the *individual*. The world's networks are now providing enormous unexplored opportunities for *groups and communities*. Providing all citizens with the means to become co-creators of new ideas, knowledge, and products in personally meaningful activities presents one of the most exciting innovations and transformations, with profound implications in the years to come.

This paper has described reasons why cultures of participation supported by meta-design are desirable. Despite the fact that some EUD environments and their supporting research have been around for years and some success models exist (Lieberman et al., 2006), there is evidence that the impact of academic research efforts in this area has been limited.

We do know, however, that digital media are powerful catalysts of cultural change. The challenge for the EUD research community is not only understanding, supporting, and participating in existing cultures, but also shaping, transforming, and fostering new cultures. Humans all over the world have the opportunity today not only to be exposed to cultures of consumerism (Postman, 1985), but to become active contributors in cultures of participation. Without an analytic model and a demystification of media to deeply understand

and explain new emerging phenomena and environments, however, we will only be able to treat cultures of participation as curiosities or transient fads (Benkler, 2006). The potential impact of cultures of participation supported by meta-design is substantial: they erode monopolistic positions held by professions, educational institutions, and experts, and they increase the diversity of perspectives on the way the world is and the way it could be. They require new metaphors, new levels of discourse, and new environments to think, reflect, and support working, learning, and collaboration for alternative and more democratic futures.

ACKNOWLEDGMENT

I thank the members of the Center for LifeLong Learning & Design at the University of Colorado, who have made major contributions to the ideas described in this paper. I specifically would like to thank: (1) *Hal Eden* who is the major architect and developer of the EDC; (2) *Stefan Carmien* who created and evaluated the MAPS environment; (3) *John Bacus* from Google Boulder who provided unique insights into the design of the 3D modeling effort; (4) *Andrew Gorman* who analyzed the SCN environment; and (5) *Holger Dick* and *Hal Eden* who have developed the CreativeIT environment. In addition, I have learned much over the years by interacting with my professional colleagues and collaborators in the EUD and EUSE communities. I would like to thank Anders Mørch, Mary Beth Rosson, Volker Wulf, and Steffen Budweg for helping me to improve an earlier version of this article with their feedback The research was supported in part by

(1) grants from the National Science Foundation, including: (a) IIS-0613638 *"A Meta-Design Framework for Participative Software Systems"*, (b) IIS-0709304 *"A New Generation Wiki for Supporting a Research Community in 'Creativity and IT'"* and (c) IIS-0843720 *"Increasing Participation and Sustaining a Research Community in 'Creativity and IT'"*;

(2) Google research award *"Motivating and Empowering Users to Become Active Contributors: Supporting the Learning of High-Functionality Environments"*; and

(3) SAP research project *"Giving All Stakeholders a Voice: Understanding and Supporting the Creativity and Innovation of Communities Using and Evolving Software Products."*

REFERENCES

Alexander, C. (1964). *The synthesis of form.* Cambridge, MA: Harvard University Press

Alexander, C. (1984). The state of the art in design methods. In N. Cross (Ed.), *Developments in design methodology* (pp. 309-316). New York: John Wiley & Sons.

Andersen, R., & Mørch, A. (2009). Mutual development: A case study in customer-initiated software product development. In V. Pipek, M. B. Rossen, B. deRuyter, & V. Wulf (Eds.), *End-user development* (pp. 31-49). Heidelberg, Germany: Springer.

Anderson, C. (2006). *The long tail: Why the future of business is selling less of more.* New York: Hyperion.

Arias, E. G., Eden, H., Fischer, G., Gorman, A., & Scharff, E. (2000). Transcending the individual human mind—creating shared understanding through collaborative design. *ACM Transactions on Computer-Human Interaction, 7*(1), 84–113. doi:10.1145/344949.345015

Benkler, Y. (2006). *The wealth of networks: How social production transforms markets and freedom.* New Haven: Yale University Press.

Benkler, Y., & Nissenbaum, H. (2006). Commons-based peer production and virtue. *Political Philosophy*, *14*(4), 394–419. doi:10.1111/j.1467-9760.2006.00235.x

Brand, S. (1995). *How buildings learn: What happens after they're built*. New York: Penguin Books.

Brown, J. S. (2005). *New learning environments for the 21st century.* Retrieved from http://www.johnseelybrown.com/newlearning.pdf

Brown, J. S., Duguid, P., & Haviland, S. (1994). Toward informed participation: Six scenarios in search of democracy in the information age. *The Aspen Institute Quarterly*, *6*(4), 49–73.

Bruner, J. (1996). *The culture of education.* Cambridge, MA: Harvard University Press.

Budweg, S., Draxler, S., Lohmann, S., Rashid, A., & Stevens, G. (2009). Open design spaces supporting user innovation. *Proceedings of the International Workshop on Open Design Spaces; International Reports on Socio-Informatics, 6*(2). Retrieved from http://www.iisi.de/fileadmin/IISI/upload/IRSI/IRSIV6I2.pdf

Burnett, M., Cook, C., & Rothermel, G. (2004). End-user software engineering. *Communications of the ACM, 47*(9), 53–58. doi:10.1145/1015864.1015889

Carmien, S. P., & Fischer, G. (2008, April). Design, adoption, and assessment of a socio-technical environment supporting independence for persons with cognitive disabilities. In *Proceedings of CHI 2008*, Florence, Italy, (pp. 597-607). ACM Publishing.

Carr, N. (2008). *Is Google making us stupid?* Retrieved from http://www.theatlantic.com/doc/200807/google

Costabile, M. F., Mussio, P., Provenza, L. P., & Piccinno, A. (2009). Supporting end users to be co-designers of their tools. In V. Pipek, M. B. Rossen, B. deRuyter, & V. Wulf (Eds.), *End-user development* (pp. 70-85). Heidelberg, Germany: Springer.

Davis, R. (1984). Interactive transfer of expertise. In B. G. Buchanan, & E. H. Shortliffe (Eds.), *Rule-based expert systems: The Mycin experiments of the Stanford Heuristic Programming Project* (pp. 171-205). Reading, MA: Addison-Wesley.

dePaula, R., Fischer, G., & Ostwald, J. (2001, March). Courses as seeds: Expectations and realities. In P. Dillenbourg, A. Eurelings, & K. Hakkarainen (Eds.), *Proceedings of the European Conference on Computer-Supported Collaborative Learning*, Maastricht, the Netherlands (pp. 494-501).

Doctorow, C. (2006). *Response to Jaron Lanier's "Digital Maoism: The hazards of the new online collectivism"*. Retrieved from http://www.edge.org/discourse/digital_maoism.html

Eden, H. (2002, January). Getting in on the (Inter) Action: Exploring affordances for collaborative learning in a context of informed participation. In G. Stahl (Ed.), *Proceedings of the Computer Supported Collaborative Learning (CSCL 2002) Conference*, Boulder, CO (pp. 399-407). Lawrence Erlbaum.

Eisenberg, M., & Fischer, G. (1994, April). Programmable design environments: Integrating end-user programming with domain-oriented assistance. In *Proceedings of Chi 1994: Human factors in computing Systems,* Boston (pp. 431-437). ACM Publishing.

Engeström, Y. (2001). Expansive learning at work: Toward an activity theoretical reconceptualization. *Journal of Education and Work, 14*(1), 133–156. doi:10.1080/13639080123238

Fischer, G. (1994). Turning breakdowns into opportunities for creativity. *Knowledge-Based Systems. Special Issue on Creativity and Cognition, 7*(4), 221–232.

Fischer, G. (2000). Social creativity, symmetry of ignorance and meta-design. *Knowledge-Based Systems Journal. Special Issue on Creativity & Cognition, 13*(7-8), 527–537.

Fischer, G. (2001, August 11-14). Communities of interest: Learning through the interaction of multiple knowledge systems. In *Proceedings of the 24th Annual Information Systems Research Seminar in Scandinavia (IRIS'24)*, Ulvik, Norway (pp. 1-14).

Fischer, G. (2002). Beyond 'couch potatoes': From consumers to designers and active contributors. *Firstmonday*. Retrieved from http://firstmonday.org/issues/issue7_12/fischer/

Fischer, G. (2005, April 12-15). Distances and diversity: Sources for social creativity. In *Proceedings of Creativity & Cognition,* London (pp. 128-136). ACM Publishing.

Fischer, G. (2006, May 23-26). Distributed intelligence: Extending the power of the unaided, individual human mind. In *Proceedings of Advanced Visual Interfaces (Avi) Conference,* Venice, Italy (pp. 7-14). ACM Publishing.

Fischer, G. (2007, September 10-14). Meta-design: Expanding boundaries and redistributing control in design. In C. Baranauskas, P. Palanque, A. Abascal, S. Diniz, & J. Barbosa (Eds.), *Human-Computer Interaction INTERACT 2007: 11th IFIP TC 13 International Conference,* Rio de Janeiro, Brazil (LNCS 4662, pp. 193-206).

Fischer, G., & Giaccardi, E. (2006). Meta-design: A framework for the future of end user development. In H. Lieberman, F. Paternò, & V. Wulf (Eds.), *End user development* (pp. 427-457). New York: Springer.

Fischer, G., Giaccardi, E., Eden, H., Sugimoto, M., & Ye, Y. (2005). Beyond binary choices: Integrating individual and social creativity. *International Journal of Human-Computer Studies. Special Issue on Computer Support for Creativity, 63*(4-5), 482–512.

Fischer, G., & Girgensohn, A. (1990, April 1-5). End-user modifiability in design environments. In *Proceedings of the Conference on Human Factors in Computing Systems (Chi 1990),* Seattle, WA (pp. 183-191). ACM Publishing.

Fischer, G., & Ostwald, J. (2002, June 23-25). Seeding, evolutionary growth, and reseeding: Enriching participatory design with informed participation. In *Proceedings of the Conference on Participatory Design (PDC'02)*, Malmö University, Sweden (pp. 135-143).

Fischer, G., Piccinno, A., & Ye, Y. (2008, September 25-26). The ecology of participants in co-evolving socio-technical environments. In P. Forbrig & F. Paternò (Ed.), *Engineering interactive systems: Proceedings of the 2nd Conference on Human-Centered Software Engineering,* Pisa, Italy (LNCS 5247, pp. 279-286).

Fischer, G., Scharff, E., & Ye, Y. (2004). Fostering social creativity by increasing social capital. In M. Huysman & V. Wulf (Eds.), *Social capital and information technology* (pp. 355-399). Cambridge, MA: MIT Press.

Fischer, G., & Sugimoto, M. (2006). Supporting self-directed learners and learning communities with sociotechnical environments. [RPTEL]. *International Journal Research and Practice in Technology Enhanced Learning, 1*(1), 31–64. doi:10.1142/S1793206806000020

Fogli, D. (2009). End-user development for e-government website content creation. In V. Pipek, M. B. Rossen, B. deRuyter, & V. Wulf (Eds.), *End-user development* (pp. 126-145) Heidelberg, Germany: Springer.

Gantt, M., & Nardi, B. A. (1992, June 3-7). Gardeners and gurus: Patterns of cooperation among cad users. In P. Bauersfeld, J. Bennett, & G. Lynch (Eds.), *Proceedings of the Conference on Human Factors in Computing Systems (Chi 1992),* Monterey, CA (pp. 107-117). ACM Publishing.

Giaccardi, E. (2004). *Principles of metadesign: Processes and levels of co-creation in the new design space*. Unpublished doctoral dissertation, CAiiA-STAR, School of Computing, Plymouth, UK.

Girgensohn, A. (1992). *End-User modifiability in knowledge-based design environments*. Unpublished doctoral dissertation, University of Colorado at Boulder.

Gorman, A., & Fischer, G. (2009, June 25-27). Toward an analytic framework for understanding and fostering peer-support communities in using and evolving software products. In *Proceedings of the International Conference Communities and Technologies (C&T 2009),* University Park, PA (pp. 1-9). ACM Publishing.

Habraken, J. (1972). *Supports: An alternative to mass housing.* North Shields, UK: Urban International Press.

Hagel, J., & Brown, J. S. (2008). *Innovation on the edge: How SAP seeds innovation.* Retrieved from http://www.businessweek.com/print/innovate/content/jul2008/id20080723_353753.htm

Illich, I. (1971). *Deschooling society.* New York: Harper and Row.

Janis, I. (1972). *Victims of groupthink.* Boston: Houghton Mifflin.

Kellogg, W. A. (2007, September 24). *Supporting collaboration in distributed teams: Implications for e-research.* Paper presented at the Ecscw Workshop "Realising and Supporting Collaboration in E-Research", Limerick, Ireland. Retrieved from http://www.e-researchcommunity.org/docs/ecscw07/submissions/Kellogg.pdf

Kittur, A., Suh, B., & Chi, E. H. (2008, November 8-12). Can you ever trust a Wiki? Impacting perceived trustworthiness in Wikipedia. In *Proceedings of the Conference on Computer Supported Cooperative Work (CSCW 2008),* San Diego, CA (pp. 477-480). ACM Publishing.

Klann, M., Paterno, F., & Wulf, V. (2006). Future perspectives in end-user development. In H. Lieberman, F. Paterno, & V. Wulf (Eds.), *End user development* (pp. 475-486). New York: Springer.

Lanier, J. (2006). *Digital Maoism: The hazards of the new online collectivism.* Retrieved from http://www.edge.org/3rd_culture/lanier06/lanier06_index.html

Leadbeater, C., & Miller, P. (2008). *The pro-am revolution — how enthusiasts are changing our economy and society.* Retrieved from http://www.demos.co.uk/files/proamrevolutionfinal.pdf

Lieberman, H., Paterno, F., & Wulf, V. (Eds.). (2006). *End user development.* New York: Springer.

McLuhan, M. (1964). *Understanding media: The extensions of man.* Cambridge, MA: MIT Press.

Mumford, E. (1987). Sociotechnical systems design: Evolving theory and practice. In G. Bjerknes, P. Ehn, & M. Kyng (Eds.), *Computers and democracy* (pp. 59-76). Aldershot, UK: Avebury.

Myers, B. A., Ko, A. J., & Burnett, M. M. (2006, April 22-27). Invited research overview: End-user programming. In *Proceedings of the Conference on Human Factors in Computing Systems (Chi 2006),* Montreal, Quebec, Canada (pp. 75-80). ACM Publishing.

O'Reilly, T. (2006). *What is Web 2.0 - design patterns and business models for the next generation of software.* Retrieved from http://www.oreillynet.com/pub/a/oreilly/tim/news/2005/09/30/what-is-web-20.html

Orr, J. (1996). *Talking about machines—an ethnography of a modern job.* Ithaca, NY: ILR Press/ Cornell University Press.

Pipek, V., Rossen, M. B., deRuyter, B., & Wulf, V. (Eds.). (2009). *End-user development.* Heidelberg, Germany: Springer.

Polanyi, M. (1966). *The tacit dimension.* Garden City, NY: Doubleday.

Postman, N. (1985). *Amusing ourselves to death—public discourse in the age of show business.* New York: Penguin Books.

Preece, J., & Shneiderman, B. (2009). The reader-to-leader framework: Motivating technology-mediated social participation. *AIS Transactions on Human-Computer Interaction, 1*(1), 13–32.

Raymond, E. S., & Young, B. (2001). *The cathedral and the bazaar: Musings on Linux and open source by an accidental revolutionary.* Sebastopol, CA: O'Reilly & Associates.

Rittel, H. (1984). Second-generation design methods. In N. Cross (Ed.), *Developments in design methodology* (pp. 317-327). New York: John Wiley & Sons.

Rittel, H., & Webber, M. M. (1984). Planning problems are wicked problems. In N. Cross (Ed.), *Developments in design methodology* (pp. 135-144). New York: John Wiley & Sons

Rogoff, B., Matsuov, E., & White, C. (1998). Models of teaching and learning: Participation in a community of learners. In D. R. Olsen & N. Torrance (Eds.), *The handbook of education and human development—new models of learning, teaching and schooling* (pp. 388-414). Oxford, UK: Blackwell.

Scharff, E. (2002). *Open source software, a conceptual framework for collaborative artifact and knowledge construction.* Unpublished doctoral dissertation, University of Colorado at Boulder.

Schön, D. A. (1983). *The reflective practitioner: How professionals think in action.* New York: Basic Books.

Shneiderman, B. (2007). Creativity support tools: Accelerating discovery and innovation. *Communications of the ACM, 50*(12), 20–32. doi:10.1145/1323688.1323689

Sieloff, C. G. (1999). 'If only Hp knew what Hp knows': The roots of knowledge management at hewlett-Packard. *Knowledge Management, 3*(1), 47–53. doi:10.1108/13673279910259385

Simon, H. A. (1996). *The sciences of the artificial* (3rd ed.). Cambridge, MA: MIT Press.

Star, S. L. (1989). The structure of ill-structured solutions: Boundary objects and heterogeneous distributed problem solving. In L. Gasser & M. N. Huhns (Eds.), *Distributed artificial intelligence* (Vol. 2, pp. 37-54). San Mateo, CA: Morgan Kaufmann Publishers.

Suchman, L. A. (1987). *Plans and situated actions.* Cambridge, UK: Cambridge University Press.

Sugimoto, M., Hosoi, K., & Hashizume, H. (2004, April 24-29). Caretta: A system for supporting face-to-face collaboration by integrating personal and shared spaces. In *Proceedings of the Conference on Human Factors in Computing Systems (Chi 2004),* Vienna, Austria (pp. 41-48). ACM Publishing.

Surowiecki, J. (2005). *The wisdom of crowds.* New York: Anchor Books.

Tapscott, D., & Williams, A. D. (2006). *Wikinomics: How mass collaboration changes everything.* New York: Penguin Group.

von Hippel, E. (2005). *Democratizing innovation.* Cambridge, MA: MIT Press.

Wenger, E. (1998). *Communities of practice—learning, meaning, and identity.* Cambridge, UK: Cambridge University Press.

Winograd, T., & Flores, F. (1986). *Understanding computers and cognition: A new foundation for design.* Norwood, NJ: Ablex Publishing Corporation.

Wulf, V., Pipek, V., & Won, M. (2008). Component-based tailorability: Enabling highly flexible software applications. *International Journal of Human-Computer Studies, 66*, 1–22.

Ye, Y., & Fischer, G. (2007, July 22-27). Designing for participation in socio-technical software systems. In C. Stephanidis (Ed.), *Universal Access in Human Computer Interaction: Coping with Diversity: Proceedings of 4th International Conference on Universal Access in Human-Computer Interaction,* Beijing, China (LNCS 4554, pp. 312-321).

This work was previously published in Journal of Organizational and End User Computing, Volume 22, Issue 1, edited by M. Adam Mahmood, pp. 52-82, copyright 2010 by IGI Publishing (an imprint of IGI Global).

Chapter 11
Investigating Technology Commitment in Instant Messaging Application Users

Y. Ken Wang
University of Pittsburgh at Bradford, USA

Pratim Datta
Kent State University, USA

ABSTRACT

Although much research in the IS field has examined IS adoption, less is known about post-adoption behavior among IS users, especially when competing alternatives are available. Incorporating commitment theory from social psychology and management science literature, this paper proposes an IS continuance model that explains why some IS technologies enjoy continued use after adoption and others are often relegated to the basement as shelfware. This paper uses a technology commitment perspective to unravel why adopted technologies experience mixed success. Specifically, the authors argue that IS continuance may be best understood by investigating user commitment toward specific technologies. Three components of technology commitment, that is, affective commitment, calculative commitment, and normative commitment, are used to formulate a research model. The model is empirically tested in the context of instant messaging software. Results show a strong support for the model and explicate commitment differentials among users across different brands of instant messaging software. The study ends with a discussion of the results and their implications for research and practice.

INTRODUCTION

What drives user intentions to continue using specific application software over other previously adopted software alternatives? In hypercompetitive environments, IS continuance, defined as the continued use of an IS technology product long after an initial acceptance decision (Bhattacherjee, 2001), is rapidly becoming relevant. From a 2001 survey of 100 companies, the CIO magazine reported that most companies use less than half of their inventory of previously adopted software (Kalin 2002) - building loyalty for one substitute to forego the use of another. Although anecdotal,

DOI: 10.4018/978-1-4666-0140-6.ch011

it is interesting to note how our adoption and early experience with Corel Wordperfect and Microsoft Works failed to dissuade us from foregoing their use for Microsoft Word. The issue becomes even more acute for freely and easily available and substitutable software, e.g., browsers, webmail applications, instant messaging applications, where alternatives run the gamut. Sadly, the question of why a user intends to continue using one software application over another remains unanswered.

From individuals to organizations, our portfolio of available technology products is rapidly growing. There is a growing body of research in the information systems (IS) literature regarding the understanding of technology adoption and use. Although technology adoption research has made great progress, a lack of empirical evidence on post-adoption use becomes increasingly critical to IS research and practice. For example, it is not uncommon for individuals to adopt multiple instant messengers with different service providers (such as Microsoft, AOL, Yahoo!, Google, Skype, etc.) but over time, users tend to precipitate towards using one or a few even when available (and already adopted) alternatives offer similar features, e.g., instant interactivity, status awareness, multi-party collaboration, conversational transcript.

The case is even more acute with software use in organizations. There is a preponderance of shareware, freeware, and demo available online or by vendors for adoption. While individuals and organizations may adopt software alternatives, users, in the post-adoption phase, choose to continue to use a certain software technology and relinquish their use of a competing alternative. In fact, a recent study found that organizational adoption and investments in software range between 30 and 40 percent of the IT budget (Gallagher, 2006). While both individuals and organizations adopt several technology products, only a few products actually experience continuous use (Selwyn, 2003). The rest remain adopted yet unused, gathering dust as "shelfware." Shelfware is a term used for software that has been adopted, but remain unused in the face of available alternatives. As such, shelfware refers only to software that has available adopted alternatives. Shelfware consists only of non-core software. Shelfware does not include core software technologies such as ERP (enterprise resource planning) or mainframe operating systems software that limit the scope of individuals and organizations in choosing available alternative and have to be captive to a single adopted software. Therefore, the scope of our discussion limits itself to shelfware only.

Shelfware is a growing concern for individuals and organizations alike. The issue is so acute that controlling shelfware is one of primary controls in any software asset management (SAM) program (Gallagher, 2006). Software that has been licensed but remains unused not only contributes to sinking costs but also adds to the total cost of ownership (TCO) without offering instrumental benefits through use. The issue however is not only contained within organizational boundaries. Individual users also incur similar degrees of over-adoption and underutilization of software. It is common to find several pieces of installed (adopted) software in our own computers that we rarely end up using. The importance placed by vendors on shelfware could easily be understood in the context of the Microsoft Windows XP operating system. Microsoft Windows XP has built in functions that trace unused icons and remark on the periodicity of use of installed (adopted) software programs in their "Add/Remove Programs" function. While the effect are conspicuous, there seems to be an absence of explanations for the disconnect between IS adoption and IS continuance. What makes us (and organizational users) adopt competing technologies yet foregoing the use of one over another? Central to unraveling shelfware reduction is the need to understanding why individuals and organizations end up using one of the many alternate (and easily/freely available) software products – an issue germane to scholars and practitioners. For research, understanding user behavior surrounding continuous use allows for an extension of the adoption model. For practice, vendors of technology products would be immensely interested in knowing how and why users choose to continue to use a certain product among a set of competing alternatives.

The remainder of this paper proceeds as follows. The next two sections review the literature on information systems (IS) continuance and commitment theories adopted from information systems, social psychology, and management science to derive the construct of technology commitment. Synthesizing commitment theory and the continuance theory, the paper constructs a theoretical model linking technology commitment to IS continuance and develops hypotheses in support of our arguments. This is followed by an empirical validation of the hypothesized model along a presentation of the results. Finally, we end with a discussion of the results and a roadmap for our ongoing research agenda. The paper closes with a discussion of the implications and limitations of the study.

LITERATURE REVIEW

To date, Davis et al.'s technology adoption model (TAM) (Davis, 1989) has been one of predominant templates used to investigate, develop, and refine user adoption and use behavior. TAM and its derivates (Legris, Ingham, & Collerette, 2003; Qingxiong Ma & Liping Liu, 2004; Szajna, 1996; Venkatesh & Davis, 2000; Venkatesh, Morris, Davis, & Davis, 2003) with their roots the theory of reasoned action (TRA) (Fishbein & Ajzen, 1975) and theory of planned behavior (TPB) (Ajzen, 1985), have proven successful in explaining users' initial acceptance of information systems (IS). However, while research has predominantly focused on the first-time use of IS, IS continuance, herein referred to as an individual's continued use of a particular technology product, has received relatively less scrutiny within the IS community (Bhattacherjee, 2001).

The diffusion of innovations theory (Rogers, 1995) provides a unique angle to the examination of technology adoption patterns. For most users in a social system, their technology decision often depends on other people's attitude and behavior. Therefore the pattern of technology adoption spread may be illustrated using a S-shaped curve, where early adopters demonstrate different adoption styles than the majority of users. Although the diffusion of innovation theory has successfully explained adoption diffusion in a social system, a closer look at individual users' continuance may provide better understanding of technology use to the IS literature.

Within existing IS literature, there are two major lines of research in respect to individual users' continued use of technologies (Hsu, Chiu, & Ju, 2004). The first line of research views continued use as an extension of acceptance. Scholars adhering to this school refer to post-acceptance as a stage of acceptance process, such as "routinization" (Cooper & Zmud, 1990; Zmud & Apple, 1992) or "confirmation" (Rogers, 1995) that assumes a deterministic view of IS continuance decisions using the same set of pre-acceptance predictors. By overly emphasizing the unidirectional causal relationships between cognitive beliefs and behavior intentions, this school overlooks social, psychological, and economic influences such as social norms and cost concerns.

The second line of research identifies new sets of predictors that lead to users' subsequent beliefs and continuance decisions. Parthasarathy et al. (1998) suggested sources of influence (external and interpersonal), perceived service attributes (usefulness and compatibility), service utilization, and network externality (complementary product usage) as antecedents that affect people's decision to discontinue use of online services (Parthasarathy & Bhattacherjee, 1998). Bhattacherjee (2001) used expectation-confirmation theory (ECT) from marketing literature to synthesize elements of IS adoption and marketing, proposing a model incorporating perceived usefulness, confirmation, and satisfaction as antecedents to IS continuance (Bhattacherjee, 2001). The ECT-based model is captive to affective factors (e.g., the confirmation of expectation from prior use and perceived usefulness as causes of users' IS continuance) but is thus limited in accommodating the impact of non-affective elements in IS continuance. Another group of researchers investigated post-adoption behavior from the perspective of automatic use (Kim & Malhotra, 2005; Kim, Malhotra, & Narasimhan, 2005; Limayem & Hirt, 2003). They argue that IS use becomes spontaneous as the frequency of use increases. Heavy IS users become less conscious in evaluating the system, therefore their continued use of IS turns out to be mostly driven by habit and automaticity as opposed to cognitive beliefs and attitudes.

Although aforementioned literature sheds light on different mechanisms that can explain users' post adoption behaviors, little has been done to examine the continuation of IS use within a single theoretical framework. To the best of our knowledge, we have found no study in the IS literature that has investigated the use of a certain technology product in the face of competing alternatives. Therefore, in this paper, we attempt to offer a different, perhaps complementing lens to unravel how IS continuance rests on the users' perceived sense of "commitment" to a certain technology. Our research shall add to the literature with the following contributions: (1) we propose and empirically investigate technology commitment as an antecedent to IS continuance, (2) we examine three components of technology commitment to provide a more comprehensive picture to account for IS continuance. Especially, by introducing calculative commitment, we emphasize the perceived cost as an important, albeit missing, link that has been overlooked in the IS literature towards understanding post-adoption behavior, (3) we apply the commitment model to measure and analyze the dynamics of user behavior across substitutable technology products.

MODEL DEVELOPMENT

IS Continuance

As noted earlier, IS continuance is defined as users' continued use of an IS technology product long after an initial acceptance decision (Bhattacherjee, 2001). Although IS continuance has been understood differently as routinization, infusion, adaptation, assimilation, etc. in the IS literature, it is generally agreed that IS continuance refers to the stage when an IS technology is adopted and repeatedly used by the user as a routine activity (Bhattacherjee, 2001; Limayem, Hirt, & Cheung, 2007). Contrary to the initial adoption when the use of technology is merely a one-time event, IS continuance requires repeated decisions of use until the users' final decision to discontinue (Limayem et al., 2007). Although the length of time to continuance may vary dependent on the nature of technologies, prior research often consider the use of a certain technology for four or more weeks constitutes a routine activity.

Technology Commitment

Commitment, as a measure of psychological attachment in a relationship, has been widely used to predict persistent behaviors, such as marriage (Arriaga & Agnew, 2001), consumer loyalty (King & Zeithaml, 2003), service retention (Bansal & Irving, 2004), and workplace performance (Sheridan, 1992), etc. The original organizational commitment draws upon the belief that employees, through interactions, form or fail to form an attachment with the organization; employees who feel a sense of attachment are committed towards a longer tenure with an organization while employees who do not feel a sense of attachment are not (Meyer & Allen, 1991; Mowday, Porter, & Steers, 1982). In the IS field, commitment has been used to study user's psychological relationships with certain information systems, such as military information systems and commercial Web sites

(Li, Browne, & Chau, 2006; Malhotra & Galletta, 2005). Given the nature of IS continuance is similar to that of many other repetitive behaviors such as consumer's repurchasing behavior (Bhattacherjee, 2001), the concept of commitment may provide a new angle to examine continued technology use beyond initial adoption.

Although the topic of commitment is widely used in the literature, the concept of commitment does not seem to have a clear cut definition. Commitment can be interpreted as a force (Meyer & Herscovitch, 2001), a tendency (Becker, 1960), a mindset (Li et al., 2006), or a relationship (Rusbult, Martz, & Agnew, 1998). The term *commitment* has been loosely used to refer to commitment process and state. Among many different interpretations of commitment, the commitment concept used by Mowday et al. (1982) and Meyer and Allen (1991) are believed to best represent an individual's commitment to a relationship.

This research introduces a technology commitment perspective to the study of post-adoption technology use. We define user's technology commitment as a *psychological bond between an individual and a technology that makes it less likely for the individual to voluntarily discontinue the use of the technology*. The definition of technology commitment confirms that formation of commitment must follow initial acceptance and a period of use of an information system. In line with Malhotra and Galetta's (2005) finding that volitional use of information systems is underpinned by notions of user commitment, this research proposes that user commitment towards an information system is an important precursor to understanding continued IS use.

The concept of commitment may be examined from two different perspectives: the attitudinal commitment perspective and the behavioral commitment perspective (Meyer & Allen, 1991; Mowday et al., 1982). Attitudinal commitment has to do with the cognitive process by which users' psychological bond with the technology evolves over time as they evaluate the technology and its alternatives through actual use, whereas behavioral commitment is interested in users' behaviors when they become "locked" to a certain technology. This research employs the attitudinal commitment perspective dedicated in studying users' IS continuance when competing systems are available.

The concept of commitment can be examined from two different perspectives: the attitudinal commitment perspective and the behavioral commitment perspective (Meyer & Allen, 1991; Mowday et al., 1982). The attitudinal commitment perspective believes that commitment is an evaluation result of a relationship (Allen & Meyer, 1990; Li et al., 2006). Commitment has to do with the attitudinal and cognitive processes by which users' psychological bond with the technology evolves over time as they evaluate the technology and its alternatives through actual use. The behavioral commitment perspective believes that commitment is a course of action (Meyer & Herscovitch, 2001). People may be committed to a behavior because of the "locked-in" situation. For example, people who are behaviorally committed to video games may have a hard time avoiding games, although they may be cognitively against games. In this paper, we employ the attitudinal commitment perspective dedicated to studying users' IS continuance when competing technologies are in place.

A closer look at the definition confirms that commitment must follow initial acceptance and use of a technology product. In a recent study of volitional use of information systems, Malhotra and Galetta (2005) found that notions of user commitment underpin volitional use of information systems. Therefore, user commitment remains an important precursor to understanding continued IS use (Malhotra & Galletta, 2005). Dixit and Pindyck, too, implicate the need for substantial user commitment because of switching costs among alternative adopted technologies (Dixit & Pindyck, 1994).

As noted earlier, technology commitment is perhaps played out at its fullest in software technologies. There are, in fact, seemingly endless competitions surrounding user loyalty or commitment related to software. Users have long been partisans by their commitment to a specific technology. There are Apple Macintosh OS loyalists; Linux loyalists; Google loyalists. While Mac loyalists are likely to have been exposed to Windows or Linux operating systems, it is a sense of commitment to Mac, even in the presence of previously adopted alternatives (i.e., Windows/ Linux), that determines continuous intention and use. Consider that a general academic institution initially adopts or licenses a variety of statistical packages, e.g., SPSS, Minitab, SAS, STATA, Systat, to name a few. Yet, over time, the institution commits to a few from the many, either by canceling licenses and updates, or simply by uninstalling the package. In the long-run, it is a sense of commitment that distinguishes continuous use behavior towards one software while foregoing other initially-adopted alternatives. In fact, a *Business Week* article by Lacy surveyed the software market only to resoundingly remark that "such fierce user loyalty may be the first spoils in the growing design renaissance in business software" (Lacy, 2006).

Facets of Attitudinal Technology Commitment

Adhering to Meyer and Allen's (1991) work on commitment, we partition attitudinal technology commitment into three components: affective commitment, normative commitment, and calculative commitment. Each of the three components respectively represents a desire, an obligation, and a need towards IS continuance

Affective commitment refers to commitment subject to a *perceived emotional attachment to, identification with, and involvement* with a corresponding entity (Meyer & Allen, 1991). Affective commitment to technology thus relates to a users' sense of attachment to a technology product driven by internal motivation and a sense of involvement and identification (Allen & Meyer, 1996; Meyer, Stanley, Herscovitch, & Topolnytsky, 2002). For example, a Web developer that *values* robust Web application development may feel more *attached* to Sun's Java Server Pages (JSP) than Microsoft's Active Server Pages (ASP) because JSP offers a richer set of objects that can be embedded in Web pages. Affective technology commitment thus refers to the user's psychological bond with a technology due to hedonic (e.g., interface characteristics, playfulness), emotional (e.g., enjoyment), and/or utilitarian (e.g., a shared sense of value) feelings towards a technology product. We can thus argue that users experiencing a sense of affective commitment to a technology product will more likely feel the need to continue their use of the technology product.

H1: Affective attitudinal commitment will have a positive influence on the user's continuance intention for a technology product

Calculative commitment has been termed differently in the literature. Its concept is related to a users' sense of attachment to an information system driven by cost concerns about discontinuing the use of an information system and switching to an alternative information system. Given the nature of calculative commitment is directly associated with continued behaviors, the original commitment literature often refers to it as *continuance commitment* (Allen & Meyer, 1990). Some scholars used a different name *calculative commitment* to refer to the same concept due to the concern that the word *continuance* does not faithfully reflect the nature of rational cost evaluation in this concept (Gilliland & Bello, 2002). This research agrees to their argument and adopts the term calculative commitment in order to avoid readers' confusion caused by the word *continuance* appearing in multiple constructs.

Calculative commitment refers to commitment subject to a *perceived awareness of costs* associated with a decision or action (Meyer & Allen, 1991). Calculative commitment to technology relates to a users' sense of attachment to a technology driven by cost concerns surrounding the choice of alternative technology products. A users' continuance cost includes financial and non-financial elements such as opportunity costs, substitution costs, learning curves, sunk costs, and contractual obligations. Calculative commitment to a technology product often depends on the costs of training, investment, and opportunities (Meyer & Allen, 1997). For example, in IS research, calculative commitment is often traceable in projects where lock-ins lead to commitment escalation, even when the project might be perceived as being in trouble (Abrahamsson, 2002).

Calculative commitment is cognition-specific. Festinger's (1957) cognitive dissonance theory contends that when people invest tremendous effort in a specific goal, they tend to increase their evaluation of the goal correspondingly so that the dissonance created between the effort and the original goal can be eliminated (Festinger, 1957; Harmon-Jones & Mills, 1999). We argue that calculative commitment subsumes prior experience and efforts of the user in relation to the technology. The cognitive dissonance theory suggests that one's commitment is influenced by the effort one has invested even though such efforts may not be relevant to the goal. For example, a user who has been trained in a Microsoft® Visual Basic environment for four years of college may be committed, albeit reluctantly, to the technology and continue to use it even if competing alternatives (e.g., Java or C#) could have been more promising for future development requirements. Users' concerns of costs stemming from discontinued use will increase their commitment and thus facilitate their intended affiliation to the technology.

H2: Calculative attitudinal commitment will have a positive influence on the user's continuance intention for a technology product.

Normative commitment refers to commitment subject to a *perceived obligation* to continue to serve a corresponding entity (Meyer & Allen, 1991). In contrast with affective commitment, normative commitment to technology is related to *external motivations (obligations)* that induce users to remain attached to a technology. As Meyer and Allen suggested, normative commitment is present when the pressure, or "debt", is in place (Meyer & Allen, 1991). Users internalize normative pressures and become committed in conformity with social norms. When the external pressure disappears, normative commitment may become trivial. For example, a user may feel attached to Microsoft® Visual Studio.NET environment mainly because a majority of team members uses it to develop web applications, even though he or she may be affectively partial to a competing technology product, such as Adobe Dreamweaver. Because normative commitment to technology refers to a user's psychological bond with a technology due to perceived obligation or pressure from people around him or her, this notion of social conformance can influence the user's intention to continue to use a technology product.

H3: Normative attitudinal commitment will have a positive influence on the user's continuance intention for an IS technology product.

The concepts of attitudinal technology commitment and IS continuance do not occur in a vacuum but are underpinned by brand-specific technology products[1]. For example, research on user commitment always uses a particular technology (e.g., Pillbury's discontinuous use of Intranets) as the underlying frame of reference. Because each technology product is perceived differently by users, inherent technology product characteristics may, by themselves, positively impact user's continuance intentions. In addition, in the context of instant messaging applications, the brand of technology products is also an important consideration in technology use. Users formulate commitment to technologies based on their affective, normative, and calculative attitudes toward the technology. However, brand-specific technology products moderate the relationship between users' commitment and their continuance intention. As a moderator, we argue that different brand-specific technology products vary the existing relationship between commitment and continuance intentions. For example, users who are in favor of Apple's brand may be more likely to continue to use his or her 1st generation iPhone even if the users are not affectively committed to the product due to lack of some features, such as GPS navigation.

When technology substitutes (alternatives) are available under the same technology category, (e.g., Adobe Photoshop, Corel Draw, GIMP, under image editor category) user commitment is traceably different across brand-specific technology products, affecting their continuous use behavior, e.g., *The New York Times* (2006) report on continuous use of Internet Explorer over competing technology products such as Opera or Mozilla. Because this research focuses on understanding IS continuance in the context of *competing alternatives*, we use brand-specific technology products as the underlying context. Because users have varied perceptions of different technology products, we believe that brand-specific technology products alternatives moderate the relationship between commitment and continuance such that the strength of the relationship between users' attitudinal commitment and IS continuance intention will be different across brand-specific technology product alternatives.

H4a: The strength of the relationship between affective attitudinal commitment and IS continuance intention will show significant differences across brand-specific technology products.

H4b: The strength of the relationship between calculative attitudinal commitment and IS continuance intention will show significant differences across brand-specific technology products.

H4c: The strength of the relationship between normative attitudinal commitment and IS continuance intention will show significant differences across brand-specific technology products.

The hypothesized model is shown in Figure 1.

RESEARCH METHODOLOGY

Survey Design

A survey design is used to empirically validate the research model. Given that the objective of this study is to understand anteceding factors to IS continuance, we chose to use a questionnaire-based survey to gather data from current technology users. Because previous studies on commitment have generally been captive to employee turnover, this study sought to develop and refine attitudinal technology commitment measures to gauge user perceptions first hand.

Two key considerations went into the selection of the technology and sample: One was ascertaining that the user sample knew that there were competing alternatives for the technology that they were currently using. The other was that users must have previously adopted one or more of the competing alternatives before opting to continuously use one of the available technology choices. In that vein, a comparative assessment of competing technologies was used to gain a better understanding on how aspects of a certain brand (instance) technology contribute to continuous IS use.

Figure 1. Research model

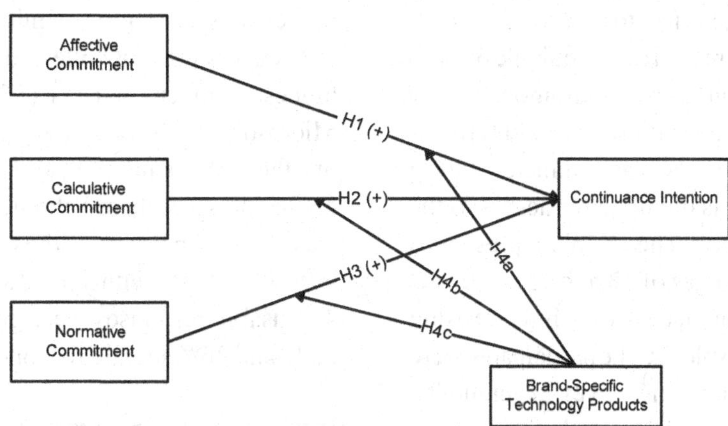

In light of the aforementioned considerations, we chose to study instant messaging applications (as instantiations of the competing technologies). First, instant messaging is a popular technology. For example, a survey of instant messaging technologies found that AOL Instant Messenger (AIM®) had 100 million registered (subscribed/downloaded) users and 53 million active (continuous) users while Microsoft® MSN Messenger (presently, Microsoft® Live Messenger) had around 27 million active users out of 120 million (Nielsen-Natratings, 2006). Altogether, total worldwide users of IM technologies amounted to approximately 350 million. Second, as the previous figures reveal, there is a distinct difference between the initial base of adopters and the active (continuous users). This difference supports the basic contentions and premise forwarded by this paper. Third, instant messaging technologies offer a wide variety of competing products, e.g., AIM®, Microsoft® MSN Messenger, and Yahoo! Messenger ™, among others. All competing products were easy to download and install, and shared a similar set of features. Fourth, instant messaging technologies are free, easy to download and install, and have very little footprint. Moreover, instant messaging has also made inroads into organizations as a popular alternative for existing modes of communication (e.g., email, collaborative portals such as Lotus Notes), thus offering added credence.

We used an online questionnaire-based survey to collect data on user perceptions of technology commitment for IM technologies. An online questionnaire-based survey was used for data collection because the method provides a non-intrusive way to assess user perceptions. Furthermore, the survey setting using a popular technology increases our ability to generalize the findings.

Data Collection

The empirical data are collected from in a large public university in the pacific northwest of the U.S. The participants were students enrolled in sophomore or junior level courses. Participation was voluntary and extra credit participants were awarded extra credit. All participants had experience with more than two IM clients but were more inclined to continue using one over other adopted IM substitutes. The data set shows that 93% of all participants reported to use two IM clients and the rest 7% reported to use more than two IM clients. Among all participants, 32.3% reported to use Microsoft® MSN Messenger as their primary[2] IM client; 56.3% reported to use AIM® as their primary IM client; the rest reported to use Yahoo! or other messengers as their primary IM client.

The study was carried out in a computer lab on campus. Participants had to enter their student IDs to receive extra credit. To assure single participant responses, the survey program automatically rejects multiple entries with the same ID. In addition, because the survey was conducted during lab hours, participants did not have access to the survey outside of class. The sample represents a population between ages of 18 and 23.

All participants had access to the Internet using Microsoft Internet Explorer. The participants were asked to complete an online survey using the lab computers. Except for demographic questions, the survey consisted of multiple Likert-type questions. Responses to each item were measured on a 7-point scale with point anchors from 1 (strongly disagree) to 7 (strongly agree). Likert-type questions. Responses to each item were measured on a 7-point scale with point anchors from 1 (strongly disagree) to 7 (strongly agree). There are a few reasons that 7-point scale is used in this study. First, using 7-point Likert scales becomes a convention in the IS literature. For example, this study adopted a 7-point scale from Bhattacherjee (2001) for measuring users' IS continuance intention. Malhotra et al. (2005) also used 7-point scales to measure user commitment. Therefore, we consistently follow such convention in the IS literature so that the results are comparable across studies. Second, although the number of points in a scale is positively related with reliability, scales with more than 7 points may cause respondents to be confused such that people may not be able to correctly mark their point of view on a scale greater than 7. Therefore, 7-point scales provide a balance between accuracy and reliability (Miller, 1956). Third, 7-point scales provide a neutral point where people are not forced to bias their responses to positive or negative answers (Devellis, 2003).

At the onset of the survey, participants were asked to choose *one* instant messenger product (such as Microsoft® MSN Messenger, AIM®, Yahoo! Messenger™, etc.) that they actively and continuously use. Their choice generated personalized survey questions (refer to Appendix). Data from participants who had never initially adopted instant messengers was not collected. AIM® showed the highest number of users (56.3%) followed by Microsoft® MSN Messenger (32.3%) and Yahoo! or other IM clients (3.9%). Data collected from participants that chose Yahoo! and other IM clients was dropped because of the constraints imposed by testing effects with limited sample size. Finally, 412 usable responses were generated with 64% male and 36% female respondents.

Instrument Generation

Instrument development followed a scale development procedure proposed by Devellis (Devellis, 2003). Initial items were adapted from the literature (Bhattacherjee, 2001; Li, Chau, & Lou, 2005; Malhotra & Galletta, 2005; Mowday et al., 1982).). Initial commitment items were adapted from Mowday et al.'s Organizational Commitment Questionnaire (OCQ) (Mowday, et al., 1982). There are two types of OCQ forms widely used in employee's commitment test – a longer 15-item version and a shorter 9-item version. The original item bank for measuring TC was generated based upon a modified version of the 15-item OCQ. Two pre-tests were administered for the purpose of item prescreening, face validity test, and scale optimization. Face validity refers to the extent to which a set of items assesses what they appear to measure (Devellis, 2003). In this particular research, the transformation of measuring context from organization to technology calls for a careful review of the face validity of the commitment scale. Two graduate students were asked to independently evaluate the items and the inter-rater correlation is greater than 0.8 on screened items. As a result, 6 items (AC01-AC03, CC01-CC03) are identified for measuring affective commitment and calculative commitment. Given that the OCQ does not explicitly measure normative commitment, another set of items from Li et al. (2005) were adapted. The operational definitions of the

Table 1. Operational definition of constructs

Construct	Operational Definition	Measurement
Affective Commitment	An individual's emotional attachment to a technology product	Adapted from Mowday et al. (1982)
Calculative Commitment	An individual's perceived costs from deciding to discontinue using the existing technology or choosing a competing technology product.	Adapted from Mowday et al. (1982)
Normative Commitment	An individual's belief that people important to him or her will think he or she should continue or discontinue using a technology product	Adapted from Li et al (2005)
Continuance Intention	An individual's intention to voluntarily continue using a technology	Bhattacherjee (2001)

constructs are summarized as in Table 1. The scale items are listed in the Appendix.

Data Analysis

Instrument Validation

The collected data set was analyzed using SPSS 13 (Norušis, 2006) and EQS 6.1 (Build 83) (Bentler, 2004; Byrne, 2006) statistical software packages. Descriptive statistics including skewness and kurtosis were calculated and reported. Skewness represents the degree to which the data is symmetrically distributed around its mean. Positive skewness indicates a distribution with an asymmetric tail extending towards the positive values. Negative skewness indicates a distribution with an asymmetric tail extending towards the negative values (Tabachnick & Fidell, 2000). As a rule of thumb, if the absolute value of skewness is less than 2, it is determined that the data set is symmetrically distributed around its mean. In this study, all items have met this criterion.

Kurtosis is a measure of how "sharp" the data is distributed in its peak. High kurtosis value means more variance is caused by extreme values. A normally distributed data set should yield kurtosis equal to 0. As long as the absolute value of kurtosis is not exceeding 3, the normality of the data set is satisfactory. Therefore, in this study skewness and kurtosis do not appear to raise a concern in the analysis.

Rigorous instrument validation is one necessary prerequisite toward quality IS research. Guided by Straub et al. (2004), the data analysis began with a set of mandatory validity checks, including *content validity check, reliability check, convergent validity check, and discriminant validity check.*

Composite reliability is a measure of the overall reliability of a collection of items that are used to manifest a latent construct variable (Raykov, 1997). Composite reliability can be calculated using the following formula:

$$Composite\ Reliability = \frac{\sum^2(s\tan dardized\,loadings)}{\sum^2(s\tan dardized\,loadings) + \sum indicator\ measurement\,error}$$

Content validity is recommended when new constructs are developed or existing constructs are adopted in new context (Cronbach, 1971). The purpose of content validity is to ensure that the instruments correctly represent the content of the constructs to be measured. Content validity can be accessed through a careful review of the literature review and/or rigorous peer review of the instrument. In this study, the instrument scales are adapted from existing validated instruments on a strong theoretical basis. Some newly developed items went through multiple rounds of peer review and data collections. Therefore, the instrument in this study has achieved satisfactory content validity.

Table 2. Descriptive data

Construct	Item	Mean	Std. Dev.	Skewness	Kurtosis	Item-Total Corr.	Composite Reliability
AC	AC01	2.473	1.321	0.998	1.072	0.910	0.940
	AC02	2.663	1.423	0.885	0.525	0.930	
	AC03	2.609	1.351	0.862	0.873	0.936	
CC	CC01	4.913	1.721	-0.503	-0.655	0.887	0.945
	CC02	4.971	1.753	-0.666	-0.403	0.899	
	CC03	4.731	1.697	-0.333	-0.844	0.876	
NC	NC01	2.214	1.429	1.621	2.525	0.938	0.947
	NC02	2.517	1.556	1.269	1.280	0.918	
	NC03	2.493	1.503	1.221	1.132	0.919	
CI	CI01	2.546	1.346	1.307	1.941	0.860	0.875
	CI02	3.049	1.601	0.883	0.271	0.909	
Note: AC-Affective Commitment; CC-Calculative Commitment; NC- Normative Commitment; CI-Continuance Intention							

Reliability check is used to ensure the measurement is internally consistent and replicable. A common means of assessing reliability is through the measure of composite reliability. It is recommended that the composite reliability to be greater than 0.70 (Nunnally, 1978). The descriptive data suggest satisfactory reliability. All composite reliability measures are over the 0.70 benchmark.

EXPLORATORY FACTOR ANALYSIS

Exploratory factor analysis (EFA) is a statistical procedure often used to reveal underlying latent factors predicted by a set of manifested variables. EFA is used when no theory or predication is made prior to the analysis, particularly because no conclusion can be drawn from EFA unless further theory development or confirmatory analysis supports the finding. In this study, although all measurement scales are theoretically grounded, conducting EFA is a step to reduce weak or cross-loaded items.

EFA was conducted using SPSS 13 statistical software package. The items were entered in three groups: the commitment constructs, the antecedent constructs, and the dependent constructs. In each group, all items are entered at the same time and allowed to rotate using the varimax method. The items for each proposed construct should load on the same factor with their loadings greater than 0.60. On the other hand, the cross loadings of these items on other factors should not exceed 0.40 (Byrne, 2006; Byrne & Crombie, 2003).

Convergent and discriminant analyses were performed for construct validity in EFA. *Convergent validity* check is used to test whether the measurement items that should theoretically measure a construct demonstrate strong correlations to each other. Convergent validity can be usually assessed using three criteria (Byrne, 2006; Fornell & Larcker, 1981): 1) all factor loadings are significant and greater than 0.70; 2) composite reliabilities for each construct are over 0.80; and 3) average variance extracted (AVE) are over 0.50, or the square root of AVEs are over 0.71. The result shows that: 1) all factor loadings are above the

Table 3. Construct correlations

	AC	CC	NC	CI
AC	**0.915**			
CC	0.240	**0.923**		
NC	0.448	0.244	**0.925**	
CI	0.648	0.271	0.514	**0.882**
Note: AC-Affective Commitment; CC-Calculative Commitment; NC-Normative Commitment; CI-Continuance Intention Diagonal is the squared root of construct Average Variance Extracted (AVE)				

0.70 level (Table 4); 2) all composite reliabilities are over 0.80 (Table 2); and 3) all square root of AVEs are over 0.70 (Table 3). Therefore, this study has adequate convergent validity.

Discriminant validity tests whether the measurement items that should be theoretically *unrelated* demonstrate weak correlations to each other. Discriminant validity is usually assessed by 1) the cross factor loadings below the 0.30 level (Table 4); 2) comparing construct correlations with the square root of AVEs (Table 3) from individual constructs (Fornell & Larcker, 1981) expecting that the square root of AVE is greater than the construct correlations. Table 4 indicates that all theory suggested items correctly loaded on their respective latent constructs with weak cross factor loadings to other unrelated items. Table 3 provides positive support for discriminant validity by indicating smaller construct correlations than the square root of AVEs. Therefore, the study has adequate discriminant validity.

A Kaiser-Meyer-Olkin (KMO) test and a Bartlett's tests were also conducted to examine the sampling adequacy and sphericity. The KMO test measures sampling adequacy by evaluating whether the partial correlations among variables are small enough. It is suggested that a KMO measure greater than 0.7 indicates satisfactory sampling adequacy in a factor analysis (Meyers, Gamst, & Guarino, 2005; Pallant, 2007). The

Table 4. Exploratory factor analysis

Construct	Item	Rotated Component Matrix			
		1	**2**	**3**	**4**
AC	AC01	0.236	**0.825**	0.107	0.278
	AC02	0.175	**0.896**	0.103	0.176
	AC03	0.161	**0.885**	0.090	0.253
CC	CC01	0.069	0.115	**0.911**	0.043
	CC02	0.102	0.081	**0.921**	0.086
	CC03	0.113	0.071	**0.899**	0.110
NC	NC01	**0.918**	0.161	0.076	0.143
	NC02	**0.859**	0.198	0.113	0.206
	NC03	**0.877**	0.184	0.119	0.169
CI	CI01	0.237	0.331	0.079	**0.783**
	CI02	0.246	0.322	0.154	**0.765**
Note; AC-Affective Commitment; CC-Calculative Commitment; NC- Normative Commitment; CI-Continuance Intention					

Bartlett's test examines sphericity by testing a null hypothesis that the correlation matrix is an identity matrix[3] (Meyers et al., 2005). A significant Bartlett's test indicates strong correlation among variables in the factor model and confirms the overall model (Tabachnick & Fidell, 2000). The result shows that the KMO measure of sampling adequacy is 0.85 and the observed 0.00 significance level of Bartlett's test as satisfactory.

THE STRUCTURAL MODEL

This study uses Structural Equation Modeling (SEM) to test our hypotheses and the overall fit between the data and the model. Structural equation modeling is a confirmatory statistical technique that uses covariance matrices for validating a theory-driven structural model against empirical data (Brown, 2006; Byrne, 2006). This technique has been widely applied in IS research. SEM testing and analysis provides intuitive indicators for model fit and path significance, demonstrating the extent to which a proposed structural model accounts for the covariance in a collected data set (Straub et al., 2004). Research employing SEM testing and analysis often reports a group of fit indices but researchers have not reached a consensus as to what indices are required in a SEM testing and analysis report. On the other hand, statistical software packages have their own reporting criteria resulting in some indices incomparable across reports generated by different software packages. Given this study employs EQS 6.1 as the statistical tool for data analysis, the reporting procedure will follow the guideline set forth by Byrne (2006). The major indices to be reported include Comparative Fit Index (CFI), the chi-square χ^2 value, the ratio of χ^2 to degree of freedom, Standardized Root Mean Square Residual (SRMR), and Root Mean Square Error of Approximation (RMSEA).

CFI is a direct measure of the fitness of the observed covariance and the predicted covariance. It is suggested that a good fit model should demonstrate CFI greater than 0.90 (Byrne, 2006; Byrne & Crombie, 2003). The χ^2 value is another measure of fit, however since the χ^2 value is sensitive to the model size, it is suggested that the ratio of χ^2 to degree of freedom be used in lieu of the direct χ^2 value. A χ^2/df less than 3 is believed to be a better indicator (Byrne, 2006; Straub, et al., 2004). SRMR and RMSEA are measures of the standardized difference between the observed covariance and predicted covariance. Good models should have an SRMR less than 0.08 and RMSEA of 0.05 or less. This study reports all above indicators in the analysis.

Table 5 provides a summary of the fit indices. The χ^2/df = 1.459 (χ^2 = 55.447, df = 38) suggests a good fit between the collected data and the model prediction. Other fit indices also support this conclusion. The CFI is 0.995, SRMR is 0.033, and the RMSEA is 0.033 with the 90% confidence interval between.010 and.053. Furthermore, the structural model explains 70.9% of variance in IS continuance intention among users. Results evidently support technology commitment as a precursor to IS continuance intentions.

The path coefficients between three exogenous constructs and one endogenous construct were also tested in the overall structural model (Figure 2). All path coefficients are significant and show support for H1, H2, and H3. Affective commit-

Table 5. Fit indices of the research model

	Case	df	χ2	CFI	SRMR	RMSEA	90% CI of RMSEA	R-sqr
Research Model	412	38	55.447	0.995	0.026	0.033	(.010,.051)	0.709

Figure 2. Path diagram, all users

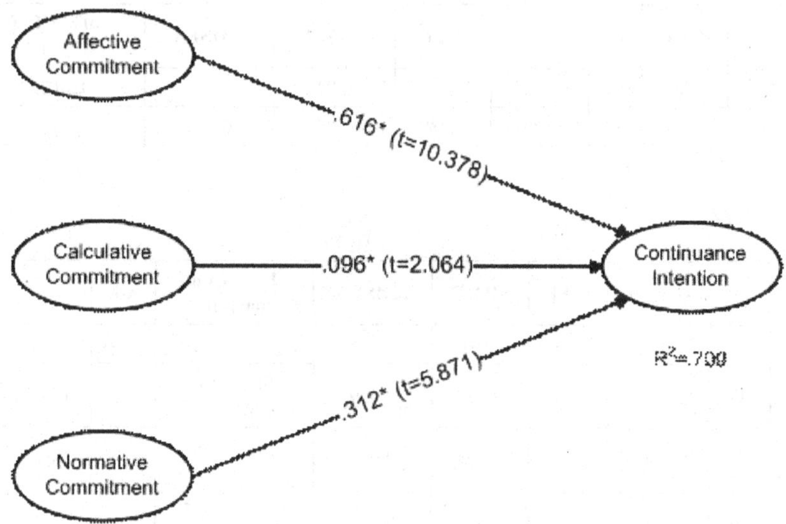

ment appears to have the strongest direct effect (0.616, t=10.378, p<0.001) on continuance intentions, followed by normative commitment (0.312, t=2.064, p<0.05) and a weak direct effect of calculative commitment (0.096, t=5.871, p<0.001). Consistent with empirical research on the three components of the commitment model (Meyer et al., 2002), correlations among exogenous variables were also conducted and findings do not suggest any significant overlaps between the commitment components.

Test of Moderation Effects

In order to test moderating effects of technology product on the relationship between commitment and IS continuance intentions, participants were split into the two major groups (AIM® users (n = 232) and MSN users (n = 133)). Individual model fits are shown in Table 5. Both groups yielded good fit indices (Table 5) which laid the foundation for the test of moderating effect of brand-specific technology products on the commitment continuance relationship.

A multi-group invariance test procedure (Byrne, 2006; Byrne & Crombie, 2003) was used to test the moderation effects (Table 6). Byrne's test procedure consists of a series of hierarchical model comparisons with stepwise constraints on item loadings, factor variances, factor covariances, error residuals, and path coefficients. Every subsequent step increases the constraints on the model and compares it to the previous set of imposed constraints to check for significance. If the model fit does not change significantly between two contiguous steps, it is concluded that the two groups are equivalent at that comparison level. Group differences surface when the model fit changes significantly with each subsequent stepwise constraint. In Table 7, steps 1-6 are foundational and used for stepwise comparisons while steps 7-9 are based on hypothesized group differences.

Table 7 reveals that brand-specific moderation (as shown as in group differences) gathers significance with normative and continuance commitment. The perceptible difference from the moderating influence of technology product lies in the relationship between calculative commitment and IS continuance intention. While AIM users show a moderate positive relationship between calculative commitment and IS continuance

Table 6. Fit indices of sub groups

	Case	df	χ2	CFI	SRMR	RMSEA	90% CI of RMSEA	R-sqr
MSN Messenger Users	133	38	56.284	0.978	0.04	0.06	(.020,.092)	0.789
AOL IM Users	232	38	53.897	0.988	0.04	0.043	(.006,.067)	0.683

Table 7. Invariance test

Step	Test	df	χ2	CFI	SRMR	RMSEA	Model Comparison	Δdf	Δχ2	ΔCFI	Sig.
1	Configural	76	110.182	0.985	0.040	0.035					
2	Metric	83	128.24	0.980	0.052	0.039	Step 2 vs. Step 1	7	18.058	-0.005	n.s
3	Factor Variance	86	141.373	0.975	0.084	0.042	Step 3 vs. Step 2	3	13.133	-0.005	n.s
4	Factor Covariance	89	150.368	0.972	0.098	0.044	Step 4 vs. Step 3	3	8.995	-0.003	n.s
5	Residual	101	177.699	0.966	0.106	0.046	Step 5 vs. Step 4	12	27.331	-0.006	n.s
6	Path Coefficient	104	194.994	0.960	0.109	0.049	Step 6 vs. Step 5	3	17.295	-0.006	n.s
7	Release AC-CI	103	192.697	0.960	0.103	0.049	Step 6 vs. Step 5	1	-2.297	0.000	n.s
8	Release CC-CI	103	189.176	0.962	0.109	0.048	Step 6 vs. Step 5	1	-5.818	0.002	<0.05
9	Release NC-CI	103	180.773	0.966	0.104	0.046	Step 6 vs. Step 5	1	-14.221	0.006	<0.001

Note: Because we are interested in the moderation effect of brand-specific differences rather than the direct effect of commitment components, therefore the insignificant path is not a concern in the analysis.
Step(n+1) and Step(n) comparisons are iterative stepwise comparisons using added constraints. Steps 7-9 are confirmatory and look at iterative model differences between the residuals test and the path coefficients.

intention, the relationship becomes negative and non-significant for MSN Messenger users. Among other differences, affective commitment has a greater main effect on IS continuance intentions among MSN users while normative commitment has a greater main effect on IS continuance intentions among AIM users. As hypothesized, path coefficients across technology products show some significant differences (Figure 3 and Figure 4). Steps 7 to 9 (Table 7) reveal that the release of constraints on normative commitment to continuance intention and calculative commitment to continuance intention makes significant change of the model χ^2. Results offer support for H4b, and H4c but not H4a.

DISCUSSION

Technology Commitment

The results confirm the role of technology commitment as a predictor of IS continuance intention. Especially, the findings confirm that affective commitment is particularly important for the user to choose an information system over available substitutes. This finding is consistent with the consensus in the IS literature that affective commitment has the strongest association with behavioral intention (Allen & Meyer, 1996; Li et al., 2006). Participant responses provide further support to our observations (emphases added).

Figure 3. Path Diagram, AIM® users

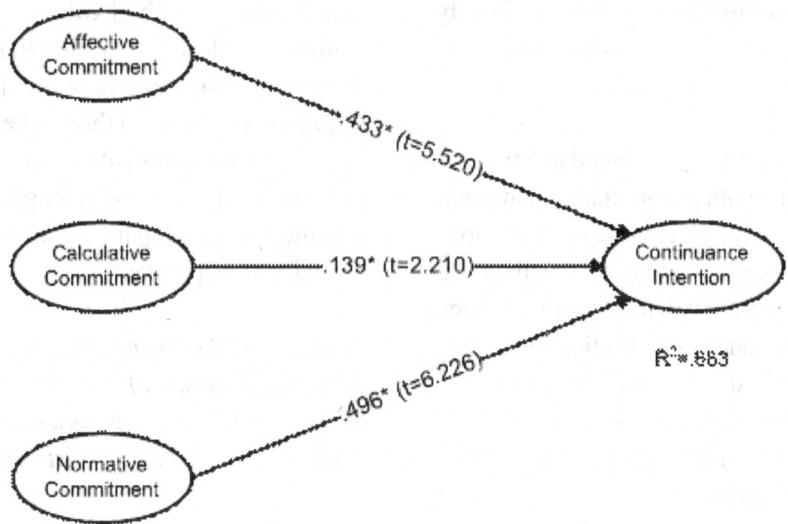

I **love** *[a particular Instant Messenger software]. It's* **the best** *I have ever used. I* **would highly recommend** *it to anyone.*

A weaker but significant relationship is confirmed between normative commitment and IS continuance intentions. The findings suggest that peer pressure has considerable effects on normative commitment, and IM users tend to value normative commitment positively in the formation of their continuance intention. In the comments, participants demonstrated mixed attitude toward the norm and it seems that overall their continuance is independent of perceived norm.

Figure 4. Path diagram, Microsoft® MSN messenger users

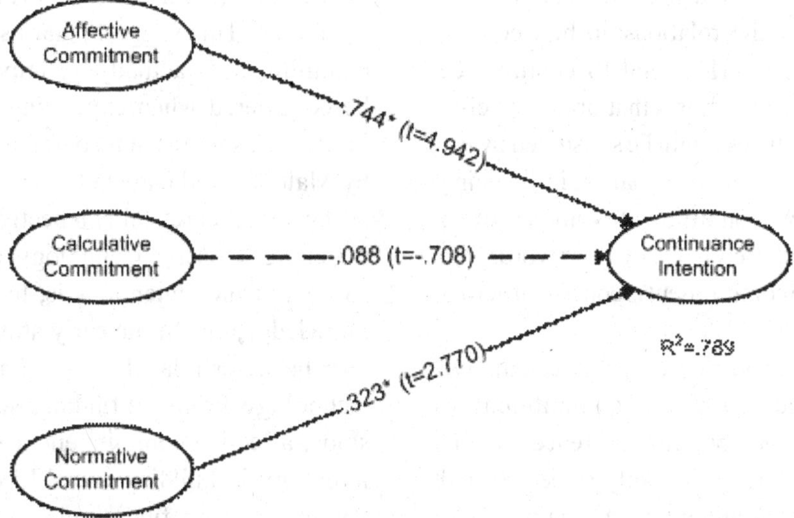

I'm using [a particular Instant Messenger software] **because lots of my friends and family are on it**. *I can't make them all switch* **so I have to use** *it.*

Calculative commitment is found to have significant relationship with IS continuance intention but the path weight is relatively low. Such relationship reflects that users are concerned with costs, especially switching costs when discontinuance decisions are to be made. The finding highlights the importance of cost as an element of commitment. In the case of instant messenger software, perceptions of costs, although low because of the ease of substitution, still appear significant due to the difficulty of notifying others of the new account. This conclusion is confirmed by user's responses:

...**It is an effort to provide people with a new account.** *But I heard there are new technologies and you can talk to people on [another particular Instant Messenger software]. That'll be cool. But I'm lazy you know...*

Brand-specific technology differences are found to significantly moderate the relationships between two commitment components (i.e., calculative commitment and normative commitment, H4b and H4c) and users' IS continuance intention, but not the relationship between affective commitment (H4a) and IS continuance intention. The finding shows that brand-specific technology differences might be subsumed by users' affective commitment so that the influencing power of affective commitment is not sensitive to brand-specific differences. In other words, the effect of affective commitment is consistent across technology brands.

On the other hand, the effect of calculative commitment and normative commitment is moderated by brand-specific differences. Users of certain brands are more likely to be affected by calculative commitment and normative commitment than those of other brands. For example, although in general high calculative and normative commitment lead to high intention to continuance, in the case when one is psychologically against a specific brand, even though he or she may perceive high commitment to that brand technology product due to cost and peer pressure, his or her intention to continuance may still be low. One participant responded:

The reason I don't wanna use [a particular Instant Messenger software] is because **I am not a fan of** *[the brand]* **anymore as a company**. *Although I have friends using it, I just don't use.*

This is interesting finding suggesting external variables such as technology differences, personal differences, and environment differences may be directions for future research.

Overall Model

Results from the data collected from an initial survey reveal that users' perceived technology commitment is a strong predictor for IS continuance intentions. Not only do we find that the proposed model achieves good fit, but we also find that technology commitment components contribute towards explaining a great proportion of the variance (in this case, 71%) in IS continuance intentions. This suggests that users' technology commitment is actually an important aspect to be considered when explaining IS continuance intentions, somewhat resonating with arguments by Malhotra and Galetta (2005).

From a theoretical perspective, the notion of matching a user's technology commitment to IS continuance intentions is, to the best of our knowledge, one of the early attempts to unravel user behavior related to the continued use of a technology. From the findings suggested by this study, affective commitment seems particularly important in building users' IS continuance intentions. Such a finding also receives intuitive support, perhaps because users would intend to keep using technology products that they like (affective), independent of influences (normative) or conditions (continuance). The weak relationship between calculative commitment and IS continuance intentions confirms that users are not particularly favorable towards any mandates, coercion, and compliance posed by the technology per se (e.g., scheduled updates, patches, fixes), especially when the technology is free and openly available. However, user intentions gain ground if they feel that using a technology provides a sense of membership.

Lessons Learned

Findings from this study of technology commitment and information systems continuance draw our attention to several important issues. First, technology commitment is an important precursor to IS continuance, explaining over 70 percent of the variance in a users' intention to continuous use of a technology. This finding is rather disillusioning. The observed role of technology commitment allows us to realize that adoption and continued use of a technology are distanced constructs. Bhattacherjee (2001) argues that intention to use does not necessarily lead to continued use of a technology.

The use of instant messaging software, even with the relatively high number of alternatives and apparently negligible switching costs, is still subject to user commitment. That is, even application technologies such as instant messengers remain adopted yet unused. Consider the lifecycle of an instant messenger application called ICQ. Users initially adopted ICQ and used it for a period, then forsook ICQ for other adopted alternatives such as MSN Messenger and Yahoo Messenger. We argue that central to this punctuated lifecycle is a lack of technology commitment While there have been anecdotal references to social norms (particularly network externalities) as an important driver of instant messaging software adoption, vendors must realize that continuance intentions rely on user-specific commitment to the messaging software. To combat issues with social norms and network externalities, Yahoo! Messenger and MSN Messenger have recently started the reuse of IM contacts across applications, therefore mitigating concerns of social norms and externalities, and underscoring the success of the applications based on commitment.

Further, easily available alternatives, negligible learning costs, and quick installations offered by IM software echo marginal lock-in effects among users. Easy substitutability often weighs heavily on vendors because it lowers barriers to entry thus increasing competition. To counter this issue, IM vendors are revisiting their deployment and design strategies. For example, Google embeds its IM in its popular webmail to reduce user costs of even installing the IM application. If users can chat without running IM software as a separate service, it could free users from using IM software that needs to be installed singly. In an age where most applications, are resource intensive, moving IM technologies from a client-based to a hosted (managed) service could possibly increase a user's calculative commitment

However, a reexamination of IS continuance in the context for brand-specific technology products offers some interesting observations. MSN messenger users' seem to be indifferent to the relationship between calculative commitment and continuance intentions. Additionally, MSN messenger users' IS continuance seems to be driven more by affective continuance in relation to AIM users. IS continuance among AIM users places a different emphasis on anteceding components of commitment. IS continuance for AIM users is anteceded by different perceptions of commitment than MSN Messenger users: mainly with a lower level of affective and relatively higher levels of normative and calculative commitment. Calculative commitment is stronger for AIM users, perhaps because the immobility of contacts raises switching costs, compelling users to continue using AIM, even when users do not particularly like the application. Further, the stronger impact of normative commitment on continuance for AIM can be explained by the larger critical mass of AIM users. It could thus be surmised that technologies with negligible learning costs could benefit from increasing affective and normative commitment.

Implications for Theory and Practice

This study has implications for IS research in a few ways. First, this study is one of few attempts to use the notion of technology commitment as an ontological shift to explain users' continuous use of technologies. This study goes beyond the adoption phase to look at routinization of technology use (Zmud & Apple, 1992) given multiple adopted alternatives. By doing so, the paper tries to look at perceived behavioral control in the face of discontinuous use of technology. Second, this paper tries to understand the influence of brand-specific technology differences on user intentions, thus shifting the research plane from inter-technology influences to intra-technology influences. Third, the treatment of technology commitment as a multi-faceted construct allows for the incorporation of a varied set of commitment components, from emotion to social desirability and obligation. Third, this study offers a systematic development of instruments, refined and validated though empirical evidence for reference by future research. Finally, in receipt of strong empirical support, the technology commitment model offers an extrapolative framework with a degree of predictive validity for other forms of technologies and technology products.

Additionally, understanding IS continuance has important implications for practice. The fierce competition among IS vendors is often a function of competing technology products. Take for example the statistical software industry that often relies on revenues from individual and site licenses. While SAS, SPSS, and Minitab may each claim significant brand-specific product differentiation advantages, all three programs offer a similar set of features. Subsequently, based on anecdotal member interests, organizations may agree to initially adopt and use all three software programs. However, users in organizations opt to use only one of the available installed options. Adopted software becomes shelfware when firms realize unused software as an expense lost as license fees, initial adoption expenses, training, or even the total cost of ownership. As a result, adopted yet underused technology products cost organizations in the U.S. millions of dollars every year (Markus & Keil, 1994). Given that evolving business models in this competitive landscape vie for continuous use rather than initial acceptance of a technology product, it becomes crucial for organizations to understand the preconditions for IS continuance intentions guiding future technology adoption choices.

It is imperative that vendors consider user commitment in designing and deploying IS technologies. Stimulating affect is no longer a sufficient condition for ascertaining IS continuance. Vendors must pay considerable attention to other facets of commitment, especially normative and calculative commitment. In a world that is getting more and more socially networked, building software solutions that can leverage on existing social networks or allow creating newer networks becomes important. For example, YouTube and FaceBook have garnered unprecedented popularity by designing and strategically positioning their products to leverage on the social network of users.

Additionally, creating lock-in effects can help increase continued IS use. For example, Linux distributions are commonly free. However, companies that bundle support services with freely distributable packages are more likely to create lock-in effects for users transitioning to the Linux platform. In the absence of support, user commitment for the latter (i.e., Linux distributions with support) is likely to be more calculative, leading to higher continuance. In short, vendors may find it prudent to bundle helpful services that are absent in competing products to increase substitution costs and elevate IS continuance. Further, vendors can employ these facets of commitment to scrutinize the performance and sustainability of past technologies, particularly technologies that have fallen to user disfavor.

Limitations and Future Research Directions

The study is not without limitations. First, the subjects were undergraduate students and their perceptions of commitment and continuance may not be reflective of a broader population. It is particularly important to review technology commitment in an organizational setting where users are perhaps more rational and display less of a bandwagon effect (Abrahamson & Rosenkoph, 1993). Second, preliminary findings from this research are captive to instant messaging technologies only and need to be validated in light of other competing technology products. For example, it would be extremely insightful to observe how vendors tend to condition user commitment over time by offering free software in face of costly alternatives. For example, Microsoft uses its academic alliance to offer otherwise expensive software such as Visual Studio, Visio, and even Windows Vista for free. Apart from the vendor's espoused altruistic motives, free software creates both economic and cognitive lock-in effects among students. In the same vein of thought, it would be useful to study future effects on technology commitment and use. Third, because IS continuance is a concept rooted in continued use, a cross sectional treatment may not portray inherent nuances, necessitating a longitudinal study. Often, commitment may be regarded as being time sensitive, captive to perceptions of novelty or otherwise. A longitudinal study could help separate these effects to pronounce a better understanding of the mechanics of technology commitment.

Another limitation of this study is its lack of consideration of intrinsic user characteristics. Intrinsic and somewhat invariant user-charateristics such as habit, inertia, resistance to change, etc., often contribute to post-adoption IS continuance. Habit has been studied as the moderator on the relationship between user's intention to use and their actual use behaviors (Kim & Malhotra, 2005; Limayem et al., 2007). However how habit would influence users' psychological attachment to a technology remains under-investigated. Inertia and resistance to change reflects a human tendency to maintain the status quo regardless of individual's attitudes. Research has reported empirical support on the moderating role of inertia between consumer's affect and loyalty (Anderson & Srinivasan, 2003). A high level of inertia decreases the influencing power of affect on loyalty. Therefore, users' psychological attachment to a technology may be collectively determined by their commitment, loyalty, and inertia. Future research may continue to explore such psychological mechanism as well as other possible drivers of users' psychological attachment [4] to a technology as a prelude to continuance.

Finally, although a variety of research models have been proposed and studied regarding technology use in the IS discipline, TAM remains to be the foundation of many alternative models. The two factors posited in TAM, i.e. perceived usefulness (PU) and perceived ease of use (PEOU) mainly reflect users' evaluation of the utilitarian and hedonic characteristics of a technology at initial adoption. However, post-adoption technology use is rather a dynamic process than a cross sectional status. Future research may consider investigating the dynamically changing context of the factors in adoption models, such as newly upgraded products and feature, changes of norm and use environment, and other circumstantial changes. A model comparison, ideally longitudinal, between TAM, the commitment model, and other alternative models may provide insightful information as to why post-adoption technology use behavior undergoes change.

CONCLUSION

One can ascribe various reasons to limit the growth of shelfware in users and organizations, and technology commitment offers a fresh perspective in unraveling how a user's sense of loyalty guides the continuous use of a technology. As the consumer-driven business model becomes more and more popular, organizations have to consider the importance of user commitment as a way to gauge user satisfaction and loyalty. What explains user commitment to technologies such as the Apple's iPod, Google.com search, or Microsoft Office Suite instead of competing technologies such as Creative's Zen, Ask.com Search, or Corel Office Suite? Instantiated by an investigation of instant messaging software, this study confirms the importance of different components of technology commitment in explaining continuous use. The use of technology commitment also highlights the importance of IS continuance as a way to ascertain returns beyond initial adoption, surfacing how various forms of user commitment drive user behavior.

As technology competition intensifies, the sustainability of firms will largely rely on the commitment of its user base. It is therefore essential to pay particular attention towards increasing affective and normative technology commitment among users to continue their IS use. In a competitive landscape, the potential of affective commitment on IS continuance intentions is compelling – a fact that vendors may wish to consider in their design and delivery of technology products. The commitment perspective further allows for a retrospective interpretation of why certain technologies remain popular over time and why some perish. Finally, commitment also paves the way towards enhancing customer relationship management (CRM) by gauging commitment rather than failing to retain users after initial adoption.

REFERENCES

Abrahamson, E., & Rosenkoph, L. (1993). Institutional and Competitive Bandwagons: Using Mathematical modeling as a Tool to Explore Innovation Diffusion. *Academy of Management Review*, *18*(3), 487–517. doi:10.2307/258906

Abrahamsson, P. (2002). *The Role of Commitment in Software Process Improvement*. Oulu, Finland: University of Oulu.

Ajzen, I. (1985). From intentions to actions: a theory of planned behavior. In Kuhl, J., & Beckmann, J. (Eds.), *Action Control: From Cognition to Behavior* (pp. 11–39). New York: Springer.

Allen, N. J., & Meyer, J. P. (1990). The measurement and antecedents of affective, continuance, and normative commitment to the organization. *Journal of Occupational Psychology*, *63*, 1–18.

Allen, N. J., & Meyer, J. P. (1996). Affective, Continuance, and Normative Commitment to the Organization: An Examination of Construct Validity. *Journal of Vocational Behavior*, *49*, 252–276. doi:10.1006/jvbe.1996.0043

Anderson, R. E., & Srinivasan, S. S. (2003). E-Satisfaction and E-Loyalty: A contingency Framework. *Psychology and Marketing*, *20*(2), 123. doi:10.1002/mar.10063

Arriaga, X. B., & Agnew, C. R. (2001). Being Committed: Affective, Cognitive, and Conative Components of Relationship Commitment. *Personality and Social Psychology Bulletin*, *27*(9), 1190–1203. doi:10.1177/0146167201279011

Bansal, H. S., & Irving, P. G. (2004). A Three-Component Model of Customer Commitment to Service Providers. *Journal of Academy of Marketing*, *32*(3), 234–250. doi:10.1177/0092070304263332

Becker, H. S. (1960). Notes on the concept of commitment. *American Journal of Sociology, 66*(1), 32–42. doi:10.1086/222820

Bentler, P. M. (2004). *EQS 6 Structural Equations Program Manual*. Encino, CA: Multivariate Software, Inc.

Bhattacherjee, A. (2001). Understanding information systems continuance: An expectation-confirmation model. *Management Information Systems Quarterly, 25*(3), 351. doi:10.2307/3250921

Brown, T. A. (2006). *Confirmatory Factor Analysis for Applied Research* (1st ed.). New York: The Guilford Press.

Byrne, B. M. (2006). *Structural Equation Modeling with EQS, Basic Concepts, Applications, and Programming* (2nd ed.). Mahwah, NJ: Lawrence Erlbaum Associates.

Byrne, B. M., & Crombie, G. (2003). Modeling and Testing Change: An Introduction to the Latent Growth Curve Model. *Understanding Statistics, 2*(3), 177–203. doi:10.1207/S15328031US0203_02

Cooper, R. B., & Zmud, R. W. (1990). Information technology implementation research: a technological diffusion approach. *Management Science, 36*(2), 123,117.

Cronbach, L. J. (1971). Test Validation. In Thorndike, R. L. (Ed.), *Educational Measurement* (2nd ed.). Washington, DC: American Council on Education.

Davis, F. D. (1989). Perceived Usefulness, Perceived Ease of Use, and User Acceptance of Information Technology. *Management Information Systems Quarterly, 13*(3), 318. doi:10.2307/249008

Devellis, R. F. (2003). *Scale Development* (2nd ed.). Thousand Oaks, CA: Sage Publications.

Dixit, A., & Pindyck, R. (1994). *Investment Under Uncertainty*. Princeton, NJ: Princeton University Press.

Festinger, L. (1957). *A theory of cognitive dissonance*. Stanford, CA: Stanford University Press.

Fishbein, M., & Ajzen, I. (1975). *Beliefs, Attitude, Intention and Behavior: An Introduction to Theory and Research*. Reading, MA: Addison-Wesley.

Fornell, C., & Larcker, D. F. (1981). Evaluating Structural Equations with Unobservable Variables and Measurement Error. *JMR, Journal of Marketing Research, 18*, 39–50. doi:10.2307/3151312

Gallagher, A. (2006). *A Guide to Eliminating Software*. CIO Magazine, Analyst Corner.

Gilliland, D. I., & Bello, D. C. (2002). Two Sides to Attitudinal Commitment: The Effect of Calculative and Loyalty Commitment on Enforcement Mechanisms in Distribution Channels. *Journal of the Academy of Marketing Science, 30*(1), 24–43. doi:10.1177/03079450094306

Harmon-Jones, E., & Mills, J. (1999). *Cognitive Dissonance: Progress on a pivotal theory in social psychology*. Washington, DC: American Psychological Association. doi:10.1037/10318-000

Hsu, M. H., Chiu, C. M., & Ju, T. L. (2004). Determinants of Continued Use of the WWW: An Integration of Two Theoretical Models. *Industrial Management & Data Systems, 104*(9), 766–775. doi:10.1108/02635570410567757

Kim, S. S., & Malhotra, M. K. (2005). A Longitudinal Model of Continued IS Use: An Integrative View of Four Mechanisms Underlying Postadoption Phenomena. *Management Science, 51*(5), 741–755. doi:10.1287/mnsc.1040.0326

Kim, S. S., Malhotra, N. K., & Narasimhan, S. (2005). Two Competing Perspectives on Automatic Use: A Theoretical and Empirical Comparison. *Information Systems Research, 16*(4), 418–432. doi:10.1287/isre.1050.0070

King, A. W., & Zeithaml, C. P. (2003). Measuring organizational knowledge: A conceptual and methodological framework. *Strategic Management Journal*, *24*(8), 763. doi:10.1002/smj.333

Lacy, S. (2006, May 3). The Friendly Face of Business Software. *Business Week.*

Legris, P., Ingham, J., & Collerette, P. (2003). Why do people use information technology? A critical review of the technology acceptance model. *Information & Management*, *40*(3), 191. doi:10.1016/S0378-7206(01)00143-4

Li, D., Browne, G. J., & Chau, P. Y. K. (2006). An Empirical Investigation of Web Site Use Using a Commitment-Based Model. *Decision Sciences*, *37*(3), 427–444. doi:10.1111/j.1540-5414.2006.00133.x

Li, D., Chau, P. Y. K., & Lou, H. (2005). Understanding Individual Adoption of Instant Messenging: An Empirical Investigation. *Journal of the Association for Information Systems*, *6*(4), 102–129.

Limayem, M., & Hirt, S. G. (2003). Force of Habit and Information Systems Usage: Theory and Initial Validation. *Journal of the Association for Information Systems*, *4*, 65–97.

Limayem, M., Hirt, S. G., & Cheung, C. M. K. (2007). *How Habit Limits the Predictive Power of Intention: The Case of Information Systems Continuance*. MIS Quarterly.

Malhotra, Y., & Galletta, D. (2005). A multidimensional Commitment Model of Volitional Systems Adoption and Usage Behavior. *Journal of Management Information Systems*, *22*(1), 117–151.

Markus, L., & Keil, M. (1994). If We Build It, They Will Come: Designing Information Systems That People Want to Use. *Sloan Management Review*, 11–25.

Meyer, J. P., & Allen, N. J. (1991). A three-component conceptualization of organizational commitment. *Human Resource Management Review*, *1*, 61–89. doi:10.1016/1053-4822(91)90011-Z

Meyer, J. P., & Allen, N. J. (1997). *Commitment in the Workplace: Theory, Research, and Application*. Thousand Oaks, CA: Sage Publication.

Meyer, J. P., & Herscovitch, L. (2001). Commitment in the Workplace: Toward a General Model. *Human Resource Management Review*, *11*(3), 299–326. doi:10.1016/S1053-4822(00)00053-X

Meyer, J. P., Stanley, D. J., Herscovitch, L., & Topolnytsky, L. (2002). Affective, Continuance, and Normative Commitment to the Organization: A Meta-Analysis of Antecedents, Correlates, and Consequences. *Journal of Vocational Behavior*, *61*, 20–52. doi:10.1006/jvbe.2001.1842

Meyers, L. S., Gamst, G., & Guarino, A. J. (2005). *Applied Multivariate Research: Design and Interpretation*. Thousand Oaks, CA: SAGE.

Miller, G. A. (1956). The Magical Number Seven, Plus or Minus Two: Some Limits on Our Capacity for Processing Information. *Psychological Review*, *63*, 81–97. doi:10.1037/h0043158

Mowday, R. T., Porter, L. W., & Steers, R. M. (1982). *Employee-Organization Linkage - The Psychology of Commitment, Absenteeism, and Turnover*. New York: Academic Press.

Nielsen-Natratings (2006). *A Survey Report on Instant Messaging*.

Norušis, M. J. (2006). *SPSS Base 13.0 Guide to Data Analysis*. Upper Saddle River, NJ: Prentice Hall.

Nunnally, J. C. (1978). *Psychometric Theory*. New York: McGraw-Hill.

Pallant, J. (2007). SPSS Survival Manual: A Step by Step Guide to Data Analysis Using SPSS for Windows (Version 15).

Parthasarathy, M., & Bhattacherjee, A. (1998). Understanding Post-Adoption Behavior in the Context of Online Services. *Information Systems Research*, *9*(4), 362. doi:10.1287/isre.9.4.362

Qingxiong Ma, T., & Liping Liu. (2004). The Technology Acceptance Model: A Meta-Analysis of Empirical Findings. *Journal of Organizational and End User Computing*, *16*(1), 59.

Raykov, T. (1997). Estimation of Composite Reliability for Congeneric Measures. *Applied Psychological Measurement*, *21*(2), 173–184. doi:10.1177/01466216970212006

Rogers, E. M. (1995). *Diffusion of Innovations* (4th ed.). New York: Free Press.

Rusbult, C. E., Martz, J. M., & Agnew, C. R. (1998). The investment model scale: Measuring commitment level, satisfaction level, quality of alternatives, and investment size. *Personal Relationships*, *5*(4), 357–391. doi:10.1111/j.1475-6811.1998.tb00177.x

Selwyn, N. (2003). Apart for technology: understanding people's non-use of information and communication technologies in everyday life. *Technology in society*, *25*, 99–106. doi:10.1016/S0160-791X(02)00062-3

Sheridan, T. B. (1992). *Telerobotics, Automation, and Human Supervisory Control*. Cambridge, MA: The MIT Press.

SPSS. I. (2006). *SPSS 15.0 Base User's Guide*. Upper Saddle River, NJ: Prentice Hall.

Straub, D. W., Boudreau, M. C., & Gefen, D. (2004). Validation Guidelilnes of IS Positivist Research. *Communications of the Association for Information Systems*, *13*, 380–426.

Szajna, B. (1996). Empirical Evaluation of the Revised Technology Acceptance Model. *Management Science*, *42*(1), 85,88.

Tabachnick, B. G., & Fidell, L. S. (2000). *Using Multivariate Statistics*. New York: Allyn & Bacon.

Venkatesh, V., & Davis, F. D. (2000). A Theoretical Extension of the Technology Acceptance Model: Four Langitudinal Field Studies. *Management Science*, *46*(2), 186. doi:10.1287/mnsc.46.2.186.11926

Venkatesh, V., Morris, M. G., Davis, G. B., & Davis, F. D. (2003). User Acceptance Of Information Technology: Toward A Unified View. *Management Information Systems Quarterly*, *27*(3), 425.

Zmud, R. W., & Apple, L. E. (1992). Measuring Information Technology Infusion. *Production and Innovation Management*, *9*(2), 148–155. doi:10.1016/0737-6782(92)90006-X

ENDNOTES

1. In the scope of our discussion, it is helpful to distinguish between technology types and technology products. Technology types are different technologies that do not share a common feature set (e.g. browsers vs. web servers). Technology products are products that share a common set of features but are different by virtue of their branding, version, or other (e.g. Apache web server versus IIS web server).
2. Primary IM client is defined as the IM client that has been used most frequently by an individual user.
3. An identity matrix is matrix in which all of the diagonal elements are 1 and all off diagonal elements are 0. An identity matrix suggests that the factor model is inappropriate and a significant Bartlett's test should reject the null hypothesis (SPSS, 2006).
4. We thank the Associate Editor for his/her insightful comment on this issue.

This work was previously published in Journal of Organizational and End User Computing, Volume 22, Issue 4, edited by M. Adam Mahmood, pp. 70-94, copyright 2010 by IGI Publishing (an imprint of IGI Global).

APPENDIX: INSTRUMENT FOR MEASURING TECHNOLOGY COMMITMENT

Affective Commitment

AC01 I am extremely glad that I chose [Name of Specific Instant Messenger].
AC02 I find [Name of Specific Instant Messenger] to be the best among available substitutes.
AC03 Deciding to use [Name of Specific Instant Messenger] was definitely a right choice for me.

Calculative Commitment

CC01 Discontinue using [Name of Specific Instant Messenger] would require considerable personal sacrifice.
CC02 I would have to give up a lot by abandoning [Name of Specific Instant Messenger].
CC03 Many changes would have to occur in my present circumstances if I discontinue using [Name of Specific Instant Messenger].

Normative Commitment

NC01 Many of my friends use [Name of Specific Instant Messenger].
NC02 Of the friends I communicate with frequently, many use [Name of Specific Instant Messenger].
NC03 A large percentage of my friends use [Name of Specific Instant Messenger].

Continuance Intention

CI01 I predict I will continue to use [Name of Specific Instant Messenger] as I do now.
CI02 I will keep using [Name of Specific Instant Messenger] as long as updates are available.

Section 3
End-User Computing:
Evidence from Practice

Chapter 12
Appropriation Infrastructure:
Mediating Appropriation and Production Work

Gunnar Stevens
University of Siegen and Fraunhofer FIT, Germany

Volkmar Pipek
University of Siegen and Fraunhofer FIT, Germany

Volker Wulf
University of Siegen and Fraunhofer FIT, Germany

ABSTRACT

End User Development offers technological flexibility to encourage the appropriation of software applications within specific contexts of use. Appropriation needs to be understood as a phenomenon of many collaborative and creative activities. To support appropriation, we propose integrating communication infrastructure into software application that follows an "easy-to-collaborate"-principle. Such an appropriation infrastructure stimulates the experience sharing among a heterogeneous product community and supports the situated development of usages. Taking the case of the BSCWeasel groupware, we demonstrate how an appropriation infrastructure can be realized. Empirical results from the BSCWeasel project demonstrate the impact of such an infrastructure on the appropriation and design process. Based on these results, we argue that the social construction of IT artifacts should be tightly integrated in the material construction of IT artifacts in bridging design and use discourses.

INTRODUCTION

We interpret the appropriation of information technology not as a phenomenon that somehow happens once a software application is in its 'application field', but as a network of activities that users continuously perform in order to make a software 'work' in a new work environment, shaping the artifact as a material as well as a meaningful object. Existing practices evolve and result in new practices. Technical flexibility to redesign the application according to specific local needs play a major role in enabling appropriation work. Appropriation work may lead to software usages

DOI: 10.4018/978-1-4666-0140-6.ch012

that go beyond what has been envisioned by the designers of the software application (cf. Pipek, 2005). It is a specific part of an IT artifact's usage, but it remains also linked (through the artifact's materiality) with its design process and the designer's work environments. Appropriation work needs to be understood as a core concept in the field of End User Development (EUD).

To deal appropriately with the combined efforts of users and designers to successfully establish a software tool usage that satisfies the needs of practice requires a fundamental shift in perspectives on the concepts of 'design' and 'use'. If the target of a design process is not a technology/software/tool, but a certain *usage* (that is stimulated by a certain new technology/software/tool), traditional notions of design processes and product structures become problematic. When does the development of usages start, when does it stop? Is it a continuous or a discrete process? Who initiates 'design' phases—the developer side or the user side? For which parts in shaping a usage are professional designers responsible, and for which parts the 'users' (they may be considered as professional usage designers just with a different expertise profile)? Which competencies and experiences are necessary to perform certain activities of appropriation work?

We see the cracks in the idea of a strict separation of design and use spheres everywhere in practice: In the necessity for software development in cycles, in the frequent software updating procedures, in continuous helpline support provided by software manufacturers, in the differentiation of user roles (scale between end users and power/lead users), in software development contract structures that include 'maintenance', in the practice of user forums in the Internet (that may have been provided by software manufacturers, but also third parties), and also in scientific conceptualizations e.g. with regard to 'tailoring' functions that support design-in-use (Henderson & Kyng, 1991), with regard to integrating users into software design (e.g. Floyd et al., 1989), with regard to professionalization structures in design and the problems they may cause (e.g. Suchman, 2002) or with regard to the integration of user-driven innovation in (re-)design processes (e.g. von Hippel & Katz, 2002). In fact, the blurring notions of design and use spheres point towards collaboration necessities and opportunities which, we claim should become a central research area in the field of End User Development.

We will first connect our perspective to the scientific discourse on the technical and symbolic dimension of appropriation. Based on a dialectic perspective of artifacts and usages, we will describe a framework to support the communicative appropriation among the diverse actors in a product community. We have implemented a first example of an appropriation infrastructure when designing the BSCWeasel groupware. To evaluate the utility of appropriation infrastructures, empirical results from the BSCWeasel project are presented.

APPROPRIATION IN AND OF PRODUCTION WORK

"[P]roduction and consumption are not completely separate spheres of existence but rather are mutually constitutive of one another. What happens to a product in consumption has effects for producers and so on, in an ongoing cycle of commodification—where producers make new products or different versions of old products as a result of consumers' activities—and appropriation—where consumers make those products meaningful, sometimes making them achieve a new 'register' of meaning that affects production in some way. In this sense, the meanings that products come to have are constructed in this process of dialogue - albeit rarely an equal one in terms of power relations - between production and consumption" (du Gay et al., 1997, p. 103).

Forms of Appropriation

In the first notion, appropriation is the work to make things work (Pipek, 2005; Balka & Wagner, 2006). It is fitting of the technology at hand into pre-existing culture and into local patterns of use and life rhythms (Silverstone & Haddon, 1996). Appropriation characterizes the socialization of material objects "to use it constructively, to incorporate it into one's life for better or worse" (Poole & DeSanctis, 1989, p. 150).

Historically the concept of appropriation grounds in Marx's evolutionary anthropology, where *man is constituted by labor as the self-realization of man in nature through the appropriation of nature* (cf. Márkus, 1978; Röhr, 1979). In the Marxian tradition appropriation is no mechanical process, but a kind of *situated development* in front of an open future that shapes both subject and object. In particular, is not only a productive achievement, but a formative event as well (cf. Honneth, 1995). Artifacts as expression of human labor inherit the twofold character, they present a *dialectic unity of material and symbolic constructed objects*. In particular in its dialectic man-*made* objects *used* by man the mediate between appropriation and production work. Further, the facility to appropriate rests on two essential powers of man:

- To give objects another form (or literarily changing the material construction), and
- To give objects another meaning (or literarily changing the symbolic construction).

In everyday life we do not distinguish between the material and symbolic construction of artifacts, until they become present-at-hand. In such moments we got aware of the contingency of the relation between material object (e.g. a stone) and meaningful object (e.g. a hammer). In such moments the artifact is not given as a unity, but as a contradiction between material and symbolic construction. To overcome this contradiction the situated development has to create a new unity between the internal and external object. This can be done for example in tailoring the material construction of the artifact. However, in practice, often the contradiction will be solved by work-arounds, which cause a change of the meaning of the objects by using them differently. The evolution of the material and symbolic construction are interwoven, but long-term studies about the appropriation of IT systems demonstrated that usages can evolve to some extend independently from the evolution of the material artifact (cf. Orlikowski, 1995; Karsten & Jones, 1998; Ngwenyama, 1998; Pipek & Wulf, 1999; Wulf, 1999; Törpel et al., 2003).

The salient point in the dialectic view on appropriation is that *giving the artifact another form* and *giving the artifact another meaning* are not two independent sets of phenomena. Instead, they express just two different forms of the same challenge, namely to carry out a situated development in order to fit the artifact into the local context. In consequence, End User Development should support both essential powers of situated development, e.g. by increasing the tailorability to express a change of the material construction and by increasing the communication means to express a change of the symbolic construction. In other words, EUD should not only take the material, but also the symbolic dimension of appropriation work into account.

The symbolic dimension of appropriation work is mainly studied in the Cultural Studies (cf. Hepp, 2004, ch. 7). The Cultural Studies are in a Marxian tradition (Hall 1980), but they are also influenced by de Certeau's (1984) notion of appropriation as button-up power to response structures of domination in society (cf. Poster, 1992). Reading de Certeau's work sensitizes researchers to explore in detail the appropriation practices of consumers in everyday life as a kind of "production in use" (Storey, 2006). In their survey on Cultural Studies, Barker and Willis (2008) highlight the existence of *creative consumption*, where users are not passive, but play an active, creative role in the symbolic production of the artifact. Hepp (2004) states that communication serves as a catalyst for appropriation in the social context.

EUD can learn from the research on consumption practices that communication is not an additional, but an essential part of appropriation (cf. Holly et al., 2001; Karnowski, 2008). Furthermore, the dialectic constitution of artifacts makes aware that we can distinguish two genres in the communicative construction of artifact:

- The production genre, and
- The consumption genre.

With the production genre we mean communication that is about the material construction of artifacts (e.g. discussing different technical options to design cassette players without speakers; cf. du Gay et al., 1997). With the consumption genre we mean communication that is about the symbolic construction of artifacts (e.g. talking about using a cassette player with headphones to create a public privacy; cf. du Gay et al., 1997).

Typically users and designer prefer a different genre in the communicative construction of the product. Technicians among each other normally prefer the production genre in artifact-centered communication, e.g. when they discuss design decisions and design rationales (Reeves & Shipman, 1992). In opposite, the users prefer the consumption genre in the communicative appropriation of commodities (du Gay et al., 1997; Karnowski, 2008). The difference in the preferences is also an expression of the fact that designer must solve in the production work the challenge to give usages a material form, while in the appropriation work users have to create usages out of the material objects present-at-hand. These different views on the same object can be the source of conflict and misunderstanding, e.g. in participatory design. For example, in their ethnographic study on the direct communication between technicians and users, Hasu and Engeström (2000) found a clash of culture, which was also manifested in a clash of communication genres: While users prefer to talk about the construction of usages, technicians prefer to talk about the construction of material objects.

However, to argue that a preference exists does not mean that producers cannot talk about artifacts in terms of usages and visa versa that consumers cannot talk about artifacts in terms of design. For example consumer advertising typically rest on the consumption genre to carry out the producer-consumer communication (du Gay et al., 1997; Karnowski, 2008). Inversely, research on tailorability demonstrates that in specific situations users choose the production genre, e.g. when they share their customizing knowledge to fit technology into the local context (cf. Mackay, 1990; Trigg & Bødker, 1994). This demonstrates that in the communicative appropriation both genres are relevant.

Appropriation in the Ongoing Cycle of Production

Marx makes us aware about the historical contingency of in organizing the division of labor and the mediation appropriation and production. Under the dominated condition of society appropriation and production work are largely separated from each other. A result of this fragmentation is that innovation emerged in appropriation cannot be incorporated in the ongoing cycle of production. This raises the question if the individual 'production in use' can be reconnected to superior streams of production?

The reconnection of situated appropriation and organizational development has been addressed by Orlikowski and Hofman (1997). From the management perspective, they classify the relation into three categories: appropriations that are *anticipated*, *opportunity-based* or *emergent* in relation to the superior organizational development. Anticipated appropriations are planned and therefore do not affect the organizational plan.

Contrary, opportunity-based appropriation occurs spontaneously, but once the opportunity is clear they present enrichment for the organizational development. Emergent appropriations present a residual category of all spontaneously effects that leave undetected or do not fit to the superior organizational development. Orlikowski and Hofman (1997) make aware that situated innovations can emerge in appropriation that cannot be planned by definition. This is one of the consequences they draw to argue for agile management, so that the results of appropriation work can be better integrated into superior development processes.

Also the research on Software Engineering explores opportunities to reconnect appropriation into an evolutionary software production. For example Floyd et al.'s (1989) STEPS model argues that software should be evolutionary with a stronger focus on user-designer collaboration to integrate the needs that emerged during appropriation. Wulf and Rohde (1995) enhance this conception. They argue that software should be tailorable and that the tailoring activities should be reconnected to the superior cycles of software production. However, neither Floyd et al. (1989) nor Wulf and Rohde (1995) address the question, how the mediation of appropriation and production work can be software-technically supported. An extension in that direction was suggested by Finck et al. (2004), elaborating the concept of e-participation as an approach of distributed participation design (Danielsson et al., 2008).

Coming from a different angle, Fischer discussed end-user modifiability (Fischer & Girgensohn, 1990) as a mean to support on the empower end users to change the artifact in its material construction. Later Fischer and Ostwald (2002) developed with SER (Seeding, Evolutionary Growth and Reseeding) a model that outline, how the local evolutions can be reconnect to the general development stream. The different works on end-user modifiability and participatory oriented design are currently integrated on a conceptual level by the Meta-design framework (Fischer & Giaccardi, 2006).

Agile software processes, like SCRUM or eXtreme Programming (XP), provide extreme short release cycles and allow customers to change requirements at any time during the design process. However, XP does not explicitly the appropriation work, so that the model does not make any suggestions about a shared infrastructure to foster mutual learning processes. Instead, the programmers just get indirect feedback mediated by a "costumer on site"-principle (Beck, 1999), although it is difficult to find these customers in practice (Rumpe & Schröder, 2001).

A pragmatic application of agile methods is offered by the development process of the Eclipse platform, called the Eclipse way (cf. Gamma et al., 2005; Lippert, 2006). The Eclipse way combines diverse strategies to organize a community based production system:

- The use of agile methods to increase the ability of the major development stream to respond on new opportunities (Gamma et al., 2005; Lippert, 2006),
- The use of a "everything is a plugin" principle (Gamma & Beck, 2004) to support the fitting of the technology into heterogeneous contexts and enabling individual development threads,
- The use of a contribution circle (Gamma & Beck, 2004) with increasing commitment and reward to major development stream to create a gentle slope of participation, and
- The use of strategies for user community involvement (Gamma et al., 2005; Lippert, 2006) to reconnect results of appropriation work into the major development stream.

In particular, Eclipse takes care that development of the common product is carried out in an open and transparent manner (Schwartz et al., 2009). We illustrate this new production forms taking out in Eclipse on one example. In 2003/2004 Eclipse evolves from version 2.1 to version 3.0. Originally, Eclipse was designed as a universal tool integration platform (e.g. used as number one Java IDE). One major innovation of version 3.0 was the re-construction of Eclipse to make it to a highly tailorable Rich Client platform (RCP) (e.g. now used by IBM Lotus Notes). This evolution of a product is a good example of a user driven innovation (von Hippel & Katz, 2002), because the re-design was triggered by an user of Eclipse. In the public bug tracking system of Eclipse he suggests to "enable Eclipse to be used as a rich client"[1]. In reaction, this topic was discoursed in the Eclipse community, which is partially documented by the 52 comments made in bug tracking system. In the end, the idea was taken up in the strategic roadmap of Eclipse and an open discussion about the consequences organized by the Eclipse Project Management Committee (PMC): "The nature and scope of some of the key plan items are such that the only feasible solutions would break compatibility. Since *breaking changes are a disruption to the Eclipse community*, they cannot be taken lightly. We (the Eclipse PMC) will have *an open discussion with the community* before approving a proposed breaking change for inclusion in 3.0" (Eclipse Foundation, 2004, emphasis original).

Products as Boundary Objects in the Cycle of Production

Eclipse gives an excellent illustration of Silverstone and Haddon's (1996) remark that "[i]nnovation is a process which involves both producers and consumers in a dynamic interweaving of activities which are solely determined neither by the forces of technological change nor by the eccentricities of individual choice" (Silverstone & Haddon, 1996, p. 44). Moreover, the case demonstrates how new technologies and production conditions enable new forms to organize appropriation and production work mediated by the product as a boundary object.

However, Eclipse is insofar an exceptional case as the user community is dominated by software engineers. This homogeneity in the cultures of designers and users makes it easier to mediate between situated appropriation and global production work. For example the homogeneity of the diverse social worlds lowers the burden to compensate the symmetry of ignorance (Fischer, 1999) between the agents. In addition, the public communication can mainly rely on the production genre, so that the translation of genres is reduces.

The idea of *open development grounded in a product community* as it is realized in the praxis of Eclipse has therefore to be developed further in order to be applicable in other domains. In particular, mass-production in general is confronted that the product connects heterogeneous actors across diverse social worlds for better or worse. In particular, in the ongoing cycle of production product and product community becomes mutual constitutive for each other, creating a dynamically evolving system. The product community of such evolving system consist of diverse social groups that embodiments of particular interpretations. The members of a social group "share the same set of meanings, attached to a specific artifact" (Pinch & Bijker, 1987, p. 30). Heuristically, we assume that users and producers constituting the most relevant social groups of a product community.

Du Gay (1997) defined such system as circuit of culture, focusing in relationship of *mutual* determination of social formation in the ongoing cycle of commodification. We are especially interested in the circumstances that in that system the product gains a duality of evolving boundary objects. The notion of duality characterizes the issue that products become the medium and outcome of the diverse communicative constructions (cf. Orlikowski, 1992; Bijker, 1995). The notion of boundary objects characterizes the issue that the product has different meanings in different social worlds but that their structure is common enough to more than one world to make them recognizable means of translation (cf. Star

& Griesemer, 1989; Star, 1990). In addition, the objects are not static, but evolve in the ongoing cycle of production (implicitly expressed in the notion of duality).

In other words, the division of production and consumption creates in cycle of production the need to mediate diverse meaning constructions. At the same time the product, in serving as a boundary objects, creates the recognizable means of translation. In particular, in the ongoing cycle of production the material construction must socially re-constructed in terms of design as well as in terms of usage. In doing so, the consumption and production genre mediated and this also means that the different genres have to be translated to each other.

A specific feature of digital goods is that discussion *about* the artifact can be *embedded* in the artifact (Reeves & Shipman, 1992; Pipek, 2005). This means digital products do not only provide the *means of translation*, but can also provide the *spaces for communication.*

AN INFRASTRUCTURE FOR APPROPRIATION SUPPORT

Our research is guided by user perspective in supporting appropriation work as a part of the ongoing cycle of production. In particular, we argue, like Orlikowski and Hofman (1997), appropriation and production work should be integrated in an holistic approach. However, we inverse the perspective of Orlikowski and Hofman (1997). Their research was guided by the question how situated development can be integrated into a superior development processes. Instead we ask how the diverse artifact-centered communication can be integrated in the local context of appropriation work. Form this stance we deduce a set on demands:

- Firstly the tailorability of artifact should by enhanced by means for communicative appropriation.
- Secondly the means for communication should be accessible, when the artifact becomes present-at-hand. Like the “easy to develop”-principle of EUD (Liebermann et al., 2006), the support for the communicative appropriation should follows an “easy to collaborate”-principle.
- Thirdly, a support for appropriation should provide means for both genres of communicative appropriation. This means to support the talking about the material construction of the artifact at hand (production genre) as well as talking about usages of the artifact at hand (consumption genre).
- Fourthly, situated development activities are embedded and affects from the ongoing cycle of production. Therefore means for communicative appropriation should not only support usage discourses among users, but also design discourse among users and designer.

Figure 1 illustrates our model of an appropriation infrastructure. We assume that different users, power users, or system administrators work with tailorable software and that the superior production processes are flexible enough to respond to activities of the product community.

In order to realize the “easy to collaborate”-principle we further elaborated ideas of End User Development to lower the burden to switch between using and designing the technology at hand (cf. Wulf & Golombek, 2001). In particular, we adopt the idea of Application Units (Mørch, 1995; Mørch & Mehandjiev, 2000) to *embed* discussion *about* a software feature into the software feature.

Mørch define Application Units as the “smallest self-contained units to be useful in the design and implementation of end-user tailorable applications” (Mørch, 1995, p. 45). The innovation of Application Units is that tailoring environment can be activated from the place where the unit is used. In addition, the tailoring environment does not only contain the source code of the unit, but

Figure 1. Conceptual view on an infrastructure for appropriation support

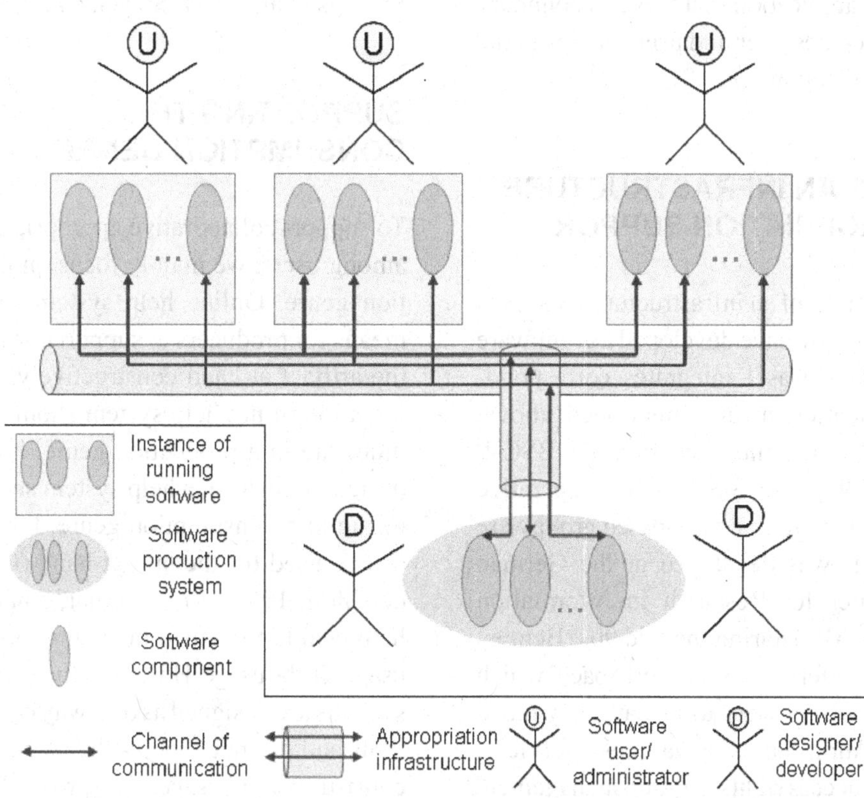

also design rationales to support the appropriation of the unit. Mørch and Mehandjiev (2000) highlight that this present as form of developers and users collaboration, helping the user to understand also complex software applications. Our design conception enlarges the initial idea of Application Units in two dimensions:

- Enlarging the scope of communication.
- Enlarging the genres of communication.

The Application Unit concept provides only a one-way communication between designer and user. In order to enlarge the scope of communication, we create a direct link to a world wide information space that integrates the diverse communication about the unit of application in the local context of appropriation work. Further, the Application Unit concept mainly focuses on the production genre, but do not address the consumption genre. In order to enlarge the genres of communication we also include means to discuss usages of the application unit in question.

As mentioned products are outcome of and medium for a product community, where the software serves as boundary objects to translate diverse constructions of meanings. The specific features of software allow the social construction into material construction to integrate. In order to make use of these new socio-technical opportunities we elaborated on the idea of Application Units and combined it with the results of the research on appropriation mentioned above. The intention of our design conception is to support 'infrastructuring' of software, which means from our perspective here that we support to switch easily between the material and the social construction of the units of application that serve as boundary objects between designer and user spheres in the cycle(s) of production.

DESIGNING AN INFRASTRUCTURE FOR APPROPRIATION SUPPORT

To explore the idea of an infrastructure for appropriation support, we have developed a groupware application BSCWeasel integrates corresponding communication means mentioned above. BSCWeasel is a rich client based on the BSCW platform. BSCW (Basic Support for Cooperative Work) was one of the first web-based groupware applications. It was developed at the German National Center for Research in Information Technology (GMD) during the mid 90s (Bentley et al., 1995). It offers a 'shared workspace' which supports a group of users to up- and download documents. Additionally, awareness services, differentiated access rights, a group management tool, email distribution lists, a discussion forum, and a shared calendar complement the functionality of the groupware.

We have developed BSCWeasel as a Eclipse RCP (McAffer & Lemieux, 2005). Eclipse is a development environment for component-based applications. Eclipse RCP presents the core set of component of Eclipse, which allows running component-based applications on a variety of different operating systems. Moreover, the Eclipse Foundation promotes the growth of the Eclipse Ecosystem which allows benefiting from the results of a large community of developers (see above).

BSCWeasel started as an open source project in spring 2004 (cf. http://www.bscweasel.de). So far we still follow the basic client server architecture of BSCW where the clients interact with a BSCW server. The Eclipse based software architecture increase the tailoring options of the BSCWeasel compared with BSCW web based solution (cf. Stevens et al., 2004; Stevens, 2005).

SUPPORTING THE CONSUMPTION GENRE

To support collaborative appropriation activities among users, we mainly focus on the consumption genre. Online help systems are a typical means for producers to support consumers to use the artifact at hand constructively. The primary intention of not help system should not to communicate in a production genre, how artifact is designed. Instead, a help system should communicate in a consumption genre, how the artifact can be used for the task at hand (Carroll & van der Meij, 1998). In particular, context sensitive help enable to embed the communication about usages in the usage. However, currently online help systems are designed as one-way communication tools and did not support the social creativity in construction of usages very well. Therefore we suggest to augment context sensitive help features by functionalities of a community system. In our work, we draw on Wikis to augment help functions. Wikis are widely spread and allow editing texts in a collaborative manner.

We decided to represent the traditional help text of each function within a Wiki. Users can extend, change or annotate these texts. They can create different local descriptions of purpose, usage, or outcome of a function and exchange knowledge concerning the appropriation of this function within their local practices. Access to the Wiki needs to be highly contextualized at the user interface to select those Wiki entries which are associated with the current usage. In our approach, we took the state of the application as a proxy for the actual context of use. By means of the Meta Object Protocol and runtime reflection (Kiczales et al., 1991), we linked Wiki/help pages technically to specific states of the application.

Figure 2. Highlighting the point of interest: (left) from a user perception (right) from a computational perceptive (the tool tip refers to information that can be gathered by algorithmic reflection on current state of the application)

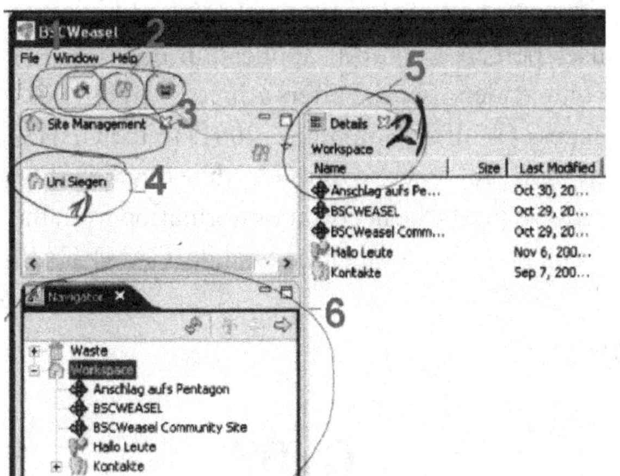

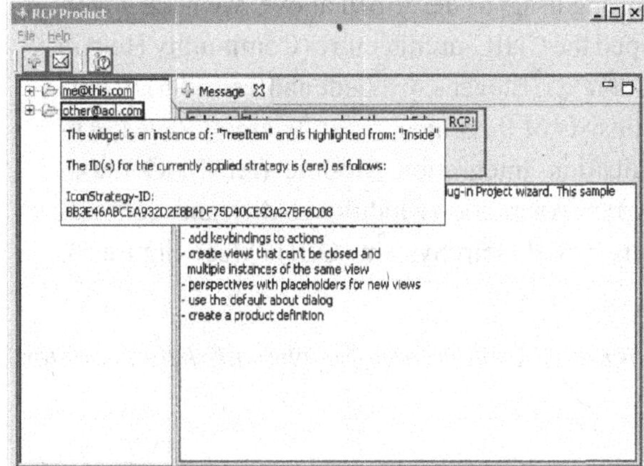

From a user's perspective, a Wiki page refers to a function perceived by the users at the interface of the application, and therefore, supports appropriation discourses among communities of users (also addressing diversifying sub-communities). The user first selects the object in question and then presses F1 to open the corresponding help/wiki page. So, the software application offers a built-in communication channel among users and therefore acts as a boundary object for contextualizing the discussion among the community that are interested in that feature.

The Wiki discourse infrastructure was realized using standardized software interfaces, but the realization of context sensitivity is more challenging. We used context identifiers in the applications source code to anchor wiki widgets in a certain functionality area. However, this implementation strategy turned out to be hard to maintain since designers may either forget to write help texts for an identifier or place the context identifier at the wrong position in the source code.

However, the situatedness of work activities (Suchman, 1987) is a tough challenge for the underlying assumption that the execution position in the code is an appropriate measure for the current work context. Still manual maintenance of context identifiers would be quite error prone, as well. Therefore, we studied in which way users make sense of the "set of pixels generated and managed by a computational process that is the result of the computer interpretation of a program P" (Costabile et al., 2007).

In our empirical studies of users' perception we present the users several screenshots of known and unknown programs and ask them to highlight their point of interest (cf. Figure 2 left). In these studies, we observe that the way users give the pixel a meaning is related to the widget hierarchy of the interface. Based on this observation we created an algorithm which identifies function compounds as they are perceived by the users and maps them with stable context identifies. The calculation of the stable context identifier use the runtime reflection feature to gather information that allows a computational identification of the point of interest (cf. Grüttner, 2007). The identified widget was highlighted as a potential point of interest at the interface (cf. Figure 2). The tool tip in Figure 2 shows some of the information that was available for that widget via runtime reflection. In particular it shows the calculated context identifier that is used as a shared reference point it offers access to the corresponding public Wiki page (cf. Figure 4).

To implement the communication channels among users as described above, we have developed the CHIC-architecture (Community Help in Context) (Stevens & Wiedenhöfer, 2006). CHIC consists of three generic software modules: Application Integration Module (AIM), Context-Aware Adaptation Module (CAM), and Community-based Help System (CBHS) (see Figure 3).

The Application Integration Module (AIM) integrates CHiC into an existing application and the user interacts with CHiC using it. When the user asks for help by pressing F1, it highlights the user perceived unit of application mapped to a context identifier and offers a direct "single-click" access (Wulf & Golombek, 2001) to the CBHS-System. In order to provide this functionality, AIM requests the necessary information from the Context-Aware Adaptation Module (CAM). CAM

Figure 3. Architecture of community help in context (ChiC)

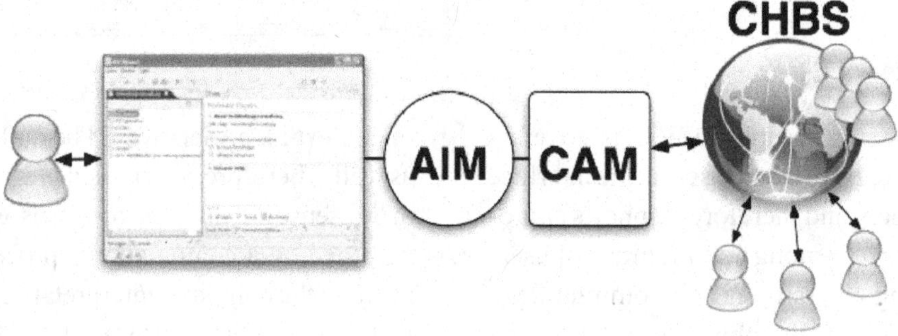

Figure 4. Changing the selected interface element triggers a recalculation of the help entries (1). A click on one of the help entries opens the Wiki page via the internal web browser (2).

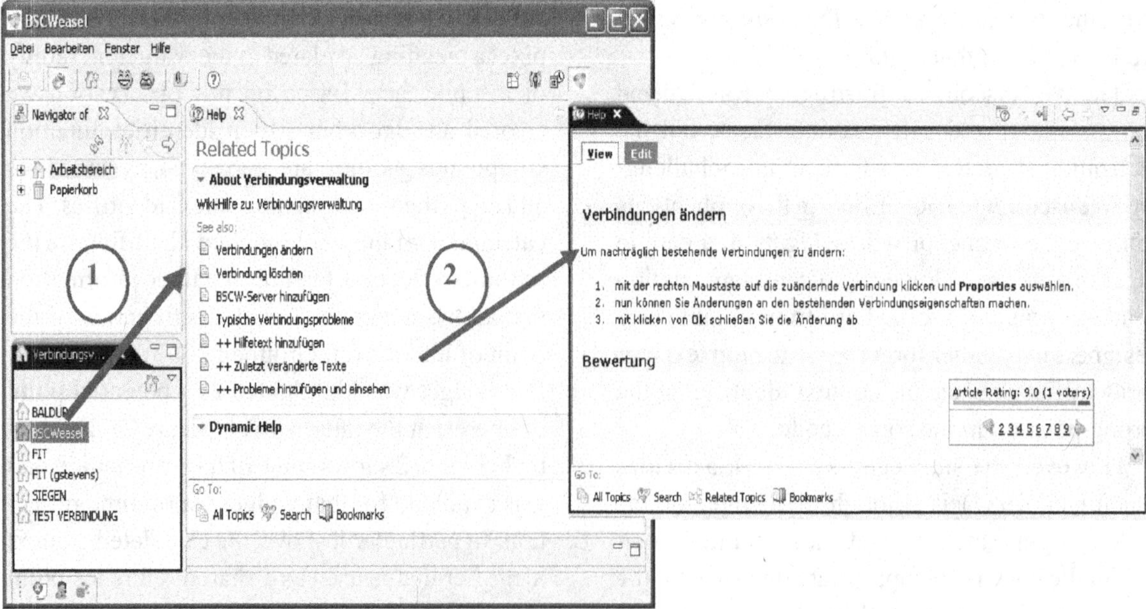

mainly calculates the context identifier and mediates between AIM and CBHS. The CBHS can be any community system, like a Wiki, which provides an infrastructure for help discourses.

In the BSCWeasel case, we use the Eclipse framework to integrate the Wiki help into the application context. We benefit from the Eclipse architecture which allows adding new help items dynamically. A help item implements the interface IHelpResource which delivers the subject labels of help texts and the URLs of the corresponding Wiki pages. The subject labels of help items are displayed as links in the help window of Eclipse. When a user clicks on the label, Eclipse opens the internal web browser and loads the associated web page (cf. Figure 4). To realize CAM under Eclipse, we extended the IContextProvider. IContextProvider is invoked whenever the state of the application has changed. CAM uses this trigger to inspect the actual system state and requests CBHS to return a set of help entries.

The CBHS module was realized by integrating the Atlassian Confluence Wiki[2] because it provides a commenting function, several notification mechanisms like mail, RSS, and the recently changed pages. Moreover, it provides a well defined Web Service API.

SUPPORTING THE PRODUCTION GENRE

In order to reconnect the appropriation work to production, we offer a collaboration support for users and designers. In this case we mainly focus on the production genre and integrated a professional requirements tracking system into the BSCWeasel application. However, in order to lower the burden of communication we have equipped the tool with a specific interface for the users.

With regard to designers' needs, our goal was increase the responsibility of production work by minimizing the overhead from the administration of direct user feedback together with other sources of requirements. To encourage contributions from a wide variety of different users, we wanted to provide a gentle slope of increasingly more complex levels of participation (McLean et al., 1990; Beck & Gamma, 2003) in the requirements specification process. Legitimate peripheral participation in the requirements specification process is supported by allowing end users to just mark shortcomings in their current interface. However, lead users can use the system to discuss and test newly designed features in interaction with the professional designers who can use the system also for their work (e.g. design planning and scheduling).

To realize this part of the appropriation infrastructure, we came up with a hybrid approach which combines an external requirements tracking system with an Eclipse plugin which is integrated into the BSCWeasel user interface. The plugin provides specific views on the requirements tracking system. Technologically we drew on the Web Service API/remote method invocation interface of the requirements tracking system to integrate its user interface into the BSCWeasel application.

We decide to use a professional requirements tracking system, called JIRA. JIRA is a web based application supporting the interaction among developers. JIRA allows saving requirements in textual form, which can be annotated with attachments, e.g. log files or screenshots. Users of JIRA can discuss these requirements, prioritize and vote for them. A configurable workflow allows processing these requirements within the team of developers. The functionality of JIRA can be used via a web-based interface or it can be integrated into 3rd party products via the Web Service API.

The integration into BSCWeasel was realized implementing an Eclipse plugin called PaDU (Participatory Design in Use). PaDU packages JIRA's Web Service API and makes it available for Eclipse RCP applications. If a requirement is submitted to JIRA or information is retrieved from JIRA, PaDU will carry it out via the XML RPC. To lower the barriers for users, PaDU uses

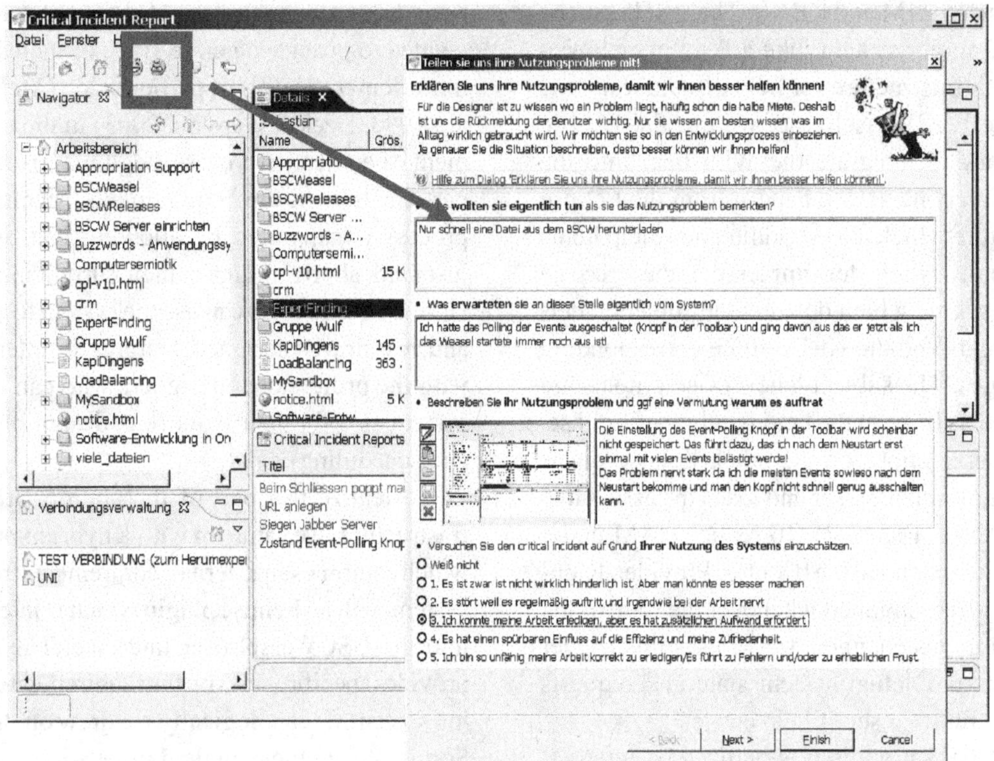

Figure 5. PaDU's access point is in the button bar which activates the requirements tracking system

the integrated web browser of Eclipse. When the user wants to see detailed information about his contribution, PaDU will open the corresponding web page.

PaDU allows contributing to the design process directly from the BSCWeasel user interface. PaDU integrates two buttons into the user interface of the BSCWeasel application (see Figure 5). The buttons help distinguishing between critical incidents (a subjective breakdown of tool usage) and use innovations (a new way of using existing functionality or a new idea for interesting functionality). These buttons are always visible and they are used as access points to document problems or suggest new design ideas.

When a user presses one of these buttons, a multi-page dialog window appears. The dialog is adapted from the critical incident dialog (Castillo, 1997) by Hartson et al (1996). Beyond purely textual descriptions of the requirements, we integrated features which allow for ostensive and deictic references to the software artefact in order to clarify design ideas. We have, for instance, extended the dialog window to enable users to add screenshots, annotate them textually or graphically, and attach own sketches. PaDU automatically takes a snapshot of the current state of the BSCWeasel interface at the moment it is activated. A drawing tool is available to edit the screenshots.

Designers can deal with the contributions of the users in the same way they do with any other requirements documented in the system. They can discuss these requirements, prioritize them and vote for them. To offer accountability with regard to their inputs, users can see all activities that happen in the requirements tracking system. Via their interface, users can track the state of their contributions. They are informed via email in case someone comments on their input. They can also set up links to other entries in order to be informed about the state of their procedure. Additionally, designers can send a direct email to a user to clarify open issues.

However, the discourse culture which emerged in the BSCWeasel project was slightly different. Instead of writing an email, questions to a contributor were attached as a comment. The contributor received an email containing this comment and had the option to answer to the email by adding a new comment. As a result, a public discourse around certain requirement emerged.

We understand design to be a communicative process which needs to be transparent to those who want to participate.[3] In order to satisfy this requirement users and designers should have similar rights with regard to inspecting the requirements database and adding comments. To support users in becoming familiar with the web interface and to increase their awareness of the design process, PaDU's start page contains all the contributions made by this particular user.

Additionally, we save a user's contributions locally. So, writing a design suggestion can happen before it is published within the requirement tracking system. Users can see all of their ideas in a list. A double click on published design ideas opens the web browser and shows the corresponding web page in the requirement tracking system. The web page shows contribution in detail, the state of the contribution in the overall design process, and discussions and comments added in reaction to the contribution.

EVALUATION STUDY

Both prototypes which we described here were implemented based on the Eclipse plugin framework. Together with further applications that are being used at the periphery of other implementations (e.g. email clients), they form an infrastructure to support appropriation work in the late phase of usage design. Any application which operates on the same infrastructural background (Eclipse) would be able to use our concepts.

To evaluate our concepts, we implemented them into the BSCWeasel client. BSCWeasel was developed by a research group of a German university. The core group consisted of two developers which were complemented temporarily by different student teams. Contrary to most work in the area of product-oriented flexibility, we applied an agile development process which was directed towards short release cycles and an immediate evaluation in practice.

In May 2005 an initial version of BSCWeasel was used by the developers and their student team. Later versions were announced towards the research group at the university (about 15 members) and towards two groups at a research institute in applied computer science (about 15 researchers) 100 km away from the university. All researchers were basically familiar with BSCW, though the system was applied to rather different degrees. The appropriation process of BSCWeasel was analyzed via the discussion threads provided by PaDU and CHIC. Moreover, observations and informal interviews were carried out to explore the appropriation of BSCWeasel further on. Additionally, two studies were conducted based on the ISO 9241-10/12 standards to improve the usability of the application. The first study was carried out in April 2005 with nine users. It focused on the basic functionality of BSCWeasel. In January 2006, a second study with six users looked particularly into the usability of the CHiC and PaDU functionality.

With regard to the appropriation of BSCWeasel at the university and the research institute, we know about 10 regular users. They were intense users of BSCW before and identified specific BSCWeasel functions to be incorporated into their practice. The individual "killer" functions were not part of the BSCW thin client and covered a wide range of functionality. Some of them were requested via PaDU—like the option to download more than one file or complete folder structures, or a synchronized view on local and remote directory structures. Other functions were communicated directly towards the team of developers.

About half of the BSCWeasel users have made use of PaDU. From September 2005 to July 2007 130 design requirements were expressed via PaDU. Due to the relatively small number of active users the design team was rather reactive towards their suggestions. About 50% of these proposals got implemented.

In evaluating our experiences, we will focus on two main issues. First, we will investigate into the impact of the infrastructure in reconnecting appropriation work to the superior production work. Secondly, we will look into the relations and interferences among the different functions of the appropriation infrastructure.

Grounding Design in Appropriaton

After the roll-out of PaDU, the designers got more feedback from users. Since PaDU items were stored in the Bug Tracking System, the feedback was more systematic and easier to handle and became an integral part of the coordination work carried out by the designers.

PaDU is mainly used by users to make designers aware of a usability problem and/or feature request, however discussions among designers and users happened rarely, which may be due to the fact that PaDU does not disclose the users' identity. However, we found frequent instances in which contributions made in PaDU triggered a reflection process within the design team, e.g. discussing design alternatives related to a concrete user experience. Sometimes designers react to a user comment, when requirements expressed by the users were not clear (e.g. a designer wrote: "Well, technically this is a little thing [to implement the feature request]. However, for the moment is not yet clear to me how you would like to use it") or different solutions were possible (e.g. asking which of different options to implement an "open file with …" feature would be needed).

Most of the contributions made by the users referred to cases in which they were able to accomplish their task, often by means of a workaround, but wanted a better support from BSCWeasel. The snapshot annotation tool was typically used to point to the referred area in the user interface. The suggested redesign would render more control or efficiency to their work. For example, with regard to the upload function a user made the following proposal: "It would be a nice thing to know the data volume ahead of an upload. In this case one would know how long it takes and whether there is sufficient space available".

Analyzing the contributions made via PaDU, we found little design requirements which went far beyond the given functionality, and most of the suggestions were rooted in practical experiences using BSCWeasel in the users' daily work. Accessing PaDU directly from their context of use seems to stimulate users to focus on present-at-hand technology when contributing. It seems to result in incremental rather than highly innovative suggestions for redesign.

However, these contributions, based on practical experience, had a considerable impact on the design process. One of the developers came up with the following bon mot: "If programming is understood as 'theory building' [cf. (Naur, 1985)], PaDU helps making it a 'grounded theory' [cf. (Glaser & Strauss, 1967)]".

Nevertheless, PaDU should be perceived as an additional instrument to improve distributed, continuous Participatory Design and not as a replacement for traditional, creativity oriented Participatory Design instruments like Future workshops.

Integrating Different Functions in an Appropriation Infrastructure

When integrating the different parts of the appropriation infrastructure and studying them simultaneously, we became aware of the phenomena of interference. The lacking integration of users' communication channels with those channels between users and designers created problems. The actual segregation of the different appropriation support functionalities—such as help, adaptation, or requirements articulation—seems to be dysfunctional.

We observe that CHiC was mainly used as a traditional help system with only little discussions among users going on. It seems that CHiC and PaDU cannibalized each other since both could be applied when BSCWeasel was not present-at-hand. This fact became obvious in the second usability study. An interviewee stated that he is occasionally uncertain whether to address other users or better the developers. He had a problem in connecting the BSCWeasel client with the BSCW server. Reflecting on his problem, he was not sure whether it was caused by bad design or inappropriate use. So he could not decide easily whether to discuss his problem in PaDU or CHiC. In another case a user explained that she put a question into PaDU but later cancelled it. She was not sure whether this issue was just her personal problem, ("just not knowing enough about the system"), or if the issue was more generally relevant for the design of BSCWeasel. These findings seem to indicate a need for a deeper integration of PaDU and CHiC.

Another example for lacking integration is the gap between flexibilization at the level of the user interface compared to the level of the component structure of the application and its missing integration into a communication infrastructure. Eclipse's "viewer" concept offers an elegant solution for the composition of interface elements compared to user interfaces of web-based clients augmented by applets. All interface elements can be integrated into a combined view, called perspective. We observed that this feature was applied by the users to individualize their user interface. However, Eclipse still suffers from the fact that this interface layer of a user centric composition is not connected to the underlying component structure. So, the underlying structure is not visible and cannot directly explore from the user interface taking the actual use context into account. Obviously, lacking references between software structure and user interface leads to confusion and does not support users in understanding the linkage between the user interface and the software architecture (de Souza et al., 2001).

As a result, users may develop a mental model which diverges strongly from the software architecture. It leads specifically to problem in cases where applications, such as Eclipse IDE or BSC-Weasel, are composed by hundreds of components provided by different vendors. During our usability study we found an example for these phenomena. It turned out that users assumed that our chat tool (a 3rd party component) and the BSCW system where tightly coupled because the interface elements were integrated. In another case we observed an Eclipse IDE user who had problems in finding out which vendor was responsible for a specific view which he had added to his user interface. He was looking for more information about the object in question.

Moreover, Eclipse suffers from lacking integration of the component management features into a community-oriented communication infrastructure. The Eclipse community starts to become aware of this problem. In particular, some commercial companies like Innoopract have started to extend Eclipse with a component repository service with thousand of plug-ins. They support end users to assemble their personal Eclipse configuration out of the repository in an easy way. Furthermore one can observe that traditional centralized provisioning strategies will be enhanced by concepts that support a grassroots diffusion of composition and tailored artifacts.

TOWARDS THE NEXT GENERATION OF APPROPRIATION INFRASTRUCTURES

With the first version of the Appropriation Infrastructure, we developed an infrastructure to support the communicative appropriation in a product community based on the Eclipse plugin architecture. The solution supplements the easy-to-develop principle of traditional EUD (Liebermann et al., 2006) by an easy-to-collaborate principle. Integrating this infrastructure into BSCWeasel it was possible to collect practical experience by means of an empirical case study covering the infrastructure's appropriation in three research groups. Based on the lessons learned, we give an outline on the further elaboration of the concept.

The central conceptual idea of the Appropriation Infrastructure is grounded in the analytical consideration that the material construction of a product becomes an object and translator of the diverse communicative constructions in the community that are constituted by the product. From this analytical consideration we deduce that the artifact present-at-hand serves as an entry point and the discourses referring to the material object. The case study confirms this concept and therefore the next version should keep this idea. In particular, the case study shows that there is need, for collaboration in the appropriation of technology and that the ongoing cycle of production can be supported by integrating the design context into the use context. In addition, the case study shows that situations where the artifacts becomes present-at-hand triggers an artifact centered reflection. It was demonstrated that appropriation work can be supported when an appropriation infrastructure is interwoven into the actual use context.

Nevertheless the case study also has demonstrated that in some points the chosen design decision should be reconsidered. In particular, the first version treated wicked use situations mainly as single events, which leads to an event centric splitting of communicative appropriation.

As a consequence the first version does not well support the evolutionary character of such situations and of corresponding situated development traces. For example, the first version has split the communicative genres into CHiC and PaDU as separated features. However, the case study has shown that in wicked use situations it is difficult for the user to choose the appropriate communication feature. Wicked use situation should therefore not treated as isolated events, but - metaphorically spoken – as the birth of situated development traces that growth and evolves over the time. For example in the beginning a user might talk-back with the artifact present-at-hand personally; yet in the evolution, the need can also arise to integrate colleagues or other parties of the product community. The evolutionary character also affects the building of common ground to translate and negotiate the different construction of meaning. In particular, the common ground is not just medium, but also outcome of social construction which co-evolve with the development traces.

The Appropriation Infrastructure should therefore be re-conceptualized in a manner that the evolutionary character of appropriation work will supported in a wider extend than BSCWeasel has done so far. Such re-conceptualization should take into account that the situated development traces are related to following activities of appropriation work:

- Consulting help systems,
- Making requirement inquiry and (re-)design contributions,
- Tailoring and updating an application.

In the first version was implicitly guided by a metaphor of communication channels. This metaphor should be replaced by a design metaphor of rooms. This metaphor is better suited to take care of evolutionary character of situated development traces: Rooms have a temporal-spatial expansion that did not only provide a space to communicate, but also a common ground for communication. In addition, temporal-spatial structure of rooms constitutes a social environment that can evolve either by changing the interior design or by changing the rules to access the environment.

Table 1. Classification of EUD purposes, shaping the interior design of the rooms for doing EUD

		Cooperation structure in doing EUD		
		1. personal centric	**2. group centric**	**3. public centric**
Effect scope of construction change	**1. personal scope**	• individual reflection and adaptation	• individualization supported by a self organized group • individualization supported by a friend/colleague	• individualization supported by a public community
	2. closed, group scope		• collectivization of commonly used configuration / convention	• collectivization supported by a public community
	3. open, public scope			• product development in a open design space

The elaboration of a context-aware room concept for collaborative appropriation can profit from the practical experience we gain in our case study. In particular, the case study has demonstrate that from a user perspective, a room concept should offer three different types of rooms for doing EUD, namely private, self-organized, as well as a public one. It should also be possible to change character of a room as well as moving development traces from one room to another. In addition a room concept should also take the research on cooperative tailoring into account (Kahler, 2001; Pipek & Kahler, 2006). One of the results of this research is to distinguish between the agents, who tailor and the agents, who are affected by the tailoring.

Based on this distinction the different room types can by classified by a two dimensional scheme, where the first dimension characterize the cooperation structure that should be supported by the room. The second dimension characterize on the intended scope of validity of the tailoring activities. In each dimension we can further distinguish if the room should support *personal*, *self-organized* or *public* collaboration, which are leads to a 3x3-matrix with nine entries. However, taken into account that users only want to be a designer in personally relevant activities (Fischer, 2002) only the upper diagonal is relevant for EUD in a narrow sense. An overview of the different room types is presented in Table 1.

Modular Composition

This section gives a brief outline of a component-oriented concept of a generic architecture for the next version of an Appropriation Infrastructure. The architecture reflects detected mention needs on a further development of the first version. The major goal of a modular architecture is an efficient implementation of software-technical that satisfies the mentioned demands. In particular, the room for collaborative appropriation should be tightly integrated into the software artifact to be accessible in wicked use situations. It should provide following features:

1. The infrastructure should provide rooms for personal, self-organized group and public for doing EUD
2. The rooms should provide tools to create as well as explore adaptations and ideations
3. The infrastructure should be context aware, so that the room for reflection is directly accessible from the place of action

The presentation of the architecture focuses on high level aspects of supporting appropriation work, but omits some technical details.

The architecture is split into a shared or backend part of the infrastructure (cf. Figure 6), and a local or client part that integrates the infrastructure into the application context. The right side of the figure

Figure 6. Diagram of the architecture for a next generation of appropriation Infrastructures

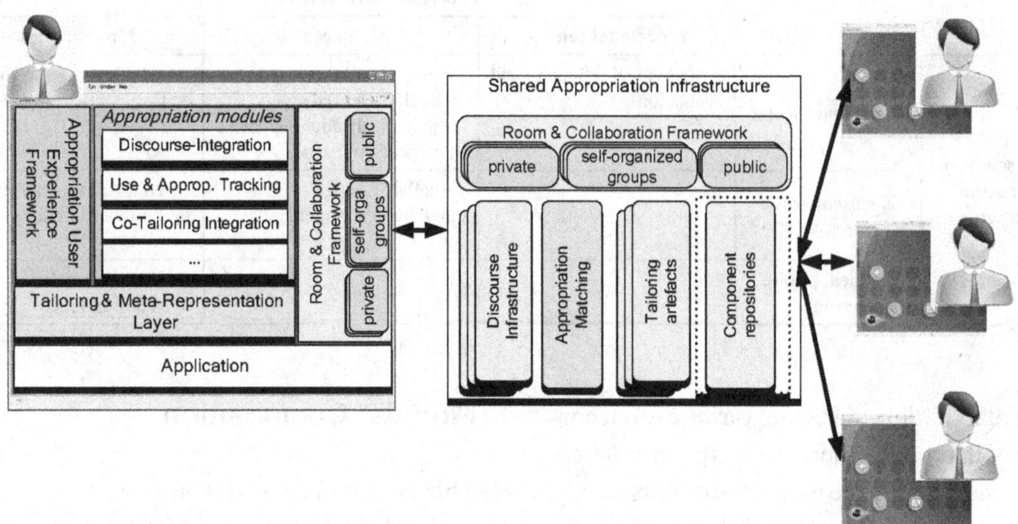

represents other agents of the product community, connected to the appropriation infrastructure. This architecture describes a logical perspective on the infrastructure and does not yet constitute the physical/technical design.

Appropriation User Experience Framework (AUEF)

The AUEF module is responsible for interweaving the shared infrastructure into the skin of the boundary object, and to guarantee a consistent user experience regardless of the modular composition. In doing so, the visual presentation, the responsible computational mechanism as well as the corresponding discussions are supposed to refer co-referentially to each other (cf. de Souza et al., 2001). This simplifies the transition between usage, usage discourse and artifact modification. In particular, the design should enable direct access to the relevant EUD rooms. Because of the fact that different heuristic strategies exist to connect design- and use context, the Appropriation User Experience Framework should provide an extension point that allows to plug-in additional and domain-specific connecting strategies.

Discourse Infrastructure (DT)

The function of the DT module is to foster the social process of sense making and negotiation around the used technology. Discourses can be related to one's own application usage, intertwined with experiences of other actors or negotiations of common interpretations. It should include reference to related components, as well as to additional components and configurations and patches. Moreover, it has to integrate the various discourses into the local context. The DT module is split into two parts: a local and a shared part. The role of the shared part is to store and manage the actors' discourses. The role of the local part is mainly to integrate discourses into the application, which means, to present discourses to the user in an adequate manner, in relation to the use context. In addition, it should enable and encourage the users to actively join discourses.

Cooperative Tailoring (CT)

The CT module will be responsible for dealing with the technical aspects of a cooperative provisioning solution. The main role of its shared part is to offer management repositories which store and manage ready-made components as well as tailoring artifacts.

The local part embeds the shared repository into the application context and should support a cooperative tailoring model. It should provide local access to the shared infrastructure, so that ready-made components and tailoring artifacts can be installed locally. Additionally, it should provide means to share local adaptations with others using the shared part of the infrastructure.

Room and Collaboration Framework (RCF)

The RCF module is responsible to provide user management and access control functionalities. Additionally, it maps the logical room concept to the physical layer of distributed computing. In particular, the RCF should offer the different types rooms as outlined in Table 1. So, the RCF should offer personal, group-organized, and public rooms in or the users to actively join discourses.

Additional Appropriation Support Features

Beside communication support, an appropriation infrastructure should support appropriation by automatically generated user recommendations. It underlines the importance of analyzing individual and collective histories of usage (Bell et al., 2006). A general architecture splits the evaluation of histories of usage into the tracking, which is in the local embedding and the matching, which is located on the shared part the Appropriation Infrastructure. The feature of appropriation matching interlinks the different histories of usage, and derives recommendations. The feature can either recommend relevant appropriation practices or recommend "similar" users in the product community. In both cases, it is important to analyze the behavior of the user in order to adjust the system to them. A realization might use collaborative filter-algorithms (Burke, 2002) to support the user in finding interesting extensions and expertise related to his actual use context.

Beside these different appropriation modules, the architecture should contain a set of common modules (e.g. component management and configuration framework). A modular conception of an Appropriation Infrastructure, as it is laid out here, should increase the extensibility and evolvability of the framework. For example, it should be possible to plug in new modules for domain-specific approaches to appropriation support.

CONCLUSION

Support for appropriation work has to be understood as a core challenge in the field of End User Development. From the perspective of appropriation work, the concept of design needs to be re-interpreted. It should be understood as supporting the development of usages, not tools. In such a perspective, activities of end users such as configurating, tailoring, sense making, or negotiating conventions of usage have to be linked to the work performed by software developers. Appropriation and production work are dialectic moments in development of usage, while in situated development it is mainly driven by actors and stakeholders from local context, not from the production sphere. These activities can be considered as inherently collaborative and should be explicitly supported by appropriate infrastructures build into the applications.

A first implementation of an Appropriation Infrastructure has been trying out in practice. This has demonstrated that such technological infrastructure can support the bridging *appropriation* and *production work*. Nevertheless, the practical experience has also demonstrate that our research needs to be extended to a on a technological level (see thoughts on next generation Appropriation Infrastructure) as well as on a theoretical level (e.g. connecting it to the discourse around 'infrastructuring' (Star & Bowker, 2002; Pipek & Wulf, in press) and '*open design spaces*' (Budweg et al., 2009). Ultimately we hope to be able to establish a methodological perspective on end user development understood as software (usage!) design which is not dominated by the traditions of programmers but respects the work of all social groups of a product community is involved.

We conclude this paper with a refinement of the definition of EUD, picking up the consideration that EUD should support a continuous co-evolution of both, the system and the user (Fischer & Ostwald, 2002; Costabile et al., 2007). In times where software development methodology conceptions like 'perpetual beta' (Wikipedia, 2008) becomes general accepted the designers, co-workers and other stakeholders of the software artifacts are essential participants in the continuous co-evolution. This also means that personal and shared design activities as highly interwoven. A definition of EUD should be reflected this issue, thus we suggest a refinement as follows: *EUD denotes a set of methods, tools and techniques to support end users to enforce their interests in the continuous co-evolutionary process by modifying individual artifacts or participating in the modification of shared artifacts.*

ACKNOWLEDGMENT

We would like to thank IBM for supporting our work by means of an Eclipse Innovation Award. We are also grateful to the German Science Foundation (DFG) and the German Ministry of Research and Education (BMBF) for research funding in the field of End User Development (EUD).

REFERENCES

Balka, E., & Wagner, I. (2006). Making Things Work: Dimensions of Configurability as Appropriation Work. In [New York: ACM Publishing.]. *Proceedings of CSCW, 2006*, 229–238.

Barker, C., & Willis, P. (2008). *Cultural Studies: Theory and Practice*. Thousand Oaks, CA: Sage.

Beck, K. (1999). *Extreme Programming Explained: Embrace Change*. Reading, MA: Addison-Wesley Professional.

Beck, K., & Gamma, E. (2003). *Contributing to Eclipse: Principles, Patterns and Plugins*. Reading, MA: Addison-Wesley.

Bell, M., Hall, M., Chalmers, M., Gray, P., & Brown, B. (2006). Domino: Exploring Mobile Collaborative Software Adaptation. In *Pervasive Computing: Proceedings of the 4th International Pervasive Computing Conference* (LNCS 3968, pp. 153-168).

Bentley, R., Horstmann, T., Sikkel, K., & Trevor, J. (1995). Supporting Collaborative Information Sharing with the World Wide Web: The BSCW Shared Workspace System. In *Proceedings of the 4th International WWW Conference* (pp. 63-74).

Bijker, W. (1995). *Of bicycles, bakelites and bulbs: Toward a Theory of Sociotechnical Change*. Cambridge, MA: MIT Press.

Budweg, S., & Draxler, S. (Eds.). (2009). Open Design Spaces Supporting User Innovation: Perspectives and Challenges [Special issue]. *IRSI Report on Open Design Spaces Supporting User Innovation, 6*(2).

Burke, R. D. (2002). Hybrid Recommender Systems: Survey and Experiments. *User Modeling and User-Adapted Interaction, 12*(4), 331–370. doi:10.1023/A:1021240730564

Carroll, J., & van der Meij, H. (1998). Principles and Heuristics for Designing Minimalist Instruction. In Carroll, J. (Ed.), *Minimalism beyond the Nurnberg funnel* (pp. 19–54). Cambridge, MA: MIT Press.

Castillo, J. (1997). *The User-Reported Critical Method for Remote Usability Evaluation*. Blacksburg, VA: Virginia Polytechnic Institute and State University.

Costabile, M. F., Fogli, D., Mussio, P., & Piccinno, A. (2007). Visual Interactive Systems for End-User Development: A Model-based Design Methodology. *IEEE Transactions on SMC - Part A. Systems and Humans, 37*(6), 1029–1046.

Danielsson, K., Naghsh, A. M., Gumm, D., & Warr, A. (2008). Distributed participatory design. In *CHI '08 Extended Abstracts on Human Factors in Computing Systems* (pp. 3953-3956). New York: ACM Publishing.

de Certeau, M. (1984). *The Practice of Everyday Life*. Berkeley, CA: University of California Press.

de Souza, C. S., Barbosa, S. D. J., & da Silva, S. R. P. (2001). Semiotic engineering principles for evaluating end-user programming environments. *Interacting with Computers, 13*(4), 467–495. doi:10.1016/S0953-5438(00)00051-5

du Gay, P., Hall, S., Janes, L., MacKay, H., & Negus, K. (1997). *Doing Cultural Studies: The Story of the Sony Walkman*. London: Sage.

Eclipse Foundation. (2004). *Eclipse Project 3.0 Plan (Final)*. Portland, OR: Author.

Finck, M., Gumm, D., & Pape, B. (2004). *Using Groupware for Mediated Feedback*. Paper presented at the Participation Design Conference, Toronto, Ontario, Canada.

Fischer, G. (1999). *Symmetry of Ignorance, Social Creativity and Meta-Design*. Paper presented at the 3rd ACM Conference on Creativity and Cognition, Loughborough, UK.

Fischer, G. (2002). Beyond "Couch Potatoes": From Consumers to Designers and Active Contributors. *First Monday, 7*(12).

Fischer, G., & Giaccardi, E. (2006). Meta-Design: A Framework for the Future of End User Development. In Lieberman, H., Paternò, F., & Wulf, V. (Eds.), *End User Development* (pp. 427–458). New York: Springer. doi:10.1007/1-4020-5386-X_19

Fischer, G., & Girgensohn, A. (1990). *End-user modifiability in design environments*. Paper presented at CHI'90.

Fischer, G., & Ostwald, J. (2002). *Seeding, Evolutionary Growth, and Reseeding: Enriching Participatory Design with Informed Participation*. Paper presented at the Participatory Design Conference, Malmö, Schweden.

Floyd, C., Reisin, F.-M., & Schmidt, G. (1989). STEPS to Software Development with Users Source. In *Proceedings of the 2nd European Software Engineering Conference* (LNCS 387, pp. 48-64).

Gamma, E., & Beck, K. (2004). *Contributing to Eclipse: Principles, patterns, and plug-ins*. Reading, MA: Addison-Wesley.

Gamma, E., & Wiegand, J. (2005). *The eclipse way - processes that adapt*. Paper presented at EclipseCon 2005.

Glaser, B. G., & Strauss, A. L. (1967). *The Discovery of Grounded Theory. Strategies for Qualitative Research*. Piscataway, NJ: Aldine Transaction.

Grüttner, M. (2007). Entwicklung eines generischen Visualisierungs- und Interaktionskonzepts für kontextsensitive Hilfesysteme und prototypische Implementierung für das Eclipse RCP-Framework. In *Wirtschaftsinformatik*. Siegen, Germany: University of Siegen.

Hall, S. (1980). Cultural Studies: Two paradigms. *Media Culture & Society, 2*, 57–72. doi:10.1177/016344378000200106

Hartson, H. R., Castillo, J. C., Kelso, J., & Neale, W. (1996). *Remote Evaluation: The Network as an Extension of the Usability Laboratory*. In Proceedings of CHI'96: Human Factors in Computing Systems (pp. 228-235).

Hasu, M., & Engeström, Y. (2000). Measurement in Action: An Activity-Theoretical Perspective on Producer-User Interaction. *International Journal of Human-Computer Studies, 53*(1), 61–89. doi:10.1006/ijhc.2000.0375

Henderson, A., & Kyng, M. (1991). There's no place like home: Continuing Design in Use. In *Design at work: Cooperative Design of Computer Systems* (pp. 219–240). Mahwah, NJ: Lawrence Erlbaum.

Hepp, A. (2004). *Cultural Studies und Medienanalyse*. Wiesbaden, Germany: Verlag für Sozialwissenschaften.

Holly, W., Püschel, U., & Bergmann, J. (2001). *Der sprechende Zuschauer: Wie wir uns Fernsehen kommunikativ aneignen* [The talking audience: On the communicative appropriation of television]. Wiesbaden, Germany: Westdeutscher Verlag.

Honneth, A. (1995). Domination and Moral Struggle: The Philosophical Heritage of Marxism Reviewed. In Wright, C. W. (Ed.), *The Fragmented World of the Social: Essays in Social and Political Philosophy* (pp. 3–15). Albany, NY: SUNY Press.

Kahler, H. (2001). *Suporting Collaborative Tailoring*. Rosklide, Denmark: Department of Communication, Journalism and Computer Science, Universiy of Roskilde.

Karnowski, V. (2008). *Das Mobiltelefon im Spiegel fiktionaler Fernsehserien: Symbolische Modelle der Handyaneignung* [The mobile phone in reflection of TV series: Symbolic models about mobile appropriation]. Wiesbaden, Germany: VS Verlag.

Karsten, H., & Jones, M. (1998). The long and winding road: Collaorative IT and organisational change. In *Proceedings of the International Conference on Computer Supported Work (CSCW'98)*, Seattle, WA (pp. 29-38). New York: ACM Press.

Kiczales, G., des Rivières, J., & Bobrow, D. G. (1991). *The Art of the Meta-Object Protocol*. Cambridge, MA: MIT Press.

Liebermann, H., Paternò, F., & Wulf, W. (Eds.). (2006). *End User Development*. New York: Springer. doi:10.1007/1-4020-5386-X

Lippert, M. (2006). Eclipse Core - Unter der Haube, Teil 2: Ein Blick auf den Entwicklungsprozess des Eclipse-Plattform-Projekts. *Eclipse Magazine, 6*.

Mackay, W. E. (1990). *Users and customizable Software: A Co-Adaptive Phenomenon*. Cambridge, MA: MIT Press.

Márkus, G. (1978). *Marxism and Anthropology: The Concept of Human Essence in the Philosophy of Marx*. Assen, The Netherlands: Van Gorcum.

McAffer, J., & Lemieux, J.-M. (2005). *Eclipse Rich Client Platform: Designing, Coding, and Packaging Java Applications*. Reading, MA: Addison-Wesley.

McLean, A., Carter, K., Lövstrand, L., & Moran, T. (1990). User tailorable systems: Pressing the issues with buttons. In *Proceedings of CHI '90,* Seattle, WA (pp. 175-182). New York: ACM Publishing.

Mørch, A. (1995). Application units: Basic building blocks of tailorable applications. *Human-Computer Interaction*, 45–62.

Mørch, A., & Mehandjiev, N. D. (2000). Tailoring as Collaboration: The Mediating Role of Multiple Representations and Application Units. *Computer Supported Cooperative Work, 9*(1), 75–100. doi:10.1023/A:1008713826637

Naur, P. (1985). Programming as Theory Building. *Microprocessing and Microprogramming, 15*, 253–261. doi:10.1016/0165-6074(85)90032-8

Ngwenyama, O. K. (1998). Groupware, social action and organizational emergence: on the process dy-namics of computer mediated distributed work. *Accounting. Management and Information Technologies*, *8*(4), 123–143.

Orlikowski, W. (1995). *Evolving with Notes: Organizational Change around Groupware Technology*. Cambridge, MA: MIT Center for Coordination Science.

Orlikowski, W. J. (1992). The Duality of Technology: Rethinking the Concept of Technology in Organizations. *Organization Science - Focused Issue. Management of Technology*, *3*(3), 398–427.

Orlikowski, W. J., & Hofman, J. D. (1997). An Improvisational Model for Change Management: the Case of Groupware. *Sloan Management Science*, *38*(2), 11–21.

Pinch, T., & Bijker, W. (1987). The social construction of facts and artifacts: Or how the sociology of science and the sociology of technology might benefit each other. In Bijker, W., Hughes, T., & Pinch, T. (Eds.), *The social construction of technological systems: New directions in the sociology and history of technology* (pp. 17–50). Cambridge, MA: MIT Press.

Pipek, V. (2005). *From Tailoring to Appropriation Support: Negotiating Groupware Usage*. Oulu, Finland: Department of Information Processing Science, University of Oulu.

Pipek, V., & Kahler, H. (2006). Supporting Collaborative Tailoring. In Lieberman, H., Paternò, F., & Wulf, V. (Eds.), *End User Development* (pp. 315–346). New York: Springer. doi:10.1007/1-4020-5386-X_15

Pipek, V., & Wulf, V. (1999). *A Groupware's Life*. Paper presented at ECSCW '99.

Pipek, V., & Wulf, V. (in press). Infrastructuring: Towards an Integrated Perspective on the Design and Use of Information Technology. *Journal of the Association of Information System (JAIS): Special Issue on e-Infrastructure*.

Poole, M. S., & DeSanctis, G. (1989). Use of Group Decision Support Systems as an appropriation process. In *Proceedings of the Twenty-Second Annual Hawaii International Conference on System Sciences* (pp. 149-157).

Poster, M. (1992). The Question of Agency: Michel de Certeau and the History of Consumerism. *Diacritics*, *22*(2), 94–107. doi:10.2307/465283

Reeves, B., & Shipman, F. (1992). Supporting communication between designers with artifact-centered evolving information spaces. In *Proceedings of the Conference on Computer-Supported Cooperative Work (CSCW'92)* (pp. 394-401). New York: ACM Publishing.

Röhr, W. (1979). *Aneignung und Persönlichkeit (Appropriation and Personality)*. Berlin, Germany: Akademie Verlag.

Rumpe, B., & Schröder, A. (2001). *Quantitative Untersuchung des Extreme Programming Prozesses* (Tech. Rep. TUM-I01). Munich, Germany: Munich University of Technology.

Schwartz, T., Meurer, J., & Stevens, G. (2009). *Nutzerinnovation im Eclipse Fall aus der Perspektive einer unternehmerischen Arbeitspraxis*. P aper presented at Open Design Spaces (ODS): Innovation durch Nutzerbeteiligung, Workshop im Rahmen der TagungMensch und Computer 2009.

Silverstone, R., & Haddon, L. (1996). Design and the Domestication of Information and Communication Technologies: Technical Change and Everyday Life. In Mansell, R., & Silverstone, R. (Eds.), *Communication by Design: The Politics of Information and Communication Technologies* (pp. 44–74). Oxford, UK: Oxford University Press.

Star, S. L. (1990). The structure of ill-structured solutions: Boundary objects and heterogeneous distributed problem solving. In *Distributed artificial intelligence* (*Vol. 2*, pp. 37–54). San Francisco: Morgan Kaufmann.

Star, S. L., & Bowker, G. C. (2002). How to infrastructure. In Lievrouw, L. A., & Livingstone, S. (Eds.), *Handbook of New Media - Social Shaping and Consequences of ICTs* (pp. 151–162). London, UK: Sage.

Star, S. L., & Griesemer, J. R. (1989). Institutional Ecology, 'Translations' and Boundary Objects: Amateurs and Professionals in Berkeley's Museum of Vertebrate Zoology, 1907-39. *Social Studies of Science*, *19*, 387–420. doi:10.1177/030631289019003001

Stevens, G. (2005). *BSCWeasel - How to make an existing Groupware System more flexible*. Paper presented at ECSCW 2005, Paris, France.

Stevens, G., Budweg, S., & Pipek, V. (2004). *The "BSCWeasel" and Eclipse-powered Cooperative End User Development*. Paper presented at the Workshop: Eclipse as a Vehicle for CSCW Research, CSCW 2004.

Stevens, G., & Wiedenhöfer, T. (2006). CHIC - a pluggable solution for community help in context. In [New York: ACM Publishing.]. *Proceedings of NORDICHI*, *06*, 212–221.

Storey, J. (2006). *Cultural theory and popular culture: an introduction*. Upper Saddle River, NJ: Pearson Education.

Suchman, L. (1987). *Plans and situated actions: The problem of human-machine communication*. Cambridge, UK: Cambridge University Press.

Suchman, L. (2002). Located accountabilities in technology production. *Scandinavian Journal of Information Systems*, *14*(2), 91–105.

Törpel, B., Pipek, V., & Rittenbruch, M. (2003). Creating Heterogeneity - Evolving Use of Groupware in a Network of Freelancers. *Special Issue of the Int. Journal on CSCW on Evolving Use of Groupware*, *12*(4), 381–409.

Trigg, R., & Bødker, S. (1994). *From implementation to design: tailoring and the emergence of systematization in CSCW*. Paper presented at CSCW'94.

von Hippel, E., & Katz, R. (2002). Shifting Innovation to Users via Toolkits. *Management Science*, *48*(7), 821–833. doi:10.1287/mnsc.48.7.821.2817

Wikipedia. (2008). *Perpetual beta*. Retrieved from http://en.wikipedia.org/wiki/Perpetual_beta

Wulf, V. (1999). Evolving Cooperation when Introducing Groupware – A Self-Organization Perspective. *Cybernetics & Human Knowing*, *6*(2), 55–75.

Wulf, V., & Golombek, B. (2001). Direct Activation: A Concept to Encourage Tailoring Activities. *Behaviour & Information Technology*, *20*(4), 249–263. doi:10.1080/01449290110048016

Wulf, V., & Rohde, M. (1995). *Towards an Integrated Organization and Technology Development*. Paper presented at DIS'95.

ENDNOTES

1. Cf.:https://bugs.eclipse.org/bugs/show_bug.cgi?id=36967 (21.3.2009)
2. http://www.atlassian.com/software/confluence/
3. This aspect distinguish our approach, e.g. from the concept of remote evaluation promoted by Hartson et al. (1996). In their work end users should only deliver information of shortcomings in the design. However, their participation in the design-related discussions of these shortcomings is not technically supported.

This work was previously published in Journal of Organizational and End User Computing, Volume 22, Issue 2, edited by M. Adam Mahmood, pp. 58-81, copyright 2010 by IGI Publishing (an imprint of IGI Global).

Chapter 13
Entering the Clubhouse:
Case Studies of Young Programmers Joining the Online Scratch Communities

Yasmin B. Kafai
University of Pennsylvania, USA

Deborah A Fields
University of California, Los Angeles, USA

William Q. Burke
University of Pennsylvania, USA

ABSTRACT

Previous efforts in end-user development have focused on facilitating the mechanics of learning programming, leaving aside social and cultural factors equally important in getting youth engaged in programming. As part of a 4-month long ethnographic study, we followed two 12-year-old participants as they learned the programming software Scratch and its associated file-sharing site, scratch.mit.edu, in an after-school club and class. In our discussion, we focus on the role that agency, membership, and status played in their joining and participating in local and online communities of programmers.

1 INTRODUCTION

With the advent of Web 2.0, the boundaries between consumers and producers of software have become less distinct (Fischer, 2009). Youth are at the forefront of those participating in social networking sites, contributing media content in various forms. More and more youth regularly act as content creators and informal programmers (Lenhart & Madden, 2007). Be it modifying a cell phone ring or creating content for a social Web site like MySpace, youth employ varying computational skills to tailor media to their own needs and tastes. And while modifying a cell phone ring is hardly the same as writing a compression algorithm, youth are nonetheless regularly encountering and navigating programmable media. To fully participate in Web 2.0 communities requires new competencies of youth (Jenkins, Clinton, Purushotm, Robison, & Weigel, 2006) involving

DOI: 10.4018/978-1-4666-0140-6.ch013

more technical and creative dimensions (Kafai & Fields, 2009; Peppler & Kafai, under review).

While the popularity of file-sharing sites suggests that young end-user designers join and participate in large numbers, in the particular case of programming the situation is often different. Much research has documented over and over again that most youth do not know what programming is, do not have access to programming skills, and perceive it as overly technical and thus not for them (Margolis, 2008). Social and cultural dynamics such as agency, membership, and status are thus instrumental in getting novices into programming (Kelleher & Pausch, 2005; Margolis, 2008; Margolis & Fisher, 2002). The focus of this paper will be how young programmers negotiate their entry into the club—an online community of programmers—its title making reference to the landmark research by Margolis and Fisher (2002).

A recently developed file-sharing site for informal programmers, scratch.mit.edu, allows us to examine in more depth how youth become engaged as end-user designers in Web 2.0 in the particular context of Scratch and its associated file-sharing site. As part of a 4-month long ethnographic study, we followed two 12-year-old participants, Lucetta and Matthew, as they learned the programming software Scratch (Resnick et al., in press) and then joined scratch.mit.edu both in an after-school club and in a class. Participation in Scratch shares many similarities and challenges with professional communities and thus we can study this process among the incoming generation of users.

BACKGROUND

Traditionally end-user development has been concerned with professionals and how they can customize tools to accomplish their work. Much of the research has either studied what problems end-user designers encounter in this process or how to design tools that would be supportive of their endeavors (e.g., Lieberman, Paterno, & Wulf, 2006). This research has been largely separate from efforts that have covered the same territory, albeit with young end-users, in school contexts. Here end-user development has been concerned with designing environments and tools that support novices in learning of programming (Guzdial, 2004). Ultimately, end-user development for professionals was seen as facilitating the modification of tools, whereas the focus for youth was on designing tools for ease-of-use, taking into account the differences in motivation, background, and developing expertise between young learners and adult professionals (Soloway, Guzdial, & Hay, 1994).

The research on learning programming and designing novice programming languages and environments has a long tradition (for an extensive overview see Kelleher & Pausch, 2005). Early studies focused mostly on understanding the design and ease-of-use of specific programming concepts such as loops, conditionals, or recursion (e.g., Soloway & Spohrer, 1989). Several efforts concentrated on designing scaffolds for beginning programmers to ease syntax and control problems (Guzdial, 1995; Jackson, Krajcik, & Soloway, 1998) or have developed new genres of interfaces that generated scripts based on users' interactions (e.g., Cypher, 1993). Perhaps the most longstanding effort has been design of programming languages for students based on an object-oriented programming paradigm which has now has become an industry standard: Logo and Smalltalk were the predecessors of today's Agentsheets, Alice, and Scratch (Guzdial, 2004).

When Kelleher and Pausch (2005) reviewed the development of programming environments and languages for novice programmers, they found that most efforts aimed at making the mechanics of programming more manageable. But more importantly, Kelleher and Pausch identified "the lack of a social context for programming, and the lack of compelling context in which to learn programming" (p. 132) as key impediments to getting programming novices involved and supported. They argued that these social and cultural barriers are "harder to address than mechanical ones because they are harder to identify and some cannot be addressed through programming systems." As the most recent designed novice programming language, Scratch facilitates many mechanical aspects of programming (see description below). In particular media-manipulation features provide the compelling context appealing to youth's interests in digital media, but Scratch also features a networked community and file-sharing site (scratch.mit.edu)—much like many professional communities which can be accessed by end-users for assistance, feedback, and sharing work (Resnick et al., in press).

In previous research, we examined the introduction of Scratch in a local context of a community technology center and identified the roles of mentors (Kafai, Desai, Peppler, Chiu, & Moya, 2008), ease of media manipulation (Peppler & Kafai, 2007), and community organization support as key factors in getting youth interested in programming (Kafai, Peppler, & Chiu, 2007). We also documented that learning programming is possible in an informal context that lacks the direct instruction and support often present in classrooms or professional training workshops (Maloney, Peppler, Kafai, Resnick & Rusk, 2008). Now that an online file-sharing site extends the community of programmers beyond a local setting, we wanted to examine what it takes to enter and participate as programmers in the Scratch programming online community.

More specifically, we focus on how young software designers develop personal agency with programming, move toward membership in a programming community, and gain status as experts amongst their peers. These three aspects emphasize an individual's sense of self in creating things (Black, 2006; Hull & Katz, 2006), centralized participation amongst a group of people (Lave & Wenger, 1991), and how individuals are recognized by their peers (Gee, 2000). In other words, we are studying how new Scratch users express themselves in their programs, how they begin to participate in an online community of Scratch programmers, and how they began to establish their own statuses as expert programmers. Incorporating Scratch in both an after-school and classroom setting provided us with a unique opportunity to view how young end-user designers interacted with programmable technology in two spaces with different affordances in terms of support.

2 SETTINGS, PARTICIPANTS, TOOL & METHODS

2.1 Settings

This was the first time we had introduced Scratch into a school setting, having up until this time used the program largely at youth-oriented technology clubs, such as the Computer Clubhouses (Kafai, Peppler, & Chapman, 2009). For four months in 2008, we were engaged in ethnographic research at a metropolitan laboratory school located in Southern California. From February to March, we started with an after-school Scratch Club, an optional extracurricular program that met two to three times a week for an hour at a time. In April and May, we continued during regular school hours, setting up a Scratch class where kids worked in groups of two or three during a set of six hour-long math classes. In both the club and the class members participated in the media-sharing Scratch Web site, which forms a third setting to our research.

2.2 Case Studies

A total of 47 middle-school youth, ages 10-12, participated in the study and were representative of the school's diverse population of African-American, Caucasian, Asian, Latino, and Middle Eastern descent students. Our analyses here center upon two of the four sixth graders who used Scratch across both the club and the classroom settings. The first, Lucetta, was 12 years old at the time of the study. About 5'5" in height, and of African American and Caucasian descent, Lucetta was quiet at times, jubilant at other times, and always inquisitive. She was one of the first and most regular Club members at the school. The second case study centers upon Matthew, a later arrival to the Club. Eleven years of age at that time and also of African-American descent, Matthew had learned about Scratch from his group of anime- and videogame-loving friends, and was excited to pursue it in both the club and classroom settings. Each of these two users' distinct personalities were reflected by their divergent interests in the program and their techniques for operating the Scratch technology, and over the course of using the program, each subsequently developed their own unique status as an expert.

2.3 Programming Environment and Site

In simple terms, Scratch can be described as a visual programming environment to effectively create games, animations, art, and other interactive media. Scratch allows designers to create games, animations, art and aesthetics, sound design, and stories (Resnick, Kafai, & Maeda, 2003; Resnick & Silverman, 2005) by manipulating media through a process of dragging-and-dropping command blocks of code then stacking these blocks together to form coding scripts (see Figure 1). On the far left side of the Scratch screen is the series of nearly 90 programming command blocks, allowing the user to manipulate sound, images, motion, and other input. In the lower right side of the screen, there is a cache of Sprites, which can be any imported or hand-drawn characters or objects in the video game. The middle panel represents the particular command blocks that the user has selected and stacked. Once they are double-clicked with the mouse, these stacked scripts activate various selected images and sounds on the Scratch Stage (in Figure 1, a musical animation featuring ocean-life characters of starfish & sea urchin) creating basic games, animations, and types of geometric art that can grow increasingly complex and nuanced depending upon a user's ability to stack and coordinate a range of command blocks (Maloney et al., 2008).

No small part of Scratch's initial appeal is based upon the informal ease with which users can begin to creatively play with the software to create games, animations, and art that are representative of their own interests and talents. Simply knowing how to "drag and drop" items with the mouse is enough to get any user started, and the program offers many sample projects for the new user to tinker with in the process of acquainting oneself with the software. Re-appropriating others' creations on Scratch for one's own purposes is one of the primary ways new users familiarize themselves with the technology. The name of the program itself, "Scratch", refers to the remix practice of DJs who would appropriate various songs into a single track by way of "scratching" multiple records.

Like in other Web 2.0 applications, Scratch designers are encouraged to share their projects with each other and build off of each other's ideas and creations. Since its public launch in May of 2007, the Scratch Web site (http://scratch.mit.edu) has been the primary means for users to share their work with one another (see Figure 2). With over 320,000 projects shared to date, the Scratch Web site is a vibrant online community with over 1,000 new projects being uploaded every day.

Described as the "YouTube of interactive media," the Scratch Web site allows designers to not only upload their creations but also download and remix others' projects, as well as post comments, "friend" other designers, and start discussion threads (Resnick et al., in press). The goal, of course, is for Scratch users to not only collaborate with one another online but to also find

Figure 1. Screenshot of the Scratch interface with the musical project Ocean Music Box

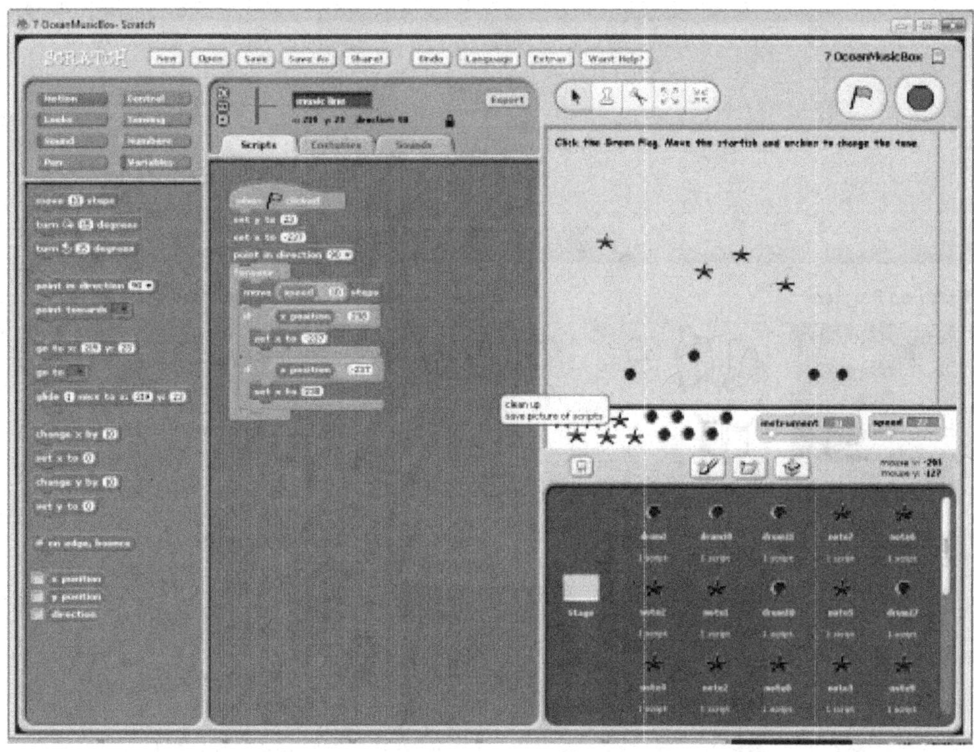

affinity groups through the site based on common interests and design techniques.

2.4 Data Collection

Ethnographic field notes were recorded daily in the after-school setting to capture the overall activity of interactions using the Scratch software. In addition, two video cameras were used to record student interactions in real time in both the Club and class settings. These were set up to focus on particular groups and individual students over the course of the study, and their results were subsequently activity-logged and analyzed. Third, both in the middle of March and at the end of May, a total of 21 students—including Lucetta and Matthew—were selected by the research team to be briefly interviewed about their individual experiences using the Scratch software. In March, this group of interviewees was small in size and consisted of 6 regular attendees of the Scratch Club. In May, the number was larger—15 students altogether, each of whom had worked with a partner (or two partners, in one case) within the classroom setting. In each 10-15 minute interview—both in March and in May—these participants were asked what worked, what proved to be a struggle, if they received help from others, whether they would use Scratch again, and how they saw themselves as new programmers.

2.5 Findings

In the first section, we will focus on Lucetta's and Matthew's use of Scratch in the club setting, highlighting each one's individual agency as they became part of the larger Scratch community online as well as established their styles of programming. Lucetta and Matthew each approached Scratch in a unique way, based on

Figure 2. Screenshot of the Scratch.mit.edu, the file sharing site

(a) the projects they were interested in creating and (b) their particular style of navigating the software. Their divergent creative interests and navigation styles highlight the multiple ways Scratch can be used by end-user developers with different needs, interests, and comfort levels. In the second section, we turn our attention to the classroom environment and examine how Lucetta and Matthew developed reputations as "experts" in Scratch based on their experience from the technology club. While both Lucetta and Matthew became widely recognized and respected by their peers as Scratch experts, each youth acted on this status of "expert" differently.

2.6 Scratch Club

Lucetta

Scratch initially was introduced to the school through the after-school Scratch club. Meeting three days a week, the club had a slow start with only two kids showing up for its first meeting in early February. Lucetta was one of these first two. Arriving on that first day with her hair in two braids, Lucetta had never used Scratch before but was ready to learn and was not hesitant to ask questions, such as how to delete certain Sprites. At the first club meeting, she began experimenting with the various Sprites, stacking scripts at random before double-clicking upon them to test their effects. Lucetta's enthusiasm for Scratch added an air of excitement to the club during that first week when membership was still growing.

Figure 3. Screenshot of the Scratch interface with Lucetta's first creation, "Mr. Wiggles"

Exploring the variety of audio features available in the Scratch media library, Lucetta finally settled on a playful—if repetitive—song entitled "Eggs." The goofy and endearing melody added to the club atmosphere that first day and over subsequent sessions, and with its instantly familiar beat, "Eggs" acted as something of a theme song for those six weeks in the club

It also was clear during that first week that Lucetta, in particular, appeared determined to start and finish a whole project in Scratch before moving on to any others. Working on a project she named "Mr. Wiggles" (see Figure 3), Lucetta created an underwater scene in which the central Sprite was an octopus that moved back and forth to the "Eggs" music. However, she had a hard time coordinating multiple images of the creature to create an even back and forth movement without the octopus turning upside down. While all the club "newbies" were encouraged during this first session to visit the Scratch Web site and explore other projects to facilitate their own creations, no club member opted to share and go online—seemingly as hesitant to let others view their early software designs as they were to explore the work of others.

This hesitancy to visit the Scratch Web site continued over the entire first week. While membership to the after-school club had grown to seven participants by the end of the week, new members shared what they were working on with each other but never joined the online community. "Yay, I got it to work!" Lucetta exclaimed of her "Mr. Wiggles" project mid-way through the second session, and it was clear that her persistence with this single project had paid off. Since this was one of the first projects to be completed and it had a jazzy tune that played over and over again, everyone in the club knew about Mr. Wiggles. In fact, two other club members subsequently sampled (to varying degrees) from Lucetta's initial creation in their own attempts to orientate themselves with the Scratch software.

Taylor was the first of these two club members. Joining the club at the beginning of its second week, she was introduced to Scratch by Lucetta, who showed Taylor her "Mr. Wiggles" project by way of an introduction to Scratch. At the researcher's suggestion the two girls then painstakingly took a screenshot of the scripts of "Mr. Wiggles" and Taylor created matching scripts in her first project, replacing the octopus Sprite with that of a hippo moving back and forth on the stage. Taylor added wings to her hippo Sprite and created multiple costumes to give the impression of flapping wings. She also used a different background and different music, and on her second day created a different ending to her project—namely, having the hippo land and settle on a large daisy. While Taylor's final project ultimately looked quite different than Lucetta's underwater creation, many of its operating scripts were identical, and the girls' collaboration helped introduce other club members to the idea that users could take scripts from one project to solve a dilemma in another project. However, despite continued efforts on the part of the club facilitator, members continued to see collaboration largely in terms of working together in the club; even into the second week of the club, few members had opted to go to the Scratch Web site to share and download creations online.

While Taylor's sampling of Lucetta's "Mr. Wiggles" project was a collaborative effort, another club member, Craig, opted to borrow directly from Lucetta without initially giving her due credit. At the end of week three, Craig entered the club reporting that he had made a project just like "Mr. Wiggles" and uploaded it to the Scratch Web site. While Craig said he had created the project by himself at home, it was an obvious copy—using the same Sprite, having it go back and forth, and utilizing an ocean background. The scripts were not all identical (as in Taylor's project) because Craig did not have a screen shot of the commands from which to copy, but the entire concept was a blatant and purposeful imitation. However the other club members quickly called Craig out on his slight. "You're making me feel guilty!" Craig protested, but he subsequently credited Lucetta under the project notes section. Lucetta, for her part, did not appear upset. "It's really a compliment that you copied my project," she informed Craig from across the room. At this, Craig protested that it was not meant as a compliment, but Lucetta had made her point and the rest of the club was there to witness it. Interestingly, despite the momentary friction it caused, this incident was a major step in getting members to access the Scratch Web site, with three youth creating Scratch Web site accounts that day and three more club members making Web site accounts by the start of the fourth week (for more on sampling others' creations work to foster collaboration, see Perkel 2008).

Over the next few weeks club members gradually began using more and more features of the Scratch Web site. At first they only used the site to socialize and to browse: uploading their projects, "friending" each other, working on their Web site images, commenting on each others' projects, and browsing projects listed on the main homepage. Then members began to do more focused browsing based on their personal interests—looking for different games, anime movies, or solutions to challenges they faced in their own projects. It was during the fifth week that yet another shift from socializing to downloading and remixing occurred. For instance, Ben wanted to create a laser effect on a gun in the game he had been working on for a couple weeks. He went to the Scratch Web site and found a game that had a similar effect, downloaded it, took a screenshot of the commands pertaining to the laser and used those in his project. Other club members browsed projects, downloaded ones they liked, and made changes to them they thought would be interesting.

The incident with Craig also helped secure Lucetta's reputation as a knowledgeable Scratch user among her peers. As a member of the club since its inception, Lucetta was instrumental in raising enthusiasm for the program at the school. Yet despite the enthusiasm she helped to instill, Lucetta seemed to consider herself anything but dynamic. "I'm just slow," she mentioned during week three, "always the last one to go." This sentiment appeared to be shared by her mother, who, picking up Lucetta up after one club session, remarked that she was not surprised to learn of her daughter's patience with Scratch. Being slow, she continued, her daughter always worked very carefully. This carefulness very much was evident in the trial-and-error methodology Lucetta chose to employ in the creation of her "Mr. Wiggles" project. While she clearly enjoyed working with her peers, she also maintained a certain focus on whatever project she currently undertook, tinkering with the scripts and Sprites until she achieved the desired effect. Such focus earned her the respect of her peers in the club. While some kids quickly downloaded already created projects, tinkered with them briefly, and then moved onto another sample project, Lucetta consistently worked bottom-up with each of her projects until she was able to get them "just right." Though she sometimes used images she found online to make Sprites and participated on the Scratch Web site by uploading projects and commenting on others' projects, Lucetta did not remix projects from the Scratch site. Nor did she leave any projects unfinished, as some members did when they got excited about a new idea. Instead her style was to come up with an idea and work it all the way through. Often after she finished one idea she would come up with another idea to add on to the project. Lucetta's expertise was evident in the fact that she could explain exactly why she chose each coding brick and how they fit together. This know-how was a primary factor leading toward Lucetta's status as an "expert" among her peers. Consequently, as evident in Taylor's and Craig's samplings, the "Mr. Wiggles" animation acted as a touchstone for other club members to work off of as they attempted to navigate the Scratch software.

Matthew

Unlike Lucetta, Matthew arrived to the Scratch club somewhat knowledgeable of Scratch because of some friends who shared an interest in the program as well as anime and video games. Matthew was taller than the rest of his schoolmates, and he often seemed a bit awkward with his lanky arms and legs. However, upon first entering the club during its second week of operation in mid-February, Matthew had a swagger to his walk and exhibited a distinct "I-know-what-I'm-doing" attitude. While the majority of his fellow members started their club experience by sampling Sprites largely from Scratch's own built-in media library, Matthew immediately went outside of the program and began Googling sprites from his favorite anime shows on the Internet which he then attempted to import into Scratch. When the club facilitator remarked on his seeming familiarity with Scratch and its capacity to import other forms of digital media, Matthew appeared nonchalant, "Aw, it's just a big thing. It didn't come out right." Despite this initial—and perhaps feigned—nonchalance, Matthew's excitement for Scratch matched that of Lucetta, though their style of programming projects was quite different.

The shift in the club to using the Scratch Web site had a dramatic effect on Matthew's use of Scratch. Like many of his peers—especially Craig—he initially was bent on creating video games with the software, but upon discovering a ninja animation on the Scratch Web site that was based on his favorite anime series, *Naruto*, Matthew focused his efforts on building upon the animation's storyline. In fact, the Scratch Web site enabled Matthew to find others who shared his interests in anime and built that into their projects. Whereas Lucetta acclimated herself to Scratch using a trail-and-error approach and initially avoided going online for ideas and support, Matthew more quickly embraced Scratch's capacity to share content, sampling not only from others' Scratch projects but from other sources of digital media as well, such as iTunes and YouTube, from which he recorded music onto Scratch. In contrast to Lucetta's working simpler projects through start to finish, Matthew built upon an extremely complex project, even though he never completed his ambitious undertaking.

Figure 4. Screenshot of the anime "Ninja Showdown," upon which Matthew developed his own project

Entitled "Ninja Showdown 2," the animation Matthew remixed was a highly complex mini-movie depicting multiple pairs of combatant ninjas, recounting important events and characters in the storyline of *Naruto* as the ninjas battled back and forth leaping and using special powers (see Figure 4). It was a very challenging project that contained over 40 Sprites and 150 scripts. Impressed by the competing figures, Matthew initially grew interested in changing the background music then decided there was an important ninja battle missing from the movie. For the next several weeks he worked on the scene, building off of the existing sprites.

By the end of the club, Matthew had made significant inroads to creating an additional scene to the Ninja Showdown, tailored in an alternative song based on music he recorded from YouTube, and re-titled the project as "Ninja Showdown II Remix," and added his username to the credits at the beginning of the movie. While he participated in the Scratch Web site by browsing, downloading, and remixing projects as well as by "friending" creators whose projects he liked, Matthew was never confident enough to post anything on the Scratch Web site, feeling there was still much work to be done before he was ready to share online. This is probably partly a result of choosing to do a very ambitious project and wanting it to be complete before posting it. Nevertheless, in the post-club interview in mid-March, he expressed a new confidence based on his time in the club. "So I've never really gotten to do computer animation," he remarked, "so I kind of get like I kind have a feel of what that's like now."

Scratch Class

While Scratch club came to a close in mid-March, we introduced Scratch in the sixth grade classes at the school just over a month later in late April. This was the first time Scratch had been formally introduced during the school day, and the format was decidedly more structured than the club as students had to make a "geometric art" project for math rather than having free-play with Scratch. Scratch was used by sixth graders—four of whom had been previous club members —though this time there was a total of 47 students over two classes as opposed to the dozen or so kids that were regulars at the after-school club. In the class, students worked in groups of two or three, and they were expected to work on a single geometric art project over the 3 weeks—a total of six hour-long classes—set aside for Scratch. While students were encouraged to get up from their seats to roam the room, most groups relied on their immediate partners to generate ideas.

Based on the participants from the club who were now also in the class, it quickly became evident that some kids had considerably more experience using Scratch than others. The more experienced Scratch participants—including Lucetta and Matthew—were considered the "experts," and those "newbies" first encountering Scratch were encouraged by both the classroom teacher and the accompanying class facilitators to reach out to their more experienced peers as they worked on their projects. This distinction between expert and newbie was present from day one and continued throughout the entire six classes; kids quickly identified and shared with each other which of their peers knew how to do what. While a select number of groups had a mix of experts and newbies, most were entirely new to the program and would often track down a more expert member from across the room to get help in a particular area. Students also participated in a number of 10-minute "gallery walks" in which they walked the classroom, exploring others' works-in-progress. These gallery walks further illustrated the multiple ways Scratch could be used. Whether it was a football simulation game, a garden animation scene, or a colorful work of interactive geometric art, participants could see what their peers were working on and how they approached the software, as well as make note of which design aspects they themselves may want to incorporate into their own projects.

Lucetta

Paired up with another 6th grader named Nikki who was entirely new to Scratch, Lucetta modeled a very inclusive leadership, unobtrusively working with her partner and helping others in the class at the same time. Over the six class sessions, the girls traded control of the computer's mouse and keyboard quite seamlessly, ensuring each had the opportunity to work the controls of the program without even having to ask for them. While Lucetta already had made a number of Scratch animations during her club days, she was careful to listen to all of Nikki's ideas, and the two often laughed at their various early proposals. "I got to listen to her ideas," Lucetta remarked in the post-class interview of her partner Nikki, "and then we got to see which ones worked. That way, we both got what we wanted." The girls' final project—an animation involving a man calling himself "supergirl" who flew across the screen followed by two blooming flowers made from triangles and squares—was an amalgamation of both their ideas. "She had come up with the supergirl thing," Lucetta explained, "I wanted him to actually make the flowers. But then it was too hard, so we just had the flowers come." Lucetta was also inclusive of Nikki when her own expertise was called upon by another group. Numerous times over the six classes, Lucetta was called over by a fellow group looking for assistance, and many times Nikki accompanied her as well. Even when Nikki did not come along, Lucetta was careful not to be gone too long, always returning to her partner within a few minutes of being called away—such periodic monitoring of more experienced programmers has been observed in other student software design teams (Ching & Kafai, 2008). While Lucetta clearly relished her status of expert and was always happy to quietly oblige another group, she never referred to herself as an expert and seemed to be happy to be considered just another Scratch user.

It is interesting to note that the club members' expertise was limited in a couple of ways. For instance, while club members were considered "experts" relative to their classmates, they were largely unfamiliar with the kinds of scripts needed to complete the geometric art project—scripts about drawing with the "pen" or stamping images. By the end of the project, Lucetta commented that these were now her favorite scripts. Additionally, because of Internet limits in the classroom, Lucetta could not always use her increased awareness of Scratch's capabilities. "Are we allowed to go online and get pictures? Are we allowed to go online?" Lucetta wondered aloud during the first class session in April, to which Nikki stared blankly back at her partner, entirely unaware that incorporating downloads from the Internet was a possibility with Scratch.

Matthew

In contrast to Lucetta, Matthew did not originally get along so well with his partners and was not initially treated as an "expert" with Scratch. Partly because of pre-existing personality conflicts, his first partners tended to ignore him. In fact, once when his partners were stuck, they asked the teacher for help and the teacher said, "So did you ask Matthew who's an expert?" This was the first time Matthew had been called an expert in relation to Scratch, and he quickly embraced it. When his first partners rebuffed him, Matthew moved around the room making suggestions to other groups who were new to Scratch. The next day when his first partners solicited then ignored his Scratch advice Matthew exclaimed, "Why are you looking at me like I'm an idiot?! I'm the expert!" Other groups in the class backed up this formal naming of Matthew as expert and one group suggested, "(H)e really should be in our group because he's helping us a lot and he's really good at Scratch." By the end of the second class, it was clear this new group was a much better fit for Matthew, as they nurtured his expert status instead of resenting it, though it still took time for them to integrate Matthew into their work.

Over the remaining four classes, Matthew built on his prior experience in the Scratch club to help guide his partners' use of the technology, and the trio ended up creating an animation involving an exploding car Sprite which was one of the most intricate and well-received projects created in the class. Matthew's partners teased out his expertise, bouncing their ideas off of him. They would try out a potential script, while Matthew would pick out any errors in their thought process. Matthew was clearly pleased with their progress—the bravado he initially flashed that second day in the class was now vindicated by his far more subdued role as mentor to his two partners. Uploading his group's final project to the Scratch Web site at the close of the classroom sessions, Matthew appeared to have attained not only a newfound confidence with the Scratch software but also with himself as a leader. Indeed, in his post-interview Matthew said that one of the parts of the project he liked best was that, "It kind of felt like leadership skills—because I can naturally use the computer." So his relative expertise in Scratch also helped him to think of himself as a leader with his peers.

3 DISCUSSION

Our study set out to examine a new group of end-user designers—young programmers—and how they negotiate their entry into a local as well as a global online community of software designers—and to identify how agency, membership, and status amongst the young programmers affect their participation. Collaborative programming activities are increasingly important in professional communities (Wulf, 1999). While professional end-user designers obviously work under different constraints that concern the focus of their design tasks and tools, participation in online networks for sharing artifacts and ideas is of relevance in both youth and professional communities. Agency certainly played a key role in club members' identification with Scratch, an attribute that may very well develop more naturally within an informal, non-prescriptive learning environment. Designed specifically for such informal learning environments (Kafai et al., 2007), Scratch's success with young end-users is not simply making the technical aspects more manageable but closely correlates with the software's ability to allow users to engage with the program on their own terms. To an extent, Scratch's informality in social practice replicates the ubiquitous informal programming environments that youth encounter daily and know so well, be it personalizing their cell phones or updating their statuses on MySpace.

The cases of Lucetta and Matthew demonstrate this in the different kinds of programs they made. Lucetta gravitated toward cute musical projects that often used animals in them, coinciding with her interests in animals at the time; Matthew was drawn toward video games and anime, embracing the opportunity to make his own animation based on his favorite anime series. Even in the class, where there was a more structured project, the groups were able to integrate their interests or styles into Scratch through football, music video, or abstract art themes. Participants thrived on the feeling that they could make anything they wanted and incorporated their various outside interests into their Scratch projects. As an extension of this, they became excited to participate in a larger Web community where they found others with similar interests. The Web community furthered both Lucetta and Matthew's membership in a programming community in different ways. Lucetta friended other users, commented on projects, and uploaded her own projects, taking advantage of the social community on the site. This fit her cooperative social style, mixing with others while sharing an interest in Scratch. In contrast, Matthew embraced the potential of remixing, though there were other aspects of participation that he did not take up such as sharing his own project for validation and feedback from the community.

However, Lucetta's initial resistance to migrating online and Matthew's own reluctance to upload his club project to the Scratch Web site, also suggest to us that establishing membership in a larger programming community is not as easily achieved as we had hoped. To return to the social barriers identified by Kelleher and Pausch (2005), when it comes to introducing programming to novice users, establishing a meaningful and comfortable social context in which to learn programming can be the most significant hurdle. While in both the club and class settings, youth freely and easily interacted with each other and then eventually took ample advantage of Scratch's online community, most of them seemed to need an initial level of comfort with the online environment before participating in the site. And even after club members began using the site frequently and young programmers began remixing others' work via the Scratch Web site, other youngsters remained much more cautious about the remixing process and stayed on the sideline while their peers actively explored it. Such hesitancy to plunge into online communities is clearly a topic that needs further investigation. Too often the popular media paints a picture of all youth actively participating in a wealth of virtual communities with abandon, yet in the cases of Lucetta and Matthew, we witnessed some real hesitancy to engage in the online community for various reasons, and these reasons—be it the anonymity of such sites or a sense that one is not "expert" enough to participate—warrant further analyses. Simply surfing through the discussion forums of a number of other social and gaming Web sites also targeting youth audiences, it quickly seems evident that only a small minority of users actually run and regularly populate these communities. Meanwhile a significant majority simply looks on and doesn't contribute.

Finally, in regard to status, the migration of Scratch from the club to the class enabled Lucetta and Matthew to stand out as experts in programming. Our reference to Lucetta and Matthew as "experts" is of course defined in relation to their classmates' understanding and experiences with Scratch. By no means do we mean to imply that their proficiency in Scratch programming is comprehensive at this point; rather it is intended to denote their relative familiarity or fluency with the Scratch environment. As in previous research we see here a form of an informal "peer pedagogy" (Ching & Kafai, 2008) emerging that showcases their ability to support and monitor their less experienced peers in Scratch design. More importantly, it provides an indication that the level of expertise required to help others can be quite fluid. In our particular case, a few months of design work with Scratch and a few projects positioned Lucetta and Matthew to provide valuable assistance to their team members as well as the larger class. By extension, this suggests that assistance in end-user design can come from more advanced users as well as experts.

Over time at both the Scratch club and classroom, we witnessed a great deal of informal practices that seem to have migrated into young designers' activities. For instance, the prominent remixing and repurposing, especially in the club, could conceivably lead to some clashes with school culture that still values individual work overall. In fact, we did see ambivalent attitudes of some club members such as Craig towards crediting the original designs of their adaptations (see Perkel, 2008). By the same token, the approach of searching out completed scripts to be adopted into their own programs mirrors the way many programmers now search online for existing applets as a starting point for their programs. One might bemoan the fact that young designers no longer start from scratch with Scratch and thus might miss out on important learning opportunities. We, on the other hand, see this as a promising practice for young end-user designers that facilitates their entry while at the same time adopting more "expert strategies." In fact, these approaches to adopting and repurposing others' software designs might provide a promising training ground for later professional practice. Experience and expertise of what it means to successfully enter, participate and navigate collaborative portals such as Scratch is something that needs to be nurtured early on.

ACKNOWLEDGMENT

The work reported in this paper was supported by a grant from the National Science Foundation (NSF-0325828) to the first author and an UCLA Research Mentorship to the second author. We wish to thank the coordinators, teachers and students at the Corinne Seeds University Elementary School for their participation.

REFERENCES

Black, R. W. (2006). Language, culture, and identity in online fanfiction. *E-Learning, 3*(2), 170-184. Retrieved April 28, 2008, from http://www.wwwords.co.uk/elea/content/pdfs/3/issue3_2.asp#6

Ching, C., & Kafai, Y. (2008). Peer pedagogy: Student collaboration and reflection in a learning through design project. *Teachers College Record, 110*(12), 2601–2632.

Cypher, A. (Ed.). (1993). *Watch what I do: Programming by example*. Cambridge, MA: MIT Press.

Fischer, G. (2009). End-user development and meta design: Foundations for cultures of participation. In V. Pipek, M. B. Rosson, B. de Ruyter, & V. Wulf (Eds.), *End-user development* (pp. 3-14). New York: Springer.

Gee, J. P. (2000). Identity as an analytic lens for research in education. *Review of Research in Education, 25*, 99–125.

Guzdial, M. (1995). Software-realized scaffolding to facilitate programming for science learning. *Interactive Learning Environments*, *4*(1), 1–44. doi:10.1080/1049482940040101

Guzdial, M. (2004). Programming environments for novices. In S. Fincher & M. Petre (Eds.), *Computer science education research* (pp. 127-154). London: Routledge Falmer. Hull, G. A., & Katz, M. L. (2006). Creating an agentive self: Case studies of digital storytelling. *Research in the Teaching of English, 41*(1), 43-81.

Jackson, S., Krajcik, J., & Soloway, E. (1998, April 18-23). The design of guided learner-adaptable scaffolding in interactive learning environments. In *Proceedings of the SIGCHI Conference on Human Factors in Computing Systems,* Los Angeles (pp. 187-194). ACM Publishing.

Jenkins, H., Clinton, K., Purushotm, R., Robison, A., & Weigel, M. (2006). *Confronting the challenges of participation culture: Media education for the 21st century* (White Paper). Chicago: The John D. and Catherine T. MacArthur Foundation.

Kafai, Y. B., Desai, S., Peppler, K., Chiu, G., & Moya, J. (2008). Mentoring partnerships in a community technology center: A constructionist approach for fostering equitable service learning. *Mentoring & Tutoring, 16*(2), 191–205. doi:10.1080/13611260801916614

Kafai, Y. B., & Fields, D. (2009). Cheating in virtual worlds: Transgressive designs for learning. *Horizon, 17*(1), 12–20. doi:10.1108/10748120910936117

Kafai, Y. B., Peppler, K., & Chapman, R. (2009). *The computer clubhouse: Constructionism and creativity in youth communities*. New York: Teachers College Press.

Kafai, Y. B., Peppler, K., & Chiu, G. (2007). High tech programmers in low income communities: Seeding reform in a community technology center. In C. Steinfield, B. Pentland, M., Ackerman, &. N. Contractor (Eds.), *Communities and technologies* (pp. 545-564). New York: Springer.

Kelleher, C., & Pausch, R. (2005). Lowering the barriers to programming: A taxonomy of programming environments and languages for novice programmers. *ACM Computing Surveys, 37*(2), 83–137. doi:10.1145/1089733.1089734

Lave, J., & Wenger, E. (1991). *Situated learning and legitimate peripheral participation*. Cambridge, UK: Cambridge University Press.

Lenhart, A., & Madden, M. (2007). *Social networking Web sites and teens: An overview*. Washington, DC: Pew Internet and American Life Project.

Lieberman, H., Paterno, F., & Wulf, V. (Eds.). (2006). *End user development*. New York: Springer.

Maloney, J., Peppler, K., Kafai, Y. B., Resnick, M., & Rusk, N. (2008, March). *Programming by choice: Urban youth learning programming with Scratch*. Paper presented at the SIGCSE 2008 Conference, Portland, OR.

Margolis, J. (2008). *Stuck in the shallow end: Education, race, and computing*. Cambridge, MA: MIT Press.

Margolis, J., & Fisher, A. (2002). *Unlocking the clubhouse: Women in computing*. Cambridge, MA: MIT Press.

Peppler, K. A., & Kafai, Y. B. (2007). From SuperGoo to Scratch: Exploring creative digital media production in informal learning. *Learning, Media and Technology, 32*(2), 149–166. doi:10.1080/17439880701343337

Peppler, K. A., & Kafai, Y. B. (Manuscript submitted for publication). Creative bytes: The technical, creative, and critical practices of media arts production. *Journal of the Learning Sciences*.

Perkel, D. (2008). No I don't feel complimented: A young artist's take on copyright. *Digital Youth Research*. Retrieved from http://digitalyouth.ischool.berkeley.edu/node/105.Resnick, M., Kafai, Y. B., & Maeda, J. (2003). *ITR: A networked, media-rich programming environment to enhance technological fluency at after-school centers in economically disadvantaged communities.* Washington, DC: National Science Foundation.

Resnick, M., Maloney, J., Hernandez, A. M., Rusk, N., Eastmond, E., & Brennan, K. (in press). Scratch: Programming for everyone. *Communications of the ACM.*

Resnick, M., & Silverman, B. (2005, June 8-10). Some reflections on designing construction kits for kids. In *Proceedings of the 2005 Interaction Design and Children Conference,* Boulder, CO (pp. 117-122). ACM Publishing.

Soloway, E., Guzdial, M., & Hay, K. (1994). Learner-centered design: The challenge for HCI in the 21st century. *Interaction, 1*(22), 36–48. doi:10.1145/174809.174813

Soloway, E., & Spohrer, J. C. (Eds.). (1989). *Studying the novice programmer*. Hillsdale, NJ: Lawrence Erlbaum Associates.

Wulf, V. (1999, November 14-17). "Let's see your search-tool!" On the collaborative use of tailored artifacts. In *Proceedings of the Conference on Supporting Group Work (Group'99),* Phoenix, AZ (pp. 50-60). ACM Publishing.

This work was previously published in Journal of Organizational and End User Computing, Volume 22, Issue 2, edited by M. Adam Mahmood, pp. 21-35, copyright 2010 by IGI Publishing (an imprint of IGI Global).

Chapter 14
Enterprise Systems Training Strategies:
Knowledge Levels and User Understanding

Tony Coulson
California State University, San Bernardino, USA

Lorne Olfman
Claremont Graduate University, USA

Terry Ryan
Claremont Graduate University, USA

Conrad Shayo
California State University, San Bernardino, USA

ABSTRACT

Enterprise systems (ESs) are customizable, integrated software applications designed to support core business processes. This paper reports research contrasting the relative effectiveness of two strategies for ES end-user training that differentially reflect the Sein, Bostrom, and Olfman (1999) hierarchical knowledge-level model. One strategy— procedural—involves training that targets the three lowest knowledge levels of the model (command-based, tool-procedural, and business-procedural); the other—tool-conceptual—involves training that also includes a higher knowledge level (tool-conceptual). A non-equivalent quasi-experimental design was used for groups of senior business students being trained to use an authentic ES. Performance measures were administered during training and ten days after training concluded. Both experiments demonstrated that training involving the tool-conceptual knowledge level leads to superior mental models, compared with training oriented toward lower knowledge levels, as expressed in the recollection and communication of ES concepts. Tool-conceptual knowledge-level training can be used to promote understanding and communication, and should be incorporated into training strategies for ES.

DOI: 10.4018/978-1-4666-0140-6.ch014

Figure 1. Hierarchical knowledge-level model (adapted from Sein et al. 1999)

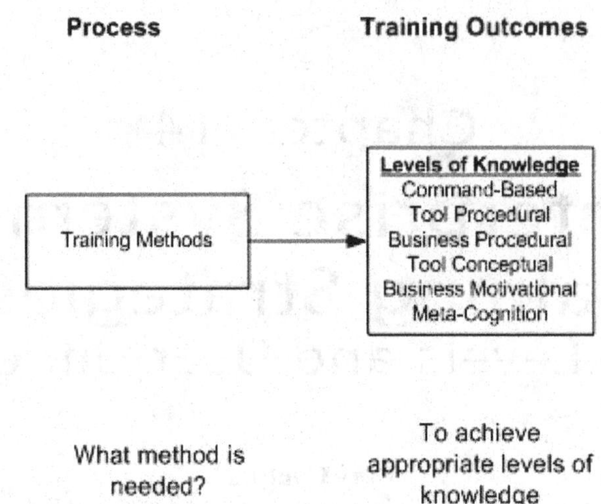

INTRODUCTION

Enterprise systems (ESs) are customizable, integrated software applications designed to support core business processes. Enterprise systems such as ERP, CRM and SCM often take years to implement, but unfortunately a significant number of ES implementations fail (Viehland & Shakir, 2005). Successful training strategies can help reduce failure (Wheatley, 2000). This study seeks to advance research in ES end-user training, examining strategies that could lead to more effective use of ESs and increase the chances of ES implementation success.

A large body of training research exists that relates to ES end-user training. From this literature, the Sein, Bostrom and Olfman (1999) hierarchical knowledge-level model (Figure 1) can serve as the basis for alternate ES training methods[1]. The model can be used to develop specific training approaches and methods across a wide variety of end-user training settings.

According to this model, training strategies should consider the types of trainees and IT tools on which they will be trained. The training methods should be designed using these inputs with the goal of achieving desired levels of knowledge, instead of focusing narrowly on skills and procedures (Sein et al., 1999). Table 1 characterizes ES end-user training outcomes in terms of knowledge levels.

End-user training provided by ES vendors is traditionally classroom based and focused on the interface and transaction procedures (Wheatley, 2000). In terms of knowledge level outcomes (Table 1), typical ES training focuses on a small portion of potential knowledge levels, specifically: the syntax and semantics of the command-based knowledge level; the combining of commands to complete tasks in the tool-procedural knowledge level; and sometimes the application of tools to a given business process in the business-procedural level (Sein et al., 1999; Wheatley, 2000; Olfman et al., 2001; Shupe & Behling, 2006).

This research contrasts existing ES training methods with a new training strategy that encompasses a broader range of knowledge levels. As shown in Figure 2, this study provides some trainees with traditional ES training covering the first three knowledge levels (command-based, tool-procedural, and business-procedural) and other trainees with ES training that adds the tool-conceptual knowledge level.

Table 1. Knowledge level outcomes for training (adapted from Sein et al. 1999)

Knowledge Level	Focus	ES System Focus
Command Based	Syntax and semantics	Learning the nuances of the system interface
Tool Procedural	Combining commands to complete tasks	Learning the steps to enter and recall transaction data
Bus. Procedural	Application of tool procedures to a task	Learning to complete and entire business process (i.e. procurement)
Tool Conceptual	The big picture of what to do with the tool	Understanding workflow of the whole process and the organizational impacts
Bus. Motivational	Reason to use	Business purpose of the system (e.g. integration, competitive necessity)
Meta-Cognition	Learning to learn	Continuous learning cycle, ways to approach the learning system

The specific research question surrounding end users' learning of ES software is:

Will end users whose training aims at the tool-conceptual knowledge level (plus traditional knowledge levels) develop more accurate mental models than those whose training aims only at traditional knowledge levels? This question has practical implications with respect to designing effective training for ES. It also has theoretical implications in that the Sein et al. knowledge level model has not been validated empirically.

In the following sections, the major constructs, their impacts and respective hypotheses are discussed further.

PREVIOUS RESEARCH, RESEARCH FRAMEWORK, AND CONSTRUCTS

A strong base of research exists concerning end-user training methods and outcomes. Many topics, including mental models and training strategies, have been studied in efforts to improve training

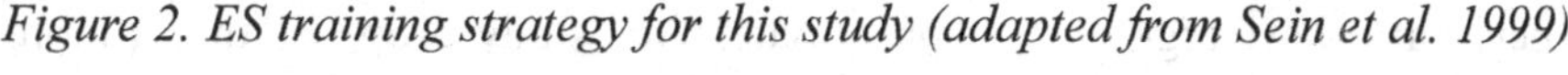
Figure 2. ES training strategy for this study (adapted from Sein et al. 1999)

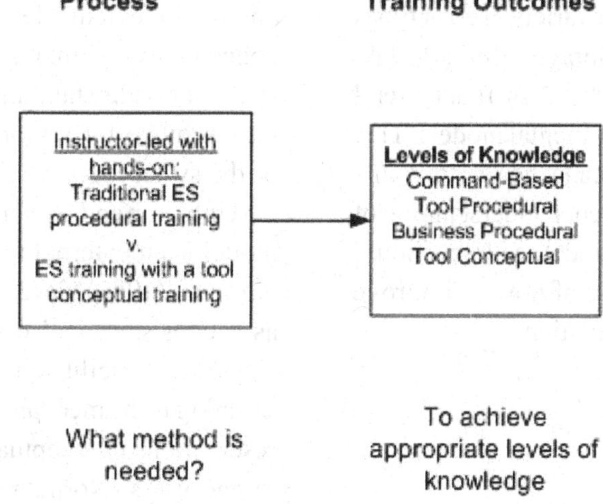

outcomes. This section examines mental models, the variables associated with Figure 1 (training strategy), and their applicability to the study at hand.

Mental Models

The concept of mental models has been a point of research within the field of cognitive psychology for many decades (Johnson-Laird, 1983). A definition of a mental model developed by Wilson and Rutherford (1989) incorporates research from many fields of study and provides a good overall definition of the construct:

A mental model is a representation formed by a user of a system and/or task, based on previous experience as well as current observation, which provides most (if not all) of their subsequent system understanding and consequently dictates the level of task performance (p. 619).

An accurate mental model of the target system is an important component to any training research because it is a desired outcome of training (Staggers & Norcio, 1993). Studies have found that end users who have more accurate mental models, as measured by mental model transfer effects, do better quality work (Bayman & Mayer, 1984; Gist et al., 1989), take less time to perform tasks (Borgman, 1986; Sein et al., 1987; Panko & Sprague, 1997), and produce a smaller variety of error types (Allwood, 1990; Panko & Sprague 1997; Peslak, Subramanian, & Clayton, 2007, 2008) than do end users who have less accurate mental models. This makes it important to understand the determinants of mental model accuracy. Better understanding of the determinants of mental model accuracy should lead to better understanding of how to improve the success of ES implementations.

Training Strategies and Mental Models

As stated above, system understanding and prior knowledge influence the formation of mental models (Wilson & Rutherford, 1989). Researchers have sought to determine effective training strategies to convey appropriate content, resulting in accurate mental models (Olfman & Mandviwalla, 1994; Ifenthaler, 2005). Of particular interest to this study is the effectiveness of traditional ES procedural training in conveying system understanding and knowledge. In terms of the training strategy framework, typical vendor-supplied ES training focuses on three knowledge levels: command-based, tool-procedural, and business-procedural.

Procedural training is focused on carrying out tasks, the content often being a sequence of action steps (Anderson, 1989). By introducing procedural training to end users, they may internalize the "how to" steps, creating a collection of rules in their mental model from which to draw upon (Kieras & Polson, 1985; Anderson, 1989; Olfman & Mandviwalla, 1994; Santhanam & Sein, 1994; Ifenthaler, 2005). The end user is left to abstract the conceptual understanding of the broader system from the procedures given (Anderson, 1989). However, given the complex, integrated nature of ESs, this method of training may be inappropriate. This study proposes that a more sophisticated training method, one that conveys another knowledge level, such as the addition of conceptual content, may be more suitable for ES. End-user understanding of the wide scope of ES may provide for a more accurate mental model of the system as a whole.

Unlike an end-user mental model, a conceptual model is an external representation of a system. Norman (1983) describes a conceptual model as a consistent and complete representation of a system to facilitate understanding or teaching. Training is the mechanism by which external representations (conceptual models) are introduced to end users (Norman, 1983). By introducing a conceptual model to end users through training, they may internalize the conceptual models into their mental model, thereby updating and filling in gaps in experience and understanding (Johnson-Laird, 1983; Norman, 1983; Sein & Bostrom, 1989; Bostrom et al., 1990; Staggers & Norcio, 1993; Santhanam & Sein, 1994). Conceptual training uses metaphorical techniques to convey the workings of a system. For ES, this could take the form of describing the overall structure and integrated workflow of the system and instructing end users on a new system by drawing analogies in terms of a system they are already familiar with (i.e., database software). In terms of the training strategy framework, this approach would include an additional knowledge level in traditional ES training, namely, a tool-conceptual component.

A competing theory suggests that procedural training and conceptual training lead to similar outcomes and that the learning styles of the trainees are often the stronger determinant of success (Borgman, 1986; Olfman & Mandviwalla, 1994; Ifenthaler, 2005). However, the existing research focuses on narrow applications, such as library database searches (Borgman, 1986), e-mail (Santhanam & Sein, 1994), graphical interfaces (Olfman & Mandviwalla, 1994), and database (Shayo & Olfman, 2000). ESs contain elements of all the aforementioned applications *and* requires business domain knowledge. The complex nature of ESs may be more suited to a training technique that draws upon elements of an end user's existing knowledge, rather than one that potentially requires the learning of hundreds of specific procedures and tasks. Therefore, those end users exposed to the additional tool-conceptual knowledge level are expected to have more accurate mental models of an ES than those receiving traditional procedural training.

Problem Conceptualization and Propositions

The literature suggests that when end users are exposed to new applications, such as an ES, they often struggle to understand the new environment (O'Leary, 2000). As evidenced by a large failure rate and ineffective use of ES applications, end users have not been successful in transitioning to these fully integrated application systems (Wheatley, 2000). While no prior research has explicitly examined factors that impact the accuracy of mental models in an ES environment, the human computer interaction literature has identified a number of factors, including instructor-led training, that lead to improved mental model development (Staggers & Norcio, 1993). In research surrounding training strategies, conceptual model training has been related to improved mental models and performance (Shayo & Olfman, 2000). Moreover, the Sein et al. (1999) knowledge level model predicts that users whose training exposes them to the tool conceptual level of training will be able to use the target software more effectively than if they had not.

The research reported in this paper explores the relative contributions of two training strategies to the accuracy of an end user's mental model of an ES. It is proposed that providing a tool-conceptual knowledge level to end users, in addition to traditional procedural training, results in more accurate mental models.

Research Proposition. End-users receiving training in four knowledge levels (command-based, tool-procedural, business-procedural, tool-conceptual training) are expected to develop more accurate mental models than those receiving training in three knowledge levels (command-based, tool-procedural, business-procedural).

This proposition is tested in the context of training experimental subjects in the use of an Enterprise System.

Figure 3. Research design

EXPERIMENT 1 (E1)									
E1	Week 1		Week 2		Week 3		Week 4		
Before	S_1	S_2	S_3	S_4	S_5	S_6	S_7	S_8	After
O_{m1}	X_1 O_{m2}	X_2 O_{m3}	X_3 O_{m4}	X_4 ...				O_{m5}	O_{m6}
O_{m1}	X_1 O_{m2}	Y_1 O_{m5a}	Y_2 O_{m3}	Y_3 O_{m4}	Y_4 ...			O_{m5b}	O_{m6}
EXPERIMENT 2 (E2)									
E2	Week 1		Week 2		Week 3		Week 4		
Before	S_1	S_2	S_3	S_4	S_5	S_6	S_7	S_8	After
O_{m1}	X_1	X_2	X_3	X_4 ...				O_{m5}	O_{m6}
O_{m1}	X_1	Y_1	Y_2	Y_3	Y_4 ...			O_{m5}	O_{m6}

where O_{mi} = Mental model assessments (measures $_a$ & $_b$ are the same test taken at different times)
S_i = Session

Procedural Training (X_i) Treatment
X_1 = Command Based Training
X_2 = Tool Procedural Training
X_3 = Business Procedural Training
X_4 = Tool/Business Procedural (complete workflow: S_4 - S_8)

Tool Conceptual Training (Y_i) Treatment
Y_1 = Tool Conceptual Training (workflow concept)
Y_2 = Tool Procedural Training
Y_3 = Business Procedural Training
Y_4= Tool/Business Procedural (complete workflow: S_5 - S_8)

METHODS

Research Design

A laboratory experiment using a quasi-experimental design (non-equivalent groups) were used in this study. The experiment used six measures applied to two training treatment groups (procedural (PT) vs. tool-conceptual (TCT)), one in each of two undergraduate classes. Because participants in the research were not randomly assigned to treatment groups, but had been enrolled in their classes prior to the studies, the design is quasi-experimental (Figure 3) (Mark, Cook, & Cook, 1984).

One classroom of participants was randomly assigned to the procedural treatment group (X_i – PT), and the other to the tool-conceptual treatment group (Y_i - TCT). Training took place over a five-week period of eight class sessions. A mental model pre-test, O_{m1}, was gathered prior to experimental manipulations to control for differences in the quasi-experiment. Immediately following each of four experimental treatments, the dependent variable (mental model accuracy) was measured (O_{m2}-O_{m5}). Ten days after all treatments were completed, a final measurement of the dependent variable occurred (O_{m6}).

Hypotheses

Based on the Research Proposition stated above, the following hypotheses were derived:

H1: The mean scores on the mental model posttests starting in session 2 (O_{m3}, O_{m4}, $O_{m5a/b}$)[2] will be higher for end users who received Tool-conceptual Training (TCT) than those who received Procedural Training (PT).

H2: The mean scores on the mental model test after all treatments (O_{m6}) will be higher for end users who received TCT than those who received PT (E1 & E2).

Table 2. Summary of treatment content and hours for PT and TCT groups

	PT (X_i)		TCT (Y_i)	
	Treatment	**Hours/Classes**	**Treatment**	**Hours/Classes**
Command-Based	Intro to Enterprise One; navigation	2/1	Intro to Enterprise One; navigation	2/1
Tool-conceptual			System integration and workflow concepts	2/1
Tool-procedural	Data entry; choosing records; creating records	2/1	Data entry; choosing records; creating records; "Integration/Data Entry relations"	2/1
Business-procedural	Advanced record location; reports; work with customer records	2/1	Advanced record location; reports; work with customer records; workflow	2/1
Tool/Business-procedural	Procure to pay: A/P, distribution, inventory	10/5	Procure to pay: A/P, distribution, inventory; "Workflow references"	8/4
All		16/8		16/8

Subjects

A total of 77 senior undergraduate business students from a southwestern state university participated. For each experiment, data was gathered during two separate class sections of a senior-level information management and corporate policy course; each class section receiving different treatments (PT and TCT). Subjects were advised of the research prior to its beginning. They were identified for the purpose of grading, but their responses for the study were not associated with identifying information. During treatments, the participants were allowed to take notes, but not to share them nor use them during mental model measurements. All participants signed an "honor code" and non-disclosure statement that included the above controls.

Procedure

The experiment involved training students on a fully functional ES application as part of the class requirements. In both experiments, one course section (referred to as the TCT group) received additional conceptual material about the system, that is, tool-conceptual information; the other section (referred to as the PT group) did not. The PT group received training as if they had gone to a commercially available ES training center. The TCT group also received similar procedural training, with the addition of tool-conceptual information. Both groups were treated with five weeks of training (a total of 16 hours and eight sessions), and an equalizing session was conducted at the end for the PT group. The training sessions and content are summarized in Table 2.

Both treatment groups were permitted to ask only questions related to the ES interface and the specific procedures in order to maintain consistency. Mental model measures occurred immediately after the administration of treatments (with the exception of O_{m6}) so as to avoid time-lapse effects.

Prior to the initial treatment, a pre-test mental model measure (O_{m1}) was administered. A teach-back short answer test—in which a participant explains concepts as if he (she) were teaching them—was given following each treatment to assess the accuracy of the participant's mental model. Because the groups (TCT and PT) received slightly

Table 3. Variables and measures

Variable Type	Variable Name	Measures of Variable	Measurement Method	Scoring
DV:				
	End-user Mental Model	Mental model accuracy	Teach-back quiz	Teach Back: score range 4 to 28
IV:				
	Training Group	Treatment of traditional ES procedural training OR ES training with tool-conceptual information	Non-equivalent groups were treated with either PT or TCT	
CV:				
	Pre-treatment measure (O_{m1})	Beginning mental model	Teach-back quiz	Teach Back: score range 4 to 28

different training treatments, the measures were normalized to avoid possible distortion of scores.

The same trainer taught all course sections. The trainer—one of the researchers—was experienced with the target software and ES application training. To reduce the risk of experimenter expectancy, the training sessions were scripted to match the content found in commercially-available training.

The target software was Oracle's Enterprise One® demo version, commonly used by the software vendor for training purposes. This version is a fully functional ES, including demo data for a bicycle manufacturing operation. The demo data was refreshed after each class to reduce cross-contamination between course sections and to ensure a consistent software environment.

Measures

The measures and variables are summarized in Table 3.

Control Variables and Measures

Preliminary Quiz: The purpose of the preliminary quiz was to provide a mental model equivalency test of the treatment groups (O_{m1}). The measure was developed by the authors following question formats similar to those used in previous studies (e.g., Shayo 1995).

Dependent Variables and Measures

Mental model accuracy was assessed using a "teach-back" short answer quiz (O_m) similar to Shayo and Olfman (2000). The "teach-back" instrument asked participants four questions to explain operations and concepts surrounding the target software (i.e., the ES), as if they were teaching it to someone who had not worked with the system before (see Figure 4 for an example of one of the questions). Content analysis similar to that of Shayo and Olfman (2000) was used to code participants' answers to determine the accuracy of their mental models of the ES. Two independent raters, the experimenter and a faculty member familiar with ESs assessed inter-rater reliability. Sampling 15% of the responses to each instrument (O_{m1} to O_{m6}), the level of agreement between the raters was: 90% for O_{m1}, 93% for O_{m2}, 93% for O_{m3}, 95% for O_{m5a}, 93% for O_{m4}, 97% for O_{m5b} and 96% for O_{m6}. Disagreements between raters were resolved by: 1) the first rater (the experimenter) reviewing the participant's response; and 2) re-scoring or

Figure 4. Sample teach-back question

Question 2:

Imagine you are teaching an ES (i.e., JD Edwards Enterprise One) to someone who is a complete novice about computers (does not have experience with database, word processors or spreadsheets).
a) How would you describe an ES (i.e., JD Edwards Enterprise One) to her/him?
b) How would you describe the process of entering a record?

confirming the original score. The maximum possible score for the teach-back instrument was 28 (7 points for each response) and the minimum was 4 (1 point for each response).

Independent Variables and Measures

Training was conducted for the PT and TCT groups via a combination of instructor-led lectures (using Microsoft PowerPoint) and hands-on exercises. The treatments for both groups started with the same command-based overview of the user interface (X_1). As described below, the two groups received different treatments.

PT group sessions S_2 and S_3 consisted of tool-procedural (X_2) and business-procedural (X_3) training. The tool-procedural segment (X_2) featured procedural steps for the data entry and recall of address book records. These techniques included query-by-example record lookup and proper steps for entering information. The business-procedural (X_3) segment featured procedural steps for locating report data (using Boolean logic) and expansion of address book information required for other modules. The final segment (X_4) was built over five sessions (S_4-S_8). This treatment covered the procedures and tasks required to complete an entire procurement of inventory items including: supplier address book, purchase order details, receiving, and voucher payment.

TCT group session S_2 consisted of tool-conceptual training (Y_1). Topics included business process workflow (using a procurement example) and ES integration. Sessions S_3 and S_4 consisted of tool-procedural (Y_2) and business-procedural (Y_3) training similar to PT group sessions X_2 and X_3. The final segment of TCT (Y_4) was built over the four remaining sessions (S_5-S_8). Similar to the PT group, this segment covered the procedures and tasks required to complete an entire procurement process. TCT group treatments also included examples relating back to the tool-conceptual information (Y_1).

Data Analyses

All analyses were conducted using SPSS v11.1, using an alpha level of .05. Correlations were used as a preliminary analysis to investigate the relations between mental model measures, domain knowledge, application knowledge, and training groups.

For hypotheses 1, two one-way ANCOVAs were run to determine mean score differences between the TCT and PT groups, using O_{m1} as a covariate.

RESULTS

Analyses

Overview of the Analyses

Correlations were used as a preliminary analysis to investigate the relations between mental model measures and training groups. To reduce the number of analyses to be conducted, only those measures of the dependent variable (mental model measures) that were significantly related to

Table 4. Significant correlations: mental model measures and independent variables

		Experiment 1	Experiment 2
	Measure	Group	Group
	O_{m1}		
	O_{m2}		-
	O_{m5a} [a]		-
	O_{m3}	0.24	-
	O_{m4}	***0.36***	-
	$O_{m5b/5}$		.37
	O_{m6}	0.23	.33

Note:
[a]O_{m5a} for the TCT group in E1 was run prior to O_{m4}
Italic bold denotes p <.01, otherwise p <.05.

the independent variables (training groups) were included in subsequent analyses.

The results presented follow the general order the hypotheses. All analyses were ANCOVA designs where the covariate was a preliminary measure of a participant's mental model (O_{m1}). The sample size (N) for each treatment sample is given because participant population varied slightly between treatments.

All data were screened to identify univariate outliers. Reliability analyses for each of the resulting teach-back measures for E1 were: O_{m1} = 0.69, O_{m2} = 0.71, O_{m3} = 0.84, O_{m4} = 0.78, O_{m5a} = 0.76, O_{m5b} = 0.71, O_{m6} = 0.82.

Table 4 shows correlations used to determine those measures that were significantly related to the independent variables (PT and TCT group) or the covariate (O_{m1}). The means, standard deviations and significance for all variables are presented in Table 5.

Preliminary Analyses

Prior to all analyses, data were screened to meet homogeneity of variance requirements for ANCOVA (Tabachnick, 1989). In all cases, the sample met the homogeneity of variance requirements (cell ratio max ratio = 4:1, variance max ratio = 16:1, minimum cell size = 5). The overall analysis procedures for the main effects are summarized in Table 6. Results are summarized in Table 7.

Hypothesis 1 (H1)

The mean scores on the mental model post-tests starting in session 2 (O_{m3}, O_{m4}, $O_{m5a/b}$) will be higher for end users who received TCT than those who received PT.

A one-way ANCOVA was used with PT and TCT groups as the independent variable, mental model measures (teach back quiz, where significant, O_{m3}, O_{m4}, O_{m5}) as the dependent variable, and O_{m1} as the covariate. Based on the correlations in Table 4, analyses were run using O_{m3} and O_{m4}, as they showed significant correlations.

Om3: The first ANCOVA was performed to determine significant differences between PT (N = 31) and TCT (N = 44) groups using O_{m3} as the dependent variable and O_{m1} as the covariate ($F_{1, 72}$ = 27.56, p =.000). This analysis revealed a significant difference between the PT and TCT groups ($F_{1, 72}$ = 9.73, p =.003, effect size (eta square) =.119, observed power.868). Resulting mean score differences showed the TCT group (mean = 14.86) had higher mean scores than the PT group (mean = 12.87). With this mental model observation (O_{m3}), the hypothesis is confirmed.

Table 5. Means, standard deviations and significance for subject groups

Experiment 1	PT Group		TCT Group		Whole Sample	
	(*N*=32)		(*N*=45)		(*N*=77)	
	Mean	SD	Mean	SD	Mean	**SD**
O_{m1}	7.09	3.11	6.35	2.46	6.66	**2.75**
O_{m2}	8.94	2.83	8.16	2.32	8.48	**2.55**
O_{m3}	***12.87***	***3.16***	***14.86***	***4.63***	14.04	**4.18**
O_{m4}	***12.69***	***3.11***	***15.68***	***4.39***	14.42	**4.15**
O_{m5a}			11.64	3.30	11.64	**3.30**
O_{m5b}	20.00	3.61	20.49	4.73	20.29	**4.28**
O_{m6}	***17.50***	***4.44***	***20.07***	***6.09***	18.99	**5.57**
Experiment 2	PT Group		TCT Group		Whole Sample	
	(*N*=22)		(*N*=20)		(*N*=42)	
	Mean	SD	Mean	SD	Mean	**SD**
O_{m1}	9.23	3.31	10.10	3.28	9.64	**3.28**
O_{m5}	**15.71**	**4.67**	**18.95**	**3.68**	17.29	**4.47**
O_{m6}	**16.67**	**4.37**	**19.50**	**3.80**	18.05	**4.30**

Note:
O_{m1} was used as a covariate in the analysis unless otherwise specified
Bold denotes p <.05; ***italic bold*** denotes p <.01.

Om4: An ANCOVA was performed to determine significant differences between PT (N = 32) and TCT (N = 44) groups using O_{m4} as the dependent variable and O_{m1} as the covariate ($F_{1,73}$ = 8.70, p=.004). This analysis revealed a significant difference between the PT and TCT groups ($F_{1,73}$ = 14.61, p =.000, effect size (eta square) =.167, observed power.965). The results indicate that the TCT group (mean = 15.68) had higher mean scores than the PT group (mean = 12.69,). With O_{m4}, the hypothesis is also confirmed.

Table 6. Hypotheses analyses

	Main Effect Hypothesis	**Variables**	**Analysis**
1a.	Experiment 1: The mean scores on the mental model post-tests starting in session 2 (O_{m3}, O_{m4}, $O_{m5a/b}$) will be higher for end users who received TCT than those who received PT.	IV: Group (TCT, PT); DV: Mental Model measures (O_{m3}, O_{m4}, O_{m5})	One-way ANCOVA with O_{m1} as the covariate
1b.	Experiment 2: The mean scores on the mental model post-test (O_{m5}) will be higher for end users who received TCT than those who received PT.	IV: Group (TCT, PT); DV: Mental Model measure (O_{m5})	One-way ANCOVA with O_{m1} as the covariate
2.	E1 & E2: The mean scores on the mental model test after all treatments (O_{m6}) will be higher for end users who received TCT than those who received PT.	IV: Group (TCT, PT); DV: Mental Model measure (O_{m6})	One-way ANCOVA with O_{m1} as the covariate

Table 7. Hypothesis results

Hypothesis	Instrument	F	Df	p	eta	power	Reject / Confirm
1a.	O_{m3}	9.73	1, 72	0.00	0.12	0.87	Confirm
	O_{ml} *Covariate*	*27.56*	*1, 72*	*0.00*	*0.27*	*0.99*	
	O_{m4}	14.61	1, 73	0.00	0.17	0.97	Confirm
	O_{ml} *Covariate*	*8.70*	*1, 73*	*0.00*	*0.11*	*0.83*	
1b.	O_{m5}	5.15	1, 39	0.03	0.12	0.60	Confirm
	O_{ml} *Covariate*	*15.35*	*1, 39*	*0.00*	*0.29*	*0.97*	
2.	E1: O_{m6}	9.71	1, 73	0.00	0.12	0.87	Confirm
	O_{ml} *Covariate*	*27.17*	*1, 73*	*0.00*	*0.27*	*0.99*	
	E2: O_{m6}	4.41	1, 39	.043	0.104	0.53	Confirm
	O_{ml} *Covariate*	*18.14*	*1,39*	*0.00*	*0.32*	*0.99*	

Hypothesis 2 (H2)

The mean scores on the mental model test after all treatments (O_{m6}) will be higher for end users who received TCT than those who received PT.

E1 Om6: A one-way ANCOVA was used with PT (N = 32) and TCT (N = 44) groups as the independent variable, mental model measure O_{m6} (r =.23) as the dependent variable, and O_{m1} as the covariate ($F_{1, 73}$ = 27.17, p =.000). This analysis revealed a significant difference between the PT and TCT groups ($F_{1, 73}$ = 9.71, p =.003, effect size (eta square) =.117, observed power.868). Resulting mean score differences, with O_{m1} as the covariate showed the TCT group (mean = 20.07) had higher mean scores than the PT group (mean = 17.50). The TCT group showed a significantly higher score after all training tasks than the PT group.

Therefore, hypothesis 2 is confirmed; the TCT group had significantly higher O_{m6} scores than the PT group.

DISCUSSION

The study proposed that end users receiving training in four knowledge levels (command-based, tool-procedural, business-procedural, tool-conceptual training) will have more accurate mental models over time when compared with those receiving training in three knowledge levels (command-based, tool-procedural, business-procedural).

Approximately 80% of the participants came into the study with very little knowledge of ES software. Scores on the O_{ml} pretest averaged around 30 percent. By the end of the ES training session, scores on O_{m6} averaged around 70 percent. While not a goal of the study, it is noteworthy to emphasize that learning did occur. Overall mental model scores increased for both training groups (PT and TCT).

Significant differences were found between groups. Specifically, in support of Hypothesis 1, later measures (O_{m3} and O_{m4}) reveal that participants in the TCT group demonstrated a significantly more accurate mental model than participants in the PT group. In support of hypothesis 2, the post treatment measure in (O_{m6}) revealed similarly significant results.

The teach-back measures were designed to model real-world training expectations. Specifically, when companies need to train their staff on a new ES implementation, it is costly and infeasible to send everyone to training. Rather, companies typically send a select group of individuals to training with the expectation that they will train others when they return (Davenport, 2001). The teach-back method focuses on participants' ability to recall information from their mental model and communicate it in their own words (e.g., O_{m2}, question 2 "How would you describe the workings of ES (i.e., Enterprise One) to her/him?"). Therefore, assessing participants' ability to recall and communicate information they have learned is an important trait, as the participants will make use of it when they are expected to train others. Any training method that promotes this skill is valuable.

With respect to hypotheses 1 and 2, TCT participants showed significantly higher levels of mental model accuracy. In other words, the participants were able to describe system concepts more effectively having had the TCT training; the only exception being the O_{m5} teach-back measure. O_{m5} was taken approximately two weeks (four sessions) after O_{m4} for the TCT group and five sessions after O_{m4} for the PT group. The time taken to train and the quantity of material presented appear to have equalized the groups' mental model accuracy with the teach-back (recall) measure. However, ten days after the O_{m5} measure, and no further training, O_{m6} re-confirmed the previous significant findings of O_{m3} and O_{m4}.

One explanation for the difference between the O_{m5} and O_{m6} results could be the complexity of the questions. Business procurement operations were the focus throughout the sessions leading up to O_{m5}. Questions in measure O_{m5} focused on the procurement process that had been learned over two weeks. However in O_{m6}, the measure asked questions related to the sales process. The objective of the O_{m6} sales process questions was to test the strength of the participants' learning since the sales process is a change in perspective (selling, versus buying) rather than a change in process. The O_{m6} teach-back measure indicates that participants in the TCT group have a deeper understanding than the PT group. Although both groups were able to improve their mental models, the type of training seems to have had impact on the depth of that improvement.

This result is consistent with mental model research involving computer applications (Davis & Bostrom, 1993). Santhanam and Sein (1994) use assimilation theory to describe mental model formation through the induction of new schema or knowledge structures. Specifically, assimilation theory describes learning in terms of three steps: 1) reception; 2) availability; and 3) activation (Ausubel, 1968). Reception refers to a participant's willingness to learn and attend to the teachings. The availability step refers to the participant's existing knowledge or concepts that can be used to aid in the assimilation of information. Lastly, the activation step refers to the participants' ability to make connections between the new information and existing knowledge. Assimilation theory research suggests that in cases where pre-existing knowledge is unavailable within the participant's mental model, the introduction of conceptual information can improve learning results (Ausubel, 1968; Davis & Bostrom, 1993; Santhanam & Sein, 1994). In this study, as demonstrated by the participant's low scores on the initial mental model measure (O_{m1}), it is evident that they did not have strong pre-existing ES knowledge available to them to aid in the assimilation process. The TCT group was explicitly taught ES conceptual models whereas the PT group had to construct their own based on their minimal pre-existing understanding of ESs. It seems reasonable that the conceptual models that were taught to the TCT group improved the assimilation learning process by providing accurate information to be integrated into the participants' mental models. The depth of learning for the TCT group was also improved as evidenced when the degree of far-transfer difficulty, challenging the participants' ability to draw upon existing knowledge as a reasoning aid and apply it to new situations, was increased in O_{m6}. The TCT group was able to draw upon their integrated mental models more effectively than the PT group.

CONCLUSION

Overall, the study offers important insights into how different training methods affect end users over time. In particular, it provides some valuable information for real-world ES training strategy development.

Implications for ES Training Strategies

This study was based on the Sein et al. (1999) training strategy framework. The study was designed to impart specific levels of ES knowledge to two participant groups in different manners. Both methods followed a traditional ES procedural training approach, which focus on the first three knowledge levels in the framework; but one method added tool-conceptual information. The objective was to test the Sein et al. framework, which posits that a more accurate mental model can be imparted to trainees by providing training at a higher knowledge level. In general, the study found that by adding a tool-conceptual knowledge level to traditional training, the end users developed more accurate mental models. Specifically, it was found that conceptual training improves the end user's ability to recall and articulate ES concepts. By using the knowledge level framework and incorporating tool-conceptual knowledge into an organization's training design, organizations may see an improvement in overall ES implementation results. For example, because ES training is very expensive, those within an organization that attend ES training are often asked to train others in the organization when they return. This study shows that adding a tool-conceptual knowledge level to their training improves their ability to recall and re-articulate their understanding of the system. Building knowledge levels that enable more effective understanding and communication of concepts learned could be a valuable asset to any company's training and implementation strategy.

Limitations

While attempts were made to ensure a sound study design based on the use of existing similar measures and established training techniques, this study, like any quasi-experiment, is not without limitations.

Internal Validity

In general, the internal validity of this study is strong. The study had extremely low levels of mortality (2 participants) and did not appear to suffer from maturation or instrumentation difficulties.

One threat to internal validity was experimenter expectancy. One of the authors was also the trainer, thereby having the power to influence results. To mitigate this risk, the training sessions were scripted based on actual training materials used in commercial training. The "trainer" only varied from the scripts to answer participant questions. Only questions directly related to the target system procedures were answered.

External Validity

To improve external validity, the study was designed to replicate real world ES training. Presentations, documentation and the actual ES were similar to those found in commercially available classes. The main threats to external validity are the timing, pace, and context of the training sessions and the participants in the study.

In real world ES training, end users often travel to the training center and receive all their training over a short period of time. For example, a class on procurement might be a week long with end users training eight hours per day. The training in the study occurred over five weeks, with two-hour sessions each time. To mitigate this particular threat, the instructor attempted to mimic the proportion of hands-on and lecture time that the end users (students) would experience in typical training. After class practice sessions were limited so as to not allow participants a disproportionate amount of practice time.

Another threat to external validity is the participant pool. This study was incorporated into a university course curriculum. The participants are not necessarily representative of a true ES training session. Specifically, most of the participants had limited business experience and different motivations to participate than one would find in commercially available ES training. Unlike a work environment, these participants were not required to use the system as part of their jobs after the training. Although not part of the hypotheses, participant data surrounding the degree of business experience was collected. However there was no significant impact of business experience on the study outcomes as is also supported by another study (Coulson, Zhu, Stewart & Rohm, 2004).

Directions for Future Research

This study provides some interesting insights into the difficult task of training end users on complex application software. Future research should include an evaluation of hands-on learning. In this study the participants were given a proportional amount of hands-on practice with the system, similar to what they would have in a commercially available ES class. However, while the measures sought to assess their mental model accuracy, no attempts were made to evaluate the participant's ability to perform the tasks.

Prior research suggests that mental model accuracy leads to better performance as measured by time and errors (Borgman, 1986; Sein et al., 1987; Panko & Sprague, 1997). Exploring hands-on results could provide some interesting findings pertaining to the accuracy of the mental models and training strategies. Specifically, this could enable evaluation of the appropriateness of prior hands-on performance research in different types of applications (Windows, database) and determine if those results are compatible with the complex ES environment.

This research found that adding one additional knowledge level to training improves learning. Further tests of the knowledge level model should be conducted. One approach could be to test the value of the knowledge level model for a different type of software using the same methodology applied in the current study. Another could be to add coverage of yet another knowledge level to ES training.

Overall, this study provides a strong case for ES vendors, implementers, and trainers to provide ES conceptual training prior to typical procedural training. Tool-conceptual information provides a platform to develop further ES understanding. Specifically, we found the end users' ability to recall and articulate their understanding to be significantly improved by incorporating conceptual training. Adapting conceptual models into ES training strategies could improve the propagation of training and ultimately save an organization time and money.

ACKNOWLEDGMENT

The authors would like to acknowledge the contribution of Dr. C. E. Tapie Rohm of California State University, San Bernardino, for their input into the original study on which this paper was based.

REFERENCES

Allwood, C. (1990). Learning and using text-editors and other application programs. In Falzon, P. (Ed.), *Cognitive ergonomics: Understanding, learning, and designing human computer interaction* (pp. 85–10). New York: Academic Press.

Anderson, J. R. (1989). A theory of human knowledge. *Artificial Intelligence*, *40*, 313–351. doi:10.1016/0004-3702(89)90052-0

Ausubel, D. P. (1968). *Educational Psychology: A Cognitive View*. New York: Holt, Reinhart and Winston.

Bayman, P., & Mayer, R. E. (1984). A diagnosis of beginning programmers misconceptions of BASIC programming statements. *Communications of the ACM, 26*, 677–679. doi:10.1145/358172.358408

Borgman, C. (1986). The user's mental model of an information retrieval system: An experiment on prototype online retrieval catalog. *International Journal of Man-Machine Studies, 10*, 625–637.

Bostrom, R. P., & Olfman, L. (1990). The importance of learning style in end-user training. *Management Information Systems Quarterly, 14*(1), 101–119. doi:10.2307/249313

Coulson, T., Zhu, J., Stewart, W., & Rohm, C. E. T. (2004). The importance of database application knowledge in successful ERP training. *Communications of the IIMA, 4*(3).

Davenport, T. H. (2001). *Mission critical: Realizing the promise of Enterprise Systems*. Boston, MA: Harvard Business School Press.

Davis, S. A., & Bostrom, R. P. (1993). Training end users: An experimental investigation of the roles of computer interface and training methods. *Management Information Systems Quarterly, 17*(1), 61–85. doi:10.2307/249510

Dixon, W. J., & Tukey, J. W. (1968). Approximate behavior of the distribution of winsorized t (Trimming/Winsorization 2). *Technometrics, 10*, 83–98. doi:10.2307/1266226

Gist, M. E., & Schwoerer, C. (1989). Effects of alternative training methods on self-efficacy and performance in computer software training. *The Journal of Applied Psychology, 74*(6), 884–891. doi:10.1037/0021-9010.74.6.884

Ifenthaler, D., & Seel, N. M. (2005). The measurement of change: learning-dependent progression of mental models. *Technology, Instruction. Cognition and Learning, 2*(4), 317–336.

Johnson-Laird, P. N. (1983). *Mental models: Towards a cognitive science of language, inference, and consciousness*. Cambridge, MA: Harvard University Press.

Kieras, D. E., & Polson, P. G. (1985). An approach to the formal analysis of user complexity. *International Journal of Man-Machine Studies, 22*, 365–394. doi:10.1016/S0020-7373(85)80045-6

Mark, M., Cook, T. D., & Cook, F. (1984). Randomized and quasi-experimental designs in evaluation research. In Rutman, L. (Ed.), *Evaluation Research methods: A basic guide*. Beverly Hills, CA: Sage.

Norman, D. A. (1983). Some observations on mental models. In *Mental Models* (pp. 15–35). Hillsdale, NJ: Lawrence Erlbaum Associates.

O'Leary, D. E. (2000). *Enterprise resource planning systems: Systems, life cycles, electronic commerce, and risk*. Cambridge, UK: Cambridge University Press.

Olfman, L., Bostrom, R. P., & Sein, M. K. (2001). *Training with a business focus: A best practice*. Bitworld.

Olfman, L., Bostrom, R. P., & Sein, M. K. (2006). Developing Training Strategies with an HCI Perspective. In Zhang, P., & Galletta, D. (Eds.), *Human-Computer Interaction and Management Information Systems - Foundations*. Armonk, NY: Sharpe Inc.

Olfman, L., & Mandviwalla, M. (1994, December). Conceptual versus procedural software training for graphical user interfaces: A longitudinal field experiment. *Management Information Systems Quarterly*, 405–426. doi:10.2307/249522

Panko, R. R., & Sprague, R. (1997). *Experiments in spreadsheet development: Task difficulty, level of expertise, and error rate*. Unpublished manuscript http://www/cba.hawaii.edu/panko/papers// ss/Imexpert.htm

Preslak, A. R., Subramanian, G. H., & Clayton, G. E. (2007). 2008). The phases of ERP software implementation and maintenance: A model for predicting preferred ERP use. *Journal of Computer Information Systems*, 25–33.

Santhanam, R., & Sein, M. K. (1994). Improving end-user proficiency: Effects of conceptual training and nature of interaction. *Information Systems Research*, *5*(4), 378–399. doi:10.1287/isre.5.4.378

Sein, M. K., & Bostrom, R. P. (1989). Individual Differences and Conceptual Models in Training Novice End-Users. *Human-Computer Interaction*, *4*(3), 197–229. doi:10.1207/s15327051hci0403_2

Sein, M. K., Bostrom, R. P., & Olfman, L. (1987). Training end users to compute: cognitive, motivational and social issues. *INFOR*, *25*, 236–255.

Sein, M. K., Bostrom, R. P., & Olfman, L. (1999). Rethinking end-user training strategy: Applying a hierarchical knowledge level model. *Journal of End User Computing*, *11*(1), 32–39.

Shayo, C. (1995). Role of conceptual and mental models in motivating end users to learn new but related software packages. Unpublished doctoral dissertation, Claremont Graduate School, Claremont, CA.

Shayo, C., & Olfman, L. (2000). The role of training in preparing end users to learn related software. *Journal of End User Computing*, *12*(1), 3–13.

Shupe, C., & Behling, R. (2006, July/August). Developing and implementing a strategy for technology deployment. *The Information Management Journal*, 52-57.

Staggers, N., & Norcio, A. F. (1993). Mental models: Concepts for human-computer interaction research. *International Journal of Man-Machine Studies*, *38*, 587–605. doi:10.1006/imms.1993.1028

Tabachnick, B. G., & Fidell, L. S. (1989). *Using Multivariate Statistics*. New York: Harper Collins.

Viehland, D., & Shakir, M. (2005, spring). Making sense of enterprise systems implementations. *University of Auckland Business Review*, 28-34.

Wheatley, M. (2000). *ES training stinks*. CIO.

Wilson, J. R., & Rutherford, A. (1989). Mental models: Theory and application in human factors. *Human Factors*, *31*(6), 617–634.

ENDNOTES

1 After the time this research was conducted, Olfman, Bostrom, and Sein (2006) revised the model by adding a seventh level. The new level is called "Business Conceptual", which more clearly specifies sections of the Tool Conceptual and Business Motivational levels in the original model. We do not believe our research is affected by this change because our focus is on Tool Conceptual training versus lower levels.

2 O_{m2} was not included in the hypothesis because both groups had received the same initial training X_1, so no differences would be expected. A post hoc test (not reported in this paper) showed that this was true.

This work was previously published in Journal of Organizational and End User Computing, Volume 22, Issue 3, edited by M. Adam Mahmood, pp. 22-39, copyright 2010 by IGI Publishing (an imprint of IGI Global).

Chapter 15
The Influence of Perceived Source Credibility on End User Attitudes and Intentions to Comply with Recommended IT Actions

Allen Johnston
University of Alabama, USA

Merrill Warkentin
Mississippi State University, USA

ABSTRACT

Through persuasive communications, information technology (IT) executives hope to align the actions of end users with the expectations of senior management and of the firm regarding technology usage. One highly influential factor of persuasive effectiveness is the source of the persuasive message. This study presents a conceptual model for explaining the influence of source credibility on end user attitudes and behavioral intentions to comply with organizationally motivated, recommended IT actions within a decentralized, autonomous environment. The results of this study suggest that the elements of source competency, trustworthiness, and dynamism are significant determinants of attitudes and behavioral intentions to engage in recommended IT actions. These findings reveal the importance of these elements of effective communication in persuading end users to follow recommended IT activities and advance IT acceptance and adoption research through the application of persuasive communication theory to the domain.

DOI: 10.4018/978-1-4666-0140-6.ch015

INTRODUCTION

A growing priority among information technology (IT) executives concerns the alignment of end users with strategies and goals relating to the acquisition and use of technology within the firm (Peterson, 2004; Changchit, 2006; Hong, Thong, & Tam, 2006). This is an issue of IT governance and involves all activities that ensure the organization's technology plans are executed and its policies are implemented (Sambamurthy & Zmud, 1999; Peterson, 2004; Johnston & Hale, 2008). Often, the IT governance posture assumed by the organization mirrors that of its enterprise governance model (Warkentin & Johnston, 2008). For some, that means the IT decision-making responsibilities are centralized within a single administrative unit that is charged with the administration of IT for the entire firm. For others, their IT function takes on a more decentralized structure in which decision making responsibilities are distributed on either a departmental or individual level. Within a decentralized environment, end users have autonomy over their respective computing facilities and information assets. As such, the successful implementation of IT within the firm rests largely on the interactions that occur between end users and systems and the degree to which these activities match the desires of management or the needs of the firm as a whole (Ahuja & Thatcher, 2005; Warkentin & Johnston, 2008).

Senior executives create written policies and procedures in order to manage the frequency, purpose and manner in which end users interact with IT within the firm. Unfortunately, these documents are often incomplete, outdated, or ambiguous, leaving users with no clear direction (Lichtenstein & Swatman, 1997). For many firms, the mere presence of written usage policies is insufficient in eliciting a desired usage behavior among users (Foltz, Cronan, & Jones, 2005). In such cases, secondary communication channels are needed and are available through the dialogue between managers and users found in training and policy awareness programs, as well as in daily informal discussions. Even for those firms that have well-established policy and procedural documents, these supportive communications serve to reaffirm the desires of management (Siponen, Pahnila, & Mahood, 2006).

A key element of this supportive communication is the use of persuasion (Siponen, 2000). Persuasion is commonly cited as an effective method for controlling the actions of others (Fishbein & Ajzen, 1975; Siponen, 2000). Particularly in the context of actions involving IT acceptance and use, persuasive arguments can address both the cognitive and social dimensions of the interaction. IT acceptance theories maintain that IT use is a cognitive event in which the human component appraises the benefits possible from the synergy of man and technology and assesses the technology's ability to facilitate the attainment of goals (Davis, 1989; Robey, 1979; Compeau & Higgins, 1995). Such appraisals include ease of use, usefulness, effort expectancy, performance expectations, self-efficacy, and compatibility, among others (Venkatesh, Morris, Davis, & Davis, 2003; Agarwal & Venkatesh, 2002; Moore & Benbasat, 1991). IT acceptance and use are also social phenomena in which the relationship between the human and system follows the rules of social behavior (Banville & Landry, 1989; Compeau & Higgins, 1995). As part of this social relationship, the human component may consider a system's approachability and likeability (Schaumburg, 2001).

The use of persuasion for modeling end user and IT interaction, however, is not a panacea. As Cacioppo and Petty (1984) describe, there are many factors, or combinations of factors, that influence the manner in which individuals respond to persuasion. For instance, one's perception of self-efficacy can have a direct influence on his or her attitudes and intentions to respond in a constructive manner to persuasive messages (Bandura, 1977; Witte, 1992; Thompson, Compeau, & Higgins, 2006). Specifically in the context of IT acceptance and use, if an individual is confident in his or her ability to engage in IT activities, he or she will have a more positive attitude and will more likely participate in the activities if properly motivated (Marakas, Yi, & Johnson, 1998). Other factors include one's ability to process persuasive arguments and to later recall them accurately (Cacioppo & Petty, 1989), the quality of the message (Cacioppo & Petty, 1980), and frequency of exposure (Cacioppo & Petty, 1980, 1989).

One highly influential factor of persuasive effectiveness concerns the source of the persuasive message (Petty & Cacioppo, 1984). Susan Cramm (2005) may have stated it best, "Persuasion is a process that starts with credibility." While eloquently articulated, Cramm's statement is not profound. In fact, numerous prior studies have empirically linked source credibility with the outcome of a message. When the desired outcome is a change in attitudes or behaviors, prior research suggests that high-credibility sources are more influential than low-credibility sources (Hovland & Weiss, 1951; Maddux & Rogers, 1980; Wittaker & Meade, 1968). Moreover, when the message is difficult for the recipient to understand, source credibility is of even greater importance (Jones, Sinclair, & Courneya, 2003).

While there is ample evidence to support the influential role of source credibility on attitudes and behavioral intentions, no study has yet to examine these relationships within the specific context of recommended IT actions in support of organizational policy. Are end users more likely to show favorable attitudes toward system tasks if persuaded to do so by highly credible sources? Further, which specific dimensions of the source's credibility are most influential on end users attitudes toward system interaction? These are the questions that drive this research.

The current study decomposes source credibility into separate constructs representing competency, trustworthiness, and dynamism; thereby allowing for separate measures of influence on end user attitudes and intentions to comply with recommended IT actions. This study, therefore, presents a conceptual model for explaining the influence of three distinct dimensions of source credibility on end user attitudes and behavioral intentions to comply with recommended IT actions within a decentralized, autonomous environment. The following sections describe the theoretical development of the model, its associated hypotheses, and the two-stage method used to test them. Following a description of the findings, the results are discussed, limitations are presented, and implications are made for the contribution of this study to both academia and practice.

CONCEPTUAL BACKGROUND AND MODEL DEVELOPMENT

Much prior research in the social, psychological, and behavioral sciences has been devoted to the study of the antecedents of technology acceptance and use. The early works of Fishbein and Ajzen (1975), Davis (1989), and Compeau and Higgins (1995) established attitude and behavioral intention as indicators of an individual's acceptance and use of technology. In fact, Davis' Technology Acceptance Model (TAM) was the first to model perceived usefulness and perceived ease of use as predictors of behavioral intention specifically within the context of information technologies. Based primarily on Fishbein and Ajzen's Theory of Reasoned Action (TRA), TAM has been instrumental in the development of future models that have increased our ability to predict technology acceptance, use, and continuance.

Acceptance models have continued to evolve and increase in predictive ability and complexity. For instance, Venkatesh and Davis (2000) introduced TAM2 as an extension of TAM through the incorporation of subjective norms into the model. Other models utilized in the study of behavioral intent to accept and use IT include the Theory of Planned Behavior (Ajzen, 1991), the Combined Theory of Planned Behavior and TAM (Riemenschneider, Harrison, & Mykytyn, 2003), the Model of PC Utilization (Thompson, Higgins, & Howell, 1991), the Social Cognitive Theory (SCT) (Bandura, 1986), and the Unified Theory of Acceptance and Use of Technology (Venkatesh et al., 2003), to name a few. Each of these theories provides their own unique contribution to the research stream. SCT, in particular, gives support for the interplay between a person's behavior and their environment – including sources of persuasion (Bandura, 1986, 1997). However, even with our current understanding of how IT may be introduced and ultimately diffused throughout an organization, effectively persuading end users to engage IT in a manner consistent with organizational expectations remains a difficult task.

Toward this challenge, the senior officials of a firm will establish goals and objectives for the proper use of IT within their organization (Straub & Welke, 1998). This is done as a means of controlling end user – IT interaction, thereby providing some assurance as to the outcome of the relationship. These goals and objectives are articulated in the form of policies and procedures within which elements of persuasive communications are present. Additionally, other communications between the policy makers and the user community serve to reinforce the goals and reaffirm the commitment of the users to the desires of the firm (Siponen, 2000; Siponen, Pahnila, & Mahmood, 2006). Persuasive communications play a key role in this dialogue.

One of five components that McGuire (1978) identifies as an essential element of persuasive communications, message source has been the focus of numerous studies among a wide variety of disciplines (Pornpitakpan, 2004). Source credibility has been the specific variable of interest among a number of these studies and has involved many different dimensions such as expertise and trustworthiness (Berlo & Lemert, 1961; O'Keefe, 1990; Pornpitakpan, 2004), physical attractiveness (Chaiken, 1979; Eagly & Chaiken, 1975), gender (Kenton, 1989), competency (Berlo & Lemert, 1961), and dynamism (Berlo & Lemert, 1961; Hewgill & Miller, 1965).

The prominent contention among scholars regarding source credibility is that a highly credible source will more effectively persuade an audience than a low credibility source (Friestad & Wright, 1994; Lirtzman & Shuv-Ami, 1986; Maddux & Rogers, 1980). When approached within the framework of persuasive communications, credible sources have been found to be more effective than non-credible sources in inducing favorable attitudes (Mugny, Tafani, Falomir, Juan, & Layat, 2000) and behavioral compliance (Crisci & Kassinove, 1973). Specifically, the perceived credibility of the source has been determined to be positively correlated with a message recipient's intentions to accept and apply recommendations as posited by the communicator (Suzuki, 1978; Bannister, 1986).

One frequently cited scale for measuring source credibility is the Leathers Source Credibility Scale (Leathers, 1992). Capturing the dimensions of competency, trustworthiness, and dynamism, the scale has proven reliable within a number of domains (Berlo & Lemert, 1961; Leathers, 1992; Powell & Wanzenried, 1995). Competence refers to the degree to which a communicator is perceived as competent of producing correct assertions, while trustworthiness refers to the degree to which a message recipient perceives those assertions as being valid (Hovland, Janis, & Kelly, 1953). Dynamism refers to the degree to which a message recipient "admires and identifies with the source's attractiveness, power or forcefulness, and energy" (Larson, 1992, p. 226). Each of these dimensions are cited as motivators for attitudinal change and, as such, serve to form the basis for explaining end user attitudes associated with recommended IT actions provided via organizationally-derived persuasive messages.

Figure 1. Conceptual model

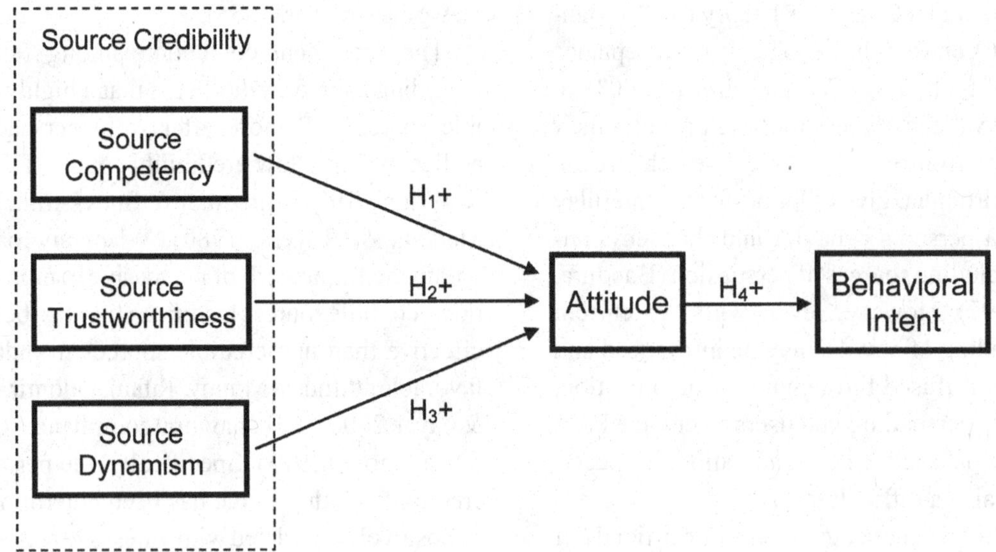

RESEARCH MODEL

Based on the three dimensions of source credibility as defined by Berlo and Lemert, (1961) and conceptualized within the Leathers Personal Source Credibility Scale (Leathers, 1992), a research model (Figure 1) is proposed that aligns attitude and behavioral intent as outcome variables for source competency, source trustworthiness, and source dynamism. The hypotheses related to each relationship are included in the model.

Source Competency

Competency is an important dimension of source credibility (Berlo & Lemert, 1961). Studies have found perceptions of a message source's competency to be positively associated with message acceptance (Hilibrand, 1964; Berlo, Lemert, & Mertz, 1969; Pornpitakpan, 2004). Consider, for example, a persuasive argument originating from the office of the Chief Information Officer (CIO) for an organization in which the end user is employed, and another coming from an Intern. The message could be instructions for the adoption and use of a particular development application, compliance with a particular IT policy or standard, or the use of a anti-malware software tool. As these are all technology-oriented tasks, a person with a higher ranking within the organizations is typically perceived as having earned the position through a history of competent behaviors. It is therefore expected that the CIO will be regarded as an authority by those end users within his or her organization. This trait should result in a more positive reception of the CIO's message. Alternatively, a message originating from an Intern is likely to be discarded based on perceptions of his or her lack of competence. To that end:

H_1: Perceptions of source competency will have a significant positive effect on an end user's attitude toward recommended IT actions.

Source Trustworthiness

A second dimension of source credibility, the trustworthiness of a persuasive argument's source is also expected to have a significant impact on an end user's attitude toward the message (Berlo

& Lemert, 1961). Hovland et al. (1953) describe trustworthiness as the degree to which a message recipient believes a communicator's message as being valid and that the message source is motivated to provide accurate information (Kelman & Hovland, 1953). These authors contend that highly trustworthy sources' arguments are more readily accepted than that of low trustworthy sources (Hovland & Weiss, 1951) and that the trustworthy sources are presumed to provide truthful message content. Priester and Petty (1995) suggest that messages from untrustworthy sources come under greater scrutiny than those from their trustworthy counterparts.

When we consider, for example, a message from an IT manager asking end users to perform a particular set of behaviors in order to secure their respective computers, the source of the message will be evaluated as to the degree to which they are perceived as being trustworthy and that the advice is not erroneous or a waste of time. It is therefore reasoned that:

H_2: Perceptions of source trustworthiness will have a significant positive effect on an end user's attitude toward recommended IT actions.

Source Dynamism

Perceptions of source dynamism refer to the degree to which a source is able to project an image of energy, power, forcefulness or attractiveness (Larson, 1992). Berlo and Lemert (1961), Berlo, Lemert, and Mertz (1969) and Whitehead (1968) were among the first to site this quality as a critical dimension of source credibility, and their contention was later confirmed by Applbaum and Anatol (1979). McEwen and Greenberg (1970) related the intensity of the communicated message to perceptions of dynamism – finding high intensity messages were more readily associated with highly dynamic sources. As such, it is expected that these qualities enable an advocate for certain IT activities to be more effective in terms of establishing favorable attitudes toward compliance with them. For example, a person delivering the message of anti-spyware software adoption and use will be more influential in his or her delivery if he or she is energetic, forceful and composed in the delivery. As such:

H_3: Perceptions of source dynamism will have a significant positive effect on an end user's attitude toward recommended IT actions.

The hypothesized relationship between attitude and behavioral intent as shown in the model as H_4, is derived from the Theory of Planned Behavior (Ajzen, 1988, 1991), in which attitude is determined to be a direct antecedent of behavioral intent. Prior research contends that attitudes are based on cognitive evaluations of the positives and negatives associated with the element of interest (Ajzen, 1988). Within the context of IT usage, these elements of interest concern the relationship between end users and computer technology or implementation practices (Melone, 1990). Further, previous research has demonstrated that an individual's attitude can have a significant impact on his or her computer usage behavior (Al-Gahtani & King, 1999; Fishbein & Ajzen, 1975; Igbaria, 1990; Igbaria & Chakrabarti, 1990; Robey, 1979). In fact, in tests of the Theory of Reasoned Action (Fishbein & Ajzen, 1975) and the Theory of Planned Behavior (Ajzen, 1985), attitude was found to be the strongest predictor of behavioral intent (Venkatesh et al., 2003), with intention serving as a "proximal determinant of behavior" (Smith et al., 2008, p. 315). When placed in the context of this study, the following hypothesis is formed:

H_4: Attitude will have a significant positive effect on an end user's behavioral intentions to comply with recommended IT actions.

METHODOLOGY

As a means for testing the influence of source credibility on attitude, leading to behavioral intent, the authors employed a two-stage research design. The first stage of this research involved the collection and analysis of data from 275 IT users at a large public university in the southeastern United States. Initially, 780 IT users were randomly selected from the general population of student, staff, and faculty IT users to participate in the study. The respondents were screened so as to ensure that they had some degree of autonomous control over their computer and its data. A total of 311 subjects agreed to participate and 275 produced usable data (35% response rate). Approximately 61% were male with 63% being from the College of Business. A majority (73%) was between the ages of 18 and 29, reflecting the sampling frame, which was largely drawn from computer-savvy student, staff, and faculty groups.

As clarified in the following section, a Solomon four-group research design (Campbell & Stanley, 1963) was implemented in which respondents were randomly assigned to four groups and exposed to treatment and survey conditions as necessitated by their group assignment. ANOVA results from this phase of the study were used to test for internal and external validity. The second stage of this research used structural equation modeling to empirically test the conceptual model and its associated hypotheses described in the previous section. Following a description of the instrument and video treatment utilized in the first phase of the study, each of the two stages is described in detail.

Instrument Development

Five variables and their respective dimensions were measured in this study - behavioral intent, attitude, and source credibility (competence, trustworthiness, and dynamism). The variables were measured using multi-item scales drawn from validated measures in IS acceptance and Social Psychology research, and were rearticulated to relate specifically to the context of a particular recommended IT action - anti-spyware software usage. Additionally, descriptive demographic questions including gender, experience with anti-spyware software, age, education, and department were included in the instrument and measured as categorical variables. Also included in this instrument were three screening questions used to identify those respondents that had a vested interest in the security of their computer facilities. The research instrument is presented in Appendix A.

The two dependent variables of interest in this study are attitude and behavioral intent. Attitude, while an independent variable for the determination of behavioral intent, is also a dependent variable that is explained by the dimensions of source credibility. Attitude represents a user's cognitive and affective disposition toward recommended IT actions – those actions in which the user is expected to interface with information technology (in this case anti-spyware technology). Behavioral intent represents a user's probability of complying with recommended IT actions. Within the broad context of IT, the recommended actions most often asked of end users involves the acceptance and use of a particular technology or the engagement in a particular set of activities involving technology. Within the more refined context of this study, the recommended action is the adoption and use of anti-spyware software. Table 1 provides definitions for each of the constructs involved in this study and does so within the context of anti-spyware software usage where appropriate.

In addition to demographic information, the survey instrument included semantic differential scale items used to measure source credibility. First established and validated by Berlo and Lemert's (1961) factor analytic research on source credibility, the scales were later tested as part of Leathers Personal Credibility Scale (Leathers, 1992) and include 12 items to conceptualize the three dimensions of competence, trustworthiness and dynamism. Chronbach's alpha results of the

Table 1. Variables of Interest

Variable	Definition
attitude	the inclination an end user possesses to react positively or negatively toward recommended IT actions to avert spyware
behavioral intent	the self-reported probability that an end user will engage in recommended IT actions to avert spyware
source credibility	the degree to which a message source is considered to be competent, trustworthy, and dynamic regarding a specific topic of communication
source competency	the degree to which a message source is perceived as being qualified, authoritative, or adequate
source trustworthiness	the degree to which a message source is perceived as being reliable or deserving of trust
source dynamism	the degree to which a message source is perceived as being able to project an image of energy, power, forcefulness or attractiveness

Leathers Personal Credibility Scale, as reported by Powell and Wanzenried (1995), range from 0.88 to 0.94 over four different testing periods. As such, these values indicate good reliability.

Scale items intended to measure attitude and behavioral intent were drawn from the work of Venkatesh et al. (2003) in their development of the Unified Theory of Acceptance and Use of Technology (UTAUT) model. Based on tests at three different time periods, Chronbach's alpha measures for attitude and behavioral intent were.84 and.92, respectively. These values also indicated good reliability.

Tests for convergent and discriminant validity were performed using Principle Components Analysis (PCA). Component loadings were examined to ensure that items loaded cleanly on those constructs to which they were intended to load, and did not cross-load on constructs to which they should not have loaded (Straub, Boudreau, & Gefen, 2004). Generally, convergent validity is demonstrated if the item loadings are in excess of.70 on their respective components, and if discriminant validity is demonstrated if the component loadings are less than.40 on unintended components (Gefen, Straub, & Boudreau, 2000). This was the case for all items except item 1 of the attitude scale. It was removed from analysis, and the PCA was repeated. As Table 2 depicts, the resultant outcome demonstrates good convergent and discriminant validity.

Reliability measures were also good for all variables. Also shown in Table 2, the standard coefficient of internal consistency, Chronbach's α, for constructs ranged from α =.961 for behavioral intent to α =.888 for attitude.

Treatment Development

A streaming video of a university IT official advocating the use of anti-spyware software was prepared. Within the video, the IT official recited a rehearsed, scripted message (Appendix B) which highlighted the dangers of spyware and advocated the use of anti-spyware software as an effective activity for its remediation. The streaming video was made available in the three most common formats, Real Player, QuickTime, and Windows Media Player, and in both high and low resolution.

Several studies point to the potentially conflicting relationship between source credibility and message credibility (Yalch & Elmore-Yalch, 1984; Wiener, LaForge, and Goolsby, 1990). This relationship is referred to as source-message incongruity and describes situations in which an individual's attitudes about a message influence

Table 2. Examination of convergent and discriminant validity

	Behavioral Intent (α =.961)	Attitude (α =.888)	Source Competency (α =.934)	Source Trustworthiness (α =.915)	Source Dynamism (α =.905)
BI1	**0.931**	0.010	0.080	0.012	0.022
BI2	**0.950**	0.045	0.006	0.087	0.046
BI3	**0.980**	0.011	0.130	0.054	0.020
AT2	0.045	**0.853**	0.036	0.033	0.162
AT3	0.002	**0.936**	0.042	0.013	0.094
AT4	0.074	**0.907**	0.080	0.040	0.059
AT5	0.000	**0.929**	0.057	0.028	0.079
SC1	0.036	0.103	**0.817**	0.265	0.264
SC2	0.015	0.087	**0.831**	0.181	0.300
SC3	0.108	0.060	**0.840**	0.351	0.208
SC4	0.137	0.017	**0.837**	0.314	0.162
ST1	0.092	0.088	0.191	**0.824**	0.170
ST2	0.011	0.014	0.266	**0.792**	0.141
ST3	0.019	0.096	0.184	**0.830**	0.214
ST4	0.004	0.057	0.212	**0.831**	0.186
ST5	0.087	0.020	0.183	**0.816**	0.178
SD1	0.025	0.075	0.099	0.264	**0.802**
SD2	0.037	0.100	0.321	0.184	**0.819**
SD3	0.049	0.171	0.252	0.216	**0.787**
SD4	0.061	0.123	0.229	0.189	**0.856**

BI = Behavioral Intent; AT = Attitude; SC = Source Competency; ST = Source Trustworthiness; SD = Source Dynamism

his/her perceptions of the message source. Wiener, LaForge, and Goolsby (1990), however, suggest that strong messages, messages that are informative, positive, and direct, lead subjects to focus on peripheral cues such as source credibility in forming their attitudes as opposed to focusing on the message itself. Given this knowledge, the message articulated within the video was subjected to a panel of experts in the field of marketing to gauge its ability to convey the appropriate message to end users regarding spyware amelioration through human computer interaction in a strong, direct, informative and positive manner. The expert panel consisted of 8 faculty and Ph.D. students in the area of Marketing. Upon review, the panel made suggestions for message clarity and content, which included the reordering of statements and intensifying the language used to describe the spyware threat.

Phase One

As a means for controlling for issues of internal and external validity, the first phase of this study involved a quasi-experimental Solomon four-group design (Campbell & Stanley, 1963) (see Figure 2). By controlling for internal and external validity, the researchers are assured of equivalence between groups and hold a high degree of confidence that the posttest observed measures are in fact caused by the message as opposed to issues of history, maturation effect, or

Figure 2. Solomon four-group design

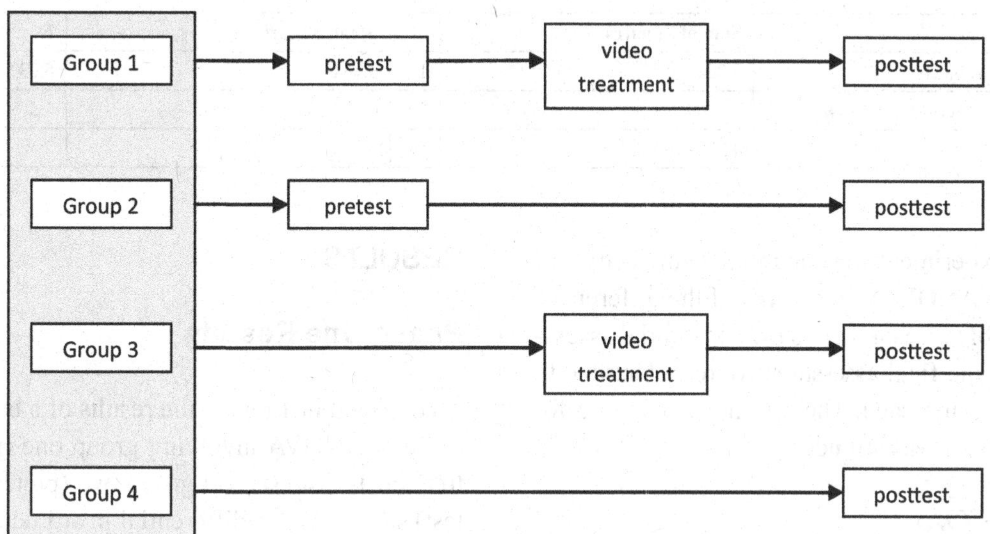

testing. Problems relating to history, maturation, and testing are addressed by the use of a control group that is not exposed to the video message. As long as participants are randomly assigned to groups 1 and 2, any impact by these contaminants is felt by both groups. Comparisons of differentials between the various groups would convey any interaction between the testing and stimulus while giving some assurance that the video message is in fact the root of changes in the outcome variables (Babbie, 2004).

This design required four groups of subjects to be randomly assigned from the general pool of end user participants. Approximately 780 end users from various colleges and departments within the University were contacted via email asking if they would be willing to voluntarily participate in a research project. Within the email was a link to a website that served as the medium for conducting this research. If a participant followed the link, the first screen he or she encountered on the website was an electronic consent form. If the participant elected to participate in the experiment by selecting the appropriate link on the consent form, the next screen viewed was dependent upon the experimental group to which he or she was randomly assigned. For this first phase of the research the participants were randomly assigned to four groups such that each group had an n of at least 30.

In addition to the collection of demographic information concerning age, experience, gender, and department, the experimental procedure involved a preliminary assessment of self-reported perceptions of attitude toward recommended IT actions to avert spyware. This pretest was conducted using two of the randomly assigned groups of participants, groups one and two. Only if the participant was randomly assigned to either of these groups would he or she have viewed a pretest instrument designed to measure attitude. Next, the video message was presented to groups one and three. Immediately following the video, these participants were asked to verify that they had in fact viewed the video. Those respondents that were unable to view the video were dismissed from the study. Finally, a posttest measure of attitude was taken of all groups, including a fourth group, group four, that had not been subjected to either the pretest or the treatment. The results

Table 3. Validity test: between-subjects ANOVA for groups one and two

	Sum of Squares	df	Mean Square	F	Sig.
Between-Subjects	3.384	1	3.384	5.037	.029
Within-Subjects	38.969	58	0.672		
Total	42.353	59			

of the experiment were analyzed using between-subjects ANOVA to determine if the differences in variable measurements from the initial assessment to the final assessment were in fact due to the video message. The dependent variable for the analysis was attitude.

Phase Two

The second phase of this research involved testing the conceptual model depicted in Figure 1 and its associated hypotheses. As the figure illustrates, attitude is positioned as a mediating variable between the dimensions of source credibility and behavioral intent. Results of these tests are provided in the following section. For this phase of the study, the initial sample of 30 respondents assigned to group 1 was augmented with an additional sample of 155 respondents, bringing the total n for group 1 to 185. The larger sample space was necessary so as to provide an adequate number of responses for structural equation modeling tests of the conceptual model. Accounting for those users that were either unable or unwilling to view the video and removing incomplete and careless responses for those that did complete the survey, the final number of valid responses for both phase one and phase two of the study was 275. This represents a 35% response rate.

RESULTS

Phase One Results

As depicted in Table 3, the results of a between-subjects ANOVA involving group one (pretest-treatment-posttest) and group two (pretest-posttest) suggested the differential in attitude was in fact caused by the application of the video message. The significance of.029 implied that, at a.05 level of significance, the difference in self-reported attitude between groups one and three was caused by the presence of the video treatment. A similar test involving group three (treatment-posttest) and group four (posttest) responses also indicated that the difference in attitude between the groups was caused by the presence of the video treatment (see Table 4).

To verify that the changes in attitude were not the result of testing conditions (use of a pretest), ANOVA tests were conducted with the same dependent variable attitude, but with the independent categorical variable, pretest (1=yes, 0=no). These tests were conducted using a random sample of 30 responses from group one (pretest-treatment-posttest) and 30 responses from group three (treatment-posttest). The results (see Table 5) confirmed that the group responses did not differ as a result of the pretest condition. A simi-

Table 4. Validity test: between-subjects ANOVA for groups three and four

	Sum of Squares	df	Mean Square	F	Sig.
Between-Subjects	2.166	1	2.166	5.093	.028
Within-Subjects	24.668	58	0.425		
Total	26.834	59			

Table 5. Validity test: between-subjects ANOVA for groups one and three

	Sum of Squares	df	Mean Square	F	Sig.
Between-Subjects	1.838	1	1.838	2.945	.091
Within-Subjects	36.188	58	0.624		
Total	38.025	59			

Table 6. Validity Test: Between-Subjects ANOVA for Groups Two and Four

	Sum of Squares	df	Mean Square	F	Sig.
Between-Subjects	0.523	1	0.523	1.181	.282
Within-Subjects	25.667	58	0.443		
Total	26.189	59			

lar test was performed involving 30 responses from group two (pretest-posttest) and group four (posttest). The results of this test, shown in Table 6, also confirmed that the pretest did not significantly impact the changes in attitude.

Based on these findings, it is clear that the outcome variable, attitude, was significantly altered due to the presence of a video message. Additionally, the application of a pretest did not significantly alter the posttest responses.

Phase Two Results

For phase two of the research design, a component-based technique for structural equation modeling, partial least squares (PLS), were used to test the conceptual model and its associated hypotheses. As indicated in Table 7 and as illustrated in Figure 3, the results of the analysis indicate the model is able to explain approximately 27% ($R^2 = 0.27$) of the variance in attitude and 41% of the variance in behavioral intent ($R^2 = 0.41$).

Further analysis reveals that each dimension of source credibility formed significant relationships with attitude (see Table 7). The relationship between source competency and attitude was significant at a 0.01 level of significance ($p < 0.01$), while the relationship between source trustworthiness and attitude and that of source dynamism and attitude were significant at a 0.05 level of significance ($p < 0.05$). The most influential predictor of attitude was source competency (β =.298), followed by source dynamism (β =.128) and source trustworthiness (β =.114).

In terms of hypotheses, the results indicate support for H_1, H_2, and H_3, meaning that each dimension of source credibility has a significant positive effect on an end user's attitude toward

Table 7. PLS analysis results of conceptual model test

Hypothesis (with direction)	Path Coefficient (β)	T-value	P-value	Supported?
H_1: Source Competency → Attitude	.298	6.009	$p < 0.01$	Supported
H_2: Source Trustworthiness → Attitude	.114	2.080	$p < 0.05$	Supported
H_3: Source Dynamism → Attitude	.128	3.055	$p < 0.05$	Supported
H_4: Attitude → Behavioral Intent	.641	8.765	$p < 0.01$	Supported

Figure 3. Conceptual model testing results

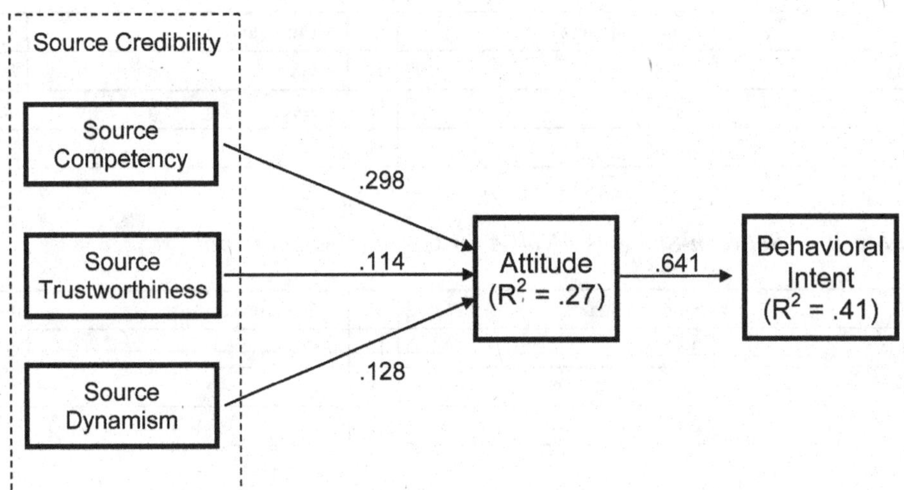

the recommended IT actions. Therefore, as an end user's perceptions of the competency, trustworthiness, and dynamism of the message source increase, so to does his or her attitude toward the recommended action. As for the relationship between attitude and behavioral intent, PLS analysis reveals a significant relationship ($p<.01$), thereby lending support for H_4.

Limitations

This study provides an initial examination of the role of source credibility in modifying attitudes and intentions to comply with recommended IT actions, and does so by means of a Solomon four-group research design. As with any research, however, there are a few limitations that should be addressed in future research activities.

While the trustworthiness of the source of a message is positioned as one of three dimensions of the Leathers Personal Credibility Scale (Leathers, 1992), the audience's propensity to trust others was not accounted for. Considered an antecedent of trust in dyadic and group relationships, trust is often characterized and measured as a perception an individual has in others as to their ability, integrity, and benevolence. Trust propensity is also an inherent characteristic of an individual, a quality that predicates the degree to which the individual will be influenced through trust-building exercises (Rotter, 1980). Although absent from this study, an individual's inclination to trust others should be included in future research regarding the effectiveness of messages involving recommended IT actions. No doubt, the ambiguity associated with appropriate technology usage plays a significant role in shaping the attitudes and intentions of individuals engaging in certain IT activities. If these individuals are not inclined to trust the sources that issue warnings or provide guidance, it is unlikely that they will value them highly.

Another limitation in this study is found in the organizational environment of the sample frame. While fulfilling the role desired by this study, that of end users having stake in the protection of computer technology, the faculty, staff, and students of a university operate in an environment unlike that found in the corporate world. University settings are inherently insecure (Warkentin & Johnston, 2006). As a result, the attitudes and behavioral intentions of the employees and students toward IT usage recommendations could be skewed to some degree by the "open" nature of university computing environments. While numerous previous studies concerning technology adoption and usage have involved higher education employees or students (Warkentin, Davis, & Bekkering, 2004; Aytes & Connolly, 2004), the use of this convenience sample represents a possible threat to the generalizability of the findings.

Finally, it should be mentioned that source credibility is a heavily researched and well-documented topic. This study focuses on those dimensions salient to the identification and measurement of perceptions of credibility appropriate to the context. To this end, dimensions such as source expertise, persistence, timing and message variables such as discrepancy and evidence were omitted from this investigation. While these aspects of credibility are important, parsimony of the conceptual model dictates their absence and provides an opportunity for future extensions of this research.

DISCUSSION AND CONCLUSION

Cumulatively, the findings of this research are consistent with the earlier works concerning persuasive communication and suggest that positive relationships between source credibility and attitudes and behavioral intent persist within the domain of IT acceptance and use. The credibility of the source of persuasive messages is important in that when exposed to persuasive messages in support of organizational policy, end users will draw upon their perceptions of the competence, trustworthiness, and dynamism of the message source. Specifically, messages distributed within an organization in support of acceptable and appropriate uses of computer technology should be conveyed by those leaders perceived as having a high degree of competency and trustworthiness, and should be delivered in a highly dynamic and engaging manner.

The results of this study give credence to the role of a "champion" within the organization, specifically alluding to the influence this person may have in motivating employees to engage in actions involving IT (Beath, 1991; Reich & Benbasat, 2000). Leaders can influence the actions of others when it comes to technology usage (Youngjin, 2006). For upper-level administrators, such as CIOs, the qualities they must possess should include an aptitude for developing and delivering effective statements and reminders for appropriate technology use. But, for these efforts to succeed, these leaders must be able to first engender a substantial level of trust and perceived competency among their subordinates. In doing so, the attitudes of IT users toward recommended technology procedures and actions will be favorable and the downstream effects of intent to proceed with IT activities will be positive as well. Beyond the top-level management, line IT personnel must also possess an ability to interact with end users in a manner that fosters trust and distinguishes them as competent sources of information. Future research should consider these various relationships and how message source credibility in influenced by the organizational role of the advocating source.

The finds of this research lend support to the idea that image and reputation are important characteristics that IT personnel, both high-level and otherwise, must strive to strengthen and protect. In terms of technology adoption and diffusion, IT personnel are leaders within the end user community. As this research demonstrates, for others to follow, the IT personnel must be conscience of the manner in which they lead. As long the communication between the IT personnel and the end users is formal, it is controllable in terms of how it leverages the elements of competency, trustworthiness, and dynamism. However, in an informal setting, communication is less thought-out and structured, thereby exposing the IT personnel to potential marks against these valued characteristics. Future research should be directed toward the temporal and structural aspects of communications and their impact on source credibility. This research charge is especially pertinent to IT environments in which many levels of personnel exist and many outlets and forms of communication are present.

The findings of this research also serve to underscore the idea that human-computer interaction is not just a technological phenomenon – it includes a social component in which the perception of humans regarding computer interaction may be manipulated by communications with credible sources. It is not enough that users simply understand the technology and are capable of competent behavior. Social interactions among peers, colleagues, administrators, and trusted others do influence end user attitudes and intentions for technology use, and attention must be given to the credibility of those in communicative roles.

REFERENCES

Agarwal, R., & Venkatesh, V. (2002). Assessing a firm's web presence: A heuristic evaluation procedure for the measurement of usability. *Information Systems Research, 13*(2), 168–186. doi:10.1287/isre.13.2.168.84

Ahuja, M. K., & Thatcher, J. B. (2005). Moving beyond intentions and toward the theory of trying: Effects of work environment and gender on post-adoption information technology use. *Management Information Systems Quarterly, 29*(3), 427–459.

Ajzen, I. (1985). From intentions to actions: A theory of planned behavior. In Kuhl, J., & Beckmann, J. (Eds.), *Action Control: From Cognition to Behavior*. New York: Springer Verlag.

Ajzen, I. (1988). Attitude structure and behavior relations. In Partkanis, A. R., Berckler, S. T., & Greenwald, A. G. (Eds.), *Attitude Structure and Function*. Hillsdale, NJ: Erlbaum.

Ajzen, I. (1991). The theory of planned behavior. *Organizational Behavior and Human Decision Processes, 50*(2), 179–211. doi:10.1016/0749-5978(91)90020-T

Al-Gahtani, S. S., & King, M. (1999). Attitudes, satisfaction and usage: Factors contributing to each in the acceptance of information technology. *Behaviour & Information Technology, 18*(4), 277–297. doi:10.1080/014492999119020

Applebaum, R. L., & Anatol, K. W. E. (1979). The relationships among job satisfaction, organizational norms, and communicational climate among employees in an academic organization. *Journal of Applied Communication Research, 7*(2), 83–90. doi:10.1080/00909887909365196

Aytes, K., & Connolly, T. (2004). Computer security and risky computing practices: A rational choice perspective. *Journal of Organizational and End User Computing, 16*(3), 22–40.

Babbie, E. (2004). *The practice of social research* (10th ed.). Belmont, CA: Wadsworth/Thomson Learning.

Bandura, A. (1977). Self-efficacy: Toward a unifying theory of behavioral change. *Psychological Review, 84*(2), 191–215. doi:10.1037/0033-295X.84.2.191

Bandura, A. (1986). *Social foundations of thought and action: A social cognitive theory*. Englewood Cliffs, NJ: Prentice Hall.

Bandura, A. (1997). *Self-efficacy: The exercise of control*. New York: W. H. Freeman.

Bannister, B. D. (1986). Performance outcome feedback and attributional feedback: Interactive effects on recipient responses. *The Journal of Applied Psychology, 71*, 203–210. doi:10.1037/0021-9010.71.2.203

Banville, C., & Landry, M. (1989). Can the field of MIS be disciplined? *Communications of the ACM, 32*(1), 48–60. doi:10.1145/63238.63241

Beath, C. M. (1991). Supporting the information technology champion. *Management Information Systems Quarterly*, *15*(3), 355–371. doi:10.2307/249647

Berlo, D. K., & Lemert, J. B. (1961, December). *An empirical test of a general construct of credibility.* Paper presented at the SAA Conference, New York, NY.

Berlo, D. K., Lemert, J. B., & Mertz, R. J. (1969). Dimensions for evaluating the acceptability of message sources. *Public Opinion Quarterly*, *33*(4), 563–576. doi:10.1086/267745

Cacioppo, J. T., & Petty, R. E. (1980). Persuasiveness of communication is affected by exposure frequency and message quality: A theoretical and empirical analysis of persisting attitude change. *Current Issues & Research in Advertising*, *3*(1), 97–122.

Cacioppo, J. T., & Petty, R. E. (1984). The elaboration likelihood model of persuasion. *Advances in Consumer Research. Association for Consumer Research (U. S.)*, *11*(1), 673–675.

Cacioppo, J. T., & Petty, R. E. (1989). Effects of message repetition on argument processing, recall, and persuasion. *Basic and Applied Social Psychology*, *10*(1), 3–12. doi:10.1207/s15324834basp1001_2

Campbell, D., & Stanley, J. (1963). *Experimental and quasi-experimental designs for research.* Chicago: Rand McNally.

Chaiken, S. (1979). Communicator physical attractiveness and persuasion. *Journal of Personality and Social Psychology*, *37*(8), 1387–1397. doi:10.1037/0022-3514.37.8.1387

Changchit, C. (2006). New information technology adoption: Are you ready for it? *Journal of Electronic Commerce in Organizations*, *4*(4), pi-iv.

Compeau, D., & Higgins, C. A. (1995b). Computer self-efficacy: Development of a measure and initial test. *Management Information Systems Quarterly*, *19*(2), 189–211. doi:10.2307/249688

Cramm, S. (2005). *The soft side of persuasion.* Retrieved February 15, 2006, from http://www.cio.com/research/leadership/edit/ec051705_persuasion.html

Crisci, R., & Kassinove, H. (1973). Effect of perceived expertise, strength of advice, and environmental setting on parental compliance. *The Journal of Social Psychology*, *89*, 245–250.

Davis, F. D. (1989). Perceived usefulness, perceived ease of use, and user acceptance of information technology. *Management Information Systems Quarterly*, *13*(3), 318–340. doi:10.2307/249008

Eagly, A. H., & Chaiken, S. (1975). An attribution analysis of the effect of communicator characteristics on opinion change: The case of communicator attractiveness. *Journal of Personality and Social Psychology*, *32*(1), 136–144. doi:10.1037/h0076850

Fishbein, M., & Ajzen, I. (1975). *Belief, attitude, intention and behavior*. Reading, MA: Addison-Wesley.

Foltz, C. B., Cronan, T. P., & Jones, T. W. (2005). Have you met your organization's computer usage policy? *Industrial Management & Data Systems*, *105*(2), 137–146. doi:10.1108/02635570510583280

Friestad, M., & Wright, P. (1994). The persuasion knowledge model: How people cope with persuasion attempts. *The Journal of Consumer Research*, *21*(1), 1–31. doi:10.1086/209380

Gefen, D., Straub, D., & Boudreau, M. (2000). Structural equation modeling techniques and regression: Guidelines for research practice. *Communications of AIS*, *7*(7), 1–78.

Hewgill, M. A., & Miller, G. (1965). Source credibility and response to fear-arousing communications. *Speech Monographs*, *32*(2), 95–101. doi:10.1080/03637756509375436

Hilibrand, M. (1964). *Source credibility and the persuasive process*. Unpublished doctoral dissertation, Harvard University, Cambridge, MA.

Hong, S., Thong, J. Y. L., & Tam, K. Y. (2006). Understanding continued information technology usage behavior: A comparison of three models in the context of mobile internet. *Decision Support Systems*, *42*(3), 1819–1834. doi:10.1016/j.dss.2006.03.009

Hovland, C., Janis, I. L., & Kelly, H. (1953). *Communication and persuasion*. New Haven, CT: Yale University Press.

Hovland, C., & Weiss, W. (1951). The influence of source credibility on communication effectiveness. *Public Opinion Quarterly*, *15*, 635–650. doi:10.1086/266350

Igbaria, M. (1990). End-user computing effectiveness: A structural equation model. *OMEGA International Journal of Management Science*, *18*(6), 637–652. doi:10.1016/0305-0483(90)90055-E

Igbaria, M., & Chakrabarti, A. (1990). Computer anxiety and attitudes towards microcomputer use. *Behaviour & Information Technology*, *9*, 229–241. doi:10.1080/01449299008924239

Johnston, A. C., & Hale, R. (2008). *Improved security through information security governance*. Communications of the ACM.

Jones, L. W., Sinclair, R. C., & Courneya, K. S. (2003). The effects of source credibility and message framing on exercise intentions, behaviors, and attitudes: An integration of the elaboration likelihood model and prospect theory. *Journal of Applied Social Psychology*, *33*(1), 179–196. doi:10.1111/j.1559-1816.2003.tb02078.x

Kelman, H. C., & Hovland, C. I. (1953). Reinstatement of the communicator in delayed measurement of opinion change. *Journal of Abnormal and Social Psychology*, *48*(3), 327–335. doi:10.1037/h0061861

Kenton, S. B. (1989). Speaker credibility in persuasive business communication: A model which explains gender differences. *Journal of Business Communication*, *26*(2), 143–157. doi:10.1177/002194368902600204

Larson, C. U. (1992). *Persuasion: Reception and responsibility* (6th ed.). Belmont, CA: Wadsworth Publishing Company.

Leathers, D. G. (1992). *Successful nonverbal communications: Principles and applications*. New York: Macmillan.

Lichtenstein, S., & Swatman, P. M. C. (1997). Internet acceptable usage policy for organizations. *Information Management & Computer Security*, *5*(5), 182–190. doi:10.1108/09685229710367726

Lirtzman, S. I., & Shuv-Ami, A. (1986). Credibility of source of communication on products' safety hazards. *Psychological Reports*, *58*, 707–718.

Maddux, J. E., & Rogers, R. W. (1980). Effects of source expertness, physical attractiveness, and supporting arguments on persuasion: A case of brains over beauty. *Journal of Personality and Social Psychology*, *39*, 235–244. doi:10.1037/0022-3514.39.2.235

Marakas, G. M., Yi, M. Y., & Johnson, R. D. (1998). The multilevel and multifaceted character of computer self-efficacy: Toward clarification of the construct and an integrative framework for research. *Information Systems Research*, *9*(2), 126–163. doi:10.1287/isre.9.2.126

McEwen, W. J., & Greenberg, B. S. (1970). The effects of message intensity on receiver evaluations of source, message and topic. *The Journal of Communication*, *20*(4), 340–350. doi:10.1111/j.1460-2466.1970.tb00892.x

McGuire, W. J. (1978). An information-processing model of advertising effectiveness. In Davis, H. L., & Silk, A. J. (Eds.), *Behavioral and management sciences in marketing* (pp. 156–180). New York: Wiley.

Melone, N. P. (1990). A theoretical assessment of the user satisfaction construct in information systems research. *Management Science*, *36*(1), 76–91. doi:10.1287/mnsc.36.1.76

Moore, G. C., & Benbasat, I. (1991). Development of an instrument to measure the perceptions of adopting an information technology innovation. *Information Systems Research*, *2*(3), 192–222. doi:10.1287/isre.2.3.192

Mugny, G., Tafani, E., Falomir, P., Juan, M., & Layat, C. (2000). Source credibility, social comparison, and social influence. *Revue Internationale de Psychologie Sociale*, *13*, 151–175.

O'Keefe, D. J. (1990). *Persuasion: Theory and research.* Newbury Park, CA: Sage.

Peterson, R. (2004). Crafting information technology governance. *Information Systems Management*, *21*(4), 7–22. doi:10.1201/1078/44705.21.4.20040901/84183.2

Petty, R. E., & Cacioppo, J. T. (1984). Source factors and the elaboration likelihood model of persuasion. *Advances in Consumer Research. Association for Consumer Research (U. S.)*, *11*(1), 668–672.

Pornpitakpan, C. (2004). The persuasiveness of source credibility: A critical review of five decade's evidence. *Journal of Applied Social Psychology*, *34*(2), 243–281. doi:10.1111/j.1559-1816.2004.tb02547.x

Powell, F. C., & Wanzenried, J. W. (1995). Do current measures of dimensions of source credibility produce stable outcomes in replicated tests? *Perceptual and Motor Skills*, *81*(2), 675–687.

Priester, J. R., & Petty, R. E. (1995). Source attributions and persuasion: Perceived honesty as a determinant of message scrutiny. *Personality and Social Psychology Bulletin*, *21*(6), 637–654. doi:10.1177/0146167295216010

Reich, B. H., & Benbasat, I. (2000). Factors that influence the social dimension of alignment between business and information technology objectives. *Management Information Systems Quarterly*, *24*(1), 81–113. doi:10.2307/3250980

Riemenschneider, C. K., Harrison, D. A., & Mykytyn, P. P. (2003). Understanding it adoption decisions in small business: Integrating current theories. *Information & Management*, *40*(4), 269–285. doi:10.1016/S0378-7206(02)00010-1

Robey, D. (1979). User attitudes and management information systems use. *Academy of Management*, *22*(3), 527–538. doi:10.2307/255742

Rotter, J. B. (1980). Interpersonal trust, trustworthiness, and gullibility. *The American Psychologist*, *35*(1), 1–7. doi:10.1037/0003-066X.35.1.1

Sambamurthy, V., & Zmud, R. W. (1999). Arrangements for information technology governance: A theory of multiple contingencies. *Management Information Systems Quarterly*, *23*(2), 261–290. doi:10.2307/249754

Schaumburg, H. (2001). Computers as tools or as social actors? The users' perspective on anthropomorphic agents. *International Journal of Cooperative Information Systems*, *10*(1-2), 217–234. doi:10.1142/S0218843001000321

Siponen, M., Pahnila, S., & Mahmood, A. (2006, November). Factors influencing protection motivation and IS security policy compliance. *Innovations in Information Technology*, 1.

Siponen, M. T. (2000). A conceptual foundation for organizational information security awareness. *Information Management & Computer Security*, *8*(1), 31–41. doi:10.1108/09685220010371394

Smith, J. R., Terry, D. J., Manstead, A. S., Louis, W. R., & Wolfs, D. K. J. (2008). The attitude-behavior relationship in consumer conduct: The role of norms, past behavior, and self-identity. *The Journal of Social Psychology*, *148*(3), 311–333. doi:10.3200/SOCP.148.3.311-334

Straub, D. W., Boudreau, M. C., & Gefen, D. (2004). Validation guidelines for IS positivist research. *Communications of AIS*, *13*, 380–427.

Straub, D. W., & Welke, R. J. (1998). Coping with systems risk: Security planning models for management decision making. *Management Information Systems Quarterly*, *22*(4), 441–469. doi:10.2307/249551

Suzuki, K. (1978). Acceptance and rejection of a suggestion. *The Japanese Psychological Research*, *20*, 60–70.

Thompson, R., Compeau, D., & Higgins, C. (2006). Intentions to use information technologies: An integrative model. *Journal of Organizational and End User Computing*, *18*(3), 25–46.

Thompson, R. L., Higgins, C. A., & Howell, J. M. (1991). Personal computing: Toward a conceptual model of utilization. *Management Information Systems Quarterly*, *15*(1), 125–143. doi:10.2307/249443

Venkatesh, V., & Davis, F. D. (2000). A theoretical extension of the technology acceptance model: Four longitudinal field studies. *Management Science*, *46*(2), 186–204. doi:10.1287/mnsc.46.2.186.11926

Venkatesh, V., Morris, M. G., Davis, G. B., & Davis, F. D. (2003). User acceptance of information technology: Toward a unified view. *Management Information Systems Quarterly*, *27*(3), 425–478.

Warkentin, M., Davis, K., & Bekkering, E. (2004). Introducing the Check-Off Password System (COPS): An advancement in user authentication methods and information security. *Journal of Organizational and End User Computing*, *16*(3), 41–58.

Warkentin, M., & Johnston, A. C. (2006). IT security governance and centralized security controls. In Warkentin, M., & Vaughn, R. (Eds.), *Enterprise Information Assurance and System Security: Managerial and Technical Issues* (pp. 16–24). Hershey, PA: IGI Global.

Warkentin, M., & Johnston, A. C. (2008). IT governance and organizational design for security management. In Baskerville, R., Goodman, S., & Straub, D. W. (Eds.), *Information Security Policies and Practices*. Armonk, NY: M. E. Sharpe.

Whitehead, J. L. Jr. (1968). Factors of source credibility. *The Quarterly Journal of Speech*, *54*, 59–63. doi:10.1080/00335636809382870

Wiener, J. L., LaForge, R. W., & Goolsby, J. R. (1990, May). Personal communication in marketing: An examination of self-interest contingency relationships. *JMR, Journal of Marketing Research*, *27*, 227–231. doi:10.2307/3172849

Wittaker, J. O., & Meade, R. D. (1968). Retention of opinion change as a function of differential source credibility. *International Journal of Psychology*, *3*, 103–108. doi:10.1080/00207596808247232

Witte, K. (1992). Putting the fear back into fear appeals: The extended parallel process model. *Communication Monographs*, *59*, 329–349. doi:10.1080/03637759209376276

Yalch, R. F., & Elmore-Yalch, R.. The effect of numbers on the route to persuasion. *The Journal of Consumer Research*, *11*, 522–527. doi:10.1086/208988

Youngjin, K. (2006). Supporting distributed groups with group support systems: A study of the effects of group leaders and communication modes on group performance. *Journal of Organizational and End User Computing*, *18*(2), 20–37.

APPENDIX A

Section 1: General Purpose

Think about your usage and maintenance responsibilities for a specific computer system. Please select a single score from 1 to 5 where, 1 – means you **Strongly Disagree** with the statement, and 5 – means you **Strongly Agree** with the statement (Table 8).

Section 2: Spyware Threat Concerns (administered to all groups)

The following statements concern spyware and spyware protection. Anti-spyware use refers to installing, running, updating, and/or configuring the software. Please select a single score from 1 to 5 where, 1 – means you **Strongly Disagree** with the statement, and 5 – means you **Strongly Agree** with the statement (Table 9).

Section 3: Message Feedback (not administered to groups 2 and 4, as these groups were not exposed to the video treatment)

Please indicate with a check mark in the appropriate box the term that best captures your beliefs concerning the *competence* of the IT Official (Table 10).

Please indicate with a check mark in the appropriate box the term that best captures your beliefs concerning the *trustworthiness* of the IT Official (Table 11).

Please indicate with a check mark in the appropriate box the term that best captures your beliefs concerning the *dynamism* of the IT Official (Table 12).

Section 4: Demographic Information (administered to all groups) (Table 13)

The demographic information in this section will only be used in aggregate form and will not be used to identify individual respondents. Please select only one item in each category. Experience refers to your experience using anti-spyware software. Department refers to the department in which you are employed or are enrolled as a student.

Thank you for participating in this study.

Table 8.

	Strongly Disagree (1)		Neutral (3)		Strongly Agree (5)
I maintain important data on a specific computer	[]	[]	[]	[]	[]
I am responsible for the detection, prevention and/or removal of spyware from that computer.	[]	[]	[]	[]	[]
I am concerned for the security of the data on that computer	[]	[]	[]	[]	[]

Table 9.

	Strongly Disagree (1)		Neutral (3)		Strongly Agree (5)
Behavioral Intent (1-3) – Venkatesh et al., 2003	[]	[]	[]	[]	[]
I intend to use the anti-spyware software in the next 3 months	[]	[]	[]	[]	[]
I predict I will use anti-spyware software in the next 3 months	[]	[]	[]	[]	[]
I plan to use anti-spyware software in the next 3 months	[]	[]	[]	[]	[]
Attitude (4-8) – Venkatesh et al., 2003					
Using the anti-spyware is a good idea	[]	[]	[]	[]	[]
Anti-spyware software makes work more interesting	[]	[]	[]	[]	[]
Working with anti-spyware is fun	[]	[]	[]	[]	[]
I like working with anti-spyware software	[]	[]	[]	[]	[]
Working with anti-spyware software is enjoyable	[]	[]	[]	[]	[]

Table 10.

Neutral								
9. Experienced	___	___	___	___	___	___	___	Inexperienced
10. Expert	___	___	___	___	___	___	___	Ignorant
11. Trained	___	___	___	___	___	___	___	Untrained
12. Competent	___	___	___	___	___	___	___	Incompetent

Table 11.

Neutral								
13. Just	___	___	___	___	___	___	___	Unjust
14. Kind	___	___	___	___	___	___	___	Cruel
15. Admiral	___	___	___	___	___	___	___	Contemptible
16. Honest	___	___	___	___	___	___	___	Dishonest
17. Fair	___	___	___	___	___	___	___	Unfair

Table 12.

Neutral								
18. Aggressive	___	___	___	___	___	___	___	Meek
19. Bold	___	___	___	___	___	___	___	Timid
20. Energetic	___	___	___	___	___	___	___	Tired
21. Extroverted	___	___	___	___	___	___	___	Introverted

Table 13.

Gender	[] male	Experience	[] < 6 months	Age	[] 18 to 29
	[] female		[] 6-12 months		[] 30 to 39
			[] > 1 year to 2 years		[] 40 to 49
			[] > 2 years to 3 years		[] 50 to 59
			[] > 3 years		[] 60 and over
Education	[] high school	Department	[] COBI		
	[] some college		[] CVM		
	[] bachelor's degree		[] ITS		
	[] master's degree		[] CE		
	[] doctorate		[] other		
	[] other				

APPENDIX B

From the ITS

Re: Spyware

Date: July 1, 2006

Currently, 91% of all home PCs are infected with some kind of spyware. Spyware is a form of software that can install itself on computer systems with or without the consent of the computer's operator. Even anti-virus software, such as Norton Anti-virus, is useless in stopping a spyware attack. The effects of spyware may be disastrous, as some form of it may lead to fraud or identity theft.

Anti-spyware software provides a proven method for protecting against spyware. This software works automatically to detect and remove existing installations of spyware and to proactively guard against future intrusions. The software is easy to install and most come with an intuitive interface that provides a clear and consistent method for fine tuning the performance of the software to match the desires of the user.

It is recommended that all faculty, staff, and students of the University take the appropriate steps to obtain and install anti-spyware software. Freeware copies of the software are available on the University's ITS web site.

This work was previously published in Journal of Organizational and End User Computing, Volume 22, Issue 3, edited by M. Adam Mahmood, pp. 1-21, copyright 2010 by IGI Publishing (an imprint of IGI Global).

Chapter 16
Organizing End-User Training:
A Case Study of an E-Bank and its Elderly Customers

Harri Oinas-Kukkonen
University of Oulu, Finland

Sari Hohtari
Kemi-Tornio University of Applied Sciences, Finland

Samuli Pekkola
Tampere University of Technology, Finland

ABSTRACT

Introducing information systems into organizations initiates a change in human behaviors, which is often perceived as obtrusive and distracting. End-user training may help manage this challenge by getting the users familiar with the system and its functionality. However, end-user training is not easy, nor self-evident, as shown in this paper. This is problematic, particularly when organization-wide standards for how to provide training are missing or when the group of end-users is two-layered, that is, both the customers and the staff must be trained. In this paper, the authors describe a qualitative case study of how the end-user training on an e-Bank was organized, and how the training was delivered to its elderly customers. The training model by Simonsen and Sein (2004) is utilized and extended to cover the systems development cycle. The authors argue that an approach that integrates the end-user training with the systems development improves organizational implementation. As a result, this paper makes practical suggestions about the issues related to organizing end-user training.

INTRODUCTION

Information systems development is often an outcome of an organizational change that is initiated by rapid advances in technology, widening markets or development of the organization's operations (Truex et al., 1999). In responding to market challenges, attention must be paid to factors related to both the organizational functions and user behavior. One success factor for organizational implementation is the support and advice provided upon the introduction of a change.[1] In the information system (IS) context, this may take place in the form of *user training*, which has been

DOI: 10.4018/978-1-4666-0140-6.ch016

identified as one of the fundamental elements for successful adoption of a new system (Davis & Olson, 1985). Providing training in connection with an organizational change ensures that an organization will be capable of functioning in a new manner. New ways of acting and using information systems need to be learned. User training becomes critical in particular when dealing with the resistance towards new systems (Piderit, 2000).

This is certainly the case with electronic services, which companies and organizations have started to offer more and more. Recently, companies and organizations have started to offer more and more electronic services. There are even banks that operate entirely electronically. Mattila (2001), for one, identified that typical e-bank users are currently well-educated, middle-aged persons with high income. However, as banking services are offered to a growing extent to other groups of customers as well, the potential user groups are becoming more and more diverse. This heterogeneity of users becomes a challenge in requirements elicitation and systems configuration (Tuunanen, 2005; Chiasson & Green, 2007). Furthermore, it is quite likely that those who are not well-equipped to conduct business through the Internet may encounter difficulties. It is an important issue to study to what extent services are truly provided for everyone regardless of age and computing skills.

Oinas-Kukkonen and Hakala (2006) and Oinas-Kukkonen and Mantila (2009) suggest that paying the bills is the most important use of Internet by the elderly, even more important than Web browsing or emailing. Karjaluoto (2002) states that customer advisory services occupy a key position in increasing the popularity of e-banking, while Mattila et al. (2003) suggest that the training of end-users is the major deficit in e-banking. All this emphasizes the need for studying this phenomenon in more detail. However, although several e-banking studies have been undertaken from a number of viewpoints, relatively little attention has been paid to user training at the introduction stage of the system. The significance of such training may be examined from the organizational viewpoint as a part of adopting a new information system into use (Lucas et al., 1990; Smithson & Hirchheim, 1998). As learning new ways of working with an information system depends upon mastery of the system itself, systematic, well-organized user training becomes highly relevant.

This paper provides a qualitative case study on how end-user training has been organized in a bank. In addition to traditional services, the bank also offers its customers electronic services such as checking the balance on/via the Internet and paying bills. These activities, the simplest and the most common actions of a bank, may become difficult if the user group is not technically advanced – as is often the case with elderly customers. In this paper we focus on training and how it has been planned and implemented in connection with e-banking services, and how elderly users have been taken into account. To do this, we will expand and test the framework by Simonsen and Sein (2004) with a process model covering the development phases of e-banking as well.

The paper is structured as follows. The related research on end-user training is summarized. The process model that is developed and adapted for our study is introduced. The case organization and research methods is also described. The phases preceding the actual end-user training are discussed, and the actual end-user training phase is examined.

RELATED RESEARCH AND TRAINING MODELS

Training attempts to ensure that users are capable of using a new information system and acting in the new situation (Eason, 1998). Training also motivates them to use the system (Eason, 1998) provided there is continuity of training until the users have a sufficient degree of familiarity with it. The instructions used in training should be aimed at those coming into contact with the system, i.e., its principal users, other interested parties who benefit from the system, and those engaged in operating and maintaining it. Instructions also need to be provided for those responsible for training others as they need a solid basic knowledge of the system. According to Sahay and Robey (1996), technical support and user clubs may become important for successful adoption, the latter being a useful form of peer support after the adoption phase.

User's beliefs and attitudes belong to key constructs to study IS usage. They may change as users gain first-hand experience (Bhattacherjee & Premkumar, 2004). Thatcher and Perrewé (2002) discuss the role of individual differences in computer self-efficacy, suggesting that information technology (IT) managers should design training programs that more effectively increase the computer self-efficacy of end-users with different dispositional characteristics. An observational learning model for computer software training and skill acquisition has been developed (Yi & Davis, 2003), and the importance of system users' motivations and commitment has been emphasized (Malhotra & Galletta, 2006). These are all in line with Gupta and Bostrom (2006), who pointed out the need for approaching training from both IS and education viewpoints.

End-user training is related to technology acceptance (for technology acceptance model, see Davis, 1989; Venkatesh et al., 2003). End-user training aims at lowering the threshold for use of the systems, so that those systems are accepted. This is particularly relevant in situations in which technologies are used voluntarily. In e-banking, for instance, the same basic services can be obtained both from the bank desk and through the Internet. It can be assumed that if one exploits e-banking, one has already accepted the technology – at least to some extent.

IT-aided learning has gained a lot of interest recently. Although Zhang et al. (2004) have questioned whether e-learning really could replace the traditional classroom setting; there are several studies that argue for the efficiency of IT-aided learning (c.f., Alavi et al., 1995; Alavi et al., 2002). The main problem with e-learning remains poor pedagogies, unattractive and non-compelling learning materials, lack of personal teaching and tools to evaluate the learning outcomes, limited interactions with fellow students and teachers, and usability issues (Wahlstedt et al., 2008; Zhang et al., 2004). However, there are several benefits, such as 24/7 access to the learning material, that may outnumber the cons (c.f., Zhang et al., 2004).

Nelson et al. (1995) noted that a systematic approach for organizing user training is needed. This entails greater awareness of different phases of the learning process, beginning with a survey of the training needs. This will be followed by defining the aims for the training and describing the user groups to be trained. After this, the steps within each task will have to be defined, along with the subject matter of the training, i.e. content. The topics selected will then have to be analyzed in such a manner that they can be taught step-by-step, yielding a detailed plan of the content and implementation of the training. The training should not be planned and implemented in isolation from the organization's other activities but in collaboration with the system designers and project managers, as it will be more effective if all stakeholders participate in planning both development and training. Training should also be arranged systematically and on an ongoing basis, allowing for different personalities and preferences (Bostrom et al., 1990).

Compeau et al. (1995) put forward a three-phase training model. The process begins with a survey of training needs and continues with the development of a method, planning and designing of the training environment and selection of the persons to be trained. After the training takes place, it is evaluated, support services for users are arranged, and the training plans undergo appropriate adjustments. The whole process will be greatly affected by the characteristics of the people to be trained, the software involved, the tasks of the trainers and the organization itself. These factors should already be taken into consideration at the planning stage. Mahapatra and Lai (2005) further point out that users rarely access the training material after the system implementation. In fact, the greatest challenges for large organizations are related to the planning and implementation of user training (Niederman & Webster, 1998). Niederman and Webster (1998) consequently suggest that the Compeau et al. (1995) model is highly useful although its phases and steps will have to be modified according to the characteristics of particular information technologies.

Simonsen and Sein (2004) provide another interesting observation. In their evaluation of the user training strategy adopted by one organization, the organization was obliged to invest in training in order to preserve its competitive position. Under such conditions, a uniform, comprehensive strategy is required as a basis for efficient training. This should be a part of the organization's overall strategy, as user training is one of the critical factors for the functioning of an organization.

THEORETICAL END-USER TRAINING MODEL

For the purposes of our study, we construct an integrated end-user training (EUT) process model. In order to cope with the change introduced by the implementation of an IS into organization, we extend the Simonsen and Sein (2004) training model to cover also the phases of the information systems development (ISD) cycle. We did this for two reasons that were pointed out earlier. First, training is an inseparable part of organizational change and implementation. Thus, it needs to be planned concurrently with the planning of organizational implementation of an IS. Second, understanding the systems requirements requires realistic feedback from its actual users. That feedback cannot be obtained without the system first being introduced in the organization. In other words, the training needs to begin concurrently with the requirements elicitation. Both of these reasons reinforce the need for merging the planning of EUT and the planning and development of IS.

ISD Model

Information systems development is usually perceived to range from systems analysis and design (requirements elicitation, systems design), to systems development (technical implementation) and its testing. These phases and their activities are well defined in ISD literature (e.g., Avison & Fitzgerald, 2003; Fitzgerald et al., 2003).

Simonsen and Sein Model

Simonsen and Sein validated and further developed the Olfman et al. (2003) training model. It comprises four phases: a survey of training needs, definition of the responsibility for training, definition of the content of the training, and evaluation. Each phase has several components, ranging from the assessment of training needs and the designs of training organization and training materials to the training of different groups of users and the process of its evaluation. Altogether, similarly to ISD process, the phases are quite straightforward. We shall discuss this in more detail in the next section.

Integrated End-User Training Model

The Simonsen and Sein model does not consider the phases preceding the organizational implementation phase. Rather, it focuses solely on the organizational implementation. However, as argued earlier, such an approach is not suitable – in fact both Olfman et al. (2003) and Simonsen and Sein (2004) identified several weaknesses of their models. Under these circumstances, we extend this model so that testing proceeds and converges as a spiral through the IS development phases. Figure 1 illustrates the integration of the EUT and ISD

Figure 1. Integration of the EUT process and ISD process

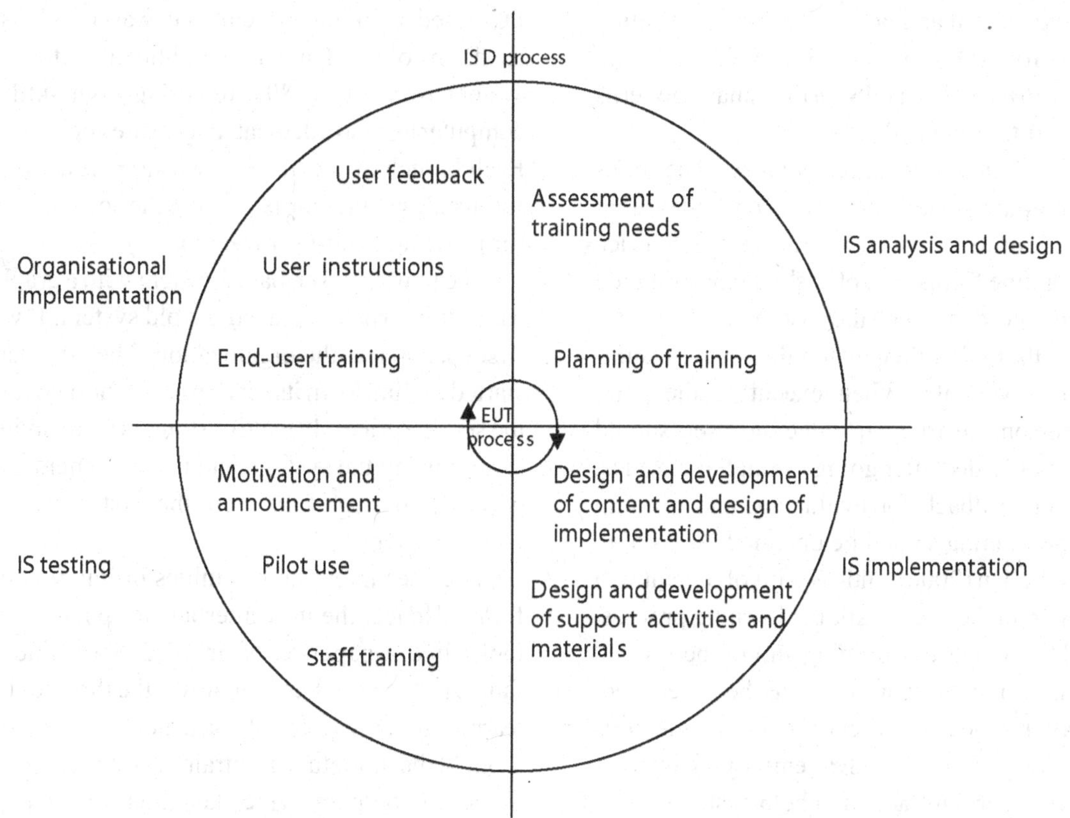

processes. The ISD phases can be found outside of the circle, whereas the EUT phases can be found inside of the circle. In practice, this means that some phases of EUT are started already with IS design and analysis.

The relationship between ISD and EUT varies according to the ISD phases:

1. *IS analysis and design.* The process begins with the assessment of training needs and planning of user training as an integral part of defining systems requirements. The requirements definition schemes enable the system to be outlined at a level that allows an analysis of the training needs of future users, e.g., by means of questionnaires or interviews in connection with the definition of system requirements.
2. *IS implementation.* More detailed IS design refines the training plan. This allows training aims, content, and implementation to be considered. The design process is governed by the IS implementation phase. Support activities, such as telephone advisory services and supporting material, should be planned and designed accordingly.
3. *IS testing.* Before the actual user training, staff training may be arranged, focusing on pedagogical, cognitive, and technical skills. The end-user training begins with a pilot study of an appropriately selected group of users. This enables adjustments before the actual training begins. Motivating end-users and the timing of training need to be carefully considered. The most suitable timing seems to be very shortly before adopting the system

as the window of opportunity for end-user enthusiasm and/or making changes is quite narrow (Orlikowski, 1992; Pekkola et al., 2006). Again, the IS testing phase governs staff training and pilot use.

4. *Organizational implementation.* The training plan should address current e-learning platforms, such as Internet and e-Service training forms. The plan should be designed in accordance with the customers' computer skills so that they match the level of training available. When executing the plan, personal instruction for the end-users should be provided after going through the basics, and feedback for evaluating and refining the training should be obtained. According to Yellen (2006), end-user involvement will help in the organizational learning process. The actual user training should be refined until a saturation point has been reached, after which self-directed end-user methods may be defined, such as employing interactive user interfaces and help systems.

RESEARCH SETTINGS

The target organization of this study/research is a Scandinavian banking concern. The bank operates commercially in three sectors: (1) retail banking, (2) business and corporate clients, and (3) asset management and life assurance. It offers a variety of services to its customers, who range from private persons and companies to private and public-sector organizations. Although the bank has an extensive network of outlets, it has made an active effort to develop e-banking services, such as paying bills or checking balances through the internet. The designing of the services began in the 1980s. The investigated system was brought into use in the late 1990s. Even though the system had 4.2 million Internet users in the summer of 2005, it was still continuously developed at the time of writing.

The e-Bank system was built on top of the old PC-based banking system that was previously used. The old system was a traditional text-based system from the 1980s, requiring high skill in computer use and a dedicated software application. Each branch office had its own support advisors for installing and implementing the software and for providing end-user training.

The new browser-based system with a graphical user interface replaced the old system. It was first used inside the organization. Then the bank started to slim down its service personnel and raise the service prices. Private customers were invited to start using the system, and the customers with good computing skills were the first to use the e-bank system.

The user interface resembles ordinary paper forms. Hence, the user interface for paying bills looks like a paper-based invoice. This kind of familiarity was believed to lower the threshold of learning the new system. In fact, the bank originally thought that no actual user training was necessary. Thus, no company-wide standards, practices or instructions were published.

During 2003 and 2004, the bank was improving its cost-effectiveness by adjusting the service personnel and the prices. The main strategy was to get more and more customers to use the e-bank. Although 57.5% of the bank's customers had used e-banking services during the preceding three months, there was one group of customers with marginal use of e-banking. This was elderly customers (above 55 years of age). Only 29.1% of those had used e-banking services. Consequently, from this group the portion of users was expected to increase rapidly. The branch offices started to develop their own strategies to approach the customers. They informed them through the branch Web sites and/or by personal letters, and focused their training activities according to the customers' needs. They also stopped using the local support advisors.

Yet, it was soon evident that focusing training merely on customers, i.e. the end-users, was not

Table 1. Interviewees and their backgrounds

Interviewee	*Age*	*Title*
D1	40-50	CIO
D2	40-50	System designer
D3	30-40	System designer
PT1	30-40	Service manager
PT2	40-50	Service manager
S1	50-60	Customer service advisor
S2	50-60	Customer service advisor
S3	30-40	Customer service advisor
S4	50-60	Customer service advisor
S5	50-60	Customer service advisor
S6	40-50	Customer service advisor
S7	30-40	Customer service advisor
PS1	50-60	Public sector representative, adult education manager
PS2	40-50	Public sector representative, lecturer in adult education

enough. People providing training for the customers needed to be trained as well. Thus, there were really two groups of end-users: 'customers' (elderly end-users), and customer service advisors (the staff of the bank).

Data Collection and Analysis

The data for the study was gathered though qualitative theme interviews. The questions were derived according to our model, and tested by local service personnel and management before actual interviews. The questions were then revised and modified so that there were different questions for different groups. Additional questions were asked when needed. The questionnaire can be found in Appendix 1.

The interviewees were chosen according to their areas of expertise. Initially, eight people were interviewed, covering the planning and implementation stages of our model. Three of those represented systems design, two planning and pilot testing for the training, and three were trainers from the local level (one in a managerial position, and two from customer service personnel). During the interviews, several new issues emerged, so that the number of interviewees was increased. Four people from two other geographical areas and two representatives of a public sector training organization were also interviewed to see whether the findings are generalizable. Table 1 describes the interviewees and their backgrounds.

The interviews were conducted during the summer and autumn of 2004. Each interviewee was first contacted by telephone to be informed about the purpose and content of the study and to schedule a telephone interview. During the systems development stages, the questions were sent and returned by email, after which a more detailed telephone interview was conducted. The local training personnel were interviewed as a group. The local training interviewees were given the topics beforehand via e-mail, after which the group interview was held on the organization's premises during working hours. Eventually, the number of interviewees totaled 14.

Data analysis was conducted by following the principles of grounded theory (Urquhart, 2001). In other words, we went through the interviews several times in order to identify central themes.

The process continued until theoretical saturation of the data was considered achieved. Then the findings were compared to the literature to ensure the validity of study.

Reflections from Practice to EUT Model: IS Analysis and Design

In the IS analysis and design phase, no detailed *training plan* was produced for the whole organization. Instead only some rough guidelines for personnel and customer training were set. While the bank personnel's *training needs* were defined through a survey, no customers were involved. This forced each branch office to develop local, more detailed plans.

Reflections from Practice to EUT Model: IS Implementation

There had been no *organization-wide plans* for how training should be organized. Consequently, neither the content nor its implementation was clearly defined but user training was taking place without any systematic attention to its content or practical implementation. Training practices had simply evolved over time locally.

Local call support centers provided user support for both staff and customers. In addition, various manuals, written locally, were used to support the training. For example, manuals in a branch office comprised a 17-page booklet for Internet training, an 8-page 'instant guide,' short guidebooks, a Power Point presentation, and help pages in the e-banking Web site. The guidebooks provided brief instructions for signing in and paying bills, while Power Point presentations basically described the main functions of the e-bank. As each branch had their own manuals, the need for short standardized booklets became evident as they would help in minimizing multiple versions and making the most important information more easily available.

The help tool in the e-banking Web site contained user instructions in a textual but unprintable form. These instructions did not refer to the system interface directly but provided mere general information. For instance, the guidelines for paying a bill were: "To pay a bill, use the function Payment/New Payment." None of the support materials provided information on what to do in the case of an error or problem. Similarly, the guidelines for information security were incomplete, with one exception, namely Internet training.

Reflections from Practice to EUT Model: IS Testing

Along with the new system, new user groups emerged. In the past, the main user group was the bank clerks. As the range of banking services expanded, traditional activities were replaced by sales activities and customer advisory services. As the sales are often based on personal contacts, involving the assessment of customer's needs and the identification of services that correspond with those needs, the requirements for training also changed:

S4: If you ask me, the whole matter is very simple: The staff has not had enough training in using the systems, nor teaching or guiding others.[2]

User training relied on the staff's personal interest and earlier experiences with the systems. This strategy stems from the experiences of using previous information systems in the bank. Initially, local computer experts acted as links towards the central organization. Over the years this practice had been abandoned. Local commercial transaction experts, well informed on both the systems and their training, had substituted them. These experts provided training for the rest of the staff on a hierarchical principle, i.e., the person attending training was expected to teach others. These sessions were arranged irregularly, forcing the employees to rely on each other instead.

Each branch office was in charge of organizing customer service training. Although the processes slightly differed, they shared a number of features. Each branch office had their own trainers using guidelines from the Intranet and their own slides. These guidelines contained details on the latest changes, on which they might affect, and answers to frequently asked questions. No other training was provided. Hints and instructions from meetings and training days were the only help to market e-banking services and to guide the customers with their questions on e-banking.

P2: I hold the courses. Each branch office names a person who is responsible for additional teaching (the personal part). As the number of courses has increased it was decided that no one person (myself) could be circulating between the branch offices. Instead it was necessary for the local areas to develop their local expertise by ensuring that there is always someone capable to run such courses. Also, all members in my sales group have now run these courses, first teaching small parts and then in situations in which two of them were jointly responsible for an entire course. The shortage of resources is a problem, and it is true that some branches have found it difficult to find people to attend the courses.

The shortage of resources had other problems as well. New employees had to learn their work practices by doing them and the system by using it. The staff became familiar with the system only after a lengthy period of independent study and/or use.

S7: I moved here from another banking group about a year ago and found myself on customer service straight away. At first, I had a mentor who introduced the main systems. Then I was left on my own. The mentor came every now and then to ask me how it was going on, but couldn't be there all the time. They believed that as I had done this work before in another bank, I would be able to do it here as well. The systems were quite different, however. It is quite possible to learn that way, of course, but it took a year before I could manage everything smoothly. It would have been better if there had been a computer where I could have practiced with the systems and under guidance.

All systems were subject to *pilot testing*. Although it was not formally organized training was not arranged for the staff, the e-bank was introduced to them. The staff was able to experiment with it relatively freely. It was believed that as they learned to use it in a routine manner and solved any problems, they would also be able to advise and guide the customers in system use. Some of these pilot testing periods had been very long, up to 18 months. This may have increased the staff's involvement, the amount of feedback gathered and received, and the number of defects detected. To some extent, these also affected the content of the guidelines and manuals.

The changes were published to customers as press releases. Notifications were announced through the e-banking system, on open Web pages, in the organization's customer magazine, or by some other means. Handouts, brochures and guidebooks also were used when necessary. These sources of information supported the customer services staff as well. However, the staff requested more detailed information about the changes to ensure their competence to advise the customers and to market the services.

Reflections from Practice to EUT Model: Organizational Implementation and End-User Training

Organizational implementation and the adoption into use by customers are relatively similar

Table 2. The implementation of end-user training at three branch offices

	Branch office 1	*Branch office 2*	*Branch office 3*
Instructor of e-banking training	Financial transactions expert	Bank's customer service advisors	Local polytechnic students
Instructor of Internet training	Local college teacher	None	None (the issues addressed at the e-banking course)
Content of training	Principles of the Internet, e-mail, e-banking services	Paying of bills, investments, value-added services	Internet, e-banking
Material used in training	Material from the bank's pilot projects, bank's Intranet and printed material	Material produced in house	Material designed by the students
Implementation	Small groups or personal tuition at bank branches	Public lecture with video display + 20-30 min personal tuition arranged separately	Public lecture + personal practice afterwards with demo ID's
Duration and timing	4h, mostly in the evenings, some courses at midday	1.5h (each part 30 min)	4h, in the evenings

processes. At the time of the study, there was polemic by the general audience regarding high bank charges. The branch offices had thus been encouraged to provide extensive user training. That was typically either training of basic *Internet use* or more focused training of *e-Banking*. Nevertheless, as the branch offices acted independently, the implementation of training varied considerably, as illustrated in Table 2. Yet, the training was still somewhat similar at different branch offices.

At first, a few dozens of end-users participated in the training sessions at each branch office. The participants were chosen according to their age group and interests for training. Both Branch office 1 and 3 offered more generic training on internet use, while Branch office 2 had difficulties in co-operating with the local Internet firms and educational institutions leading the bank to arrange only courses concentrating on e-Banking.

Branch office 1 sent invitations to a course in e-Banking by post, asking preregistration. The courses generated a great interest. They were targeted to the bank's local club for the elderly (aged 55-65 years) and held on the bank's premises on three evenings. The instructors were the local bank manager and the leader of the club, who used a laptop computer and a video display. The training consisted of two parts: a general introduction to e-Banking and different kinds of services, and some practical exercises, e.g. paying bills. At the beginning, a short summary of how to use personal identification numbers, an 'instant guide' to e-Banking, and a guide to the bank's telephone services were given. Then the participants walked through the e-Bank by using the material, computer, and telephone paying a fictitious bill and asking the balance of an account. After this, personal guidance was given, allowing the participants to use the services by using either their own codes or a demonstration code. Each course was intended to last for 1.5 hours, but they went up to 3 hours according to the participants' needs.

End-User Training

The aim of the organization was *"to increase the use of Internet services and the proportion of its transactions" (D1)*. Consequently, informing the customers about the new possibilities and maintaining and increasing customer satisfaction and loyalty were considered very important. The bank wanted to appear as an organization bearing responsibility for its elderly members. Customers who had not learned to use computers at their work were perceived as particularly important as there was a fear of alienating them from the information society.

S1: Training is important for society. It can help the elderly to stay in touch with developments. Learning something new may improve their self-confidence.

All this set the motivation for the training of using the e-Bank. Because the target users were elderly, the customer service advisors were anxious to point out their particular needs -- for instance, that more time should be devoted to guiding the elderly, teaching should proceed more slowly, and things should be explained more thoroughly. In addition, the target end-users were often found to face difficulties with the basic use of the computer. For instance, scroll bars and double-clicking the mouse caused troubles. Furthermore, different services and technologies require different approaches to teaching. For example, with the telephone it is quite easy to check the balance, but it was much more difficult to pay a bill. All this emphasizes teachers' physical proximity with the students, clear articulation, repetitiveness, a user interface with large icons and instructions with large, clear pictures, and unobtrusiveness, making it difficult to organize training over distances.

As the initial training was provided for only a small segment of "early adopters," the larger customer base with even fewer computer skills remained outside of the training. Reaching them was predicted to be particularly challenging:

S3: How can I begin to teach someone who doesn't know how to use the machine? Using a mouse, using a computer – we don't have the time to teach things like that. Should we in the bank be expected to teach the basics of computer use?

Such teaching was anyhow provided upon request. In those situations the training would start with Internet use, possibly implemented by local colleges, before proceeding to e-Banking.

The way to organize the training courses was important. A course needs to be arranged so that customers are able to study in the company of people of their own age, have their own computer terminal, and that the instructor acknowledges the role of age for learning. It was expected that the staff relied on their own experience when advising elderly and treated them as peers in systems use. For example, in the study the customer service advisors were an average of 54 years of age. They consequently belonged to more or less the same age group as their customers. Also, in order to answer the questions and solve problems more quickly, the involvement of two instructors in teaching and advising the participants was regarded as important. Under these circumstances, they were capable of developing more personal relationships with the customers.

S3: Customers got to know the instructors better at the personal advice stage and formed a relationship with them. This made it easier to ask for advice later. When they came to the bank they would chat about things that had happened recently and incidentally ask for advice.

Bank transactions were regarded as a very personal matter, potentially increasing the threshold to participate in large-scale training sessions. Yet, the elderly do not often have the courage to make investments or other transactions online without guidance.

S1: The elderly are reluctant to practice at home. They are afraid that if something goes wrong the money will disappear from their account.

This finding, with the fact that at the time there were more ATM users or inactive users than active e-Bank users, encouraged the bank to *train people to use value-added services*, not just perform basic transactions. Nevertheless, in addition to value-added services, it was considered important to remind users that there were still multiple ways of making the payments, and that earlier ways would not disappear.

P1: The same thing is true here as with many other new things: after the first rush of pioneers there is a lull before the other customers awaken to the possibilities, and a short time passes again before they are ready to adopt the service in question or approve the product. Our modern banking services offer many ways of carrying out everyday transactions. It may be nice to call in at the bank sometimes, but on another day one might not have the time or energy, and then it's useful if one has learned to use alternative services early enough.

However, if an elderly customer is interested in the e-Bank, it is advisable that the bank *first assesses the customer's situation and only then sets out to market its services* (from this basis). For well-motivated users who are familiar with computer use, the bank can then suggest its electronic services.

S1: Customers can be motivated towards using e-Banking facilities by presenting these as a privilege which they have earned. Good arguments may include keeping up with the times, accessing other services and privileges, and the role of computers as a means of communication. One can also refer to local circumstances in some cases, such as the sparse network of branch offices in [remote places of the country], or the long distance from the nearest bank. Bank transactions over the phone can be made virtually anywhere.

Posters, advertisements, and articles, among others, targeted to the elderly played an important role in *motivating customers* and in shaping their attitudes. Nearly every issue of the bank magazine over the preceding four years (that is, since the first training course) had articles and/or direct reports on Internet or e-Bank courses. These articles were mostly down-to-earth stories, often written by elderly users themselves. Online services were utilized to offer information on taxation, for an instance, to the customers.

User Instructions and Feedback

The same booklets as for staff training were utilized for the *users' personal guidance sessions,* taking place at a branch office. For example, if a customer asked about the bill payment option, the service advisor would show how to do it by using one of the bank's terminals. Sometimes, for a pre-booked e-Bank training session, the customer service advisers used their own computers and demonstration codes. After this, real transactions would be made through a customer terminal by using the real personal ID.

S5: I provide instruction for customers who have booked a time in advance in my own room and the customer service advisors use terminals intended for customer use. I presume this is common practice at all branches.

The inclusion of *customer training in ordinary advisory work* was thought to be problematic as the elderly users were reluctant to ask for help or advice if there were long queues in the bank. Local offices were thus publicizing training courses. *Non-stop training and advice without a prior booking* might be feasible during certain periods, such as for a week or for a month. The other opportunity is to appoint one service person to be responsible for training, accepting bookings in advance.

S3: Financial matters are very personal things for elderly people, and one barrier to asking for advice and guidance is the location of the customer terminal in an open banking hall where everyone can see and hear what is going on. It is difficult to give advice in such a situation.

In addition to the personal nature of bank transactions, the quote also points out the importance of *convenient location of customer service terminals*. The area should be sufficiently large, and there should be table space on both sides for books and papers. The space should also protect privacy.

Similarly to customer service advisors, the customers were able to give *feedback* about the system through the Internet or through the phone. However, this feedback and statistics about the organized training were collected infrequently. Although the bank claimed they had used user feedback and training experiences for improving the e-Banking and its content, such information was not collected or documented systematically.

D2: Reports on user training were received on different areas, and the telephone support service for both customers and staff kept a note of all contacts and FAQs. There were dozens of staff calls and e-mails every day, as well as a large number of questions regarding the Internet bank in the customer feedback.

DISCUSSION

In this paper we have emphasized the need for end-user training throughout system development and introduction into its use, as opposed to Simonsen and Sein (2004) and Compeau et al. (1995). Organizations should consequently pay attention to end-user training already at the systems analysis and design phase. This becomes crucial if the end-users' direct involvement is difficult during the systems development (c.f., Tuunanen, 2005). Furthermore, an assumption that routine use and ability to solve basic usage-related problems make it possible to advise and guide the customers without any specific training, is usually incorrect as seen in the case.

The case clearly demonstrated that the training provided by the organization for its elderly customers was not sufficient for them to cope with electronic banking and services independently. This finding is not novel (c.f., Bostrom et al., 1990), although general ignorance of similar findings before make it worth repeating. It also seems to be that there were great differences between different branch offices in customer training. This may be explained by the strong role of local managers in planning the training, indicating the lack of systematic approach on organizational level (c.f., Nelson et al., 1995). Nevertheless, because the banks operate on a national and international scale, they should consider whether to strive for greater uniformity in their customer training.

The most common training method focused on personal guidance, lasting about 20 minutes per person and involving the payment of some bills. Yet, as the customer service advisers expressed, the training of end-users during an ordinary working day was considered problematic due to very limited resources. An alternative was an "e-Banking school" where instructions were given to small customer groups at a time. If customers are inadequately prepared in computer basics, training in e-Banking may be difficult or even impossible. This suggests that it would be worthwhile for banks to promote Internet training in conjunction with local adult education institutions, for instance, to allow them to concentrate on tailored training in e-Banking. If this kind of collaboration is established, it may be a source of goodwill and good publicity for the bank.

The extended end-user training model emphasizes the broadening of user-training from mere introduction into use to cover the whole systems development lifecycle. The best practices identified by Simonsen and Sein (2004), Nelson et al. (1995) and Bostrom et al. (1990) are still relevant, although they should now be considered to cover also the systems analysis and design phases. This study found that organization-wide training strategy and training-need evaluation were incompletely implemented. This caused problems for introduction into use. Thus, Simonsen and Sein (2004) findings need to be extended to a process model covering the whole systems development lifecycle. This way the end-users are encouraged/trained to live with the new system from its very beginning. Their motivation and commitment are increased when both systems development and educational issues are considered in training (Gupta & Bostrom, 2006).

The key steps for the planning of end-user training may be summarized as:

1. Build a strategy for user training for the whole organization as well its customers throughout the system development life cycle.
2. Make clear plans for training with respect to both content and implementation, covering all user groups.
3. Develop material for both basic Internet use and the electronic service use. If the user group is heterogeneous, consider the differences between user groups.
4. Provide training for customer service advisors to ensure an adequate skill level.
5. Provide Internet training for customers with poor computer skills.
6. Provide electronic service training as a continuation to Internet training for those with proper basic skills. With more skilled customers, learning may be directed towards more advanced transactions.
7. Collect end-user feedback in order to improve training and electronic services.

The role of customer service advisors was found crucial for supporting elderly users, even if the staff felt that they did not receive enough training. Instead, they had to learn the system mainly by themselves. Support materials did help them greatly in their daily work. Quite understandably, helping the elderly users was perceived as challenging. Without well-motivated and committed staff, the system would have been much more difficult, if not impossible, to take into use.

LIMITATIONS AND FUTURE RESEARCH

As in any case study, this study suffers from the relatively low generalizability. As we have studied only one bank, and three of its branch offices, the critique is certainly legitimate. However, we argue the findings are still valuable and at least to some extent generalizable. This is because of several reasons. First, organizing end-user training in situations where there are two levels of users, customer service advisors and customers, is by no means atypical. Second, the findings are not limited to banks or other financial institutions as the EUT model is not related to the line of business. Third, the three different branch offices were quite different from each other although they also had several commonalities. Consequently, adding new offices would not have added many new findings. Fourth, elderly customers are just one group of users. Although they had some special demands, those bear no implications to the training process. Consequently, the process model for training can be used for other user groups as well.

However, these issues point to the need for future research. As the case study only presents a set of findings on how the end-user training was organized, it needs to be validated by a larger set of empirical studies ranging from banks to other organizations operating nationally and internationally. Other practices also need to be mapped against it. Third, there is a need to provide even more detailed instructions for organizing the training. Those details can be obtained from other studies.

SUMMARY AND CONCLUSION

This paper extended and tested the EUT process model by Simonsen and Sein (2004). The training should be integrated with the different phases of systems development, and actual training should take place as part of organizational implementation. In general, developing end-user training processes on a continuous base should be a natural way of working for organizations.

There are several implications for both research and practice. First, there is a need for deeper understanding of the interrelationship between training and ISD. Our work provides a basis to further studies. Second, end-user training has gained relatively little attention in IS literature. With the fast pace of development of different services and technologies, and the broadening of their target user groups, there is evidently more need to understand the relationships between users, developers and technologies (c.f., Iivari et al., in press), also from the training point of view. For practitioners, the training process model provides a basis for planning how end-user training should be organized. Our findings from the bank and its elderly customers may help practitioners also in other sectors and for other groups of users.

In conclusion, previous models of end-user training have become inadequate in the current era of modern information technology. Our proposed process model covering the ISD phases may provide more proper results in organizing the end-user training. However, further studies are needed to confirm this claim. In addition, the notion of two kinds of end-users, in our case customer service advisors and elderly customers, underlines the need for a new training model and in-depth studies about the role of training and the ways to organize it. We believe this work lays a foundation for further work on this research stream.

REFERENCES

Alavi, M., Marakas, G. M., & Yoo, Y. (2002). A comparative study of distributed learning environments on learning outcomes. *Information Systems Research, 13*(4), 404–415. doi:10.1287/isre.13.4.404.72

Alavi, M., Wheeler, B. C., & Valacich, J. (1995). Using IT to reengineer business education: An exploratory investigation of collaborative telelearning. *Management Information Systems Quarterly, 19*(3), 293–312. doi:10.2307/249597

Alter, S., & Ginzberg, M. (1978). Managing uncertainty in MIS implementation. *Sloan Management Review, 20*(1), 23–31.

Avison, D., & Fitzgerald, G. (2003). *Information systems development: Methodologies, techniques and tools* (2nd ed.). New York: McGraw Hill.

Bhattarcherjee, A., & Premkumar, G. (2004). Understanding changes in belief and attitude toward information technology usage: A theoretical model and longitudinal test. *Management Information Systems Quarterly, 28*(2), 229–254.

Bostrom, R. P., Olfman, L., & Sein, M. K. (1990). The importance of learning style in end-user training. *Management Information Systems Quarterly, 14*(1), 101–119. doi:10.2307/249313

Chiasson, M. W., & Green, L. W. (2007). Questioning the IT artefact: User practices that can, could, and cannot be supported in packaged-software designs. *European Journal of Information Systems, 16*(5), 542–554. doi:10.1057/palgrave.ejis.3000701

Compeau, D., Olfman, L., Sein, M., & Webster, J. (1995). End-user training and learning. *Communications of the ACM, 38*(7), 24–26. doi:10.1145/213859.214791

Davis, F. D. (1989). Perceived ease of use, and user acceptance of information technology. *Management Information Systems Quarterly, 13*(3), 319–340. doi:10.2307/249008

Davis, G. B., & Olson, M. H. (1985). *Management information systems: Conceptual foundations, structure and development*. New York: McGraw-Hill.

Dickie, J. (2006). Invest in CRM beyond applications. *Customer Relationship Management, 10*(9), 20.

Eason, K. (1988). *Information technology and organisational change*. London: Taylor & Francis.

Fitzgerald, B., Russo, N. L., & Stolterman, E. (2003). *Information systems development: Methods in action*. New York: McGraw Hill.

Gupta, S., & Bostrom, R. P. (2006, April 13-15). End-user training methods: what we know, need to know. In *Proceedings of the 2006 ACM SIGMIS CPR Conference on Computer Personnel Research*, Claremont, CA (pp. 172-182). New York: ACM Press.

Iivari, J., Isomäki, H., & Pekkola, S. (in press). User – the great unknown of systems development: Reasons, forms, challenges, experiences and intellectual contributions of user involvement. *Information Systems Journal*.

Karjaluoto, H. (2002). *Electronic banking in Finland: Consumer beliefs, attitudes, intentions, and behaviors*. Unpublished doctoral dissertation, University of Jyväskylä, Finland.

Lucas, H. C. Jr, Ginzberg, M. J., & Schultz, R. L. (1990). *Information systems implementation: testing a structural model*. Norwood, NJ: Ablex Publishing Corporation.

Mahapatra, R., & Lai, V. (2005). Evaluating end-user training programs. *Communications of the ACM, 48*(1), 66–70. doi:10.1145/1039539.1039540

Malhotra, Y., & Galletta, D. F. (2004). Building systems that users want to use. *Communications of the ACM, 47*(12), 89–94. doi:10.1145/1035134.1035139

Mattila, M. (2001). *Essays on customers in the dawn of interactive banking*. Unpublished doctoral dissertation, University of Jyväskylä, Finland.

Mattila, M., Karjaluoto, H., & Pento, T. (2003). Internet banking adoption among mature customers: Early majority or laggards? *Journal of Services Marketing, 17*(5), 514–528. doi:10.1108/08876040310486294

Nelson, R. R., Whitner, E. M., & Philcox, H. H. (1995). The assessment of end-user training needs. *Communications of the ACM, 38*(7), 27–38. doi:10.1145/213859.214793

Niederman, F., & Webster, J. (1998). Trends in end-user training: A research agenda. In *Proceedings of the 1998 ACM SIGCPR Conference on Computer Personnel Research*, Boston (pp. 224-232).

Oinas-Kukkonen, H., & Hakala, K. (2006). Internet services for the underprivileged: Computer courses for the elderly and unemployed at a residents' meeting room. In *Proceedings of the IFIP International Federation for Information Processing*, Boston (Vol. 226, pp. 324-336). New York: Springer.

Oinas-Kukkonen, H., & Mantila, L. (2009, March 12-14). Lisa, Lisa, the machine says I have performed an illegal action. Should I tell the police…? A survey and observations of inexperienced elderly Internet users. In *Proceedings of the Southern Association for Information Systems Conference*, Charleston, SC (pp. 146-151).

Olfman, L., Bostrom, R. P., & Sein, M. K. (2003, April). A best-practice based model of information technology learning strategy formulation. In *Proceedings of the ACM SIGMIS CPR Conference on Computer Personnel Research*, Philadelphia (pp. 75-86).

Orlikowski, W. J. (1992). Learning from Notes: Organizational issues in groupware implementation. In *Proceedings of the Computer-Supported Cooperative Work Conference (CSCW '92)* (pp. 362-369). New York: ACM Press.

Pekkola, S., Kaarilahti, N., & Pohjola, P. (2006, August 1-5). Towards formalised end-user participation in information systems development process: Bridging the gap between participatory design and ISD methodologies. In *Proceedings of the Participatory Design Conference (PDC '2006)*, Trento, Italy (pp. 21-30). New York: ACM Press.

Piderit, S. K. (2000). Rethinking resistance and recognising ambivalence: A multidimensional view of attitudes towards an organisational change. *Academy of Management Review*, *25*(4), 783–794. doi:10.2307/259206

Sahay, S., & Robey, D. (1996). Organizational context, social interpretation, and the implementation and consequences of geographic information systems. *Accounting. Management & Information Technology*, *6*(4), 255–282. doi:10.1016/S0959-8022(96)90016-8

Simonsen, M., & Sein, M. K. (2004, April 22-24). Conceptual frameworks in practice: Evaluating end- user training strategy in an organization. In *Proceedings of the ACM SIGMIS CPR Conference on Computer Personnel Research*, Tucson, AZ (pp. 14-24).

Smithson, S., & Hirshheim, R. (1998). Analyzing information systems evaluation: Another look at an old problem. *European Journal of Information Systems*, *7*(3), 158–174. doi:10.1057/palgrave.ejis.3000304

Thatcher, J. B., & Perrewé, P. L. (2002). An empirical examination of individual traits as antecedents to computer anxiety and computer self-efficacy. *Management Information Systems Quarterly*, *26*(4), 381–396. doi:10.2307/4132314

Truex, D. P., Baskerville, R., & Klein, H. (1999). Growing systems in emergent organisations. *Communications of the ACM*, *42*(8), 117–123. doi:10.1145/310930.310984

Tuunanen, T. (2005). *Requirements elicitation for wide audience end-users*. Unpublished doctoral dissertation, Helsinki School of Economics, Finland.

Urquhart, C. (2001). An Encounter with Grounded Theory: Tackling the Practical and Philosophical Issues. In Trauth, E. (Ed.), *Qualitative Research in Information Systems: Issues and Trends* (pp. 104–140). Hershey, PA: IGI Global.

Venkatesh, V., Morris, M., Davis, G. B., & Davis, F. D. (2003). User acceptance of information technology: Toward a unified view. *Management Information Systems Quarterly*, *27*(3), 425–478.

Wahlstedt, A., Pekkola, S., & Niemelä, M. (2008). From e-learning space to e-learning place. *British Journal of Educational Technology*, *39*(6), 1020–1030. doi:10.1111/j.1467-8535.2008.00821_1.x

Yellen, R. E. (2006). A new look at learning for the organization. *Information & Management*, *19*(3), 20–23.

Yi, M. Y., & Davis, F. M. (2003). Developing and validating an observational learning model of computer software training and skill acquisition. *Information Systems Research*, *14*(2), 146–169. doi:10.1287/isre.14.2.146.16016

Zhang, D., Zhao, J. L., Zhou, L., & Nunamaker, J. F. (2004). Can e-learning replace classroom learning? *Communications of the ACM*, *47*(5), 75–79. doi:10.1145/986213.986216

ENDNOTES

1. According to Alter and Ginzberg (1978) not all the challenges of introducing an information system into use can be recognized in

advance, but the probability of a successful introduction can be greatly enhanced by analysing potential problems and planning alternative strategies for tackling them.

[2] The letters indicate the subject groups being interviewed (D=development, PT=pilot testing, S=service personnel and management, PS=public service representative).

APPENDIX 1. INTERVIEW QUESTIONS

Development staff:

- Have you made a plan for end-user training during software design process?
- In what phase of software design process did you start planning the end-user training? Who made the plan? Did the plan include the training material and user instructions? Have you used pedagogical specialists for the planning of training?
- What kind of a plan do you have? Do you have company-wide standards, practices or instructions? How have you paid attention to different groups of users?
- Have you provided user training for your personnel? When and how did you put the training into practice? What kind of material have you used during this training?
- Do you have company-wide instructions for end-users? What kind of a material the personnel had to use in the end-user training?
- Did you make any pilot tests (training, materials etc.)?

Service personnel and management:

- Who is in charge of the end-user training in your office? Have you provided end-user training for your own staff?
- Did you get trained about the e-bank?
- Did you get trained to teach the end-users?
- What kind of a material do you have to teach the end-users? Are the instructions company-wide or local?
- How did you inform the customers about the e-bank and the end-user training?

This work was previously published in Journal of Organizational and End User Computing, Volume 22, Issue 4, edited by M. Adam Mahmood, pp. 95-112, copyright 2010 by IGI Publishing (an imprint of IGI Global).

Chapter 17
A Path Analysis of the Impact of Application-Specific Perceptions of Computer Self-Efficacy and Anxiety on Technology Acceptance

Bassam Hasan
The University of Toledo, USA

Mesbah U. Ahmed
The University of Toledo, USA

ABSTRACT

Perceptions of computer self-efficacy (CSE) and computer anxiety are valuable predictors of various computer-related behaviors, including acceptance and utilization of information systems (IS). Although both factors are purported to have general and application-specific components, little research has focused on the application or system-specific component, especially in IS acceptance contexts. Thus, little is known about the effects of application-specific beliefs on IS acceptance or how such effects compare with the effects of more general CSE and computer anxiety beliefs. Accordingly, a research model comprising application CSE, application anxiety, perceived ease of use, perceived usefulness, attitude, and intention was proposed and tested via path analysis. The results demonstrated that the direct impacts of application CSE and application anxiety on perceived ease of use and perceived usefulness were almost equal, but in opposite directions. However, the indirect effect of application CSE on attitude and intention was stronger than that of application anxiety.

DOI: 10.4018/978-1-4666-0140-6.ch017

INTRODUCTION

Much research aimed at understanding factors contributing to or hindering acceptance and utilization of information systems (IS) has accumulated over the past three decades. Among the myriad of the examined variables, computer self-efficacy (CSE) (Compeau et al., 1999; Hu et al., 2003) and computer anxiety (Brown et al., 2004; Igbaria & Chakrabarti, 1990; Venkatesh, 2000) have been found to be valuable predictors of users' acceptance and utilization of various computer systems. However, while CSE (Johnson, 2005; Marakas, Yi, & Johnson, 1998) and computer anxiety (Brown et al., 2004) are hypothesized to have general (application-independent) and more specific (application-dependent) components, this distinction has not been adequately addressed in past research. Thus, the effects of application-specific CSE and anxiety on IS acceptance remain vague and poorly understood and it is unknown whether such effects differ from the effects of the more general and broader constructs of CSE and computer anxiety. Therefore, this study aims to fill this void and provide better understanding of the impact of CSE and computer anxiety at the application level on users' decision to accept and use an IS.

The distinction between general and application-specific computer beliefs is vital for several reasons. First, beliefs at the general level (e.g., CSE and anxiety) represent trait-oriented beliefs that are difficult to change, whereas beliefs at the application level are considered state-oriented and treatable beliefs. Second, this distinction is more consistent with the theoretical basis of the two constructs. Social cognitive theory (SCT) suggests that self-efficacy is a malleable construct that operates at a general and task-specific level (Bandura, 1986; Gist, 1987) and, similarly, the theory of reasoned action (TRA) (Ajzen, 1991) posits that the prediction of a behavior can be greatly improved when the antecedents and the behavior are associated with the same task or object. Finally, the differentiation allows assessments of such beliefs to exclude evaluations of cross-domain efficacies and anxieties that may facilitate or hinder successful performance of a behavior (Marakas et al., 1998). Moreover, reviews of IS acceptance studies indicate that the mixed results reported in the literature can be attributed to the lack of task specifity when evaluating IS acceptance and suggest that more attention should be given to specific tasks and applications in studying IS acceptance (e.g., Lee, Kozar, & Larsen, 2003).

Based on the aforementioned limitations, the present study attempts to achieve two main objectives. First, it extends previous research by examining CSE and computer anxiety at the application level rather than the general level. The second objective is to combine both factors in a single research model as external factors to TAM and examine their direct and indirect effects on systems acceptance. In summary, this study empirically tests relationships among the following variables: application CSE, application computer anxiety, perceived ease of use, perceived usefulness, attitude, and behavioral intention.

RESEARCH BACKGROUND AND HYPOTHESES

The technology acceptance model (TAM) (Davis, 1989; Davis et al., 1989) provides a theoretical basis for studying IS acceptance. TAM models IS acceptance and use as a function of users' beliefs about perceived ease of use and perceived usefulness of the target system. Reviews and meta-analytic studies of TAM provide ample support for TAM's ability to explain and predict technology acceptance and utilization (King & He, 2006; Legris et al., 2003; Ma & Liu, 2004; Mahmood et al., 2001). Although TAM captures the impact of external factors on IS acceptance through their direct effects on perceptions of ease of use and usefulness (Davis, Bagozzi, & Warshaw, 1989),

Figure 1. Research model

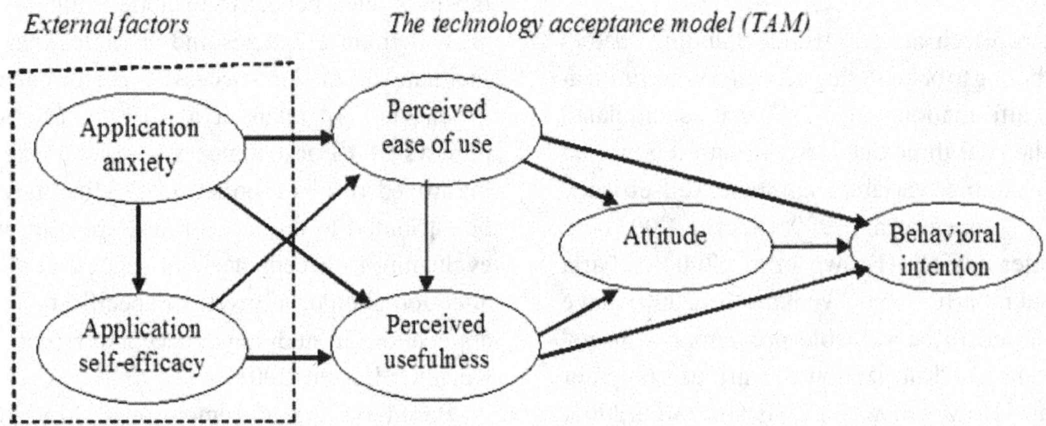

external factors effecting TAM have not been adequately examined in past research (Hsu & Lu, 2004; Taylor & Todd, 1995). As was pointed out earlier, the literature indicates that additional research is needed to investigate which and how external variables influence TAM's core variables and subsequent acceptance behavior (Lee et al., 2003).

Figure 1 presents the proposed research model underlying the current study. As the research model suggests, application CSE is posited to have direct positive effects on perceived usefulness and perceived ease of use. Application anxiety is hypothesized to have negative effects on perceived ease of use, perceived usefulness, and application CSE. The external variables (i.e., CSE and anxiety) are explained in more detail below.

Computer Self-Efficacy

Adapted from the broader concept of self-efficacy (Bandura, 1986), computer self-efficacy (CSE) refers to people's perceptions about their abilities to use a computer successfully (Compeau & Higgins, 1995). CSE has been examined as an antecedent to various computer-related outcomes including: IS acceptance including perceived ease of use and perceived usefulness (Chau, 2001; Venkatesh & Davis, 1996).

Marakas et al. (1998) demonstrated that CSE was a multilevel construct with general and application-specific components. They defined general computer self-efficacy as "an individual's judgment of efficacy across multiple computer application domains" (p. 129) whereas application-specific CSE refers to perceptions of efficacy in performing specific computing tasks related to a particular computer application. Thus, unlike general CSE which refers to a generalized and system-independent trait, application-specific CSE refers to judgments of self-efficacy toward a specific software package or computing domain.

Application CSE demonstrated diverse effects on IS-related outcomes. For instance, it demonstrated positive effects on systems acceptance and performance in computer training (Johnson & Marakas, 2000). Application CSE (i.e., Lotus 123 and Windows 95) was found to have positive effect on perceived ease of use of both applications (Agarwal, Sambamurthy, & Stair, 2000). Finally, Yi, and Hwang (2003) found that application (Blackboard) CSE had positive effect on ease of use and actual use of the Blackboard system. Thus, application CSE is expected to have direct and indirect effects on perceived ease of use, perceived usefulness, attitude, and behavioral intention.

Computer Anxiety

Computer anxiety refers an emotional fear or discomfort experienced by people when they use a computer system (Chiu & Wang, 2008). Computer anxiety has demonstrated negative effects on ability to learn computing skills (Harrison & Rainer, 1992), affect toward computers (Compeau & Higgins, 1995), computer usage (Igbaria & Iivari, 1995), and intention to use web-based learning (Chiu & Wang, 2008). Furthermore, computer anxiety demonstrated negative impacts on determinants of IS acceptance including perceived ease of use (Bronson, 2002; Venkatesh, 2000), perceived usefulness (Igbaria, 1993), relative advantage (Karahanna et al., 2002) and intention to use a system (Igbaria, 1992; Igbaria & Iivari, 1995).

Although the widespread prevalence of computers in all aspects of society at the present time may insinuate that computer anxiety has faded away, recent studies suggest that computer anxiety still represents a prevalent problem and various groups of people have varying levels of computer anxiety (Havelka, Beasley, & Broome, 2004). Moreover, other studies suggest that the growing proliferation of computers only changed the nature of the construct (Dyck et al., 1998) and the problem of computer anxiety is expected to exacerbate as a result of increased computer proliferation and rapid technology changes (Beckers & Schmidt, 2001; Chua, Chen, & Wong, 1999). This may suggest that the scope of computer anxiety may have shifted from general anxiety toward computers in general to anxiety towards specific applications or situations (Dyck et al., 1998).

Computer anxiety is conceptualized as a multifaceted construct (Beckers & Schmidt, 2001). Earlier work by Igbaria and his colleagues (1989, 1995) also indicate that computer anxiety can be divided into trait anxiety (a stable and generalized predisposition to be anxious or nervous toward an object) or state anxiety (an ephemeral response to a specific situation). Past studies have found that general computer anxiety and application-specific anxiety are two distinct constructs that exert different effects on IS-related behaviors (Brown et al., 2004; Thatcher et al., 2007). Accordingly, application computer anxiety is expected to have direct and indirect effects on perceived ease of use, perceived usefulness, attitude, and intention.

Social cognitive theory (Bandura, 1986) suggests an inverse, bidirectional relationship between self-efficacy and anxiety. A similar reciprocal relationship between CSE and computer anxiety had been suggested in IS research (Marakas et al., 1998). Empirical findings seem to support the reciprocal relationship between CSE and computer anxiety. For instance, while some studies found that CSE had a negative influence on computer anxiety (e.g., Igbaria & Iivari, 1995), other studies found that computer anxiety had a negative impact on computer self-efficacy (e.g., Thatcher & Perrewé, 2002). Moreover, Venkatesh (2000) asserts that depending on which of the two variables (computer anxiety or computer self-efficacy) serves as the stimulus, an effect on the other variable may be observed. Thus, application computer anxiety is presented as the stimulus that is expected to have a negative impact on application CSE.

TAM Variables

TAM models IS acceptance as a function of users' assessments of perceived ease of use and perceived usefulness. Davis (1989) maintains that, everything else being equal, the easier a system is to use, the less effort one will need to operate it, and the more likely it will actually be used. However, in additional research to validate and refine TAM, Davis, Bagozzi, and Warshaw (1989) found that perceived ease of use had a significant effect on perceived usefulness. They suggested that perceived ease of use might be a determinant of perceived usefulness rather than a parallel to it.

Users' decisions to adopt and use a system are driven mostly by the functions it performs for them and the extent to which these functions will help them perform their jobs better (1989). Davis (1989) labeled this concept as perceived usefulness and found that perceived usefulness was a significant determinant of IS acceptance. This finding was further substantiated in replication and meta-analytic studies (Adams, Nelson, & Todd, 1992; Legris, Ingham, & Collerette, 2003; Mahmood, Hall, & Swanberg, 2001). Attitude toward a behavior (e.g., using a computer) refers to the degree to which an individual has a favorable or unfavorable evaluation of that behavior (Ajzen, 1991). TAM suggests that a person's attitude toward using a computer system is determined by his/her beliefs about the usefulness and ease of use of the system in question. At the same time, TAM theorizes that attitude is a direct determinant of intention to use the system.

TAM has been successfully used to explain acceptance of various computer systems such as microcomputers (Chau, 2001), world wide web (Agarwal & Karahanna, 2000), online-learning (Saadé & Bahli, 2005), Internet-based applications (Shih, 2004), ERP (Amoako-Gyampah & Salam, 2004), and workstations (Lucas & Spitler, 2000). Furthermore, TAM was successfully used to explain IS acceptance behavior among diverse user groups such as: students (Agarwal & Karahanna, 2000; Chau, 2001), Internet customers (Henderson & Divett, 2003).

The relationship between intention and actual behavior has been validated in various settings towards a variety of behaviors. For instance, in studying knowledge sharing in an organizational setting, Bock and Kim (2002) found that attitude toward knowledge sharing was a significant determinant of intention to share knowledge with other employees. With respect to IS acceptance behavior, Hsu and Lu (2004) found that attitude toward playing an online game had strong effect on intention to play an online game. A number of other studies have found empirical support of the positive correlation between attitude and intention to use (Adams et al., 1992; Mathieson, 1991). Thus, perceived ease of use and perceived usefulness are expected to demonstrate direct and indirect effects on attitude and intention.

METHODOLOGY

Subjects and Procedure

Data for this study were collected from 191 undergraduate business students at a Midwestern university. Of the 191 participants, 81 were females (42.4%) and 101 were males (52.9). The remaining 9 participants (4.7%) did not indicate their gender. Thirty-three participants indicated their age was below 20 years; 133 indicated their age between 20 and 25, and 21 participant indicated their age over 25. The remaining 4 participants did not indicate their age. All majors in the college of business were represented in the sample.

Participants were enrolled in four sections of a computer information systems course. In this course, students were required to use Microsoft's Excel 2003 to perform various statistical procedures and techniques. In this course, students were taught how to use Excel's statistical functions to perform various statistical tests such as regression, correlation, and other statistical procedures. Students were initially given an explanation on the statistical concepts and then Excel was used to demonstrate that concept. Thus, our study focused on Excel's statistical component. That is, all the research variables were measured with respect to Excel's 2003 statistical features. Excel's statistical component was selected for two primary reasons. First, students' had little previous experience with this component of Excel and, as a result, they were expected to form their application-related beliefs based on their use of and interactions with Excel statistical features. In fact, students rated their past experience in Excel as 5.76 on a scale ranging from 1 (*very little experience*) to 10 (*very experienced*) and most of their experience involved simple calculations in Excel. Second, since there are many other applications that can be used to perform the same statistical procedures that students used in Excel, the results can be extended to similar applications.

In each of the four sections, instructors were asked whether their students can participate in the study. All instructors agreed and indicated that students can participate in the last class session of the semester. Student participation was anonymous and voluntary and students were assured that their participation or responses would not affect their performance in the class. While instructors were not present in the classrooms, four graduate students distributed and collected the questionnaires in the four sections.

Measurements

The study uses well-established and previously validated measurement instruments. Application CSE was measured by 4 items adapted from the work of Johnson and Marakas (2000). Statements on this instrument assessed subjects' confidence their ability to perform certain statistical procedures in Excel. Sample statements from this measure include: 1. "I would be able to perform descriptive statistics (e.g., mean, std. deviation) in Excel" and 2. "I would be able to perform regression analysis in Excel".

Application computer anxiety was measured by four items from the instrument used by Brown et al. (2004). Sample items from this measure include: 1. "I feel tense while doing data analysis in Excel" and 2. "I would be comfortable performing statistical analysis in Excel". The remaining variables: perceived ease of and perceived usefulness were measured by three and four items, respectively from the work of Davis (1989), attitude (4 items) and behavioral intention (3 items) were measured based on the work of Ajzen (1991). The responses to all items were recorded on a 7-point Likert scale with end points of 1 (*strongly disagree*) and 7 (*strongly agree*).

RESULTS

Table 1 presents the means and standard deviations of the study variables. The variability of application anxiety and application CSE were slightly higher than those of other variables. In addition, Table 1 presents the internal consistency reliability (alpha) estimates. All alpha values ranged from 0.79 to 0.96, suggesting high internal consistency. Table 2 presents the correlations among the study variables. With the exception of the correlation between application anxiety and attitude ($r = -0.112$, $p = 0.203$), all correlations were significant and in the expected direction. Moreover, all correlation estimates are within the acceptable range and below the 0.80 threshold, suggesting that multi-collinearity is not a concern (Bryman & Cramer, 1994).

Path analysis was used to empirically test the direct and indirect relationships depicted in the research model. Path analysis is a popular regression-based procedure that is used to provide quantitative estimates of proposed relationships between sets of variables that are explicitly formulated in a causal model (Billings & Wroten, 1978).Thus, path analysis uses standardized regression coefficients (betas) to indicate the strength and direction of relationships among independent and dependent variables.

Table 3 presents partial results of the path analysis for application CSE, perceived ease of use, and perceived usefulness. As can be seen in Table 3, application anxiety demonstrated negative, significant effects on application CSE (beta = -0.705, $p <.001$) and perceived ease of use (beta = -0.221 $p <.001$). Contrary to expectations, the impact of application anxiety on perceived usefulness was minimal and insignificant (beta =.029, $p = 0.26$). With respect to indirect effects,

Table 1. Descriptive statistics

	Mean	S.D.	# Items	Alpha
Application Anxiety	12.75	5.5	3	0.79
Application CSE	22.70	7.67	5	0.90
Perceived Ease of use	12.27	4.71	3	0.94
Perceived Usefulness	18.13	6.35	4	0.96
Attitude	18.75	4.03	4	0.85
Intention	13.02	4.87	3	0.93

Table 2. Correlations among study variables

	1	2	3	4	5	6
1. Application Anxiety	1.00	-0.504**	-0.513**	-0.358**	-0.112	-0.325**
2. Application CSE		1.00	0.707**	0.571**	0.373**	0.494**
3. Perceived Ease of use			1.00	0.696**	0.449**	0.722*
4. Perceived Usefulness				1.00	0.405**	0.700**
5. Attitude					1.00	0.540**
6. Intention						1.00

application anxiety demonstrated substantial indirect negative effects on both perceived ease of use and usefulness. Application anxiety explained about 25% of the variability in application CSE.

Application CSE demonstrated positive, significant effects on perceived ease of use (beta = 0.597, *p <.001*) and perceived usefulness (beta = 0.151, *p <.05*). In addition, application CSE demonstrated substantial indirect effect on perceived usefulness through its direct effects on application anxiety and perceived ease of use. The impact of perceived ease of use on perceived usefulness was significant and positive (beta = 0.607, *p <.001*). Application anxiety and application CSE explained about 54% of the variance in perceived ease of use. Likewise, the amount of variance in perceived usefulness that was explained by the three variables (application anxiety, application CSE, and perceived ease of use) was about 50%.

Table 4 presents the results of path analysis for attitude and behavioral intention. As Table 4 indicates, application anxiety demonstrated substantial, negative indirect effects on attitude

Table 3. Results of path analysis

	Application CSE			PEOU			PU		
	Direct	Indirect	Total	Direct	Indirect	Total	Direct	Indirect	Total
App. Anxiety	-0.705**		-0.705	- 0.221**	-0.301	-0.522	0.029	-0.392	-0.363
App. CSE				0.597**		0.597	0.151*	0.220	0.371
PEOU							0.607**		0.607
R^2		0.254			0.538			0.501	

*** p < 0.01; * p < 0.05*

Table 4. Results of path analysis

	Attitude			Behavioral intention		
	Direct	Indirect	Total	Direct	Indirect	Total
App. Anxiety		- 0.226	-0.226		-0.240	-0.240
App. CSE		0.318	0.318		0.518	0.518
PEOU	0.008	0.371	0.378	0.382**	0.156	0.538
PU	0.611**		0.611	0.370**	0.097	0.467
Attitude				0.159*		0.159
R^2		0.381			0.652	

** $p < 0.01$; * $p < 0.05$

and intention. In contrast, the indirect effects of application CSE on attitude and intention were substantial and positive. While perceived ease of use demonstrated positive impact on behavioral intention (beta = 0.382, $p <.001$), its impact on attitude was minimal and insignificant (beta = 0.008, $p <.994$). For perceived usefulness, its direct effects on attitude (beta = 0.611, $p <.001$) and behavioral intention (beta = 0.370, $p <.001$) were both positive and significant whereas its indirect effect on behavioral intentions was relatively small. Finally, attitude demonstrated a significant, positive effect on behavioral intention (beta = 0.159, $p <.001$). The amount of variability in perceived ease of use explained by the predictor variables was about 38% and that of perceived usefulness was about 65%. A summary of the research results and path coefficients are depicted in Figure 2.

To further examine the somewhat weak relationship between attitude and behavioral intention, we excluded attitude from the regression model and tested perceived ease of use and perceived usefulness as direct predictors of behavioral intention and the results are presented in Table 5. As Table 5 shows, the amount of variability did not slump greatly and stood at about 59% (a decrease of about 6%). Furthermore, the beta coefficients for perceived ease of usefulness and perceived ease of use were modestly affected by the exclusion of attitude as from the regression model, with beta for perceived ease of use increas-

*Figure 2. Research results (**p<0.001; *p<0.05)*

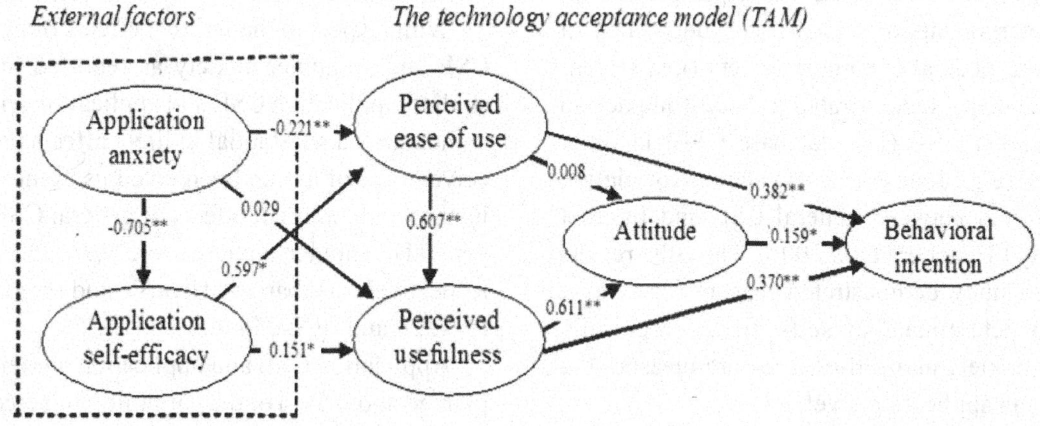

Table 5. Predictors of intention (excluding attitude)

	B	T	Sig T
Perceived ease of use	0.448	6.714	0.000
Perceived usefulness	0.386	5.790	0.000
R^2	0.589		

ing and that of perceived usefulness decreasing more precipitously.

DISCUSSION

The present study focused on the role of CSE and computer anxiety beliefs at the application level in the context of systems acceptance and utilization. Although similar attempts have been done in past research, we were unable to find any studies which examined these two application-specific factors simultaneously as external variables to determinants of IS acceptance as posited in the technology acceptance model. Accordingly, the proposed research model aimed to assess the direct and indirect effects of application CSE and application anxiety on users' decisions to accept and use an IS.

The results provide support for the research model and its hypothesized relationships. Application computer anxiety demonstrated a strong direct effect on application CSE (*beta = -0.705, p < 0.001*), providing support for social cognitive theory's (Bandura's, 1986) perspective on the determinants of self-efficacy judgments. In contrast, general computer anxiety (i.e., system independent) demonstrated a modest impact on application CSE (i.e., database CSE) in other studies (e.g., Johnson, 2005) and no correlation was found between general CSE and Internet anxiety (Thatcher et al., 2007). Thus, the results of this study demonstrated that anxiety was a sound determinant of self-efficacy, especially when anxiety and self-efficacy are measured at the same application level.

Compared with previous studies focusing on general CSE and computer anxiety, this study provides better insights into the direct effects of application CSE and computer anxiety. For instance, while Igbaria and Iivari (1995) found that general CSE had a moderate effect on perceived ease of use (*beta = 0.29, p <0.01*), application CSE demonstrated a strong impact on perceived ease of use (*beta = 0.59, p < 0.01*) in this study, almost double the impact reported by Igbaria and Iivari (1995). Other studies found that application CSE had a strong impact on perceived ease of use (e.g., Agarwal et al., 2000; Yi & Hwang, 2003). This suggests that application CSE seems to be a better predictor of perceived ease of use than general CSE. Likewise, application CSE represents a stronger predictor of perceived usefulness; the results showed that the impact of application CSE on perceived usefulness was significant (*beta = 0.151, p < 0.05*), whereas general CSE demonstrated a much smaller and insignificant effect on perceived usefulness (Igbaria & Iivari, 1995). Overall, the results show that application-specific beliefs may offer better prediction of behavior than general beliefs (Saeed & Abdinnour-Helm, 2008).

With respect to the indirect effects of general CSE and computer anxiety as reported in past studies, application CSE and application anxiety demonstrated substantial indirect effects on perceived ease of use and perceived usefulness For instance, the indirect effects of general CSE and general computer anxiety were *0.16* and *-0.13* respectively in Igbaria and Iivari's study compared to *0.220* and *-0.392* in this study.

Application CSE and application anxiety explained about 54% of the variability in perceived ease of use and about 50% of the variability in perceived usefulness (with perceived ease use included as a predictor). In contrast, general CSE and general computer anxiety (with computer experience and organizational support included as predictor variables) explained about 26% of variability in perceived ease of use and about 30% of the variability in perceived usefulness as reported by Igbaria and Iivari (1995). Thus, our results are consistent with the notion that more proximal (i.e., application-specific) beliefs represent better predictors of a behavior than distal (i.e., general) beliefs (Brown et al., 2004).

For TAM, the results deviated slightly from findings reported in past research. For example, while perceived ease of use demonstrated a strong, significant effect on behavioral intention, it demonstrated a very small and insignificant impact on attitude. However, when attitude was excluded from the regression model and perceived ease of use and perceived usefulness were used as predictors of intention, perceived ease of use demonstrated a stronger effect (*beta, 0.382,* $p<0.001$) on behavioral intention than did perceived usefulness (*beta, 0.370,* $p<0.001$). Similar results have been reported by Liu and Ma (2006) who examined the impact of perceived system performance (PSP), perceived ease of use, and perceived usefulness on behavioral intention. They found that the relationship between perceived ease of use and behavioral intention was dependent on the presence or absence of PSP. That is, when on PSP was present, perceived ease of use had no significant impact on behavioral intention and when PSP was absent, perceived ease of use had a significant impact on behavioral intention. They attributed this relationship to the conditional independence phenomenon. That is, the role of perceived ease of use in IS acceptance behavior may be captured by other factors.

Another possible explanation for the above findings is that the effect of perceived ease of use may have been captured by perceived usefulness. This explanation is supported by the results of a recent review of TAM studies which found that perceived ease of use plays indirect role in technology acceptance through its direct effect on perceived usefulness (King & He, 2006). Moreover, Hsu and Chiu (2004) found that the effect of perceived usefulness on attitude was stronger than the effects of other predictor variables (perceived playfulness, perceived risk, and general Internet self-efficacy). The results of this study corroborate this finding and show that the impact of perceived usefulness was much stronger than that of perceived ease of use.

The above findings offer several implications. The study demonstrated the value of using application-specific beliefs as determinants of IS acceptance. Thus, practitioners can assess users' beliefs of anxiety and CSE about the target (or comparable) system early in the IS adoption process. The results of such evaluation can be used to develop some intervention program to focus on lowering anxiety or enhancing CSE judgments. Past studies point out several methods to manipulate computer anxiety and CSE. For instance, Johnson (2005) found that past experience, positive feedback, proper training, and setting challenging goals in training exert positive impact on application CSE. For application anxiety, Brown et al. (2004) found that increasing users' familiarity with the system or similar systems from the same computing domain decrease application anxiety. Their results also demonstrated a positive relationship between general and application computer anxiety, suggesting that all approaches used to decrease general computer anxiety will also decrease application computer anxiety.

From a research perspective, the study extended previous research by distinguishing between general and application-specific beliefs about CSE and computer anxiety. Thus, the results provide additional empirical evidence the malleability of the self-efficacy construct as suggested to social cognitive theory. Furthermore, given that CSE and computer anxiety at the application-level received little attention relative the more broad and general beliefs of CSE and computer anxiety, this study sought to fill this void by focusing on application-level CSE and computer anxiety as direct determinants of IS acceptance. Finally, contributing to TAM's literature, the study combined both application-level constructs as external variables to the technology acceptance model (TAM) and shed light on their direct and indirect effects on TAM's main constructs and contributes to calls for the inclusion of external variables into acceptance research to seek additional explanatory power for technology acceptance (Lee et al., 2003; Lucas & Spitler, 2000).

LIMITATIONS AND FUTURE RESEARCH

Like most studies, this study is not without limitations that should be pointed out and recognized when interpreting the results. The first limitation pertains to the use of a student sample in an educational setting. However, a recent review of 88 TAM studies substantiated the value of using student subjects as surrogates for professional IS users (King & He, 2006) and this approach was consistent with most studies similar to the present study (e.g., Brown et al., 2004; Chau, 2001; Hsu & Chiu, 2004; Lin & Lu, 2000; Premkumar, Ramamurthy, & Liu, 2008; Saeed & Abdinnour-Helm, 2008).

Another possible limitation relates to the sample characteristics. For example, gender and age have been found to have various effects on individuals' behavior in computing settings. In a recent study, Djamasbi and Loiacono (2008) found that males and females reacted differently to computer-based feedback in a decision support system (DSS) task. Future studies may examine the impact of individual characteristics on application-specific beliefs or control the effects in studying computer-related behavior.

Finally, a potential limitation concerns the use of behavioral intention as a surrogate for actual system use. While this approach was consistent with past study which used intention as a surrogate for actual system usage (e.g., Chau, 2001; Yi et al., 2006), our results are somewhat analogous to other studies which examined actual system use (e.g., Igbaria & Iivari, 1995). In addition, behavioral intention had been found to be a significant predictor of actual system use (Hsu & Chiu, 2004; Venkatesh et al., 2003) and a recent meta-analytic study of TAM-based studies found a significant relationship between behavioral intention and actual system use (Schepers & Wetzels, 2007).

The study provides interesting areas for future research. For instance, future research should consider testing the research model using other technology. Such research attempts are certainly needed to enhance the generalization of the results of this study. In addition, such research will also allow the comparison of results across applications and whether results can be generalized across similar applications.

The determinants of application-specific CSE and anxiety represent another valuable area for future research. The results of this study demonstrated that the effects of application-specific beliefs may diverge from the effects of the broader and more general beliefs. Thus, given that determinants of general CSE and computer anxiety have received extensive attention in past research, it is interesting to examine the impact of those determinants of application-specific beliefs. The four sources of efficacy factors identified in Bandura's (1986) social cognitive theory and the large number of empirical studies of CSE and computer anxiety provide appropriate foundation on which to develop and test research models of determinants of application-specific CSE and anxiety.

While this study examined behavioral intention to general system use, the recent work by Saeed and Abdinnour-Helm (2008) distinguish between types of system usage: extended and exploratory usage. They defined extended use as the frequency with which different features of the system are used and exploratory usage as the extent to which users can use the system in novel and innovative ways. Thus, future research can use the research model presented in this study to examine the effects of application-specific beliefs on the two types of post adoption usage.

REFERENCES

Adams, D. A., Nelson, R. R., & Todd, P. A. (1992). Perceived usefulness, ease of use, and usage of information. *Management Information Systems Quarterly, 16*(2), 227–247. doi:10.2307/249577

Agarwal, R., & Karahanna, E. (2000). Time flies when you're having fun: Cognitive absorption and beliefs about information technology usage. *Management Information Systems Quarterly, 24*(4), 665–694. doi:10.2307/3250951

Agarwal, R., Sambamurthy, V., & Stair, R. (2000). The evolving relationship between general and specific computer self-efficacy: An empirical assessment. *Information Systems Research, 11*(4), 418–430. doi:10.1287/isre.11.4.418.11876

Ajzen, I. (1991). The theory of planned behavior. *Organizational Behavior and Human Decision Processes, 50*, 179–211. doi:10.1016/0749-5978(91)90020-T

Amoako-Gyampah, K., & Salam, A. F. (2004). An extension of the technology acceptance model in an ERP implementation environment. *Information & Management, 41*(6), 731–745. doi:10.1016/j.im.2003.08.010

Bandura, A. (1986). *Social foundations of thought and action: A social cognitive theory*. Upper Saddle River, NJ: Prentice-Hall.

Beckers, J. J., & Schmidt, H. G. (2001). The structure of computer anxiety: A six-factor model. *Computers in Human Behavior, 17*(1), 35–49. doi:10.1016/S0747-5632(00)00036-4

Billings, R., & Wroten, S. (1978). Use of path analysis in industrial/organizational psychology: criticisms and suggestions. *The Journal of Applied Psychology, 63*(6), 677–688. doi:10.1037/0021-9010.63.6.677

Bock, G. W., & Kim, Y.-G. (2002). Breaking the myths of rewards: an exploratory study of attitudes about knowledge sharing. *Information Resources Management Journal, 15*(2), 14–21. doi:10.4018/irmj.2002040102

Brown, S. A., Fuller, R., & Vician, C. (2004). Who's afraid of the virtual world? The role of anxiety in computer-mediated communication use and satisfaction. *Journal of the Association for Information Systems, 5*(2), 81–109.

Bryman, A., & Cramer, D. (1994). *Quantitative data analysis for social scientists*. New York: Routledge.

Chau, P. Y. K. (1996). An empirical investigation on factors affecting the acceptance of CASE by systems developers. *Information & Management, 30*(6), 269–280. doi:10.1016/S0378-7206(96)01074-9

Chau, P. Y. K. (2001). Influence of computer attitude and self-efficacy on IT usage behavior. *Journal of End User Computing, 13*(1), 26–33. doi:10.4018/joeuc.2001010103

Chiu, C.-M., & Wang, E. T. G. (2008). Understanding Web-based learning continuance intention: The role of subjective task value. *Information & Management, 45*(3), 194–201. doi:10.1016/j.im.2008.02.003

Chua, S. L., Chen, D., & Wong, A. (1999). Computer anxiety and its correlates: A meta-analysis. *Computers in Human Behavior, 15*(5), 609–623. doi:10.1016/S0747-5632(99)00039-4

Compeau, D. R., & Higgins, C. A. (1995). Application of social cognitive theory to training for computer skills. *Information Systems Research*, *6*(1), 118–143. doi:10.1287/isre.6.2.118

Compeau, D. R., & Higgins, C. A. (1999). Social cognitive theory and individual reactions to computing technology: A longitudinal study. *Management Information Systems Quarterly*, *23*(2), 145–159. doi:10.2307/249749

Davis, F. D. (1989). Perceived usefulness, perceived ease of use, and user acceptance of information technology. *Management Information Systems Quarterly*, *13*(3), 319–340. doi:10.2307/249008

Davis, F. D., Bagozzi, R. P., & Warshaw, P. R. (1989). User acceptance of computer technology: A comparison of two theoretical models. *Management Science*, *35*(8), 982–1003. doi:10.1287/mnsc.35.8.982

Djamasbi, S., & Loiacono, E. T. (2008). Do men and women use feedback provided by their decision support systems (DSS) differently? *Decision Support Systems*, *44*(4), 854–869. doi:10.1016/j.dss.2007.10.008

Dyck, J. L., Gee, N. R., & Smither, J. A. (1998). The changing construct of computer anxiety for younger and older adults. *Computers in Human Behavior*, *14*(1), 61–77. doi:10.1016/S0747-5632(97)00032-0

Gist, M. E. (1987). Self-efficacy: Implications for organizational behavior and human resource management. *Academy of Management Review*, *12*(3), 472–485. doi:doi:10.2307/258514

Hackbarth, G., Grover, V., & Yi, M. Y. (2003). Computer playfulness and anxiety: Positive and negative mediators of the system experience effect on perceived ease of use. *Information & Management*, *40*(3), 221–232. doi:10.1016/S0378-7206(02)00006-X

Havelka, D., Beasley, F., & Broome, T. (2004). A study of computer anxiety among business students. *Mid-American Journal of Business*, *19*(1), 63–71. doi:10.1108/19355181200400007

Henderson, R., & Divett, M. (2003). Perceived usefulness, ease of use and electronic supermarket use. *International Journal of Human-Computer Studies*, *59*(3), 383–395. doi:10.1016/S1071-5819(03)00079-X

Hsu, C. L., & Lu, H. P. (2004). Why do people play on-line games? An extended TAM with social influences and flow experience. *Information & Management*, *41*(7), 853–868. doi:10.1016/j.im.2003.08.014

Hsu, M.-H., & Chiu, C.-M. (2004). Internet self-efficacy and electronic service acceptance. *Decision Support Systems*, *38*(3), 369–381. doi:10.1016/j.dss.2003.08.001

Hu, P. J. H., Clark, T. H. K., & Ma, W. W. (2003). Examining technology acceptance by school teachers: A longitudinal study. *Information & Management*, *41*(2), 227–241. doi:10.1016/S0378-7206(03)00050-8

Igbaria, M., & Chakrabarti, A. (1990). Computer anxiety and attitudes towards microcomputer use. *Behaviour & Information Technology*, *9*(3), 229–241. doi:10.1080/01449299008924239

Igbaria, M., & Iivari, J. (1995). Effects of self-efficacy on computer usage. *Omega-International Journal of Management Science*, *23*(6), 587–605. doi:10.1016/0305-0483(95)00035-6

Johnson, R. A. (2005). An empirical investigation of sources of application-specific computer-self-efficacy and mediators of the efficacy: Performance relationship. *International Journal of Human-Computer Studies*, *62*(6). doi:10.1016/j.ijhcs.2005.02.008

Johnson, R. D., & Marakas, G. M. (2000). The role of behavioral modeling in computer skills acquisition: Toward refinement of the model. *Information Systems Research, 11*(4), 402–417. doi:10.1287/isre.11.4.402.11869

King, W. R., & He, J. (2006). A meta-analysis of the technology acceptance model. *Information & Management, 43*(6), 740–755. doi:10.1016/j.im.2006.05.003

Lee, T. Y., Kozar, K. A., & Larsen, K. R. T. (2003). The technology acceptance model: Past, present, and future. *Communications of the Association for Information Systems, 12*(50), 752–780.

Legris, P., Ingham, J., & Collerette, P. (2003). Why do people use information technology? A critical review of the technology acceptance model. *Information & Management, 40*(3), 191–204. doi:10.1016/S0378-7206(01)00143-4

Lin, J. C., & Lu, H. P. (2000). Towards an understanding of the behavioural intention to use a Web site. *International Journal of Information Management, 20*(3), 197–208. doi:10.1016/S0268-4012(00)00005-0

Liu, L., & Ma, Q. (2006). Perceived system performance: A test of an extended technology acceptance model. *The Data Base for Advances in Information Systems, 37*(2-3), 51–59.

Lucas, H. C., & Spitler, V. K. (2000). Implementation in a world of workstations and networks. *Information & Management, 38*(2), 119–128. doi:10.1016/S0378-7206(00)00059-8

Ma, Q., & Liu, L. (2004). The technology acceptance model: A meta-analysis of empirical findings. *Journal of Organizational and End User Computing, 16*(1), 59–72. doi:10.4018/joeuc.2004010104

Mahmood, M. A., Hall, L., & Swanberg, D. L. (2001). Factors affecting information technology usage: A meta-analysis of the empirical literature. *Journal of Organizational Computing and Electronic Commerce, 11*(2), 107–130. doi:10.1207/S15327744JOCE1102_02

Marakas, G. M., Yi, M. Y., & Johnson, R. (1998). The multilevel and multifaceted character of computer self-efficacy: Toward a clarification of the construct and an integrative framework for research. *Information Systems Research, 9*(2), 126–163. doi:10.1287/isre.9.2.126

Mathieson, K. (1991). Predicting user intentions: Comparing the technology acceptance model with the theory of planned behavior. *Information Systems Research, 2*(3), 173–191. doi:10.1287/isre.2.3.173

Premkumar, G., Ramamurthy, K., & Liu, H. N. (2008). Internet messaging: An examination of the impact of attitudinal, normative, and control belief systems. *Information & Management, 45*(7), 451–457. doi:10.1016/j.im.2008.06.008

Saadé, R., & Bahli, B. (2005). The impact of cognitive absorption on perceived usefulness and perceived ease of use in on-line learning: An extension of the technology acceptance model. *Information & Management, 42*(2), 317–327. doi:10.1016/j.im.2003.12.013

Saeed, K. A., & Abdinnour-Helm, S. (2008). Examining the effects of information system characteristics and perceived usefulness on post adoption usage of information systems. *Information & Management, 45*(1), 376–386. doi:10.1016/j.im.2008.06.002

Schepers, J., & Wetzels, M. (2007). A meta analysis of the technology acceptance model: Investigating subjective norm and moderation effects. *Information & Management, 44*(1), 90–103. doi:10.1016/j.im.2006.10.007

Shih, H. P. (2004). An empirical study on predicting user acceptance of e-shopping on the Web. *Information & Management*, *41*(3), 351–368. doi:10.1016/S0378-7206(03)00079-X

Taylor, S., & Todd, P. A. (1995). Understanding information technology usage: A test of competing models. *Information Systems Research*, *6*(2), 144–176. doi:10.1287/isre.6.2.144

Thatcher, J. B., Loughry, M. L., Lim, J., & McKnight, D. H. (2007). Internet anxiety: An empirical study of the effects of personality, beliefs, and social support. *Information & Management*, *44*(4), 353–363. doi:10.1016/j.im.2006.11.007

Thatcher, J. B., & Perrewé, P. L. (2002). An empirical examination of individual traits as antecedents to computer anxiety and computer self-efficacy. *Management Information Systems Quarterly*, *26*(4), 381–395. doi:10.2307/4132314

Venkatesh, V. (2000). Determinants of perceived ease of use: Integrating perceived behavioral control, computer anxiety and enjoyment into the technology acceptance model. *Information Systems Research*, *11*(4), 342–365. doi:10.1287/isre.11.4.342.11872

Venkatesh, V., & Davis, F. D. (1996). A model of the antecedents of perceived ease of use: Development and test. *Decision Sciences*, *27*(3), 451–481. doi:10.1111/j.1540-5915.1996.tb01822.x

Yi, M. U., & Im, K. S. (2004). Predicting computer task performance: Personal goal and self-efficacy. *Journal of Organizational and End User Computing*, *16*(2), 28–37. doi:10.4018/joeuc.2004040102

Yi, M. Y., & Hwang, Y. (2003). Predicting the use of web-based information systems: Self-efficacy, enjoyment, learning goal orientation, and the technology acceptance model. *International Journal of Human-Computer Studies*, *59*(4), 431–449. doi:10.1016/S1071-5819(03)00114-9

Yi, M. Y., Jackson, J. D., Park, J. S., & Probst, J. C. (2006). Understanding information technology acceptance by individual professionals: Toward an integrative view. *Information & Management*, *43*(3), 350–363. doi:10.1016/j.im.2005.08.006

This work was previously published in Journal of Organizational and End User Computing, Volume 22, Issue 3, edited by M. Adam Mahmood, pp. 82-95, copyright 2010 by IGI Publishing (an imprint of IGI Global).

Compilation of References

Abrahamson, E., & Rosenkoph, L. (1993). Institutional and Competitive Bandwagons: Using Mathematical modeling as a Tool to Explore Innovation Diffusion. *Academy of Management Review*, *18*(3), 487–517. doi:10.2307/258906

Abrahamsson, P. (2002). *The Role of Commitment in Software Process Improvement*. Oulu, Finland: University of Oulu.

Adams, B., Berner, E. S., & Wyatt, J. R. (2004). Best practice. Applying strategies to overcome user resistance in a group of clinical managers to a business software application: A case study. *Journal of Organizational and End User Computing*, *16*(4), 55–64.

Adams, D. A., Nelson, R. R., & Todd, P. A. (1992). Perceived usefulness, ease of use, and usage of information. *Management Information Systems Quarterly*, *16*(2), 227–247. doi:10.2307/249577

Agarwal, R., & Karahanna, E. (2000). Time flies when you're having fun: Cognitive absorption and beliefs about information technology usage. *Management Information Systems Quarterly*, *24*(4), 665–694. doi:10.2307/3250951

Agarwal, R., Sambamurthy, V., & Stair, R. (2000). The evolving relationship between general and specific computer self-efficacy: An empirical assessment. *Information Systems Research*, *11*(4), 418–430. doi:10.1287/isre.11.4.418.11876

Ahadi, H. (2004). An Examination of the Role of Organizational Enablers in Business Process Reengineering and the Impact of Information Technology. *Information Resources Management Journal*, *17*(4), 1–19.

Ahuja, M. K., & Thatcher, J. B. (2005). Moving beyond intentions and toward the theory of trying: Effects of work environment and gender on post-adoption information technology use. *Management Information Systems Quarterly*, *29*(3), 427–459.

Ajzen, I. (1985). From intentions to actions: a theory of planned behavior. In Kuhl, J., & Beckmann, J. (Eds.), *Action Control: From Cognition to Behavior* (pp. 11–39). New York: Springer.

Ajzen, I. (1985). From intentions to actions: A theory of planned behavior. In Kuhl, J., & Beckmann, J. (Eds.), *Action Control: From Cognition to Behavior*. New York: Springer Verlag.

Ajzen, I. (1988). Attitude structure and behavior relations. In Partkanis, A. R., Berckler, S. T., & Greenwald, A. G. (Eds.), *Attitude Structure and Function*. Hillsdale, NJ: Erlbaum.

Ajzen, I. (1991). The theory of planned behavior. *Organizational Behavior and Human Decision Processes*, *50*, 179–211. doi:10.1016/0749-5978(91)90020-T

Akrich, M. (1992). The De-Scription ofTechnical Objects. In Bijker, W., & Law, J. (Eds.), *Shaping Technology/Building Society. Studies in Sociotechnical Change* (pp. 205–224). Cambridge, MA: The MIT Press.

Alavi, M., Marakas, G. M., & Yoo, Y. (2002). A comparative study of distributed learning environments on learning outcomes. *Information Systems Research*, *13*(4), 404–415. doi:10.1287/isre.13.4.404.72

Alavi, M., Wheeler, B. C., & Valacich, J. (1995). Using IT to reengineer business education: An exploratory investigation of collaborative telelearning. *Management Information Systems Quarterly*, *19*(3), 293–312. doi:10.2307/249597

Albion, P. R. (1999). Heuristic evaluation of educational multimedia: from theory to practice. In *Proceedings of the 16th annual conference of the Austrasian Society for Computers in Learning in Tertiry Education (ASCILITE)*.

Alexander, C. (1964). *The synthesis of form*. Cambridge, MA: Harvard University Press

Alexander, C. (1984). The state of the art in design methods. In N. Cross (Ed.), *Developments in design methodology* (pp. 309-316). New York: John Wiley & Sons.

Al-Gahtani, S. S., & King, M. (1999). Attitudes, satisfaction and usage: Factors contributing to each in the acceptance of information technology. *Behaviour & Information Technology*, *18*(4), 277–297. doi:10.1080/014492999119020

Allen, N. J., & Meyer, J. P. (1990). The measurement and antecedents of affective, continuance, and normative commitment to the organization. *Journal of Occupational Psychology*, *63*, 1–18.

Allen, N. J., & Meyer, J. P. (1996). Affective, Continuance, and Normative Commitment to the Organization: An Examination of Construct Validity. *Journal of Vocational Behavior*, *49*, 252–276. doi:10.1006/jvbe.1996.0043

Allwood, C. (1990). Learning and using text-editors and other application programs. In Falzon, P. (Ed.), *Cognitive ergonomics: Understanding, learning, and designing human computer interaction* (pp. 85–10). New York: Academic Press.

Alter, S., & Ginzberg, M. (1978). Managing uncertainty in MIS implementation. *Sloan Management Review*, *20*(1), 23–31.

Alvesson, M. (1990). On the Popularity of Organizational Culture. *Acta Sociologica*, *33*(1), 31–49. doi:10.1177/000169939003300103

Amoako-Gyampah, K., & Salam, A. F. (2004). An extension of the technology acceptance model in an ERP implementation environment. *Information & Management*, *41*(6), 731–745. doi:10.1016/j.im.2003.08.010

Andersen, R. (2008). *Customer-initiated product development: A case study of adaptation and co-configuration*. Unpublished masters' thesis, University of Oslo, Norway.

Andersen, R., & Mørch, A. (2009). Mutual development: A case study in customer-initiated software product development. In V. Pipek, M. B. Rossen, B. deRuyter, & V. Wulf (Eds.), *End-user development* (pp. 31-49). Heidelberg, Germany: Springer.

Andersen, R., & Mørch, A. I. (2009, March 2-4). Mutual development: A case study in customer-initiated software product development. In V. Pipek, M. B. Rosson, B de Ruyter, & V. Wulf (Eds.), *End-User Development: Proceedings of the 2nd International Symposium on End-User Development*, Siegen, Germany (LNCS 5435, pp. 31-49).

Anderson, C. (2006). *The long tail: Why the future of business is selling less of more*. New York: Hyperion.

Anderson, J. R. (1989). A theory of human knowledge. *Artificial Intelligence*, *40*, 313–351. doi:10.1016/0004-3702(89)90052-0

Anderson, R. E., & Srinivasan, S. S. (2003). E-Satisfaction and E-Loyalty: A contingency Framework. *Psychology and Marketing*, *20*(2), 123. doi:10.1002/mar.10063

Andriessen, J. H. E. (2003). *Working with groupware. Understanding and evaluating collaboration technology*. London: Springer.

Apel, K.-O. (1972). The a priori of communication and the foundations of the humanities. *Man and World*, *51*, 3–37. doi:10.1007/BF01253016

Applebaum, R. L., & Anatol, K. W. E. (1979). The relationships among job satisfaction, organizational norms, and communicational climate among employees in an academic organization. *Journal of Applied Communication Research*, *7*(2), 83–90. doi:10.1080/00909887909365196

Ardichvili, A., Page, V., & Wentling, T. (2003). Motivation and barriers to participation in virtual knowledge-sharing communities of practice. *Journal of Knowledge Management*, *7*(1), 64–77. doi:10.1108/13673270310463626

Arias, E. G., Eden, H., Fischer, G., Gorman, A., & Scharff, E. (2000). Transcending the individual human mind—creating shared understanding through collaborative design. *ACM Transactions on Computer-Human Interaction*, *7*(1), 84–113. doi:10.1145/344949.345015

Armstrong, C. P., & Sambamurthy, V. (1999). Information Technology Assimilation in Firms: The Influence of Senior Leadership and IT Infrastructures. *Information Systems Research, 10*(4), 304–327. doi:10.1287/isre.10.4.304

Arriaga, X. B., & Agnew, C. R. (2001). Being Committed: Affective, Cognitive, and Conative Components of Relationship Commitment. *Personality and Social Psychology Bulletin, 27*(9), 1190–1203. doi:10.1177/0146167201279011

Artman, H. (2002). Procurer usability requirements: negotiations in contract development. In O. Bertelsen, S. Bødker, & K. Kuutti (Eds.), *Proceedings of the second Nordic conference on Human-computer interaction* (pp. 61-70). New York: ACM Press.

Åsand, H.-R., & Mørch, A. I. (2006). Super users and local developers: The organization of end-user development in an accounting company. *Journal of Organizational and End User Computing, 18*(4), 1–21.

Asaro, P. (2000). Transforming Society by Transforming Technology: the science and politics of participatory design. *Accounting. Management and Information Technologies, 10*(4), 257–290. doi:10.1016/S0959-8022(00)00004-7

Aucella, A. (1997). Ensuring Success with Usability Engineering. *Interaction, 4*(3), 19–22. doi:10.1145/255392.255395

Ausubel, D. P. (1968). *Educational Psychology: A Cognitive View*. New York: Holt, Reinhart and Winston.

Avison, D., & Fitzgerald, G. (2003). *Information systems development: Methodologies, techniques and tools* (2nd ed.). New York: McGraw Hill.

Avison, D., & Myers, M. (1995). Information systems and anthropology: an anthropological perspective on IT and organizational culture. *Information Technology & People, 8*(3), 43–56. doi:10.1108/09593849510098262

Aytes, K., & Connolly, T. (2004). Computer security and risky computing practices: A rational choice perspective. *Journal of Organizational and End User Computing, 16*(3), 22–40.

Babbie, E. (2004). *The practice of social research* (10th ed.). Belmont, CA: Wadsworth/Thomson Learning.

Bacon, L. D. (1997). *Using Amos for structural equation modeling in market research*. Retrieved from ftp://hqftp1.spss.com/pub/web/wp/AMOSMRP.pdf

Balka, E., & Wagner, I. (2006). Making Things Work: Dimensions of Configurability as Appropriation Work. In [New York: ACM Publishing.]. *Proceedings of CSCW, 2006*, 229–238.

Bandura, A. (1977). Self-efficacy: Toward a unifying theory of behavioral change. *Psychological Review, 84*(2), 191–215. doi:10.1037/0033-295X.84.2.191

Bandura, A. (1986). *Social foundations of thought and action: A social cognitive theory*. Upper Saddle River, NJ: Prentice-Hall.

Bandura, A. (1997). *Self-efficacy: The exercise of control*. New York: W. H. Freeman.

Banker, R. D., Bardham, I. R., Chang, H., & Lin, S. (2006). Plant Information Systems, Manufacturing Capabilities, and Plant Performance. *Management Information Systems Quarterly, 30*(2), 315–337.

Banker, R. D., Kauffman, R. C., & Morey, R. C. (1990). Measuring Gains in Operational Efficiency from Information Technology: A Study of the Positran Deployment at Hardee's Inc. *Journal of Management Information Systems, 7*(2), 29–54.

Bannister, B. D. (1986). Performance outcome feedback and attributional feedback: Interactive effects on recipient responses. *The Journal of Applied Psychology, 71*, 203–210. doi:10.1037/0021-9010.71.2.203

Bannon, L. (1991). From human factors to human actors: The role of psychology and human-computer interaction studies in system design. In J. Greenbaum & M. Kyng (Eds.), *Design at Work. Cooperative Design of Computer Systems* (pp. 25-44). Mahwah, NJ: New Jersey: Lawrence Erlbaum Associates.

Bansal, H. S., & Irving, P. G. (2004). A Three-Component Model of Customer Commitment to Service Providers. *Journal of Academy of Marketing, 32*(3), 234–250. doi:10.1177/0092070304263332

Bansler, J. P., & Havn, E. (1994, May 30-31). Information systems development with generic systems. In W. Baets (Ed.), *Proceedings of the 2nd European Conference on Information Systems,* Nijenrode, the Netherlands (pp. 30-31). Nijenrode University Press.

Banville, C., & Landry, M. (1989). Can the field of MIS be disciplined? *Communications of the ACM, 32*(1), 48–60. doi:10.1145/63238.63241

Barker, C., & Willis, P. (2008). *Cultural Studies: Theory and Practice*. Thousand Oaks, CA: Sage.

Barley, S. R. (1986). Technology as an occasion for structuring: Evidence from observations of CT scanners and social order of radiology departments. *Administrative Science Quarterly, 31*, 78–108. doi:10.2307/2392767

Barley, S. R., & Tolbert, P. S. (1997). Institutionalization and structuration: studying the links between action and institution. *Organization Studies, 18*(1), 93–117. doi:10.1177/017084069701800106

Barnes, S. J., & Vidgen, R. (2001). An evaluation of cyber-bookshops: the WebQual method. *International Journal of Electronic Commerce, 6*(1), 11–30.

Barney, J. B. (1991). Firm Resources and Sustained Competitive Advantage. *Journal of Management, 17*(1), 99–120. doi:10.1177/014920639101700108

Barney, J. B. (2001). Is the Resource-Based View a Useful Perspective for Strategic Management Research? Yes. *Academy of Management Journal, 26*(1), 41–56. doi:10.2307/259393

Barton, A. J. (2005). Cultivating Informatics Competencies in a Community of Practice. *Nursing Administration Quarterly, 29*(4), 323–328.

Barua, A., Kriebel, C. H., & Mukhopadhyay, T. (1995). Information Technologies and Business Value - an Analytic and Empirical-Investigation. *Information Systems Research, 6*(1), 3–23. doi:10.1287/isre.6.1.3

Barua, A., & Lee, B. (1997a). An Economic Analysis of the Introduction of an Electronic Data Interchange System. *Information Systems Research, 8*(4), 398–422. doi:10.1287/isre.8.4.398

Barua, A., & Lee, B. (1997b). The Information Technology Productivity Paradox Revisited: A Theoretical and Empirical Investigation in the Manufacturing Sector. *International Journal of Flexible Manufacturing Systems, 9*(2), 145–166. doi:10.1023/A:1007967718214

Barua, A., & Mukhopadhyay, T. (2000). Information Technology and Business Performance: Past, Present, and Future. In Zmud, R. W. (Ed.), *Framing the Domains of IT Management: Projecting the Future through the Past* (pp. 65–84). Cincinnati, OH: Pinnaflex Educational Resources, Inc.

Bayman, P., & Mayer, R. E. (1984). A diagnosis of beginning programmers misconceptions of BASIC programming statements. *Communications of the ACM, 26*, 677–679. doi:10.1145/358172.358408

Beath, C. M. (1991). Supporting the information technology champion. *Management Information Systems Quarterly, 15*(3), 355–371. doi:10.2307/249647

Beaton, J., Jeong, S. Y., Xie, Y., Stylos, J., & Myers, B. A. (2008, September 15-19). Usability challenges for enterprise service-oriented architecture APIs. In *Proceedings of the the 2008 IEEE Symposium on Visual Languages and Human-Centric Computing (VL/HCC '08),* Herrsching am Ammersee, Germany (pp. 193-196). Washington, DC: IEEE Computer Society.

Beaton, J., Myers, B. A., Stylos, J., Jeong, S. Y., & Xie, Y. (2008). Usability evaluation for enterprise SOA APIs. In *Proceedings of the 2nd International Workshop on Systems Development in SOA Environments (SDSOA 2008, ICSE 2008),* Leipzig, Germany, (pp. 29-34). ACM Publishing.

Becerra-Fernandez, I., Gonzalex, A., & Sabherwal, R. (2004). *Knowledge Management: Challenges, Solutions and Technologies*. Upper Saddle River, NJ: Prentice Hall.

Becker, H. S. (1960). Notes on the concept of commitment. *American Journal of Sociology, 66*(1), 32–42. doi:10.1086/222820

Beckers, J. J., & Schmidt, H. G. (2001). The structure of computer anxiety: A six-factor model. *Computers in Human Behavior, 17*(1), 35–49. doi:10.1016/S0747-5632(00)00036-4

Beck, K. (1999). *Extreme Programming Explained: Embrace Change*. Reading, MA: Addison-Wesley Professional.

Beck, K., & Gamma, E. (2003). *Contributing to Eclipse: Principles, Patterns and Plugins*. Reading, MA: Addison-Wesley.

Beckwith, L., Inman, D., Rector, K., & Burnett, M. (2007, September 23-27). On to the real world: Gender and self-efficacy in Excel. In *Proceedings of the IEEE Symposium on Visual Languages and Human-Centric Computing (VL/HCC 2007)*, Coeur d'Alene, ID (pp. 119-126). Washington, DC: IEEE Computer Society.

Beckwith, L., Sorte, S., Burnett, M., Wiedenbeck, S., Chintakovid, T., & Cook, C. (2005, September 20-24). Designing features for both genders in end-user programming environments. In *Proceedings of the 2005 IEEE Symposium on Visual Languages and Human-Centric Computing (VL/HCC 2005)*, Dallas, TX (pp. 153-160). Washington, DC: IEEE Computer Society.

Beckwith, L., Burnett, M., Grigoreanu, V., & Wiedenbeck, S. (2006). Gender HCI: What about the software? *Computer*, *39*(11), 83–87. doi:10.1109/MC.2006.382

Bell, M., Hall, M., Chalmers, M., Gray, P., & Brown, B. (2006). Domino: Exploring Mobile Collaborative Software Adaptation. In *Pervasive Computing: Proceedings of the 4th International Pervasive Computing Conference* (LNCS 3968, pp. 153-168).

Bellini, C. G. B., & Vargas, L. M. (2003). Rationale for Internet-Mediated Communities. *Cyberpsychology & Behavior*, *6*(1), 3–14. doi:10.1089/109493103321167929

Benbasat, I., Goldstein, D., & Mead, M. (1987, September). The Case Study Strategy in Studies of Information Systems. *Management Information Systems Quarterly*, 368–386.

Bender, D. H. (1986). Financial Impact of Information Processing. *Journal of Management Information Systems*, *3*(2), 22–32.

Benigno, V., & Trentin, G. (2000). The evaluation of online courses. *Journal of Computer Assisted Learning*, *16*, 259–270. doi:10.1046/j.1365-2729.2000.00137.x

Benkler, Y. (2006). *The wealth of networks: How social production transforms markets and freedom*. New Haven: Yale University Press.

Benkler, Y., & Nissenbaum, H. (2006). Commons-based peer production and virtue. *Political Philosophy*, *14*(4), 394–419. doi:10.1111/j.1467-9760.2006.00235.x

Bentler, P. M. (2004). *EQS 6 Structural Equations Program Manual*. Encino, CA: Multivariate Software, Inc.

Bentley, R., Horstmann, T., Sikkel, K., & Trevor, J. (1995). Supporting Collaborative Information Sharing with the World Wide Web: The BSCW Shared Workspace System. In *Proceedings of the 4th International WWW Conference* (pp. 63-74).

Berger, P., & Luckmann, T. (1967). *The social construction of reality*. New York: Doubleday.

Berg, M. (1999a). Accumulating and coordinating: Occasions for information technologies in medical work. *Computer Supported Cooperative Work*, *8*(4), 373–401. doi:10.1023/A:1008757115404

Berg, M., & Goorman, E. (1999b). The contextual nature of medical information. *International Journal of Medical Informatics*, *56*, 51–60. doi:10.1016/S1386-5056(99)00041-6

Berlo, D. K., & Lemert, J. B. (1961, December). *An empirical test of a general construct of credibility.* Paper presented at the SAA Conference, New York, NY.

Berlo, D. K., Lemert, J. B., & Mertz, R. J. (1969). Dimensions for evaluating the acceptability of message sources. *Public Opinion Quarterly*, *33*(4), 563–576. doi:10.1086/267745

Bernard, P. J., Hammond, N. V., Morton, J., & Long, J. B. (1981). Consistency and compatibility in human-computer dialogue. *International Journal of Man-Machine Studies*, *15*(1), 87–134. doi:10.1016/S0020-7373(81)80024-7

Beyer, H., & Holtzblatt, K. (1998). *Contextual Design: Defining Customer-Centered Systems*. San Francisco, CA: Morgan Kaufmann Publishers, Inc.

Bharadwaj, A. S., Sambamurthy, V., & Zmud, R. W. (1999b). IT Capabilities: Theoretical Perspectives and Empirical Operationalization. In *Proceedings of the 20th International Conference on Information Systems*, Charlotte, NC (pp. 378-385).

Bharadwaj, A. S. (2000). A Resource-Based Perspective on Information Technology Capability and Firm Performance: An Empirical Investigation. *Management Information Systems Quarterly*, *24*(1), 169–196. doi:10.2307/3250983

Bharadwaj, A. S., Bharadwaj, S. G., & Konsynski, B. R. (1999a). Information Technology Effects on Firm Performance as Measured by Tobin's q. *Management Science*, *45*(7), 1008–1024. doi:10.1287/mnsc.45.7.1008

Bhattacherjee, A. (2001). Understanding information systems continuance: An expectation-confirmation model. *Management Information Systems Quarterly*, *25*(3), 351. doi:10.2307/3250921

Bhattarcherjee, A., & Premkumar, G. (2004). Understanding changes in belief and attitude toward information technology usage: A theoretical model and longitudinal test. *Management Information Systems Quarterly*, *28*(2), 229–254.

Bhatt, G. D., & Grover, V. (2005). Type of Information Technology Capabilities and Their Role in Competitive Advantage: An Empirical Study. *Journal of Management Information Systems*, *22*(2), 253–277.

Bias, R., & Reitmeyer, P. (1995). Usability Support Inside and Out. *Interaction*, *2*(2), 29–32. doi:10.1145/205350.205355

Bieber, M., Engelbart, D., Furuta, R., Hiltz, S. R., Noll, J., & Preece, J. (2002). Toward Virtual Community Knowledge Evolution. *Journal of Management Information Systems*, *18*(4), 11–35.

Bijker, W. (1995). *Of bicycles, bakelites and bulbs: Toward a Theory of Sociotechnical Change*. Cambridge, MA: MIT Press.

Billingsley, P. (1995). Starting from Scratch: Building a Usability Program at Union Pacific Railroad. *Interaction*, *2*(4), 27–30. doi:10.1145/225362.225366

Billings, R., & Wroten, S. (1978). Use of path analysis in industrial/organizational psychology: criticisms and suggestions. *The Journal of Applied Psychology*, *63*(6), 677–688. doi:10.1037/0021-9010.63.6.677

Bjerknes, G., & Bratteteig, T. (1987). Florence in wonderland. System development with nurses. In G. Bjerknes, P. Ehn, & M. Kyng (Ed.), *Computers and democracy. A Scandinavian challenge* (pp. 279-295). Aldershot, UK: Avebury.

Black, R. W. (2006). Language, culture, and identity in online fanfiction. *E-Learning, 3*(2), 170-184. Retrieved April 28, 2008, from http://www.wwwords.co.uk/elea/content/pdfs/3/issue3_2.asp#6

Blackwell, A. (2002, September 3-6). First steps in programming: A rationale for attention investment models. In *Proceedings of the 2002 IEEE Symposium on Visual Languages and Human-Centric Computing (VL/HCC 2002),* Arlington, VA (pp. 2-10). Washington, DC: IEEE Computer Society.

Bloch, J. (2001). *Effective java programming language guide*. Reading, MA: Addison-Wesley.

Bloomer, S., & Croft, R. (1997). Pitching Usability to Your Organization. *Interaction*, *4*(6), 18–26. doi:10.1145/267505.267510

Bock, G. W., & Kim, Y.-G. (2002). Breaking the myths of rewards: an exploratory study of attitudes about knowledge sharing. *Information Resources Management Journal*, *15*(2), 14–21. doi:10.4018/irmj.2002040102

Bock, G.-W., Zmud, R. W., Kim, Y.-G., & Lee, J.-N. (2005). Behavioral Intention Formation in Knowledge Sharing: Examining the Roles of Extrinsic Motivators, Social-Psychological Forces, and Organizational Climate. *Management Information Systems Quarterly*, *29*(1), 87–111.

Bødker, S., & Buur, J. (2002). The Design Collaboratorium – a Place for Usability Design. *ACM Transactions on Computer-Human Interaction*, *9*(2), 152–169. doi:10.1145/513665.513670

Boissel, J.-P., Amsallem, E., Cucherat, M., Nony, P., & Haugh, M. (2004). Bridging the gap between therapeutic research results and physician prescribing decisions: knowledge transfer, a prerequisite to knowledge translation. *European Journal of Clinical Pharmacology, 60*(9), 609–616. doi:10.1007/s00228-004-0816-2

Boivie, I., Gulliksen, J., & Göransson, B. (2006). The lonesome cowboy: a study of the usability designer role in systems development. *Interacting with Computers, 18*(4), 601–634. doi:10.1016/j.intcom.2005.10.003

Booth, J., Tolson, D., Hotchkiss, R., & Schofield, I. (2007). Using action research to construct national evidence-based nursing care guidance for gerontological nursing. *Journal of Clinical Nursing, 16*(5), 945–953. doi:10.1111/j.1365-2702.2007.01773.x

Borgholm, T., & Madsen, K. (1999). Cooperative Usability Practices. *Communications of the ACM, 42*(5), 91–97. doi:10.1145/301353.301438

Borgman, C. (1986). The user's mental model of an information retrieval system: An experiment on prototype online retrieval catalog. *International Journal of Man-Machine Studies, 10*, 625–637.

Borofsky, R. (Ed.). (1994). *Assessing Cultural Anthropology*. New York: McGraw-Hill, Inc.

Bostrom, R. P., & Olfman, L. (1990). The importance of learning style in end-user training. *Management Information Systems Quarterly, 14*(1), 101–119. doi:10.2307/249313

Bostrom, R. P., Olfman, L., & Sein, M. K. (1990). The importance of learning style in end-user training. *Management Information Systems Quarterly, 14*(1), 101–119. doi:10.2307/249313

Braa, K., & Sandahl, T. (2000). Introducing digital documents in work practices challenges and perspectives. *Group Decision and Negotiation, 9*(3), 189–203. doi:10.1023/A:1008783106613

Brand, S. (1995). *How buildings learn: What happens after they're built*. New York: Penguin Books.

Bratteteig, T. (1997, August 9-12). Mutual learning: Enabling cooperation in systems design. In K. Braa & E. Monteiro (Eds.), *Proceedings of the 20th Information Systems Research Seminar in Scandinavia,* Hankø, Norway (pp. 1-20). Department of Informatics, University of Oslo, Norway.

Brewer, J., & Bassoli, A. (2006, May 23). Reflections of gender, reflections on gender: Designing ubiquitous computing technologies. In *Proceedings of Gender and Interaction: Real and Virtual Women in a Male World Workshop at AVI 2006,* Venice, Italy (pp. 9-12).

Brooks, F., & Scott, P. (2006). Exploring knowledge work and leadership in online midwifery communication. *Journal of Advanced Nursing, 55*(4), 510–520. doi:10.1111/j.1365-2648.2006.03937.x

Brown, J. S. (2005). *New learning environments for the 21st century.* Retrieved from http://www.johnseelybrown.com/newlearning.pdf

Brown, A. (1995). Managing Understandings: Politics, Symbolism, Niche Marketing and the Quest for Legitimacy in IT Implementation. *Organization Studies, 16*(6), 951–969. doi:10.1177/017084069501600602

Brown, J. S., & Duguid, P. (1998). Organizing Knowledge. *California Management Review, 40*(3), 90–111.

Brown, J. S., & Duguid, P. (2001). Knowledge and organization: A social-practice perspective. *Organization Science, 12*(2), 198–213. doi:10.1287/orsc.12.2.198.10116

Brown, J. S., Duguid, P., & Haviland, S. (1994). Toward informed participation: Six scenarios in search of democracy in the information age. *The Aspen Institute Quarterly, 6*(4), 49–73.

Brown, S. A., Fuller, R., & Vician, C. (2004). Who's afraid of the virtual world? The role of anxiety in computer-mediated communication use and satisfaction. *Journal of the Association for Information Systems, 5*(2), 81–109.

Brown, T. A. (2006). *Confirmatory Factor Analysis for Applied Research.* New York: Guilford Press.

Bruner, J. (1996). *The culture of education.* Cambridge, MA: Harvard University Press.

Bryman, A., & Cramer, D. (1994). *Quantitative data analysis for social scientists.* New York: Routledge.

Brynjolfsson, E., & Hitt, L. (1996). Paradox Lost? Firm-level Evidence on the Returns to Information Systems Spending. *Management Science*, *42*(4), 541–558. doi:10.1287/mnsc.42.4.541

Brynjolfsson, E., Malone, T. W., Gurbaxani, V., & Kambil, A. (1994). Does Information Technology Lead to Smaller Firms. *Management Science*, *40*(12), 1628–1644. doi:10.1287/mnsc.40.12.1628

Budweg, S., & Draxler, S. (Eds.). (2009). Open Design Spaces Supporting User Innovation: Perspectives and Challenges [Special issue]. *IRSI Report on Open Design Spaces Supporting User Innovation, 6*(2).

Budweg, S., Draxler, S., Lohmann, S., Rashid, A., & Stevens, G. (2009). Open design spaces supporting user innovation. *Proceedings of the International Workshop on Open Design Spaces; International Reports on Socio-Informatics, 6*(2). Retrieved from http://www.iisi.de/fileadmin/IISI/upload/IRSI/IRSIV6I2.pdf

Burke, R. D. (2002). Hybrid Recommender Systems: Survey and Experiments. *User Modeling and User-Adapted Interaction*, *12*(4), 331–370. doi:10.1023/A:1021240730564

Burnett, M., Chekka, S., & Pandey, R. (2001, September 5-7). FAR: An end-user language to support cottage e-services. In *Proceedings of the IEEE Symposia on Human-Centric Computing Languages and Environments,* Stresa, Italy (pp. 195-202). Washington, DC: IEEE Computer Society.

Burnett, M., Cook, C., & Rothermel, G. (2004). End-user software engineering. *Communications of the ACM*, *47*(9), 53–58. doi:10.1145/1015864.1015889

Burrell, G., & Morgan, G. (1979). *Sociological Paradigms and Organizational Analysis. Elements of the Sociology of Corporate Life*. London: Heinemann Educational Books Ltd.

Byrd, T. A. (2001). Information Technology, Core Competencies, and Sustained Competitive Advantage. *Information Resources Management Journal*, *14*(2), 27–36.

Byrd, T. A., Lewis, B. R., & Bryan, R. W. (2006). The Leveraging Influence of Strategic Alignment on IT Investment: An Empirical Examination. *Information & Management*, *43*(3), 308–321. doi:10.1016/j.im.2005.07.002

Byrd, T. A., & Marshall, T. E. (1997). Relating Information Technology Investment to Organizational Performance: A Causal Model Analysis. *Omega-International Journal of Management Science*, *25*(1), 43–56. doi:10.1016/S0305-0483(96)00040-0

Byrd, T. A., & Turner, D. E. (2001). An Exploratory Analysis of the Value of the Skills of IT Personnel: Their Relationship to IS Infrastructure and Competitive Advantage. *Decision Sciences*, *32*(1), 21–54. doi:10.1111/j.1540-5915.2001.tb00952.x

Byrne, B. M. (2006). *Structural Equation Modeling with EQS, Basic Concepts, Applications, and Programming* (2nd ed.). Mahwah, NJ: Lawrence Erlbaum Associates.

Byrne, B. M., & Crombie, G. (2003). Modeling and Testing Change: An Introduction to the Latent Growth Curve Model. *Understanding Statistics*, *2*(3), 177–203. doi:10.1207/S15328031US0203_02

Cabitza, F., & Simone, C. (2006, October). *"You Taste Its Quality": Making sense of quality standards on situated artifacts*. Paper presented at the 1st Mediterranean Conference on Information Systems (MCIS'06), Venice, Italy. Association for Information Systems.

Cabitza, F., & Simone, C. (2007, September 24-28). "... and do it the usual way": fostering awareness of work conventions in document-mediated collaboration. In *Proceedings of the 10th European Conference on Computer Supported Cooperative Work (ECSCW'07),* Limerick, Ireland (pp. 24-28). Dordrecht, The Netherlands: Springer.

Cabitza, F., & Simone, C. (2008, June 17-19). Supporting practices of positive redundancy for seamless care. In *Proceedings of the 21st IEEE International Symposium on Computer-Based Medical Systems (CBMS'08),* Jyväskylä, Finland (pp. 470-475). Washington, DC: IEEE Computer Society.

Cabitza, F., & Simone, C. (2009, June 25-27). Active artifacts as bridges between context and community knowledge sources. In *Proceedings of the 4th International Conference on Communities and Technologies (C&T2009),* Univeristy Park, PA (pp. 115-124). ACM Publishing.

Cabitza, F., & Simone, C. (in press). PRODOC: An electronic patient record to foster process-oriented practices In *Proceedings of the 11th European Conference on Computer Supported Cooperative Work (ECSCW2009),* Vienna, Austria. Dordrecht, The Netherlands: Springer.

Cabitza, F., Locatelli, M., Sarini, M., & Simone, C. (2006, March 13-17). CASMAS: Supporting collaboration in pervasive environments. In *Proceedings of the 4th Annual IEEE International Conference on Pervasive Computing and Communications (PerCom2006),* Pisa, Italy (pp. 286-295). Washington, DC: IEEE Computer Society.

Cabitza, F., Sarini, M., & Simone, C. (2007, November 4-7). Providing awareness through situated process maps: the hospital care case. In *Proceedings of the 2007 International ACM SIGGROUP Conference on Supporting Group Work (GROUP '07),* Sanibel Island, FL (pp. 41-50). ACM Publishing.

Cabitza, F., Simone, C., & Sarini, M. (2009). Leveraging coordinative conventions to promote collaboration awareness. *Computer Supported Cooperative Work, 18*(4), 301–330. doi:10.1007/s10606-009-9093-z

Cabrera, A., Cabrera, E., & Barajas, S. (2001). The key role of organizational culture in a multi-system view of technology-driven change. *International Journal of Information Management, 21*(3), 245–261. doi:10.1016/S0268-4012(01)00013-5

Cacioppo, J. T., & Petty, R. E. (1980). Persuasiveness of communication is affected by exposure frequency and message quality: A theoretical and empirical analysis of persisting attitude change. *Current Issues & Research in Advertising, 3*(1), 97–122.

Cacioppo, J. T., & Petty, R. E. (1984). The elaboration likelihood model of persuasion. *Advances in Consumer Research. Association for Consumer Research (U. S.), 11*(1), 673–675.

Cacioppo, J. T., & Petty, R. E. (1989). Effects of message repetition on argument processing, recall, and persuasion. *Basic and Applied Social Psychology, 10*(1), 3–12. doi:10.1207/s15324834basp1001_2

Campbell, D., & Stanley, J. (1963). *Experimental and quasi-experimental designs for research.* Chicago: Rand McNally.

Carmel, E. (1997). American Hegemony in Packaged Software Trade and the "Culture of Software". *The Information Society, 13*(1), 125–142. doi:10.1080/019722497129322

Carmel, E., & Sawyer, S. (1998). Packaged software development teams: what makes them different? *Information Technology & People, 11*(1), 7–19. doi:10.1108/09593849810204503

Carmien, S. P., & Fischer, G. (2008, April). Design, adoption, and assessment of a socio-technical environment supporting independence for persons with cognitive disabilities. In *Proceedings of CHI 2008*, Florence, Italy, (pp. 597-607). ACM Publishing.

Carr, N. (2008). *Is Google making us stupid?* Retrieved from http://www.theatlantic.com/doc/200807/google

Carr, N. G. (2003). IT Doesn't Matter. *Harvard Business Review, 81*(5), 41–49.

Carroll, J., & Rosson, M. (1987). Paradox of the active user. In J. Carrol (Ed.), *Interfacing thought: Cognitive aspects of human-computer interaction* (pp. 80-111). Cambridge, MA: MIT Press.

Carroll, J., & van der Meij, H. (1998). Principles and Heuristics for Designing Minimalist Instruction. In Carroll, J. (Ed.), *Minimalism beyond the Nurnberg funnel* (pp. 19–54). Cambridge, MA: MIT Press.

Castillo, J. (1997). *The User-Reported Critical Method for Remote Usability Evaluation.* Blacksburg, VA: Virginia Polytechnic Institute and State University.

Catarci, T., Matarazzo, G., & Raiss, G. (2002). Driving usability into the public administration: the Italian experience. *International Journal of Human-Computer Studies, 57*(2), 121–138. doi:10.1016/S1071-5819(02)91014-1

Chaiken, S. (1979). Communicator physical attractiveness and persuasion. *Journal of Personality and Social Psychology, 37*(8), 1387–1397. doi:10.1037/0022-3514.37.8.1387

Changchit, C. (2006). New information technology adoption: Are you ready for it? *Journal of Electronic Commerce in Organizations, 4*(4), pi-iv.

Chan, Y. E., Huff, S. L., Copeland, D. G., & Barclay, D. W. (1997). Business Strategic Orientation, Information Systems Strategic Orientation and Strategic Alignment. *Information Systems Research*, *8*(2), 125–150. doi:10.1287/isre.8.2.125

Chau, P. Y. K. (1996). An empirical investigation on factors affecting the acceptance of CASE by systems developers. *Information & Management*, *30*(6), 269–280. doi:10.1016/S0378-7206(96)01074-9

Chau, P. Y. K. (2001). Influence of computer attitude and self-efficacy on IT usage behavior. *Journal of End User Computing*, *13*(1), 26–33. doi:10.4018/joeuc.2001010103

Chau, P. Y. K., & Hu, P. J.-H. (2001). Information Technology Acceptance by Individual Professionals: A Model Comparison Approach. *Decision Sciences*, *32*(4), 699–718. doi:10.1111/j.1540-5915.2001.tb00978.x

Chau, P. Y. K., & Hu, P. J.-H. (2002). Investigating healthcare professionals' decisions to accept telemedicine technology: an empirical test of competing theories. *Information & Management*, *39*(4), 297–311. doi:10.1016/S0378-7206(01)00098-2

Chen, A. N. K., & Edgington, T. M. (2005). Assessing Value in Organizational Knowledge Creation: Consideration for Knowledge Workers. *Management Information Systems Quarterly*, *29*(2), 279–309.

Chen, Y., & Lou, H. (2002). Toward an understanding of the behavioral intention to use a groupware application. *Journal of End User Computing*, *14*(4), 1–16.

CHI (Catholic Health Initiatives) Corporate Website. (2005). Retrieved December 21, 2006, from http://www.catholichealthinit.org/body.cfm?id=37785&action=detail&ref=1634

CHI (Catholic Health Initiatives) Corporate Website. (2008). Retrieved January 22, 2009, from http://www.catholichealthinit.org/default.cfm

Chiasson, M. W., & Green, L. W. (2007). Questioning the IT artefact: User practices that can, could, and cannot be supported in packaged-software designs. *European Journal of Information Systems*, *16*(5), 542–554. doi:10.1057/palgrave.ejis.3000701

Chickering, A., & Ehrmann, S. (1996). *Implementing the Seven Principles: Technology as Lever*. AAHE Bulletin.

Chickering, A., & Gamson, Z. F. (1987). *Seven Principles for Good Practice in Undergraduate Education*. AAHE Bulletin.

Ching, C., & Kafai, Y. (2008). Peer pedagogy: Student collaboration and reflection in a learning through design project. *Teachers College Record*, *110*(12), 2601–2632.

Chin, W. W. (1998). The Partial Least Squares Approach to Structural Equation Modeling. In Marcoulides, G. A. (Ed.), *Modern Methods for Business Research* (pp. 295–336). London: Lawrence Erlbaum.

Chiu, C.-M., & Wang, E. T. G. (2008). Understanding Web-based learning continuance intention: The role of subjective task value. *Information & Management*, *45*(3), 194–201. doi:10.1016/j.im.2008.02.003

Choi, B., & Lee, H. (2003). An empirical investigation of KM styles and their effect on corporate performance. *Information & Management*, *40*(5), 403–417. doi:10.1016/S0378-7206(02)00060-5

Choi, M. (2006). Communities of practice: an alternative learning model for knowledge creation. *British Journal of Educational Technology*, *37*(1), 143–146. doi:10.1111/j.1467-8535.2005.00486.x

Chou, C. (2003). Interactivity and interactive functions in web-based learning systems: A technical framework for designers. *British Journal of Educational Technology*, *34*(3), 265–279. doi:10.1111/1467-8535.00326

Chua, S. L., Chen, D., & Wong, A. (1999). Computer anxiety and its correlates: A meta-analysis. *Computers in Human Behavior*, *15*(5), 609–623. doi:10.1016/S0747-5632(99)00039-4

Chwelos, P., Benbasat, I., & Dexter, A. S. (2001). Research Report: Empirical Test of an EDI Adoption Model. *Information Systems Research*, *12*(3), 304–321. doi:10.1287/isre.12.3.304.9708

Clarke, S. (2004). Measuring API usability. *Dr. Dobb's Journal, May 2004,* S6-S9.

Clarke, T., & Hermens, A. (2001). Corporate developments and strategic alliances in e-learning. *Education + Training, 43*(4), 256-267.

Clement, A. (1994). Computing at Work: Empowering Action By 'Low-level Users'. *Communications of the ACM, 37*(1), 52–63. doi:10.1145/175222.175226

Clemons, E. K., & Row, M. C. (1991). Sustaining IT Advantage: The Role of Structural Differences. *Management Information Systems Quarterly, 15*(3), 275–292. doi:10.2307/249639

Clifford, J., & Marcus, G. (Eds.). (1986). *Writing culture: the poetics and politics of ethnography*. Berkeley, CA: University of California Press.

Cole, M., O'Keefe, R. M., & Siala, H. (2000). From the user interface to the consumer interface. *Information Systems Frontiers, 1*, 349–361. doi:10.1023/A:1010009923913

Compeau, D. R., & Higgins, C. A. (1995). Application of social cognitive theory to training for computer skills. *Information Systems Research, 6*(1), 118–143. doi:10.1287/isre.6.2.118

Compeau, D. R., & Higgins, C. A. (1999). Social cognitive theory and individual reactions to computing technology: A longitudinal study. *Management Information Systems Quarterly, 23*(2), 145–159. doi:10.2307/249749

Compeau, D., & Higgins, C. A. (1995b). Computer self-efficacy: Development of a measure and initial test. *Management Information Systems Quarterly, 19*(2), 189–211. doi:10.2307/249688

Compeau, D., Olfman, L., Sein, M., & Webster, J. (1995). End-user training and learning. *Communications of the ACM, 38*(7), 24–26. doi:10.1145/213859.214791

Conner, M. (2005). Communities of practice in health care: a personal reflection. *Work Based Learning in Primary Care, 3*(4), 347–350.

Cooper, R. B., & Zmud, R. W. (1990). Information technology implementation research: a technological diffusion approach. *Management Science, 36*(2), 123,117.

Cooper, A. (1999). *The inmates are running the asylum: Why high-tech products drive us crazy and how to restore the sanity*. Indianapolis, IN: Sams.

Cooper, C., & Bowers, J. (1995). Representing the users: Notes on the disciplinary rhetoric of human-computer interaction. In Thomas, P. (Ed.), *The Social and Interactional Dimensions of Human-Computer Interfaces* (pp. 48–66). Cambridge, MA: Cambridge University Press.

Cooper, R. B., & Zmud, R. W. (1990). Information technology implementation research: A technological diffusion approach. *Management Science, 36*(2), 123–139. doi:10.1287/mnsc.36.2.123

Costabile, M. F., Mussio, P., Provenza, L. P., & Piccinno, A. (2009). Supporting end users to be co-designers of their tools. In V. Pipek, M. B. Rossen, B. deRuyter, & V. Wulf (Eds.), *End-user development* (pp. 70-85). Heidelberg, Germany: Springer.

Costabile, M., Foglia, D., Fresta, G., Mussio, P., & Piccinno, A. (2003, October 28-31). Building environments for end-user development and tailoring. In *Proceedings of the IEEE Symposium on Human Centric Computing Languages and Environments,* Auckland, New Zealand (pp. 31-38). Washington, DC: IEEE Computer Society.

Costabile, M. F., Fogli, D., Mussio, P., & Piccinno, A. (2007). Visual Interactive Systems for End-User Development: A Model-based Design Methodology. *IEEE Transactions on SMC - Part A. Systems and Humans, 37*(6), 1029–1046.

Coulson, T., Zhu, J., Stewart, W., & Rohm, C. E. T. (2004). The importance of database application knowledge in successful ERP training. *Communications of the IIMA, 4*(3).

Cramm, S. (2005). *The soft side of persuasion*. Retrieved February 15, 2006, from http://www.cio.com/research/leadership/edit/ec051705_persuasion.html

Crisci, R., & Kassinove, H. (1973). Effect of perceived expertise, strength of advice, and environmental setting on parental compliance. *The Journal of Social Psychology, 89*, 245–250.

Cronbach, L. J. (1971). Test Validation. In Thorndike, R. L. (Ed.), *Educational Measurement* (2nd ed.). Washington, DC: American Council on Education.

Cron, W. L., & Sobol, M. G. (1983). The Relationship Between Computerization and Performance: A Strategy for Maximizing the Economic Benefits of Computerization. *Information & Management*, *6*, 171–181. doi:10.1016/0378-7206(83)90034-4

Cross, J., Earl, M. J., & Sampler, J. (1997). Transformation of the IT Function at British Petroleum. *Management Information Systems Quarterly*, *21*(4), 401–423. doi:10.2307/249721

Cwalina, K., & Abrams, B. (2005). *Framework design guidelines*. Upper-Saddle River, NJ: Addison-Wesley.

Cypher, A. (Ed.). (1993). *Watch what I do: Programming by example*. Cambridge, MA: MIT Press.

Czarniawska-Joerges, B. (1992). *Exploring Complex Organizations. A Cultural Perspective*. Newbury Park, CA: Sage Publications.

Damodaran, L. (1996). User involvement in the systems designs process - a practical guide for users. *Behaviour & Information Technology*, *15*(16), 363–377. doi:10.1080/014492996120049

Danielsson, K., Naghsh, A. M., Gumm, D., & Warr, A. (2008). Distributed participatory design. In *CHI '08 Extended Abstracts on Human Factors in Computing Systems* (pp. 3953-3956). New York: ACM Publishing.

Davenport, T. H. (2001). *Mission critical: Realizing the promise of Enterprise Systems*. Boston, MA: Harvard Business School Press.

Davis, R. (1984). Interactive transfer of expertise. In B. G. Buchanan, & E. H. Shortliffe (Eds.), *Rule-based expert systems: The Mycin experiments of the Stanford Heuristic Programming Project* (pp. 171-205). Reading, MA: Addison-Wesley.

Davis, F. (1989). Perceived usefulness, perceived ease of use, and user acceptance of information technology. *Management Information Systems Quarterly*, *13*(3), 319–340. doi:10.2307/249008

Davis, F. D. (1989). Perceived ease of use, and user acceptance of information technology. *Management Information Systems Quarterly*, *13*(3), 319–340. doi:10.2307/249008

Davis, F. D., Bagozzi, R. P., & Warshaw, P. R. (1989). User acceptance of computer technology: A comparison of two theoretical models. *Management Science*, *35*(8), 982–1003. doi:10.1287/mnsc.35.8.982

Davis, G. B., & Olson, M. H. (1985). *Management information systems: Conceptual foundations, structure and development*. New York: McGraw-Hill.

Davison, R., & Martinsons, M. (2002). Empowerment or enslavement? A case of process-based organizational change in Hong Kong. *Information Technology & People*, *15*(1), 42–59. doi:10.1108/09593840210421516

Davis, S. A., & Bostrom, R. P. (1993). Training end users: An experimental investigation of the roles of computer interface and training methods. *Management Information Systems Quarterly*, *17*(1), 61–85. doi:10.2307/249510

de Certeau, M. (1984). *The Practice of Everyday Life*. Berkeley, CA: University of California Press.

de Souza, C. S., Barbosa, S. D. J., & da Silva, S. R. P. (2001). Semiotic engineering principles for evaluating end-user programming environments. *Interacting with Computers*, *13*(4), 467–495. doi:10.1016/S0953-5438(00)00051-5

Deci, E. L., & Ryan, R. M. (2000). The "what" and "why" of goal pursuits: Human needs and the self-determination of behavior. *Psychological Inquiry*, *11*(4), 227–268. doi:10.1207/S15327965PLI1104_01

Deci, E. L., Ryan, R. M., & Koestner, R. (1999). A meta-analytic review of experiments examining the effects of extrinsic rewards on intrinsic motivation. *Psychological Bulletin*, *125*(6), 627–668. doi:10.1037/0033-2909.125.6.627

Dehning, B., Richardson, V. J., & Zmud, R. W. (2003). The Value Relevance of Announcements of Transformational Information Technology Investments. *Management Information Systems Quarterly*, *27*(4), 637–656.

Dent, J. (1991). Accounting and Organizational Cultures: A Field Study of the Emergence of a New Organizational Reality. *Accounting, Organizations and Society*, *16*(8), 705–732. doi:10.1016/0361-3682(91)90021-6

Denzin, N., & Lincoln, Y. (2000). Introduction: The Discipline and Practice of Qualitative Research. In Denzin, N., & Lincoln, Y. (Eds.), *Handbook of Qualitative Research* (2nd ed., pp. 1–34). Thousand Oaks, CA: Sage.

dePaula, R., Fischer, G., & Ostwald, J. (2001, March). Courses as seeds: Expectations and realities. In P. Dillenbourg, A. Eurelings, & K. Hakkarainen (Eds.), *Proceedings of the European Conference on Computer-Supported Collaborative Learning*, Maastricht, the Netherlands (pp. 494-501).

DeSanctis, G., & Poole, M. S. (1994). Capturing the complexity in advanced technology use: adaptive structuration theory. *Organization Science*, *5*(2), 121–132. doi:10.1287/orsc.5.2.121

DeSanctis, G., Poole, M. S., Dickson, G. W., & Jackson, B. M. (1993). Interpretive analysis of team use of group technologies. *Journal of Organizational Computing*, *3*(1), 1–29. doi:10.1080/10919399309540193

Devellis, R. F. (2003). *Scale Development* (2nd ed.). Thousand Oaks, CA: Sage Publications.

Dickie, J. (2006). Invest in CRM beyond applications. *Customer Relationship Management*, *10*(9), 20.

Dittrich, Y., & Vaucouleur, S. (2008, May 13). Practices around customization of standard systems. In L.-T. Chen et al. (Eds.), *Proceedings of the 2008 International Workshop on Cooperative and Human Aspects of Software Engineering,* Leipzig Germany (pp. 37-40). ACM Publishing.

Divitini, M., & Simone, C. (2000). Supporting different dimensions of adaptability in workflow modeling. *Computer Supported Cooperative Work*, *9*(3), 365–397. doi:10.1023/A:1008751210054

Dixit, A., & Pindyck, R. (1994). *Investment Under Uncertainty*. Princeton, NJ: Princeton University Press.

Dixon, W. J., & Tukey, J. W. (1968). Approximate behavior of the distribution of winsorized t (Trimming/Winsorization 2). *Technometrics*, *10*, 83–98. doi:10.2307/1266226

Djamasbi, S., & Loiacono, E. T. (2008). Do men and women use feedback provided by their decision support systems (DSS) differently? *Decision Support Systems*, *44*(4), 854–869. doi:10.1016/j.dss.2007.10.008

Doctorow, C. (2006). *Response to Jaron Lanier's "Digital Maoism: The hazards of the new online collectivism"*. Retrieved from http://www.edge.org/discourse/digital_maoism.html

Dourish, P. (2001). Seeking a foundation for context-aware computing. *Special Issue on Context-Aware Computing HCI Journal*, *16*(2), 229–241.

Dourish, P., Edwards, W. K., LaMarca, A., Lamping, J., Petersen, K., & Salsibury, M. (2000). Extending document management systems with user-specific active properties. *ACM Transactions on Information Systems*, *18*(2), 140–170. doi:10.1145/348751.348758

Douthwaite, B., Keatinge, J. D. H., & Park, J. R. (2001). Why promising technologies fail: The neglected role of user innovation during adoption. *Research Policy*, *30*(5), 819–836. doi:10.1016/S0048-7333(00)00124-4

du Gay, P., Hall, S., Janes, L., MacKay, H., & Negus, K. (1997). *Doing Cultural Studies: The Story of the Sony Walkman*. London: Sage.

Dubé, L., Bourhis, A., & Jacob, R. (2005). The impact of structuring characteristics on the launching of virtual communities of practice. *Journal of Organizational Change*, *18*(2), 145–166. doi:10.1108/09534810510589570

Dube, L., & Robey, D. (1999). Software Stories: Three Cultural Perspectives on the Organizational Practices of Software Development. *Accounting. Management and Information Technologies*, *9*(4), 223–259. doi:10.1016/S0959-8022(99)00010-7

Dubois, A., & Gadde, L. (2002). Systematic combining: an abductive approach to case research. *Journal of Business Research*, *55*(7), 553–560. doi:10.1016/S0148-2963(00)00195-8

Dupouët, O., & Yildizoğlu, M. (2006). Organizational performance in hierarchies and communities of practice. *Journal of Economic Behavior & Organization*, *61*(4), 668–690. doi:10.1016/j.jebo.2004.07.011

Dyck, J. L., Gee, N. R., & Smither, J. A. (1998). The changing construct of computer anxiety for younger and older adults. *Computers in Human Behavior*, *14*(1), 61–77. doi:10.1016/S0747-5632(97)00032-0

Dymock, D., & McCarthy, C. (2006). Towards a learning organization? Employee perceptions. *The Learning Organization*, *13*(5), 525–536. doi:10.1108/09696470610680017

Eagly, A. H., & Chaiken, S. (1975). An attribution analysis of the effect of communicator characteristics on opinion change: The case of communicator attractiveness. *Journal of Personality and Social Psychology*, *32*(1), 136–144. doi:10.1037/h0076850

Eason, K. (1988). *Information technology and organisational change*. London: Taylor & Francis.

Eclipse Foundation. (2004). *Eclipse Project 3.0 Plan (Final)*. Portland, OR: Author.

Eden, H. (2002, January). Getting in on the (Inter)Action: Exploring affordances for collaborative learning in a context of informed participation. In G. Stahl (Ed.), *Proceedings of the Computer Supported Collaborative Learning (CSCL 2002) Conference*, Boulder, CO (pp. 399-407). Lawrence Erlbaum.

Ehn, P., & Kyng, M. (1991). Cardboard computers: Mocking-it-up or hands-on the future. In J. Greenbaum & M. Kyng (Eds.), *Design at work: Cooperative design of computer systems* (pp. 169-195). Hillsdale, NJ: Lawrence Erlbaum.

Ehrlich, S. F. (1987). Strategies for encouraging successful adoption of office communication systems. *ACM Transactions on Office Information Systems*, *5*(4), 340–357. doi:10.1145/42196.42198

Eisenberg, M., & Fischer, G. (1994, April). Programmable design environments: Integrating end-user programming with domain-oriented assistance. In *Proceedings of Chi 1994: Human factors in computing Systems,* Boston (pp. 431-437). ACM Publishing.

Eisenhardt, K. (1989). Building Theories from Case Study Research. *Academy of Management Review*, *14*(4), 532–550. doi:10.2307/258557

Ellis, B., Stylos, J., & Myers, B. (2007, May 19-27). The factory pattern in API design: A usability evaluation. In *Proceedings of the 29th International Conference on Software Engineering (ICSE 2007),* Minneapolis, MN (pp. 302-312). Washington, DC: IEEE Computer Society.

Engeström, Y. (2001). Expansive learning at work: Toward an activity theoretical reconceptualization. *Journal of Education and Work*, *14*(1), 133–156. doi:10.1080/13639080123238

Engeström, Y. (2004). New forms of learning in co-configuration work. *Journal of Workplace Learning*, *16*(1-2), 11–21. doi:10.1108/13665620410521477

Engeström, Y. (2007). Enriching the theory of expansive learning: Lessons from journeys toward co-configuration. *Mind, Culture, and Activity*, *14*(1-2), 23–29.

Eriksson, J., & Dittrich, Y. (2007). Combining tailoring and evolutionary software development for rapidly changing business systems. *Journal of Organizational and End User Computing*, *19*(2), 47–64.

Ethiraj, S. K., & Levinthal, D. (2004). Modularity and innovation in complex systems. *Management Science*, *50*, 159–173. doi:10.1287/mnsc.1030.0145

EUSPRIG. (2009). *Spreadsheet mistakes news stories*. Retrieved July 19, 2009, from http://www.eusprig.org/stories.htm

Evans, J. R., & Haase, I. M. (2001). Online business in the twenty-first century: An analysis of potential target markets. *Internet Research: Electronic Networking Applications Policy*, *11*(3), 246–260. doi:10.1108/10662240110396432

Fellenz, C. (1997). Introducing Usability into Smaller Organizations. *Interaction*, *4*(5), 29–33. doi:10.1145/264044.264047

Festinger, L. (1957). *A theory of cognitive dissonance*. Stanford, CA: Stanford University Press.

Finck, M., Gumm, D., & Pape, B. (2004). *Using Groupware for Mediated Feedback*. Paper presented at the Participation Design Conference, Toronto, Ontario, Canada.

Fischer, G. (1999). *Symmetry of Ignorance, Social Creativity and Meta-Design*. Paper presented at the 3rd ACM Conference on Creativity and Cognition, Loughborough, UK.

Fischer, G. (2001, August 11-14). Communities of interest: Learning through the interaction of multiple knowledge systems. In *Proceedings of the 24th Annual Information Systems Research Seminar in Scandinavia (IRIS'24)*, Ulvik, Norway (pp. 1-14).

Fischer, G. (2002). Beyond 'couch potatoes': From consumers to designers and active contributors. *Firstmonday*. Retrieved from http://firstmonday.org/issues/issue7_12/fischer/

Fischer, G. (2005, April 12-15). Distances and diversity: Sources for social creativity. In *Proceedings of Creativity & Cognition,* London (pp. 128-136). ACM Publishing.

Fischer, G. (2006, May 23-26). Distributed intelligence: Extending the power of the unaided, individual human mind. In *Proceedings of Advanced Visual Interfaces (Avi) Conference,* Venice, Italy (pp. 7-14). ACM Publishing.

Fischer, G. (2007, September 10-14). Meta-design: Expanding boundaries and redistributing control in design. In C. Baranauskas, P. Palanque, A. Abascal, S. Diniz, & J. Barbosa (Eds.), *Human-Computer Interaction INTERACT 2007: 11th IFIP TC 13 International Conference,* Rio de Janeiro, Brazil (LNCS 4662, pp. 193-206).

Fischer, G. (2009). End-user development and meta design: Foundations for cultures of participation. In V. Pipek, M. B. Rosson, B. de Ruyter, & V. Wulf (Eds.), *End-user development* (pp. 3-14). New York: Springer.

Fischer, G., & Giaccardi, E. (2006). Meta-design: A framework for the future of end user development. In H. Lieberman, F. Paternò, & V. Wulf (Eds.), *End user development* (pp. 427-457). New York: Springer.

Fischer, G., & Girgensohn, A. (1990, April 1-5). End-user modifiability in design environments. In *Proceedings of the Conference on Human Factors in Computing Systems (Chi 1990),* Seattle, WA (pp. 183-191). ACM Publishing.

Fischer, G., & Ostwald, J. (2002). *Seeding, Evolutionary Growth, and Reseeding: Enriching Participatory Design with Informed Participation.* Paper presented at the Participatory Design Conference, Malmö, Schweden.

Fischer, G., & Ostwald, J. (2002, June 23-25). Seeding, evolutionary growth, and reseeding: Enriching participatory design with informed participation. In T. Binder, J. Gregory, & I. Wagner (Eds.), *Proceedings of the 2002 Participatory Design Conference,* Malmo, Sweden (pp. 135-143). Palo Alto, CA: CPSR.

Fischer, G., & Scharff, E. (2000, August). Meta-design: Design for designers. In D. Boyarski & W. A. Kellogg (Eds.), *Proceedings of the 3rd International Conference on Designing Interactive Systems,* New York (pp. 396-405). ACM Publishing.

Fischer, G., Piccinno, A., & Ye, Y. (2008, September 25-26). The ecology of participants in co-evolving socio-technical environments. In P. Forbrig & F. Paternò (Ed.), *Engineering interactive systems: Proceedings of the 2nd Conference on Human-Centered Software Engineering,* Pisa, Italy (LNCS 5247, pp. 279-286).

Fischer, G., Scharff, E., & Ye, Y. (2004). Fostering social creativity by increasing social capital. In M. Huysman & V. Wulf (Eds.), *Social capital and information technology* (pp. 355-399). Cambridge, MA: MIT Press.

Fischer, G. (1994). Turning breakdowns into opportunities for creativity. *Knowledge-Based Systems. Special Issue on Creativity and Cognition, 7*(4), 221–232.

Fischer, G. (2000). Social creativity, symmetry of ignorance and meta-design. *Knowledge-Based Systems Journal. Special Issue on Creativity & Cognition, 13*(7-8), 527–537.

Fischer, G. (2002). Beyond "Couch Potatoes": From Consumers to Designers and Active Contributors. *First Monday, 7*(12).

Fischer, G. (This issue). End-user development and meta-design: Foundations for cultures of participation. *Journal of Organizational and End User Computing.*

Fischer, G., & Giaccardi, E. (2006). Meta-Design: A Framework for the Future of End User Development. In Lieberman, H., Paternò, F., & Wulf, V. (Eds.), *End User Development* (pp. 427–458). New York: Springer. doi:10.1007/1-4020-5386-X_19

Fischer, G., Giaccardi, E., Eden, H., Sugimoto, M., & Ye, Y. (2005). Beyond binary choices: Integrating individual and social creativity. *International Journal of Human-Computer Studies. Special Issue on Computer Support for Creativity, 63*(4-5), 482–512.

Fischer, G., Giaccardi, E., Ye, Y., Sutcliffe, A. G., & Mehandjiev, N. (2004). Meta-design: A manifesto for end-user development. *Communications of the ACM, 47*(9), 33–37. doi:10.1145/1015864.1015884

Fischer, G., & Sugimoto, M. (2006). Supporting self-directed learners and learning communities with socio-technical environments. [RPTEL]. *International Journal Research and Practice in Technology Enhanced Learning, 1*(1), 31–64. doi:10.1142/S1793206806000020

Fishbein, M., & Ajzen, I. (1975). *Belief, attitude, intention and behavior*. Reading, MA: Addison-Wesley.

Fishbein, M., & Ajzen, I. (1975). *Beliefs, Attitude, Intention and Behavior: An Introduction to Theory and Research.* Reading, MA: Addison-Wesley.

Fitzgerald, B., Russo, N. L., & Stolterman, E. (2003). *Information systems development: Methods in action.* New York: McGraw Hill.

Fitzpatrick, G. (2004). Integrated care and the working record. *Health Informatics Journal, 10*(4), 291–302. doi:10.1177/1460458204048507

Floyd, C., Reisin, F.-M., & Schmidt, G. (1989). STEPS to Software Development with Users Source. In *Proceedings of the 2nd European Software Engineering Conference* (LNCS 387, pp. 48-64).

Floyd, I. R., Jones, M. C., Rathi, D., & Twidale, M. B. (2007, January 3-7). Web mash-ups and patchwork prototyping: User-driven technological innovation with Web 2.0 and open source software. In *Proceedings of the 40th Annual Hawaii International Conference on System Sciences,* Big Island, HI (pp. 86-96). Washington, DC: IEEE Computer Society.

Fogli, D. (2009). End-user development for e-government website content creation. In V. Pipek, M. B. Rossen, B. deRuyter, & V. Wulf (Eds.), *End-user development* (pp. 126-145) Heidelberg, Germany: Springer.

Fok, L., Fok, W., & Hartman, S. (2001). Exploring the relationship between total quality management and information systems development. *Information & Management, 38*(6), 355–371. doi:10.1016/S0378-7206(00)00075-6

Foltz, C. B., Cronan, T. P., & Jones, T. W. (2005). Have you met your organization's computer usage policy? *Industrial Management & Data Systems, 105*(2), 137–146. doi:10.1108/02635570510583280

Fornell, C., & Larcker, D. F. (1981). Evaluating Structural Equations with Unobservable Variables and Measurement Error. *JMR, Journal of Marketing Research, 18*, 39–50. doi:10.2307/3151312

Forward, A., & Lethbridge, T. C. (2002, November 8-9). The relevance of software documentation, tools, and technology: A survey. In *Proceedings of DocEng 2002,* McLean, VA (pp. 26-33). ACM Publishing.

Fox, R. (Ed.). (1991). *Recapturing Anthropology. Working in the Present.* Santa Fe, NM: School of American Research Press.

Foy, P. S. (1999). Knowledge Management in Industry. In Liebowitz, J. (Ed.), *Knowledge Management Handbook.* Boca Raton, FL: CRC Press.

French, C. (2003, June 3). TransAlta says clerical snafu costs it $24 million. *Globe and Mail.*

Friendly, L. (1995, June 1-2). The design of distributed hyperlinked programming documentation. In *Proceedings of the International Workshop on Hypermedia Design,* Montpellier, France, (pp. 151-173). London: Springer.

Friestad, M., & Wright, P. (1994). The persuasion knowledge model: How people cope with persuasion attempts. *The Journal of Consumer Research, 21*(1), 1–31. doi:10.1086/209380

Furumo, K., & Melcher, A. (2006). The importance of social structure in implementing ERP systems: A case study using adaptive structuration theory. *Journal of Information Technology Case and Application Research, 8*(2), 39–58.

Gabbay, J., & le May, A. (2004). Evidence based guidelines or collectively constructed "mindlines?" Ethnographic study of knowledge management in primary care. *British Medical Journal, 329*(7473), 1013–1017. doi:10.1136/bmj.329.7473.1013

Gabbay, J., le May, A., Jefferson, H., Webb, D., Lovelock, R., Powell, J., & Lathlean, J. (2003). A case study of knowledge management in multi-agency consumer-informed 'communities of practice': implications for evidence-based policy development in health and social services. *Health: An Interdisciplinary Journal for the Social Study of Health. Illness & Medicine, 7*(3), 283–310.

Gagné, M., & Deci, E. L. (2005). Self-determination theory and work motivation. *Journal of Organizational Behavior, 26*(4), 331–362. doi:10.1002/job.322

Gallagher, A. (2006). *A Guide to Eliminating Software.* CIO Magazine, Analyst Corner.

Gallivan, M., & Srite, M. (2005). Information Technology and Culture: Merging Fragmented and Holistic Perpectives of Culture. *Information and Organization, 15*(2), 295–338. doi:10.1016/j.infoandorg.2005.02.005

Gamma, E., & Wiegand, J. (2005). *The eclipse way - processes that adapt*. Paper presented at EclipseCon 2005.

Gamma, E., & Beck, K. (2004). *Contributing to Eclipse: Principles, patterns, andplug-ins*. Reading, MA: Addison-Wesley.

Gantt, M., & Nardi, B. A. (1992, June 3-7). Gardeners and gurus: Patterns of cooperation among cad users. In P. Bauersfeld, J. Bennett, & G. Lynch (Eds.), *Proceedings of the Conference on Human Factors in Computing Systems (Chi 1992),* Monterey, CA (pp. 107-117). ACM Publishing.

Garavan, T. N., Carbery, R., & Murphy, E. (2007). Managing intentionally created communities of practice for knowledge sourcing across organisational boundaries. *The Learning Organization, 14*(1), 34–49. doi:10.1108/09696470710718339

Garrison, D. R. (1997). Self-directed learning: Toward a comprehensive model. *Adult Education Quarterly, 48*(1), 18–33. doi:10.1177/074171369704800103

Garrison, D. R., & Cleveland-Innes, M. (2005). Facilitating Cognitive Presence in Online Learning: Interaction Is Not Enough. *American Journal of Distance Education, 19*(3), 133–148. doi:10.1207/s15389286ajde1903_2

Gee, J. P. (2000). Identity as an analytic lens for research in education. *Review of Research in Education, 25*, 99–125.

Geertz, C. (1973). *The interpretation of cultures: selected essays*. New York: Basic Books.

Gefen, D., Straub, D., & Boudreau, M. (2000). Structural equation modeling techniques and regression: Guidelines for research practice. *Communications of AIS, 7*(7), 1–78.

Ghosh, B., & Scott, J. E. (2005). Comparing knowledge management in health-care and technical support organizations. *IEEE Transactions on Information Technology in Biomedicine, 9*(2), 162–168. doi:10.1109/TITB.2005.847202

Giaccardi, E. (2004). *Principles of metadesign: Processes and levels of co-creation in the new design space*. Unpublished doctoral dissertation, CAiiA-STAR, School of Computing, Plymouth, UK.

Giddens, A. (1984). *Constitution of society outline of the theory of structuration*. Cambridge, UK: Polity Press.

Gilliland, D. I., & Bello, D. C. (2002). Two Sides to Attitudinal Commitment: The Effect of Calculative and Loyalty Commitment on Enforcement Mechanisms in Distribution Channels. *Journal of the Academy of Marketing Science, 30*(1), 24–43. doi:10.1177/03079450094306

Girgensohn, A. (1992). *End-User modifiability in knowledge-based design environments*. Unpublished doctoral dissertation, University of Colorado at Boulder.

Gist, M. E. (1987). Self-efficacy: Implications for organizational behavior and human resource management. *Academy of Management Review, 12*(3), 472–485. doi:doi:10.2307/258514

Gist, M. E., & Schwoerer, C. (1989). Effects of alternative training methods on self-efficacy and performance in computer software training. *The Journal of Applied Psychology, 74*(6), 884–891. doi:10.1037/0021-9010.74.6.884

Gladstone, B. M., Volpe, T., & Boydell, K. M. (2007). Issues encountered in a qualitative secondary analysis of help-seeking in the prodrome to psychosis. *The Journal of Behavioral Health Services & Research, 34*(4), 431–442. doi:10.1007/s11414-007-9079-x

Glaser, B. G., & Strauss, A. L. (1967). *The Discovery of Grounded Theory. Strategies for Qualitative Research*. Piscataway, NJ: Aldine Transaction.

Gleitman, H., Fridlund, A. J., & Reisberg, D. (1999). *Psychology* (5th ed.). New York: W. W. Norton & Company.

Goh, S. C. (2003). Improving organizational learning capability: lessons from two case studies. *The Learning Organization, 10*(4), 216–227. doi:10.1108/09696470310476981

Gorman, A., & Fischer, G. (2009, June 25-27). Toward an analytic framework for understanding and fostering peer-support communities in using and evolving software products. In *Proceedings of the International Conference Communities and Technologies (C&T 2009),* University Park, PA (pp. 1-9). ACM Publishing.

Gray, W. D., & Salzman, M. C. (1998). Damaged merchandise? A review of experiments that compare usability evaluation methods. *Human-Computer Interaction, 13*, 203–261. doi:10.1207/s15327051hci1303_2

Greenbaum, J., & Kyng, M. (Eds.). (1991). *Design at Work. Cooperative Design of Computer Systems*. Mahwah, NJ: Lawrence Erlbaum Associates.

Grigoreanu, V., Cao, J., Kulesza, T., Bogart, C., Rector, K., Burnett, M., et al. (2008, September 15-19). Can feature design reduce the gender gap in end-user software development environments? In *Proceedings of the the 2008 IEEE Symposium on Visual Languages and Human-Centric Computing (VL/HCC'08),* Herrsching am Ammersee, Germany (pp. 149-156). Washington, DC: IEEE Computer Society.

Grint, K., & Woolgar, S. (1997). *The Machine at Work. Technology, Work and Organization.* Cambridge, MA: Polity Press.

Grudin, J., & Pruitt, J. (2002). Personas, Participatory Design and Product Development: An Infrastructure of Engagement. In T. Binder, J. Gregory, & I. Wagner (Eds.), *Proceedings of Participatory Design Conference* (pp. 144-161). Palo Alto, CA: CPSR.

Grudin, J. (1991a). Interactive Systems: Bridging the Gaps between Developers and Users. *IEEE Computer, 24*(4), 59–69.

Grudin, J. (1991b). Systematic Sources of Suboptimal Interface Design in Large Product Development Organizations. *Human-Computer Interaction, 6*(2), 147–196. doi:10.1207/s15327051hci0602_3

Grudin, J. (1994). Eight challenges for developers. *Communications of the ACM, 37*(1), 93–105. doi:10.1145/175222.175230

Grudin, J. T. (1989). Why groupware applications fail: problems in design and evaluation. *Office Technology and People, 4*(3), 245–264.

Grüttner, M. (2007). Entwicklung eines generischen Visualisierungs- und Interaktionskonzepts für kontextsensitive Hilfesysteme und prototypische Implementierung für das Eclipse RCP-Framework. In *Wirtschaftsinformatik.* Siegen, Germany: University of Siegen.

Gulliksen, J., Boivie, I., & Göransson, B. (2006). Usability professionals – current practices and future development. *Interacting with Computers, 18*(4), 568–600. doi:10.1016/j.intcom.2005.10.005

Gupta, S., & Bostrom, R. P. (2006, April 13-15). End-user training methods: what we know, need to know. In *Proceedings of the 2006 ACM SIGMIS CPR Conference on Computer Personnel Research,* Claremont, CA (pp. 172-182). New York: ACM Press.

Guzdial, M. (2004). Programming environments for novices. In S. Fincher & M. Petre (Eds.), *Computer science education research* (pp. 127-154). London: Routledge Falmer. Hull, G. A., & Katz, M. L. (2006). Creating an agentive self: Case studies of digital storytelling. *Research in the Teaching of English, 41*(1), 43-81.

Guzdial, M. (1995). Software-realized scaffolding to facilitate programming for science learning. *Interactive Learning Environments, 4*(1), 1–44. doi:10.1080/1049482940040101

Habraken, J. (1972). *Supports: An alternative to mass housing.* North Shields, UK: Urban International Press.

Hackbarth, G., Grover, V., & Yi, M. Y. (2003). Computer playfulness and anxiety: Positive and negative mediators of the system experience effect on perceived ease of use. *Information & Management, 40*(3), 221–232. doi:10.1016/S0378-7206(02)00006-X

Hagel, J., & Brown, J. S. (2008). *Innovation on the edge: How SAP seeds innovation.* Retrieved from http://www.businessweek.com/print/innovate/content/jul2008/id20080723_353753.htm

Hair, J. F., Anderson, J. C., Tatham, R. L., & Black, W. C. (1994). *Multivariate Data Analysis.* Upper Saddle River, NJ: Prentice Hall.

Hall, A., & Walton, G. (2004). Information overload within the health care system: a literature review. *Health Information and Libraries Journal, 21*(2), 102–108. doi:10.1111/j.1471-1842.2004.00506.x

Hall, S. (1980). Cultural Studies: Two paradigms. *Media Culture & Society, 2,* 57–72. doi:10.1177/016344378000200106

Hardstone, G., Hartswood, M., Procter, R., Slack, R., Voss, A., & Rees, G. (2004, November 6-10). Supporting informality: Team working and integrated care records. In *Proceedings of the International Conference on Computer Supported Cooperative Work (CSCW '04),* Chicago (pp. 142-151). ACM Publishing.

Harkness, W. L., Kettinger, W. J., & Segars, A. H. (1996). Sustaining Process Improvement and Innovation in the Information Services Function: Lessons Learned at the Bose Corporation. *Management Information Systems Quarterly*, *20*(3), 349–368. doi:10.2307/249661

Harmon-Jones, E., & Mills, J. (1999). *Cognitive Dissonance: Progress on a pivotal theory in social psychology*. Washington, DC: American Psychological Association. doi:10.1037/10318-000

Harper, G., & Utley, D. (2001). Organizational Culture and Successful Information Technology Implementation. *Engineering Management Journal*, *13*(2), 11–15.

Harrington, S., & Ruppel, C. (1999). Practical and value compatibility: their roles in the adoption, diffusion, and success of telecommuting. In P. De & J. DeGross (Eds.), *Proceedings of the 20th International Conference of Information Systems* (pp. 103-112). Atlanta, GA: AIS.

Harris, S. E., & Katz, J. L. (1991). Organizational Performance and IT Investment Intensity in the Insurance. *Organization Science*, *2*(3), 263–295. doi:10.1287/orsc.2.3.263

Hartson, H. R., Castillo, J. C., Kelso, J., & Neale, W. (1996). *Remote Evaluation: The Network as an Extension of the Usability Laboratory*. In Proceedings of CHI'96: Human Factors in Computing Systems (pp. 228-235).

Hasu, M., & Engeström, Y. (2000). Measurement in Action: An Activity-Theoretical Perspective on Producer-User Interaction. *International Journal of Human-Computer Studies*, *53*(1), 61–89. doi:10.1006/ijhc.2000.0375

Havelka, D., Beasley, F., & Broome, T. (2004). A study of computer anxiety among business students. *Mid-American Journal of Business*, *19*(1), 63–71. doi:10.1108/19355181200400007

Heath, C., & Lu, P. (1996, November 16-20). Documents and professional practice: 'Bad' organisational reasons for 'good' clinical records. In *Proceedings of the International Conference on Computer Supported Cooperative Work (CSCW'96),* Boston (pp. 354-363). ACM Publishing.

Heaton, H. (1998). Secondary analysis of qualitative data. *Social Research Update, 22*. Retrieved February 24, 2009, from http://sru.soc.surrey.ac.uk/SRU22.html

Heeter, C. (1989). Implications of New Interactive Technologies for Conceptualizing Communication. In Salvaggio, J. L., & Bryant, J. (Eds.), *Media use in the information age: emerging patterns of adoption and consumer use* (pp. 217–235). Hillsdale, NJ: Lawrence Erlbaum.

Henderson, A., & Kyng, M. (1991). There's no place like home: Continuing Design in Use. In *Design at work: Cooperative Design of Computer Systems* (pp. 219–240). Mahwah, NJ: Lawrence Erlbaum.

Henderson, J. C., & Sifonis, J. G. (1988). The Value of Strategic IS Planning: Understanding Consistency, Validity, and IS Markets. *Management Information Systems Quarterly*, *12*(2), 187–200. doi:10.2307/248843

Henderson, R., & Divett, M. (2003). Perceived usefulness, ease of use and electronic supermarket use. *International Journal of Human-Computer Studies*, *59*(3), 383–395. doi:10.1016/S1071-5819(03)00079-X

Hepp, A. (2004). *Cultural Studies und Medienanalyse*. Wiesbaden, Germany: Verlag für Sozialwissenschaften.

Hewgill, M. A., & Miller, G. (1965). Source credibility and response to fear-arousing communications. *Speech Monographs*, *32*(2), 95–101. doi:10.1080/03637756509375436

Hilibrand, M. (1964). *Source credibility and the persuasive process*. Unpublished doctoral dissertation, Harvard University, Cambridge, MA.

Hinds, P. S., Vogel, R. J., & Clarke-Steffen, L. (1997). The possibilities and pitfalls of doing a secondary analysis of a qualitative data set. *Qualitative Health Research*, *7*(3), 408–424. doi:10.1177/104973239700700306

Hippel, E. V., & Katz, R. (2002). Shifting Innovation to Users via Toolkits. *Management Science*, *48*(7), 821–833. doi:10.1287/mnsc.48.7.821.2817

Hirschheim, R., & Klein, H. (1989). Four Paradigms of Information Systems Development. *Communications of the ACM*, *32*(10), 1199–1216. doi:10.1145/67933.67937

Hitt, L. M., & Brynjolfsson, E. (1996). Productivity, Business Profitability, and Consumer Surplus: Three Different Measures of Information Technology Value. *Management Information Systems Quarterly*, *20*(2), 121–142. doi:10.2307/249475

Hitt, L. M., Wu, D. J., & Zhou, X. (2002). Investment in Enterprise Resource Planning: Business Impact and Productivity Measures. *Journal of Management Information Systems*, *19*(1), 71–98.

Holly, W., Püschel, U., & Bergmann, J. (2001). *Der sprechende Zuschauer: Wie wir uns Fernsehen kommunikativ aneignen* [The talking audience: On the communicative appropriation of television]. Wiesbaden, Germany: Westdeutscher Verlag.

Holsapple, C. W., & Lee-Post, A. (2006). Defining, assessing, and promoting e-learning success: An information systems perspective. *Decision Sciences Journal of Innovative Education*, *4*(1), 67–85.

Hong, S., Thong, J. Y. L., & Tam, K. Y. (2006). Understanding continued information technology usage behavior: A comparison of three models in the context of mobile internet. *Decision Support Systems*, *42*(3), 1819–1834. doi:10.1016/j.dss.2006.03.009

Honneth, A. (1995). Domination and Moral Struggle: The Philosophical Heritage of Marxism Reviewed. In Wright, C. W. (Ed.), *The Fragmented World of the Social: Essays in Social and Political Philosophy* (pp. 3–15). Albany, NY: SUNY Press.

Horton, S. (2000). *Web Teaching Guide – A Practical Approach to Creating Course Web Sites*. New Haven, CT: Yale University Press.

Hovland, C., Janis, I. L., & Kelly, H. (1953). *Communication and persuasion*. New Haven, CT: Yale University Press.

Hovland, C., & Weiss, W. (1951). The influence of source credibility on communication effectiveness. *Public Opinion Quarterly*, *15*, 635–650. doi:10.1086/266350

Hsu, M. K. (2007). *Structural equation modeling with Amos*. Retrieved from ftp://hqftp1.spss.com/pub/web/wp/Amos and SEM in the Services Sector.pdf

Hsu, C. L., & Lu, H. P. (2004). Why do people play online games? An extended TAM with social influences and flow experience. *Information & Management*, *41*(7), 853–868. doi:10.1016/j.im.2003.08.014

Hsu, M. H., Chiu, C. M., & Ju, T. L. (2004). Determinants of Continued Use of the WWW: An Integration of Two Theoretical Models. *Industrial Management & Data Systems*, *104*(9), 766–775. doi:10.1108/02635570410567757

Hsu, M.-H., & Chiu, C.-M. (2004). Internet self-efficacy and electronic service acceptance. *Decision Support Systems*, *38*(3), 369–381. doi:10.1016/j.dss.2003.08.001

Huang, N.-T., Wei, C.-C., & Chang, W.-K. (2007). Knowledge management: modeling the knowledge diffusion in community of practice. *Kybernetes*, *36*(5-6), 607–621. doi:10.1108/03684920710749703

Hu, L.-T., & Bentler, P. M. (1999). Cutoff Criteria for Fit Indexes in Covariance Structure Analysis: Conventional Criteria versus New Alternatives. *Structural Equation Modeling*, *6*(1), 1–55. doi:10.1080/10705519909540118

Hung, D., & Chen, D.-T. (2003). Learning within the context of communities of practice: a re-conceptualization of tools, rules, and roles of the activity system. *Educational Media International*, *39*(3-4), 247–255.

Hung, D., Chen, D.-T., & Koh, T. S. (2006). The reverse LPP process for nurturing a community of practice. *Educational Media International*, *43*(4), 299–314. doi:10.1080/09523980600926267

Hu, P. J. H., Clark, T. H. K., & Ma, W. W. (2003). Examining technology acceptance by school teachers: A longitudinal study. *Information & Management*, *41*(2), 227–241. doi:10.1016/S0378-7206(03)00050-8

Huselid, M. A. (1995). The Impact of Human Resource Management Practices on Turnover, Productivity, and Corporate Financial Performance. *Academy of Management Journal*, *38*(3), 635–672. doi:10.2307/256741

Hutchings, A., & Knox, S. (1995). Creating Products - Customer Demand. *Communications of the ACM*, *38*(5), 72–80. doi:10.1145/203356.203370

Ifenthaler, D., & Seel, N. M. (2005). The measurement of change: learning-dependent progression of mental models. *Technology, Instruction. Cognition and Learning*, *2*(4), 317–336.

Igbaria, M. (1990). End-user computing effectiveness: A structural equation model. *OMEGA International Journal of Management Science*, *18*(6), 637–652. doi:10.1016/0305-0483(90)90055-E

Igbaria, M., & Chakrabarti, A. (1990). Computer anxiety and attitudes towards microcomputer use. *Behaviour & Information Technology*, *9*, 229–241. doi:10.1080/01449299008924239

Igbaria, M., & Iivari, J. (1995). Effects of self-efficacy on computer usage. *Omega-International Journal of Management Science*, *23*(6), 587–605. doi:10.1016/0305-0483(95)00035-6

Igbaria, M., Zinatelli, N., Cragg, P., & Cavaye, A. L. M. (1997). Personal Computing Acceptance Factors in Small Firms: A Structural Equation Model. *Management Information Systems Quarterly*, *21*(3), 279–305. doi:10.2307/249498

Iivari, N. (2006b). Understanding the Work of an HCI Practitioner. In A. Morch, K. Morgan, T. Bratteig, G. Ghosh, & D. Svanaes (Eds.), *Proceedings of fourth Nordic Conference on Human Computer Interaction* (pp. 185-194). New York: ACM.

Iivari, J., & Hirschheim, R. (1996). Analyzing information systems development: a comparison and analysis of eight IS development approaches. *Information Systems*, *21*(7), 551–575. doi:10.1016/S0306-4379(96)00028-2

Iivari, J., Isomäki, H., & Pekkola, S. (in press). User – the great unknown of systems development: Reasons, forms, challenges, experiences and intellectual contributions of user involvement. *Information Systems Journal*.

Iivari, N. (2006a). 'Representing the User' in Software Development – A Cultural Analysis of Usability Work in the Product Development Context. *Interacting with Computers*, *18*(4), 635–664. doi:10.1016/j.intcom.2005.10.002

Illich, I. (1971). *Deschooling society.* New York: Harper and Row.

Inkpen, A. C., & Tsang, E. W. K. (2005). Social Capital Networks and Knowledge Transfer. *Academy of Management Review*, *30*(1), 146–165.

International Standard ISO 13407. (1999). *Human-centered design processes for interactive systems.* Geneva, Switzerland: International Organization for Standardization.

International Standard ISO 9241-11. (1998). *Ergonomic requirements for office work with visual display terminals (VDT)s - Part 11 Guidance on usability*. Geneva, Switzerland: International Organization for Standardization.

Jackson, S., Krajcik, J., & Soloway, E. (1998, April 18-23). The design of guided learner-adaptable scaffolding in interactive learning environments. In *Proceedings of the SIGCHI Conference on Human Factors in Computing Systems,* Los Angeles (pp. 187-194). ACM Publishing.

Jackson, B., & Anagnostopoulou, K. (2001). Making the right connections: Improving quality in online learning. In Stephenson, J. (Ed.), *Teaching and learning online: Pedagogies for new technologies* (pp. 53–66). Sterling, VA: Stylus Publishing.

Janis, I. (1972). *Victims of groupthink.* Boston: Houghton Mifflin.

Javenpaa, S. L., & Leidner, D. E. (1998). An Information Company in Mexico: Extending the Resource-Based View of the Firm to A Developing Country Context. *Information Systems Research*, *9*(4), 342–361. doi:10.1287/isre.9.4.342

Jenkins, H., Clinton, K., Purushotm, R., Robison, A., & Weigel, M. (2006). *Confronting the challenges of participation culture: Media education for the 21st century* (White Paper). Chicago: The John D. and Catherine T. MacArthur Foundation.

Jeppesen, L. B. (2004). *Profiting from innovative user communities: How firms organize the production of user modifications in the computer industry* (Working Papers 2003-2004). Copenhagen, Denmark: Copenhagen Business School, Department of Industrial Economics and Strategy.

Jeppesen, L. B., & Molin, M. J. (2003). Consumers as co-developers: Learning and innovation outside the firm. *Technology Analysis and Strategic Management*, *15*(3), 363–384. doi:10.1080/09537320310001601531

Jiang, J. J., Muhanna, W. A., & Klein, G. (2000). User resistance and strategies for promoting acceptance across system types. *Information & Management*, *37*(1), 25–36. doi:10.1016/S0378-7206(99)00032-4

Johnson-Laird, P. N. (1983). *Mental models: Towards a cognitive science of language, inference, and consciousness*. Cambridge, MA: Harvard University Press.

Johnson, R. A. (2005). An empirical investigation of sources of application-specific computer-self-efficacy and mediators of the efficacy: Performance relationship. *International Journal of Human-Computer Studies, 62*(6). doi:10.1016/j.ijhcs.2005.02.008

Johnson, R. D., & Marakas, G. M. (2000). The role of behavioral modeling in computer skills acquisition: Toward refinement of the model. *Information Systems Research, 11*(4), 402–417. doi:10.1287/isre.11.4.402.11869

Johnston, A. C., & Hale, R. (2008). *Improved security through information security governance*. Communications of the ACM.

Jonassen, D. (1995). Supporting communities of learners with technology: A vision for integrating technology with learning in schools. *Educational Technology, 35*(4), 60–63.

Jones, M., & Karsten, H. (2003). *Review: Structuration theory and information systems research*. Retrieved February 10, 2009, from http://www.jbs.cam.ac.uk/research/working_papers/2003/wp0311.pdf

Jones, S. (2006). *SOA anti-patterns*. Retrieved from http://www.infoq.com/ articles/ SOA-anti-patterns

Jones, L. W., Sinclair, R. C., & Courneya, K. S. (2003). The effects of source credibility and message framing on exercise intentions, behaviors, and attitudes: An integration of the elaboration likelihood model and prospect theory. *Journal of Applied Social Psychology, 33*(1), 179–196. doi:10.1111/j.1559-1816.2003.tb02078.x

Jones, M. R., & Karsten, H. (2008). Giddens's structuration theory and information systems research. *Management Information Systems Quarterly, 32*(1), 127–157.

Kaarst-Brown, M., & Robey, D. (1999). More on Myth, Magic and Metaphor. Cultural Insights into the Management of Information Technology in Organizations. *Information Technology & People, 12*(2), 192–217. doi:10.1108/09593849910267251

Kaasbøll, J., & Øgrim, L. (1994). Super-users: Hackers, management hostages or working class heroes? A study of user influence on redesign in distributed organizations. In P. Kerola, A. Juustila, & J. Järvinen (Eds.), *Proceedings of the 17th Information Systems Research Seminar in Scandinavia,* Syöte, Finland (pp. 784-798). Department of Information Processing Science, University of Oulu, Finland.

Kafai, Y. B., Peppler, K., & Chapman, R. (2009). *The computer clubhouse: Constructionism and creativity in youth communities*. New York: Teachers College Press.

Kafai, Y. B., Peppler, K., & Chiu, G. (2007). High tech programmers in low income communities: Seeding reform in a community technology center. In C. Steinfield, B. Pentland, M., Ackerman, &. N. Contractor (Eds.), *Communities and technologies* (pp. 545-564). New York: Springer.

Kafai, Y. B., Desai, S., Peppler, K., Chiu, G., & Moya, J. (2008). Mentoring partnerships in a community technology center: A constructionist approach for fostering equitable service learning. *Mentoring & Tutoring, 16*(2), 191–205. doi:10.1080/13611260801916614

Kafai, Y. B., & Fields, D. (2009). Cheating in virtual worlds: Transgressive designs for learning. *Horizon, 17*(1), 12–20. doi:10.1108/10748120910936117

Kahler, H. (2001). *Suporting Collaborative Tailoring*. Rosklide, Denmark: Department of Communication, Journalism and Computer Science, Universiy of Roskilde.

Kanstrup, A. M., & Christiansen, E. (2006, October 14-18). Selecting and evoking innovators: Combining democracy and creativity. In A. Mørch, K. Morgan, T. Bratteteig, G. Ghosh, & D. Savanaes (Eds.), *Proceedings of the 4th Nordic Conference on Human-Computer Interaction,* Oslo, Norway (pp. 321-330). ACM Publishing.

Kantner, L., & Rosenbaum, S. (1997). Usability studies of WWW sites: Heuristic evaluation vs. laboratory testing. In *Proceedings of SIGDOC*, Snowbird, UT (pp. 153-160).

Kanungo, S., Sadavarti, S., & Srinivas, Y. (2001). Relating IT strategy and organizational culture: An empirical study of public sector units in India. *The Journal of Strategic Information Systems, 10*(1), 29–57. doi:10.1016/S0963-8687(01)00038-5

Karasek, R. A. (1979). Job demand, job decision latitude, and mental strain: Implications for job redesign. *Administrative Science Quarterly*, *24*(2), 285–308. doi:10.2307/2392498

Karat, J. (1997). Evolving the Scope of User-Centered Design. *Communications of the ACM*, *40*, 33–38. doi:10.1145/256175.256181

Karjaluoto, H. (2002). *Electronic banking in Finland: Consumer beliefs, attitudes, intentions, and behaviors*. Unpublished doctoral dissertation, University of Jyväskylä, Finland.

Karnowski, V. (2008). *Das Mobiltelefon im Spiegel fiktionaler Fernsehserien: Symbolische Modelle der Handyaneignung* [The mobile phone in reflection of TV series: Symbolic models about mobile appropriation]. Wiesbaden, Germany: VS Verlag.

Karsten, H., & Jones, M. (1998). The long and winding road: Collaorative IT and organisational change. In *Proceedings of the International Conference on Computer Supported Work (CSCW'98)*, Seattle, WA (pp. 29-38). New York: ACM Press.

Kearns, G. S., & Lederer, A. L. (2003). A Resource-Based View of Strategic Alignment: How Knowledge Sharing Creates Competitive Advantage. *Decision Sciences*, *34*(1), 1–26. doi:10.1111/1540-5915.02289

Keesing, R., & Strathern, A. (1998). *Cultural Anthropology. A Contemporary Perspective* (3rd ed.). Fort Worth, TX: Harcourt Brave College Publishers.

Keil, M., & Carmel, E. (1995). Customer-Developer Links in Software Development. *Communications of the ACM*, *38*(5), 33–44. doi:10.1145/203356.203363

Kelleher, C., Pausch, R., & Kiesler, S. (2007, April 28-May 3). Storytelling Alice motivates middle school girls to learn computer programming. In *Proceedings of the ACM Conference on Human Factors in Computing Systems (CHI 2007)*, San Jose, CA (pp. 1455-1464). ACM Publishing.

Kelleher, C., & Pausch, R. (2005). Lowering the barriers to programming: A taxonomy of programming environments and languages for novice programmers. *ACM Computing Surveys*, *37*(2), 83–137. doi:10.1145/1089733.1089734

Kellogg, W. A. (2007, September 24). *Supporting collaboration in distributed teams: Implications for e-research.* Paper presented at the Ecscw Workshop "Realising and Supporting Collaboration in E-Research", Limerick, Ireland. Retrieved from http://www.e-researchcommunity.org/docs/ecscw07/submissions/Kellogg.pdf

Kelman, H. C., & Hovland, C. I. (1953). Reinstatement of the communicator in delayed measurement of opinion change. *Journal of Abnormal and Social Psychology*, *48*(3), 327–335. doi:10.1037/h0061861

Kenton, S. B. (1989). Speaker credibility in persuasive business communication: A model which explains gender differences. *Journal of Business Communication*, *26*(2), 143–157. doi:10.1177/002194368902600204

Kerlinger, F. N. (1986). *Foundations of Behavioral Research*. New York: Harcourt Brace Jovanovich.

Kettinger, W. J., Grover, V., Subashish, A. H., & Segars, A. H. (1994). Strategic Information Systems Revisited: A Study in Sustainability and Performance. *Management Information Systems Quarterly*, *12*(3), 31–58. doi:10.2307/249609

Kiczales, G., des Rivières, J., & Bobrow, D. G. (1991). *The Art of the Meta-Object Protocol*. Cambridge, MA: MIT Press.

Kieras, D. E., & Polson, P. G. (1985). An approach to the formal analysis of user complexity. *International Journal of Man-Machine Studies*, *22*, 365–394. doi:10.1016/S0020-7373(85)80045-6

Kilby, T. (2001). The direction of Web-based training: A practitioner's view. *The Learning Organization*, *8*(5), 194–199. doi:10.1108/EUM0000000005912

Kimble, C., & Hildreth, P. (2005). Dualities, distributed communities of practice and knowledge management. *Journal of Knowledge Management*, *9*(4), 102–113. doi:10.1108/13673270510610369

Kim, S. S., & Malhotra, M. K. (2005). A Longitudinal Model of Continued IS Use: An Integrative View of Four Mechanisms Underlying Postadoption Phenomena. *Management Science*, *51*(5), 741–755. doi:10.1287/mnsc.1040.0326

Kim, S. S., Malhotra, N. K., & Narasimhan, S. (2005). Two Competing Perspectives on Automatic Use: A Theoretical and Empirical Comparison. *Information Systems Research, 16*(4), 418–432. doi:10.1287/isre.1050.0070

King, N. (1994). Template analysis. In G. Symon & C. Cassell (Eds.), *Qualitative methods and analysis in organizational research: A practical guide* (pp. 118-134). London: Sage.

King, A. W., & Zeithaml, C. P. (2003). Measuring organizational knowledge: A conceptual and methodological framework. *Strategic Management Journal, 24*(8), 763. doi:10.1002/smj.333

King, W. R., Grover, V., & Hufnagel, E. H. (1989). Using Information and Information Technology for Sustainable Competitive Advantage: Some Empirical Evidence. *Information & Management, 17*, 87–93. doi:10.1016/0378-7206(89)90010-4

King, W. R., & He, J. (2006). A meta-analysis of the technology acceptance model. *Information & Management, 43*(6), 740–755. doi:10.1016/j.im.2006.05.003

Kira, M., & Forslin, J. (2008). Seeking regenerative work in the post-bureaucratic transition. *Journal of Organizational Change Management, 21*(1), 76–91. doi:10.1108/09534810810847048

Kittur, A., Suh, B., & Chi, E. H. (2008, November 8-12). Can you ever trust a Wiki? Impacting perceived trustworthiness in Wikipedia. In *Proceedings of the Conference on Computer Supported Cooperative Work (CSCW 2008)*, San Diego, CA (pp. 477-480). ACM Publishing.

Klann, M., Paterno, F., & Wulf, V. (2006). Future perspectives in end-user development. In H. Lieberman, F. Paterno, & V. Wulf (Eds.), *End user development* (pp. 475-486). New York: Springer.

Klaus, T., Wingreen, S., & Blanton, J. E. (2007). Examining user resistance and management strategies in enterprise system implementations. In *Proceedings of the ACM SIGMIS CPR Conference on Computer Personnel Research*, St. Louis, MO (pp. 55-62).

Klein, H., & Myers, M. (1999). A Set of Principles for Conducting and Evaluating Interpretive Field Studies in Information Systems. *Management Information Systems Quarterly, 23*(1), 67–94. doi:10.2307/249410

Knight, W. (2008). *Supernatural powers become contagious in PC game*. Retrieved April 28, 2008, from http://www.newscientist.com/article.ns?id=dn6857

Knowles, M. S. (1975). *Self-directed learning. A guide for learners and teachers*. Englewood Cliffs, NJ: Prentice Hall.

Ko, A. J., & Myers, B. (2004, April 24-29). Designing the whyline: A debugging interface for asking questions about program behavior. In *Proceedings of the ACM Conference on Human Factors in Computing Systems (CHI 2004)*, Vienna, Austria (pp. 151-158). ACM Publishing.

Ko, A. J., Abraham, R., Beckwith, L., Blackwell, A., Burnett, M., Erwig, M., et al. (2009 under review). The state of the art in end-user software engineering.

Ko, A. J., Myers, B. A., & Aung, H. H. (2004, September 26-29). Six learning barriers in end-user programming systems. In *Proceedings of the IEEE Symposium on Visual Languages and Human-Centric Computing*, Rome, Italy (pp. 199-206). Washington, DC: IEEE Computer Society.

Kohlbacher, F., & Mukai, K. (2007). Japan's learning communities in Hewlett-Packard Consulting and Integration. *The Learning Organization, 14*(1), 8–20. doi:10.1108/09696470710718311

Kouroubali, A. (2002). Structuration theory and conception-reality gaps: Addressing cause and effect of implementation outcomes in health care information systems. In *Proceedings of the 35th Hawaii International Conference on System Sciences*. Washington, DC: IEEE.

Kroeber, A., & Kluckhohn, C. (1952). *Culture: a critical review of the concepts and definitions*. Cambridge, MA: Harvard University Press.

Kujala, S. (2003). User involvement: a review of the benefits and challenges. *Behaviour & Information Technology, 22*(1), 1–16. doi:10.1080/01449290301782

Kujala, S. (2007). Effective user involvement in product development by improving the analysis of user needs. *Behaviour & Information Technology, 27*(6), 457–473. doi:10.1080/01449290601111051

Kulesza, T., Wong, W., Stumpf, S., Perona, S., White, R., Burnett, M., et al. (2009, February 8-11). Fixing the program my computer learned: Barriers for end users, challenges for the machine. In *Proceedings of the 13th International Conference on Intelligent User Interfaces,* Sanibel Island, FL (pp. 187-196). ACM Publishing.

Kuzel, A. J. (2000). Sampling in qualitative inquiry. In Crabtree, B. F., & Miller, W. L. (Eds.), *Doing qualitative research* (2nd ed., pp. 31–44). Thousand Oaks, CA: Sage.

Kvale, S. (1989). To validate is to question. In Kvale, S. (Ed.), *Issues of validity in qualitative research* (pp. 73–92). London: Chartwell Bratt.

Kwon, T. H., & Zmud, R. W. (1987). Unifying the fragmented models of information systems implementation. In Bolan, R. J., & Hirschheim, R. A. (Eds.), *Critical issues in information systems research* (pp. 227–251). New York: John Wiley.

Kyng, M. (1994). Scandinavian Design: Users in Product Development. In B. Adelson, S. Dumais, & J. Olson (Eds.), *Proceedings of the Conference on Human Factors in Computing Systems* (pp. 3-9). New York: ACM.

Kyng, M. (1998). Users and computers: A contextual approach to design of computer artifacts. *Scandinavian Journal of Information Systems, 10*(1-2), 7–44.

Labbate, E. (1996). Usability and pedagogical issues in user interface design. Retrieved from http://www.technosphere.net/usability_in_uid.htm.

Lacy, S. (2006, May 3). The Friendly Face of Business Software. *Business Week.*

Lanier, J. (2006). *Digital Maoism: The hazards of the new online collectivism.* Retrieved from http://www.edge.org/3rd_culture/lanier06/lanier06_index.html

LaPelle, N. (2004). Simplifying Qualitative Data Analysis Using General Purpose Software Tools. *Field Methods, 16*(1), 85–108. doi:10.1177/1525822X03259227

Larson, C. U. (1992). *Persuasion: Reception and responsibility* (6th ed.). Belmont, CA: Wadsworth Publishing Company.

Lave, J., & Wenger, E. (1991). *Situated learning and legitimate peripheral participation.* Cambridge, UK: Cambridge University Press.

Lave, J., & Wenger, J. (1991). *Situated learning: Legitimate peripheral participation.* Cambridge, MA: Cambridge University Press.

Lawhead, P. B., Alpert, E., Bland, C. G., Carswell, L., Cizmar, D., DeWitt, J., et al. (1997). The web and distance learning: What is appropriate and what is not. In *Proceedings of ITiCSE'97 Working Group Reports and Supplemental* (pp. 27-37). New York: ACM.

Leadbeater, C., & Miller, P. (2008). *The pro-am revolution — how enthusiasts are changing our economy and society.* Retrieved from http://www.demos.co.uk/files/proamrevolutionfinal.pdf

Leathers, D. G. (1992). *Successful nonverbal communications: Principles and applications.* New York: Macmillan.

Lecerof, A., & Paterno, F. (1998). Automatic support for usability evaluation. *IEEE Transactions on Software Engineering, 24,* 863–887. doi:10.1109/32.729686

Lee, B., & Barua, A. (1999). An Integrated Assessment of Productivity and Efficiency Impacts of Information Technology Investments: Old Data, New Analysis and Evidence. *Journal of Productivity Analysis, 12*(1), 21–43. doi:10.1023/A:1007898906629

Lee, J. Sr, & Valderrama, K. (2003). Building Successful Communities of Practice. *Information Outlook, 7*(5), 28–32.

Lee, T. Y., Kozar, K. A., & Larsen, K. R. T. (2003). The technology acceptance model: Past, present, and future. *Communications of the Association for Information Systems, 12*(50), 752–780.

Legris, P., Ingham, J., & Collerette, P. (2003). Why do people use information technology? A critical review of the technology acceptance model. *Information & Management, 40*(3), 191–204. doi:10.1016/S0378-7206(01)00143-4

Leidner, D., & Kayworth, T. (2006). A Review of Culture in Information Systems Research: Towards a Theory of IT-Culture Conflict. *Management Information Systems Quarterly, 30*(2), 357–399.

Lenhart, A., & Madden, M. (2007). *Social networking Web sites and teens: An overview.* Washington, DC: Pew Internet and American Life Project.

Lenz, R., & Reichert, M. (2007). IT support for healthcare processes – premises, challenges, perspectives. *Data & Knowledge Engineering, 61*(1), 39–58. doi:10.1016/j.datak.2006.04.007

Lesser, E. L., & Storck, J. (2001). Communities of Practice and organizational performance. *IBM Systems Journal, 40*(4), 831–841. doi:10.1147/sj.404.0831

Lett, J. (1987). *The Human Enterprise. A Critical Introduction to Anthropological Theory.* Boulder, CO: Westview Press Inc.

Levi Strauss & Co. (2009). *History of the Levi's 501 jeans.* Retrieved June 14, 209, from http://www.levistrauss.com/Downloads/history_of_levis_501_jeans.pdf

Lewin, K. (1952). Group decision and social change. In Newcombe, G. E., & Hartley, E. L. (Eds.), *Readings in social psychology* (pp. 459–473). New York: Henry Holt.

Lewis, J. R. (1995). IBM computer usability satisfaction questionnaires: psychometric evaluation and instructions for use. *International Journal of Human-Computer Interaction, 7*(1), 57–78. doi:10.1080/10447319509526110

Lichtenstein, S., & Swatman, P. M. C. (1997). Internet acceptable usage policy for organizations. *Information Management & Computer Security, 5*(5), 182–190. doi:10.1108/09685229710367726

Li, D., Browne, G. J., & Chau, P. Y. K. (2006). An Empirical Investigation of Web Site Use Using a Commitment-Based Model. *Decision Sciences, 37*(3), 427–444. doi:10.1111/j.1540-5414.2006.00133.x

Li, D., Chau, P. Y. K., & Lou, H. (2005). Understanding Individual Adoption of Instant Messenging: An Empirical Investigation. *Journal of the Association for Information Systems, 6*(4), 102–129.

Lieberman, H. (Ed.). (2001). *Your wish is my command: Programming by example.* San Francisco: Morgan Kaufmann Publishers.

Lieberman, H., Paterno, F., & Wulf, V. (Eds.). (2006). *End-user development: Empowering people to flexibly employ advanced information and communication technology.* New York: Springer.

Liebermann, H., Paternò, F., & Wulf, W. (Eds.). (2006). *End User Development.* New York: Springer. doi:10.1007/1-4020-5386-X

Lim, J. H., Richardson, V. J., & Roberts, T. L. (2004). Information Technology Investment and Firm Performance: A Meta-Analysis. In *Proceedings of the Thirty-Seventh Hawaii International Conference on System Sciences,* HI (pp. 1-10).

Limayem, M., & Hirt, S. G. (2003). Force of Habit and Information Systems Usage: Theory and Initial Validation. *Journal of the Association for Information Systems, 4,* 65–97.

Limayem, M., Hirt, S. G., & Cheung, C. M. K. (2007). *How Habit Limits the Predictive Power of Intention: The Case of Information Systems Continuance.* MIS Quarterly.

Lin, J. C., & Lu, H. P. (2000). Towards an understanding of the behavioural intention to use a Web site. *International Journal of Information Management, 20*(3), 197–208. doi:10.1016/S0268-4012(00)00005-0

Lin, N. (2001). *Social Capital.* Cambridge, UK: Cambridge University Press.

Lippert, M. (2006). Eclipse Core - Unter der Haube, Teil 2: Ein Blick auf den Entwicklungsprozess des Eclipse-Plattform-Projekts. *Eclipse Magazine, 6.*

Lirtzman, S. I., & Shuv-Ami, A. (1986). Credibility of source of communication on products' safety hazards. *Psychological Reports, 58,* 707–718.

Little, G., Lau, T., Cypher, A., Lin, J., Haber, E., & Kandogan, E. (2007, April 28-May 3). Koala: Capture, share, automate, personalize business processes on the web. In *Proceedings of the ACM Conference on Human Factors in Computing Systems (CHI 2007),* San Jose, CA (pp. 943-946). ACM Publishing.

Liu, L., & Ma, Q. (2006). Perceived system performance: A test of an extended technology acceptance model. *The Data Base for Advances in Information Systems, 37*(2-3), 51–59.

Lorence, D., & Abraham, J. (2006). Comparative Analysis of Medical Web Search Using Generalized vs. Niche Technologies. *Journal of Medical Systems, 30*(3), 211–219. doi:10.1007/s10916-005-7990-y

Lorigo, L., Pan, B., Hembrooke, H., Joachims, T., Granka, L., & Gay, G. (2006). The influence of task and gender on search and evaluation behavior using Google. *Information Processing & Management, 42*(4), 1123–1131. doi:10.1016/j.ipm.2005.10.001

Loveman, G. W. (1994). An Assessment of the Productivity Impact of the Information Technologies. In Allen, T. J., & Scott Morton, M. S. (Eds.), *Information Technology and the Corporation of the 1990's: Research Studies* (pp. 84–110). New York: Oxford University Press.

Lowenstein, G. (1994). The psychology of curiosity. *Psychological Bulletin, 116*(1), 75–98. doi:10.1037/0033-2909.116.1.75

Lucas, H. C. Jr, Ginzberg, M. J., & Schultz, R. L. (1990). *Information systems implementation: testing a structural model.* Norwood, NJ: Ablex Publishing Corporation.

Lucas, H. C., & Spitler, V. K. (2000). Implementation in a world of workstations and networks. *Information & Management, 38*(2), 119–128. doi:10.1016/S0378-7206(00)00059-8

Mackay, W. E. (1990). *Users and customizable Software: A Co-Adaptive Phenomenon.* Cambridge, MA: MIT Press.

Maddux, J. E., & Rogers, R. W. (1980). Effects of source expertness, physical attractiveness, and supporting arguments on persuasion: A case of brains over beauty. *Journal of Personality and Social Psychology, 39*, 235–244. doi:10.1037/0022-3514.39.2.235

Mahapatra, R., & Lai, V. (2005). Evaluating end-user training programs. *Communications of the ACM, 48*(1), 66–70. doi:10.1145/1039539.1039540

Mahmood, M. A., Hall, L., & Swanberg, D. L. (2001). Factors affecting information technology usage: A meta-analysis of the empirical literature. *Journal of Organizational Computing and Electronic Commerce, 11*(2), 107–130. doi:10.1207/S15327744JOCE1102_02

Majchrzak, A., Beath, C. M., Ricardo, L., & Chin, W. W. (2005). Managing Client Dialogues During Information Systems Design to Facilitate Client Learning. *Management Information Systems Quarterly, 29*(4), 653–672.

Malhotra, Y., & Galletta, D. (2005). A multidimensional Commitment Model of Volitional Systems Adoption and Usage Behavior. *Journal of Management Information Systems, 22*(1), 117–151.

Malhotra, Y., & Galletta, D. F. (2004). Building systems that users want to use. *Communications of the ACM, 47*(12), 89–94. doi:10.1145/1035134.1035139

Maloney, J., Peppler, K., Kafai, Y. B., Resnick, M., & Rusk, N. (2008, March). *Programming by choice: Urban youth learning programming with Scratch.* Paper presented at the SIGCSE 2008 Conference, Portland, OR.

Ma, Q., & Liu, L. (2004). The technology acceptance model: A meta-analysis of empirical findings. *Journal of Organizational and End User Computing, 16*(1), 59–72. doi:10.4018/joeuc.2004010104

Marakas, G. M., Yi, M. Y., & Johnson, R. (1998). The multilevel and multifaceted character of computer self-efficacy: Toward a clarification of the construct and an integrative framework for research. *Information Systems Research, 9*(2), 126–163. doi:10.1287/isre.9.2.126

Marakas, G. M., Yi, M. Y., & Johnson, R. D. (1998). The multilevel and multifaceted character of computer self-efficacy: Toward clarification of the construct and an integrative framework for research. *Information Systems Research, 9*(2), 126–163. doi:10.1287/isre.9.2.126

Margolis, J. (2008). *Stuck in the shallow end: Education, race, and computing.* Cambridge, MA: MIT Press.

Margolis, J., & Fisher, A. (2002). *Unlocking the clubhouse: Women in computing.* Cambridge, MA: MIT Press.

Mark, M., Cook, T. D., & Cook, F. (1984). Randomized and quasi-experimental designs in evaluation research. In Rutman, L. (Ed.), *Evaluation Research methods: A basic guide.* Beverly Hills, CA: Sage.

Márkus, G. (1978). *Marxism and Anthropology: The Concept of Human Essence in the Philosophy of Marx.* Assen, The Netherlands: Van Gorcum.

Markus, L., & Keil, M. (1994). If We Build It, They Will Come: Designing Information Systems That People Want to Use. *Sloan Management Review*, 11–25.

Markus, M. L., Majchrzak, A., & Gasser, L. (2002). A design theory for systems that support emergent knowledge processes. *Management Information Systems Quarterly*, *26*, 199–232.

Markus, M., & Mao, Y. (2004). Participation in Development and Implementation - Updating an Old, Tired Concept for Today's IS Contexts. *Journal of the Association for Information Systems*, *5*(11-12), 514–544.

Marsh, H. W., Hau, K.-T., & Wen, Z. (2004). In Search of Golden Rules: Comment on Hypothesis-Testing Approaches to Setting Cutoff Values for Fit Indexes and Dangers in Overgeneralizing Hu and Bentler's (1999) Findings. *Structural Equation Modeling*, *11*(3), 320–341. doi:10.1207/s15328007sem1103_2

Mata, F. J., Fuerst, W. L., & Barney, J. B. (1995). Information Technology and Sustained Competitive Advantage: A Resource-Based Analysis. *Management Information Systems Quarterly*, *19*(4), 487–505. doi:10.2307/249630

Mathieson, K. (1991). Predicting user intentions: Comparing the technology acceptance model with the theory of planned behavior. *Information Systems Research*, *2*(3), 173–191. doi:10.1287/isre.2.3.173

Mattila, M. (2001). *Essays on customers in the dawn of interactive banking*. Unpublished doctoral dissertation, University of Jyväskylä, Finland.

Mattila, M., Karjaluoto, H., & Pento, T. (2003). Internet banking adoption among mature customers: Early majority or laggards? *Journal of Services Marketing*, *17*(5), 514–528. doi:10.1108/08876040310486294

Mayhew, D. (1999a). Strategic Development of Usability Engineering Function. *Interaction*, *6*(5), 27–34. doi:10.1145/312683.312706

Mayhew, D. (1999b). *The usability engineering lifecycle: a practitioner's handbook for user interface design*. San Francisco, CA: Morgan Kaufmann Publishers, Inc.

McAffer, J., & Lemieux, J.-M. (2005). *Eclipse Rich Client Platform: Designing, Coding, and Packaging Java Applications*. Reading, MA: Addison-Wesley.

McDermott, R. (1999). Why Information Technology Inspired But Cannot Deliver Knowledge Management. *California Management Review*, *41*(4), 103–117.

McDermott, R. (2002). Measuring the impact of communities. *Knowledge Management Review*, *5*(2), 26–29.

McEwen, W. J., & Greenberg, B. S. (1970). The effects of message intensity on receiver evaluations of source, message and topic. *The Journal of Communication*, *20*(4), 340–350. doi:10.1111/j.1460-2466.1970.tb00892.x

McFarland, D. J., & Hamilton, D. (2006). Adding contextual specificity to the technology acceptance model. *Computers in Human Behavior*, *22*(3), 427–447. doi:10.1016/j.chb.2004.09.009

McGuire, W. J. (1978). An information-processing model of advertising effectiveness. In Davis, H. L., & Silk, A. J. (Eds.), *Behavioral and management sciences in marketing* (pp. 156–180). New York: Wiley.

McLean, A., Carter, K., Lövstrand, L., & Moran, T. (1990). User tailorable systems: Pressing the issues with buttons. In *Proceedings of CHI '90*, Seattle, WA (pp. 175-182). New York: ACM Publishing.

McLuhan, M. (1964). *Understanding media: The extensions of man.* Cambridge, MA: MIT Press.

Mehandjiev, N., Sutcliffe, A. G., & Lee, D. (2006). Organisational views of end-user development. In H. Lieberman, F. Paterno, & V. Wulf (Eds.), *End user development: Empowering people to flexibly employ advanced information and communication technology* (pp. 371-399). New York: Springer.

Mehandjiev, N., & Bottaci, L. (Eds.). (2004). End-user development [special issue]. *Journal of End User Computing*, *10*(2).

Melis, E., Weber, M., & Andres, E. (2003). Lessons for (Pedagogic) Usability of eLearning Systems. *World Conference on E-Learning in Corporate, Government, Healthcare, &. Higher Education*, (1): 281–284.

Melone, N. P. (1990). A theoretical assessment of the user satisfaction construct in information systems research. *Management Science*, *36*(1), 76–91. doi:10.1287/mnsc.36.1.76

Melville, N., Kraemer, K., & Gurbaxani, V. (2004). Information Technology and Organizational Performance: An Integrative Model of IT Business Value. *Management Information Systems Quarterly*, *28*(2), 283–321.

Menon, N. M., Lee, B., & Eldenburg, L. (2000). Productivity of Information Systems in the Healthcare Industry. *Information Systems Research, 11*(1), 83–92. doi:10.1287/isre.11.1.83.11784

Meyer, J. P., & Allen, N. J. (1991). A three-component conceptualization of organizational commitment. *Human Resource Management Review, 1*, 61–89. doi:10.1016/1053-4822(91)90011-Z

Meyer, J. P., & Allen, N. J. (1997). *Commitment in the Workplace: Theory, Research, and Application*. Thousand Oaks, CA: Sage Publication.

Meyer, J. P., & Herscovitch, L. (2001). Commitment in the Workplace: Toward a General Model. *Human Resource Management Review, 11*(3), 299–326. doi:10.1016/S1053-4822(00)00053-X

Meyer, J. P., Stanley, D. J., Herscovitch, L., & Topolnytsky, L. (2002). Affective, Continuance, and Normative Commitment to the Organization: A Meta-Analysis of Antecedents, Correlates, and Consequences. *Journal of Vocational Behavior, 61*, 20–52. doi:10.1006/jvbe.2001.1842

Meyers, L. S., Gamst, G., & Guarino, A. J. (2005). *Applied Multivariate Research: Design and Interpretation*. Thousand Oaks, CA: SAGE.

Mezirow, J. (1997). Trasformative learning: theory to practice. In Cranton, P. (Ed.), *Trasformative learning in action: Insights from practice. New Directions for Adult and Continuing Education*. San Franciso, CA: Jossey-Bass Publishers.

Miles, M. B., & Huberman, A. M. (1994). *Qualitative data analysis. An expanded sourcebook* (2nd ed.). Thousand Oaks, CA: Sage.

Miller, G. A. (1956). The Magical Number Seven, Plus or Minus Two: Some Limits on Our Capacity for Processing Information. *Psychological Review, 63*, 81–97. doi:10.1037/h0043158

Miller, W. L., & Crabtree, B. F. (1992). Primary care research: A multimethod typology and qualitative road map. In Crabtree, B. F., & Miller, W. L. (Eds.), *Doing qualitative research* (2nd ed., pp. 3–28). Thousand Oaks, CA: Sage.

Mohrman, S. A., Tenkasi, R. V., Lawler, E. E. III, & Ledford, J. G. G. (1995). Total Quality Management: Practice and Outcomes in the Largest US Firms. *Employee Relations, 17*(3), 26–41. doi:10.1108/01425459510086866

Moore, G. C., & Benbasat, I. (1991). Development of an instrument to measure the perceptions of adopting an information technology innovation. *Information Systems Research, 2*(3), 192–222. doi:10.1287/isre.2.3.192

Moore, M. G. (1999). Three types of interaction. *American Journal of Distance Education, 3*(2), 1–6. doi:10.1080/08923648909526659

Mørch, A. I. (1995, July 3-7). Application units: Basic building blocks of tailorable applications. In B. Blumenthal, J. Gornostaev, & C. Unger (Eds.), *Proceedings of the 5th International Conference on East-West Human-Computer Interaction,* Moscow, Russia (LNCS 1015, pp. 45-62).

Mørch, A. I., Nygård, K. A., & Ludvigsen, S. R. (2009). Adaptation and generalisation in software product development. In H. Daniels, A. Edwards, Y. Engestrom, T. Gallagher, & S. R. Ludvigsen, (Eds.), *Activity theory in practice: Promoting learning across boundaries* (pp. 184-205). London: Routledge.

Mørch, A. (1995). Application units: Basic building blocks of tailorable applications. *Human-Computer Interaction*, 45–62.

Mørch, A. (1996). Evolving a generic application into a domain-oriented design environment. *Scandinavian Journal of Information Systems, 8*(2), 63–90.

Mørch, A. I., & Mehandjiev, N. D. (2000). Tailoring as collaboration: The mediating role of multiple representations and application units. *Computer Supported Cooperative Work, 9*(1), 75–100. doi:10.1023/A:1008713826637

Mørch, A. I., Stevens, G., Won, M., Klann, M., Dittrich, Y., & Wulf, V. (2004). Component-based technologies for end-user development. *Communications of the ACM, 47*(9), 59–62. doi:10.1145/1015864.1015890

Mørch, A., & Mehandjiev, N. D. (2000). Tailoring as Collaboration: The Mediating Role of Multiple Representations and Application Units. *Computer Supported Cooperative Work, 9*(1), 75–100. doi:10.1023/A:1008713826637

Mowday, R. T., Porter, L. W., & Steers, R. M. (1982). *Employee-Organization Linkage - The Psychology of Commitment, Absenteeism, and Turnover*. New York: Academic Press.

Mugny, G., Tafani, E., Falomir, P., Juan, M., & Layat, C. (2000). Source credibility, social comparison, and social influence. *Revue Internationale de Psychologie Sociale, 13*, 151–175.

Mukhopadhyay, T., Lerch, F. J., & Mangal, V. (1997). Assessing the Impact of Information Technology on Labor Productivity: A Field Study. *Decision Support Systems, 19*(2), 109–122. doi:10.1016/S0167-9236(96)00044-9

Muller, M., & Carey, K. (2002). Design as a Minority Discipline in a Software Company: Toward Requirements for a Community of Practice. In [CHI Letters]. *Proceedings of the Conference on Human Factors in Computing Systems, 4*(1), 383–390.

Mulrow, C. D., & Lohr, K. N. (2001). Proof and policy from medical research evidence. *Journal of Health Politics, Policy and Law, 26*(2), 249–266. doi:10.1215/03616878-26-2-249

Mumford, E. (1987). Sociotechnical systems design: Evolving theory and practice. In G. Bjerknes, P. Ehn, & M. Kyng (Eds.), *Computers and democracy* (pp. 59-76). Aldershot, UK: Avebury.

Mumford, E. (1983). *Designing Human Systems for New Technology. The ETHICS Method*. Manchester, UK: Manchester Business School.

Munkvold, B. E. (2003). *Implementing collaboration technologies in industry. Case examples and lessons*. London: Springer.

Myers, B. A., Ko, A. J., & Burnett, M. M. (2006, April 22-27). Invited research overview: End-user programming. In *Proceedings of the Conference on Human Factors in Computing Systems (Chi 2006)*, Montreal, Quebec, Canada (pp. 75-80). ACM Publishing.

Myers, B., Weitzman, D., Ko, A., & Chau, D. H. (2006, April 22-27). Answering why and why not questions in user interfaces. In *Proceedings of the ACM Conference on Human Factors in Computing Systems*, Montreal, Quebec, Canada (pp. 397-406). ACM Publishing.

Myers, B. A., Pane, J. F., & Ko, A. (2004). Natural programming languages and environments. *Communications of the ACM, 47*(9), 47–52. doi:10.1145/1015864.1015888

Nahm, A. Y., Vonderembse, M. A., & Koufteros, X. A. (2004). The impact of organizational culture on time-based manufacturing and performance. *Decision Sciences, 35*(4), 579–607. doi:10.1111/j.1540-5915.2004.02660.x

Nandhakumar, J., & Jones, M. (1997). Designing in the Dark: the Changing User-Developer Relationship in Information Systems Development. In J. DeGross & K. Kumar (Eds.), *Proceedings of the 18th International Conference of Information Systems* (pp. 75-86). Atlanta, GA: AIS.

Nardi, B. (1993). *A small matter of programming: Perspectives on end-user computing*. Cambridge, MA: MIT Press.

Naur, P. (1985). Programming as Theory Building. *Microprocessing and Microprogramming, 15*, 253–261. doi:10.1016/0165-6074(85)90032-8

Nedic, D., & Olsen, E. A. (2007). *Customizing an open source web portal framework in a business context: Integrating participatory design with an agile approach*. Unpublished master's thesis, University of Oslo, Norway.

Nelson, K. M., & Cooprider, J. G. (1996). The Contribution of Shared Knowledge to IS Group Performance. *Management Information Systems Quarterly, 20*(4), 409–429. doi:10.2307/249562

Nelson, R. R., Whitner, E. M., & Philcox, H. H. (1995). The assessment of end-user training needs. *Communications of the ACM, 38*(7), 27–38. doi:10.1145/213859.214793

Neo, B. S. (1988). Factors Facilitating the Use of Information Technology for Competitive Advantage: An Exploratory Study. *Information & Management, 15*(4), 191–201. doi:10.1016/0378-7206(88)90045-6

Ngwenyama, O. K. (1998). Groupware, social action and organizational emergence: on the process dy-namics of computer mediated distributed work. *Accounting. Management and Information Technologies, 8*(4), 123–143.

Niederman, F., & Webster, J. (1998). Trends in end-user training: A research agenda. In *Proceedings of the 1998 ACM SIGCPR Conference on Computer Personnel Research*, Boston (pp. 224-232).

Nielsen, J. (1993). *Usability engineering.* Boston, MA: Academic Press.

Nielsen, J. (1993). *Usability engineering.* Boston: Academic Press.

Nielsen, J. (1993). *Usability Engineering.* San Francisco, CA: Morgan Kaufmann.

Nielsen, J. (1994). Heuristic evaluation. In Nielsen, J., & Mack, R. L. (Eds.), *Usability Inspection Methods* (pp. 25–62). New York: John Wiley and Sons.

Nielsen, J. (2000). *Designing web usability.* Indianapolis, IN: New Riders Publishing.

Nielsen, J., & Mack, R. (Eds.). (1994). *Usability inspection methods.* New York: John Wiley & Sons.

Nielsen-Natratings (2006). *A Survey Report on Instant Messaging.*

Norman, D. A. (1983). Some observations on mental models. In *Mental Models* (pp. 15–35). Hillsdale, NJ: Lawrence Erlbaum Associates.

Norman, D. A. (2008). Workarounds and hacks: The leading edge of innovation. *Interaction, 15*(4), 47–48. doi:10.1145/1374489.1374500

Norušis, M. J. (2006). *SPSS Base 13.0 Guide to Data Analysis.* Upper Saddle River, NJ: Prentice Hall.

Nunamaker, J. F., Jr., & Chen, M. (1990). Systems Development in Information Systems Research. In *Proceedings of the Twenty-third Annual Hawaii International Conference on System Sciences* (Vol. 3, pp. 631-640).

Nunamaker, J. F. Jr. (1997). Future research in group support systems: Needs, some questions and possible directions. *International Journal of Human-Computer Studies, 47*(3), 357–385. doi:10.1006/ijhc.1997.0142

Nunnally, J. C. (1978). *Psychometric Theory.* New York: McGraw-Hill.

Nunnaly, J., & Bernstein, I. (1994). *Psychometric Theory.* New York: McGraw-Hill.

Nygaard, K. (1984). User-oriented Languages. In *Proceedings of the International Conference on Medical Informatics Europe (MIE 1984)* (pp. 38-44). Berlin, Germany: Springer-Verlag.

Nygård, K. A., & Mørch, A. I. (2007, November 5-9). The role of boundary crossing for knowledge advancement in product development. In T. Hirashima, U. Hoppe, & S. S. C. Young (Eds.), *Proceedings of the 15th International Conference Computers in Education,* Hiroshima, Japan (pp.183-186). Amsterdam, The Netherlands: IOS Press.

Oinas-Kukkonen, H., & Hakala, K. (2006). Internet services for the underprivileged: Computer courses for the elderly and unemployed at a residents' meeting room. In *Proceedings of the IFIP International Federation for Information Processing,* Boston (Vol. 226, pp. 324-336). New York: Springer.

Oinas-Kukkonen, H., & Mantila, L. (2009, March 12-14). Lisa, Lisa, the machine says I have performed an illegal action. Should I tell the police...? A survey and observations of inexperienced elderly Internet users. In *Proceedings of the Southern Association for Information Systems Conference,* Charleston, SC (pp. 146-151).

O'Keefe, D. J. (1990). *Persuasion: Theory and research.* Newbury Park, CA: Sage.

O'Leary, D. E. (2000). *Enterprise resource planning systems: Systems, life cycles, electronic commerce, and risk.* Cambridge, UK: Cambridge University Press.

Olfman, L., Bostrom, R. P., & Sein, M. K. (2003, April). A best-practice based model of information technology learning strategy formulation. In *Proceedings of the ACM SIGMIS CPR Conference on Computer Personnel Research,* Philadelphia (pp. 75-86).

Olfman, L., Bostrom, R. P., & Sein, M. K. (2001). *Training with a business focus: A best practice.* Bitworld.

Olfman, L., Bostrom, R. P., & Sein, M. K. (2006). Developing Training Strategies with an HCI Perspective. In Zhang, P., & Galletta, D. (Eds.), *Human-Computer Interaction and Management Information Systems - Foundations.* Armonk, NY: Sharpe Inc.

Olfman, L., & Mandviwalla, M. (1994, December). Conceptual versus procedural software training for graphical user interfaces: A longitudinal field experiment. *Management Information Systems Quarterly,* 405–426. doi:10.2307/249522

Ong, C.-S., Lai, J.-Y., & Wang, Y.-S. (2004). Factors affecting engineers' acceptance of asynchronous e-learning systems in high-tech companies. *Information & Management, 41*(6), 795–804. doi:10.1016/j.im.2003.08.012

OpenDoc Design Team. (1993). *OpenDoc technical summary*. Apple Computer.

O'Reilly, T. (2006). *What is Web 2.0 - design patterns and business models for the next generation of software*. Retrieved from http://www.oreillynet.com/pub/a/oreilly/tim/news/2005/09/30/what-is-web-20.html

Organ, D. W., Podsakoff, P. M., & MacKenzie, S. B. (2006). *Organizational citizenship behavior: Its nature, antecedents, and consequences*. Thousand Oaks, CA: Sage.

Orlikowski, W. J. (1992). Learning from Notes: Organizational issues in groupware implementation. In *Proceedings of the Computer-Supported Cooperative Work Conference (CSCW '92)* (pp. 362-369). New York: ACM Press.

Orlikowski, W. (1995). *Evolving with Notes: Organizational Change around Groupware Technology*. Cambridge, MA: MIT Center for Coordination Science.

Orlikowski, W. J. (1992). The Duality of Technology: Rethinking the Concept of Technology in Organizations. *Organization Science - Focused Issue. Management of Technology, 3*(3), 398–427.

Orlikowski, W. J. (1993). Learning from notes: Organizational issues in groupware implementation. *The Information Society, 9*(3), 237–250. doi:10.1080/01972243.1993.9960143

Orlikowski, W. J. (2000). Using technology and constituting structures: A practice lens for studying technology in organizations. *Organization Science, 11*(4), 404–428. doi:10.1287/orsc.11.4.404.14600

Orlikowski, W. J., & Hofman, J. D. (1997). An Improvisational Model for Change Management: the Case of Groupware. *Sloan Management Science, 38*(2), 11–21.

Orlikowski, W. J., & Robey, D. (1991). Information technology and the structuring of organizations. *Information Systems Research, 2*(2), 143–169. doi:10.1287/isre.2.2.143

Orr, J. (1996). *Talking about machines—an ethnography of a modern job*. Ithaca, NY: ILR Press/Cornell University Press.

Ortner, S. (Ed.). (1999). *The Fate of Culture. Geertz and Beyond*. Berkeley, CA: University of California Press.

Østerlund, C., & Carlile, P. (2005). Relations in Practice: Sorting Through Practice Theories on Knowledge Sharing in Complex Organizations. *The Information Society, 21*(2), 91–107. doi:10.1080/01972240590925294

Ouchi, W., & Wilkins, A. (1985). Organizational Culture. *Annual Review of Sociology, 11*, 457–483. doi:10.1146/annurev.so.11.080185.002325

Pallant, J. (2007). SPSS Survival Manual: A Step by Step Guide to Data Analysis Using SPSS for Windows (Version 15).

Palmer, J. W. (2002). Web site usability, design, and performance metrics. *Information Systems Research, 13*, 151–167. doi:10.1287/isre.13.2.151.88

Pane, J. F., & Myers, B. A. (2006). More natural programming languages and environments. In H. Lieberman, F. Paternò, & V. Wulf (Ed.), *End user development* (pp. 31-50). New York: Springer.

Pane, J., Myers, B., & Miller, L. (2002, September 3-6). Using HCI techniques to design a more usable programming system. In *Proceedings of the 2002 IEEE International Conference on Human-Centric Computing Languages and Environments (HCC'2002)*, Arlington, VA (pp. 198-206). Washington, DC: IEEE Computer Society.

Panko, R. R., & Sprague, R. (1997). *Experiments in spreadsheet development: Task difficulty, level of expertise, and error rate*. Unpublished manuscript http://www/cba.hawaii.edu/panko/papers//ss/Imexpert.htm

Parboosingh, J. T. (2002). Physician Communities of Practice: Where Learning and Practice Are Inseparable. *The Journal of Continuing Education in the Health Professions, 22*(4), 230–236. doi:10.1002/chp.1340220407

Pardo, T. A., Cresswell, A. M., Thompson, F., & Zhang, J. (2006). Knowledge sharing in cross-boundary information system development in the public sector. *Information Technology Management, 7*(4), 293–313. doi:10.1007/s10799-006-0278-6

Parthasarathy, M., & Bhattacherjee, A. (1998). Understanding Post-Adoption Behavior in the Context of Online Services. *Information Systems Research, 9*(4), 362. doi:10.1287/isre.9.4.362

Patton, M. Q. (1990). *Qualitative evaluation and research methods* (2nd ed.). Newbury Park, CA: Sage.

Pearrow, M. (2000). *Web Site Usability*. Rockland, MA: Charles River Media.

Pekkola, S., Kaarilahti, N., & Pohjola, P. (2006, August 1-5). Towards formalised end-user participation in information systems development process: Bridging the gap between participatory design and ISD methodologies. In *Proceedings of the Participatory Design Conference (PDC '2006)*, Trento, Italy (pp. 21-30). New York: ACM Press.

Peppler, K. A., & Kafai, Y. B. (2007). From SuperGoo to Scratch: Exploring creative digital media production in informal learning. *Learning, Media and Technology, 32*(2), 149–166. doi:10.1080/17439880701343337

Peppler, K. A., & Kafai, Y. B. (Manuscript submitted for publication). Creative bytes: The technical, creative, and critical practices of media arts production. *Journal of the Learning Sciences.*

Perkel, D. (2008). No I don't feel complimented: A young artist's take on copyright. *Digital Youth Research.* Retrieved from http://digitalyouth.ischool.berkeley.edu/node/105.Resnick, M., Kafai, Y. B., & Maeda, J. (2003). *ITR: A networked, media-rich programming environment to enhance technological fluency at after-school centers in economically disadvantaged communities.* Washington, DC: National Science Foundation.

Peterson, R. (2004). Crafting information technology governance. *Information Systems Management, 21*(4), 7–22. doi:10.1201/1078/44705.21.4.20040901/84183.2

Petty, R. E., & Cacioppo, J. T. (1984). Source factors and the elaboration likelihood model of persuasion. *Advances in Consumer Research. Association for Consumer Research (U. S.), 11*(1), 668–672.

Piccoli, G., & Ives, B. (2005). Review: IT-Dependent Strategic Initiatives and Sustained Competitive Advantage: A Review and Synthesis of the Literature. *Management Information Systems Quarterly, 29*(4), 747–776.

Piderit, S. K. (2000). Rethinking resistance and recognising ambivalence: A multidimensional view of attitudes towards an organisational change. *Academy of Management Review, 25*(4), 783–794. doi:10.2307/259206

Pinch, T., & Bijker, W. (1987). The social construction of facts and artifacts: Or how the sociology of science and the sociology of technology might benefit each other. In Bijker, W., Hughes, T., & Pinch, T. (Eds.), *The social construction of technological systems: New directions in the sociology and history of technology* (pp. 17–50). Cambridge, MA: MIT Press.

Pipek, V., & Wulf, V. (1999). *A Groupware's Life*. Paper presented at ECSCW '99.

Pipek, V., & Wulf, V. (in press). Infrastructuring: Towards an Integrated Perspective on the Design and Use of Information Technology. *Journal of the Association of Information System (JAIS): Special Issue on e-Infrastructure.*

Pipek, V., Rossen, M. B., deRuyter, B., & Wulf, V. (Eds.). (2009). *End-user development.* Heidelberg, Germany: Springer.

Pipek, V. (2005). *From Tailoring to Appropriation Support: Negotiating Groupware Usage*. Oulu, Finland: Department of Information Processing Science, University of Oulu.

Pipek, V., & Kahler, H. (2006). Supporting Collaborative Tailoring. In Lieberman, H., Paternò, F., & Wulf, V. (Eds.), *End User Development* (pp. 315–346). New York: Springer. doi:10.1007/1-4020-5386-X_15

Plaskoff, J. (2003). Intersubjectivity and community building: learning to learn organizationally. In Easterby-Smith, M., & Lyles, M. A. (Eds.), *The Blackwell Handbook of Organizational Learning and Knowledge Management* (pp. 161–184). Oxford, UK: Blackwell Publishing.

Pliskin, N., Romm, T., Lee, A., & Weber, Y. (1993). Presumed Versus Actual Organizational Culture: Managerial Implications for Implementation of Information Systems. *The Computer Journal, 36*(2), 1–10. doi:10.1093/comjnl/36.2.143

Polanyi, M. (1966). *The tacit dimension.* Garden City, NY: Doubleday.

Pollock, N., & Williams, R. (2008). *The biography of the enterprise-wide system or how SAP conquered the world.* London: Routledge.

Poltrock, S., & Grudin, J. (1994). Organizational Obstacles to Interface Design and Development: Two Participant – Observer Studies. *ACM Transactions on Computer-Human Interaction, 1*(1), 52–80. doi:10.1145/174630.174633

Poole, M. S., & DeSanctis, G. (1989). Use of Group Decision Support Systems as an appropriation process. In *Proceedings of the Twenty-Second Annual Hawaii International Conference on System Sciences* (pp. 149-157).

Poole, M. S., & DeSanctis, G. (2004). Structuration theory in information systems research: Methods and controversies. In Whitman, M. E., & Woszczynski, A. B. (Eds.), *The handbook of information systems research* (pp. 206–249). Hershey, PA: IGI Global.

Pornpitakpan, C. (2004). The persuasiveness of source credibility: A critical review of five decade's evidence. *Journal of Applied Social Psychology, 34*(2), 243–281. doi:10.1111/j.1559-1816.2004.tb02547.x

Porter, M. E., & Millar, V. E. (1985). How Information Gives You Competitive Advantage. *Harvard Business Review, 64*(4), 149–160.

Poster, M. (1992). The Question of Agency: Michel de Certeau and the History of Consumerism. *Diacritics, 22*(2), 94–107. doi:10.2307/465283

Postman, N. (1985). *Amusing ourselves to death—public discourse in the age of show business.* New York: Penguin Books.

Powell, F. C., & Wanzenried, J. W. (1995). Do current measures of dimensions of source credibility produce stable outcomes in replicated tests? *Perceptual and Motor Skills, 81*(2), 675–687.

Powel, T. A. (2000). *The Complete Reference. Web Design.* New York: Osborne/McGraw-Hill.

Preece, J., & Shneiderman, B. (2009). The reader-to-leader framework: Motivating technology-mediated social participation. *AIS Transactions on Human-Computer Interaction, 1*(1), 13–32.

Premkumar, G., Ramamurthy, K., & Liu, H. N. (2008). Internet messaging: An examination of the impact of attitudinal, normative, and control belief systems. *Information & Management, 45*(7), 451–457. doi:10.1016/j.im.2008.06.008

Preslak, A. R., Subramanian, G. H., & Clayton, G. E. (2007). 2008). The phases of ERP software implementation and maintenance: A model for predicting preferred ERP use. *Journal of Computer Information Systems*, 25–33.

Priester, J. R., & Petty, R. E. (1995). Source attributions and persuasion: Perceived honesty as a determinant of message scrutiny. *Personality and Social Psychology Bulletin, 21*(6), 637–654. doi:10.1177/0146167295216010

Purho, V. (2000). Heuristic inspections for documentation-10 recommended documentation heuristics. *STC Usability SIG Newsletter, 6*(4).

Qingxiong Ma, T., & Liping Liu. (2004). The Technology Acceptance Model: A Meta-Analysis of Empirical Findings. *Journal of Organizational and End User Computing, 16*(1), 59.

Quinn, C. N. (1996). Pragmatic evaluation: Lessons from usability. In *Proceedings of the 13th Annual Conference of the Australasian Society for Computers in Learning in Tertiry Education (ASCILITE).*

Rai, A., Patnayakuni, R., & Patnayakuni, N. (1997). Technology investment and business performance. *Communications of the ACM, 40*(7), 89–97. doi:10.1145/256175.256191

Randell, R. (2004, November 6-10). Accountability in an alarming environment. In *Proceedings of the International Conference on Computer Supported Cooperative Work (CSCW '04),* Chicago (pp. 125-131). ACM Publishing.

Raquel, B. F. (2001). Using protocol analysis to evaluate the usability of a commercial Web site. *Information & Management, 39*, 151–163. doi:10.1016/S0378-7206(01)00085-4

Ravichandran, T., & Lertwongsatien, C. (2005). Effect of Information Systems Resources and Capabilities on Firm Performance: A Resource-Based Perspective. *Journal of Management Information Systems, 21*(4), 237–276.

Raykov, T. (1997). Estimation of Composite Reliability for Congeneric Measures. *Applied Psychological Measurement, 21*(2), 173–184. doi:10.1177/01466216970212006

Raymond, E. S., & Young, B. (2001). *The cathedral and the bazaar: Musings on Linux and open source by an accidental revolutionary.* Sebastopol, CA: O'Reilly & Associates.

Reeves, B., & Shipman, F. (1992). Supporting communication between designers with artifact-centered evolving information spaces. In *Proceedings of the Conference on Computer-Supported Cooperative Work (CSCW '92)* (pp. 394-401). New York: ACM Publishing.

Reich, B. H., & Benbasat, I. (1990). An Empirical Investigation of Factors Influencing the Success of Customer-Oriented Strategic Systems. *Information Systems Research, 1*(3), 325–347. doi:10.1287/isre.1.3.325

Reich, B. H., & Benbasat, I. (2000). Factors That Influence the Social Dimension of Alignment Between Business and Information Technology Objectives. *Management Information Systems Quarterly, 24*(1), 81–113. doi:10.2307/3250980

Repenning, A., & Ioannidou, A. (2006, September 4-8) AgentCubes: Raising the ceiling of end-user development in education through incremental 3D. In *Proceedings of the 2006 IEEE Symposium on Visual Languages and Human-Centric Computing (VL/HCC 2006),* Brighton, UK (pp. 27-31). Washington, DC: IEEE Computer Society.

Resnick, M., & Silverman, B. (2005, June 8-10). Some reflections on designing construction kits for kids. In *Proceedings of the 2005 Interaction Design and Children Conference,* Boulder, CO (pp. 117-122). ACM Publishing.

Resnick, M., Maloney, J., Hernandez, A. M., Rusk, N., Eastmond, E., & Brennan, K. (in press). Scratch: Programming for everyone. *Communications of the ACM.*

Riemenschneider, C. K., Harrison, D. A., & Mykytyn, P. P. (2003). Understanding it adoption decisions in small business: Integrating current theories. *Information & Management, 40*(4), 269–285. doi:10.1016/S0378-7206(02)00010-1

Rittel, H. (1984). Second-generation design methods. In N. Cross (Ed.), *Developments in design methodology* (pp. 317-327). New York: John Wiley & Sons.

Rittel, H., & Webber, M. M. (1984). Planning problems are wicked problems. In N. Cross (Ed.), *Developments in design methodology* (pp. 135-144). New York: John Wiley & Sons

Roach, S. (1987). *America's Technology Dilemma: A Profile of the Information Economy.* New York: Morgan Stanley.

Roach, S. (1988). Technology and the Service Sector: The Hidden Competitive Challenge. *Technological Forecasting and Social Change, 34*(4), 387–403. doi:10.1016/0040-1625(88)90006-6

Roach, S. (1991). Services Under Siege - The Restructuring Imperative. *Harvard Business Review, 69,* 82–91.

Robey, D. (1979). User attitudes and management information systems use. *Academy of Management, 22*(3), 527–538. doi:10.2307/255742

Robey, D., & Azevedo, A. (1994). Cultural Analysis of the Organizational Consequences of Information Technology. *Accounting. Management & Information Technology, 4*(1), 23–37. doi:10.1016/0959-8022(94)90011-6

Rode, J. A., Toye, E. F., & Blackwell, A. F. (2004). The fuzzy felt ethnography - understanding the programming patterns of domestic appliances. *Personal and Ubiquitous Computing, 8,* 161–176. doi:10.1007/s00779-004-0272-0

Rogers, E. (1995). *Diffusion of Innovations* (5th ed.). New York: Free Press.

Rogers, E. M. (1995). *Diffusion of Innovations* (4th ed.). New York: Free Press.

Rogoff, B., Matsuov, E., & White, C. (1998). Models of teaching and learning: Participation in a community of learners. In D. R. Olsen & N. Torrance (Eds.), *The handbook of education and human development—new models of learning, teaching and schooling* (pp. 388-414). Oxford, UK: Blackwell.

Rohde, M., Klamma, R., Jarke, M., & Wulf, V. (2007). Reality is our laboratory: communities of practice in applied computer science. *Behaviour & Information Technology, 26*(1), 81–94. doi:10.1080/01449290600811636

Röhr, W. (1979). *Aneignung und Persönlichkeit (Appropriation and Personality).* Berlin, Germany: Akademie Verlag.

Rosenbaum, S., Rohn, J., & Humburg, J. (2000). A Toolkit for Strategic Usability: Results from Workshops, Panels, and Surveys. In *Proceedings of the Conference on Human Factors in Computing Systems (CHI Letters)* (Vol. 2, No. 1, pp. 337-344). New York: ACM.

Ross, J. W., Beath, C. M., & Goodhue, D. L. (1996). Develop Long-Term Competitiveness Through IT Assets. *Sloan Management Review*, *38*(1), 31–42.

Rosson, M., Ballin, J., & Nash, H. (2004, September 26-29). Everyday programming: Challenges and opportunities for informal web development. In *Proceedings of the 2004 IEEE Symposium on Visual Languages and Human-Centric Computing (VL/HCC 2004),* Rome, Italy (pp. 123-130). Washington, DC: IEEE Computer Society.

Rosson, M., Ballin, J., & Rode, J. (2005, September 21-24). Who, what, and how? A survey of informal and professional web developers. In *Proceedings of the 2005 IEEE Symposium on Visual Languages and Human-Centric Computing (VL/HCC 2005),* Dallas, TX (pp. 199-206). Washington, DC: IEEE Computer Society.

Rosson, M., Sinha, H., Bhattacharya, M., & Zhao, D. (2007, September 23-27). Design planning in end-user web development. In *Proceedings of the IEEE Symposium on Visual Languages and Human-Centric Computing (VL/HCC 2007),* Coeur d'Alene, ID (pp. 189-196). Washington, DC: IEEE Computer Society.

Rosson, M., & Carroll, J. (2002). *Usability Engineering: Scenario-based Development of Human-Computer Interaction*. San Francisco, CA: Morgan-Kaufman.

Rothermel, K., Cook, C., Burnett, M., Schonfeld, J., Green, T., & Rothermel, G. (2000, June 4-11). WYSIWYT testing in the spreadsheet paradigm: An empirical evaluation. In *Proceedings of the 22nd International Conference on Software Engineering,* Limerick, Ireland (pp. 230-239). ACM Publishing.

Rothermel, G., Burnett, M., Li, L., DuPuis, C., & Sheretov, A. (2001). A methodology for testing spreadsheets. *ACM Transactions on Software Engineering*, *10*(1), 110–147. doi:10.1145/366378.366385

Rotter, J. B. (1980). Interpersonal trust, trustworthiness, and gullibility. *The American Psychologist*, *35*(1), 1–7. doi:10.1037/0003-066X.35.1.1

Rumpe, B., & Schröder, A. (2001). *Quantitative Untersuchung des Extreme Programming Prozesses* (Tech. Rep. TUM-I01). Munich, Germany: Munich University of Technology.

Ruppel, C., & Harrington, S. (2001). Sharing Knowledge through Intranets: A Study of Organizational Culture and Intranet Implementation. *IEEE Transactions on Professional Communication*, *44*(1), 37–52. doi:10.1109/47.911131

Rusbult, C. E., Martz, J. M., & Agnew, C. R. (1998). The investment model scale: Measuring commitment level, satisfaction level, quality of alternatives, and investment size. *Personal Relationships*, *5*(4), 357–391. doi:10.1111/j.1475-6811.1998.tb00177.x

Ruthruff, J., Phalgune, A., Beckwith, L., Burnett, M., & Cook, C. (2004, September 26-29). Rewarding good behavior: End-user debugging and rewards. In *Proceedings of the 2004 IEEE Symposium on Visual Languages and Human-Centric Computing (VL/HCC 2004),* Rome, Italy (pp. 115-122). Washington, DC: IEEE Computer Society.

Ryan, R. M., & Deci, E. L. (2000). Intrinsic and extrinsic motivations: classic definitions and new directions. *Contemporary Educational Psychology*, *25*(1), 54–67. doi:10.1006/ceps.1999.1020

Ryu, S., Ho, S. H., & Han, I. (2003). Knowledge sharing behavior of physicians in hospitals. *Expert Systems with Applications*, *25*(1), 113–122. doi:10.1016/S0957-4174(03)00011-3

Saadé, R., & Bahli, B. (2005). The impact of cognitive absorption on perceived usefulness and perceived ease of use in on-line learning: An extension of the technology acceptance model. *Information & Management*, *42*(2), 317–327. doi:10.1016/j.im.2003.12.013

Sabherwal, R. (1999). The Relationship Between Information System Planning Sophistication and Information System Success: An Empirical Assessment. *Decision Sciences*, *30*(1), 137–166. doi:10.1111/j.1540-5915.1999.tb01604.x

Sabherwal, R., & Chan, Y. E. (2001). Alignment between Business and IS Strategies: A Study of Prospectors, Analyzers, and Defenders. *Information Systems Research*, *12*(1), 11–33. doi:10.1287/isre.12.1.11.9714

Sabherwal, R., & King, W. R. (1995). An Empirical Taxonomy of the Decision-Making Processes Concerning Strategic Applications of Information Systems. *Journal of Management Information Systems, 11*(4), 177–214.

Saeed, K. A., & Abdinnour-Helm, S. (2008). Examining the effects of information system characteristics and perceived usefulness on post adoption usage of information systems. *Information & Management, 45*(1), 376–386. doi:10.1016/j.im.2008.06.002

Sahay, S., & Robey, D. (1996). Organizational context, social interpretation, and the implementation and consequences of geographic information systems. *Accounting. Management & Information Technology, 6*(4), 255–282. doi:10.1016/S0959-8022(96)90016-8

Sambamurthy, V., & Zmud, R. W. (1999). Arrangements for information technology governance: A theory of multiple contingencies. *Management Information Systems Quarterly, 23*(2), 261–290. doi:10.2307/249754

Sandars, J., & Heller, R. (2006). Improving the implementation of evidence-based practice: a knowledge management perspective. *Journal of Evaluation in Clinical Practice, 12*(3), 341–346. doi:10.1111/j.1365-2753.2006.00534.x

Sandberg, J. (2005). How do we justify knowledge produced within interpretive approaches? *Organizational Research Methods, 8*(1), 41–68. doi:10.1177/1094428104272000

Santhanam, R., & Hariono, E. (2003). Issues Liking Information Technology Capability to Firm Performance. *Management Information Systems Quarterly, 27*(1), 125–143.

Santhanam, R., & Sein, M. K. (1994). Improving end-user proficiency: Effects of conceptual training and nature of interaction. *Information Systems Research, 5*(4), 378–399. doi:10.1287/isre.5.4.378

Scaffidi, C., Shaw, M., & Myers, B. (2005, September 20-24). Estimating the numbers of end users and end user programmers. In *Proceedings of the 2005 IEEE Symposium on Visual Languages and Human-Centric Computing (VL/HCC 2005),* Dallas, TX (pp. 207-214). Washington, DC: IEEE Computer Society.

Scharff, E. (2002). *Open source software, a conceptual framework for collaborative artifact and knowledge construction.* Unpublished doctoral dissertation, University of Colorado at Boulder.

Schaumburg, H. (2001). Computers as tools or as social actors? The users' perspective on anthropomorphic agents. *International Journal of Cooperative Information Systems, 10*(1-2), 217–234. doi:10.1142/S0218843001000321

Schein, E. (1985). *Organizational culture and leadership* (2nd ed.). San Francisco, CA: Jossey-Bass.

Schepers, J., & Wetzels, M. (2007). A meta analysis of the technology acceptance model: Investigating subjective norm and moderation effects. *Information & Management, 44*(1), 90–103. doi:10.1016/j.im.2006.10.007

Schermelleh-Engel, K., Moosbrugger, H., & Müller, H. (2003). Evaluating the Fit of Structural Equation Models: Tests of Significance and Descriptive Goodness-of-Fit Measures. *Methods of Psychological Research Online, 8*(2), 23–74.

Schmidt, K., & Simone, C. (1996). Coordination mechanisms: Towards a conceptual foundation of CSCW systems design. *Computer Supported Cooperative Work, 5*(2-3), 155–200. doi:10.1007/BF00133655

Schön, D. A. (1983). *The reflective practitioner: How professionals think in action.* New York: Basic Books.

Schwandt, T. (2000). Three Epistemological Stances for Qualitative Inquiry: Interpretivism, Hermeneutics, and Social Constructionism. In Denzin, N., & Lincoln, Y. (Eds.), *Handbook of Qualitative Research* (2nd ed., pp. 189–214). Thousand Oaks, CA: Sage Publications Inc.

Schwartz, T., Meurer, J., & Stevens, G. (2009). *Nutzerinnovation im Eclipse Fall aus der Perspektive einer unternehmerischen Arbeitspraxis.* P aper presented at Open Design Spaces (ODS): Innovation durch Nutzerbeteiligung, Workshop im Rahmen der TagungMensch und Computer 2009.

Seale, C. (1999). *The quality of qualitative research.* London: Sage.

Segars, A. H., & Grover, V. (1998). Strategic Information Systems Planning Success: An Investigation of the Construct and its Measurement. *Management Information Systems Quarterly, 22*(2), 139–163. doi:10.2307/249393

Sein, M. K., & Bostrom, R. P. (1989). Individual Differences and Conceptual Models in Training Novice End-Users. *Human-Computer Interaction*, *4*(3), 197–229. doi:10.1207/s15327051hci0403_2

Sein, M. K., Bostrom, R. P., & Olfman, L. (1987). Training end users to compute: cognitive, motivational and social issues. *INFOR*, *25*, 236–255.

Sein, M. K., Bostrom, R. P., & Olfman, L. (1999). Rethinking end-user training strategy: Applying a hierarchical knowledge level model. *Journal of End User Computing*, *11*(1), 32–39.

Sellen, A. J., & Harper, R. H. R. (2003). *The myth of the paperless office*. Cambridge, MA: MIT Press.

Selwyn, N. (2003). Apart for technology: understanding people's non-use of information and communication technologies in everyday life. *Technology in society*, *25*, 99–106. doi:10.1016/S0160-791X(02)00062-3

Sethi, V., & King, W. R. (1994). Development of Measures to Assess the Extent to Which an Information Technology Application Provides Competitive Advantage. *Management Science*, *40*(12), 1601–1627. doi:10.1287/mnsc.40.12.1601

Shayo, C. (1995). Role of conceptual and mental models in motivating end users to learn new but related software packages. Unpublished doctoral dissertation, Claremont Graduate School, Claremont, CA.

Shayo, C., & Olfman, L. (2000). The role of training in preparing end users to learn related software. *Journal of End User Computing*, *12*(1), 3–13.

Sheridan, T. B. (1992). *Telerobotics, Automation, and Human Supervisory Control*. Cambridge, MA: The MIT Press.

Shih, H. P. (2004). An empirical study on predicting user acceptance of e-shopping on the Web. *Information & Management*, *41*(3), 351–368. doi:10.1016/S0378-7206(03)00079-X

Shneiderman, B. (1998). *Designing the User Interface: Strategies for Effective Human-Computer Interaction*. Reading, MA: Addison-Wesley.

Shneiderman, B. (2007). Creativity support tools: Accelerating discovery and innovation. *Communications of the ACM*, *50*(12), 20–32. doi:10.1145/1323688.1323689

Shupe, C., & Behling, R. (2006, July/August). Developing and implementing a strategy for technology deployment. *The Information Management Journal*, 52-57.

Sieloff, C. G. (1999). 'If only Hp knew what Hp knows': The roots of knowledge management at hewlett-Packard. *Knowledge Management*, *3*(1), 47–53. doi:10.1108/13673279910259385

Siggelkow, N. (2007). Persuasion with case studies. *Academy of Management Journal*, *50*(1), 20–24.

Silius, K., & Tervakari, A.-M. (2003). The Usefulness of Web-based Learning Environments. The Evaluation tool into the Portal of Finnish Virtual University. In *Proceedings of the International Conference on Network Universities and e-Learning*. Retrieved from http://www.hsh.no/menu/

Silverman, D. (2006). *Interpreting qualitative data* (3rd ed.). Thousand Oaks, CA: Sage.

Silverstone, R., & Haddon, L. (1996). Design and the Domestication of Information and Communication Technologies: Technical Change and Everyday Life. In Mansell, R., & Silverstone, R. (Eds.), *Communication by Design: The Politics of Information and Communication Technologies* (pp. 44–74). Oxford, UK: Oxford University Press.

Simon, H. A. (1996). *The sciences of the artificial* (3rd ed.). Cambridge, MA: MIT Press.

Simonsen, M., & Sein, M. K. (2004, April 22-24). Conceptual frameworks in practice: Evaluating end- user training strategy in an organization. In *Proceedings of the ACM SIGMIS CPR Conference on Computer Personnel Research*, Tucson, AZ (pp. 14-24).

Siponen, M., Pahnila, S., & Mahmood, A. (2006, November). Factors influencing protection motivation and IS security policy compliance. *Innovations in Information Technology*, 1.

Siponen, M. T. (2000). A conceptual foundation for organizational information security awareness. *Information Management & Computer Security*, *8*(1), 31–41. doi:10.1108/09685220010371394

Skinner, B. (2004). Web alert: news and views within healthcare -- managing the information overload. *Quality in Primary Care, 12*(4), 289–292.

Skyrme, D. J. (2001). *Capitalizing on Knowledge: from E-business to K-business*. Oxford, UK: Butterworth-Heinemann.

Smircich, L. (1983). Concepts of Culture and Organizational Analysis. *Administrative Science Quarterly, 28*(3), 339–358. doi:10.2307/2392246

Smith, J. R., Terry, D. J., Manstead, A. S., Louis, W. R., & Wolfs, D. K. J. (2008). The attitude-behavior relationship in consumer conduct: The role of norms, past behavior, and self-identity. *The Journal of Social Psychology, 148*(3), 311–333. doi:10.3200/SOCP.148.3.311-334

Smith, L. J. (2001). Content and delivery: A comparison and contrast of electronic and traditional MBA marketing planning courses. *Journal of Marketing Education, 23*(1), 35–44. doi:10.1177/0273475301231005

Smithson, S., & Hirshheim, R. (1998). Analyzing information systems evaluation: Another look at an old problem. *European Journal of Information Systems, 7*(3), 158–174. doi:10.1057/palgrave.ejis.3000304

Soloway, E., & Spohrer, J. C. (Eds.). (1989). *Studying the novice programmer*. Hillsdale, NJ: Lawrence Erlbaum Associates.

Soloway, E., Guzdial, M., & Hay, K. (1994). Learner-centered design: The challenge for HCI in the 21st century. *Interaction, 1*(22), 36–48. doi:10.1145/174809.174813

Spinuzzi, C. (2002). A Scandinavian Challenge, a US Response: Methodological Assumptions in Scandinavian and US Prototyping Approaches. In *Proceedings of the 20th annual international conference on Computer documentation* (pp. 208-215). New York: ACM.

SPSS. I. (2006). *SPSS 15.0 Base User's Guide*. Upper Saddle River, NJ: Prentice Hall.

Squires, D. (1997). An heuristic approach to the evaluation of educational multimedia software. In *Proceedings of the Computer Assisted Learning Conference*, University of Exeter, Exeter, UK. Retrieved from http://www/media/uwe.ac.uk/masoud/cal-97/papers/squires.htm

Staggers, N., & Norcio, A. F. (1993). Mental models: Concepts for human-computer interaction research. *International Journal of Man-Machine Studies, 38*, 587–605. doi:10.1006/imms.1993.1028

Stake, R. E. (1994). Case studies. In Denzin, K. N., & Lincoln, Y. S. (Eds.), *Handbook of qualitative research* (pp. 236–247). Thousand Oaks, CA: Sage.

Star, S. L. (1989). The structure of ill-structured solutions: Boundary objects and heterogeneous distributed problem solving. In L. Gasser & M. N. Huhns (Eds.), *Distributed artificial intelligence* (Vol. 2, pp. 37-54). San Mateo, CA: Morgan Kaufmann Publishers.

Star, S. L. (1990). The structure of ill-structured solutions: Boundary objects and heterogeneous distributed problem solving. In *Distributed artificial intelligence* (*Vol. 2*, pp. 37–54). San Francisco: Morgan Kaufmann.

Star, S. L., & Bowker, G. C. (2002). How to infrastructure. In Lievrouw, L. A., & Livingstone, S. (Eds.), *Handbook of New Media - Social Shaping and Consequences of ICTs* (pp. 151–162). London, UK: Sage.

Star, S. L., & Griesemer, J. R. (1989). Institutional Ecology, 'Translations' and Boundary Objects: Amateurs and Professionals in Berkeley's Museum of Vertebrate Zoology, 1907-39. *Social Studies of Science, 19*, 387–420. doi:10.1177/030631289019003001

Stevens, G. (2005). *BSCWeasel - How to make an existing Groupware System more flexible*. Paper presented at ECSCW 2005, Paris, France.

Stevens, G., & Wiedenhöfer, T. (2006, October 14-18). CHIC - a pluggable solution for community help in context. In A. Mørch et al. (Eds), *Proceedings of the 4th Nordic Conference on Human-Computer Interaction,* Oslo, Norway (pp. 212-221). ACM Publishing.

Stevens, G., & Wulf, V. (2002, November 16-20). A new dimension in access control: Studying maintenance engineering across organizational boundaries. In E. F. Churchill, J. McCarthy, C. Neuwirth, & T. Rodden (Eds.), *Proceedings of the 2002 Conference on Computer Supported Cooperative Work (CSCW 2002),* New Orleanes (pp. 196-205). ACM Publishing.

Stevens, G., Budweg, S., & Pipek, V. (2004). *The "BSC-Weasel" and Eclipse-powered Cooperative End User Development*. Paper presented at the Workshop: Eclipse as a Vehicle for CSCW Research, CSCW 2004.

Stevens, L. (2000, October). Incentives for Sharing. *Knowledge Management*, 54-60.

Stevens, G., & Wiedenhöfer, T. (2006). CHIC - a pluggable solution for community help in context. In [New York: ACM Publishing.]. *Proceedings of NORDICHI, 06*, 212–221.

Stevenson, W. J. (2005). *Operations Management*. New York: McGraw-Hill.

Storck, J., & Hill, P. (2000). Knowledge diffusion through strategic communities. *Sloan Management Review*, *41*(2), 63–74.

Storey, J. (2006). *Cultural theory and popular culture: an introduction*. Upper Saddle River, NJ: Pearson Education.

Straub, D. W. (1989). Validating Instruments in MIS research. *Management Information Systems Quarterly*, *13*, 147–169. doi:10.2307/248922

Straub, D. W., Boudreau, M. C., & Gefen, D. (2004). Validation Guidelilnes of IS Positivist Research. *Communications of the Association for Information Systems*, *13*, 380–426.

Straub, D. W., & Welke, R. J. (1998). Coping with systems risk: Security planning models for management decision making. *Management Information Systems Quarterly*, *22*(4), 441–469. doi:10.2307/249551

Stumpf, S., Rajaram, V., Li, L., Burnett, M., Dietterich, T., Sullivan, E., et al. (2007, January 28-31). Toward harnessing user feedback for machine learning. In *Proceedings of the 12th International Conference on Intelligent User Interfaces,* Honolulu, HI (pp. 82-91). ACM Publishing.

Stumpf, S., Sullivan, E., Fitzhenry, E., Oberst, I., Wong, W., & Burnett, M. (2008, January 13-16). Integrating rich user feedback into intelligent user interfaces. In *Proceedings of the 13th International Conference on Intelligent User Interfaces,* Gran Canaria, Spain (pp. 50-59). ACM Publishing.

Stylos, J., & Clarke, S. (2007, May 19-27). Usability implications of requiring parameters in objects' constructors. In *Proceedings of the 29th International Conference on Software Engineering (ICSE 2007),* Minneapolis, MN (pp. 529-539). Washington, DC: IEEE Computer Society.

Stylos, J., & Myers, B. A. (2008, November 9-14). The implications of method placement on API learnability. In *Proceedings of the 16th ACM SIGSOFT Symposium on Foundations of Software Engineering (FSE 2008),* Atlanta, GA (pp. 105-112). ACM Publishing.

Stylos, J., Busse, D. K., Graf, B., Ziegler, C., Ehret, R., & Karstens, J. (2008, September 15-19). A case study of API design for improved usability. In *Proceedings of the the 2008 IEEE Symposium on Visual Languages and Human-Centric Computing (VL/HCC'08),* Herrsching am Ammersee, Germany (pp. 189-192). Washington, DC: IEEE Computer Society.

Stylos, J., Faulring, A., Yang, Z., & Myers, B. A. (2009, September 20-24). *Improving API documentation using API usage information*. Paper presented at the 2009 IEEE Symposium on Visual Languages and Human-Centric Computing (VL/HCC'09), Corvallis, OR. (pp. 119-126).

Subrahmaniyan, N., Beckwith, L., Grigoreanu, V., Burnett, M., Wiedenbeck, S., Narayanan, V., et al. (2008, April 5-10). Testing vs. code inspection vs.... What else? Male and female end users' debugging strategies. In Proceedings of the *ACM Conference on Human Factors in Computing Systems (CHI 2008),* Florence, Italy (pp. 617-626). ACM Publishing.

Subrahmaniyan, N., Burnett, M., & Bogart, C. (2008, September 16-17). Software visualization for end-user programmers: Trial period obstacles. *ACM Symposium on Software Visualization,* Herrsching am Ammersee, Germany (pp. 135-144). ACM Publishing.

Subrahmaniyan, N., Kissinger, C., Rector, K., Inman, D., Kaplan, J., Beckwith, L., et al. (2007, September 23-27). Explaining debugging strategies to end-user programmers. In *Proceedings of the 2007 IEEE Symposium on Visual Languages and Human-Centric Computing (VL/HCC 2007),* Coeur d'Alene, ID (pp. 127-134). Washington, DC: IEEE Computer Society.

Suchman, L. A. (1987). *Plans and situated actions.* Cambridge, UK: Cambridge University Press.

Suchman, L. (1987). *Plans and situated actions: The problem of human-machine communication*. Cambridge, UK: Cambridge University Press.

Suchman, L. (1995). Making Work Visible. *Communications of the ACM, 38*(9), 56–64. doi:10.1145/223248.223263

Suchman, L. (2002). Located accountabilities in technology production. *Scandinavian Journal of Information Systems, 14*(2), 91–105.

Sugimoto, M., Hosoi, K., & Hashizume, H. (2004, April 24-29). Caretta: A system for supporting face-to-face collaboration by integrating personal and shared spaces. In *Proceedings of the Conference on Human Factors in Computing Systems (Chi 2004),* Vienna, Austria (pp. 41-48). ACM Publishing.

Sundholm, L. H. (2000). *Self-determination in organisational change*. Jyväskylä, Finland: University of Jyväskylä.

Surowiecki, J. (2005). *The wisdom of crowds.* New York: Anchor Books.

Suzuki, K. (1978). Acceptance and rejection of a suggestion. *The Japanese Psychological Research, 20*, 60–70.

Szajna, B. (1996). Empirical Evaluation of the Revised Technology Acceptance Model. *Management Science, 42*(1), 85,88.

Tabachnick, B. G., & Fidell, L. S. (1989). *Using Multivariate Statistics*. New York: Harper Collins.

Tallon, P. P., Kraemer, K., & Gurbaxani, V. (2000). Executives' Perceptions of the Business Value of Information Technology: A Process-Oriented Approach. *Journal of Management Information Systems, 16*(4), 145–173.

Tang, F., Mu, J., & Maclachlan, D. L. (2008). Implication of network size and structure on organizations' knowledge transfer. *Expert Systems with Applications, 34*(2), 1109–1114. doi:10.1016/j.eswa.2006.12.020

Tang, H., & Ng, J. H. K. (2006). Googling for a diagnosis? Use of Google as a diagnostic aid: internet based study. *British Medical Journal, 333*(7579), 1143–1145. doi:10.1136/bmj.39003.640567.AE

Tapscott, D., & Williams, A. D. (2006). *Wikinomics: How mass collaboration changes everything.* New York: Penguin Group.

Taylor, S., & Todd, P. A. (1995). Understanding information technology usage: A test of competing models. *Information Systems Research, 6*(2), 144–176. doi:10.1287/isre.6.2.144

Teece, D. J., Pisano, G., & Shuen, A. (1997). Dynamic Capabilities and Strategic Management. *Strategic Management Journal, 18*(7), 509–533. doi:10.1002/(SICI)1097-0266(199708)18:7<509::AID-SMJ882>3.0.CO;2-Z

Teh, G. P. L. (1999). Assessing Student Perceptions of Internet-based Online Learning Environment. *International Journal of Instructional Media, 26*(4), 397–402.

Thatcher, J. B., Loughry, M. L., Lim, J., & McKnight, D. H. (2007). Internet anxiety: An empirical study of the effects of personality, beliefs, and social support. *Information & Management, 44*(4), 353–363. doi:10.1016/j.im.2006.11.007

Thatcher, J. B., & Perrewé, P. L. (2002). An empirical examination of individual traits as antecedents to computer anxiety and computer self-efficacy. *Management Information Systems Quarterly, 26*(4), 381–395. doi:10.2307/4132314

Thomke, S., & Hippel, E. V. (2002, April). Customers as Innovators – A New Way to Create Value. *Harvard Business Review*, 74–81.

Thompson, R. L., Higgins, C. A., & Howell, J. M. (1991). Personal computing: Toward a conceptual model of utilization. *Management Information Systems Quarterly, 15*(1), 125–143. doi:10.2307/249443

Thompson, R., Compeau, D., & Higgins, C. (2006). Intentions to use information technologies: An integrative model. *Journal of Organizational and End User Computing, 18*(3), 25–46.

Thorne, S. (1994). Secondary analysis in qualitative research: Issues and implications. In Morse, J. M. (Ed.), *Critical issues in qualitative research methods* (pp. 263–279). Thousand Oaks, CA: Sage.

Tilson, R., Dong, J., Martin, S., & Kiele, E. (1998). Factors and principles affecting the usability of four E-commerce sites. In *Proceedings of the 4th Conference on Huamn Factors and the Web*, Basking Ridge, NJ.

Took, R. (1990). Putting Design into Practice: Formal Specification and the User Interface. In Harrison, M., & Thimbleby, H. (Eds.), *Formal Methods in Human-Computer Interaction* (pp. 82–96). Cambridge, UK: Cambridge University Press.

Törpel, B., Pipek, V., & Rittenbruch, M. (2003). Creating Heterogeneity - Evolving Use of Groupware in a Network of Freelancers. *Special Issue of the Int. Journal on CSCW on Evolving Use of Groupware*, *12*(4), 381–409.

Trigg, R., & Bødker, S. (1994). *From implementation to design: tailoring and the emergence of systematization in CSCW*. Paper presented at CSCW'94.

Truex, D. P., Baskerville, R., & Klein, H. (1999). Growing systems in emergent organisations. *Communications of the ACM*, *42*(8), 117–123. doi:10.1145/310930.310984

Tudor, L. (1998). Human Factors: Does Your Management Hear You? *Interaction*, *5*(1), 16–24. doi:10.1145/268986.268989

Tuunanen, T. (2005). *Requirements elicitation for wide audience end-users*. Unpublished doctoral dissertation, Helsinki School of Economics, Finland.

Ulrich, K. T., & Eppinger, S. D. (1999). *Product Design and Development* (2nd ed.). New York: McGaw-Hill.

Urquhart, C. (2001). An Encounter with Grounded Theory: Tackling the Practical and Philosophical Issues. In Trauth, E. (Ed.), *Qualitative Research in Information Systems: Issues and Trends* (pp. 104–140). Hershey, PA: IGI Global.

Van Biervliet, A., & Edwards-Shafer, P. (2004). Consumer Health Information on the Web: Trends, Issues, and Strategies. *Medsurg Nursing*, *13*(2), 91–96.

van Maanen, J., & Barley, S. (1984). Occupational communities: Culture and control in Organizations. In Staw, B., & Cummings, L. (Eds.), *Research in Organizational Behavior 6* (pp. 287–365). Greenwich, CT: JAI Press.

Van Schaik, P., Flynn, D., Van Wersch, A., Douglass, A., & Cann, P. (2004). The acceptance of a computerized decision-support system in primary care: A preliminary investigation. *Behaviour & Information Technology*, *23*(5), 321–326. doi:10.1080/01449290410006669941

Venkatesh, V. (2000). Determinants of perceived ease of use: Integrating perceived behavioral control, computer anxiety and enjoyment into the technology acceptance model. *Information Systems Research*, *11*(4), 342–365. doi:10.1287/isre.11.4.342.11872

Venkatesh, V., & Agarwal, R. (2006). Turning visitors into customers: A usability-centric perspective on purchase behavior in electronic channels. *Management Science*, *52*(3), 367–382. doi:10.1287/mnsc.1050.0442

Venkatesh, V., & Davis, F. D. (1996). A model of the antecedents of perceived ease of use: Development and test. *Decision Sciences*, *27*(3), 451–481. doi:10.1111/j.1540-5915.1996.tb01822.x

Venkatesh, V., & Davis, F. D. (2000). A Theoretical Extension of the Technology Acceptance Model: Four Langitudinal Field Studies. *Management Science*, *46*(2), 186. doi:10.1287/mnsc.46.2.186.11926

Venkatesh, V., & Davis, F. D. (2000). A theoretical extension of the technology acceptance model: Four longitudinal field studies. *Management Science*, *46*(2), 186–204. doi:10.1287/mnsc.46.2.186.11926

Venkatesh, V., Morris, M. G., Davis, G. B., & Davis, F. (2003). User Acceptance of Information Technology: Toward a Unified View. *Management Information Systems Quarterly*, *27*(3), 425–478.

Venkatesh, V., & Ramesh, V. (2006). Web and wireless site usability: understanding differences and Modeling use. *Management Information Systems Quarterly*, *30*(1), 181–206.

Vestal, W. (2003). Ten traits for a successful Community of Practice. *KM Review*, *5*(6), 6.

Vestal, W. (2006). Sustaining: communities of practice. *KM World*, *15*(3), 8–40.

Victor, B., & Boynton, A. C. (1998). *Invented here: Maximizing your organization's internal growth and profitability*. Boston: Harvard Business School Press.

Viehland, D., & Shakir, M. (2005, spring). Making sense of enterprise systems implementations. *University of Auckland Business Review*, 28-34.

Volkoff, O., Strong, D. M., & Elmes, M. B. (2002, August). Between a rock and a hard place: Boundary spanners in an ERP implementation. In D. R. Banker, H. Chang, & Y.-C. Kao (Eds.), *Proceedings of the 8th Americas Conference on Information Systems*, Dallas, TX (pp. 958-962). Atlanta, GA: Association for Information Systems.

von Hippel, E. (2005). *Democratizing innovation*. Cambridge, MA: MIT Press.

von Hippel, E. (2001). Innovation by user communities: Learning from open-source software. *MIT Sloan Management Review*, *42*(4), 82–86.

von Hippel, E., & Katz, R. (2002). Shifting Innovation to Users via Toolkits. *Management Science*, *48*(7), 821–833. doi:10.1287/mnsc.48.7.821.2817

von Lubitz, D., & Wickramasinghe, N. (2006). Network centric healthcare and bioinformatics: Unified operations within three domains of knowledge. *Expert Systems with Applications*, *30*(1), 11–23. doi:10.1016/j.eswa.2005.09.069

Vredenburg, K., Mao, J., Smith, P., & Casey, T. (2002). A survey of user-centered design practice. In [CHI Letters]. *Proceedings of the Conference on Human Factors in Computing Systems*, *2*(1), 471–478.

Wade, M., & Hulland, J. (2004). The Resource-Based View and Information Systems Research: Review, Extension, and Suggestions for Future Research. *Management Information Systems Quarterly*, *28*(1), 107–142.

Wahlstedt, A., Pekkola, S., & Niemelä, M. (2008). From e-learning space to e-learning place. *British Journal of Educational Technology*, *39*(6), 1020–1030. doi:10.1111/j.1467-8535.2008.00821_1.x

Walczak, S. (2003). A Multiagent Architecture for Developing Medical Information Retrieval Agents. *Journal of Medical Systems*, *27*(5), 479–498. doi:10.1023/A:1025668124244

Walsham, G. (1995). Interpretive case studies in IS research: nature and method. *European Journal of Information Systems*, *4*(2), 74–81. doi:10.1057/ejis.1995.9

Walsham, G., & Han, C. K. (1993). Information systems strategy formation and implementation: The case of a central government agency. *Accounting. Management & Information Technology*, *3*(3), 191–209. doi:10.1016/0959-8022(93)90016-Y

Ward, M. M., Jaana, M., Behensky, J. A., Vartak, S., & Wakefield, D. S. (2006). Clinical Information System Availability and Use in Urban and Rural Hospitals. *Journal of Medical Information Systems*, *30*(6), 429–438.

Warkentin, M., Davis, K., & Bekkering, E. (2004). Introducing the Check-Off Password System (COPS): An advancement in user authentication methods and information security. *Journal of Organizational and End User Computing*, *16*(3), 41–58.

Warkentin, M., & Johnston, A. C. (2006). IT security governance and centralized security controls. In Warkentin, M., & Vaughn, R. (Eds.), *Enterprise Information Assurance and System Security: Managerial and Technical Issues* (pp. 16–24). Hershey, PA: IGI Global.

Warkentin, M., & Johnston, A. C. (2008). IT governance and organizational design for security management. In Baskerville, R., Goodman, S., & Straub, D. W. (Eds.), *Information Security Policies and Practices*. Armonk, NY: M. E. Sharpe.

Wasko, M. M., & Faraj, S. (2005). Why Should I Share? Examining Social Capital and Knowledge Contribution in Electronic Networks of Practice. *Management Information Systems Quarterly*, *29*(1), 35–57.

Weber, R. P. (1990). *Basic content analysis*. Beverly Hills, CA: Sage.

Weedon, C. (2004). *Identity and Culture: Narratives of Difference and Belonging*. New York: Open University Press.

Weill, P. (1990). Strategic Investment in Information Technology - an Empirical- Study. *Information Age*, *12*(3), 141–147.

Weill, P. (1992). The Relationship Between Investment in Information Technology and Firm Performance: A Study of the Valve Manufacturing Sector. *Information Systems Research*, *3*(4), 307–333. doi:10.1287/isre.3.4.307

Weill, P., Surbramani, M., & Broadbent, M. (2002). Building IT Infrastructure for Strategic Agility. *Sloan Management Review*, *44*(1), 57–66.

Wenger, E. (1998). *Communities of practice—learning, meaning, and identity.* Cambridge, UK: Cambridge University Press.

Wenger, E. (1998). *Communities of Practice. Learning, Meaning, and Identity*. Cambridge, MA: Cambridge University Press.

Wenger, E. (2004). Knowledge management as a doughnut: Shaping your knowledge strategy through communities of practice. *Ivey Business Journal*, *68*(3), 1–8.

West, R. E., Waddoups, G., & Graham, C. R. (2007). Understanding the experience of instructors as they adopt a course management system. *Educational Technology Research and Development*, *55*(1), 1–26. doi:10.1007/s11423-006-9018-1

Wheatley, M. (2000). *ES training stinks*. CIO.

Wheeler, B. C., Dennis, A. R., & Press, L. I. (1999). Groupware Comes to the Internet: Charting a New World. *The Data Base for Advances in Information Systems*, *30*(3-4), 8–21.

Whitehead, J. L. Jr. (1968). Factors of source credibility. *The Quarterly Journal of Speech*, *54*, 59–63. doi:10.1080/00335636809382870

Wiener, J. L., LaForge, R. W., & Goolsby, J. R. (1990, May). Personal communication in marketing: An examination of self-interest contingency relationships. *JMR, Journal of Marketing Research*, *27*, 227–231. doi:10.2307/3172849

Wikipedia. (2008). *Perpetual beta*. Retrieved from http://en.wikipedia.org/wiki/Perpetual_beta

Wilcox, E., Atwood, J., Burnett, M., Cadiz, J., & Cook, C. (1997, March 22-27). Does continuous visual feedback aid debugging in direct-manipulation programming systems? *ACM Conference on Human Factors in Computing Systems (CHI 1997),* Atlanta, GA (pp. 258-265). ACM Publishing.

Wild, R. H., Griggs, K. A., & Downing, T. (2002). A framework for e-learning as a tool for knowledge management. *Industrial Management & Data Systems*, *102*(7), 371–380. doi:10.1108/02635570210439463

Wilson, A., Burnett, M., Beckwith, L., Granatir, O., Casburn, L., Cook, C., et al. (2003, April 5-10). Harnessing curiosity to increase correctness in end-user programming. In *Proceedings of the ACM Conference on Human Factors in Computing Systems (CHI 2003),* Fort Lauderdale, FL (pp. 305-312). ACM Publishing.

Wilson, J. R., & Rutherford, A. (1989). Mental models: Theory and application in human factors. *Human Factors*, *31*(6), 617–634.

Winkelman, W. J., & Choo, C. W. (2003). Provider-sponsored virtual communities for chronic patients: improving health outcomes through organizational patient-centered knowledge management. *Health Expectations*, *6*(4), 352–358. doi:10.1046/j.1369-7625.2003.00237.x

Winograd, T., & Flores, F. (1986). *Understanding computers and cognition: A new foundation for design.* Norwood, NJ: Ablex Publishing Corporation.

Winthereik, B. R., & Vikkelso, S. (2005). ICT and integrated care: Some dilemmas of standardising inter-organisational communication. *Computer Supported Cooperative Work*, *14*(1), 43–67. doi:10.1007/s10606-004-6442-9

Wittaker, J. O., & Meade, R. D. (1968). Retention of opinion change as a function of differential source credibility. *International Journal of Psychology*, *3*, 103–108. doi:10.1080/00207596808247232

Witte, K. (1992). Putting the fear back into fear appeals: The extended parallel process model. *Communication Monographs*, *59*, 329–349. doi:10.1080/03637759209376276

Won, M., Stiemerling, O., & Wulf, V. (2006). Component-based approaches to tailorable systems. In H. Lieberman, F. Paternò, & V. Wulf (Ed.), *End user development* (pp. 115-141). New York: Springer.

Wright, R. W., Brand, R. A., Dunn, W., & Spindler, K. P. (2007). How to Write a Systematic Review. *Clinical Orthopaedics and Related Research*, *455*, 23–29. doi:10.1097/BLO.0b013e31802c9098

Wulf, V. (1999, November 14-17). "Let's see your search-tool!" On the collaborative use of tailored artifacts. In *Proceedings of the Conference on Supporting Group Work (Group '99),* Phoenix, AZ (pp. 50-60). ACM Publishing.

Wulf, V., & Rohde, M. (1995). *Towards an Integrated Organization and Technology Development.* Paper presented at DIS'95.

Wulf, V. (1999). Evolving Cooperation when Introducing Groupware–A Self-Organization Perspective. *Cybernetics & Human Knowing, 6*(2), 55–75.

Wulf, V., & Golombek, B. (2001). Direct Activation: A Concept to Encourage Tailoring Activities. *Behaviour & Information Technology, 20*(4), 249–263. doi:10.1080/01449290110048016

Wulf, V., Paterno, F., & Lieberman, H. (Eds.). (2006). *End user development.* New York: Springer.

Wulf, V., Pipek, V., & Won, M. (2008). Component-based tailorability: Enabling highly flexible software applications. *International Journal of Human-Computer Studies, 66*(1), 1–22.

Wulf, V., Stiemerling, O., & Pfeifer, A. (1999). Tailoring groupware for different scopes of validity. *Behaviour & Information Technology, 18*(3), 199–212. doi:10.1080/014492999119084

Yalch, R. F., & Elmore-Yalch, R.. The effect of numbers on the route to persuasion. *The Journal of Consumer Research, 11*, 522–527. doi:10.1086/208988

Yamazaki, H. (2004). East Meets West in Japanese Communities: Combining face-to-face with virtual communications in CoPs. *KM Review, 7*(2), 24–27.

Ye, Y., & Fischer, G. (2007, July 22-27). Designing for participation in socio-technical software systems. In C. Stephanidis (Ed.), *Universal Access in Human Computer Interaction: Coping with Diversity: Proceedings of 4th International Conference on Universal Access in Human-Computer Interaction,* Beijing, China (LNCS 4554, pp. 312-321).

Yellen, R. E. (2006). A new look at learning for the organization. *Information & Management, 19*(3), 20–23.

Yi, M. U., & Im, K. S. (2004). Predicting computer task performance: Personal goal and self-efficacy. *Journal of Organizational and End User Computing, 16*(2), 28–37. doi:10.4018/joeuc.2004040102

Yi, M. Y., & Davis, F. M. (2003). Developing and validating an observational learning model of computer software training and skill acquisition. *Information Systems Research, 14*(2), 146–169. doi:10.1287/isre.14.2.146.16016

Yi, M. Y., & Hwang, Y. (2003). Predicting the use of web-based information systems: Self-efficacy, enjoyment, learning goal orientation, and the technology acceptance model. *International Journal of Human-Computer Studies, 59*(4), 431–449. doi:10.1016/S1071-5819(03)00114-9

Yi, M. Y., Jackson, J. D., Park, J. S., & Probst, J. C. (2006). Understanding information technology acceptance by individual professionals: Toward an integrative view. *Information & Management, 43*(3), 350–363. doi:10.1016/j.im.2005.08.006

Yin, R. K. (2003a). *Applications of case study research* (2nd ed.). Thousand Oaks, CA: Sage.

Yin, R. K. (2003b). *Case study research: design and methods* (3rd ed.). Thousand Oaks, CA: Sage.

Youngjin, K. (2006). Supporting distributed groups with group support systems: A study of the effects of group leaders and communication modes on group performance. *Journal of Organizational and End User Computing, 18*(2), 20–37.

Zaharias, P. (2005). Call for Papers: E-Learning Design and Usability. *ISWorld.*

Zboralski, K., Salomo, S., & Gemuenden, H. G. (2006). Organizational Benefits of Communities of Practice: A Two-Stage Information Processing Model. *Cybernetics and Systems, 37*(6), 533–552. doi:10.1080/01969720600734461

Zhang, D., Zhao, J. L., Zhou, L., & Nunamaker, J. F. (2004). Can e-learning replace classroom learning? *Communications of the ACM, 47*(5), 75–79. doi:10.1145/986213.986216

Zhang, P., & Li, N. (2005). The Intellectual Development of Human-Computer Interaction Research: A Critical Assessment of the MIS Literature (1990-2002). *Journal of the Association for Information Systems, 6*, 227–291.

Zmud, R. W., & Apple, L. E. (1992). Measuring Information Technology Infusion. *Production and Innovation Management, 9*(2), 148–155. doi:10.1016/0737-6782(92)90006-X

About the Contributors

Ashish Dwivedi is the Deputy Director, Centre for Systems Studies at Hull University Business School, UK. Previously, he was the Deputy Graduate Research Director at Hull University Business School, and was also associated with the management of the high-tech Management Learning Laboratory). His primary research interests are in knowledge management (in which he obtained his PhD), supply chain management healthcare management and information and communication technologies. He has published 4 books and over 50 journal and conference papers. He has served as an Invited reviewer and Guest Editor for several journals, including the IEEE Transactions on Information Technology in Biomedicine.

Steve Clarke received a BSc in Economics from The University of Kingston Upon Hull, an MBA from the Putteridge Bury Management Centre, The University of Luton, and a PhD in human centred approaches to information systems development from Brunel University – all in the United Kingdom. He is Emeritus Professor of Information Systems in the University of Hull Business School.

Steve has extensive experience in management systems and information systems consultancy and research, focusing primarily on the identification and satisfaction of user needs and issues connected with knowledge management. His research interests include: social theory and information systems practice; strategic planning; and the impact of user involvement in the development of management systems. Major current research is focused on approaches informed by critical social theory.

* * *

Mesbah U. Ahmed is a professor in the Information Operations and Technology Management department at the University of Toledo. His current research and teaching interests are in the area of systems development, and data warehousing. He has published in Decision Sciences, MIS Quarterly, Journal of Operations Management, International Journal of Data Warehousing and Mining, Journal of Database Management, and Information & Management.

Jack Kimenker Beaton is a Usability Scientist at Nokia Inc. in Boston, Massachusetts. His research interests include the design of usable interactions for programmers, and mobile device users, in industrialized countries and emerging markets. He received a Master's degree in Human-Computer Interaction from Carnegie Mellon University in 2007 and a BA in Cultural Anthropology from the University of Maryland, Baltimore County in 2004.

Margaret Burnett is a Professor of Computer Science at the School of Electrical Engineering and Computer Science at Oregon State University. Her current research focuses on end-user programming, end-user software engineering, information foraging theory as applied to programming, and gender issues in those contexts. She has a long history of research in these issues and others relating to human issues of programming. She is also the principal architect of the Forms/3 and the FAR visual programming languages and, together with Gregg Rothermel, of the WYSIWYT testing methodology for end-user programmers. She is the founding Project Director of the EUSES Consortium, a multi-institution collaboration to help End Users Shape Effective Software.

Daniela Busse is a Director for User Research in SAP Lab's central User Experience organization in Palo Alto (CA), with over 13 years of experience in Product Definition and Design, using User Research to inform enquiry, ideation, and productization. Prior to joining the SAP Labs UX team, she led incubation projects at a global innovation team in SAP's Office of the CEO, and was also Principal Investigator on a number of SAP Research funded projects. Her early experiences with research & design were formed working closely with product planning and development as part of the Microsoft Office Design Group in Redmond (WA). Her current focus at SAP Labs is Research for Sustainability. She received her M.A. in Psychology and Computing Science from the University of Glasgow (UK), as well as her Ph.D. on the investigation, analysis, and cognitive modeling of accidents and preventable deaths in complex systems, with special focus on Intensive Care Unit system design and optimization.

Tony Coulson is a Professor in the College of Business and Public Administration, Department of Information & Decision Sciences at California State University, San Bernardino (CSUSB). He came to San Bernardino in 2001 after a professional career as an IT executive and graduating with a PhD in Information Systems from Claremont Graduate University. Tony's research interests include: Enterprise Systems implementation, virtual communities and systems security. Tony is the Executive Director of the Information Assurance and Security Management Center at CSUSB and recently led the effort to have the University designated as a Center of Academic Excellence in Information Assurance Education by the U.S. National Security Agency.

Pratim Datta is an Assistant Professor of Information Systems in the Department of Management and Information Systems at Kent State University. He also serves as a co-advisor to the MIS Association and as the co-chair of the Computer Information Systems Marketing Committee at Kent State University. His work has been published in the Journal of the Association of Information Systems, European Journal on Information Systems, Communications of the AIS and the ACM, IEEE Transactions, among others.

Xiaodong Deng is an Associate Professor of Management Information Systems at Oakland University. He received his Ph.D. in Manufacturing Management and Engineering from The University of Toledo. His research has appeared in Journal of Management Information Systems, Decision Sciences, Information and Management, Information Resources Management Journal, and Journal of Intelligent Manufacturing. His research interests are in post-implementation information technology learning, information systems benchmarking, and information technology acceptance and diffusion.

William J. Doll is a Professor of MIS and Strategic Management at The University of Toledo. Dr. Doll holds a doctoral degree in Business Administration from Kent State University and has published extensively on information system and manufacturing issues in academic and professional journals including Management Science, Communications of the ACM, MIS Quarterly, Academy of Management Journal, Decision Sciences, Journal of Operations Management, Information Systems Research, Journal of Management Information Systems, Omega, and Information & Management.

Arkin Efeoglu is a Business Consultant at SAP giving strategic advises for Business Process Management and service-oriented architecture. Before going into strategic Business Consulting he was leading the ES Workplace project in the service-oriented architecture solution management. In this role he ensured that SAP gave easy access for customers and partners to all productized SAP enterprise services for evaluation and adaptation. Prior to this Arkin worked for the Business Renovation Team, which is part of the Office of the CEO. In solution management there he was working on an SCM prototype. The prototype xCarrier aimed to optimize carrier selection and seamlessly integrate carrier services. Arkin holds a Masters in Business Information Systems from the University of Mannheim and received an MBA from Western Carolina University.

Ralf Ehret is a development architect at SAP. He joined SAP in April 1998 as a developer working with HR and Workforce Management software before moving on to the Business Process Renovation Team. After evaluating Smalltalk as a tool for rapid prototyping, he was analyzing business rule engines and business process management systems before he started in the summer of 2007 to evaluate the concepts of API usability on ABAP APIs of an internal rule engine together with Jeff Stylos. As a follow up since 2008 he has been part of the current "Enterprise Service API Usability Project" which is a joint effort between SAP and the HCI Institute at CMU.

Gerhard Fischer is a professor of computer science, a Fellow of the Institute of Cognitive Science, and the director of the Center for Lifelong Learning and Design (L3D) at the University of Colorado at Boulder. He is a member of the CHI Academy. His research is focused on new conceptual frameworks and new media for learning, working, and collaboration; human-computer interaction; cognitive science; distributed intelligence; social creativity; design; meta-design; domain-oriented design environments; and universal design (assistive technologies).. Over the last twenty years, he has directed research projects and has published extensively in these areas.

Bassam Hasan is an Associate Professor of Management Information Systems at The University of Toledo. He holds a Ph.D. in MIS from The University of Mississippi and MBA in CIS from Missouri State University. His research interests include management of information systems, end-user computer training, and user attitudes about computer systems. His research has been published in several IS journals and presented at various regional and national IS conferences.

Sari Hohtari, MSc, is Head of the Information and Communication Technology Degree Program at the Kemi-Tornio University of Applied Sciences, Finland. She teaches systems design, programming and electronic business. Her current research interests include systems design processes, electronic business and end-user training.

Netta Iivari has a doctoral degree in information systems from University of Oulu and a master's degree in cultural anthropology from University of Jyvaskyla. Currently, she works as an assistant professor at the Department of Information Processing Science at the University of Oulu. She received her doctoral degree in 2006, and in her thesis, she critically analyzed discourses on 'culture' and 'usability work' in the software product development context. Her research is strongly influenced by interpretive and critical research traditions. Her long lasting research interests are related to the empirical, interpretive examinations of participation of different stakeholder groups in defining, developing, shaping and framing information technologies. Currently, she is specifically interested in enabling participation of children in information technology development, as well as in the discursive construction of users and their role in open source software development.

Sae Young Jeong is a student researcher in the Human-Computer Interaction Institute in the School of Computer Science at Carnegie Mellon University. Her current research focused on end-user software engineering and information visualization. She was a senior consultant in IBM by managing Service Oriented Architecture consulting project in the enterprise. She was also a senior software architect in several domestic banks in order to develop an application framework to help developers write JAVA application more effectively. She received her M.S. in the School of Computer Science from Carnegie Mellon University, and the M.S. and B.S. degrees in electrical engineering from Korea Advance Institute of Science and Technology, South Korea.

Allen C. Johnston an Assistant Professor in the School of Business at the University of Alabama Birmingham. He holds a BS from Louisiana State University in Electrical Engineering as well as an MSIS and PhD in Information Systems from Mississippi State University. His works can be found in such outlets as Communications of the ACM, Journal of Global Information Management, Information Resources Management Journal, Journal of Information Privacy and Security, Journal of Internet Commerce, and International Journal of Information Security and Privacy. The primary focus of his research has been in the areas of technology adoption, information assurance and security, with specific concentration on the behavioral aspects of information security and privacy.

Jan Karstens is a development architect at SAP AG, Walldorf, Germany. He has several years experience in software engineering in different companies and industries. At SAP he works for the office of the Chief Technology Officer with a focus on different programming languages (including ABAP), development tools and development efficiency. He received his MS and BSc degrees from the Hasso-Plattner Institute at the University of Potsdam.

Mari Kira is an Academy Research Fellow at Helsinki University of Technology, Finland. She has a Ph.D. degree (2003) from Royal Institute of Technology, Sweden. From 2004 to 2006, she was a Marie Curie Fellow at University of Kassel, Germany, and in winter 2007/2008, she was a visiting faculty at the Leeds School of Business, University of Colorado at Boulder, USA. Her research interests focus on sustainability of individuals at work and of work organizations as a whole.

Eija Korpelainen is a doctoral student in the Doctoral Program for Multidisciplinary Research on Learning Environments, Finland. She is working at Helsinki University of Technology in the Department of Industrial Engineering and Management, Work Psychology and Leadership as a researcher and project manager. She has gained her Master of Arts in Education. The special focus of her current studies is on support needs that employees experience in adopting and using ICT systems, especially to support interaction and on-the-job training in work organizations.

Richard Mann is a PhD candidate at the University of Colorado Denver currently focusing his dissertation work on the use of information systems by diverse groups of clinical professionals. His previous degrees include a MSIS (UCD) and a MHSA (Arizona State University). He works as an Integration Engineer for Cardinal Health.

Brad A. Myers is a Professor in the Human-Computer Interaction Institute in the School of Computer Science at Carnegie Mellon University. He is an ACM Fellow, and a member of the CHI Academy, an honor bestowed on the principal leaders of the field. He is the author or editor of over 350 publications. He has been a consultant on user interface design and implementation to over 60 companies. He received a PhD in computer science at the University of Toronto, and the MS and BSc degrees from MIT during which time he was a research intern at Xerox PARC.

Harri Oinas-Kukkonen, Ph.D., is Professor of information systems at the University of Oulu, Finland. Currently, he is a Visiting Scholar at Stanford University. His research interests include the next generation of the Web, attitude and behaviour change, social and organizational knowledge management, and IT innovation creation. His research has been published in journals such as ACM Computing Surveys, Communications of the ACM, Communications of the AIS, The DATA BASE for Advances in Information Systems, European Journal of Information Systems, Information and Software Technology, Information Technology and Management, International Journal of Healthcare Information Systems and Informatics, International Journal of Human-Computer Studies, International Journal of Networking and Virtual Organizations, Journal of Digital Information, Journal of Healthcare Information Management, Netnomics: Economic Research and Electronic Networking and Software Process Improvement and Practice. In 2005, he was awarded The Outstanding Young Person of Finland award by the Junior Chamber of Commerce. He is currently editing a special issue on Persuasive technology for the Communications of the Association of Information Systems and on Social networks in socio-technical environments for the Journal of the Association of Information Systems.

Lorne Olfman is a Professor in the School of Information Systems and Technology and Fletcher Jones Chair in Technology Management at Claremont Graduate University (CGU). He came to Claremont in 1987 after graduating with a PhD in Business (Management Information Systems) from Indiana University. Lorne's research interests include: how software can be learned and used in organizations, the impact of computer-based systems on knowledge management, and the design and adoption of systems used for group work. Along with Terry Ryan, Lorne co-directs the Social Learning Software Lab (SL2). A key component of Lorne's teaching is his involvement with doctoral students; he has supervised 46 students to completion. Lorne is an active member of the Information Systems community.

Samuli Pekkola, PhD, is Professor of information and knowledge management at Tampere University of Technology, Finland, and Lecturer of information systems at the University of Jyväskylä, Finland.

His research focuses on individual users in different manifestations of information systems, and around participatory information systems development methods. His main research interests include CSCW, PD, ISD, HCI and enterprise architectures. His research has been published in journals such as The DATA BASE for Advances in Information Systems, Decision Support Systems, British Journal of Educational Technology, and Journal of Network and Computer Applications. He is an editor of Scandinavian Journal of Information Systems, and just edited a special issue on "User -- The great unknown of systems development" for the Information Systems Journal.

Terry Ryan is Associate Professor and Dean of the School of Information Systems and Technology, as well as Co-Director (with Lorne Olfman) of the Social Learning Software Lab at Claremont Graduate University. His teaching and research interests are in the design, development, implementation, and evaluation of information systems, especially those that support conversation and social learning. He has published articles in Communications of the ACM, Communications of the AIS, Data Base, Information & Management, International Journal of Human-Computer Studies, International Journal of Knowledge Management, Journal of Computer Information Systems, Journal of Database Management, and Journal of Information Systems Education.

Conrad Shayo is a Professor of Information Science at California State University San Bernardino. Over the last 28 years he has worked in various capacities as a university professor, consultant, and manager. He holds a Doctor of Philosophy Degree and a Master of Science Degree in Information Science from the Claremont Graduate University. He also holds an MBA in Management Science from the University of Nairobi, Kenya; and a Bachelor of Commerce Degree in Finance from the University of Dar-Es-Salaam, Tanzania. He has consulted for the World Bank, Swiss Agency for Development Corporation, and the US Government. His research interests are in the areas of IT assimilation, performance measurement, distributed learning, end-user computing, organizational memory, instructional design, organizational learning assessment, reusable learning objects, IT strategy, and "virtual societies." Dr. Shayo has published these and other topics in various books and journals. Currently he is involved in developing reusable learning objects and web based learning game simulations. He is also consulting in the areas of tourism promotion, joint ventures, and poverty eradication in developing countries. He is a Co-Editor (with Dr. Magid Igbaria) of the book: Strategies for Managing IS/IT Personnel.

Jeffrey Stylos is a User Experience Researcher with the Developer Division User Experience group at Microsoft. He received his PhD from the Computer Science Department at Carnegie Mellon University. His PhD focused on programming tools, documentation and redesigned APIs to help programmers more easily use APIs.

Matti Vartiainen, Ph.D is Professor of Learning Organization at Work Psychology and Leadership (Helsinki University of Technology, Department of Industrial Engineering and Management). He leads the Virtual and Mobile Work Research Unit (http://vmwork.tkk.fi) at the BIT Research Center (http://www.bit.hut.fi/). His research interests cover the fields of organizational innovations, mobile distributed work, reward systems (http://www.palkitseminen.hut.fi), knowledge and competence building, collaboration, and e-learning systems.

Steven Walczak is an Associate Professor of Information Systems at the University of Colorado Denver. He received his Ph.D. from the University of Florida and his M.S. and B.S. from the Johns Hopkins University and the Pennsylvania State University respectively. His research interests are in applied artificial intelligence systems, electronic commerce applications and functionality, and organizational knowledge management. Professor Walczak is a member of multiple editorial boards for distinguished journals in information systems, electronic commerce, and organizational learning.

Jianfeng Wang is an Assistant Professor of Business Administration at Mansfield University of Pennsylvania. He received his Ph.D. in manufacturing Management and Engineering from The University of Toledo. His research appeared in the Journal of Internet Commerce, conference proceedings of Decision Sciences Institution, and Academy of Marketing Science. His research interests are evaluation of Web-based systems, e-learning, web site usability, and marketing channels.

Y. Ken Wang is Assistant Professor of Computer Information Systems at University of Pittsburgh at Bradford. He received his Ph.D. in Business Administration from Washington State University. His research interests include information systems continuance and use, human computer interaction, virtual team, and knowledge management. His research articles have appeared in the International Resources Management Journal (IRMJ) and a number of refereed conference proceedings, such as the International Conference on Information Systems (ICIS), the Hawaii International Conference on System Sciences (HICSS), and the Americas Conference on Information Systems (AMCIS).

Merrill Warkentin is Professor of MIS at Mississippi State University. He has published over 125 research manuscripts, primarily in computer security management, eCommerce, and virtual teams, in books, proceeding, and journals such as MIS Quarterly, Decision Sciences, Decision Support Systems, Communications of the ACM, Communications of the AIS, Information Systems Journal, Information Resources Management Journal, Journal of Organizational and End User Computing, Journal of Global Information Management, and others. Professor Warkentin is the co-author or editor of four books, and is currently an Associate Editor of Information Resources Management Journal and Journal of Information Systems Security, and of the Special Issue of MIS Quarterly on Security. Dr. Warkentin has served as a consultant to numerous organizations and has served as National Distinguished Lecturer for the Association for Computing Machinery (ACM).

Yingyu ("Clare") Xie is a Masters student in the Human-Computer Interaction Institute in the School of Computer Science at Carnegie Mellon University. At CMU, she worked as a research assistant on improving API usability and the learnability of programming tools. She has been a consultant on user experience design and research to various clients including Nokia, Siemens, HP, Flir, Sony, NEC, BMCC (Beijing Mobil Communication Company), and China Alibaba. She received a BE degree from Xi'an Jiao Tong University in China.

Index

A

B

C

D

N

O

P

Q

R

S